THE THEORY OF COMMUNICATIVE ACTION

Volume 2

LIFEWORLD AND SYSTEM: A CRITIQUE OF FUNCTIONALIST REASON

Jürgen Habermas

Translated by Thomas McCarthy

D0879291

Polity Press

First published in 1981 as *Theorie des kommunikativen Handelns, Band 2: Zur Kritik der funktionalistischen Vernunft*, by Suhrkamp Verlag, Frankfurt am Main

Translator's preface and translation copyright © Beacon Press 1987

This edition first published 1987 by Polity Press in association with
Blackwell Publishers Ltd
First published in paperback 1989
Reprinted 1992, 1995

Editorial office:
Polity Press, 65 Bridge Street, Cambridge CB2 1UR, UK

Marketing and production:
Blackwell Publishers Ltd
108 Cowley Road, Oxford OX4 1JF, UK

ISBN 0 7456 0770 5 (pbk)

A CIP catalogue record for this book is available from the British Library.

Printed in Great Britain.

Contents

Volume 2: Lifeworld and System:
A Critique of Functionalist Reason

Translator's Preface

In preparing this translation, I was greatly reassured by the author's willingness to read through a first draft and suggest whatever changes he thought appropriate. The reader should be advised that, while these changes were introduced to capture more precisely his meaning or to make the translation more readable, they often resulted in minor departures from the original text. At such points, then, the correspondence between the German and English versions is not exactly that of translation.

I am indebted to Victor Lidz and Jeffrey Alexander for reading and commenting upon the translation of Chapter VII, and to Robert Burns and Carol Rose for helping with the legal terminology in Chapter VIII. I am particularly grateful to Sydney Lenit, Marina Rosiene, and Claudia Mesch for undertaking the hardly inconsiderable task of typing and retyping the manuscript.

Thomas McCarthy
Northwestern University

V

The Paradigm Shift in Mead and Durkheim: From Purposive Activity to Communicative Action

In the Marxist reception of Weber's theory of rationalization, from Lukacs to Adorno, the rationalization of society was always thought of as a reification of *consciousness*. As I have argued in Volume 1, the paradoxes to which this conceptual strategy leads show that rationalization cannot be dealt with adequately within the conceptual frame of the philosophy of consciousness. In Volume 2 I will take up the problematic of reification once again and reformulate it in terms of, on the one hand, communicative action and, on the other, the formation of subsystems via steering media. Before doing so I shall develop these basic concepts in the context of the history of social theory. Whereas the problematic of rationalization/reification lies along a "German" line of social-theoretical thought running from Marx through Weber to Lukacs and Critical Theory, the paradigm shift from purposive activity to communicative action was prepared by George Herbert Mead and Emile Durkheim. Mead (1863–1931) and Durkheim (1858–1917) belong, like Weber (1864–1920), to the generation of the founding fathers of modern sociology. Both developed basic concepts in which Weber's theory of rationalization may be taken up again and freed from the aporias of the philosophy of consciousness: Mead with his communication-theoretic foundation of sociology, Durkheim with a theory of social solidarity connecting social integration to system integration.

The ideas of reconciliation and freedom, which Adorno—who in the final analysis remained under the spell of Hegelian thought—merely circled around in a negative-dialectical fashion, stand in need of explication. They can in fact be developed by means of the concept of commu-

1

nicative rationality, toward which their use by Adorno points in any case. For this purpose we can draw upon a theory of action that, like Mead's, is concerned to project an ideal communication community. This utopia serves to reconstruct an undamaged intersubjectivity that allows both for unconstrained mutual understanding among individuals and for the identities of individuals who come to an unconstrained understanding with themselves. The limits of a communication-theoretic approach of this sort are evident. The reproduction of society as a whole can surely not be adequately explained in terms of the conditions of communicative rationality, though we can explain the symbolic reproduction of the lifeworld of a social group in this way, if we approach the matter from an internal perspective.

In what follows, I will (1) examine how Mead develops the basic conceptual framework of normatively regulated and linguistically mediated interaction; he arrives at this point by way of a logical genesis, starting from interaction mediated by gestures and controlled by instincts, and passing through the stage of symbolically mediated interaction in signal languages. (2) In the transition from symbolically mediated to normatively guided interaction, there is a gap in the phylogenetic line of development which can be filled in with Durkheim's assumptions concerning the sacred foundations of morality, the ritually preserved fund of social solidarity. (3) Taking as our guideline the idea of a "linguistification" [*Versprachlichung*] of this ritually secured, basic normative agreement, we can arrive at the concept of a rationalized lifeworld with differentiated symbolic structures. This concept takes us beyond the conceptual limitations of the Weberian theory of action, which is tailored to purposive activity and purposive rationality.

1. The Foundations of Social Science in the Theory of Communication

Early in the twentieth century, the subject-object model of the philosophy of consciousness was attacked on two fronts—by the analytic philosophy of language and by the psychological theory of behavior. Both renounced direct access to the phenomena of consciousness and replaced intuitive self-knowledge, reflection, or introspection with procedures that did not appeal to intuition. They proposed analyses that started from linguistic expressions or observed behavior and were open to intersubjective testing. Language analysis adopted procedures for rationally reconstructing our knowledge of rules that were familiar from logic and linguistics; behavioral psychology took over the methods of observation and strategies of interpretation established in studies of animal behavior.[1]

Despite their common origins in the pragmatism of Charles Sanders Peirce, these two approaches to the critique of consciousness have gone their separate ways and have, in their radical forms, developed independent of one another. Moreover, logical positivism and behaviorism purchased their release from the paradigm of the philosophy of consciousness by reducing the traditional roster of problems with a single coup de main—in one case through withdrawing to the analysis of languages constructed for scientific purposes, in the other by restricting itself to the model of the individual organism's stimulus-induced behavior. The analysis of language has, of course, freed itself from the constrictions of its dogmatic beginnings. The complexity of the problematic developed by Peirce has been regained along two paths—one running from Carnap and Reichenbach through Popper to postempiricist philosophy of science, the other from the early Wittgenstein through the late Wittgenstein and Austin to the theory of speech acts. By contrast the psychological theory of behavior has, notwithstanding occasional moves for liberalization, developed within the bounds of an objectivistic methodology. If we want to release the revolutionary power of the basic concepts of behavior theory, the potential in this approach to burst the bounds of its own paradigm, we shall have to go *back* to Mead's social psychology.

Mead's theory of communication also recommends itself as a point of intersection of the two critical traditions stemming from Peirce.[2] Although Mead took no notice of the linguistic turn in philosophy, looking back today one finds astonishing convergences between his social psychology and the analysis of language and theory of science developed in formal-pragmatic terms. Mead analyzed phenomena of consciousness from the standpoint of how they are formed within the structures of linguistically or symbolically mediated interaction. In his view, language has constitutive significance for the sociocultural form of life: "In man the functional differentiation through language gives an entirely different principle of organization which produces not only a different type of individual but also a different society."[3]

Mead presented his theory under the rubric of "social behaviorism" because he wanted to stress the note of criticism of consciousness. Social interactions form symbolic structures out of sentences and actions, and analyses can deal with them as with something objective. There are however two methodological differences separating Mead's approach from behaviorism. The model from which he starts is not the behavior of an individual organism reacting to stimuli from an environment, but an interaction in which at least two organisms react to one another and behave in relation to one another: "We are not, in social psychology, building up the behavior of the social group in terms of the behavior of the separate individuals composing it; rather, we are starting out with a given social whole of complex activities, into which we analyze (as elements) the behavior of each of the separate individuals composing it."[4] Mead rejects not only the methodological individualism of behavior theory but its objectivism as well. He does not want to restrict the concept of "behavior" to observable behavioral reactions; it is to include symbolically oriented behavior as well, and to allow for the reconstruction of general structures of linguistically mediated interactions: "Social psychology is behavioristic in the sense of starting off with an observable activity—the dynamic, ongoing social process, and the social acts which are its component elements—to be studied and analyzed scientifically. But it is not behavioristic in the sense of ignoring the experience of the individual— the inner phase of that process or activity."[5] In comparison with the aspect of behavior, the meaning embodied in social action is something nonexternal; at the same time, as something objectivated in symbolic expressions, it is publicly accessible and not, like phenomena of consciousness, merely internal: "There is a field within the act itself which is not external, but which belongs to the act, and there are characteristics of that inner organic conduct which do reveal themselves in their own attitudes, especially those connected with speech."[6]

Because Mead incorporated a nonreductionist concept of language into behaviorism, we find combined in him the two approaches critical of consciousness that otherwise went their separate ways after Peirce: the theory of behavior and the analysis of language. His communication theory is not restricted to acts of reaching understanding; it deals with communicative *action.* Linguistic symbols and languagelike symbols interest him only insofar as they mediate interactions, modes of behavior, and actions of more than one individual. In communicative action, beyond the function of achieving understanding, language plays the role of coordinating the goal-directed activities of different subjects, as well as the role of a medium in the socialization of these very subjects. Mead views linguistic communication almost exclusively under these last two aspects: the social integration of goal-directed actors, and the socialization of subjects capable of acting. He neglects the achievement of mutual understanding and the internal structures of language. In this respect, his communication theory stands in need of supplementary analyses of the sort carried out since in semantics and speech-act theory.[7]

The paradigm shift prepared by Mead's social psychology interests us here because it clears the way for a communication concept of rationality, to which I shall return later. In this section I want (*A*) to characterize the problem that serves as the point of departure for Mead's theory of communication, in order (*B*) to show how he explains the transition from subhuman interaction mediated by gestures to symbolically mediated interaction. (*C*) The results of Mead's theory of meaning can be rendered more precise by drawing upon Wittgenstein's investigations of the concept of a rule. (*D*) I would like then to show how language is differentiated in respect to the functions of mutual understanding, social integration, and socialization, and how this makes possible a transition from symbolically mediated to normatively guided interaction. (*E*) A desocialized perception of things, a norming of behavioral expectations, and a development of the identity of acting subjects serve as the basis for a complementary construction of the social and subjective worlds. Mead did not develop the basic concepts of objects, norms, and subjects from a phylogenetic perspective—as he did the basic categories of the theory of meaning—but only from an ontogenetic perspective. This gap can be closed by drawing upon Durkheim's theory of the origins of religions and ritual.

A.—Mead sets himself the task of capturing the structural features of symbolically mediated interaction. What interests him here is that symbols that can be used with the same meaning make possible an evolutionarily new form of communication. He views the *conversation of gestures* found in developed vertebrate societies as the evolutionary starting point for a development of language that leads first to the *signal-language* stage of symbolically mediated interaction and then to *propositionally differentiated speech.* Mead uses the term 'significant gesture' for simple, syntactically unarticulated symbols that have the same meaning for at least two participants in the same (i.e., sufficiently similar) contexts, for he regards such symbols as having developed from gestures. Examples would be vocal gestures that have taken on the character of languagelike signals, or the one-word utterances with which the child's acquisition of language begins, but which are usual among adult speakers as well, albeit only as elliptical forms of linguistically explicit utterances.

Calls such as "Dinner!" or "Fire!" or "Attack!" are context-dependent, propositionally nondifferentiated, and yet complete speech acts, which can be used only quasi-imperatively, quasi-expressively. One-word utterances are employed with communicative intent, but as syntactically unarticulated expressions they do not yet permit grammatical distinctions among different modes. Thus "Attack!" is a warning when, for example, the context is such that enemies have turned up suddenly and unexpectedly; the same call can be a command to confront an enemy that has suddenly appeared in this way; it can also be an expression of alarm at the fact that the unexpected enemy is threatening one's own life or the lives of close relations, and so on. In a way, the exclamation signifies all of these at once; in cases such as this we speak of a "signal."

Signals or one-word utterances can be used only situation-dependently, for singular terms by means of which objects could be identified relative to a situation and yet context-independently are lacking.[8] Signals are embedded in interaction contexts in such a way that they always serve to coordinate the actions of different participants—the quasi-indicative meaning and the quasi-expressive meaning of the utterance form a unity with the quasi-imperative meaning. Both the warning statement of the fact that enemies have suddenly and unexpectedly turned up and the express of alarm at the threat posed by their sudden appearance point to the *same* expectation of behavior—and this is given direct expression in the command to offer resistance to the unexpected enemy. For this reason there is an unmistakable relation between the meaning of a signal—in all its modal components of signification—and the sort of behavior that the sender expects from the addressee as an appropriate response.

Linguistic signals can be replaced by manufactured symbols (such as drumming or the tolling of a bell) that are languagelike without being linguistic. Likewise, the beginning of a significant action can take on signal functions (as when a leader demonstratively reaches for his weapon). In such cases we are, however, already dealing with signs that have a conventional meaning; their meaning no longer derives from a naturelike context. It is characteristic of the stage of symbolically mediated interaction that the language community in question has at its disposition only signals—primitive systems of calls and signs. For analytical purposes, Mead simplifies the situation by disregarding the fact that the meaning of a symbol holds for all the members of a language community.

He starts from the situation in which two independent participants can employ and understand the same symbol with the same meaning in sufficiently similar circumstances. To be sure, the condition that meaning conventions be fixed in the same way for a plurality of participants holds only for genuine signal languages and not for the gesture languages that are found at the subhuman level.

Mead illustrates the latter with examples of gesture-mediated interactions between animals belonging to the same species, such as a fight between two dogs. The interaction is set up in such a way that the beginnings of movement on the part of one organism are the gestures that serve as the stimulus eliciting a response on the part of the other; the beginnings of this latter movement become in turn a gesture that calls forth an adaptive response on the part of the first organism: "I have given the illustration of the dog-fight as a method of presenting the gesture. The act of each dog becomes the stimulus to the other dog for his response. There is then a relationship between these two; and as the act is responded to by the other dog, it, in turn, undergoes changes. The very fact that the dog is ready to attack another becomes a stimulus to the other dog to change his own position or his own attitude. He has no sooner done this than the change of attitude in the second dog in turn causes the first dog to change his attitude. We have here a conversation of gestures."[9]

Interaction between animals that is mediated through gestures is of central importance in genetic considerations if one starts, as Mead does, with the concept of objective or natural meaning. He borrows this concept of meaning from the practice of research into animal behavior. Ethologists ascribe a meaning to a certain pattern of behavior that they observe from a third-person perspective, without supposing that the observed behavior has this meaning (or indeed any meaning) for the reacting organism itself. They get at the meaning of behavior through the functional role that it plays in a system of modes of behavior. The familiar functional circuits of animal behavior serve as a foundation for these ascriptions of meaning: search for food, mating, attack and defense, care of the young, play, and so on. Meaning is a systemic property. In the language of the older ethnology: meanings are constituted in species-specific environments (von Uexküll), they are not at the disposition of the individual exemplar as such.

Mead traces the emergence of linguistic forms of communication using as his guideline the step-by-step transformation of objective or natural meanings of systemically ordered mean-ends relations between observed behavioral responses into the meanings that these modes of behavior take on for the participating organisms themselves. Symbolic meanings arise from a subjectivizing or internalizing of objective struc-

tures of meaning. As these structures are mainly found in the social behavior of animals, Mead tries to explain the emergence of language
through the fact that the semantic potential residing in gesture-mediated
interaction becomes symbolically available to participants through an
internalization of the language of gestures.

Mead distinguishes two steps in this process. At the first stage, a *signal
language* emerges that converts the objective meanings of typical behavior patterns into symbolic meanings and opens them up to processes
of reaching understanding among participants in interaction. This is the
transition from *gesture-mediated* to *symbolically mediated* interaction,
and Mead studies it from the standpoint of meaning theory as a semanticization of natural meanings. At the second stage, social roles make the
natural meaning of functionally specified systems of behavior—such as
hunting, sexual reproduction, care of the young, defense of territory, status rivalry, and the like—not only semantically accessible to participants
but normatively binding on them. For the time being I shall leave this
stage of *normatively regulated action* to one side and concentrate on
the stage of symbolically mediated interaction. I want to elucidate how
Mead understands his task of "explaining," by way of reconstructing the
emergence of this early stage of languagelike communication.

He begins with an analysis of gesture-mediated interaction because he
finds there the beginnings of a process of semanticization. A certain segment of the meaning structure embedded in the functional circuit of
animal behavior is already made thematic in the language of gestures:
"Meaning is thus a development of something objectively there as a relation between certain phases of the social act; it is not a psychical addition to that act and it is not an 'idea' as traditionally conceived. A gesture by one organism, the resultant of the social act in which the gesture
is an early phase, and the response of another organism to the gesture,
are the relata in a triple or three-fold relationship of gesture to first organism, of gesture to second organism, and of gesture to subsequent
phases of the given social act; and this three-fold relationship constitutes
the matrix within which meaning arises, or which develops into the field
of meaning."[10] Thus in the language of gestures the relations obtaining
between the gesture of the first organism and the action that follows
upon it, on the one side, and the response it stimulates in the second
organism, on the other, form the objective basis of the meaning that the
gesture of one participant assumes *for the other.* Because the gesture of
the first organism is embodied in the beginnings of a repeatedly occur-
ring movement, and is in that respect an indication of the state in which
the completed movement will result, the second organism can respond
as if the gesture were an expression of the intention to bring about this

result. It thereby gives to the gesture a meaning—which, to begin with, it has only for the second organism.

If we assume that the first organism undertakes a similar ascription, the situation looks as follows. Inasmuch as the second organism responds to the gesture of the first with a certain behavior, and the first organism responds in turn to the beginning of this behavioral response, each organism expresses how it interprets the gesture of the other, that is, how it understands it. In this way, each participant in the interaction connects with the gestures of the other a typical meaning—which obtains only for that participant.

When this is clear, we can specify the transformations that have to take place along the way from gesture-mediated to symbolically mediated interaction. First, gestures are transformed into symbols through replacing meanings that exist for individual organisms with meanings that are the same for both participants. Second, the behavior of participants changes in such a way that an interpersonal relation between speaker and addressee replaces the causal relation between stimulus-response-stimulus—in interacting with one another, participants now have a communicative intent. Finally, there is a transformation of the structure of interaction, in that the participants learn to distinguish between acts of reaching understanding and actions oriented to success. The problem of the transition from the stage of gesture-mediated interaction to the stage of symbolically mediated interaction is resolved in these three steps.

Mead tries to explain this transition by means of a mechanism he calls "taking the attitude of the other." Piaget and Freud also introduced learning mechanisms of internalization—one in the sense of "interiorizing" action schemata, the other in the sense of "internalizing" relations to social objects, that is, to given reference persons. Similarly, Mead conceives of internalization as making objective structures of meaning internal [*Verinnerlichung*]. Unlike the case of the reflective relations that come about when a subject turns back upon itself in order to make itself an object for itself, the model of internalization says that the subject finds itself again in something external, inasmuch as it takes into itself and makes its own something that it encounters as an object. The structure of assimilation [*Aneignung*] differs from the structure of reflection [*Spiegelung*] by virtue of its opposite direction: the self relates itself to itself not by making itself an object but by recognizing in an external object, in an action schema or in a schema of relations, something subjective that has been externalized.

To be sure, these elucidations remain tied to the model of the philosophy of consciousness. Mead takes his orientation from an older model, which was already employed by Augustine—the model of thought as an inner dialogue, a dialogue made internal: "Only in terms of gestures and significant symbols is the existence of mind or intelligence possible; for only in terms of gestures that are significant symbols can thinking— which is simply an internalized or implicit conversation of the individual with himself by means of such gestures—take place."[11]

This model illuminates the mechanism of "taking the attitude of the other" from one side only. It makes clear that the intersubjective relation between participants in interaction, who adjust to one another and recip- rocally take positions on one another's utterances, is reflected in the structure of the relation-to-self.[12] However, a higher-level subjectivity of this type, distinguished by the fact that it can turn back upon itself only mediately—via complex relations to others—alters the structure of in- teraction as a whole. The more complex the attitudes of the other are, which participants "internalize in their own experience," the more there is a shift in what connects the participants (to start with, organisms) beforehand, in virtue of systemic features—from the level of innate, spe- cies-specific, instinctual regulations to the level of intersubjectivity that is communicatively generated, consolidated in the medium of linguistic symbols, and secured finally through cultural tradition.

In his chapters on the social constitution of the self, Mead gives the mistaken impression that taking the attitude of the other and the corre- sponding internalization of objective meaning structures are to be under- stood primarily as a mechanism for generating higher-level subjectivity. But this mechanism has consequences for an entire system; its operations bear on all the components of the interaction system—on the *partici- pants* engaging in interaction, on their *expressions,* and on the *regula- tions* that secure the continued existence of the interaction system through coordinating actions to a sufficient degree. If Mead wants to use the mechanism of taking the attitude of the other to explain how sym- bolically mediated interaction arises from gesture-mediated interaction, he has to show how the regulative accomplishments of gestures, which function as economical release mechanisms for instinctually anchored discharges of movement, devolve upon communication in signal lan- guage; he has to show how an organism responding to stimuli grows into the roles of speaker and addressee, and how communicative acts differ from noncommunicative actions, that is, how processes of reaching understanding *with* one another differ from exerting influence *upon* one another with a view to consequences. This is not merely a question of the emergence of the relation-to-self that is reflected in itself, or of a higher-level subjectivity; these ideas are still tied to the subject-object model Mead is trying to overcome. It is a question of the emergence of a higher-level form of life characterized by a linguistically constituted form of intersubjectivity that makes communicative action possible. There are, however, problems with the way Mead carries out his analysis, for he does not adequately distinguish the stage of symbolically mediated interaction from the stage of linguistically mediated and normatively guided interaction. I shall begin by sketching the way in which Mead develops his theory from the three viewpoints mentioned above.

B.—Mead's basic idea is simple. In gesture-mediated interaction, the gesture of the first organism takes on a meaning for the second organism that responds to it. This response expresses how the latter interprets the gesture of the former. If, now, the first organism "takes the attitude of the other," and in carrying out its gesture already anticipates the response of the second organism, and thus its interpretation, its own gesture takes on *for it* a meaning that is like, but not yet the same as, the meaning it has *for the other.* "When, in any given social act or situation, one individual indicates by a gesture to another individual what this other individual is to do, the first individual is conscious of the meaning of his own gesture—or the meaning of his gesture appears in his own experience—in so far as he takes the attitude of the second individual toward that gesture, and tends to respond to it implicitly in the same way that the second individual responds to it explicitly. Gestures become significant symbols when they implicitly arouse in an individual making them the same responses which they explicitly arouse, or are supposed to arouse, in other individuals, the individuals to whom they are addressed."[13] Mead thinks he can explain the genesis of meanings that are the same for at least two participants by one organism internalizing the relation between its own gesture and the response of the other; the internalization comes about through one organism taking up the attitude in which the other responds to its gesture. If this were the case, it would remain only to specify the conditions under which taking the attitude of the other— that is, the process of internalizing objective meaning structures—can get under way.

On this point Mead vacillates between two lines of thought. The first rests on the thesis of inhibited or delayed reaction.[14] By virtue of a break in the direct connection between stimulus and response, intelligent conduct arises, characterized by "the ability to solve the problems of present behavior in terms of its possible future consequence."[15] The organism pauses and becomes aware of what it is doing when it arouses certain responses to its own gestures in another party. Mead does not notice that this explanation of taking the attitude of the other already draws upon a mode of reflection that will itself have to be explained in terms of an orientation to the meaning that one's own actions have for other participants—unless Mead wants to slide back into the philosophy of consciousness.

For this reason, his other line of thought—Darwinian in inspiration—is more consistent: the pressure to adapt that participants in complex interactions exert upon one another—whether from the need to cooperate or, even more so, in situations of conflict—puts a premium on the speed of reaction. An advantage accrues to participants who learn not only to interpret the gestures of others in light of their own instinctually anchored reactions, but even to understand the meaning of their own gestures in light of the expected responses of others.[16]

Furthermore, Mead stresses that acoustically perceptible gestures are especially suited for this. With vocal gestures it is easier for the organism that makes the sounds to take the attitude of the other, because the sender can hear acoustic signals as well as the receiver.[17] Thus Mead sees in the fact that phonemes, vocal gestures, are the sign-substratum of linguistic communication confirmation of his assumption that taking the attitude of the other is an important mechanism in the emergence of language.[18]

I will not go into these empirical questions here, but will restrict myself to the conceptual question of whether it is possible for Mead to reconstruct the emergence of signal language from the language of gestures by appealing to one participant's taking the attitude of another. Insofar as nothing more is meant by this than that one participant takes in advance the attitude with which the other will respond to its vocal gesture, it is not at all clear how languagelike symbols, vocal gestures with the *same* meanings, are supposed to arise from this. Mead could only explain by this the emergence of a structure with the characteristic that the first organism is stimulated by its own sounds in a way *similar* to the second. If the same gesture arouses in both a disposition to *like* (sufficiently similar) behavior, an observer can notice a concurrence in the way they interpret the stimulus, but this does not yet imply the formation of a meaning that is the same for the participants themselves. "It does not follow from the fact that the one is disposed to do the same as that to which the other is stimulated that there is something identical in relation to which both are behaving."[19] That both concur in the interpretation of the same stimulus is a state of affairs that exists in itself but *not for them.*

In many passages Mead understands the mechanism of "taking the attitude of the other" as "calling out the response in himself he calls out in another." If we understand "response" not in behaviorist terms as the reaction to a stimulus, but in the full dialogical sense as an "answer," we can give "taking the attitude of the other" the more exacting sense of internalizing yes/no responses to statements or imperatives. Tugendhat suggests this interpretation: "The reaction of the hearer which the speaker implicitly anticipates is the former's response with 'yes' or 'no' ... when one deliberates, one speaks with oneself in yes/no responses in the way that one would speak with others with whom one was discussing what should be done."[20] Apart from the fact that this way of reading Mead's text does violence to it,[21] it would rob the mechanism of taking the attitude of the other of the explanatory power that it is meant to have. Internalized dialogue cannot be constitutive for achieving understanding via identical meanings because participation in real or external dialogues already requires the use of linguistic symbols. What is more, if speakers and hearers are to be able to respond to statements and imperatives with a "yes" or a "no," they must be equipped with a propositionally differentiated language. Mead, however, locates languagelike communication one stage deeper, in the modally undifferentiated expressions of signal language.

Nevertheless, we have to look for the solution to the problem in the direction marked out by Tugendhat. Taking the attitude of the other is a mechanism that bears first on the response of the other to one's own gesture, but it gets extended to additional components of interaction. Once the first organism has learned to interpret its own gesture in the same way as the other organism, it cannot avoid making the gesture *in the expectation* that it will have a certain meaning for the second organism. This consciousness means a change in the attitude of the one organism toward the other. The first organism encounters the second as a *social* object that no longer merely reacts adaptively to the first's gesture; with its response it expresses an interpretation of that gesture. The second organism appears to the first as an interpreter of the first's own behavior; this means a change in the attitude of the latter to the former as well. The first organism behaves toward the second as toward an addressee who interprets the coming gesture in a certain way, but this means that the first produces its gesture with communicative intent. If we further assume that this holds for the other organism as well, we have a situation in which the mechanism of internalization can be applied once again: to the attitude in which the two organisms no longer simply express their gestures straightaway as adaptive behavior, but address them to one another. When they can take this "attitude of addressing the other" toward themselves as well, they learn the communication roles of hearer and speaker; each behaves toward the other as an ego that gives an alter ego something to understand.

Mead does not distinguish adequately between two categories of attitudes that one organism takes over from the other: on the one hand, reacting to its own gesture; on the other hand, addressing a gesture to an interpreter. However there are numerous passages that show he has both in mind: "The process of addressing another person is a process of addressing himself as well, and of calling out the response he calls out in the other."[22] The expression "response" changes its meaning unawares when what is presupposed is not merely the simple operation of taking the attitude of the other, but the expanded one—for then the stimulated response does indeed become an "answer." We have a situation "where one does *respond* to that which he *addresses* to another and where that response of his own becomes a part of his conduct, where he not only *hears* himself but *responds* [i.e., answers—J.H.] to himself, *talks* and *replies* to himself as truly as the other person replies to him."[23]

With the first taking of the attitude of the other, participants learn to internalize a segment of the objective meaning structure to such an extent that the interpretations they connect with the same symbol are in agreement, in the sense that each of them implicitly or explicitly responds to it in the same way. With the second taking of the attitude of the other, they learn what it means to employ a gesture with communicative intent and to enter into a reciprocal relation between speaker and hearer. Now the participants can differentiate between the social object in the role of speaker or hearer and the other as an object of external influence, between communicative acts addressed to one's counterpart and consequence-oriented actions that bring something about. And this is in turn the presupposition for a *third* way of taking the attitude of the other, which is constitutive for participants ascribing to the same gesture an *identical* meaning rather than merely undertaking interpretations that are objectively in agreement.

There is an identical meaning when ego knows how alter *should* respond to a significant gesture; it is not sufficient to expect that alter *will* respond in a certain way. According to the first two ways of taking the attitude of the other, ego can only predict—that is, expect in the sense of prognosis—how alter will act if he understands the signal. As we have seen, ego does already distinguish two aspects under which alter can respond to his gesture: (*a*) alter's response is a directed action oriented to consequences; (*b*) at the same time it expresses how alter interprets ego's gesture. Since ego has already interpreted his own gesture by way of anticipating alter's response, there is on his part a prognostic expectation in regard to (*b*), an expectation that can be disappointed. Let us suppose that ego, surprised in this regard by an unexpected response from alter, expresses his disappointment. His reaction reveals disappointment regarding a failed communication and not regarding, say, the undesirable consequences of alter's actual course of action. If we further suppose that this also holds true of alter, we have a situation in which the mechanism of internalization can be applied for a third time—now to the responses through which ego and alter mutually express disappointment at misunderstandings. In adopting toward themselves the critical attitude of others when the interpretation of communicative acts goes wrong, they develop *rules for the use of symbols.* They can now consider in advance whether in a given situation they are using a significant gesture in such a way as to give the other no grounds for a critical response. In this manner, *meaning conventions* and symbols that can be employed with the same meaning take shape.

Mead does not work out this third category of taking the attitude of the other in any precise way; he does touch upon it when explaining the emergence of meaning conventions in connection with the creative accomplishments of the lyric poet: "It is the task not only of the actor but of the artist as well to find the sort of expression that will arouse in others what is going on in himself. The lyric poet has an experience of beauty with an emotional thrill to it, and as an artist using words he is seeking for those words which will answer to his emotional attitude, and will call out in others the attitude he himself has ... What is essential to communication is that the symbol should arouse in oneself what it arouses in the other individual. It must have that sort of universality to any person who finds himself in the same situation."[24]

The creative introduction of new, evaluative, meaning conventions into an existing, already propositionally differentiated, language system is far from the emergence of a signal language. Yet it is instructive on just the point that interests us here. A poet searching for new formulations creates his innovations from the material of existing meaning conventions. He has to make intuitively present to himself the probable responses of competent speakers so that his innovations will not be rejected as mere violations of conventional usage. It remains, nonetheless, that Mead never did become sufficiently clear about the important step of internalizing the other's response to a mistaken use of symbols. This gap can be filled with Wittgenstein's analysis of the concept of a rule.

C.—The system of basic concepts that permits us to demarcate 'behavior' from observable events or states,[25] and that includes concepts such as 'disposition', 'response', 'stimulus', was made fruitful for general semiotics in the wake of Mead and Morris, and later in the framework of language theory. Morris drew upon the basic concepts of behaviorism to develop the basic semiotic concepts of sign, sign interpreter, sign meaning, and the like. He did this in such a way that the structural relation of intention and meaning could be described objectivistically, without anticipating the understanding of rule-governed behavior.[26] In laying the foundations of semiotics in behavior theory, Morris appealed to his teacher, George Herbert Mead; but he missed the real point of Mead's approach.[27] Mead understood the meaning structures built into the functional circuit of animal behavior as a feature of interaction systems that guarantees a prior, instinctually based commonality between participating organisms. The idea is that internalization of this objectively regulated pattern of behavior gradually replaces instinctual regulation with a cultural tradition transmitted via communication in language. Mead has to attach importance to reconstructing the linguistically sublimated commonality of intersubjective relations between participants in symbolically mediated interactions *from the perspective of the participants themselves.* He cannot content himself, as does Morris, with ascribing to individual organisms concurring interpretations of the same stimulus, that is, a *constancy* of meaning as viewed from the perspective of the observer. He has to demand *sameness* of meaning. The use of the same symbols with a constant meaning has to be not only given *as such;* it has to be knowable for the symbol users themselves. And this sameness of meaning can be secured only by the intersubjective validity of a rule that "conventionally" fixes the meaning of a symbol.

In this respect the transition from gesture-mediated to symbolically mediated interaction also means the constitution of rule-governed behavior, of behavior that can be explained in terms of an orientation to meaning conventions. I would like to recall here Wittgenstein's analysis of the concept of a rule, in order, first, to elucidate the connection between identical meanings and intersubjective validity—that is, between following a rule and taking a critical yes/no position on rule violations—and second, to capture more precisely Mead's proposal regarding the logical genesis of meaning conventions. In the concept of a rule, the two moments characteristic of the use of simple symbols are combined: identical meaning and intersubjective validity. The generality that constitutes the meaning of a rule can be represented in any number of exemplary actions. Rules lay down how someone produces something: material objects, or symbolic formations such as numbers, figures, and words (and we shall be dealing only with such formations). Thus one can explain the meaning of a (constructive) rule through examples. This is not done by teaching someone how to generalize inductively from a finite number of cases. Rather, one has grasped the meaning of a rule when one has learned to understand the exhibited formations as examples of something that can be seen *in* them. In certain situations a single example can suffice for this: "It is then the rules which hold true of the example that make it an example."[28] The objects or actions that serve as examples are not examples of a rule in and of themselves, so to speak; only the application of a rule makes the universal in the particular apparent to us.

Not only can the meaning of a rule be elucidated in connection with examples of it; the rule can, inversely, serve to explain the meaning of examples. One understands the meaning of a particular symbolic action—a move in a chess game, say—when one has mastered the rules governing the use of the chess pieces. Understanding a symbolic action is linked with the competence to follow a rule. Wittgenstein stresses that a pupil learning a series of numbers through examples understands the underlying rule when he can go on by himself. The "and so on" with which the teacher breaks off a series of numbers—for example, one exemplifying a geometric progression—stands for the possibility of generating an indefinite number of further instances that satisfy the rule. A pupil who has learned the rule is, by virtue of his generative ability to invent new examples, potentially a teacher himself.

The concept of rule competence refers not only to the ability to produce symbolic expressions with communicative intent and to understand them; nevertheless it is a key to our problem because we can explain what we mean by the *sameness* of meaning in connection with the ability to follow a rule.[29]

The "identity" of a meaning cannot be the same as the identity of an object that can be identified by different observers as the same object under different descriptions. This act of identifying an object about which the speakers are making certain statements already presupposes the understanding of singular terms. Symbolic meanings constitute or establish identity in a way similar to rules that establish unity in the multiplicity of their exemplary embodiments, of their different realizations or fulfillments. It is owing to conventional regulations that meanings count as identical. In this connection, it is important to recall Wittgenstein's remark that the concept of rule is interwoven with the use of the word 'same'. A subject S can follow a rule only by following the *same* rule under changing conditions of application—otherwise he is not following a rule. The meaning of 'rule' analytically entails that what S takes as a basis for his action orientation remains the same. This remaining-the-same is not the result of regularities in S's observable behavior. Not every irregularity indicates a rule violation. One has to know the rule if one wishes to determine whether someone is deviating from it. Irregular behavior can be characterized as a mistake, as the violation of a rule, only in the knowledge of the rule that has been taken as a basis for action. Consequently, the identity of a rule cannot be reduced to empirical regularities. It depends rather on intersubjective validity, that is, on the circumstances that (*a*) subjects who orient their behavior to rules deviate from them, and (*b*) they can criticize their deviant behavior as a violation of rules.

Wittgenstein's famous argument against the possibility of subjects following rules for themselves alone, so to speak, has its place here: "And to *think* one is obeying a rule is not to obey a rule. Hence it is not possible to obey a rule 'privately': otherwise thinking one was obeying a rule would be the same thing as obeying it."[30] The point of this consideration is that S cannot be sure whether he is following a rule at all if there is no situation in which his behavior is exposed to critique by T—a critique that is in principle open to consensus. Wittgenstein wants to show that the identity and the validity of rules are systematically interconnected. To follow a rule means to follow the *same* rule in *every* single case. The identity of the rule in the multiplicity of its realizations does not rest on observable invariants but on the intersubjectivity of its validity. Since rules hold counterfactually, it is possible to criticize rule-governed behavior and to evaluate it as successful or incorrect. Thus two different roles are presupposed for the participants S and T. S has the competence to follow a rule in that he avoids systematic mistakes. T has the competence to judge the rule-governed behavior of S. T's competence to judge presupposes in turn rule competence, for T can undertake the required check only if he can point out to S his mistake and, if necessary, bring about an agreement concerning the correct application of the rule. T then takes over S's role and shows him what he did wrong. Now S takes over the role of a judge and has in turn the possibility of justifying his original behavior by showing T that *he* has applied the rule incorrectly. Without this possibility of reciprocal criticism and mutual instruction leading to agreement, the identity of rules could not be secured. A rule has to possess validity intersubjectively for at least two subjects if one subject is to be able to follow the rule—that is, the *same* rule.

With this analysis of the concept of 'following a rule', Wittgenstein demonstrates that sameness of meaning is based on the ability to follow intersubjectively valid rules together with at least one other subject; both subjects must have a competence for rule-governed behavior as well as for critically judging such behavior. A single isolated subject, who in addition possessed only one of these competences, could no more form the concept of a rule than he could use symbols with identically the same meaning. If we analyze the intersubjective validity of a rule in this way, we come across two different types of expectations: (a) T's expectation that it is S's intention to carry out an action in applying a rule, and (b) S's expectation that T will recognize or admit his action as satisfying a rule.

Let S and T stand for a student and a teacher with the competence to follow rules and to judge rule-governed behavior. Let R be a rule, and m, n, q . . . be symbolic expressions that can count as instances of R in a given context. Let BE stand for the teacher's expectation of behavior, which is based on R in such a way that $q_{(R)}$, for instance, represents a fulfillment of BE. Finally J is a judgment concerning whether a certain action can be identified as $q_{(R)}$, that is, recognized as a fulfillment of BE; JE is the corresponding expectation of this [judgment of] recognition, so that *S*, when he expresses *q* in the expectation *JE*, raises a claim that *T* can recognize through *J*. *BE* and *JE* symbolize the two types of expectations—of behavior and of recognition—that I am concerned to distinguish. We can now state the conditions that must be satisfied if *R* is to be intersubjectively valid for *S* and *T*, that is, to have the same meaning for them; we shall presuppose that *S* and *T* possess the competence both to follow rules and to judge rule-following behavior. Then, to say that *S* is applying a rule *R* in a given context means

1. *S* produces the symbolic expression $q(_R)$,
2. with the intention of fulfilling *T*'s expectation of behavior *BE* in a given context,
3. while expecting in turn $JEq(_R)$ that in the given context *T* will recognize *q* as a fulfillment of his expectation of behavior.
4. *S* thereby presupposes that (1') *T* is in a position to produce $q'(_R)$ himself, if necessary,
5. by fulfilling (2') in a given context BEq';
6. *S* further presupposes that (3') in this case *T* would have the expectation $JEq'(_R)$ that q' will be recognized by *S* as fulfilling his expectation of behavior BEq'.

S has to satisfy these conditions if he wants to produce an expression that can be understood as $q(_R)$. Correspondingly, *T* has to satisfy *S*'s presuppositions (4)–(6), and has either to fulfill or fail to fulfill the expectation $JEq(_R)$, that is, to give either a "yes" or "no" response. Should *T* disappoint *S*'s expectation of recognition, he takes over in turn the role of *S* and has to satisfy conditions analogous to (1)–(3), whereas *S* then has to satisfy the corresponding presuppositions of *T* and either to fulfill or fail to fulfill the expectation $JEq(_R)$, that is, to give either a "yes" or "no" response. Should *T* disappoint *S*'s expectation of recognition, he takes over in turn the role of *S* and has to satisfy conditions analogous to (1)–(3), whereas *S* then has to satisfy the corresponding presuppositions of *T* and either fulfill or fail to fulfill the expectation $JEq(_{R'})$, that is, to say "yes" or "no." The sequence can be repeated until one of the participants fulfills the other's expectation of recognition, the two arrive at a consensus grounded on critical positions, and are certain that *R* is intersubjectively valid for them—which is to say, that it has the same meaning for them.

In our reconstruction we have assumed that *S* and *T* believe they know the meaning of *R*. Student and teacher already know what it means to follow a rule; they want only to be certain whether they know what it means to follow the specific rule *R*. We can distinguish from this the case in which someone is teaching someone else the *concept of a rule*. I shall not go into that here but shall proceed directly to the extreme case of the genesis of rule-consciousness on *both* sides—for this is the case that interests me.

I have recapitulated Wittgenstein's analysis of the concept of following a rule so as to be in a position to apply the results to the employment of communicative symbols. To this point 'q' has stood for any symbolic object produced according to a rule. In what follows I shall restrict myself to the class of symbolic objects we have called significant gestures, or signals, which coordinate the goal-directed behavior of participants in interaction.

To return to our example of a simple symbol: if a member of the tribe, *S*, shouts "Attack!" in an appropriate context, he expects those fellow members *T, U, V* ... within hearing distance to help because they understand his modally undifferentiated expression q_1 as a request for help in a situation in which he sees enemies appear unexpectedly, is alarmed by the sudden danger, and wants to set up a defense against the attackers. We shall assume that such a situation meets the conditions under which q_1 can be used as a request for assistance. A corresponding rule fixes the meaning of q_1 in such a way that addressees can judge whether "Attack!" is used correctly in a given context, or whether the one shouting has allowed himself a joke in making a systematic mistake—trying, for example, to frighten his comrades upon the arrival of a neighbor by letting out a battle cry—or whether perhaps *S* does not know how this symbolic expression is used in the language community, whether he has not yet learned the meaning conventions of the word. This example is in some respects more complex and more difficult to get hold of than that of the teacher who wants to check whether a student has learned the rule for constructing a certain number series. However, this complexity proves helpful when we turn to a genetically interesting case, namely, the situation in which *S* uses the same symbolic expression without being able to rely upon a conventional determination of its meaning, that is, in which 'q_0' does not yet have an identical meaning for the participants. On the other hand, the structure of interaction is assumed already to exhibit all the features that Mead introduces when, on the basis of a *double* taking-the-attitude-of-the-other, he equips participants with the ability to agree in their interpretations of a gesture and to use vocal gestures with communicative intent.

On our presupposition, *S* produces q_0 *not* with the intention of following a rule, and *not* in the expectation that his hearers *T, U, V* ... will recognize "q_0" as an utterance conforming to a rule. *S* can certainly *address* q_0 to his hearers in the expectation that (*a*) they will respond to it with the intention of lending assistance, and that (*b*) in so responding, they will give expression to the fact that they are interpreting "q_0" as a call for help in a situation in which *S* sees enemies appear unexpectedly, is alarmed by the sudden threat, and wants help. However, the expectations that S connects with q_0 have only the prognostic sense that T, U, V ... *will* behave in a certain way; they differ from BEq and JEq_R in that the conventional elements of meaning are still missing. S's expectations can be disappointed by the nonappearance of the *predicted* behavior, but not by incorrect behavior.

Let us recall how Mead reconstructed these nonconventional expectations of behavior: (a) S anticipates the behavior of T (lending assistance) when he has learned to take the attitude in which T responds to S's gesture; (b) S anticipates the interpretation that T expresses with his response to S's gesture (a call for help in a situation in which ...) when he has learned to take the attitude with which T, on his side, addresses gestures to him as something open to interpretation. Now what is the nature of the attitude of T which S has to take over if he is to acquire a rule-consciousness and be in a position henceforth to produce "q" *according to a rule?*

Let us assume that S's utterance "q_0" falls on deaf ears, that T, U, V ... do not rush to his aid. The failure to lend assistance is a circumstance that directly disappoints S's expectation (a). There can be trivial reasons for this: his comrades are not within hearing distance, his shouts reach only young and infirm members of the tribe, the men went to get their weapons and thereby fell into a trap, and so forth. If there are no circumstances of this sort, it is not a question of assistance *failing to appear*, but of T, U, V ... *refusing* to lend assistance. Of course, Mead's construction rules out already understanding this refusal as the voluntary rejection of an imperative; what is happening is still at the presymbolic level of interaction based on a species-specific repertoire of behavior and proceeding according to the schema of stimulus and response. Thus a refusal to lend assistance can be understood only in the sense of the situation that obtains when S's expectation (b) is disappointed: T, U, V ... did not interpret "q_0" in the expected way. Again, there can be trivial reasons for this—but they lie at a different level than in the first case. S may have been mistaken about the relevant circumstances of the situation that form the context in which q_0 is regularly (*regelmässig*) understood as a call for help; for example, he may not have recognized the strangers as members of a friendly tribe, he may have taken their gestures of greeting as gestures of attack, and so on. The fact that T, U, V ... have disappointed S's expectation (b) shows a failure of communication for which S is responsible. Those hearing the call react to this failure dismissively by refusing their assistance. The decisive step consists now in the fact that S *internalizes this dismissive reaction by T, U, V ... as a use of q_0 that is out of place.*

If S learns to adopt toward himself the negative positions that T, U,

V ... take toward him when he goes wrong "semantically" (and if *T, U, V* ... , for their part, deal with similar disappointments in like manner), the members of this tribe learn to address calls to one another in such a way that they *anticipate critical responses* in cases where q_0 is used inappropriately to the context. And on the basis of this anticipation, expectations of a new type can take shape, behavioral expectations (*c*) based on the convention that a vocal gesture is to be understood as "*q*" only if it is uttered under specific contextual conditions. With this we have reached the state of symbolically mediated interaction in which the employment of symbols is fixed by meaning conventions. Participants in interaction produce symbolic expressions guided by rules, that is, with the implicit expectation that they can be recognized by others as expressions conforming to a rule.

Wittgenstein emphasized the internal connection that holds between the competence to follow rules and the ability to respond with a "yes" or "no" to the question whether a symbol has been used correctly, that is, according to the rules. The two competences are equally constitutive for rule-consciousness; they are equiprimordial in regard to logical genesis. If we explicate Mead's thesis in the way I have suggested, it can be understood as a genetic explanation of Wittgenstein's concept of rules— in the first instance, of rules, governing the use of symbols, that determine meanings conventionally and thereby secure the sameness of meaning.[31]

D.—Mead offers only a vague description of the evolutionary point at which symbolically mediated interaction appears; the transition from gesture-mediated to symbolically mediated interaction is said to mark the threshold of anthropogenesis. In all likelihood primitive call systems developed already in the phase of hominization, that is, before the appearance of Homo sapiens. There are also indications that significant gestures, in Mead's sense—that is to say, expressions of a signal language— were used spontaneously in primate societies. When interaction became guided by symbols employed with identical meanings, the status systems typically found in vertebrate societies had to change. I cannot go into such empirical questions here.[32] What is important for our conceptual considerations is that with the concept of symbolically mediated interaction, Mead only explains how mutual understanding through use of identical meanings is possible—he does not explain how a differentiated system of language could replace the older, species-specific innate regulation of behavior.

We have followed Mead to the point where he has outfitted participants in interaction with the ability to exchange signals with communicative intent. Signal language also changes the mechanism for coordinating behavior. Signals can no longer function in the same way as gestures—as release mechanisms that "trigger" dispositionally based behavior schemes in organisms. One can imagine that the communicative employment of signs with identical meanings reacts back upon the organism's structure of drives and modes of behavior. However, with the new medium of communication—to which Mead restricts his reflections on the theory of meaning—not all the elements of the structure of interaction have been brought to the level of language. Signal languages do not yet reach into the impulses and behavioral repertoire of participants. As long as the motivational bases and the repertoire of modes of behavior are not symbolically restructured, the symbolic coordination of action remains embedded in a regulation of behavior that functions prelinguistically and rests finally on residues of instinct.

Up to this point we have looked at one-word expressions as examples of symbolically mediated interaction. This description implicitly presupposes the standpoint of a differentiated system of language. But symbolically mediated interactions require neither a *developed* syntactic organization nor a *complete* conventionalization of signs. Full-fledged language systems, by contrast, are characterized by a grammar that permits complex combinations of symbols; semantic contents have been cut loose from the substratum of natural meanings to such a degree that sounds and signs vary independent of semantic properties. Mead did not himself clearly set the stage of symbolically mediated interaction off from this higher stage of *communication* characterized by grammatical language, but he did distinguish it from a more highly organized stage of *interaction* characterized by role behavior. He goes abruptly from symbolically mediated to normatively regulated action. His interest is in the complementary construction of subjective and social worlds, the genesis of self and society from contexts of interaction that is both linguistically mediated and normatively guided. He traces the development that starts from symbolically mediated interaction only along the path that leads to normatively regulated *action*, and neglects the path that leads to propositionally differentiated *communication* in language.

This problem can be dealt with if we distinguish, more clearly than did Mead himself, between language as a medium for reaching understanding and language as a medium for coordinating action and socializing individuals. As we have seen, Mead viewed the transition from gesture-mediated to symbolically mediated interaction exclusively under the aspect of communication; he shows how symbols arise from gestures and how symbolic—intersubjectively valid—meaning conventions arise from natural meanings. This entails a conceptual restructuring of relations between participants in interaction; they encounter one another as social objects in the communicative roles of speakers and hearers, and they learn to distinguish acts of reaching understanding from actions oriented to consequences. This new structure of sociation is still coincident with the new structure of reaching understanding made possible through symbols. This is not the case with regard to further development, but Mead does not take that into his account. After he has constituted signal language, he restricts himself to aspects of action coordination and of socialization, that is, to the formative process that takes place in the medium of grammatical language and from which both social institutions and the social identity of socialized organisms proceed with equal originality.

> A person is a personality because he belongs to a community, because he takes over the institutions of that community into his own conduct. He takes its language as a medium by which he gets his personality, and then through a process of taking the different roles that all the others furnish he comes to get the attitude of the members of the community. Such, in a certain sense, is the structure of a man's personality. There are certain common responses which each individual has toward certain common things, and insofar as those common responses are awakened in the individual when he is affecting other persons he arouses his own self. The structure, then, on which the self is built is this response which is common to all, for one has to be a member of a community to be a self.[33]

Mead is here viewing socialization from an ontogenetic perspective, as a constitution of the self mediated by grammatical language; he explains this construction of an inner world once again by means of the mechanism of taking the attitude of the other. But now ego takes over not the behavioral reactions of alter but alter's already normed expectations of behavior.

The formation of identity and the emergence of institutions can now be approached along the following lines: the extralinguistic context of behavioral dispositions and schemes is in a certain sense permeated by language, that is to say, symbolically restructured. Previously, only the instruments for reaching understanding were transformed into signals, into signs with conventionally fixed meanings; at the stage of normatively guided action, however, the symbolism penetrates even into motivation and the behavioral repertoire. It creates both subjective orientations and suprasubjective orientation systems, socialized individuals, and social institutions. In this process language functions as a medium not only of reaching understanding and transmitting cultural knowledge, but of socialization and of social integration as well. These latter do, of course, take place in and through acts of reaching understanding; unlike processes of reaching understanding, however, they are not sedimented in cultural knowledge, but in symbolic structures of self and society—in competences and behavior patterns.

Self and *society* are the titles under which Mead treats the complementary construction of the subjective and social worlds. He is right to start from the assumption that these processes can get underway only when the stage of symbolically mediated interaction has been attained and it has become possible to use symbols with identical meanings. However, he does not take into consideration the fact that the instruments for reaching understanding cannot remain unaffected by this process. Signal language develops into *grammatical speech* when the medium of reaching understanding detaches itself simultaneously from the symbolically structured selves of participants in interaction and from a society that has condensed into a normative reality.

To illustrate this I shall take up once again our example of a call for help, but with two modifications: this time those involved have mastered a common, propositionally differentiated language; moreover, there is a difference in status between S and the other members of the tribe T, U, V . . . , a difference that arises from S's social role as the chief of the tribe. When S shouts "Attack!", this symbolic expression "q" counts as a communicative act with which S is moving within the scope of his social role. By uttering q, S actualizes the normative expectation that tribal members within hearing distance will obey his request for assistance by performing certain socially established actions. Together, the role-conforming utterance of the chief and the role-conforming actions of tribal members make up a nexus of interaction regulated by norms. Now that the participants can perform explicit speech acts, they will understand "q" as an elliptical utterance that could be expanded so that the hearers understand it, alternatively

1. as a report that enemies have appeared unexpectedly; or
2. as an expression of the speaker's fear in the face of imminent danger; or
3. as the speaker's command to his hearers that they lend assistance.

Those involved know that

4. S's status authorizes him to make this request, that is, that he is *entitled* to make it, and
5. T, U, V . . . are *obligated* to lend assistance.

The utterance "q" can be understood in the sense of (1) because, as we have assumed, those involved know what it means to make a statement.

Further, "q" can be understood in the sense (3) on the strength of (4) and (5), that is, when those involved know what it is to follow a norm of action. Finally, as we shall see, "q" can be understood in the sense of (2) only if, once again, (4) and (5) obtain—because a subjective world to which a speaker relates with an expressive utterance gets constituted only to the extent that his identity is formed in relation to a world of legitimately regulated interpersonal relations.

If we submit the case of communicative action embedded in a normative context to the same sort of analysis we applied to symbolically mediated interaction—in which participants are not yet in a position to resolve the meaning of the symbols exchanged into its modal components—clear differences emerge not only as regards the degree of complexity but as regards the setting of the problem. We have occupied ourselves with the conversion of communication from gestures over to language, and we have dealt with the question of the conditions for using symbols with identical meanings; now we have to trace the conversion of interaction from a prelinguistic, instinctually bound mode of steering over to a language-dependent, culturally bound mode of steering, so as to throw light on the new medium for coordinating action. This question can in turn be approached from two sides: in terms of communication theory—for in communicative action, reaching understanding in language becomes the mechanism for coordination—or, and this is the way Mead chooses, in terms of social theory and psychology.

From the point of view of communication theory, the problem looks as follows: how can ego bind alter by a speech act in such a way that alter's actions can be linked, without conflict, to ego's so as to constitute a cooperative interrelation? Returning to our example of a call for help, we can see that the actions of $S, T, U \ldots$ are coordinated via the addressees' positive or negative responses, however implicit, to the speaker's utterance. This utterance has an illocutionary *binding effect* only when it permits responses that are not simply arbitrary reactions to expressions of the speaker's will. The term 'arbitrary' is used here to characterize, for example, responses to demands or imperatives that are not normed. In our example, however, the call for help "q" allows for positive or negative responses to criticizable validity claims. Hearers can contest this utterance in three respects: depending on whether it is expanded to a statement of fact, an expression of feeling, or a command, they can call into question its truth, its sincerity, or its legitimacy. As I have explained above, these are precisely the three basic modes available in communicative action. It is easy to see in the case of the assertoric mode that the offer contained in the speech act owes its binding power to the internal relation of the validity claim to reasons; the same holds for the other two modes as well. Because, under the presuppositions of communicative action oriented to reaching understanding, validity claims cannot be rejected or accepted without reason, there is in alter's response to ego a basic *moment of insight,* and this takes the response out of the sphere of mere caprice, sheer conditioning, or adjustment—at least that is how participants themselves see it. So long as in their speech acts they raise claims to the validity of what is being uttered, they are proceeding in the expectation that they can achieve a rationally motivated agreement and can coordinate their plans and actions on this basis—without having to influence the empirical motives of the others through force or the prospect of reward, as is the case with simple impositions and the threat of consequences. With the differentiation of the basic modes, the linguistic medium of reaching understanding gains the power to *bind* the will of responsible actors. Ego can exercise this illocutionary power on alter when both are in a position to orient their actions to validity claims.

With the validity claims of subjective truthfulness and normative rightness, which are *analogous to the truth claim,* the binding/bonding effect of speech acts is expanded beyond the range of convictions with descriptive content that is marked out by utterances admitting of truth. When participants in communication utter or understand experiential sentences or normative sentences, they have to be able to relate to something in a subjective world or in their common social world in a way similar to that in which they relate to something in the objective world with their constative speech acts. Only when these worlds have been constituted, or at least have begun to be differentiated, does language function as a mechanism of coordination. This may have been a reason for Mead's interest in the genesis of those worlds. He analyzes the constitution of a world of perceptible and manipulable objects, on the one hand, and the emergence of norms and identities, on the other. In doing so he focuses on language as a medium for action coordination and for socialization, while leaving it largely unanalyzed as a medium for reaching understanding. Furthermore, he replaces the phylogenetic viewpoint with the ontogenetic; he simplifies the task of reconstructing the transition from symbolically mediated to normatively guided interaction by presupposing that the conditions for socializing interaction between parents and children are satisfied. Below I shall try to sketch out—in very broad strokes and drawing upon Durkheim's theory of social solidarity—how the tasks of phylogenetic reconstruction can be dealt with on this basis. Only then can we describe the starting point for the communicative rationalization attaching to normatively regulated action.

E.—In Mead's work the three prelinguistic roots of the illocutionary power of speech acts are not given the same weight. His chief concern is with the structure of role behavior, which he explains by showing how the child reconstructively assimilates the social world into which it is born and in which it grows up. Complementary to the construction of the social world, there is a demarcation of a subjective world; the child develops its identity by becoming qualified to participate in normatively guided interactions. Thus at the center of Mead's analysis stand the concepts of social role and identity. By contrast, the differentiation of a world of things is treated rather in passing from the perspective of social interaction. Moreover, Mead treats problems of the perception of things more in psychological terms than in the methodological attitude of conceptual reconstruction.

(a) Propositions and the perception of things. As we have seen, all of the many components of a signal are connected with the fact that ego expects a certain behavior from alter. This modally undifferentiated complex of meaning breaks up when the speaker learns how to use propositions. One can see in the structure of simple predicative sentences that the speaker divides up states of affairs into identifiable objects and properties that he can predicate or deny of them. By means of singular terms he can refer to objects that are removed in space and time from the speech situation, so as to report states of affairs independent of context, possibly in ontic and temporal modalities. Ernst Tugendhat has analyzed the means that enable us to use language in a way that is both situation related and situation transcending.[34] The mastery of singular terms frees speech acts from the imperative web, as it were, of interaction regulated extralinguistically. Formal semantics gives precedence to the analysis of two types of sentences that presuppose the concept of an objective world as the totality of the existing states of affairs: assertion sentences and intention sentences. Both types are of such a nature that they could be employed monologically, that is, without communicative intent; both express the linguistic organization of the experience and action of a subject who relates to something in the world in an objectivating attitude. Assertoric sentences express the speaker's belief that something is the case, intentional sentences the speaker's intention to perform an action so that something will be the case. Assertoric sentences can be true or false; because of this relation to truth, we can also say that they express the speaker's knowledge. It is only with respect to the feasibility and efficiency of intended actions that intentional sentences have a relation to truth. Teleological actions can be reconstructed in the form of intentional sentences that the agent could have uttered to himself; with these intentional sentences we give expression to the design of an action.

Mead paid no attention to the propositional *structure of language,* but he did analyze—from the standpoint of the psychology of perception—the cognitive *structure of experience* underlying the formation of propositions. In doing so he followed the familiar pragmatist line that the schemata for the perception of permanent objects are formed through the interplay of eye and hand in our goal-inhibited dealings with physical objects: "The original biological act is one that goes through to its consummation and has within it, at least in lower animal forms, no perceptual world of physical things. It is a world of stimuli and responses, a Minkowski world. Physical things are implemental and find their perceptual reality in manipulatory experiences which lead on to consummations. They involve the stoppage of the act and an appearance of a field that is irrelevant to passage in which alternative completions of the act may take place. The act, then, is antecedent to the appearance of things."[35]

Above all Mead stresses the "social character of perception." He develops a theory of the progressive desocialization of our dealings with physical objects, which are first encountered *as* social objects. He conceives the contact experience of the resistance of manipulable objects according to the model of taking the attitude of an alter ego: "The relationship of the perceptual field and the organism in the perspective is social, i.e., there has been excited in the organism that response of the object which the act of the organism tends to call out. Through taking this attitude of the object, such as that of resistance, the organism is in the way of calling out its own further response to the object and thus becomes an object."[36] Mead develops the basic idea of his theory in an essay entitled "The Self and the Process of Reflection," as follows:

The child gets his solutions of what from our standpoint are entirely physical problems, such as those of transportation movement, movement of things, and the like, through his social reaction to those about him. This is not simply because he is dependent, and must look to those about him for assistance during the early period of infancy, but, more important still, because his primitive process of reflection is one of mediation through vocal gestures of a cooperative social process. The human individual thinks first of all entirely in social terms. This means, as I have emphasized above, not that nature and natural objects are personalized, but that the child's reactions to nature and its objects are social reactions and that his responses imply that the actions of natural objects are social reactions. In other words, insofar as the young child acts reflectively toward his physical environment, he acts as if it were helping or hindering him, and his responses are accompanied with friendliness or anger. It is an attitude of which there are more than vestiges in our sophisticated experience. It is perhaps most evident in the irritations against the total depravity of inanimate things, in our affection for familiar objects of constant employment, and in the aesthetic attitude toward nature which is the source of all nature poetry.[37]

Mead himself did not link this theoretical perspective to experimental research.[38] But it has proved its worth in the efforts to connect Piaget's studies on the development of intelligence in young children with ideas from socialization theory. The *early* Piaget, inspired by Baldwin and Durkheim, tended in this direction anyway.[39]

We can assume that in connection with the constitution of a "perceptual world of physical objects," propositional elements are first of all differentiated out of the holistic utterances of context-bound signal languages. Drawing upon language-analytic reflections on the communicative employment of propositions, we can make clear how this interferes with the signal-language mechanism of coordinating action and shakes the foundations of symbolically mediated interaction. To the extent that participants in interaction have linguistically at their disposal an objective world to which they relate with propositions or in which they can intervene in a goal-directed manner, their action can no longer be coordinated via signals. Only so long as the descriptive elements of meaning are fused with the expressive and imperative elements do signals have the power to steer behavior. It is true that the functional circuits of animal behavior break down at the stage of symbolically mediated interaction; on the other hand, signals remain tied to dispositions and schemes of behavior. It is because they are embedded in this way that signals have a binding power that is a functional equivalent for the triggering effects of gestures. At the stage of propositionally differentiated communication—of *linguistic* communication in the narrower sense—this kind of motivation gets lost.

A speaker who utters a statement p with a communicative intent, raises the claim that the statement p is true; a hearer can respond to this with a "yes" or a "no." Thus with the assertoric mode of language use, communicative acts gain the power to coordinate actions via rationally motivated agreement. With this we have an alternative to action coordination that relies ultimately on instinctual regulation. However, the binding effect of truth claims extends only as far as participants take their action orientations from convictions with descriptive content. It does not cover the goals by which they are guided in forming action intentions.

Intention sentences are not directly tailored to communicative ends. In general, the communicative intention that competent speakers connect with an intention sentence consists in announcing their own actions, or the positive and negative consequences these might have for the addressees. An *announcement* is a speaker's declaration of intention from which hearers can draw conclusions. It gives the hearer reason to expect the announced intervention in the world and to predict the changes that the success of the action would bring. With announcements, the speaker is not looking to achieve a consensus but to exert influence on the action situation. The same holds for *imperatives*. At least in those limiting cases when they are not embedded in a normative context, imperatives likewise express only the intentions of a speaker oriented to consequences.

With announcements and imperatives, speakers want to influence the action intentions of addressees without making themselves dependent on the achievement of consensus. Imperatives express a will which the addressees can either submit to or resist. For this reason, the "yes" or "no" with which hearers respond to imperatives cannot ground the behaviorally effective intersubjective validity of symbolic utterances. They are expressions of will, or options, that require no further grounding. In that case, yes/no responses can be replaced by expressions of intention. This leads Tugendhat to the thesis that sentences of intention are "those sentences in the first person that correspond to imperatives in the second person. If someone tells me to 'go home after the lecture,' I can answer either by yes or by the corresponding sentence of intention. They are equivalent. Thus, a sentence of intention is the affirmative answer to an imperative. But instead of answering the imperative by yes or executing the action, one can answer by saying no."[40] This internal relation between imperatives and statements of intention shows that the claim connected with imperatives is not a validity claim, a claim that could be criticized and defended with reason; it is a power claim.

Neither imperatives nor announcements appear with claims that aim at rationally motivated consensus and point to criticism or grounding.[41] They do not have a binding effect but need, if they are to have any effect, to be externally connected with the hearer's empirical motives. Of themselves they cannot guarantee that alter's actions will link up with those of ego. They attest to the contingencies that enter into linguistically mediated interaction with the choice of agents acting teleologically; these contingencies cannot be absorbed by the binding force of language used in the assertoric mode alone, that is to say, by the binding force of the validity claim to propositional truth alone.[42]

The regulation of action via norms can thus be viewed as the solution to a problem that arises when the coordination of action via signal language no longer functions.

(b) Norms and role behavior. Mead analyzes the construction of a common social world from the perspective of a growing child, *A*, who understands the announcements and imperatives of a reference person, *B*, but who has yet to acquire the competence for role behavior that *B* already possesses. Let us recall the two stages in the development of interaction that Mead illustrates with the role play of children (play) and the competitive games of youth (game): "Children get together to 'play

Indian.' This means that the child has a certain set of stimuli which call out in itself the responses they would call out in others, and which answer to an Indian. In the play period the child utilizes his own responses to the stimuli which he makes use of in building a self. The response which he has a tendency to make to the stimuli organizes them. He plays that he is, for instance, offering himself something, and he buys it; he gives a letter to himself and takes it away; he addresses himself as a parent, as a teacher; he arrests himself as a policeman. He has a set of stimuli which call out in himself the sort of responses they call out in others. He takes this group of responses and organizes them into a certain whole. Such is the simplest form of being another to oneself."[43] The competitive game represents a more highly organized stage of role playing: "The fundamental difference between the game and play is that in the former the child must have the attitude of all the others involved in that game. The attitudes of the other players which the participant assumes organize into a sort of unit, and it is that organization which controls the response of the individual. The illustration used was of a person playing baseball. Each one of his own acts is determined by his assumption of the action of the others who are playing the game. What he does is controlled by his being everyone else on that team, at least insofar as those attitudes affect his own particular response. We get then an 'other' which is an organization of the attitudes of those involved in the same process."[44] I shall try now to reconstruct the conceptual genesis of role behavior along the lines sketched out by Mead.[45]

The mechanism to which Mead appeals in explaining the acquisition of role competence is, once again, taking the attitude of the other toward oneself. This time the mechanism fastens not upon behavioral reactions, nor upon behavioral expectations, but upon the positive or negative sanctions that *B* announces when he utters an imperative to *A*. The construction presupposes a socializing interaction that is characterized by differences in competence and authority and in which the participants typically satisfy the following conditions.

The reference person *B* has mastered a propositionally differentiated language and is fulfilling the social role of an educator outfitted with parental authority. *B* understands this role in the sense of a norm that *entitles* the members of the social group to expect certain actions from one another in certain situations, and that *obligates* members to meet the legitimate expectations of others. On the other hand, the child *A* is able to take part only in symbolically mediated interactions; it has learned to understand imperatives and to express desires. It can reciprocally connect the perspectives of ego and alter who stand to one another in the communicative relation of speaker and hearer. It distinguishes the perspective from which participants each "see" their com-

common situation—not only the different points of view behind their perceptions but also those behind their differing intentions, desires, and feelings. At first the growing child takes one perspective after the other; later he can also coordinate them. Obeying imperatives requires not only sociocognitive accomplishments but preparedness for action as well; we are dealing here with the symbolic structuring of dispositions to behavior. *B* connects the imperative "*q*" with the announcement of sanctions. Because *A* experiences positive sanctions when he carries out the desired action $h_{(q)}$ and negative sanctions when he does not, he grasps the connection between obeying an imperative and satisfying a corresponding interest. In obeying the imperative "*q*", *A* performs the action $h_{(q)}$, and he knows that in doing so he is at the same time avoiding the sanction threatened for disobedience and satisfying an interest of *B*. These complex accomplishments are possible only if, in knowing and acting, *A* can relate to an at least incipiently objectivated world of perceptible and manipulable objects.

It is now our task to trace the construction of the child's social world in *one* important dimension, namely, the step-by-step, sociocognitive, and moral assimilation of the objectively given structure of roles through which interpersonal relations are legitimately regulated. An institutional reality not dependent on the individual actor arises from the fact that *A*, on the way to symbolically restructuring his action orientations and dispositions, forms an identity as a member of a social group. The *first step* along this path is marked by conceptions and dispositions for particularistic expectations that are "clustered," that is to say, conditionally connected and complementarily related to one another. In a *second step*, these expectations are generalized and gain normative validity. These two steps correspond approximately to the stages Mead characterized as "play" and "game." Their reconstruction becomes clearer if we separate in each case sociocognitive development from moral development. In reconstructing the moral aspect we are also concerned only with conceptual structures; in the present context it is only the *logic* of the internalization of sanctions that interests us and not the psychodynamics of the emergence of normative validity.

Play. As *B*'s behavior toward *A* is determined by the social role of the nurturing parent, *A* learns to follow imperatives not only in connection with positive and negative sanctions but in a context of caring and of the satisfaction of his own needs. To be sure, *A* does not yet recognize the attention he receives from *B* as parental behavior regulated by norms. *A* can understand those actions by *B* only at the level at which he himself satisfies *B*'s interests by doing what *B* asks. To begin with, following imperatives means for *A* satisfying interests. In the simplest case, *B*'s expectation that *A* will obey the imperative "*q*" and *A*'s reciprocal expectation that his imperative "*r*" will be followed by *B* are connected in pairs. In the situation we have presupposed, for *B* this connection arises from norms that regulate the parent-child relationship, whereas *A* experiences the normative connection of complementary expectations in the context of parental care simply as an empirical regularity. If *A* knows that by following *B*'s imperatives he is also satisfying *B*'s interests, he can interpret the situation accordingly: in issuing and following imperatives, *B* and *A* are encouraging one another to satisfy each other's interests.

The complementarity of actions that results in the reciprocal satisfaction of interests, if it comes about by way of fulfilling reciprocal expectations, forms a cognitive scheme that *A* can learn, in the situation described above, through taking the attitude of the other toward himself. In uttering "*r*," *A* has to anticipate that *B* will fulfill this imperative in the expectation that *A* will in turn follow the imperative "*q*" uttered by *B*. Insofar as *A* takes up these attitudes of expectation toward himself, he acquires the concept of a pattern of behavior that conditionally connects the complementarily interlaced expectations of *A* and *B*.

If one considers the sociocognitive side of this process in isolation, one could get the mistaken impression that the child has a certain space for negotiation in pursuing his interests, whereas in fact it is only in this process that he learns to interpret his needs and to articulate his desires. Expectations come to the child as something external, behind which there stands the authority of the reference person. Part of the situation is the unequal disposition over means of sanction. At *this* level a further taking of the attitude of the other comes into play, and it is upon this that Mead focuses in analyzing the development of the self.

B no longer connects his announcement of sanctions only with individual imperatives but with the generalized expectation that *A* will exhibit a willingness to obey under the condition of the care he receives from *B*. *A* anticipates this threat and takes up *B*'s attitude toward himself when following *B*'s imperative "*q*." This is the basis for the internalization of roles—to begin with, of particularistic expectations that are connected in pairs. Freud and Mead realized that these patterns of behavior become detached from the context-bound intentions and speech acts of individual persons, and take on the external shape of social norms insofar as the sanctions connected with them are internalized through taking the attitude of the other, that is to say, to the degree that they are taken into the personality and thereby rendered independent of the sanctioning power of concrete reference persons.

A pattern of behavior that *A* internalizes in this sense takes on the authority of a suprapersonal will [*Willkür*]. Under this condition the pattern can be carried over to similar action situations, that is, it can be spatially and temporally generalized. Thus *A* learns to understand interactions in which he and *B* take turns issuing and following imperatives as the fulfillment of an expectation. In the process the imperativistic sense of 'expectation' changes in a peculiar way: *A* and *B* subordinate their particular wills to a combined choice that is, so to speak, delegated to the spatially and temporally generalized expectation of behavior. *A* now understands the higher-level imperative of a pattern of behavior, which both *A* and *B* lay claim to in uttering "*q*" and "*r.*"

Mead observed the process of developing a suprapersonal will [*Wille*], which is characteristic of the behavior pattern, in connection with the role playing of a child who fictively changes sides, taking now the part of the seller, now that of the buyer, playing now the policeman, now the criminal. To be sure, this is not yet a matter of social roles in the strict sense, but of concrete patterns of behavior. As long as the behavior patterns the child is practicing have not yet been generalized socially to cover all members of a group, they are valid only for situations in which *A* and *B* face one another. *A* can form the concept of a socially generalized pattern of behavior—that is, of a norm that permits everyone, in principle, to take the places of *A* and *B*—only if he once again takes the attitude of the other, but now of the "generalized other."

Game. To this point we have assumed that ego and alter, when interacting with one another, take up exactly two communicative roles, namely, those of speaker and hearer. Correspondingly, there are two coordinated perspectives of participation; the intermeshing of the interchangeable perspectives of speaker and hearer describes a cognitive structure that underlies their understanding of action situations. We have further assumed that the constitution of a world of objects has at least begun; the child must have at least a nascent ability to adopt an objectivating attitude toward perceptible and manipulable objects if it is to act intentionally and to understand imperative requests and statements of intention. To this there corresponds the perspective of an observer, which is only now introduced into the domain of interaction. As soon as this condition, which is required for the transition from "play" to "game," is fulfilled, ego can split up the communicative role of alter into the communicative roles of an *alter ego,* a participating counterpart, and a *neuter,* a member of the group present as an onlooker. With this, the communicative roles of speaker and hearer are relativized against the position of an uninvolved *third person*—they become the roles of a *first person* who is speaking, and a *second person* who is spoken to and responds. Thus there arises for interactions that take place among members of the same social group the system—expressed by the personal pronouns—of an I's possible relations to a thou or you, and to a him or her or them; conversely, others can relate to me in the role of second or third persons. With this differentiation, a new category of taking the attitude of the other becomes possible, both from the sociocognitive and from the moral points of view.

We are assuming that *A* has mastered behavior patterns that are not yet socially generalized and has now also acquired the sociocognitive ability to switch from the performative attitude (of a first person in relation to *B* as a second person) to the neutral attitude of a third person, also belonging to the group, and to transform the corresponding action perspectives (of *A* toward *B*, *B* toward *A*, *A* toward neuter (*N*), and *N* toward *A* and *B*) into one another. *A* can now *objectify* the reciprocal interconnection of participant perspectives from the perspective of an observer, that is to say, he can adopt an objectivating attitude toward his interaction with *B* and distinguish the system of intermeshed perspectives between himself and *B* from the particular situation in which he and *B* find themselves. *A* understands that anyone who might adopt ego's and alter's perspectives would have to take over the same system of perspectives. Under these conditions the concept of a concrete pattern of behavior can be generalized into the concept of a norm or action.

Up to now, what stood behind the higher-level imperative of the behavior pattern to which *A* and *B* laid claim when they uttered "*q*" or "*r*" was the combined, yet still particular, will and interests of *A* and *B*. If in his interaction with *B*, *A* now adopts the attitude that neuter takes toward *A* and *B* as an uninvolved member of their social group, he becomes aware that the positions occupied by *A* and *B* are interchangeable.

A realizes that what had appeared to him as a concrete behavior pattern, tailored to this child and to these parents, was for *B* always a norm that regulated relations between parents and children generally. With this taking of the attitude of the other, *A* forms the concept of a pattern of behavior that is socially generalized to *every* member of the group, and in which the places are not reserved for ego and alter but can in principle be taken by any member of their social group. This social generalization of a behavior pattern also affects the imperativistic sense connected with it. From now on *A* understands interactions in which *A, B, C, D* ... utter or obey the imperatives '*q*' or '*r*' as fulfilling the *collective will* [*Wille*] of the group, to which *A* and *B* now subordinate their combined will [*Willkür*].

It is important now to recall that at this stage of conceptualization *A* does not yet understand social roles or norms in the *same* sense as *B*. While the imperatives '*q*' and '*r*' no longer count directly as the de facto expression of a speaker's will, the norm of action, so far as *A* understands it to this point, expresses only the generalized choice of the others—a group-specifically generalized imperative—and *every imperative rests in the end on choice*. *A* knows only that the action consequences normed in this way have become socially expectable within the group; anyone who belongs to the group of parents or to the group of children, and who utters "*q*" or "*r*" to addressees in the other group in accord with the relevant norm in the given situation, can expect (in the sense of a prognosis) that this imperative will generally be followed. If *A* violates a socially generalized behavior pattern by not obeying the imperative "*q*" uttered by *B*, he not only harms *B*'s interests but the interests of the group as a whole as embodied in the norm. In this case *A* has to expect group sanctions that, while they may be applied by *B* in certain circumstances, originate in the authority of the group.

So far as we have reconstructed the concept of a norm of action to this point, it refers to the collective regulation of the choices of participants in interaction who are coordinating their actions via sanctioned imperatives and the reciprocal satisfaction of interests. So long as we take into consideration only the sociocognitive side of norming expectations, we arrive at the models of mutual conditioning through probabilities of success familiar to us from empiricist ethics. *A* knows what *B, C, D* . . . have in view when they base their imperatives on the higher-level imperative of a norm of action. He has, however, not yet understood the central element in the meaning of the concept of a norm of action—the obligatory character of valid norms. Only with the concept of normative validity could he overcome entirely the asymmetries built into socializing interaction.

Generalized other. Mead connects with the concept of a social role the sense of a norm that simultaneously *entitles* group members to expect certain actions from one another in certain situations and *obligates* them to fulfill the legitimate expectations of others.

If we assert our rights, we are calling for a definite response just because they are rights that are universal—a response which everyone should, and perhaps, will give. Now that response is present in our own nature; in some degree we are ready to take that same attitude toward somebody else if he makes the appeal. When we call out that response in others, we can take the attitude of the other and then adjust our own conduct to it. There are, then, whole series of such common responses in the community in which we live, and such responses are what we term "institutions". The institution represents a common response on the part of all members of the community to a particular situation . . . One appeals to the policeman for assistance, one expects the state's attorney to act, expects the court and its various functionaries to carry out the process of the trial of the criminal. One does take the attitude of all these different officials as involved in the very maintainance of property; all of them as an organized process are in some sense found in our own natures. When we arouse such attitudes, we are taking the attitude of what I have termed a "generalized other".[46]

In this passage Mead is referring to socialized adults who already know what it means for a norm to be valid; he tries to explicate this concept through the idea that the actor who asserts his rights speaks from the lofty position of the "generalized other." At the same time, he stresses that this position becomes a social reality only to the extent that the members of a social group internalize roles and norms. The authority with which the generalized other is outfitted is that of a *general* group *will*; it is not the same as the force of the generalized *will of all* individuals, which expresses itself in the sanctions the group applies to deviations. However, Mead, again like Freud, thinks that the authority of *obligatory* norms comes to be by way of the internalization of sanctions that are de facto threatened and carried out. Up to this point we have viewed the acquisition of socially generalized patterns of behavior only under its cognitive aspects. In fact, however, the growing child learns these patterns through anticipating the sanctions that come from violating a generalized imperative, thereby internalizing the power of the social group that stands behind them. The mechanism of taking the attitude of the other again operates here, on the moral level; this time, however, it fixes on the sanctioning power of the group as a norm-giving entity, and not on that of individual persons, or even of all of them. To the degree that *A* anchors the power of institutions, which first confront him as a fact, in the very structures of the self, in a system of internal, that is, moral, behavioral controls, generalized behavior patterns acquire for him the authority of a "thou shalt!"—no longer in an imperativist sense—and thus that kind of normative validity in virtue of which norms possess binding force.

We have seen how the authority that is first held by the individual reference person and then passed over to the combined wills of *A* and *B*, is built up to the generalized choice of everyone else by way of the social generalization of behavior patterns. This concept makes possible the idea of sanctions behind which there stands the collective will of a social group. This will [*Wille*] remains, to be sure, a *Willkür*, however generalized it might be. The authority of the group consists simply in the fact that it can threaten to carry out sanctions in case interests are violated. This imperativistic authority is transformed into normative authority through internalization. It is only then that there arises a "generalized other" that grounds the validity of norms.

The authority of the "generalized other" differs from authority based only on disposition over means of sanction, in that it rests on assent.

When *A* regards the group sanctions *as his own,* as sanctions he directs at himself, he has to presuppose his assent to the norm whose violation he punishes in this way. Unlike socially generalized imperatives, institutions claim a validity that rests on intersubjective recognition, on the consent of those affected by it: "Over against the protection of our lives or property, we assume the attitude of assent of all members in the community. We take the role of what may be called 'the generalized other.'"[47] Mead reconstructs the norm-conforming attitude that a speaker adopts in carrying out a regulative speech act as taking the attitude of the generalized other; with his norm-conforming attitude, *A* expresses the standpoint of a normative consensus among members of the group.

At first, the affirmative responses that carry this consensus retain an ambiguous status. On the one hand, they *no longer* simply mean the "yes" with which a compliant hearer responds to a merely imposed imperative "*q.*" As we have seen, that "yes" is equivalent to an intentional sentence referring to the required action $h(_q)$ and thus is merely the expression of a normatively unbound *Willkür.* On the other hand, these affirmative responses are *not yet* the sort of "yes" to a criticizable validity claim. Otherwise we would have to assume that the de facto validity of norms of action rests everywhere, and from the very beginning, on the rationally motivated agreement of everyone involved; this conflicts with the repressive character evinced in the fact that norms, demanding obedience, take effect in the form of social control. And yet the social control exercised via norms that are valid for specific groups is not based on repression *alone:* "Social control depends upon the degree to which the individuals in society are able to assume the attitudes of the others who are involved with them in common endeavor ... All of the institutions serve to control individuals who find in them the organization of their own social responses."[48] This sentence takes on a precise meaning if we understand "response" as an answer to the question of whether an institution or a norm is worthy of being recognized in the interest of all involved.

For the growing child this question has already been given an affirmative answer before it can pose itself to him *as* a question. The de facto power of a generalized imperative still attaches to the moment of generality in the generalized other, for the concept is constructed by way of internalizing a concrete group's power to sanction. And yet, that same moment of generality *also* already contains the claim—aiming at insight—that a norm deserves to be valid only insofar as, in connection with some matter requiring regulation, it takes into account the interests of everyone involved, and only insofar as it embodies the will that all could form in common, each in his own interest, as the will of the generalized other. This two-sidedness is characteristic of the traditional understanding of norms. Only when the power of tradition is broken to the extent that the legitimacy of existing orders can be viewed in the light of hypothetical alternatives do the members of a group dependent on cooperation—that is, on common efforts to attain collective goals— ask themselves whether the norms in question regulate the choices of members in such a way that every one of them can see his interests protected. At any rate, with the conceptualization of normatively regulated action and the constitution of a world of legitimately regulated interpersonal relations, a perspective opens up that Mead did not pursue ontogenetically but dealt with in the context of social evolution. The posttraditional understanding of norms is interwoven with a concept of communicative rationality that can become actual only to the degree that structures of the lifeworld are differentiated and members develop divergent individual interests. Before taking up this theme, we should get clear about how the construction of a subjective world complementary to that of the social world comes about.

(c) Identity and need. We have considered the process of socialization from the perspective of the growing child, to begin with only in regard to the construction of the social world that the socialized youth finally encounters as the normative reality of the generalized other. In learning how to follow norms and to take on more and more roles, he acquires the generalized ability to take part in normatively regulated interactions. After acquiring this interactive competence, the youth can also behave toward institutions in an objectivating attitude, as if they were nonnormative elements of given action situations. However, *A* could not comprehend the meaning of the word 'institution', if he had not taken over from his reference persons that attitude in which alone norms can be followed or violated. The growing child can relate to something in the social world with a communicative act only when he knows how to adopt a norm-conforming attitude and to orient his action to normative validity claims.

This know-how is of such a nature that it makes possible a reorganization of one's own behavioral dispositions: "The self . . . is essentially a social structure, and arises in social experiences."[49] The transition from symbolically mediated to normatively regulated interaction means not only a transfer to a modally differentiated way of reaching understanding, and not only the construction of a social world; it also means that motives for action are symbolically restructured. From the standpoint of socialization, this side of the process of sociation presents itself as the development of an identity. Mead deals with identity development under the rubric of a relation between the "me" and the "I." The expression 'me' designates the perspective from which the child builds up a system of internal behavior controls by adopting the expectations of the generalized other toward himself. By way of an internalization of social roles there gradually takes shape an integrated superego structure which enables the actor to orient himself to normative validity claims. At the same time as this superego—the "me"—there takes shape an "I," a subjective world of experiences to which one has privileged access: "The 'I' reacts to the self which arises through the taking of the attitudes of others. Through taking those attitudes we have introduced the 'me' and we react to it as an 'I.'"[50]

While the concept of the 'me' is fixed, Mead vacillates in his use of the expression 'I'. He presents it as something that sets itself off from the representatives of social norms in the self, and that raises the self "beyond the institutionalized individual." On the one hand, Mead understands by this the spontaneity of sudden ideas, of desires, of feelings and moods—that is to say, a reaction potential that goes beyond the orientations anchored in the superego and forms the region of the subjective vis-à-vis the objective world: "The 'me' does call for a certain sort of an 'I' insofar as we meet the obligations that are given in conduct itself, but the 'I' is always something different from what the situation calls for ... The 'I' both calls out the 'me' and responds to it."[51] On the other hand, Mead understands the "I" as the generalized capacity to find creative solutions to situations in which something like the self-realization of the person is at stake: "The possibilities in our nature, those sorts of energy which William James took so much pleasure in indicating, are possibilities of the self that lie beyond our own immediate presentation. We do not know just what they are. They are in a certain sense the most fascinating concepts that we can contemplate, so far as we can get hold of them. We get a great deal of our enjoyment of romance, of moving pictures, of art, in setting free, at least in imagination, capacities which belong to ourselves, or which we want to belong to ourselves ... It is there that novelty arises and it is there that our most important values are located. It is the realization in some sense of the self that we are continually seeking."[52] The "I" is at once the motor force and the placeholder of an individuation that can be attained only through socialization. I shall come back to the "I" as connected with self-realization.

At the moment we are interested in the "I" only as a subjectivity that sets itself off from the foil of a superego modeled after social roles: "When an individual feels himself hedged in he recognizes the necessity of getting a situation in which there shall be an opportunity for him to make his addition to the undertaking, and not simply to the conventionalized 'me.'"[53] Mead is referring to the subjective world of experiences to which an actor has privileged access and which he discloses in expressive utterances before the eyes of a public, as is evident in the following passage: "The situation in which one can let himself go, in which the very structure of the 'me' opens the door for the 'I', is favorable to self expression. I have referred to the situation in which a person can sit down with a friend and say just what he is thinking about someone else. There is a satisfaction in letting oneself go in this way. The sort of thing that under other circumstances you would not say and would not even let yourself think is now naturally uttered."[54]

Looked at from an ontogenetic standpoint, in the same measure as the child cognitively assimilates the social world of legitimately regulated interpersonal relations, builds up a corresponding system of controls, and learns to orient his action to normative validity claims, he draws an increasingly clear boundary between an *external world,* which has consolidated into an institutional reality, and an *inner world* of spontaneous experiences, which come out not through norm-conforming actions but only through communicative self-presentation.

2. The Authority of the Sacred and the Normative Background of Communicative Action

In the preceding section I gave a systematic presentation of Mead's attempt to explain, by way of reconstructing, symbolically mediated interaction and action in social roles. The first of these two stages of interaction is characterized by the emergence of a new medium of communication, the second by the norming of behavioral expectations. In the first phase, communication switches over from expressive gestures that stimulate behavior to the use of symbols; in the second, the transition to normatively regulated action means a shift to a symbolic basis for steering behavior: it is no longer only the means of communication that are symbolically restructured, but behavioral schemes and dispositions as well. As I have emphasized, Mead reconstructs this developmental step only from the ontogenetic perspective of the growing child. He has to presuppose at the level of the parents' socializing interaction the competences for speech and interaction that the child is to acquire. This methodological restriction is legitimate so long as he is dealing with the genesis of the self. Mead was fully aware, however, that in going from the individual to society,[1] he would have to take up once again the phylogenetic viewpoint that he had already adopted in explaining symbolically mediated interaction.[2] The genetic primacy of society in relation to socialized individuals follows from the basic assumptions of the theory of socialization developed by Mead, as discussed in the preceding section: "if the individual reaches his self only through communication with others, only through the elaboration of social processes by means of significant communication, then the self could not antidate the social organism. The latter would have to be there first."[3] Oddly enough, however, Mead makes no effort to explain how this normatively integrated "social organism" could have developed out of the sociative forms of symbolically mediated interaction.

He compares human society with insect and mammal societies, but these diffused anthropological considerations always lead only to a single result, namely, that signal language, intercourse via symbols employed with the same meaning, makes possible a new level of sociation: "The principle which I have suggested as basic to human social organization is that of communication involving participation in the other ... a type of communication distinguished from that which takes place among other forms which do not have this principle in their societies."[4] Even if this assumption were correct, even if primitive systems of calls did open up the path of development to Homo sapiens, it does not yet explain the emergence of institutions.

Mead also has recourse here to cognitive development, through which an objective world of perceptible and manipulable objects emerges from the functional circuit of instrumental action: "There is, as we have seen, another very important phase in the development of the human animal which is perhaps quite as essential as speech for the development of man's peculiar intelligence, and that is the use of the hand for the isolation of physical things."[5] The world of physical objects is constituted as a complex of "involvements," as Heidegger puts it in *Being and Time*.[6] Mead writes: "I have emphasized the importance of the hand and the building-up of this environment. The acts of the living form are those which lead up to consummations such as that of eating food. The hand comes in between the beginning and the end of this process. We get hold of the food, we handle it, and so far as our statement of the environment is concerned, we can say that we present it to ourselves in terms of the manipulated object. The fruit that we can have is a thing that we can handle. It may be fruit that we can eat or a representation of it in wax. The object, however, is a physical thing. The world of physical things we have about us is not simply the goal of our movement but a world which permits the consummation of the act."[7] Unlike Heidegger, who adopts this pragmatist motif for an analysis of being-in-the-world that is insensitive to the phenomena of sociation, Mead knows as well as Piaget that instrumental actions are set within the cooperative interrelations of group members and presuppose regulated interactions. The functional circuit of instrumental action cannot be analyzed independent of structures of cooperation, and cooperation requires social control regulating group activities.[8]

Now, however, Mead explains this social control, which serves "to integrate the individual and his action with reference to the organized social process of experience and behavior in which he is implicated,"[9] by reference to the moral authority of the generalized other: "The very organization of the self-conscious community is dependent upon individuals taking the attitude of the other individuals. The development of this process, as I have indicated, is dependent upon getting the attitude of the group as distinct from that of a separate individual—getting what I have termed the 'generalized other.'"[10] Oddly, Mead uses the generalized other, the phylogenesis of which is to be explained, only in the role of explanans. Even here, where it is a question of the phylogenesis of normative consensus, his clarification of the concept refers only to examples familiar from the dimension of ontogenesis, above all the example of the ball game.[11] Mead is moving in a circle: in order to explain the phylogenetic transition from symbolically mediated to normatively guided interactions, he resorts to something that figured in ontogenesis, even though the ontogenesis of this "generalized other" cannot itself be explained without recourse to phylogenesis. My criticism measures Mead against the task he set himself: to distinguish three stages of interaction, in order to elucidate their structure from within, that is, from the perspective of a participant, and to place them in a hierarchy, such that the emergence of any higher stage can be understood as a learning process that can be recapitulated from the inside. As we have seen, to render comprehensible the emergence of one complex structure from another, Mead resorts to a single "mechanism," namely, ego's taking the attitude of alter. He explains the significance of the norm-conforming attitude that an actor adopts when he takes his bearings from a social role in terms of the notion of a generalized other; this generalized other is distinguished by the authority of a general, or suprapersonal, will that has cast off the character of mere *Willkür*: the regard it meets with is not exacted by external sanctions. The authority of the generalized other functions in such a way that offenses can be sanctioned because the norms violated are valid. Thus norms do not claim validity because they are connected with sanctions; if they did, they could not *obligate* the actors to obey but only force them into submissiveness. And open repression is incompatible with the *meaning* of the validity of norms—if not with their de facto recognition. Thus Mead attributes normative validity directly to the sanction-free, that is, moral, authority of the generalized other. The latter is supposed to have arisen by way of the internalization of group sanctions. However, this explanation can hold only for ontogenesis, for groups must have first been constituted as units capable of acting before sanctions could be imposed in their name. Participants in symbolically mediated interaction can transform themselves, so to speak, from exemplars of an animal species with an inborn, species-specific environment into members of a collective with a lifeworld only to the degree that a generalized other—we might also say: a collective consciousness or a group identity—has taken shape. If one follows Mead up to this point, two questions arise.

First, it would have been reasonable to seek out the phenomena through which the structure of group identities could be clarified—that is to say, in the language of Durkheim, the expressions of collective consciousness, above all of religious consciousness. Whenever Mead treats such phenonema, he analyzes them by drawing on concepts from the development of personality, that is, he analyzes them as states of consciousness characterized by a fusion of "I" and "me," of ego and superego: "It is where the 'I' and the 'me' can in some sense fuse that there arises the peculiar sense of exaltation which belongs to the religious and patriotic attitudes in which the reaction which one calls out in others is the response which one is making himself." [12] By contrast, Durkheim analyzes religious beliefs and patriotism not as extraordinary attitudes of contemporary individuals, but as the expression of a collective consciousness rooted deep in tribal history and constitutive of the identity of groups.

Second, Mead makes no attempt to show how the oldest sacred symbols, in which the authority of the generalized other—which is prior to all normative validity—is manifested, could emerge from symbolically mediated interactions, or at least how it could be understood as a residue of this earlier stage. This religious—in the broadest sense of the term— symbolism, which is located this side of the threshold of grammatical speech, is evidently the archaic core of norm consciousness.

Thus I will next consider Durkheim's theory of religion in order to complete the program of reconstruction pursued by Mead. (*A*) In Durkheim's collective consciousness we can identify a prelinguistic root of communicative action that has a symbolic character and thus can itself be "constructed," that is, included in a reconstructive examination of normatively guided action. (*B*) Durkheim does not distinguish adequately between the commonality of ritual practice established via religious symbolism and the intersubjectivity produced by language. I shall therefore have to probe those weaknesses in his theory that provide a reason for picking up the thread of linguistic development (which Mead also let lie). (*C*) (*D*) The key is the transition from symbolically mediated interaction to grammatical speech. We can at least make plausible the idea that the familiar structures of speech acts are, from a genetic standpoint, the result of integrating three, prelinguistically rooted, cognitive, moral, and expressive relations to external nature, to collective identity, and to inner nature. Naturally, there is no claim here to be giving a causal explanation of the emergence of language.

With these steps we will have recovered at the phylogenetic level the structures that Mead *presupposed* at the level of socializing interaction: normed expectations and grammatical speech. They supplement one another to yield the structure of linguistically mediated, normatively guided interaction, which is the starting point for sociocultural development. Mead and Durkheim agree in characterizing the latter as a trend toward the linguistification of the sacred; I shall come back to this in section V.3. To the degree that the rationality potential ingrained in communicative action is released, the archaic core of the normative dissolves and gives way to the rationalization of worldviews, to the universalization of law and morality, and to an acceleration of processes of individuation. It is upon this evolutionary trend that Mead bases in the end his idealistic projection of a communicatively rationalized society.

A.—His whole life long,[13] Durkheim was concerned to explain the normative validity of institutions and values;[14] only in his later work, however, which culminated in 1912 in his sociology of religion,[15] did he succeed in unearthing the sacred roots of the moral authority of social norms. It is during this phase that Durkheim presented his views on "The Determination of Moral Facts" to the Société Française de Philosophie in 1906.[16] In that talk he defined his task as follows: "We shall show that moral rules are invested with a special authority by virtue of which they are obeyed simply because they command. We shall reaffirm, as a result of a purely empirical analysis, the notion of duty and nevertheless give a definition of it closely resembling that already given by Kant. Obligation is, then, one of the primary characteristics of the moral rule."[17] Thus the phenomenon calling for explanation is the obligatory character of social norms.

Durkheim circumscribes his problem by distinguishing the technical rules that underlie instrumental actions from the moral rules or norms that determine the consensual action of participants in interaction. And he compares the two types of rules from the standpoint of what happens when they are violated: "We shall put these various rules to the test of violation and see whether from this point of view there is not some difference between moral rules and rules of technique."[18] The violation of a valid technical rule leads to consequences that are internally connected with the action in a certain way: the intervention fails. The goal striven for is not realized, and the failure comes about automatically; there is an empirical, a lawlike relation between the rules governing action and the consequences of action. By contrast, the violation of a moral rule brings a sanction that cannot be understood as a failure that automatically follows. The relation between the rules of action and the consequences of action is conventional; on this basis, behavior conforming to norms is rewarded, behavior deviating from norms is punished. Thus, for example, we can infer empirical consequences from the idea of unhygenic behavior, whereas the idea of murder has no comparable empirical content: "It is impossible to discover *analytically* in the act of murder the slightest notion of blame. The link between act and consequence here is a *synthetic* one."[19]

It is no accident that Durkheim chooses for his comparison moral rules and not rules of statutory or positive law. In the case of legal regulations or administrative prescriptions a comparison with technical rules suggests itself,[20] for the conventional relation between legal rules and sanctions is meant to secure the observance of norms in a way similar to that in which the empirical relation between technical rules and action consequences guarantees the efficacy of an action conforming to the rule. This is true in the derivative case of legal norms sanctioned by the state, but Durkheim is interested in the original use of prestate norms. Violations of these norms are punished *because* they claim validity in virtue of moral authority; this validity does not accrue to them because external sanctions compel their observance. "The term 'moral authority' is opposed to material authority or physical supremacy."[21] The aspect of the validity of moral rules calling for explanation is precisely that they possess a binding power that, rather than itself presupposing sanctions, justifies the applications of sanctions when they are violated. This is what Durkheim is driving at with his comparison between technical and moral rules: "Thus there are rules that present this particular characteristic: we refrain from performing the acts they forbid simply because they are forbidden. This is what is meant by the obligatory character of the moral rule."[22]

The explanation provided by Durkheim in his talk is still very sketchy. To begin with, he highlights two features of "moral facts": (*a*) the mark of the impersonal that attaches to moral authority; and (*b*) the ambivalent feelings that this triggers in the actor.

(*à*) Durkheim first discusses the Kantian opposition between duty and inclination from the standpoint that the relation of moral precepts to the interests of the individual is one of tension. Imperatives of self-maintenance, interests in the satisfaction of private needs and desires—in short, action orientations that are utilitarian and related to oneself—are not as such in accord with moral requirements, which demand, rather, that the actor raise himself above himself. The selflessness of the morally acting individual corresponds to the universality of morally normed expectations, which are directed to all the members of a community: "Morality begins with membership in a group, whatever that group may be."[23]

(*b*) There is also a second standpoint from which Durkheim discusses the Kantian distinction between duty and inclination, namely, that moral commands exert a singular force upon the individual. A subject acting morally has to submit to an authority and do violence to his nature in a certain sense, but he does this in such a way that he takes on the obligation himself and makes the moral requirements his own.

Because the will of someone acting morally does not acquiesce in externally imposed force but in an authority commanding respect—an authority that "while it surpasses us, is within us"[24]—moral constraint has the character of a self-overcoming. On the other hand, Durkheim relativizes the Kantian dualism by deriving the binding power of obligations from constraint *and* attraction simultaneously. The morally good is at the same time something worth pursuing; it could not be effective as an ideal and arouse enthusiastic fervor if it did not offer the prospect of

satisfying real needs and desires. "Morality must then not only be obligatory but also desirable and desired. This *desirability* is the second characteristic of every moral act."[25]

Durkheim's next move, after this phenomenology of the moral, is to
point out the similarities between the validity of moral rules and the aura
of the sacred [in these two respects].

(ad a) In investigating mythical representations and ritual behavior in
primitive societies, we encounter a demarcation of sacred from profane
areas of life: "The sacred . . . is that which is *set apart*, that which is *separated* . . . What characterizes it, is that it cannot, without losing its nature,
be mixed with the profane. Any mixture, or even contact, *profanes* it,
that is to say, destroys its essential attributes. But this separation does not
leave the two orders of being that have been separated in this way on
the same level. We see this from the break in continuity between the
sacred and the profane. There is between them no common measure,
they are heterogeneous and incommensurable; the value of the sacred
cannot be compared with that of the profane."[26] Like the attitude toward
moral authority, the attitude toward the sacred is marked by devotion
and self-renunciation; in worshiping the sacred, in performing cultic actions, in observing ritual prescriptions, and the like, the believer re-
nounces his profane action orientations, that is, those that are utilitarian
and related to the self. Without regard for the imperatives of self-
maintenance, for personal interests, he enters into communion with all
other believers; he merges with the impersonal power of the sacred
which reaches beyond all that is merely individual.

(ad b) Further, the sacred arouses the same ambivalent attitude as
moral authority, for it is surrounded with an aura that simultaneously
frightens and attracts, terrorizes and enchants: "The sacred being is in a
sense forbidden; it is a being which may not be violated; it is also good,
loved and sought after."[27] In the aura itself is expressed the untouchabil-
ity of what is at the same time sought after, the closeness in the distance.[28] "The sacred object inspires us, if not with fear, at least with respect that keeps us at a distance; at the same time it is an object of love
and aspiration that we are drawn towards. Here then is a dual sentiment
which seems self-contradictory but does not for that cease to be real."[29]
The sacred produces and stabilizes just the ambivalence that is characteristic of the feeling of moral obligation.

Durkheim infers from these structural analogies between the sacred
and the moral that the foundations of morality are to be found in the
sacred. He puts forward the thesis that in the last analysis moral rules get
their binding power from the sphere of the sacred; this explains the fact
that moral commands are obeyed without being linked to external sanctions. Durkheim understands respect for the moral law, as well as the

inner sanctions of shame and guilt that are triggered by norm violations, as an echo of more ancient reactions rooted in the sacred: "Morality would no longer be morality if it had no element of religion. Apart from this, the horror which crime inspires is in all ways comparable to that with which a believer reacts to sacrilege. The respect which we have for the human being is distinguishable only very slightly from that which the faithful of all religions have for the objects they deem sacred."[30] Like Weber, Durkheim poses the question whether a secularized morality can at all endure: certainly not if secularization means rendering it profane in the sense of reinterpreting it in utilitarian terms—for with that the fundamental moral phenomenon of the obligatory character of valid norms would disappear (as it does in all ethics developed on empiricist assumptions).[31]

After having established the sacred foundations of morality, Durkheim attempts, in a third step, to elucidate the origins of the sacred and thereby the meaning of moral authority. At this point Durkheim's unbroken ties to the tradition of the philosophy of consciousness become noticeable. Religions are said to consist of beliefs and ritual practices. Taking beliefs as his point of departure, he conceives of religion as the experience of a collective, supraindividual consciousness. In virtue of its intentional structure, consciousness is always consciousness of something. Accordingly, Durkheim looks for the intentional object of the religious world of ideas; he inquires after the reality that is represented in concepts of the sacred. The answers that religion itself gives are clear: the divine being, the mythical order of the world, sacred powers, and the like. But for Durkheim what is concealed behind this is society—"transfigured and symbolically represented." For society, or the collectivity that group members form by association, in short, "the collective person," is of such a nature that it reaches beyond the consciousness of the individual person and yet is at the same time immanent in him. Furthermore, it has all the features of a moral authority commanding respect. Durkheim presents this argument in the style of a proof for the existence of God: "if a morality, or system of obligations and duties, exists, society is a moral being qualitatively different from the individuals it comprises and from the aggregation of which it derives."[32] According to Durkheim, this entity, society, can at first be viewed and recognized only in sacred terms.

Apart from the fact that concepts such as "collective consciousness" and "collective representation" seduce us into personalizing society, assimilating it to a subject-writ-large, the proposed explanation is circular. The moral is traced back to the sacred, and the sacred to collective representation of an entity that is itself supposed to consist of a system of binding norms. Nevertheless, with his work on the sacred foundations of morality, Durkheim opened up a path that led him to occupy himself with ethnological studies, especially of totemistic systems among Australian aborigines.[33] And these studies point in the end to a clarification of the symbolic structure of the sacred and to a nonpositivistic interpretation of collective consciousness.

Once again Durkheim starts from the division of the universe into the strictly separate domains of the sacred and the profane. He distinguishes more sharply now between beliefs and practices, between mythical world interpretations and ritual actions, between dealing with sacred objects cognitively and actively. Both, however, express the same attitude. Durkheim describes the character of the sacred as impersonal, commanding respect, overpowering and at the same time uplifting, as triggering enthusiasm, motivating the faithful to selflessness and self-overcoming, permitting them to put their own interests aside. He analyzes once more the peculiar kinship between the aspects of well-being and terror: "Of course, the sentiments inspired by the two are not identical: respect is one thing, disgust and horror another. Yet, if the gestures are to be the same in both cases, the sentiments expressed must not differ in nature. And, in fact, there is a horror in religious respect, especially when it is very intense, while the fear inspired by the malign powers is generally not without a certain reverential character. The shades by which these two attitudes are differentiated are even so slight sometimes that it is not always easy to say which state of mind the believers actually happen to be in."[34]

In light of the empirical materials, Durkheim now finds it necessary to work out more clearly the symbolic status of sacred objects. In the case of totemic animals or plants the symbolic character is evident anyhow: they are what they signify. Taboos prevent them from being treated as profane things, for example, from being consumed as food. All sacred objects—flags, emblems, decorations, tatoos, ornaments, figures, idols, or natural objects and events—share this symbolic status. They figure as signs with conventional significations, and they all have the same semantic core: they represent the power of the sacred; they are "collective ideals that have fixed themselves on material objects."[35] This formulation comes from the interesting essay in which Durkheim gives his theory of collective consciousness the shape of a theory of symbolic forms: "collective representations originate only when they are embodied in material objects, things, or beings of every sort—figures, movements, sounds, words, and so on—that symbolize and delineate them in some outward appearance. For it is only by expressing their feelings, by translating them into signs, by symbolizing them externally, that the individual consciousnesses, which are, by nature, closed to each other, can feel that they are communicating and are in unison. The things that embody the collective representations arouse the same feelings as do the mental states that they represent and, in a manner of speaking, materialize. They, too, are respected, feared, and sought after as helping powers."[36]

The medium of religious symbols provides the key to resolving the problem that Durkheim formulates as follows: how can we at one and the same time belong wholly to ourselves and just as completely to others? How can we be simultaneously within ourselves and outside of ourselves? Religious symbols have the same meaning for the members of the same group; on the basis of this uniform sacred semantics, they make possible a kind of intersubjectivity that is still this side of the communicative roles of first, second, and third persons, but is nevertheless beyond the threshold of sheer collective contagion by feelings.

Durkheim analyzes this consensus—normative at its core, prelinguistic [in the sense of propositionally differentiated language] but symbolically mediated—in connection with ritual practices. He looks upon rites as the more primordial element of religion. Religious convictions are already formulated in a grammatical language; they are the common property of a religious community whose members assure themselves of their communality in cultic action. Religious belief is always the belief of a collectivity; it proceeds from a practice that it at the same time interprets. Durkheim first describes the ritual practice itself in mentalistic terms, that is, in terms of collective consciousness: "Religious representations are collective representations which express collective reality; the rites are a manner of acting which take rise in the midst of the assembled group and which are destined to excite, maintain or re-create certain mental states in these groups."[37] But now he no longer presents religion in a positivistic manner, as a kind of theory that depicts society as a whole, in however encoded a form.[38] He gets beyond his reifying identification of the referent of belief sentences with the nexus of social life and adopts a more dynamic view. When ritual practice is seen as the more primordial phenomenon, religious symbolism can be understood as the medium of a special form of symbolically mediated interaction. Ritual practice serves to bring about communion in a communicative fashion.

It can be seen in ritual actions that the sacred is the expression of a normative consensus regularly made actual:

> There can be no society which does not feel the need of upholding and reaffirming at regular intervals the collective sentiments and the collective ideas which make its unity and its personality. Now this moral remaking cannot be achieved except by the means of reunions, assemblies and meetings where the individuals, being closely united to one another, reaffirm in common their common sentiments; hence come ceremonies which do not differ from regular religious ceremo-

nies, either in their object, the result which they produce, or the process employed to attain the results. What essential difference is there between an assembly of Christians celebrating the principal dates of the life of Christ, or Jews remembering the exodus from Egypt or the promulgation of the Decalogue, and a reunion of citizens commemorating the promulgation of a new moral or legal system or some great event in the national life?[39]

Nothing is depicted in ceremonies of this kind; they are rather the exemplary, repeated putting into effect of a consensus that is thereby renewed. It is a question of variations on one and the same theme, namely, the presence of the sacred, and this in turn is only the form in which the collectivity experiences "its unity and its personality." Because the basic normative agreement expressed in communicative action establishes and sustains the identity of the group, the fact of successful consensus is at the same time its essential content.

There is a corresponding shift in the concept of the *conscience collective*. Whereas Durkheim had first understood by this the totality of socially imposed representations shared by all members of the society, in the context of his analysis of rites the term refers less to the content than to the structure of a group identity established and renewed through identification in common with the sacred. Collective identity develops in the form of normative consensus; this is, of course, not a question of an achieved consensus, for the identities of individual group members are established equiprimordially with the identity of the group. What makes the individual into a person is that in which he agrees with all the other members of his social group—in Mead's terms, it is the "me" that represents the authority of the generalized other in the socialized adult. Durkheim's position is similar to Mead's: "we must say that what makes a man a personality is that by which he is not distinguished from other men, that which makes him a man as such, and not a certain man. The senses, the body and, in a word, all that individualizes is, on the contrary, considered by Kant as antagonistic to personality. This is because individuation is not the essential characteristic of personality."[40] The identity of the person is to begin with only a mirror image of collective identity; the latter secures social solidarity in, so to speak, a "mechanical" form.

B.—This theory is suited to close the phylogenetic gaps in Mead's construction. Collective identity has the form of a normative consensus built up in the medium of religious symbols and interpreted in the semantics of the sacred. The religious consciousness that secures identity is regenerated and maintained through ritual practice. On the other hand, Mead's communication theory can be brought in to provide tentative answers to questions left open by Durkheim's theory. I am referring to (*a*) questions concerning the emergence of religious symbolism, (*b*) questions as to how the solidarity of the collectivity, presented as monolithic, branches out in the institutional system of a society, and finally (*c*) the parallel question of how, starting from Durkheim's concept of collective identity, we can conceive the individuality of individual group members. Behind (*b*) and (*c*) are the two basic questions of classical social theory: How is social order or social integration possible? How do the individual and society stand to one another?

(*a*) If we put Durkheim's collective identity in place of Mead's generalized other, this suggests viewing the symbolism of the earliest tribal religions in the light of Mead's construction of the transition from symbolically mediated to normatively guided interaction. It was made clear above that signals—or, as Mead says, "significant gestures"—no longer function as animal gestures of expression, as triggers to which the organism reacts with a program of behavior partly learned, partly innate to its species. Even at the stage of symbolically mediated interaction, however, the coordination of action remains embedded in a regulation of behavior that functions prelinguistically and is based in the final analysis on instinctual residues. The further cognitive development advances, giving rise to an objectivating attitude by actors toward the world of perceptible and manipulable objects, the less communicative acts carried out with symbolic means can by themselves link together the actions of participants. To the extent that object perception and teleological action undergo development, propositional elements are differentiated out of signal language, elements that later take the explicit form of assertoric sentences and intentional sentences. As we have seen, speakers cannot replace the binding effects of signal languages with the communicative employment of *these* sentences. For this reason I would conjecture that there is a split in the medium of communication corresponding to the segregation of the sacred from the profane domains of life: religious signification, which makes possible a normative consensus and thereby provides the foundation for a ritual coordination of action, is the archaic part left over from the stage of symbolically mediated interaction after experiences from domains in which perceptible and manipulable objects are dealt with in a more and more propositionally structured manner flow into communication. Religious symbols are disengaged from functions of adapting and mastering reality; they serve especially to link those behavioral dispositions and instinctual energies set loose from innate programs with the medium of symbolic communication.

Durkheim's observations regarding paleosymbols in connection with ritual practices support this hypothesis:

That an emblem is useful as a rallying-center for any sort of a group it is superfluous to point out. By expressing the social unity in a material form, it makes this more obvious to all, and for that very reason the use of emblematic symbols must have spread quickly when once thought of. But more than that, this idea spontaneously arises out of the conditions of common life; for the emblem is not merely a convenient process for clarifying the sentiments society has of itself: it also serves to create these sentiments; it is one of its constituent elements. In fact, if left to themselves, individual consciousnesses are closed to each other; they can communicate only by means of signs which express their internal states. If the communication established between them is to become a real communion, that is to say, a fusion of all particular sentiments into one common sentiment, the signs expressing them must themselves be fused into one single and unique resultant. It is the appearance of this that informs the individuals that they are in harmony and makes them conscious of their moral unity. It is by uttering the same cry, pronouncing the same words, or performing the same gesture regarding the same object that they become and feel themselves to be in unison.[41]

One can see the structural similarities between ritual action and symbolically mediated interaction steered via signals. Paleosymbols have a meaning that is not yet modally differentiated, and, like signals, they possess the power to steer behavior. On the other hand, ritual actions have lost their adaptive function; they serve to establish and maintain a collective identity, on the strength of which the steering of interaction is transferred from a genetic program anchored in the individual organism over to an intersubjectively shared cultural program. This program can be transmitted only if the intersubjective unity of a communication community is secured. The group can constitute itself as a collectivity when the motivational makeup of the associated individuals is taken hold of symbolically and structured through the *same* semantic contents. The predominantly appelative-expressive character of rites suggests that instinctual residues are symbolically absorbed and sublimated—perhaps on the basis of ritualizations that characteristically turn up with animals in areas in which emotionally ambivalent reactions terminate in the replacement of one behavior pattern by a contrary one (e.g., the switchover from attack to submission).[42]

(b) If, as proposed above, we understand by collective consciousness a consensus through which the identity of the relevant collective is first established, we have to explain how this unity-bringing symbolic structure is related to the multiplicity of institutions and socialized individuals. Durkheim speaks of the birth of all great institutions from the spirit of religion.[43] To begin with, this means only that normative validity has moral foundations and that morality in turn always has its roots in the sacred; at first moral and legal norms themselves had the character of ritual prescriptions. The more institutions are differentiated, however, the looser the ties to ritual practice become. A religion does not consist in cultic activities alone. In my view, we can give a nontrivial meaning to the religious origins of institutions only if we take into account the religious world-interpretation as a connecting link between collective identity and institutions.

In societies that have attained the level of civilizations, worldviews have the function, among others, of legitimating political leadership. They offer a potential for grounding that can be used to justify a political order or the institutional framework of a society in general. Thus they lend support to the moral authority or validity of basic norms. As Weber emphasized, the legitimating power of worldviews is to be explained primarily by the fact that cultural knowledge can meet with rationally motivated approval. The situation is different with the not yet intellectually elaborated worldviews common in tribal societies; they do make available a potential for narrative explanations, but they are still so tightly interwoven with the system of institutions that they explicate it rather than subsequently legitimate it. These worldviews establish an analogical nexus between man, nature, and society which is represented as a totality in the basic concepts of mythical powers. Because these worldviews project a totality in which everything corresponds with everything else, they subjectively attach the collective identity of the group or the tribe to the cosmic order and integrate it with the system of social institutions. In the limit case, worldviews function as a kind of drive belt that transforms the basic religious consensus into the energy of social solidarity and passes it on to social institutions, thus giving them a moral authority.

What is of primary interest in analyzing the interrelation between normative consensus, worldview, and institutional system, however, is that the connection is established through channels of linguistic communication. Whereas ritual actions take place at a pregrammatical level, religious worldviews are connected with full-fledged communicative actions. The situational interpretations entering into everyday communication are fed by worldviews, however archaic; worldviews can, in turn, reproduce themselves only by way of these processes of reaching understanding. In virtue of this feedback relation they have the form of cultural knowledge, a knowledge that is based on both cognitive and socially integrative experiences. In the epistemological parts of his sociology of religion, Durkheim did not entirely neglect the role of language: "The system of concepts with which we think in everyday life is that expressed by the vocabulary of our mother tongues; for every word translates a concept."[44] But he rashly subsumes both the communality of normative consensus accomplished through ritual and the intersubjectivity of knowledge established through speech acts under the same concept of collective consciousness. For this reason it remains unclear how institutions draw their validity from the religious springs of social solidarity. We can resolve this problem only if we bear in mind that profane everyday practice proceeds by way of linguistically differentiated processes of reaching understanding and forces us to specify validity claims for actions appropriate to situations in the normative context of roles and institutions.[45] Communicative action is a switching station for the energies of social solidarity; Durkheim did not pay it sufficient heed.

(c) This neglect of the dimension of linguistic understanding also explains the unsatisfactory dualism Durkheim maintains in regard to the relation between the individual and society. As he sees it, the individual is divided into two heterogeneous components: one part that is subject to nonsocialized self-interest and the imperatives of self-preservation, and a second—moral—part that is stamped by group identity, or, in Durkheim's words: "an individual being which has its foundation in the organism, and the circle of whose activities is therefore limited, and a social being which represents the highest reality in the intellectual and moral order that we can know by observation—I mean society."[46] The split of the social universe into the domains of the profane and the sacred is repeated psychologically in the antithesis of body and soul or body and spirit, in the antagonisms between inclination and duty, sensibility and understanding. Durkheim remains tied here, more clearly than anywhere else in his work, to the mentalistic conceptualizations of the philosophy of consciousness. He distinguishes states of individual consciousness from states of collective consciousness, but both count as conscious states of the individual:

> There are in him two classes of states of consciousness that differ from each other in origin and nature, and in the ends toward which they aim. One class merely expresses our organisms and the object to which they are most directly related. Strictly individual, the states of consciousness of this class connect us only with ourselves, and we can no more detach them from us than we can detach ourselves from our bodies. The states of consciousness of the other class, on the contrary, come to us from society; they transfer society into us and connect us with something that surpasses us. Being collective, they are impersonal; they turn us toward ends that we hold in common with other men; it is through them and them alone that we can communicate with others.[47]

Individuals owe their identities as persons exclusively to their identification with, or internalization of, features of collective identity; personal identity is a mirror image of collective identity. "So it is not at all true that we are more personal as we are more individualized."[48] The only principle of individuation is the spatiotemporal location of the body and the desiring and feeling nature [*Bedürfnisnatur*] that is presented with the organism for the process of socialization—or, as Durkheim says, alluding to the classical tradition, "the passions." If one considers how strongly subjective experiences are shaped by culture, this thesis is implausible. Moreover, Durkheim himself discusses the phenomenon that Frazer had pointed to with the expression "individual totemism." In many Australian tribes there are totems not only for the clan as a whole but also for single individuals. They are represented as alter egos that function as protective patrons. Unlike collective totems, these individualized totems are not ascribed but acquired, normally by way of ritual initiation. In other cases, their acquisition is optional—the only ones who bother about a personal totem are those who want to stand out from the collective.[49] Like the universal practice of giving names, this is a device for differentiating personal identities. It makes it possible to designate a multiplicity not only of bodies but of persons. Evidently, individuality too is a socially produced phenomenon that is a result of the socialization process itself and not an expression of residual, natural needs that escape that process.

Mead conceives of personal identity exactly as Durkheim does—as a structure that results from taking over socially generalized expectations. The "me" is the organized set of attitudes that one takes over from one's reference persons.[50] Unlike Durkheim, however, Mead starts from the view that identity formation takes place through the medium of linguistic communication. And since the subjectivity of one's own intentions, desires, and feelings by no means eludes this medium, the agencies of the "I" and the "me," of ego and superego, issue from the *same* process of socialization. In this regard, Mead holds a convincing counterposition to Durkheim's: the process of socialization is at the same time one of individuation. He supports this by pointing to the diversity of position-bound perspectives that speakers and hearers adopt. As a principle of individuation he adduces not the body but a structure of perspectives that is set within the communicative roles of the first, second, and third person. By introducing the expression "me" to refer to the identity of the sociated individual, Mead is systematically connecting the role taking effective in socialization with the speech situations in which speakers and hearers enter into interpersonal relations as members of a social group. "Me" stands for the aspect that ego offers to an alter in an interaction when the latter makes a speech-act offer to ego. Ego takes this view of himself by adopting alter's perspective when alter requests something of ego, that is, of *me,* promises something to *me,* expects something of *me,* fears, hates or pleases *me,* and so forth. The interpersonal relation between the speaker and the one spoken to, I and thou, first and second person, is set up in such a way, however, that in adopting the perspective of a vis-à-vis, ego cannot steal away from his own communicative role. Taking the attitude of alter, so as to make the latter's expectations his own, does not exempt ego from the role of first person; it is *he* who, in the role of ego, has to satisfy the behavior patterns he first took over from alter and internalized.

The performative attitude that ego and alter adopt when they act communicatively with one another is bound up with the presupposition that the other can take a "yes" or "no" position on the offer contained in one's own speech act. Ego cannot relinquish this scope for freedom even when he is, so to speak, obeying social roles; for the linguistic structure of a relation between responsible actors is built into the internalized pattern of behavior itself. Thus in the socialization process an "I" emerges equiprimordially with the "me," and the individuating effect of socialization processes results from this double structure. The model for the relation between the two agencies is the "answer" of a participant in communication who takes a "yes" or "no" position. Which answer ego will give in any instance, what position he will take, cannot be known in advance—either by him or by anyone else. "Perhaps he will make a brilliant play or an error. The response to that situation ... is uncertain, and it is that which constitutes the 'I.'"[51]

Mead stresses the moment of nonpredictability and spontaneity in the way that a communicative actor plays a social role. The very structure of linguistic intersubjectivity forces the actor to be *himself* even in norm-conformative behavior. In a very basic sense, the initiative cannot be taken from a person in communicative action however guided by norms; no one can relinquish the initiative. "The I gives the sense of freedom, of initiative."[52] To take the initiative means to begin something new, to be able to do something surprising.[53] "The separation of the 'I' and the 'me' is not fictitious. They are not identical, for, as I have said, the 'I' is something that is never entirely calculable. The 'me' does call for a certain sort of an 'I' insofar as we meet the obligations that are given in conduct itself, but the 'I' is always something different from what the situation calls for ... Taken together they constitute a personality as it appears in social experience. The self is essentially a social process going on with these two distinguishable phases. If it did not have these two phases there could not be conscious responsibility, and there would be nothing novel in experience."[54]

Durkheim's difficulties in explaining how the identity of a group relates to that of its members prompted us to take up Mead's analysis of the relations between "I" and "me" for a second time. The first time we were interested in how a subjective world of experiences to which the growing child has privileged access takes shape complementary to the construction of a common social world. In that context Mead could support his choice of the term "I" by pointing to the meaning that this expression has in first-person sentences, that is, in sentences a speaker employs in the expressive mode. In the present context, the concept has a different meaning. The choice of the term "I" is here based on the meaning that this expression takes on in the illocutionary components of speech acts, where it appears together with an expression for an [indirect] object in the second person. The performative sense points to the interpersonal relation between I and thou, and thus to a structure of a linguistic intersubjectivity that exercises on the growing child an unrelenting pressure toward individuation. Communicative action turns out to be a switching station for energies of social solidarity, but this time we viewed the switch point not under the aspect of coordination but of socialization, in order to discover how the collective consciousness is communicated, via illocutionary forces, not to institutions but to individuals.

These tentative answers to two basic questions of classical social theory, which I have developed out of the thought of Durkheim and Mead, are still somewhat metaphorical; to get beyond that I shall pick up once again, from a genetic perspective, the discussion concerning the general structures of linguistic understanding. Before doing so, however, I want to pin down the results of our interpretation of Durkheim's theory of religion.

The core of collective consciousness is a normative consensus established and regenerated in the ritual practices of a community of believers. Members thereby orient themselves to religious symbols; the intersubjective unity of the collective presents itself to them in concepts of the holy. This collective identity defines the circle of those who understand themselves as members of the same social group and can speak of themselves in the first-person plural. The symbolic actions of the rites can be comprehended as residues of a stage of communication that has already been gone beyond in domains of profane social cooperation. The evolutionary gap between symbolically mediated and normatively guided interaction makes it possible to encapsulate a domain of the sacred from the practices of everyday life. Even in the most primitive societies, everyday practice already takes place at the level of grammatical language and norm-guided action, such that systems of institutions are developed, on the one hand, and structures of socialized individuals, on the other. The emergence of institutions and the formation of identities are the phylogenetic correlates to the constructions of the social and subjective worlds that Mead studied in ontogenesis.

Durkheim attempted to trace the normative validity of institutions back to a normative agreement tied to religious symbols; similarly, he traced the personal identity of individual group members back to the collective group identity expressed in those symbols. A closer look showed, however, that in both cases linguistic communication takes on an important *mediating function*. Normatively guided action presupposed grammatical speech as a medium of communication. The interrelation between collective consciousness, on the one side, and, on the other side, norms that can be applied to specific situations and personality structures that can be attributed to individuals, remains unclear so long as the structure of reaching understanding in language has not been cleared up. Religious symbolism represents one of three *prelinguistic* [in the sense of propositionally differentiated language] roots of communicative action. Only in and through communicative action can the energies of social solidarity attached to religious symbolism branch out and be imparted, in the form of moral authority, both to institutions and to persons.

What is puzzling about this root is that it is from the very beginning symbolic in nature. Cognitive dealings with perceptible and manipulable objects, and expressions of subjective experiences are in contact with external or internal nature through stimulation of our senses or through our needs and desires. They are in touch with a reality that not only transcends language but is also free of symbolic structures. Human cognitions and expressions, however shaped by language they may be, can also be traced back to the natural history of intelligent performances and expressive gestures in animals. Norm consciousness, on the other hand, has no equally trivial extralinguistic reference; for obligations there are no unambiguous natural-historical correlates, as there are for sense impressions and needs. Nevertheless, collective consciousness, the paleosymbolically supported normative consensus, and the collective identity supported by it secure for experiences of obligation contact with a reality that is, if not free of symbols, at least prelinguistic [in the strict sense of propositionally differentiated language]—they are "older" than interaction mediated by grammatical speech.

I am assuming that grammatical speech is distinguished from signal language by the differentiation and reintegration at a higher level of the assertoric, appellative, and expressive components that at first form a diffuse unity. Cognitive relations to external nature and expressive relations to internal nature, both of which have prelinguistic roots, are, on the level of speech acts, integrated with obligatory relations, which are also prelinguistic [in the strict sense] but yet symbolically rooted, and are thereby transformed. If we further assume that the history of the origin and rise of language is somehow sedimented and reflected in the formal structures of the speech act, the hypothesis of the three roots of communicative action would be open at least to an indirect check. We must, of course, keep in mind that we can carry out our formal-pragmatic description only in the horizon of a modern understanding of the world.

C.—Excursus on the Three Roots of Communicative Action. We have distinguished three structural components of speech acts: the propositional, the illocutionary, and the expressive. If we take as our basis the normal form of a speech act ('I am telling you that p'; 'I promise you that q'; 'I admit to you that r'), we can say that the propositional component is represented by a dependent sentence with propositional content ('that p'). Each such sentence can be transformed into an assertoric sentence with descriptive content. The structure of the latter can be clarified in terms of an analysis of simple predicative sentences (e.g., 'The ball is red'). The illocutionary component can be represented in normal form by a superordinated performative sentence that is constructed with the first-person pronoun (as the subject expression), a performative verb (with a predicative function), and a personal pronoun in the second person (as [indirect] object). The structure of such sentences can be clarified in terms of an analysis of the special case of institutionally bound speech acts with which an actor fulfills a single, well-circumscribed norm (e.g., betting, congratulating, marrying). The expressive component remains implicit in the normal form, but it can always be expanded into an expressive sentence. The latter is constructed with the first-person pronoun (as subject expression) and an intentional [in Husserl's sense] verb (with a predicative function), while the place of the logical object is occupied either by an object (e.g., 'I love T') or by a nominalized state of affairs (e.g., 'I fear that p'). The fact that each of these three structural components exhibits significant peculiarities speaks for their mutual independence. With each component there is connected *one* property that is constitutive for grammatically differentiated understanding in general. *Assertoric sentences* can be true or false. Truth-conditional semantics has singled them out to show the internal connection between meaning and validity. With *performative sentences* the speaker carries out an action in saying something. The theory of speech acts has used them to establish the internal connection between speaking and acting. Performative sentences are neither true nor false; the actions carried out with their help can be understood as complements to commands (such as, 'You should help A'). In comparison to assertoric sentences, *expressive sentences* have the peculiar feature that when they are meaningfully employed neither their objective reference nor their content can be contested—mistaken identification is excluded, as is criticism of a knowledge to which the speaker has privileged access. The internal connection between intention and meaning, between what is meant and what is said, can be demonstrated in connection with such first-person sentences. Furthermore, there is no logical continuum between assertoric, normative, and expressive sentences such that sentences of one category can be inferred from sentences of another category. The structural components of speech acts cannot be reduced to one another.

What interests us in the present context is the correlation of these three components of speech acts with cognitions, obligations, and expressions. If, for purposes of comparison, we bring in here the *prelinguistic correlates* familiar to us from behavioral research, we see how they are changed at the linguistic level. Perceptions and representations take on a propositional structure, as does adaptive behavior. Ritually generated solidarity, obligations to the collectivity are split up at the level of normatively regulated action into intersubjective recognition of existing norms on the one hand, and norm-conformative motives for action on the other. Spontaneous expressions linked to the body lose their involuntary character when they are replaced with or interpreted by linguistic utterances. Expressive utterances serve communicative ends; they can be employed intentionally [in Husserl's sense].

When communicative acts take the shape of grammatical speech, the symbolic structure has penetrated *all* components of interaction; the cognitive-instrumental grasp of reality and the steering mechanism that attunes the behavior of different interaction partners to one another, as well as the actors and their behavior dispositions, get connected to linguistic communication and are symbolically restructured. At the same time, this transposition of cognitions, obligations, and expressions onto a linguistic basis makes it possible in turn for the means of communication to take on new functions—in addition to the function of *reaching understanding,* those of *coordinating action* and *socializing actors* as well. Under the aspect of reaching understanding, communicative acts serve the *transmission of culturally stored knowledge*—as shown above, cultural tradition reproduces itself through the medium of action oriented to reaching understanding. Under the aspect of coordinating action, the same communicative acts serve the *fulfillment of norms* appropriate to a given context; social integration also takes place via this medium. Under the aspect of socialization, finally, communicative acts serve the construction of internal controls on behavior, in general, the *formation of personality structures;* one of Mead's fundamental insights is that socialization processes take place via linguistically mediated interaction.

If one's aim is to provide a detailed analysis of why speech acts are, in virtue of their formal properties, a suitable medium for social reproduction, it is of course not enough to demonstrate the independence of the three structural components and the connection between the propositional component and the representation of knowledge, between the illocutionary component and the coordination of action, between the expressive component and the differentiation of the internal from the external world. In the symbolic reproduction of the lifeworld, speech acts can *simultaneously* take on the functions of cultural transmission, social integration, and the socialization of individuals only if the propositional, illocutionary, and expressive components are integrated into a *grammatical unity* in each and every speech act, such that semantic content does not break up into segments but can be freely converted from component to component. I will now indicate, in very broad strokes, how each individual component is intermeshed with the other two (*a–c*) and then examine the consequences that flow, in particular, from the intermeshing of the illocutionary component with the propositional and the expressive components—consequences having to do with the relation of speech to action and the relation of speakers to themselves (*d*).

(*a*) In comparing the *propositional component* of the speech act to the other two we are struck at first by an asymmetry. For every nondescriptive sentence there is at least one descriptive sentence that reproduces its semantic content; by contrast, there are assertoric sentences whose semantic content cannot be transformed into normative, evaluative, or expressive sentences. This is true of all statement-making sentences formulated in a thing-event language.

The sentence

(1) I promise (order) you that q.

can be transformed with preservation of meaning into

(1′) He promises (orders) him that q.

where the corresponding personal pronouns refer in each case to the same person. To be sure, the semantic content is affected by the transformation insofar as it is connected with a change of mode. This has consequences on the pragmatic level. Whereas (1) already represents an explicit speech act, (1′) represents only the propositional content of a constative speech act which a speaker can reproduce (1) as a happening in the world. The two utterances are exactly comparable only if (1′) is expanded, for example, to

(1′ exp.) I am reporting to you that he has promised (ordered) him that q.

For the same reason, an ought-sentence that gives expression to the application of a norm in a situation *s*, such as,

(2) You ought in situation *s* to carry out action *a*.

can be transformed while preserving meaning only by bringing in the speaker-hearer relationship:

(2′) *S* is saying to *H* that he ought to carry out *a* in *s*.

By contrast, an ought-sentence that directly expresses the content of a norm, such as,

(3) One ought (generally) to carry out the action *a* in situations of type *s*.

is to begin with not a speech act at all. It could be transformed in the way that (1) was into (1′) only if it were supplemented by an illocutionary component, as, for example, in

(4) I hereby proclaim a norm with the content that *q*,

where a nominalized version of (3) can be inserted for '*q*'. The transformation then yields:

(4′) He is proclaiming a norm with the content that *q*.
(5′) He is describing a norm with the content that *q*.

These sentences can be expanded in the way that (1′) was to (1′ exp.). Correspondingly, experiential sentences such as

(6) I desire (fear) that *p*.

can be transformed into

(6′) He desires (fears) that *p*.

These sentences preserve meaning when the personal pronouns refer to the same person. Here too, the change of mode that has taken place becomes comprehensible only through comparing the simply and the doubly expanded versions.

(6 exp.) I hereby express (admit) the desire (the fear) that *p*.
(6′ exp.) I am reporting to you that he has expressed (admitted) the desire (the fear) that *p*.

What is true of ought-sentences can be extended mutatis mutandis to evaluative sentences.

We need not be concerned with this here; I want only to draw attention to the asymmetry in the fact the semantic content of any illocutionary or expressive speech-act component can be expressed by means of a descriptive sentence, whereas it is not at all the case that all assertoric sentences can be transformed into another mode while preserving meaning. For a sentence like

(7) This ball is red.

there is, for instance, no meaning-preserving sentence in a nonassertoric mode. This holds for all statements formulated in a thing-event language.

This asymmetry explains why we learn the linguistic expression constitutive of illocutionary or expressive components in such a way that we can employ them in the attitude of *both* the first and the third persons. This is true, for example, of predicatively employed performative and intentional [in Husserl's sense] verbs. We have not understood the meaning of 'order' or 'hate' if we do not know that (1) and (1'), (2) and (2') express the *same* semantic contents in *different* illocutionary roles. And we can only know this if we have learned the communicative roles of the first, second, and third persons, with the corresponding expressive, norm-conformative, and objectivating speaker attitudes, as a *system*— that is to say, in such a way that from the pragmatic presuppositions of an expression for the first person employed expressively (as in 6), or from a pair of expressions for the first and second persons employed performatively (as in 1), we infer the pragmatic presuppositions of an expression for the third person employed in an objectivating manner (as in 6' and 1') and, conversely, infer the former from the latter.

Propositionally differentiated language is organized in such a way that everything that can be said at all can also be said in assertoric form. Thus even those experiences of society that a speaker has in a norm-conformative attitude, and those experiences of his own subjectivity that a speaker has in an expressive attitude, can be assimilated to the assertorically expressed knowledge that comes from an objectivating treatment of external nature. When it enters into the cultural tradition, this practical knowledge is released from its ties to the illocutionary or expressive speech-act components with which it is interwoven in the communicative practice of everyday life. It gets stored there under the category of knowledge.

For the transfer of meaning from nonassertoric to assertoric speech-act components, it is important that the illocutionary and expressive components are already propositionally structured. Performative and expressive sentences can be analyzed according to the schema of combining expressions for objects with predicates that are attributed or denied of those objects. Normative, expressive, and evaluative sentences even have the grammatical form of statements, without sharing the assertoric mode of descriptive sentences.

(b) I will compare the *expressive component* of speech acts with the

other two only in a cursory way. From this side, too, we can observe an integration. For every nonexpressive component there is an intention with the same meaning (in the language of analytic philosophy: a propositional attitude). Thus, for instance, with every correctly performed constative speech act a speaker gives expression to a belief or conviction; with every correctly performed regulative speech act, to a feeling of obligation, or at least to an attitude that evinces some internal connection with valid norms. With the assertion '*p*', a speaker normally gives expression to the fact that he *believes p*; with the promise '*q*', that he *feels himself obligated* to *q* in the future; with an apology for '*r*', that he *regrets r*, and so forth.

In this way, a certain assimilation of convictions and feelings of obligation to the structure of emotional experiences take place. It is only this assimilation that makes it possible to draw clear boundaries between the internal and external worlds, such that the beliefs of someone who asserts facts can be distinguished from the facts themselves, or the feelings of someone who expresses regret or gratitude or sympathy or sheer delight by apologizing to or thanking or commiserating with or congratulating someone else can be distinguished from the corresponding illocutionary acts.

Here too there is an asymmetry. From the sincere expressions of a speaker we can infer nonexpressive speech acts that the speaker would utter under suitable conditions. If he believes '*p*', he is disposed to assert that '*p*'; if he regrets '*r*', he is disposed to apologize for '*r*'. But we cannot infer inversely from these constative or regulative speech acts that the speaker also really believes or feels what he expresses. In this respect speakers are not forced to say what they mean.[55] This asymmetry presupposes the assimilation of convictions and obligations to subjective experiences of noncognitive and nonobligatory origin; this in turn makes it possible to distance a domain of experiences with privileged access from facts, on the one hand, and norms, on the other.

(c) From the point of view of social theory, we are primarily interested in how the *illocutionary component* is joined together with the other two components of speech acts. Taking the later Wittgenstein as his point of departure, Austin embarked upon an investigation of the composition of speech acts out of illocutionary and propositional elements. The integration of these two components fixes the grammatical form of standard speech acts, which can be characterized by the dependence of a nominalized propositional sentence: '—that *p*' on a performative sentence 'I *m* you', where '*m*' stands for a predicative expression constructed with the help of a performance verb.

The form that has become usual in analytic philosophy, '*Mp*', neglects the equally structure-forming integration of the illocutionary component with the expressive. This remains concealed in the standard form because the first-person pronoun appearing in the performative sentence has two different meanings at once: on the one hand, in connection with the second-person pronoun it has the meaning that ego, as a speaker in a performative attitude, stands opposite alter; on the other hand, considered in itself, it has the meaning familiar from first-person sentences that ego, as a speaker in an expressive attitude, is expressing desires, feelings, intentions, and so forth. This *double meaning* goes unnoticed because the intentions of the speaker are not explicitly expressed in constative and regulative speech acts. This is possible, despite the assimilation of convictions and obligations to emotional experiences, because the act of uttering counts per se as self-presentation, that is, as a sufficient indicator of the speaker's intention to express some experience. For the same reason, expressive speech acts can normally be performed without illocutionary components. Only in cases of special emphasis are these components made linguistically explicit—for example, in situations in which a speaker gives solemn or forcible expression to his desires or feelings, or in contexts in which a speaker discloses, reveals, confesses his until-then silent thoughts or feelings to a surprised or mistrustful hearer. This is why avowals have a paradigmatic role in the analysis of the expressive mode of communication, similar to that of assertions and commands or promises.

In contrast to performative sentences, assertoric and first-person sentences can also be used monologically, that is, in such a way that the speaker, *in foro interno,* does not have to take on both the communicative role of speaker and hearer, as he does with language use that has become monologicized, that is, with speech acts that are *subsequently internalized.* Evidently assertoric and expressive sentences do not have by nature the force to motivate a hearer to accept a speech-act offer. This force accrues to them only through the illocutionary components that supplement them. They are embedded in contexts of communicative action only through being modalized.

Analytically we can distinguish two levels of modalization. To begin with, we can understand the illocutionary components as the linguistic representatives of the action character of speech acts. *Using* assertoric and expressive sentences means that the speaker *performs* a speech act with them. Performative sentences such as 'I assert that p', or 'I confess that p', are expressions of this action character. They make it linguistically explicit that constative and expressive speech acts have a relation to social norms like that of orders, warnings, concessions, and so on. Like such regulative speech acts—as well as all nonverbal actions—they can be subjected to normative regulation. It depends upon the normative context of a speech situation whether and, if so, to whom participants may or should make assertions or confessions.

If, however, the meaning of the modalization of assertoric or experiential sentences were exhausted therein, constative and expressive speech actions could not achieve binding effects *on their own* but only in virtue of their normative content. The illocutionary component of such speech acts would then have no motivating force; the burden of coordinating action would have to be borne instead by the prior consensus supporting the normative context.

In fact, however, a speaker can motivate a hearer to accept his offer through the illocutionary force of a constative or expressive speech act even independent of the normative context in which it is performed. As I have explained in Volume 1, this is not a question of achieving some prolocutionary effect *on* the hearer but of reaching a rationally motivated understanding *with* the hearer, an understanding that comes about on the basis of a criticizable validity claim. We can understand the illocutionary components of assertions and confessions as the linguistic representatives of claims to the validity of the corresponding assertoric or expressive sentences. They bring to expression not only the action character in general but the speaker's demand that the hearer *ought* to accept a sentence as true or sincere. In discussing Mead and Durkheim we have until now encountered the "ought" claim only in the form of normative validity, but we cannot simply equate the validity claim that the speaker connects to the assertion of a proposition (and it is on this that we shall now focus) with the validity of norms. There are, however, structural analogies between the sentence (equivalent in meaning to (3) above):

(8) It is right that a in s.

and the metalinguistic remark

(9) It is the case (is true) that p.

Unlike the illocutionary components of standard speech acts which express the fact that the speaker is raising a validity claim, (8) and (9) express the validity claim *itself,* in one case as a normative validity claim, in the other as an assertoric validity claim.

In order to see how such validity claims might have been constituted, I will start from the paradigmatic case of an institutionally bound speech act, such as marrying, and from the corresponding institutions, in this case of marriage. We shall assume that the speech act performed by the priest or the family elder at the wedding could be replaced by a ceremonial action of a nonverbal sort. The ceremony consists of a verbal or ritual action that counts in the appropriate situation as an act of marrying because it meets the institutionally set conditions for a marriage. In tribal societies the institutional complex of kinship relations is endowed with a moral authority anchored in the domain of the sacred. The institution of marriage derives its validity from the ritually protected normative consensus that Durkheim analyzes. This can be seen directly in the ceremonial character of the wedding—even when it is carried out *expressis verbis.* At any rate, it is clear that the validity of the ceremony depends on fulfilling a valid norm.

We can describe this norm by means of a sentence having the form of (8) above. We understand the expression that appears therein—"it is right"—in the sense of the concept of normative validity that Durkheim introduced in anthropological terms.[56] There is no need here to analyze further what it means to say that the moral authority of an existing institution "stems" from the so-called collective consciousness. It is enough to recall that at this stage the "ought" claim of norms cannot yet be interpreted in terms of a posttraditional understanding of norms, that is, in the sense of an agreement established in the form of intersubjective recognition of a *criticizable* validity claim. We can imagine a context in which sentence (8) is used as an authoritative utterance not meant to be criticizable. One does not understand (8) if one does not know that the addressee can disobey the command and violate the underlying norm. As soon as participants in interactions achieve mutual understanding in any grammatical language at all, they can, to be sure, appeal to the validity of norms *in various ways* and can differentiate the illocutionary force of the normative in various respects—for example, by conceding, delegating, allowing, regretting something, or by authorizing, punishing, honoring someone. The criticizability of actions in relation to existing norms by no means presupposed, however, the possibility of contesting the validity of the underlying norms themselves.

It is interesting to note the differences from the structurally analogous sentence (9). One does not understand (9) if one does not know that the speaker can adopt the sentence only in the role of a proponent, that is, in the readiness to defend '*p*' against possible objections of an opponent. It may be the case that the claim to propositional truth originally borrowed the structure of a validity claim that can be *justifiably* redeemed from the kind of claim that rests on valid norms, but it had at once to appear in a radicalized version geared to the giving of reasons in its support. This suggests that the concept of a criticizable validity claim derives from an assimilation of the truth of statements to the validity of norms (which was, to begin with, not criticizable).

Since descriptive statements appear in modalized form, and since the illocutionary components of constative speech acts can be thematized (as in (9)), it is tempting to interpret truth in structural analogy to an already available concept of normative validity. Mead and Durkheim suggest such a hypothesis—Mead because he believes anyway that the concept of an objective world is formed via a desocialization of the perception of things, and Durkheim because he traces the counterfactual determination of a spatiotemporally neutralized idea of truth back to the idealizing power residing in the notion of the sacred.

Up to this point I have neglected this element in the Durkheimian concept of the *conscience collective:* "Animals know only one world, the one which they perceive by experience, internal as well as external. Men alone have the faculty of conceiving the ideal, of adding something to the real. Now where does this singular privilege come from? ... The explanation of religion which we have proposed has precisely this advantage, that it gives an answer to this question. For our definition of the sacred is that it is something added to and above the real; now the ideal answers to the same definition; we cannot explain one without explaining the other."[57] According to Durkheim, a social group cannot stabilize its collective identity and its cohesiveness without projecting an *idealized image* of its society: "The ideal society is not outside of the real society; it is part of it. Far from being divided between them as between two poles which mutually repel each other, we cannot hold to one without holding to the other."[58] The normative consensus that is expounded in the semantics of the sacred is present to members in the form of an idealized agreement transcending spatiotemporal changes. This furnishes the model for all concepts of validity, especially for the idea of truth:

> In fact, logical thinking is always impersonal thinking, and is also thought *sub specie aeternitatis*—as though for all time. Impersonality and stability are the two characteristics of truth. Now logical life evidently presupposes that men know, at least confusedly, that there is such a thing as truth, distinct from sensuous appearance. But how have they been able to arrive at this conception? We generally talk as though it should have spontaneously presented itself to them from the moment they open their eyes to the world. However, there is nothing in immediate experience which could suggest it; everything even contradicts it. Thus the child and the animal have no suspicion of it. History shows that it has taken centuries for it to disengage and establish itself. In our Western world, it was with the great thinkers of Greece that it first became clearly conscious of itself and of the consequences which it implies; when the discovery was made, it caused an amazement which Plato has translated into magnificent language. But it is only at this epoch that the idea is expressed in philosophic formulae, it was necessarily pre-existent in the stage of an obscure sentiment.[59]

The idea of truth as a transcending validity claim derives from the idealizations inherent in collective identity: "It is under the form of collective thought that impersonal thought is for the first time revealed to humanity; we cannot see by what other way this revelation could have been made ... Hence the individual at least obscurely takes account of the fact that above his private ideas, there is a world of absolute ideas according to which he must shape his own; he catches a glimpse of a whole intellectual kingdom in which he participates, but which is greater than him. This is the first intuition of the realm of truth."[60]

The idea of truth can get from the concept of normative validity only the impersonality—supratemporal—of an idealized agreement, of an intersubjectivity related to an ideal communication community. This moment of a "harmony of minds" is *added* to that of a "harmony with the nature of things." The authority standing behind knowledge does not coincide with moral authority. Rather, the concept of truth combines the objectivity of experience with a claim to the intersubjective validity of a corresponding descriptive statement, the idea of the correspondence of sentences to facts with the concept of an idealized consensus.[61] It is only from this *combination* that we get the concept of a criticizable validity claim.

To the degree that the normative validity rooted in paleosymbols can in turn be interpreted by analogy to the truth claim, our understanding of normative sentences such as (8) is also changed. Commands can then be understood as utterances with which the speaker raises a *contestable* validity claim vis-à-vis members of a social group—and not merely the claim that a speech act conforms with a norm, where the validity of that authorizing norm itself remains untouched.

I shall not go into the validity claim of truthfulness or sincerity (which is analogous to truth) again. My aim in discussing it above was to explain how three different, indeed mode-specific, validity claims could have emerged from the integration of the narrower, paleosymbolically anchored concept or moral authority with the other components of speech acts, such that even nonregulative speech acts are invested with an illocutionary force independent of normative contexts.

(d) The illocutionary components express the fact that the speaker is explicitly raising a claim to propositional truth, normative rightness, or subjective truthfulness, as well as the particular aspects under which he is doing so. These aspects can differ more or less fundamentally. A promise with which a speaker takes on a new obligation differs from a command in which a speaker relies on existing obligations more basically than a recommendation differs from a warning. Furthermore, modes can be selected in such a way that they discriminate more or less sharply between validity claims. While a speaker raises assertoric validity claims with assertions or statements just as unmistakably as he does normative validity claims with promises and commands, the validity relation of ad-

vising and recommending, for instance, remains unclear; according to the circumstances, they can be based on either predictive or moral-practical knowledge. Culture-dependent surface differentiation between the various ways in which speakers can relate to validity claims within a given language often merely covers up a lack of discrimination among culture-invariant validity claims. We should note, finally, that normative validity is differentiated to the degree that it gets detached from the sacred foundations of moral authority and splits up into the social validity of norms that are de facto recognized, and the ideal validity of norms that deserve to be recognized. As we shall see, in the course of this process, the formal aspects of ought-validity get separated from the material aspects of cultural values embodied in forms of life.

However, the wide range of cultural and historical variation of the illocutionary forces available in individual languages does not affect the fact that at a differentiated level of linguistic communication participants in interaction gain the freedom to say "yes" or "no" to validity claims. The scope for freedom is characterized by the fact that under the presuppositions of communicative action a hearer can reject the utterance of a speaker only by denying its validity. Assent means then that the negation of the invalidity of the utterance is affirmed. Whenever participants in interactions are pursuing mutual understanding by means of whatever symbols, there are alternative possibilities of understanding, not understanding, or misunderstanding; on this basis, cooperation and conflict already assume a different character. But it is only at the level of grammatical speech that an agreement *can* take on the form of communicatively achieved consensus. Linguistic communication presupposes understanding and taking positions on criticizable validity claims. Any explicit agreement thereby has something of the nature of a disagreement that has been avoided, excluded; it is mediated through an at least implicit rejection of a contradictory utterance, that is, through a negation.[62]

If the rejection of an assertion '*p*' means that the statement '*p*' is untrue, the affirmation of '*p*' implies a negation of this rejection, that is, of the sentence: 'It is untrue that *p*'. If the rejection of the command '*q*' (where '*q*' stands for an action that is to be carried out or refrained from) means that in the given situation the command is not justified by the norm *N* invoked to authorized it, and is to this extent not right, the affirmation of '*q*' implies the negation of this rejection, that is, of the sentence: 'It is not right for the one commanding to utter *q* in *s* with reference to *N*'. If, finally, the rejection of the avowal '*r*' means that ego does not mean what he says, the affirmation of '*r*' implies the negation of this rejection, that is, of the sentence: 'Ego's utterance *r* is insincere'.

The binding effect of illocutionary forces comes about, ironically, through the fact that participants can say "no" to speech-act offers. The critical character of this saying "no" distinguishes taking a position in this way from a reaction based solely on caprice. A hearer can be "bound" by speech-act offers because he is not permitted arbitrarily to refuse them but only to say "no" to them, that is, to reject them for reasons. We are already familiar with two consequences for the structure of communication that flow from this "being able to say no."[63]

I am referring, *first* of all, to the stratification of action oriented to reaching understanding into naïve and reflexive forms of communication. Because communicative action demands an orientation to validity claims, it points from the start to the possibility of settling disagreements by adducing reasons. From this can develop institutionalized forms of argumentative speech, in which validity claims normally raised naïvely, and immediately affirmed or denied, can be made thematic as controversial validity claims and discussed hypothetically. In the *second* place, I am referring to the demarcation of action oriented to understanding from action oriented to consequences. Generally, alter is moved to link up his actions with ego's actions by a complicated mix of empirical and rational motives. Because communicative action demands an orientation to validity claims, it points from the start to the possibility that participants will distinguish more or less sharply between having an influence *upon* one another and reaching an understanding *with* one another. Thus, as we shall see, a generalized "willingness to accept" can develop along two lines: empirical ties forged by inducement and intimidation, on the one hand, and rational trust motivated by agreement based on reasons, on the other hand.

A *further* consequence of being able to say "no," which was merely suggested above, concerns the actors themselves. If one aims to reconstruct how participants learn to orient their actions explicitly to validity claims, and wants to do so by means of the mechanism of taking the attitude of the other, the model of inner dialogue, which Mead used rather too unspecifically, turns out in fact to be helpful. In anticipating from alter a negative answer to his own speech act, and raising against himself an objection that alter might raise, ego understands what it means to make a *criticizable* validity claim. As soon, then, as ego masters the orientation to validity claims, he can repeat the internalization of discursive relations once more. Now alter already encounters him with the expectation that ego is not assuming the communicative role of the first person only in a naïve manner, but will expand it, if necessary, to the role of a proponent in argumentation. If ego makes *this* attitude of alter his own, that is to say, if he views himself through the eyes of an arguing opponent and considers how he will answer to his critique, he gains a reflective relation to himself. By internalizing the role of a participant in argumentation, ego becomes capable of self-criticism. It is the relation-to-self established by this model of self-criticism that we shall call "reflec-tive." Knowing that one does not know has, since Socrates, rightly been regarded as the basis for self-knowledge.

The reflective relation-to-self takes on different shadings according to the modes of language use. Ego can take up a relation to himself by way of a critique of his own statement, his own action, or his own self-presentation. The self to which he then relates is not a mysterious some-thing; it is familiar to him from the communicative practice of daily life; it is ego himself in the communicative role of the first person, as he asserts the existence of states of affairs in an objectivating attitude, or enters into an interpersonal relation regarded as legitimate in the norm-conformative attitude, or makes a subjective experience accessible to a public in an expressive attitude. Correspondingly, ego can relate to him-self according to the model of self-criticism: as an *epistemic* subject who is capable of learning and has already acquired a certain knowledge in his cognitive-instrumental dealings with reality, or as a *practical* subject who is capable of acting and has already formed a certain character or a superego in interactions with his reference persons, or as an *affective* subject who is sensitive, "passionate" in Feuerbach's sense, and has al-ready demarcated from the external world of facts and norms a special domain of subjectivity marked by privileged access and intuitive pres-ence.

It is of course misleading to speak of three subjects. In the perspective of self-criticism, when ego adopts in relation to himself the role of a possible opponent in a debate about validity claims he has raised naïvely, he encounters a self that is, naturally, one and the same under all three aspects. Indeed, it is one and the same from the very start, so to speak; there is no need at all for a subsequent identification of the three rela-tions-to-self.

We have presupposed that ego can take up these different relations to himself only by confronting himself as a communicatively acting subject, by adopting toward himself the attitude of *another* participant in argu-mentation. He encounters himself just as he has adopted a performative attitude. It is this attitude of a first person toward a second that guaran-tees the unity in the changing modes of language use, the continuity in the transitions between objectivating, norm-conformative, and expres-sive attitudes that we continually make in communicative practice. From a genetic standpoint, the performative attitude can be understood, per-haps, as the result of a secularization and generalization of that emotion-ally ambivalent attitude toward sacred objects that originally secured the recognition of moral authority. This transformation becomes necessary to the degree that the illocutionary components of speech acts are released from their symbiotic entanglement with archaic institutions and differentiated so that assertoric and expressive sentences are also endowed with illocutionary forces, and in this way modalized and incorporated in communicative actions.

If it is the performative attitude that secures unity through changes in mode, then practical self-consciousness has a certain priority over epistemic and affective self-consciousness. The reflective relation to self is the ground of the actor's accountability. A responsible actor behaves self-critically not only in his directly moralizable actions but also in his cognitive and expressive utterances. Although accountability is at bottom a moral-practical category, it also extends to the cognitions and expressions included in the validity spectrum of action oriented to reaching understanding.

3. The Rational Structure of the Linguistification of the Sacred

We can return now to the question of how communicative action mediates between the ritually preserved fund of social solidarity and existing norms and personal identities. We looked at the sacred foundations of moral authority so as to be able to follow the phylogenetic line of development that leads from symbolically mediated to normatively guided interaction. And we discovered in the sacrally rooted validity of norms a starting point for the development from symbolically mediated interaction to language, that is, to grammatical speech. Our formal-pragmatic description of the general structure of speech acts has to draw on the pretheoretical knowledge of speakers who belong to a modern and—in a sense still to be explained more precisely—rationalized life-world. If, following Mead and Durkheim, we attempt now to locate a complex of social interaction that might be postulated as the hypothetical starting point of sociocultural development, we shall have to be careful, in depicting the connection between normatively guided action and grammatical speech, that our view is not distorted by our modern pre-understanding. As we cannot step out of an objectively given horizon of interpretation at will, we must simultaneously pose the social-evolutionary question of the direction of change in the initial constellations decisive for normatively guided action (as did both Mead and Durkheim).

In answering this question I shall be guided by the hypothesis that the socially integrative and expressive functions that were at first fulfilled by ritual practice pass over to communicative action; the authority of the holy is gradually replaced by the authority of an achieved consensus. This means a freeing of communicative action from sacrally protected normative contexts. The disenchantment and disempowering of the domain of the sacred takes place by way of a linguistification of the ritually secured, basic normative agreement; going along with this is a release of the rationality potential in communicative action. The aura of rapture and terror that emanates from the sacred, the *spellbinding* power of the holy, is sublimated into the *binding/bonding* force of criticizable validity claims and at the same time turned into an everyday occurrence. I want to develop these ideas by (A) taking up Durkheim's theory of the evolution of law and placing legal development in the context of the changing forms of social integration he observed. (B) The logic of this change in form can be clarified by means of a thought experiment based on Durkheim and (*C*) explained in terms of Mead's ideas concerning a discourse ethics. Mead's diagnosis of the irresistable advance of individuation provides a point of contact for (*D*) an excursus on identity and individuation. Finally, I would like (*E*) to mention certain reservations I have in regard to the formalistic and idealistic tendencies in Mead's social theory.

A.—The framework for Durkheim's first great work, *The Division of Labor in Society,* was the social evolution of law.[1] He offered lecture courses in the sociology of law on a number of occasions; significant parts of these lectures were published only posthumously.[2] Like Weber, Durkheim conceived of legal development as a process of disenchantment. I will not go into his attempts to classify areas of law from a social-evolutionary perspective. Archaic law is basically criminal law; he treats civil law as exemplary for modern law, with private property as its core institution and contract and inheritance as related guarantees.

The question of how the moral authority of the sacred is converted into the validity of institutions does not arise in connection with the primitive institutions of criminal law, for the latter is, to begin with, only the symbolic expression of a reaction to the violation of taboos. The original crime is sacrilege, touching the untouchable, profaning the holy. Durkheim sees in the punishment of sacrilege an expression of the horror and fear of fateful consequences; punishment is a ritual that restores the disturbed order. Condemning the sacrilege is thus merely the other side of venerating the sacred. The violation of a sacred norm counts as a crime not because sanctions are placed upon it; rather, it brings sanctions because norms are at first an apparatus for protecting sacred objects or regions. Punishment is understood as expiation:

> It is certain that at the bottom of the notion of expiation there is the idea of a satisfaction accorded to some power, real or ideal, which is superior to us. When we desire the repression of crime, it is not that we desire to avenge personally, but to avenge something sacred which we feel more or less confusedly outside and above us. This something we conceive of in different ways according to the time and the place. Sometimes it is a simple idea, as morality, duty; most often we represent it in the form of one or several concrete beings: ancestors, divinity. That is why penal law is not alone essentially religious in origin, but indeed always retains a certain religious stamp. It is because the acts that it punishes appear to be attacks upon something transcendent, whether being or concept. It is for this very reason that we explain to ourselves the need for a sanction superior to a simple reparation which would content us in the order of purely human interests.[3]

Reparation, in the sense of compensating the harm done, belongs in the profane sphere of balancing private interests. In civil law, paying damages takes the place of expiation. It is along this axis that Durkheim marks off the evolution of law. Modern law crystallizes around the balancing of private interests; it has shed its sacred character. At the same time, the authority of the sacred cannot be dropped without replacement, for the validity has to be based on something that can bind the choices of private legal persons and *obligate* the parties to a contract.

In his lectures on the sociology of law, Durkheim pursues this problem in connection with property and contract law. He elaborates on the analogies that obtain between the archaic legal institutions of property and sacred things. Property is originally borrowed from the gods. Ritual offerings are taxes paid at first to the gods, then later to the priests, and finally to the state authorities. Owing to this sacred origin, property has a magical character which it communicates to the owner—the property relation is based on a magical bond between person and thing:

> The sacred character, wherever it resides, is in its essence contagious and communicates itself to any object it comes in contact with ... The characteristic that makes a thing the property of a certain subject or individual exhibits the same contagiousness. It tends always to pass from the objects in which it resides to all those objects that come in contact with them. Property is contagious. The thing appropriated, like the sacred thing, draws to itself all things that touch it and appropriates them. The existence of this singular capacity is confirmed by a whole collection of juridical principles which the legal experts have often found disconcerting: these are the principles that decide what is called 'right of accession'.[4]

Private property is a later derivate. The rights of the gods pass first to the collectivity; property rights are then differentiated according to sub-collectivities, tribes, and families; they are tied to the status of a family member and not to an individual legal person.[5] Inheritance is thus the normal form for the transfer of property. Even the competing form of acquiring and alienating property, the contract, counts to begin with as a change of status: "Indeed, men's wills cannot agree to contract obligations if these obligations do not arise from a status in law already acquired, whether of things or of persons; it can only be a matter of modifying the status and of superimposing new relations on those already existing. The contract, then, is a source of variations which presupposes a primary basis in law, but one that has a different origin. The contract is the supreme instrument by which transfers of ownership are carried through. The contract itself cannot constitute the primary foundations on which the right of contract rests."[6]

The conspicuous formalism with which contracts are concluded, the ceremonies with which they are sealed, are reminders of the religious, noncontractual bases of the contract.

(a) At this point we encounter the key question that inspired Durkheim's investigations in the sociology of law. The contract between autonomous legal persons is the basic instrument of bourgeois private law; in modern legal theory it has been elevated to a paradigm of legal relations in general. How can such a contract bind the parties to it when the sacred foundation of law has disappeared? The standard answer to this question, from Hobbes to Weber, has been that modern law is precisely coercive law. Corresponding to the internalization of morality, there is a complementary transformation of law into externally imposed law authorized by the state and dependent on the sanctioning apparatus of the state. The legality of a contract, or generally of any relation between private legal subjects, means that legal claims can be sued for. The possibility of, as it were, automatically enforcing the fulfillment of legal claims is supposed to guarantee obedience to the law. Durkheim, however, is not satisfied with this response. Even the obedience of modern legal subjects has to have a moral core. For the legal system is part of a political order, together with which it would break down if that order could not claim legitimacy.

Thus Durkheim inquires into the legitimacy of legal relationships in the form of contracts between autonomous legal persons. He denies that a contractual relation can acquire legitimacy solely on the basis of the conditions under which the contract is concluded. The obligatory character of a contract by no means follows from the fact of an agreement voluntarily entered into by two parties in their own interests. A contract of this sort "is not sufficient unto itself, but is possible only thanks to a regulation of the contract which is originally social."[7] This regulation cannot itself be an expression of mere choice; it cannot rest on the facticity of government force; but then where do the legal foundations of a contract get their moral authority once the law has been secularized? "We have seen that the rights which have their origin in things, derive from the sacred nature of things; we need not revert to this. Therefore, all moral and juridical relations and ties which derive from a personal or from a *real* status, owe their existence to some virtue *sui generis*, inherent either in the subjects or the objects and compelling respect. But how could a virtue of this kind reside in mere inclinations of the will?"[8]

The answer—which, it is interesting to note, Durkheim elaborates in connection with the example of a labor contract—is simple: the obligatory character of a contract is based on the legitimacy of the legal regulations that underlie it; the latter count as legitimate only insofar as they express a general interest. One can test this by checking whether the

contracts they authorize actually produce a balance of interests or violate, instead, the legitimate interests of one of the parties, regardless of
the latter's formally free consent. "Thus, the coming on the scene of the
contract by mutual consent, together with an increase in human sympa-
thies, inclined the minds of men to the idea that the contract was only
moral and only to be recognized and given sanction by society, provided
it was not merely a means of exploiting one of the contracting parties, in
a word, provided it was just . . . It is not enough that the contract shall
be by consent. It has to be just, and the way in which the consent is
given is now no more than the outward criterion of the degree of equity
in the contract."[9]

From the perspective of Max Weber, it might seem as if Durkheim
wants to reclaim for formal law substantive justice plain and simple. In
fact, however, his argument points in another direction. Durkheim wants
to make clear that the obligatory character of constraints cannot be derived from the voluntary nature of an agreement between individuals
governed by their interests. The binding force of moral agreement
grounded in the sacred can be replaced only by moral agreement that
expresses in rational form what was always intended in the symbolism
of the holy: the generality of the underlying interest. Durkheim is here
following Rousseau's famous distinction:[10] the general interest is by no
means the sum of, or a compromise between, a number of individual
interests. Rather, the general interest draws its morally obligating force
from its impersonal and impartial character. "The role of the state, in fact,
is not to express and sum up the unreflective thought of the mass of the
people but to superimpose on this unreflective thought a more considered thought, which therefore cannot be other than different."[11]

In differentiated societies, collective consciousness is embodied in the
state. The latter must itself provide for the legitimacy of the force over
which it has a monopoly. "To sum up, we can therefore say that the state
is a special organ whose responsibility it is to work out certain representations which hold good for the collectivity. These representations are
distinguished from the other collective representations by their high degree of consciousness and reflection."[12] It is characteristic of the development of modern states that they change over from the sacred foundation of legitimation to foundation on a common will, communicatively
shaped and discursively clarified in the political public sphere: "Seen
from this point, a democracy may, then, appear as the political system by
which the society can achieve a consciousness of itself in its purest form.
The more that deliberation and reflection and a critical spirit play a considerable part in the course of public affairs, the more democratic the
nation. It is the less democratic when lack of consciousness, uncharted
customs, the obscure sentiments and prejudices that evade investigation,

predominate. This means that democracy ... is the form that societies are assuming to an increasing degree."[13] Durkheim sees the moral superiority of the democratic principle in the arrangements for a discursive formation of will: "Because it is a system based on reflection, it allows the citizen to accept the laws of the country with more intelligence and thus less passively. Because there is a constant flow of communication between themselves and the state, the state is for individuals no longer like an exterior force that imparts a wholly mechanical impetus. Owing to the constant exchanges between them and the state, its life becomes linked with theirs, just as their life does with that of the state."[14] To the degree that the basic religious consensus gets dissolved and the power of the state loses its sacred supports, the unity of the collectivity can be established and maintained only as the unity of a communication community, that is to say, only by way of a consensus arrived at communicatively in the public sphere.

Against the background of this conversion of the state over to a secular basis of legitimation, the development of the contract from a ritual formalism into the most important instrument of bourgeois private law suggests the idea of a "linguistification" of a basic religious consensus that has been set communicatively aflow. In archaic societies the ceremonial declarations of the parties to a contract are scarcely distinguishable from ritual actions; through the words of the participants it is the consensus-forming power of the sacred itself that speaks: "The wills can effect the bond only on condition of declaring themselves. This declaration is made by words. There is something in words that is real, natural and living and they can be endowed with a sacred force, thanks to which they compel and bind those who pronounce them. It is enough for them to be pronounced in ritual form and in ritual conditions. They take on a sacred quality by that very act. One means of giving them the sacred character is the oath, or invocation of a divine being. Through this invocation, the divine being becomes the guarantor of the promise exchanged. Thereby the promise, as soon as exchanged in this way ... becomes compulsive, under threat of sacred penalties of known gravity."[15] In modern law, by contrast, the private contract draws its binding power from its legality; but the law that gives it this legality owes its obligatory character, demanding recognition, to a legal system legitimated in the end by political will-formation. It is the achievement of mutual understanding by a communication community of citizens, their own words, that brings about the binding consensus.

(b) Durkheim treats the evolution of law in connection with a change in the form of social integration affecting society as a whole. He characterizes this trend as a departure from an initial situation in which "the individual personality is absorbed into the collective personality."[16]

Durkheim thinks of the dissolution of this mechanical solidarity of tribal members, who, assimilated one to the other, derive their own identities almost completely from the collective identity, as a process of emancipation. To the degree that social structures become differentiated, sociated individuals free themselves from a collective consciousness encompassing the whole personality structure. At the same time, they distance themselves from the basic religious consensus in which everyone is merged with everyone else. Durkheim characterizes this development from *mechanical* to *organic* solidarity at three levels. The rationalization of worldviews goes hand in hand with a generalization of moral and legal norms and with a growing individuation of individuals.

The *rationalization of worldviews* expresses itself in a process of abstraction that sublimates mythical powers into transcendent gods and finally into ideas and concepts and, at the cost of shrinking down the domain of the sacred, leaves behind a nature bereft of gods.

> In the beginning, the gods are not distinct from the universe, or rather there are no gods, but only sacred beings, without their sacred character being related to any external entity as their source ... But little by little religious forces are detached from the things of which they are first only the attributes, and become hypostatized. Thus is formed the notion of spirits or gods who, while residing here or there, as preferred, nevertheless exist outside of the particular objects to which they are more specifically attached. By that very fact they are less concrete ... The Graeco-Latin polytheism, which is a more elevated and better organized form of animism, marks new progress in the direction of transcendence. The residence of the gods becomes sharply distinct from that of men. Set upon the mysterious heights of Olympus or dwelling in the recesses of the earth, they personally intervene in human affairs only in somewhat intermittent fashion. But it is only with Christianity that God takes leave of space; his kingdom is no longer of this world. The dissociation of nature and the divine is so complete that it degenerates into antagonism. At the same time, the concept of divinity becomes more general and more abstract, for it is formed, not of sensations, as originally, but of ideas.[17]

In the end, rationalized worldviews have to compete with the authority of a fully secularized science. This gives rise to a reflective attitude toward tradition in general. A tradition that has become problematic in principle can now be continued only through the medium of permanent critique. At the same time, the traditional consciousness of time switches over to orientations toward the future.[18]

Corresponding to the abstraction of the representations of the divine, there is a *generalization of values*: "The idea of man, for example, re-

places in law, morality, religions, that of Roman, which, being more concrete, is more refractory to science."[19] The parallel development at the
level of institutionalized values consists in a *universalization of law and
morality* that brings with it a disenchantment of sacred law, that is, a de-
formalization of legal procedures. Whereas the rules of law and morality
were "linked at first to local circumstances, to particularities, ethnic, cli-
matic, etc., they free themselves little by little, and with the same stroke
become more general. What makes this increase of generality obvious is
the uninterrupted decline of formalism."[20] Together with their range of
application, the latitude for interpreting norms and the necessity of rationality justifying them also grow. "There is nothing fixed save abstract
rules which can be freely applied in very different ways. Then they
no longer have the same ascendancy nor the same force of resistance.
Indeed, if practices and formulae, when they are precise, determine
thought and movement with a necessity analogous to that of reflexes,
these general principles, on the contrary, can pass into facts only with
the aid of intelligence. But, once reflection is awakened, it is not easy to
restrain it. When it has taken hold, it develops spontaneously beyond the
limits assigned to it. One begins by putting articles of faith beyond discussion; then discussion extends to them. One wishes an explanation of
them; one asks their reasons for existing, and, as they submit to this
search, they lose part of their force."[21]

Finally, in the manifestations of *modern individualism* Durkheim sees
signs of a quasi-religious revaluation of the individual, of a "cult of personality, or individual dignity,"[22] which commands everyone, as it were,
"to be more and more of a person."[23]

The increasing individuation can be measured by both the differentiation of unique identities and the growth of personal autonomy: "To be a
person is to be an autonomous source of action. Man acquires this quality
only in so far as there is something in which is his alone and which
individualizes him, as he is something more than a simple incarnation of
the generic type of his race and his group."[24]

This autonomy is more than a capacity for *arbitrary* free choice
within an expanded and variable range of alternatives. It does not consist
in the "abstract power of choice between two opposites," but rather in
what we have called "reflective self-understanding." According to Durkheim, this increasing individuation and growing autonomy of the individual are characteristic of a new form of solidarity that is no longer secured
by prior value consensus but has to be cooperatively achieved by virtue
of individual efforts. In place of social integration through belief, we have
a social integration through cooperation. Durkheim originally thought
he could explain this organic solidarity as an effect of the social division
of labor, that is, of the differentiation of the social system. A few years

later, in the preface to the second edition of *The Division of Labor in Society,* he revised this view. The differentiation of the system does not itself give rise to the new form of solidarity; so Durkheim sees himself forced to look for help in a morality of occupational groups that he has to postulate and to illustrate by historical examples painted in utopian hues. He does not explain what mechanism could produce this new form of solidarity in place of structural differentiation.[25]

Nevertheless he does offer an interesting suggestion; in the transition from the mechanical to the organic form of solidarity, he sees a "tendency to become more rational."[26] And at the end of the book he also specifies the standard he uses when he conceives of the modernization of society as rationalization—a universalistic morality that is realized to the extent that individuals learn to act responsibly.

> If, moreover, we remember that the collective consciousness is becoming more and more a cult of the individual, we shall see that what characterizes the morality of organized societies, compared to that of segmental societies, is that there is something more human, therefore more rational, about them. It does not direct our activities to ends which do not immediately concern us; it does not make us servants of ideological powers of a nature other than our own, which follow their directions without occupying themselves with the interests of men ... The rules which constitute it do not have a constraining force which snuffs out free thought; but because they are rather made for us and, in a certain sense, by us, we are free ... We know only too well what a laborious work it is to erect this society in which each individual will have the place he merits, will be rewarded as he deserves, where everybody, accordingly, will spontaneously work for the good of all and each. Indeed, a moral code is not above another because it commands in a dryer and more authoritarian manner, or because it is more sheltered from reflection. Of course, it must attach us to something besides ourselves, but it is not necessary for it to chain us to it with impregnable bonds.[27]

In holding out this prospect, Durkheim does not avoid the pitfalls of the philosophy of history. On the one hand, he strives for the descriptive attitude of a social scientist who merely observes historical tendencies; on the other hand, in a normative attitude, he adopts the concept of a universalistic morality that seems to arise from these tendencies, at least as a generally accepted ideal, and announces pithily the duty "to make a moral code for ourselves."[28] Durkheim is evidently not clear about the methodological conditions that a descriptive account of a developmental process, conceived as a process of rationalization, has to satisfy.

Moralism is an ironic echo of his positivism.[29] As we have seen, in his later writings, particularly in his studies of the sociology of religion and law, Durkheim came close to the idea of the linguistification of a basic religious consensus that has been set communicatively aflow. From this theoretical perspective, I shall attempt to defend the changes in the form of social integration described by Durkheim as indicators of a process of rationalization. With this we return to Mead's point of explaining linguistically mediated, normatively guided interaction by way of rational reconstruction.

As was propaedeutically set forth in the first chapter of Volume 1, the conditions of rationality can be explained in terms of the conditions for a communicatively achieved, reasonable consensus. Linguistic communication that aims at mutual understanding—and not merely at reciprocal influence—satisfies the *presuppositions* for rational utterances or for the rationality of speaking and acting subjects. We have also seen why the rationality inherent in speech can become empirically effective to the extent that communicative acts take over the steering of social interactions and fulfill functions of social reproduction, of maintaining social lifeworlds. The rationality potential in action oriented to mutual understanding can be released and translated into the rationalization of the lifeworlds of social groups to the extent that language fulfills functions of reaching understanding, coordinating actions, and socializing individuals; it thereby becomes a medium through which cultural reproduction, social integration, and socialization take place. Bringing social evolution into the perspective of rationalization in this fashion, we can combine the theoretical approaches of Mead and Durkheim to construct a hypothetical initial state; from this we can hope to learn what the change to communicative action—at first narrowly circumscribed by institutions—meant for the process of hominization, and why the linguistic mediation of norm-guided action could have supplied the impetus for a rationalization of the lifeworld.

The construction I am proposing is based, on the one hand, on the limit state that Durkheim assumes for a totally integrated society, and on the other hand, on the disintegrating effects that speech acts, by virtue of the structures we have analyzed, give rise to when the symbolic reproduction of the lifeworld gets tied to communicative action. This thought experiment requires that we think of the Durkheimian zero point of society as composed of a sacred domain that does not yet *need* a linguistic mediation of ritual practice, and a profane domain that does not yet *permit* a linguistic mediation of cooperation with its own dynamics. Particularly this last assumption is artificial, but it is not completely inappropriate, inasmuch as Durkheim does not attribute any really constitutive significance to grammatical speech. Our thought experiment is intended to show that when it becomes linguistically channeled, social reproduction is subject to certain structural constraints; and that by reference to these we can—not causally explain, certainly, but—render reconstructively comprehensible, in their inner logic, the above-mentioned structural transformation of worldviews, the universalization of law and morality, and the growing individuation of socialized subjects.

B.—Let us imagine, for the moment, the limit case of a totally integrated society. Religion serves only to interpret existing ritual practices in concepts of the holy; without a strictly cognitive content, it has not yet taken on the character of a *world*view. It secures, in the sense of cultural determinism, the unity of the collectivity and largely represses conflicts that might arise from power relations and economic interests. These counterfactual assumptions signify a state of social integration in which language has only minimal significance. The prior value consensus needs, of course, to be linguistically actualized and channeled into situations of action, but the achievement of mutual understanding remains so tightly restricted to an instrumental role that the influence the structure of speech acts has on the nature and composition of the cultural tradition may be ignored. In a somewhat different context, Wittgenstein spoke of language "going on holiday"; when it is released from the discipline of everyday practice, disengaged from its social functions, it luxuriates, kicks over the the traces. We are trying to imagine a state in which language is on holiday, or at any rate, one in which language's proper weight has not yet made itself felt in social reproduction. Considerations similar to those we have introduced in connection with the function of reaching understanding can be spelled out for the functions of coordinating action and socializing individuals as well.

In a seamlessly integrated society, the religious cult is something like a total institution that encompasses and normatively integrates all actions, whether in the family or in the area of social labor, to such a degree that every transgression of a norm has the significance of a sacrilege. It is true that this basic institution can branch out into norms specific to situations and to tasks only by virtue of linguistic mediation. But in the process, communicative actions are confined to instrumental roles, so that the influence that language has on the validity and application of norms may be ignored. It is above all the third aspect of such a society that Durkheim emphasizes—the reproduction of the group identity in the personality structure of each individual member. Personality is divided into a general component that stereotypically reproduces the structures of the society and an individual, nonsocialized, residual component tied to the individual organism. This situation expresses the idea of a socialization process in which the individuating force of linguistically established intersubjectivity does not yet play any role.

Finally, the structures of worldview, institutions, and individual personality are not yet seriously separated from one another; they are fused in the collective consciousness constitutive of the identity of the group. There is a differentiation of this sort inherent in the structures of linguistic communication, but it takes effect only to the extent that communicative action has its own weight in the functions of mutual understanding, social integration, and personality formation, and dissolves the symbiotic relation in which religion and society stand. Only when the structures of action oriented to reaching understanding become effective does a linguistification of the sacred arise, determining the logic of the changing forms of social integration as described by Durkheim. Our thought experiment is meant to show that the abstraction of worldviews, the universalization of law and morality, and growing individuation can be conceived as developments that, so far as their structural aspects are concerned, set in when, in the midst of a seamlessly integrated society, the rationality potential of action oriented to reaching understanding becomes unfettered. We shall leave to one side here the empirical conditions for a dynamic of this sort.

As we have seen, in grammatical speech, propositional components are joined with illocutionary and expressive components in such a way that semantic contents can fluctuate among them. Whatever can be said at all, can also be expressed in assertoric form. With this basic feature of language in mind, we can make clear what it means for religious worldviews to connect up with communicative action. Background knowledge enters into the situation definitions of goal-oriented actors who regulate their cooperation in a consensual manner; the results of such interpretative accomplishments are stored in worldviews. As semantic contents of sacred and profane origin fluctuate freely in the medium of language, there is a fusion of meanings; moral-practical and expressive contents are combined with cognitive-instrumental contents in the form of cultural knowledge. We can distinguish two aspects of this process.

On the one hand, the normative and expressive contents of experience stemming from the domain in which collective identity is secured by ritual means can be expressed in the form of propositions and stored as *cultural knowledge*; this makes of religion a *cultural tradition* in need of being communicatively continued. On the other hand, sacred knowledge has to be *connected* to profane knowledge from the domains of instrumental action and social cooperation; this makes of religion a *worldview* with a claim to totality. To the extent that everyday communicative practice is given its proper weight, worldviews have to process the profane knowledge streaming into them, the flow of which they can less and less control; they have to bring this knowledge into a more or less consistent connection with moral-practical and expressive elements of knowledge. The structural aspects of the development of religious worldviews, which Durkheim and Weber sketched in complementary ways, can be explained by the fact that the validity basis of tradition shifts from ritual action over to communicative action. Convictions owe their authority less and less to the spellbinding power and the aura of the holy, and more and more to a consensus that is not merely reproduced but *achieved*, that is, brought about communicatively.

As we have also seen, in grammatical speech illocutionary components are joined with propositional and expressive components in such a way that an illocutionary force is connected with *every* speech act. From these illocutionary forces is constituted a concept of validity that, while it is modeled after the paleosymbolically rooted authority of the holy, is nonetheless of a genuinely linguistic nature. Keeping this basic feature of language in mind, we can make clear what it means when institutions grounded in the sacred not only act effectively in and through processes of reaching understanding—by steering, preforming, prejudging—but themselves become dependent upon the binding effect of consensus formation in language. Then social integration no longer takes place directly via institutionalized values but by way of intersubjective recognition of validity claims raised in speech acts. Communicative actions also remain embedded in existing normative contexts, but speakers can explicitly refer to the latter in speech acts and take up different stances toward them. From the fact that speech acts get their own proper illocutionary force—independent of existing normative contexts—some noteworthy consequences follow, both for the validity and for the application of norms.

The validity basis of norms of action changes insofar as every communicatively mediated consensus depends on reasons. The authority of the sacred that stands behind institutions is no longer valid per se. Sacred authorization becomes dependent instead on the justificatory accomplishments of religious worldviews. Entering into the situation interpretations of participants in communication, *cultural knowledge* takes on functions for coordinating action. So long as moral-practical elements of knowledge are mixed up with expressive and cognitive-instrumental elements in the basic concepts of mythical and religious-metaphysical worldviews, the latter can serve to explain and justify institutional systems. This means that all consonant experiences that can be consistently worked up in a worldview confirm existing institutions, whereas dissonant experiences that overload a worldview's potential for supplying reasons place belief in the legitimacy and the validity of the corresponding institutions in question. The institutional system can, however, come under pressure otherwise than through the structural transformation of worldviews; this can also happen as the result of a growing need for specification of altered and increasingly complex action situations. To the degree that communicative actors themselves take over the application of norms, the latter can become simultaneously more abstract and more specialized. The *communicatively mediated* application of action norms depends on participants coming to shared situation definitions that refer simultaneously to the objective, the normative, and the subjective facets of the situation in question. Participants in interaction must *themselves* relate the relevant norms to the given situation and tailor them to special tasks. To the degree that these interpretative accomplishments become independent from the normative context, the institutional system can deal with the growing complexity of action situations by branching out into a network of social roles and special regulations within a framework of highly abstract basic norms.

The universalization of law and morality noted by Durkheim can be explained in its structural aspect by the gradual shifting of problems of justifying and applying norms over to processes of consensus formation in language. Once a community of believers has been secularized into a community of cooperation, only a universalistic morality can retain its obligatory character. And only a formal law based on abstract principles creates a divide between legality and morality such that the domains of action, in which the responsibility for settling disputed questions of applying norms is institutionally lifted from participants, get sharply separated from those in which it is radically demanded of them.

Finally, as we have noted, in grammatical speech expressive components are joined with illocutionary and propositional components in such a way that the first-person pronoun appearing in the subject position of performative sentences has two overlapping meanings. On the one hand, it refers to ego as the speaker who has expressed his experiences in an expressive attitude; on the other hand, it refers to ego as a member of a social group who is entering into an interpersonal relation with (at least) one other member. With this basic feature of language in view, we can make clear what it means for socialization processes to be shaped by the linguistic structure of relations between a growing child and his reference persons. The structure of linguistic intersubjectivity which finds expression in the system of personal pronouns ensures that the child learns to play social roles in the first person.[30] This structural pressure blocks the simple reduplication of group identity in the personality structure of the individual; it works as a pressure toward individuation. Anyone who participates in social interaction in the communicative role of the first person must appear as an actor who demarcates from facts and norms an inner world to which he has privileged access and who, simultaneously, vis-à-vis other participants, takes initiatives that will be attributed to him as his "own" actions for which he is responsible.

The degree of individuation and the extent of responsibility vary with the scope for independent communicative action. Insofar as the socializing interaction of parents frees itself from fixed models and rigid norms, the competences transmitted in the socialization process become increasingly formal. The trend toward growing individuation and autonomy, observed by Durkheim, can be explained in its structural aspects by the fact that the formation of identities and the genesis of group membership become further and further removed from particular contexts and are shifted more and more over to the acquisition of generalized competences for communicative action.

The thought experiment briefly sketched above draws on the idea of a linguistification of the sacred to decode the *logic* of the changes in the form of social integration analyzed by Durkheim. The experiment illuminates the path along which we can make our way back from the formal–pragmatically clarified structures of action oriented to mutual understanding to the anthropologically deep-seated structures of linguistically mediated, normatively regulated action. Norm-guided interaction changes its structure to the degree that functions of cultural reproduction, social integration, and socialization pass from the domain of the sacred over to that of everyday communicative practice. In the process, the religious community that first made social cooperation possible is transformed into a communication community standing under the pressure to cooperate. Durkheim shares the social-evolutionary perspective with Mead. But he is unable to conceive the transition from forms of mechanical to forms of organic solidarity as a transformation of collective consciousness reconstructible *from within;* thus it remains unclear what entitles him to conceive of the changing form of social integration as a development toward rationality. The idea of a linguistification of the sacred is, to be sure, suggested by Durkheim, but it can be worked out only along the lines of a Meadean attempt at reconstruction. Mead does in fact definitely conceive of the communicative thawing of traditionally solid institutions based on sacred authority as a rationalization. He explicitly takes communicative action as a reference point for his utopian projection of a "rational society." His remarks on the possibility of development of modern societies, his outlines of a "rational," or, as he also writes, an "ideal" society read as if he wanted to answer the question of which structures a society would have to have if its social integration were to be completely converted over from sacred foundations to communicatively achieved consensus. I want to look next at the cultural development characterized by the differentiation of science, morality, and art.

Modern science and morality are governed by ideals of an objectivity and impartiality secured through unrestricted discussion, while modern art is defined by the subjectivism of a decentered ego's unrestricted experience of itself, freed from the constraints of knowledge and action. Inasmuch as the sacred domain was constitutive for society, neither science nor art can inherit the mantle of religion; only a morality, set communicatively aflow and developed into a discourse ethics, can replace the authority of the sacred *in this respect.* In this morality we find dissolved the archaic core of the normative, we see developed the rational meaning of normative validity.

The relationship between religion and morality can be seen in, among other things, the fact that morality gets no clear status in the construction of a structurally differentiated lifeworld. Unlike science and art, it cannot be regarded as belonging exclusively to the cultural tradition; unlike legal norms or character traits, it cannot be imputed exclusively to society or to personality. We can, of course, make an analytical separation between moral *representations* as elements of tradition, moral *rules* as elements of the norm system, and moral *consciousness* as an element of personality. But collective moral representations, moral norms, and the moral consciousness of individuals are aspects of one and the same morality. Something of the penetrating power of primordial sacred powers still attaches to morality; it permeates the since differentiated levels of culture, society, and personality in a way that is unique in modern societies.

Durkheim too credited only universalistic morality with the power to hold together a secularized society and to replace the basic, ritually secured, normative agreement on a highly abstract level. But only Mead grounded universalistic morality in such a way that it can be conceived as the result of a communicative rationalization, an unfettering of the rationality potential inherent in communicative action. In his rough sketch of a critique of Kantian ethics, he attempted to justify such a discourse ethic genetically.[31]

C.—Mead starts from an intuition common to all universalistic moral theories: the standpoint we adopt in judging morally relevant questions has to allow for the impartial consideration of the known interests of *everyone* involved, because moral norms, rightly understood, bring a *general* interest into play.[32] The utilitarians are in agreement with Kant in requiring universality of basic norms: "The utilitarian says it must be the greatest good of the greatest number; Kant says that the attitude of the act must be one which takes on the form of a universal law. I want to point out this common attitude of these two schools which are so opposed to each other in other ways: they both feel that an act which is moral must have in some way a universal character. If you state morality in terms of the result of the act, then you state the result in terms of the whole community; if in the attitude of the act, it must be in the respect for law, and the attitude must take on the form of a universal law, a universal rule. Both recognized that morality involves universality, that the moral act is not simply a private affair. A thing that is good from a moral standpoint must be a good for everyone under the same conditions."[33]

This intuition, which has been given expression in the dogmatics of world religions no less than in the topoi of common sense, is better analyzed by Kant than by the utilitarians. Whereas the latter, with their idea of the general welfare, the greatest happiness for the greatest number, are specifying a point of view from which to test the universalizability of interests, Kant proposes a principle of legislation that all moral norms have to be able to satisfy. From a generalizing compromise among fundamentally particular interests we do not get an interest outfitted with the authority of a general interest, that is, with the claim to be recognized by everyone involved as a shared interest. Thus, the utilitarian is unable to explain that moment of uncoerced, well-considered, rationally motivated consent that valid norms demand of everyone involved. Kant explains the validity of moral norms by reference to the meaning of the universality of laws of practical reason. He presents the categorical imperative as a maxim by which each individual can test whether a given or recommended norm deserves general assent, that is, counts as a law.

Mead picks up this line of thought: "We are what we are through our relationship to others. Inevitably, then, our end must be a social end, both from the standpoint of its content . . . and also from the point of view of form. Sociality gives the universality of ethical judgments and lies back of the popular statement that the voice of all is the universal voice; that is, everyone who can rationally appreciate the situation agrees."[34] Mead gives a characteristic twist to the Kantian argument by responding in social-theoretical terms to the question of why moral norms may claim social validity on the basis of their universality. The authority of moral norms rests on the fact that they embody a general interest, and the unity of the collective is at stake in protecting this interest. "It is this feel for social structure which is implicit in what is present that haunts the generous nature and causes a sense of obligation which transcends any claim that his actual social order fastens upon him."[35] On this point Mead is in accord with Durkheim. The "ought" quality of moral norms implicitly invokes the danger that any harm to the social bond means for all the members of a collectivity—the danger of anomie, of group identity breaking down, of the members common life-contexts disintegrating.

To the extent that language becomes established as the principle of sociation, the conditions of socialization converge with the conditions of communicatively produced intersubjectivity. At the same time, the authority of the sacred is converted over to the binding force of normative validity claims that can be redeemed only in discourse. The concept of normative validity is cleansed in this way of empirical admixtures; the validity of any norm means in the end only that it *could* be accepted with good reasons by *everyone* involved. In this way of viewing the matter, Mead agrees with Kant that "the 'ought' does involve universality . . . Wherever the element of the 'ought' comes in, wherever one's conscience speaks, it always takes on this universal form."[36]

The universality of a moral norm can be a criterion of its validity only if by this is meant that universal norms express in a reasonable way the common will of all involved. This condition is not met merely by norms taking on *the grammatical form* of universal ought-sentences; immoral maxims, or maxims without any moral content, can also be formulated in this way. Mead puts the point as follows: "Kant said we could only universalize the form. However, we do universalize the end itself."[37] At the same time, he does not want to surrender the advantage that comes from the formalism of Kant's ethics. He poses the problem in the following terms: "But when the immediate interests come in conflict with others we had not recognized, we tend to ignore the others and take into account only those which are immediate. The difficulty is to make ourselves recognize the other and wider interests, and then to bring them into some sort of rational relationship with the more immediate ones."[38] Faced with moral-practical questions, we are so caught up in our own interests that *the impartial consideration of all interests affected* already presupposes a moral standpoint on the part of anyone who wants to arrive at an unbiased judgment. "I think all of us feel that one must be ready to recognize the interests of others even when they run counter to our own, but that the person who does that does not really sacrifice himself, but becomes a larger self."[39] Mead makes methodological use of this insight to replace the categorical imperative with a procedure of discursive will-formation.

In judging a morally relevant conflict of action, we have to consider what general interest all those involved would agree upon if they were to adopt the moral standpoint of impartially taking into account all the interests affected. Mead then specifies this condition by way of projecting an ideal communication community:

> In logical terms there is established a *universe of discourse which transcends the specific order* within which the members of the community, in a specific conflict, place themselves outside of the community order as it exists, and agree upon changed habits of action and a restatement of values. *Rational procedure,* therefore, sets up an order within which thought operates; that abstracts in varying degrees from the actual structure of society . . . It is a *social order that in-*

cludes any rational being who is or may be in any way implicated in the situation with which thought deals. It sets up an ideal world, not of substantive things, but of proper method. Its claim is that all the conditions of conduct and all the values which are involved in the conflict must be taken into account in abstraction from the fixed forms of habits and goods which have clashed with each other. It is evident that a man cannot act as a rational member of society, except as he constitutes himself as a member of this wider common world of rational beings.[40]

What was intended by the categorical imperative can be made good by projecting a will-formation under the idealized conditions of universal discourse. Subjects capable of moral judgment cannot test each for himself alone whether an established or recommended norm is in the general interest and ought to have social force; this can only be done in common with everyone else involved. The mechanisms of taking the attitude of the other and of internalizing reach their definitive limit here. Ego can, to be sure, anticipate the attitude that alter will adopt toward him in the role of a participant in argumentation; by this means the communicative actor gains a reflective relation to himself, as we have seen. Ego can even try to *imagine* to himself the course of a moral argument in the circle of those involved; but he cannot *predict* its results with any certainty. Thus the projection of an ideal communication community serves as a guiding thread for *setting up* discourses that have to be carried through *in fact* and cannot be replaced by monological mock dialogue. Mead does not work out this consequence sharply enough because it seems trivially true to him. Its triviality is already attested to by the psychological argument to the effect that we are always tempted "to ignore certain interests that run contrary to our own interests, and to emphasize those with which we have been identified."[41] Mead does, however, also deploy an argument-in-principle. It holds only on the assumption that the justification of hypothetical norms cannot, finally, be isolated from the constructive task of forming hypotheses.

Kant and the utilitarians operated with concepts from the philosophy of consciousness. Thus they reduced the motives and aims of action, as well as the interests and value orientations on which they depended, to inner states or private episodes. They assumed that "our inclinations are toward our own subjective states—the pleasure that comes from satisfaction. If that is the end, then of course our motives are all subjective affairs."[42] In fact, however, motives and ends have something intersubjective about them; they are always interpreted in the light of a cultural tradition. Interests are directed to what is worthwhile, and "all the things worthwhile are shared experiences ... Even when a person seems to retire into himself to live among his own ideas, he is living really with the others who have thought what he is thinking. He is reading books, recalling the experiences which he has had, projecting conditions under which he might live. The content is always of a social character."[43] But if motives and ends are accessible only under interpretations dependent upon traditions, the individual actor cannot himself be the *final* instance in developing and revising his interpretations of needs. Rather, his inter- pretations change in the context of the lifeworld of the social group to which he belongs; little by little, practical discourses can also gear into this quasi-natural process. The individual is not master of the cultural interpretations in light of which he understands his motives and aims, his interests and value orientations, no more than he disposes over the tra- dition in which he has grown up. Like every monological procedure, the monological principle of Kantian ethics fails in the face of this: "From Kant's standpoint, you assume that the standard is there ... but where you have no standard, it does not help you to decide. Where you have to get a restatement, a readjustment, you get a new situation in which to act; the simple generalizing of the principle of your act does not help. It is at that point that Kant's principle breaks down."[44]

Mead develops the basic assumptions of a communicative ethics with both a systematic and an evolutionary intent. Systematically he wants to show that a universalist morality can best be grounded in this way. But he wants to explain this very fact in terms of an evolutionary theory. The basic theoretical concept of the ethics of communication is "universal discourse," the formal ideal of mutual understanding in language. Be- cause the idea of coming to a rationally motivated, mutual understanding is to be found in the very structure of language, it is no mere demand of practical reason but is built into the reproduction of social life. The more communicative action takes over from religion the burdens of social in- tegration, the more the ideal of an unlimited and undistorted communi- cation community gains empirical influence in the real communication community. Mead supports this contention, as did Durkheim, by pointing to the spread of democratic ideas, the transformation of the foundations of legitimation in the modern state. To the extent that normative validity claims become dependent on confirmation through communicatively achieved consensus, principles of democratic will-formation and univer- salistic principles of law are established in the modern state.[45]

D.—Excursus on Identity and Individuation. To this point I have made nothing of the fact that the ideal communication community provides not only a model for impartial, rational will-formation. Mead also draws on this ideal in shaping his model of nonalienated communicative inter- action, which affords reciprocal scope for spontaneous self-presentation in everyday life and demands reciprocal empathy. Looked at more closely, the ideal communication community can be seen to contain two utopian projections. Each of them stylizes one of two moments still fused together in ritual practice: the moral-practical and the expressive. Together they form the point of reference for Mead's concept of a fully individuated person.

Let us imagine individuals being socialized as members of an ideal communication community; they would in the same measure acquire an identity with two complementary aspects: one universalizing, one particularizing. On the one hand, these persons raised under idealized conditions learn to orient themselves within a universalistic framework, that is, to act autonomously. On the other hand, they learn to use this autonomy, which makes them equal to every other morally acting subject, to develop themselves in their subjectivity and singularity. Mead ascribes both autonomy and the power of spontaneous self-realization to every person who, in the revolutionary role of a participant in universal discourse, frees himself from the fetters of habitual, concrete conditions of life. Membership in the ideal communication community is, in Hegelian terms, constitutive of both the I as universal and the I as individual.[46]

Universalistic action orientations reach beyond all existing conventions and make it possible to gain some distance from the social roles that shape one's background and character: "The demand is freedom from conventions, from given laws. Of course, such a situation is only possible where the individual appeals, so to speak, from a narrow and restricted community to a larger one, that is, larger in the logical sense of having rights which are not so restricted. One appeals from fixed conventions which no longer have any meaning to a community in which the rights shall be publicly recognized, and one appeals to others . . . even if the appeal be made to posterity. In that case there is the attitude of the 'I' as over against the 'me.'"[47] Corresponding to this "appeal to the larger community" is "the larger self," precisely that autonomous subject who can orient his action to universal principles.

The "me" represents not only the particularities of moral consciousness tied to tradition, but also the constraints of a character that impedes the development of subjectivity. In this respect, too, membership in an ideal communication community has the power to burst bonds. The structures of nonalienated social intercourse provoke action orientations that reach beyond established conventions in a different way than universalistic orientations; they are aimed at filling in the spaces for reciprocal self-realization: "That capacity allows for exhibiting one's own peculiarities . . . it is possible for the individual to develop his own peculiarities, that which individualizes him."[48]

Mead illustrates these two aspects of ego-identity—self-determination and self-realization—with traits such as "self-respect" and "sense of superiority." These feelings, too, reveal the implicit reference to structures of an ideal communication community. Thus, in extreme cases a person can preserve his self-respect only when he acts in opposition to the moral judgment of all his contemporaries: "The only way in which we can react against the disapproval of the entire community is by set-ting up a higher sort of community which in a certain sense out-votes the one we find. A person may reach a point of going against the whole world about him; he may stand out by himself over against it. But to do that he has to speak the voice of reason to himself. He has to comprehend the voices of the past and of the future ... As a rule we assume that this general voice of the community is identical with the larger community of the past and the future."[49] In a parallel passage Mead speaks of the idea of "a higher and better society."[50]

It is similar with feelings of self-worth. The creative activity of the artist or scientist serves as the exemplary form of self-realization; not only they, however, but all persons have the need to be confirmed in their self-worth by outstanding accomplishments or qualities. In this way, a feeling of superiority builds up, which loses its morally questionable as-pects because the self-confirmation of the one does not take place at the cost of the self-confirmation of the other. Here, too, Mead is tacitly ori-ented to an ideal of social intercourse free of coercion, in which the self-realization of one party does not have to be bought with the mortification of the other.

Corresponding to the ideal communication community is an *ego-identity that makes possible self-realization on the basis of autono-mous action*. This identity proves itself in the ability to lend continuity to one's own life history. In the course of the process of individualization, the individual has to draw his identity behind the lines of the concrete lifeworld and of his character as attached to this background. The iden-tity of the ego can then be stabilized only through the abstract ability to satisfy the requirements of consistency, and thereby the conditions of recognition, in the face of incompatible role expectations and in passing through a succession of contradictory role systems.[51] The ego-identity of the adult proves its worth in the ability to build up new identities from shattered or superseded identities, and to integrate them with old identities in such a way that the fabric of one's interactions is organized into the unity of a life history that is both unmistakable and accountable. An ego-identity of this kind simultaneously makes possible self-determination *and* self-realization, two moments that are already at work in the tension between "I" and "me" at the stage where identity is tied to social roles. To the extent that the adult can take over and be respon-sible for his own biography, he can come back to himself in the narra-tively preserved traces of his own interactions. Only one who takes over his own life history can see in it the realization of his self. Responsibly to take over one's own biography means to get clear about *who one wants to be,* and from this horizon to view the traces of one's own interactions as *if* they were deposited by the actions of a responsible author, of a subject that acted on the basis of a reflective relation to self.

To this point I have used the concept of identity rather carelessly; in any case, I have offered no explicit justification for sometimes accepting the translation [into German] of Mead's expression 'self' with the expression *Identität,* that is, 'identity' (which comes from symbolic interactionism and psychoanalysis). Mead and Durkheim determine the identity of individuals in relation to the identity of the group to which they belong. The unity of the collective is the point of reference for the communality of all members which is expressed in the fact that they can speak of themselves and each other in the first-person plural. At the same time, the identity of the person is a presupposition for members being able to speak with one another in the first-person singular. In both cases the expression 'identity' can be justified in terms of language theory. The symbolic structures constitutive for the unity of the collective and of its individual members are connected with the employment of personal pronouns, the deictic expressions used to identify persons. The sociopsychological concept of identity most readily reminds us of a child's identifications with its reference persons, but these identification processes are in turn involved in the construction and maintenance of those symbolic structures that first make possible the identification in language of groups and persons. The psychological term may have been chosen without regard for the homonymous linguistic term. It is my view, however, that the sociopsychological concept of identity can also be expounded in terms of the theory of language.[52]

The growing child develops an identity to the extent that a *social world* to which he belongs is constituted for him, and complementary to that, a *subjective world* that is marked off from the external world of facts and norms, and to which he has privileged access. The relation of these two worlds is reflected in the relation between the two components of identity, the "I" and the "me." The "I" stands, first of all, for the expressively manifested subjectivity of a desiring and feeling nature [*Bedürfnisnatur*]; the "me" stands for a character shaped through social roles. These two concepts of self correspond in a certain way to the moments of the "id" and the "superego" in Freud's structural model. With them we can explain the two specific meanings that the word "I" takes on in spontaneous expressions of subjective experiences, on the one hand, and in institutionally bound speech acts, on the other. In expressions of subjective experiences, the pathic subject speaks out its desires and feelings, whereas in norm-conformative action it is the freedom of the practical subject that expresses itself; both forms of expression already take place, of course, without the refraction of a reflected relation to self.

As we have seen, there are other contexts in which Mead gives a further meaning to the concept of the "I." He also understands the "I" as the independent and creative initiator of fundamentally unpredictable actions. The ability to begin something new expresses both the autonomy and the individuality of speaking and acting subjects. This third concept of the self helps explain the sense of the expression "I" in institutionally unbound performative sentences. When a speaker (in the role of the first person) takes up a relation to a hearer (in the role of the second person) and thereby raises a criticizable validity claim with his speech-act offer, he appears as a responsibly acting subject. The structure of linguistic intersubjectivity that lays down the communicative roles of the person speaking, the person spoken to, and the person who is present but uninvolved, forces the participants, insofar as they want to come to an understanding with one another, to act under the presupposition of responsibility [or accountability: *Zurechnungsfähigkeit*].

The idealizations that Mead undertakes in specifying ego-identity are connected to this concept of a responsible actor. He works out the aspects of self-realization and self-determination. Under these aspects of the I-in-general and the I-as-individual, the moments of the "me" and the "I" return in reflected form, as we can now see. *Ego-identity enables a person to realize himself under conditions of autonomous action.* The actor must thereby maintain a reflected relation to himself both as a pathic and a practical self. The projection of an ideal communication community can be understood as a construction intended to explain what we mean by acting in a self-critical attitude. With his concept of universal discourse, Mead sets out his explanatory proposal in terms of the theory of communication. Between this concept of ego-identity and the problem of personal identity discussed in analytic philosophy, there is, I think, a connection that can be elucidated by semantic analysis.

Let us begin with the currently dominant view that "the connection between genuinely philosophical problems and what is meant by the term 'identity' as it has infiltrated the psychological enlightenment of the man-in-the-street is only very indirect."[53] Dieter Henrich correctly insists upon a clear distinction between the problem of numerically identifying a single person and the question of the "identity" of this person, where what is meant is that a person can appear in his actions as both autonomous and unmistakable.

In philosophical theory identity is a predicate with a special function; by means of it a particular thing or object is distinguished as such from others of the same kind; conversely, this predicate permits us to say what is really only a single object can be thematic under different conditions and in different modes of access. This sort of identity precisely does not require that the identical individuals be distinguishable from one another by special qualities. Even less does it require that they evince a basic pattern of qualities in relation to which they orient their behavior, or by means of which their behavior can be explained as a unified complex. Even a thing that behaves quite erratically, or a person who changes life styles and convictions with the weather, and each year in a different way, is characterized in this formal sense as "identical with itself". If something is a single thing, identity is to be attributed to it. It makes no sense to say that it has acquired or lost its identity. The social-psychological concept of identity has an entirely different logic. Here "identity" is a complex property that persons can acquire from a certain age onwards. They may not have this property, and they cannot possess it at all times. Once they have acquired it, they are, in virtue of it, "independent". They are able to free themselves from the influence of others; they can give to their lives a form and continuity which it previously had, if at all, only through external influence. In this sense, they are, in virtue of their "identities", autonomous individuals. We can see the associations between the philosophical and socio-psychological concepts of identity. But that does not alter the fact that they have very different meanings. Any number of individuals can be independent in exactly the same way. If that is so, they cannot be distinguished by their "identities".[54]

Henrich explicitly refers to Mead's social psychology, but he emphasizes only the *self-determination* aspect of the concept of identity. He neglects the *self-realization* aspect, under which the self can be identified not only generically, that is, as a person capable of autonomous action in general, but as an individual to whom an unmistakable life history can be attributed.[55] This second aspect is certainly not to be confused with the numerical identification of a single person. For, as Ernst Tugendhat has stressed,[56] the question of who one wants to be has the sense not of a numerical but of a qualitative identification. When person A gets clear about who he wants to be, predicative self-identification also has the sense that he distinguishes himself from all other persons as an unmistakable individual, through his life project, through the organization of a life history that he has responsibly taken on. But this rather demanding self-identification is not, at least at first glance, a necessary condition for A being numerically identified by other members B, C, D ... of the group to which he belongs.

Both Henrich and Tugendhat want to separate the concept of ego-identity from the question of how an individual person can be identified. Henrich uses the concept of identity to refer to the ability of persons to act autonomously, and that is a generic determination of persons in general. Tugendhat uses the concept of identity to refer to the ability of a person to identify himself, on the basis of a reflective self-understanding, as the person who he wants to be. Thus, we can distinguish three different meanings: numerical identification of an individual person, generic identification of a person as a speaking and acting subject in general, and the qualitative identification of a specific person with an individual life history, particular character, and so on. Rather than leaving things with the demarcation thesis of Henrich and Tugendhat, I will now use Mead's concept of identity as a guide in illuminating the semantic interconnections between these three kinds of identification. I argue for the following thesis: the predicative self-identification that a person undertakes is in certain respects a presupposition of others being able to identify him generically and numerically.

The word 'I' belongs—together with the other personal pronouns, adverbs of time and place, and demonstratives—to the class of deictic expressions. Along with names and characterizations, they make up the class of singular terms that serve to identify individual objects. "The function of a singular term consists in its use by the speaker to specify which object among all objects he is referring to; that is, he specifies the particular object among all objects to which the predicate expression is to apply that complements the singular term in a sentence."[57] Like the other deictic expressions, personal pronouns get a clear sense only in the specific context of a speech situation. With the expression 'I', the person speaking at a given time designates himself.

Among other characteristic features, one has been especially noted: a speaker who uses the word 'I' in a meaningful way can make no mistake. If, in such a case, a hearer should argue that the entity intended by the speaker is not identical to the one designated by him, or that it did not exist at all, one would have to ask him whether he understood the deictic significance of the expression 'I'.[58] Tugendhat explains this by showing that with the expression 'I', viewed in isolation, a speaker is not making an identification at all; rather, he is designating himself as a person who can be identified by others in appropriate circumstances. Tugendhat is relying here on a theory he has advanced elsewhere,[59] to the effect that every identification of an object requires a subjective and an objective component. The objective, spatiotemporal indications have to be relatable to the here and now of the speech situation; in this respect, the speaker and his situation are the ultimate reference point for all identifications. On the other hand, a description of a speech situation with deictic expressions such as 'I', 'here', and 'now' does not suffice to identify an object; the situation of the speaker must, conversely, also be relatable to objective spatiotemporal locations. Mountain climbers who have lost their way and signal an SOS back to the valley could no more identify their position with the word 'here' than a speaker could identify himself to a questioning telephone caller with the laconic answer "I". Tugendhat uses these examples to show that in this respect 'I' is like the two other fundamental deictic expressions 'here' and 'now'.

The differences are more interesting. Whereas those who have gotten lost and answer "here" do not know where they are, the person on the phone who answers "I" knows very well who he is; the information is (in general) only insufficient for the hearer. The "here" of the lost mountain climbers would suffice to identify their position if there were a search party in hearing distance who knew their own position. Even in the case of the telephone call, a spatiotemporal identification might succeed by, say, the unknown party confirming the number of his phone to the caller; the latter might then know (or be in a position to learn) that he is speaking with the person holding in his hand the phone in the downstairs hall of the house three doors down from his. The caller knows now the position of the other party, but his question—with whom is he speaking— is not yet thereby answered. He could hurry over to the nearby house to see who had just been on the phone. Let us suppose he does that, finds an unfamiliar face, and asks: "Who are you?" It follows that the unknown individual had referred the caller to an identifiable *person* with his answer "I," and not just to an *object* identifiable through observation. As a perceptible person, the unknown individual has indeed been identified; nevertheless, the question about his identity is not answered in the sense that the answer "I" had suggested. Of course, the caller could afterward report to a friend who has returned in the meantime that in his absence he had encountered a stranger in his apartment. He could provide a description of the stranger's outward appearance, and perhaps his friend could then explain who the unknown individual was. Let us suppose that the matter is not cleared up. Then the caller could, in subsequent accounts, identify the other party as the person who used a specific telephone at the given time and place. And yet, there is still a need to identify the person. For the identifiable person whom the speaker designated with "I" was not intended as an entity that could be identified on the basis of observation alone.

Peter Geach has defended the thesis that the identity predicate can be used only in connection with the general characterization of a class of objects.[60] In discussing this thesis, Deter Henrich comes to an interesting distinction between conditions and criteria of identity: "It makes no sense to say that an object appears under one description as (the same) number, under another as (different) marks. The black mark on the paper that designates the number 8 is not that number itself, as is easy to see from the fact that it can also be written as 'VIII' or 'eight'. *Conditions* of identity divide off types of objects fundamentally from one another, whereas *criteria* of identity can individuate in various ways within the domain of an object type."[61] Obviously, persons cannot be identified under the same conditions as observable objects; for them, spatio-temporal identification does not suffice. The additional conditions depend on how a person can be identified generically, that is, as a person .in general.

Whereas entities are generally determined by the fact that a speaker can say something about them, persons belong to the class of entities that can themselves assume the role of speaker and thereby employ the self-referential expression 'I'. For categorization as a person, it is not only essential that these entities be equipped with the capacity for speaking and acting and be able to say "I"; *how* they do this is crucial as well. The expression 'I' has not only the deictic meaning of reference to an object; it also indicates the pragmatic attitude or the perspective in which or from which the speaker expresses himself. An 'I' used in a first-person sentence means that the speaker is presenting himself in the expressive mode. With the perspective of the first person, he takes on the role of self-presentation in such a way that the desires, feelings, intentions, beliefs, and so forth uttered can be ascribed to him. The ascription of experiences that an observer undertakes from the perspective of a third person must rest, *in the end,* on an act of reaching understanding, where alter, from the perspective of the second person, accepts ego's expressive utterance as sincere. In this respect, the expression 'I', as used in expressive sentences, points to the homonymous expression as used in performative sentences. This means that someone in the communicative role of a speaker takes up an interpersonal relation with (at least) one other party in the communicative role of a hearer, such that they encounter one another against the background of those who are presently uninvolved but are potentially participants. The interpersonal relation tied to the perspectives of the first, second, and third persons actualizes an underlying relation of membership in a social group. It is here that we first encounter the *pronominal* meaning of the expression 'I'.

To return to our example, when the unknown party on the phone responds to the question of who he is with "I", he makes himself known as an identifiable *person,* that is, as an entity that fulfills the identity conditions for a person, that cannot be identified merely through observation. The stranger indicates that a subjective world to which he has privileged access and a social world to which he belongs have been constituted for him. He indicates that he can take part in social interactions and act communicatively in the proper ways. If he satisfies the identity conditions for a person, it is also clear how he might be identified: by a proper name.

Naturally, the name as such is not sufficient. But the institution of giv-ing names is such that a proper name functions as a guidepost by which we can orient ourselves in gathering the data that would be sufficient for identification: date and place of birth, family background, nationality, re-ligious affiliation, and so forth. These are, as a rule, the criteria on the basis of which a person is identified—for instance, when he presents a passport. The usual identity criteria refer the questioner to those situa-tions in which alone, *in the final analysis,* persons can be identified. They refer him virtually to those interactions in which the identity of the person in question was formed. When the identity of a person is unclear—when it turns out that a pass has been forged, that a person's own statements are incorrect—our inquiries lead, *in the end,* to asking neighbors, colleagues, friends, family, and, if necessary, parents whether they know the person in question. Only this sort of primary familiarity gained from common interactions—*in the last analysis* from socializing interactions—enables us to order a person spatiotemporally in a life-context whose *social* spaces and *historical* times are symbolically struc-tured.

The peculiarity of identifying persons as opposed to objects can be explained by the fact that persons do not satisfy from the start (perhaps it would be better to say: by nature) the conditions of identity, or even the criteria by which they might be identified under these conditions. They first have to acquire their identities as persons if they are to be identifiable as persons at all and, if need be, as specific persons. Since, as we have seen, persons acquire their identities through linguistically me-diated interaction, they satisfy the conditions of identity for persons, and the basic criteria of identity for specific persons, not only for others but for themselves as well. They understand themselves as persons who have learned to take part in social interactions; they understand themselves as specific persons who have been raised as daughters or sons in specific families, in specific geographical areas, in the spirit of specific religious traditions, and so on. A person can ascribe to *himself* such properties only by answering the question, *what kind of* a person he is, and not the question, *which* of all persons he is. A person satisfies the conditions and criteria of identity according to which he can be numerically distin-guished from others only when he is in a position to ascribe to himself the relevant predicates. In this respect, the predicative self-identification of a person accomplished at an elementary level is a presupposition for that person's being identifiable by others as a person in general—that is, generically—and as a specific person—that is, numerically.

Mead introduced a two-level concept of personal identity and thereby cleared up an ambiguity in the idea of "acquiring" an identity.[62] A con-ventional identity, one tied to specific roles and norms, is also "acquired," and indeed in such a way that the child internalizes the behavior patterns ascribed to him and makes them his own in a certain way. From this appropriation of an ascribed identity, Mead wants to distinguish an identity maintained under one's own direction, as it were. He works out two aspects of this ego-identity by means of a counterfactual reference to universal discourse: on the one hand, the ability to act autonomously on the basis of universalistic action orientations, and on the other hand, the ability to realize oneself in a life history to which one lends continuity by responsibly taking it over. From the viewpoint of the ideal communication community, the level of requirements for the predicative self-identification of sociated individuals changes. At the level of role identity a person understands himself in such a way that he answers the question, what kind of a person he is (has become), what character he has (has acquired) by means of ascribed predicates. At the level of ego-identity a person understands himself in a different way, namely, by answering the question, who or what kind of person he *wants* to be. In place of an orientation to the past, we have an orientation to the future, which makes it possible for the past to become a problem. This has consequences for the manner of numerical identification as well. Of course, this holds true only on the assumption that the concept of ego-identity is not an idle construction but does in fact capture the intuitions of members of modern societies to an increasing degree and does become sedimented in social expectations.

If, following Durkheim, we affirm a trend toward the linguistification of the sacred that can be seen in the rationalization of worldviews, in the universalization of law and morality, and in progressive individuation, we have to suppose that the concept of ego-identity will increasingly fit the self-understanding accompanying everyday communicative practice. In this case, we face the serious question of whether, with a new stage of identity formation, the conditions and criteria of identity do not also have to change. Normally, with the answer "I" a speaker indicates only that he can be identified generically as a speaking and acting subject and numerically by a few significant data that throw light on his background. However, when he satisfies the level of requirement of ego-identity by means of predicative self-identification, he indicates by the answer "I" (in the appropriate contexts) that he can be identified generically as an *autonomously* acting subject and numerically by such data as throw light on the continuity of a life history he has responsibly taken upon himself. At any rate, this is the direction pointed in by the Western (i.e., articulated in the Judeo-Christian tradition) concept of the immortal soul of creatures who, in the all-seeing eye of an omnipresent and eternal creator, recognize themselves as fully individuated beings.

E.—The utopian sketch of an ideal communication community could be misleading if it were taken to be the introduction to a philosophy of history; this would be to misunderstand the limited methodological status that can sensibly be attributed to it. The construction of an unlimited and undistorted discourse can serve at most as a foil for setting off more glaringly the rather ambiguous developmental tendencies in modern societies. Mead is interested in the pattern common to these tendencies— the increasing prevalence of structures of action oriented to mutual understanding or, as we put it in reference to Durkheim, the linguistification of the sacred. By this I mean the transfer of cultural reproduction, social integration, and socialization from sacred foundations over to linguistic communication and action oriented to mutual understanding. To the extent that communicative action takes on central societal functions, the medium of language gets burdened with tasks of producing substantial consensus. In other words, language no longer serves merely to *transmit* and actualize prelinguistically guaranteed agreements, but more and more to *bring about* rationally motivated agreements as well; it does so in moral-practical and in expressive domains of experience no less than in the specifically cognitive domain of dealing with an objectivated reality.

In this way Mead can interpret certain evolutionary trends (which Durkheim also has in view) as a communicative rationalization of the lifeworld. This is a matter, first, of the differentiation of structural components of the lifeworld which are tightly interwoven in the collective consciousness: culture, society, and person separate off from one another. It is also a question, second, of changes on these three levels, some of which are parallel, others complementary: sacred knowledge is superseded by a knowledge specialized according to validity claims and based on reasons; legality and morality get separated from one another as "law" and "morality" and are universalized; finally, individualism spreads along with its heightened claims to autonomy and self-realization. The rational structure of these tendencies toward linguistification can be seen in the fact that the continuation of traditions, the maintenance of legitimate orders, and the continuity of the life histories of individual persons become more and more dependent on outlooks that refer, when problematized, to yes/no positions on criticizable validity claims.

The overt simplification and level of abstraction that marks statements of this sort give rise, surely, to doubts concerning their empirical usefulness. And yet they serve to clarify what we might understand by the communicative rationalization of a lifeworld. Even in this connection, however, two qualifications are in order. Mead mentions them himself, but does not give them sufficient weight. The first has to do with Mead's fixation on the *formal* features of modern legal and moral development, and on the formal features of individualism in the domain of personality development. He neglects the other side of this formalism and does not consider the price that communicative reason has to pay for its victory in the coin of concrete ethical life [*Sittlichkeit*]. The treatment of this theme in the wake of the *Dialectic of Enlightenment* does not stand alone. Hegel's critique of the formalism of Kantian ethics today serves as the model for a theory of post-Enlightenment that goes back to Arnold Gehlen and Joachim Ritter.[63] More radical in its approach and less traditionalistic in its outcome is the critique of modernity directed at similar phenomena in the context of French poststructuralism, for example, by Foucault.[64] The other qualification relates to the scope of the reconstructive procedures preferred by Mead. He ignores the external restrictions on the logic of the change in forms of social integration that he distilled out. The functional aspects of societal development have to be set over against the structural aspects if we do not want to deceive ourselves concerning the importance of communicative reason. Today, this is the dominant theme of systems theory.[65]

The critique of ethical formalism takes exception, first of all, to the fact that preoccupation with questions of the validity of moral norms misleads us into ignoring the intrinsic value of cultural life-forms and life-styles. From the perspective of Durkheimian analysis, there is the question of what remains from the collective consciousness constitutive of the identity of tribal societies when the ritually secured, basic normative consensus about concrete values and contents evaporates into a merely procedurally secured consensus about the foundations of communicative ethics. The content has been filtered out of this procedural consensus. Cultural values that have not been abstracted into basic formal values (such as equality, freedom, human dignity, and the like) surrender their authority and stand at the disposition of processes of mutual understanding which are not prejudged. In mass culture, value contents have been deflated into stereotypical and, at the same time, manipulable elements; in the hermetic works of modern art, they have been subjectivized. To be sure, it is only at the level of culture that formal and material, normative and expressive elements can separate off from one another in this way; in everyday communicative practice, where the lifeworlds of different collectives are demarcated from each other, they are now as ever woven into concrete forms of life. Traditional, habitual forms of life find their expression in particular group identities marked by particular traditions that overlay and overlap one another, compete with one another, and so on; they are differentiated according to ethnic and linguistic, regional, occupational, and religious traditions. In modern societies these forms of life have lost the power to totalize and thus to exclude; they have been subordinated to the universalism of law and morality; but as concrete forms of life, they are subject to standards other than that of universalization.

Whether the life-form of a collectivity has turned out more or less "well," has more or less "succeeded," may be a general question we can direct at every form of life, but it is more like a clinical request to judge a patient's mental and spiritual condition than a moral question concerning a norm's or institutional system's worthiness to be recognized. Moral judgment presupposes a hypothetical outlook, the possibility of considering norms as something to which we can grant or deny social validity. The analogous assumption that we could choose forms of life in the same way is a contrast without sense. No one can reflectively agree to the form of life in which he has been socialized in the same way as he can to a norm of whose validity he has convinced himself.[66]

There is, in this respect, a parallel between the life-form of a collective and the life history of an individual. If we start from Mead's concept of ego-identity, the question arises of what remains of concrete identities tied to specific social roles and norms when adults have acquired the *generalized* ability to realize themselves autonomously. The answer was that ego-identity proves itself in the ability to integrate a series of concrete—partly disintegrated, partly superseded—identities into a life history responsibly taken upon oneself; concrete identities, displaced into the past, are in a certain sense *aufgehoben* [cancelled and preserved in a new synthesis] in the individual conduct of life. An autonomous conduct of life depends in turn on the decision—or on successively repeated and revised decisions—as to "who one wants to be." Hitherto I have adopted this existential mode of expression without comment. But this way of describing the situation stylizes what actually takes place in the form of a complex, obscure process into a conscious, spontaneously exercised choice. In any case, the answer to the question, who does one want to be, cannot be rational in the way that a moral decision can. This existential "decision" is indeed a necessary condition for a moral attitude toward one's own life history, but it is not itself the result of moral reflection. There is an indissoluble element of arbitrariness (*Willkür*) in the choice of a life project. This is to be explained by the fact that the individual cannot adopt a hypothetical attitude toward his own origins and background, that he cannot accept or reject his biography in the same way as he can a norm whose claim to validity is under discussion. There can be no comparable distance to one's own life conduct, no matter how high the degree of individualization. This is stressed by Mead himself: "One difference between primitive human society and civilized human society is that in primitive human society the individual self is much more completely determined, with regard to his thinking and his behavior, by the general pattern of the organized social activity ... In civilized society individuality is constituted rather by the individual's departure from, or modified realization of, any given social type than by his conformity, and tends to be something much more distinctive and singular and peculiar than it is in primitive human society. But even in the most modern and highly-evolved forms of human civilization the individual, however original and creative he may be in his thinking or behavior, always and necessarily assumes a definite relation to, and reflects in the structure of his self or personality, the general organized pattern of experience and activity exhibited in or characterizing the social life process in which he is involved, and of which his self or personality is essentially a creative expression or embodiment."[67]

Insofar as a person does make his decision about who he wants to be depend on rational deliberation, he orients himself not by moral standards, but by the standards of happiness and well-being that we intuitively use to judge forms of life as well. For the life conduct of an individual is entwined with the life-form of the collectivity to which he belongs. Whether a life is a good one is not decided by standards of normative rightness—though the standards of a good life are also not completely independent of moral standards. Ever since Aristotle, the philosophical tradition has dealt with this difficult-to-grasp connection between happiness and justice under the title of "the good." Life-forms, no less than life histories, crystallize around particular identities. If it is to be a good life, these identities may not contradict moral demands, but their substance cannot itself be justified from universalistic points of view.[68]

The second, more radical reservation has to do not with the formalism, but with the *idealism* of Mead's theory of society. Although Mead does not entirely leave functional considerations out of his account, he is not clear about the scope and limits of reconstructive analyses of the emergence and transformation of linguistically mediated, normatively guided interaction. The one-sidedness of his communication-theoretic approach and his structuralist procedures can be seen already in the fact that mainly those societal functions come into view that devolve upon communicative action and in which communicative action cannot be replaced by other mechanisms. The material reproduction of society—securing its physical maintenance both externally and internally—is blended out of the picture of society understood as a communicatively structured lifeworld. The neglect of economics, warfare, and the struggle for political power, the disregard for dynamics in favor of the logic of societal development are detrimental, above all, to Mead's reflections on social evolution. Precisely insofar as social integration has more and more to be secured via communicatively achieved consensus, there is a pressing question as to the limits of the integrative capacity of action oriented to reaching understanding, the limits of the empirical efficacy of rational motives. The constraints of reproducing the social system, which reach right through the action orientations of sociated individuals, remain closed off to an analysis restricted to structures of interaction. The rationalization of the lifeworld, which occupies Mead's interest, has to be located in a *systematic* history accessible only to functional analysis. In this regard, Durkheim's theory of the division of labor has the advantage that it connects the forms of social solidarity to the structural differentiation of the social system.

VI

Intermediate Reflections: System and Lifeworld

Following the thread of Mead's theory of action, we have traced the paradigm shift from purposive rationality to communicative action to a point at which the theme of intersubjectivity and self-preservation again comes to the fore. The change of paradigm *within* the theory of action deals with only one of the two basic notions left to us by the aporetic discussion of the critique of instrumental reason. The other problem is the unclarified relation between action theory and systems theory, the question of how these two conceptual strategies, pulled apart after the disintegration of idealist dialectics, can be related to and integrated with one another. The provisional answer advanced in this chapter establishes a connection with the problematic of reification as it arose in the Marxist reception of the Weberian rationalization thesis. Durkheim's theory of the division of labor provides us with a suitable point of departure.

Durkheim does mention phenomena associated with the carving up of labor processes,[1] but he uses the phrase "the division of labor" to refer to the structural differentiation of social systems. This usage can be explained in terms of the history of social theory; from John Millar and Adam Smith through Marx to Spencer, processes of system differentiation had been studied chiefly in connection with the system of social labor, that is, with the differentiation of occupational groups and socioeconomic classes. For Durkheim too the functional differentiation of occupational groups has exemplary significance: "The division of labor is not peculiar to the economic world; we can observe its growing influence in the most varied fields of society. The political, administrative, and judicial functions are growing more and more specialized."[2] On the other hand, he is inclined to measure the complexity of a society by demographic indicators, even though they are relevant primarily to differentiation processes in tribal societies: "The division of labor varies in direct ratio with the volume and density of society and, if it progresses in a continuous manner in the course of social development, it is because societies become regularly denser and generally more voluminous."[3]

In the dimension of the social division of labor Durkheim introduces a typological distinction between segmentally and functionally differentiated societies; his criterion is the similarity or dissimilarity between the differentiated units. The biological model through which he elucidates this typology explains why Durkheim calls functionally differentiated societies "organic": "They are constituted, not by a repetition of similar, homogeneous segments, but by a system of different organs each of which has a special role, and which are themselves formed of differentiated parts. Not only are social elements not of the same nature, but they are not arranged in the same manner. They are not juxtaposed linearly as the rings of an earthworm, nor entwined with one another, but coordinated and subordinated one to another around the same central organ which exercises a moderating action over the rest of the organism. This organ itself no longer has the same character as in the preceding case, for, if the others depend upon it, it, in its turn, depends upon them. No doubt, it still enjoys a special situation, and, if one chooses so to speak, a privileged position."[4] Durkheim identifies the state as the central organ; in this respect, he is still moving within the "old European" intellectual horizon of politically constituted society. On the other hand, he shares with Spencer (and with more recent functionalist theories of evolution) the view that the division of labor is not a sociocultural manifestation but a "phenomenon of general biology whose conditions must be sought in the essential properties of organized matter."[5]

With this move Durkheim arrives at an analytical level of "norm-free sociality,"[6] which can be separated from the level of reconstructive analysis of communicative action, the lifeworld, and the changing forms of social solidarity. He gives the impression of wanting to ascertain the types of social solidarity and the stages of system differentiation independent of one another, in order subsequently to correlate mechanical solidarity with segmentally differentiated societies and organic solidarity with functionally differentiated societies. On this procedure, he could leave open to begin with the question of whether there is a linear causal relation between the degree of system differentiation and the type of social integration, or whether the structures of consciousness and of society are internally related to one another as moments of a whole. But another idea interferes with this approach, namely, Durkheim's view that collective consciousness is constitutive for archaic societies whereas in modern societies the life-context is constituted by the division of labor: "Social life comes from a double source, the likeness of consciousness and the division of social labor."[7] The transition from one form of social solidarity to the other means, according to this, a transformation of the foundations of societal integration. Whereas primitive societies are integrated via a *basic normative consensus,* the integration of developed societies comes about via the *systemic interconnection of functionally specified domains of action.*

Durkheim finds this idea radically developed by Spencer. The latter believes that "social life, just as all life in general, can naturally organize itself only by an unconscious, spontaneous adaptation under the immediate pressure of needs, and not according to a rational plan of reflective intelligence. He does not believe that higher societies can be built according to a rigidly drawn program ... Social solidarity would then be nothing else than the spontaneous accord of individual interests, an accord of which contracts are the natural expression. The typical social relation would be the economic, stripped of all regulation and resulting from the entirely free initiative of the parties. In short, society would be solely the stage where individuals exchange the products of their labor, without any action properly social coming to regulate this exchange."[8] Spencer explains the unifying character of the division of labor by appeal to a systemic mechanism, namely, the market. Through it exchange relations are established into which individuals enter in accord with their egocentric calculations of utility and within the framework of bourgeois private law. The market is a mechanism that "spontaneously" brings about the integration of society not, say, by harmonizing action orientations via moral or legal rules, but by harmonizing the aggregate effects of action via functional interconnections. To Durkheim's question, how the division of labor could be both a natural law of evolution and the generative mechanism for a specific form of social solidarity,[9] Spencer gives a clear answer. In the "gigantic system of private contracts" the division of social labor steered by the nonnormative mechanism of the market is merely given normative expression.

But this answer makes Durkheim aware that he had intended his question in a different sense. It becomes clear in his exchange with Spencer that Durkheim does not want to explain organic solidarity in terms of a systemic integration of society uncoupled from the value orientations of individual actors, in terms, that is, of a norm-free regulative mechanism, an "exchange of information which takes place increasingly from one place to another through supply and demand."[10] For Durkheim finds in exchange relations nothing "that resembles a regulatory influence." Even in functionally differentiated societies, an effect of this sort can be brought about, he believes, only through the socially integrating power of moral and legal rules. Referring to Spencer's picture of a market society integrated exclusively by systemic means, Durkheim poses the rhetorical question: "Is this the character of societies whose unity is produced by the division of labor? If this were so, we could with justice doubt their stability. For if interest relates men, it is never for more than a few moments. It can create only an external link between them. In the fact of exchange, the various agents remain outside of each other, and when the business has been completed, each one retires and is left entirely on his own. Consciousnesses are only superficially in contact; they neither penetrate each other, nor do they adhere. If we look further into the matter, we shall see that this total harmony of interests conceals a latent or deferred conflict. For where interest is the only ruling force each individual finds himself in a state of war with every other since nothing comes to mollify the egos, and any truce in this eternal antagonism would not be of long duration. There is nothing less constant than interest."[11]

Even the organic form of social solidarity has to be secured by values and norms; like mechanical solidarity, it is the expression of a collective consciousness, however altered in its structure. The latter cannot be replaced by a systemic mechanism, such as the market, which coordinates the aggregate effects of interest-oriented actions: "Thus, it is wrong to oppose a society which comes from a community of beliefs to one which has a cooperative basis, according only to the first a moral character, and seeing in the latter only an economic group. In reality, cooperation also has its intrinsic morality."[12]

On this account, there would have to be a causal connection between the growing differentiation of the social system and the development of an independent morality effective for integration. But there is scarcely any empirical evidence for this thesis. Modern societies present us with a different picture. The differentiation of a highly complex market system destroys traditional forms of solidarity without at the same time producing normative orientations capable of securing an organic form of solidarity. On Durkheim's own diagnosis, democratic forms of political will-formation and universalistic morality are too weak to counter the disintegrating effects of the division of labor. He sees industrial capitalist societies driving toward a state of anomie. And he traces this anomie back to the same processes of differentiation from which a new morality is supposed to arise "as if by a law of nature." This dilemma is not unlike the Weberian paradox of societal rationalization in certain respects.

Durkheim wants to dissolve the paradox by distinguishing, first of all, normal phenomena of the division of labor from "anomic division of labor." His central example of the latter is "the conflict between capital and labor."[13] But the analysis that Durkheim carries out in Book 3 of the

Division of Labor in Society, under the title "Abnormal Forms," makes quite clear the vicious circle in which he is caught. On the one hand, he holds fast to the thesis that "in the normal state" the moral rules that make organic solidarity possible flow "from the division of labor."[14] On the other hand, he explains the dysfunctional character of certain forms of the division of labor by the absence of such normative regulations; there is no tie-in of functionally specified domains of action to morally obligatory norms: "If the division of labor does not produce solidarity in all these cases, it is because the relations of the organs are not regulated, because they are in a state of anomie."[15] Durkheim is unable to resolve this paradox. He goes on the offensive and—as the preface to the second edition of *The Division of Labor in Society* and the later lectures on professional ethics show—sets the requirement that the professional divisions of the modern occupational system *should* form the point of departure for universalistically justified normative regulations.

It is not Durkheim's answer but the way he poses the question that is instructive. It directs our attention to empirical connections between stages of system differentiation and forms of social integration. It is only possible to analyze these connections by distinguishing mechanisms for coordinating action that harmonize the *action orientations* of participants from mechanisms that stabilize nonintended interconnections of actions by way of functionally intermeshing *action consequences.* In one case, the integration of an action system is established by a normatively secured or communicatively achieved consensus, in the other case, by a nonnormative regulation of individual decisions that extends beyond the actors' consciousnesses. This distinction between a *social integration* of society, which takes effect in action orientations, and a *systemic integration,* which reaches through and beyond action orientations, calls for a corresponding differentiation in the concept of society itself. No matter whether one starts with Mead from basic concepts of social interaction or with Durkheim from basic concepts of collective representation, in either case society is conceived from the perspective of acting subjects as the *lifeworld of a social group.* In contrast, from the observer's perspective of someone not involved, society can be conceived only as a *system of actions* such that each action has a functional significance according to its contribution to the maintenance of the system.

One can join the system concept of society with the lifeworld concept, as Mead did. He related the natural or objective meanings that the biologist ascribes to the *behavior of an organism* in the system of its species-specific environment to the semanticized meanings of the corresponding *actions* as these become accessible to the actor himself within his lifeworld. As we have seen, Mead reconstructs the emergence of the sociocultural world as the transition to a stage, first, of symbolically mediated interaction and, then, of linguistically mediated interaction. In the process, natural meanings resulting from the significance of specific items in the functional circuit of animal behavior are transformed into symbolic meanings at the intentional disposition of participants in interactions. The object domain is changed by this process of semanticization, so that the ethological model of a self-regulating system, according to which every event or state is ascribed a meaning on the basis of its functional significance, is gradually replaced by the communication-theoretic model, according to which actors orient their actions by their own interpretations. Of course, this latter model of the lifeworld would be *adequate* for human societies only if that process of semanticization absorbed *all* "natural" meanings—that is, if *all* systemic interconnections in which interactions stand were brought into the horizon of the lifeworld and thereby into the intuitive knowledge of participants. This is a bold assumption, but it is an empirical matter that should not be *pre*decided at an analytical level by a conception of society set out in action-theoretical terms.

Every theory of society that is restricted to communication theory is subject to limitations that must be observed. The concept of the lifeworld that emerges from the conceptual perspective of communicative action has only limited analytical and empirical range. I would therefore like to propose (1) that we conceive of societies *simultaneously* as systems and lifeworlds. This concept proves itself in (2) a theory of social evolution that separates the rationalization of the lifeworld from the growing complexity of societal systems so as to make the connection Durkheim envisaged between forms of social integration and stages of system differentiation tangible, that is, susceptible to empirical analysis. In pursuing these aims, I shall develop a concept of forms of mutual understanding [*Verständigungsform*] in analogy to Lukacs's concept of forms of objectivity [*Gegenständlichkeitsform*], and then make use of it to reformulate the problematic of reification. With this conceptual apparatus in hand, I shall return in the concluding chapter to Weber's diagnosis of the times and propose a new formulation of the paradox of rationalization.

1. The Concept of the Lifeworld and the Hermeneutic Idealism of Interpretive Sociology

I would like to explicate the concept of the lifeworld, and to this end I shall pick up again the threads of our reflection on communication theory. It is not my intention to carry further our formal-pragmatic examination of speech acts and of communicative action; rather, I want to build upon these concepts so far as they have already been analyzed, and take up the question of how the lifeworld—as the horizon within which communicative actions are "always already" moving—is in turn limited and changed by the structural transformation of society as a whole.

I have previously introduced the concept of the lifeworld rather casually and only from a reconstructive research perspective. It is a concept complementary to that of communicative action. Like the phenomenological lifeworld analysis of the late Husserl,[1] or the late Wittgenstein's analysis of forms of life (which were not, to be sure, carried out with a systematic intent),[2] formal-pragmatic analysis aims at structures that, in contrast to the historical shapes of particular lifeworlds and life-forms, are put forward as invariant. With this first step we are taking into the bargain a separation of form and content. So long as we hold to a formal-pragmatic research perspective, we can take up questions that have previously been dealt with in the framework of transcendental philosophy—in the present context, we can focus our attention on structures of the lifeworld in general.

I should like to begin by (A) making clear how the lifeworld is related to those three worlds on which subjects acting with an orientation to mutual understanding base their common definitions of situations. (B) I will then elaborate upon the concept of the lifeworld present as a context in communicative action and relate it to Durkheim's concept of the collective consciousness. Certainly, it is not a concept that can be put to empirical use without further ado. (C) The concepts of the lifeworld normally employed in interpretive [verstehenden] sociology are linked with everyday concepts that are, to begin with, serviceable only for the narrative presentation of historical events and social circumstances. (D) An investigation of the functions that communicative action takes on in maintaining a structurally differentiated world originates from within this horizon. In connection with these functions, we can clarify the necessary conditions for a rationalization of the lifeworld. (E) This takes us to the limit of theoretical approaches that identify society with the lifeworld. I

119

shall therefore propose that we conceive of society simultaneously as a system and as a lifeworld.

A.—In examining the ontological presuppositions of teleological, normatively regulated, and dramaturgical action in Chapter I, I distinguished three different actor-world relations that a subject can take up to something in a world—to something that either obtains or can be brought about in the one objective world, to something recognized as obligatory in the social world supposedly shared by all the members of a collective, or to something that other actors attribute to the speaker's own subjective world (to which he has privileged access). These actor-world relations turn up again in the pure types of action oriented to mutual understanding. By attending to the modes of language use, we can clarify what it means for a speaker, in performing one of the standard speech acts, to take up a pragmatic relation

- to something in the objective world (as the totality of entities about which true statements are possible); or
- to something in the social world (as the totality of legitimately regulated interpersonal relations); or
- to something in the subjective world (as the totality of experiences to which a speaker has privileged access and which he can express before a public);

such that what the speech act refers to appears to the speaker as something objective, normative, or subjective. In introducing the concept of communicative action,[3] I pointed out that the pure types of action oriented to mutual understanding are merely limit cases. In fact, communicative utterances are always embedded in various world relations at the same time. Communicative action relies on a cooperative process of interpretation in which participants relate simultaneously to something in the objective, the social, and the subjective worlds, even when they *thematically stress only one* of the three components in their utterances. Speaker and hearer use the reference system of the three worlds as an interpretive framework within which they work out their common situation definitions. They do not relate point-blank to something in a world but relativize their utterances against the chance that their validity will be contested by another actor. Coming to an understanding [*Verständigung*] means that participants in communication reach an agreement [*Einigung*] concerning the validity of an utterance; agreement [*Einverständnis*] is the intersubjective recognition of the validity claim the speaker raises for it. Even when an utterance clearly belongs only to one mode of communication and sharply thematizes one corresponding validity claim, all three modes of communication and the validity claims corresponding to them are internally related to each other. Thus, it is a rule of communicative action that when a hearer assents to a thematized validity claim, he acknowledges the other two implicitly raised validity claims as well—otherwise, he is supposed to make known his dissent. Consensus does not come about when, for example, a hearer accepts the *truth of an assertion* but at the same time doubts the sincerity of the speaker or the normative appropriateness of his utterance; the same holds for the case in which a speaker accepts the *normative validity of a command* but suspects the seriousness of the intent thereby expressed or has his doubts about the existential presuppositions of the action commanded (and thus about the possibility of carrying it out). The example of a command that the addressee regards as unfeasible reminds us that participants are always expressing themselves in situations that they have to define in common so far as they are acting with an orientation to mutual understanding. An older construction worker who sends a younger and newly arrived co-worker to fetch some beer, telling him to hurry it up and be back in a few minutes, supposes that the situation is clear to everyone involved—here, the younger worker and any other workers within hearing distance. The *theme* is the upcoming midmorning snack; taking care of the drinks is a *goal* related to this theme; one of the older workers comes up with the *plan* to send the "new guy," who, given his status, cannot easily get around this request. The informal group hierarchy of the workers on the construction site is the *normative framework* in which the one is allowed to tell the other to do something. The action situation is defined *temporally* by the upcoming break and *spatially* by the distance from the site to the nearest store. If the situation were such that the nearest store could not be reached by foot in a few minutes, that is, that the plan of action of the older worker could—at least under the conditions specified—only be carried out with an automobile (or other means of transportation), the person addressed might answer with: "But I don't have a car."

The background of a communicative utterance is thus formed by situation definitions that, as measured against the actual need for mutual understanding, have to overlap to a sufficient extent. If this commonality cannot be presupposed, the actors have to draw upon the means of strategic action, with an orientation toward coming to a mutual understanding, so as to bring about a common definition of the situation or to negotiate one directly—which occurs in everyday communicative practice primarily in the form of "repair work." Even in cases where this is not necessary, every new utterance is a test: the definition of the situation implicitly proposed by the speaker is either confirmed, modified, partly suspended, or generally placed in question. This continual process of definition and redefinition involves correlating contents to worlds—according to what counts in a given instance as a consensually interpreted element of the objective world, as an intersubjectively recognized normative component of the social world, or as a private element of a subjective world to which someone has privileged access. At the same time, the actors demarcate themselves from these three worlds. With every common situation definition they are determining the boundary between external nature, society, and inner nature; at the same time, they are renewing the demarcation between themselves as interpreters, on the one side, and the external world and their own inner worlds, on the other.

So, for instance, the older worker, upon hearing the other's response, might realize that he has to revise his implicit assumption that a nearby shop is open on Mondays. It would be different if the younger worker had answered: "I'm not thirsty." He would then learn from the astonished reaction that beer for the midmorning snack is a norm held to independently of the subjective state of mind of one of the parties involved. Perhaps the newcomer does not understand the normative context in which the older man is giving him an order, and asks whose turn to get the beer it will be tomorrow. Or perhaps he is missing the point because he is from another region where the local work rhythm, that is, the custom of midmorning snack, is not familiar, and thus responds with the question: "Why should I interrupt my work *now*?" We can imagine continuations of this conversation indicating that one or the other of the parties changes his initial definition of the situation and brings it into accord with the situation definitions of the others. In the first two cases described above, there would be a regrouping of the individual elements of the situation, a Gestalt-switch; the presumed fact that a nearby shop is open becomes a subjective belief that turned out to be false; what is presumed to be a desire to have beer with the midmorning snack turns out to be a collectively recognized norm. In the other two cases, the interpretation of the situation gets supplemented with respect to elements of the social world: the low man on the pole gets the beer; in this part of the world one has a midmorning snack at 9:00 A.M. These *redefinitions* are based on suppositions of commonality in respect to the objective, social, and each's own subjective world. With this reference system, participants in communication suppose that the situation definitions forming the background to an actual utterance hold intersubjectively.

Situations do not get "defined" in the sense of being sharply delimited. They always have a horizon that shifts with the theme. A *situation* is a segment of *lifeworld contexts of relevance* [*Verweisungszusammenhänge*] that is thrown into relief by themes and articulated through goals and plans of action; these contexts of relevance are concentrically ordered and become increasingly anonymous and diffused as the spatiotemporal and social distance grows. Thus, as regards our little scene with the construction workers, the construction site located on a specific street, the specific time—a Monday morning shortly before midmorning snack—and the reference group of co-workers who are at this site constitute the null point of a spatiotemporal and social reference system, of a world that is "within my actual reach." The city around the building site, the region, the country, the continent, and so on, constitute, as regards space, a "world within my potential reach"; corresponding to this, in respect to time, we have the daily routine, the life history, the epoch, and so forth; and in the social dimension, the reference groups from the family through the community, nation, and the like, to the "world society." Alfred Schutz again and again supplied us with illustrations of these spatiotemporal and social organizations of the lifeworld.[4]

The *theme* of an upcoming midmorning snack and the *plan* of fetching some beer, with regard to which the theme is broached, mark off a situation from the lifeworld of those directly involved. This action situation presents itself as a field of actual needs for mutual understanding and of actual options for action: the expectations the workers attach to midmorning snack, the status of a newly arrived younger co-worker, the distance of the store from the construction site, the availability of a car, and the like, belong to the elements of the situation. The facts that a single-family house is going up here, that the newcomer is a foreign "guest worker" with no social security, that another co-worker has three children, and that the new building is subject to Bavarian building codes are circumstances irrelevant to the given situation. There are, of course, shifting boundaries. That becomes evident as soon as the homeowner shows up with a case of beer to keep the workers in a good mood, or the guest worker falls from the ladder as he is getting ready to fetch the beer, or the theme of the new government regulations concerning child subsidies comes up, or the architect shows up with a local official to check the number of stories. In such cases, the theme shifts and with it the horizon of the situation, that is to say, the segment of the lifeworld relevant to the situation for which mutual understanding is required in view of the options for action that have been actualized. Situations have boundaries that can be overstepped at any time—thus Husserl introduced the image of the *horizon* that shifts according to one's position and that can expand and shrink as one moves through the rough countryside.[5]

For those involved, the action situation is the center of their lifeworld; it has a movable horizon because it points to the complexity of the lifeworld. In a certain sense, the lifeworld to which participants in communication belong is always present, but only in such a way that it forms the background for an actual scene. As soon as a *context of relevance* of this sort is brought into a situation, becomes part of a situation, it loses its triviality and unquestioned solidity. If, for instance, the fact that the new worker is not insured against accidental injury suddenly enters the domain of relevance of a thematic field, it can be explicitly mentioned— and in various illocutionary roles: a speaker can state that *p;* he can deplore or conceal that *p;* he can blame someone for the fact that *p,* and so on. When it becomes part of the situation, this state of affairs can be known and problematized as a fact, as the content of a norm or of a feeling, desire, and so forth. Before it becomes relevant to the situation, the same circumstance is given only in the mode of something taken for granted in the lifeworld, something with which those involved are intuitively familiar without anticipating the possibility of its becoming problematic. It is not even "known," in any strict sense, if this entails that it can be justified and contested. Only the limited segments of the lifeworld brought into the horizon of a situation constitute a thematizable context of action oriented to mutual understanding; only they appear under the category of *knowledge.* From a perspective turned toward the situation, the lifeworld appears as a reservoir of taken-for-granteds, of unshaken convictions that participants in communication draw upon in cooperative processes of interpretation. Single elements, specific taken-for-granteds, are, however, mobilized in the form of consensual and yet problematizable knowledge only when they become relevant to a situation.

If we now relinquish the basic concepts of the philosophy of consciousness in which Husserl dealt with the problem of the lifeworld, we can think of the lifeworld as represented by a culturally transmitted and linguistically organized stock of interpretive patterns. Then the idea of a "context of relevance" that connects the elements of the situation with one another, and the situation with the lifeworld, need no longer be explained in the framework of a phenomenology and psychology of perception.[6] Relevance structures can be conceived instead as interconnections of meaning holding between a given communicative utterance, the immediate context, and its connotative horizon of meanings. Contexts of relevance are based on *grammatically regulated* relations among the elements of a *linguistically organized* stock of knowledge.

If, as usual in the tradition stemming from Humboldt,[7] we assume that there is an internal connection between structures of lifeworlds and structures of linguistic worldviews, language and cultural tradition take on a certain transcendental status in relation to everything that can become an element of a situation. Language and culture neither coincide with the formal world concepts by means of which participants in communication together define their situations, nor do they appear as something innerworldly. Language and culture are constitutive for the life-world itself. They are neither one of the formal frames, that is, the worlds to which participants assign elements of situations, nor do they appear as something in the objective, social, or subjective worlds. In performing or understanding a speech act, participants are very much moving within their language, so that they cannot bring a present utterance *before themselves* as "something intersubjective," in the way they experience an event as something objective, encounter a pattern of behavior as something normative, experience or ascribe a desire or feeling as something subjective. The very medium of mutual understanding abides in a peculiar *half-transcendence.* So long as participants maintain their per-formative attitudes, the language actually in use remains *at their backs.* Speakers cannot take up an extramundane position in relation to it. The same is true of culture—of those patterns of interpretation transmitted in language. From a semantic point of view, language does have a peculiar affinity to linguistically articulated worldviews. Natural languages con-serve the contents of tradition, which persist only in symbolic forms, for the most part in linguistic embodiment. For the semantic capacity of a language has to be adequate to the complexity of the stored-up cultural contents, the patterns of interpretation, valuation, and expression.

This stock of knowledge supplies members with unproblematic, com-mon, background convictions that are assumed to be guaranteed; it is from these that contexts for processes of reaching understanding get shaped, processes in which those involved use tried and true situation definitions or negotiate new ones. Participants find the relations between the objective, social, and subjective worlds already preinterpreted. When they go beyond the horizon of a given situation, they cannot step into a void; they find themselves right away in another, now actualized, yet *preinterpreted* domain of what is culturally taken for granted. In every-day communicative practice there are no completely unfamiliar situa-tions. Every new situation appears in a lifeworld composed of a cultural stock of knowledge that is "always already" familiar. Communicative ac-tors can no more take up an extramundane position in relation to their lifeworld than they can in relation to language as the medium for the processes of reaching understanding through which their lifeworld main-tains itself. In drawing upon a cultural tradition, they also continue it.

The category of the lifeworld has, then, a different status than the normal world-concepts dealt with above. Together with criticizable va-lidity claims, these latter concepts form the frame or categorial scaffold-ing that serves to order problematic situations—that is, situations that need to be agreed upon—in a lifeworld that is already substantively in-terpreted. With the formal world-concepts, speakers and hearers can qualify the possible referents of their speech acts so that they can relate

to something objective, normative, or subjective. The lifeworld, by contrast, does not allow for analogous assignments; speakers and hearers
cannot refer by means of it to something as "something intersubjective."
Communicative actors are always moving *within* the horizon of their
lifeworld; they cannot step outside of it. As interpreters, they themselves
belong to the lifeworld, along with their speech acts, but they cannot
· refer to "something in the lifeworld" in the same way as they can to facts,
norms, or experiences. The structures of the lifeworld lay down the
forms of the intersubjectivity of possible understanding. It is to them that
participants in communication owe their extramundane positions vis-à-
vis the innerworldly items about which they can come to an understanding. The lifeworld is, so to speak, the transcendental site where speaker
and hearer meet, where they can reciprocally raise claims that their utterances fit the world (objective, social, or subjective), and where they
can criticize and confirm those validity claims, settle their disagreements, and arrive at agreements. In a sentence: participants cannot assume *in actu* the same distance in relation to language and culture as in
relation to the totality of facts, norms, or experiences concerning which
mutual understanding is possible.

The scheme in Figure 20 is meant to illustrate that the lifeworld is
constitutive for mutual understanding *as such,* whereas the formal
world-concepts constitute a reference system for that *about which* mutual understanding is possible: speakers and hearers come to an understanding from out of their common lifeworld about something in the
objective, social, or subjective worlds.

B.—In this case graphic representation is particularly unsatisfactory. So I
shall now try to make the communication-theoretic concept of the lifeworld more precise by comparing it to the phenomenological concept—
the only one hitherto analyzed in any detail. In doing so, I shall be referring to Alfred Schutz's posthumously published manuscripts on *The
Structure of the Lifeworld,* edited and reworked by Thomas Luckmann.[8]

Up to now we have conceived of action in terms of dealing with situations. The concept of communicative action singles out above all two
aspects of this situation management: the *teleological aspect* of realizing
one's aims (or carrying out one's plan of action) and the *communicative
aspect* of interpreting a situation and arriving at some agreement. In communicative action participants pursue their plans cooperatively on the
basis of a shared definition of the situation. If a shared definition of the
situation has first to be negotiated, or if efforts to come to some agreement within the framework of shared situation definitions fail, the attainment of consensus, which is normally a condition for pursuing goals, can
itself become an end. In any case, the *success* achieved by teleological

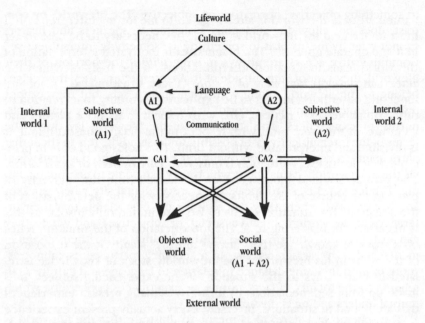

The double arrows indicate the world-relations that actors (A) establish with their utterances (CA).

Figure 20. World-Relations of Communicative Acts (CA)

action and the *consensus* brought about by acts of reaching understanding are the criteria for whether a situation has been dealt with successfully or not. A *situation* represents a segment of the lifeworld delimited in relation to a theme. A *theme* comes up in connection with the interests and aims of at least one participant; it circumscribes a domain of relevance of thematizable elements of the situation, and it is accentuated by the *plans* that participants draw up on the basis of their interpretations of the situation, in order to realize their ends. It is constitutive for communicative action that participants carry out their plans cooperatively in an action situation defined in common. They seek to avoid two risks: the risk of not coming to some understanding, that is, of disagreement or misunderstanding, and the risk of a plan of action miscarrying, that is, of failure. Averting the former risk is a necessary condition for managing the latter. Participants cannot attain their goals if they cannot meet the need for mutual understanding called for by the possibilities of acting in the situation—or at least they can no longer attain their goals by way of communicative action.

Schutz and Luckmann also distinguish these two aspects of interpreting a situation and carrying out a plan of action in a situation: "in the natural attitude the world is already given to me for my interpretation. I must understand my lifeworld to the degree necessary to be able to act in it and operate upon it."[9] The pragmatically motivated interpretation of the world leads to situation interpretations on the basis of which the actor can develop his plans of action: "Every situation has an infinite inner and outer horizon; it is to be explicated according to its relation to other situations, experiences, etc., with respect to its prior history and its future. At the same time, with respect to the details constituting it, it is divisible and interpretable without limit. This holds good only in principle. Practically, every situation is only *limitedly in need of explication.* The plan-determined interest, which is derived from the hierarchy of plans in the course of life, limits the necessity for the determination of the situation. The situation needs to be determined only insofar as this is necessary for mastering it."[10] The interpretation of the situation relies on a stock of knowledge that "always already" stands at the disposition of the actor in his lifeworld: "The lifeworldly stock of knowledge is related in many ways to the situation of the experiencing subject. It is made up from sedimentations of formerly actually present experiences that are bound to situations. Inversely, every actually present experience is inserted into the flow of lived experience and into a biography, according to the set of types and relevance found in the stock of knowledge. And finally, each situation is defined and mastered with the help of the stock of knowledge."[11]

Schutz and Luckmann hold the view that the actor constitutes the world from out of which he lives from the basic elements of this stock of knowledge.

> In every situation only a certain segment of the world is given to me. Only part of the world is in actual reach. But around this province, other provinces of restorable or attainable reach are differentiated, their spheres of reach exhibiting a temporal as well as a social structure. Further, I can operate only in one segment of the world. Around the actual zone of operation there are graduated zones that are again restorable or attainable, possessing in any case a temporal social structure. My experience of the lifeworld is also temporally arranged: inner duration is a flow of lived experience arising from present, retentive, and protentive phases, as also from memories and expectations. It is intersected by world time, biological time, and social time, and is sedimented in the unique sequence of an articulated biography. And finally, my experience is socially arranged. All experiences have a social dimension, just as the temporal and spatial arrangement of my experiences is also "socialized." As a consequence, my experience of the social world has a specific structure. The other is given to me imme-

diately as a fellow-man in the we-relation, while the mediate experiences of the social world are graduated according to degrees of anonymity and are arranged in experiences of the contemporary world, the world of predecessors, and the world of successors.[12]

The primary aim of the phenomenological analysis of lifeworld structures is to elucidate the spatiotemporal and social organization of the lifeworld; I shall not go into that here. What interests me in the present context is the fact that Schutz and Luckmann hold on to the model of the philosophy of consciousness. Like Husserl, they begin with the egological consciousness for which the general structures of the lifeworld are given as necessary subjective conditions of the experience of a concretely shaped, historically stamped, social lifeworld: "The above does not concern specific, concrete, and variable experiences, but rather the fundamental structures of experience of the lifeworld as such. In contrast to specific experiences, these fundamental structures do not enter into the grip of consciousness in the natural attitude, as a core of experience, but they are a condition of everyday experience of the lifeworld and enter into the horizon of experience."[13]

Schutz and Luckmann give an *action-theoretic* twist to the model of a generative subjectivity that constitutes the lifeworld as the transcendental frame of possible everyday experience—a model developed with an eye to basic *epistemological* questions. There is no doubt that the familiar psychological and sociological models of an isolated actor in a situation, affected by stimuli or acting according to plans,[14] gain a certain depth of focus through being connected with phenomenological analysis of lifeworlds and action situations.[15] And this is in turn the jumping-off point for a phenomenologically informed systems theory.[16] This shows, incidentally, how easy it is for systems theory to become the heir to the philosophy of consciousness. If we interpret the situation of the acting subject as the environment of the personality system, the results of phenomenological lifeworld analysis can be smoothly absorbed into a systems theory of the Luhmannian observance. This even has the advantage that one can ignore a problem on which Husserl shipwrecked in the *Cartesian Meditations,* namely, the problem of monadological production of the intersubjectivity of the lifeworld.[17] This problem does not even come up when subject-object relations are replaced by system-environment relations. On this view, personality systems are environments for one another, just as, at another level, personality systems and social systems are. The problem of intersubjectivity disappears—that is to say, the question of how different subjects can share the same lifeworld—in favor of the problem of interpenetration—that is, the question of how certain kinds of systems can form environments for each other that are conditionally contingent and attuned to one another.[18] The price for this reformulation will occupy us further on.

In this field of tension between phenomenological lifeworld analysis and sociological action theory, Schutz takes up an ambivalent position. One the one hand, he sees that Husserl did not solve the problem of intersubjectivity; under the influence of American pragmatism, especially Mead's,[19] Schutz tends to put aside the constitution of the lifeworld and to start directly from an intersubjectively constituted lifeworld. On the other hand, Schutz does not convert, say, to a communication-theoretical approach; he sticks with Husserl's intuitive method and even takes over the architectonic of transcendental phenomenology, conceiving of his own undertaking in this framework as a regional ontology of society. This explains why Schutz and Luckmann do not get at the structures of the lifeworld by grasping the structures of linguistically generated intersubjectivity directly, but rather in the mirror of the isolated actor's subjective experience. In the frame of the philosophy of consciousness, the "experiencing subject" remains the court of last appeal for analysis.

The following excursus is meant to show that the phenomenologically described basic features of the constituted lifeworld can be easily explained if we treat 'lifeworld' as a complementary concept to 'communicative action'. Schutz and Luckmann stress primarily three moments: (*a*) the naïve familiarity with an unproblematically given background, (*b*) the validity of an intersubjectively shared world, and (*c*) the at once total and indeterminate, porous, and yet delimiting character of the life-world.

(*ad a*) The lifeworld is given to the experiencing subject as unquestionable. "By the everyday lifeworld is to be understood that province of reality which the wide-awake and normal adult simply takes for granted in the attitude of common sense. By this taken-for-grantedness, we designate everything which we experience as unquestionable; every state of affairs is for us unproblematic until further notice."[20] The unproblematic character of the lifeworld has to be understood in a radical sense: qua lifeworld it cannot become problematic, it can at most fall apart. The elements of the lifeworld with which we are naïvely familiar do not have the status of facts or norms or experiences concerning which speakers and hearers could, if necessary, come to some understanding. On the other hand, the elements of an action situation concerning which participants want to reach some consensus by means of their communicative utterances must also be open to question. However, this domain of what can be thematized and problematized is restricted to an action situation that remains *encompassed* within the horizons of a lifeworld, however blurred these may be. The lifeworld forms the indirect context of what is said, discussed, addressed in a situation; it is, to be sure, in principle accessible, but it does not belong to the action situation's thematically delimited domain of relevance. The lifeworld is the intuitively present, in this sense familiar and transparent, and at the same time vast and incalculable web of presuppositions that have to be satisfied if an actual utterance is to be at all meaningful, that is, valid *or* invalid.[21] The presuppositions relevant to a situation are only a segment of this. As the example of the construction workers illustrated, only the context directly spoken to on a given occasion can fall into the whirl of problematization associated with communicative action; by contrast, *the lifeworld always remains in the background.* It is "the unquestioned ground of everything given in my experience, and the unquestionable frame in which all the problems I have to deal with are located."[22] The lifeworld is given in a mode of taken-for-grantedness that can maintain itself only this side of the threshold to basically criticizable convictions.

(*ad b*) The lifeworld owes this certainty to a social a priori built into the intersubjectivity of mutual understanding in language. Although Schutz and Luckmann, operating on the premises of the philosophy of consciousness, play down the importance of language, particularly of the linguistic mediation of social interaction, they stress the intersubjectivity of the lifeworld: "Thus, from the outset, my lifeworld is not my private world but, rather, is intersubjective; the fundamental structure of its reality is shared by us. Just as it is self-evident to me, within the natural attitude, that I can, up to a certain point, obtain knowledge of the lived experience of my fellow-men—for example, the motives of their acts—so, too, I also assume that the same holds reciprocally for them with respect to me."[23] Again the commonality of the lifeworld has to be understood in a radical sense: it is prior to any possible disagreement and cannot become controversial in the way that intersubjectively shared knowledge can; at most it can fall apart. The perspectival character of perception and interpretation, which is linked with the communicative roles of the first, second, and third person, is decisive for the structure of an action situation. The members of a collective count themselves as belonging to the lifeworld in the first-person plural, in a way similar to that in which the individual speaker attributes to himself the subjective world to which he has privileged access in the first-person singular. Communality rests, to be sure, on consensual knowledge, on a cultural stock of knowledge that members share. But it is only in the light of an actual situation that the relevant segment of the lifeworld acquires the status of a contingent reality that could also be interpreted in another way. Naturally, members live in the consciousness that new situations might arise at any time, that they have constantly to deal with new situations; but such situations cannot shatter the naïve trust in the lifeworld. Everyday communicative practice is not compatible with the hypothesis that everything could be entirely different:

> I trust that the world as it has been known by me up until now will continue further and that consequently the stock of knowledge obtained from my fellow-men and formed from my own experiences will continue to preserve its fundamental validity. We would like to designate this (in accord with Husserl) the "and so forth" idealization. From this assumption follows the further and fundamental one: that I can repeat my past successful acts. So long as the structure of the world can be taken to be constant, as long as my previous experience is valid, my ability to operate upon the world in this and that manner remains in principle preserved. As Husserl has shown, the further ideality of the "I can always do it again" is developed correlative to the ideality of the "and so forth". Both idealizations, and the assumptions of the constancy of the world's structure which are grounded upon them—the validity of my previous experience and, on the other hand, my ability to operate upon the world—are essential aspects of thinking within the natural attitude.[24]

(ad c) This immunizing of the lifeworld against total revision is connected with the third basic feature that Schutz, following Husserl, stresses: situations change, but the limits of the lifeworld cannot be transcended. The lifeworld forms the setting in which situational horizons shift, expand, or contract. It forms a context that, itself boundless, draws boundaries. "The stock of knowledge pertaining to thinking within the lifeworld is to be understood not as a context transparent in its totality, but rather as a totality of what is taken for granted, changing from situation to situation, set into relief at any given time against a background of indeterminacy. This totality is not graspable as such but is co-given in the flow of experience as a certain, familiar ground of every situationally determined interpretation."[25] The lifeworld circumscribes action situations in the manner of a preunderstood context that, however, is not addressed. The lifeworld screened out of the domain of relevance of an action situation stands undecided as a reality that is at once unquestionable and shadowy. It flows into the actual process of reaching understanding not at all, or only very indirectly, and thus it remains indeterminate. It can, of course, be drawn into the wake of a new theme and thereby into the catchment of a changed situation. We then encounter it as an intuitively familiar, preinterpreted reality. It is only in becoming relevant to a situation that a segment of the lifeworld comes into view as something that is taken for granted culturally, that rests on interpretations, and that, now that it can be thematized, has lost this mode of unquestionable givenness: "Even in the natural attitude, the relative intrans-

parency of the lifeworld can be grasped subjectively at any given time. Any specific process of interpretation can serve as an occasion for this. But only in theoretical reflection does the lived experience of the inadequacy of specific interpretations lead to an insight into the essential limitations of the lifeworldly stock of knowledge in general."[26] As long as we do not free ourselves from the naïve, situation-oriented attitude of actors caught up in the communicative practice of everyday life, we cannot grasp the limitations of a lifeworld that is dependent upon, and changes along with, a cultural stock of knowledge that can be expanded at any time. For members, the lifeworld is a context that cannot be gotten behind and cannot in principle be exhausted. Thus every understanding of a situation can rely on a global preunderstanding. Every definition of a situation is an "interpretation within the frame of what has already been interpreted, within a reality that is fundamentally and typically familiar."[27]

Every step we take beyond the horizon of a given situation opens up access to a further complex of meaning, which, while it calls for explication, is already intuitively familiar. What was until then "taken for granted," is transformed in the process into cultural knowledge that can be used in defining situations and exposed to tests in communicative action.

It is distinctive of the modern understanding of the world that the cultural tradition can be exposed to testing of this sort across its entire spectrum and in a methodical manner. Centered worldviews that do not yet allow for a radical differentiation of formal world-concepts are, at least in their core domains, immunized against dissonant experiences. This is all the more so, the less there is a chance that "the unquestionable character of my experience explodes."[28] In the experiential domain of our cognitive-instrumental dealings with external nature, "explosions" can scarcely be avoided even when absorbent worldviews restrict the scope of perceived contingencies. In the experiential domain of normatively guided interaction, however, a social world of legitimately regulated interpersonal relations detaches itself only gradually from the diffuse background of the lifeworld.

If we understand lifeworld analysis as an attempt to describe reconstructively, from the internal perspective of members, what Durkheim called the *conscience collective,* then the standpoint from which he viewed the structural transformation of collective consciousness could also prove to be instructive for a phenomenological investigation. We could then understand the differentiation processes he observed as follows: the lifeworld loses its prejudgmental power over everyday communicative practice to the degree that actors owe their mutual understanding to *their own* interpretative performances. Durkheim understands the process of the differentiation of the lifeworld as a separation of culture, society, and personality. We now have to introduce and explain these as structural components of the lifeworld.

Up to this point, borrowing from phenomenological studies, we have limited ourselves to a culturalistic concept of the lifeworld. According to this, cultural patterns of interpretation, evaluation, and expression serve as resources for the achievement of mutual understanding by participants who want to negotiate a common definition of a situation and, within that framework, to arrive at a consensus regarding something in the world. The interpreted action situation circumscribes a thematically opened up range of action alternatives, that is, of conditions and means for carrying out plans. Everything that appears as a restriction on corresponding action initiatives belongs to the situation. Whereas the actor keeps the lifeworld at his back as a resource for action oriented to mutual understanding, the restrictions that circumstances place on the pursuit of his plans appear to him as elements of the situation. And these can be sorted out, within the framework of the three formal world-concepts, into facts, norms, and experiences.

This suggests identifying the lifeworld with culturally transmitted background knowledge, for culture and language do not normally count as elements of a situation. They do not restrict the scope for action and do not fall under one of the formal world-concepts by means of which participants come to some understanding about their situation. They are not in need of any concept under which they might be grasped as elements of an action situation. It is only in those rare moments when culture and language fail as resources that they develop the peculiar resistance we experience in situations of disturbed mutual understanding. Then we need the repair work of translators, interpreters, therapists. They too have at their disposition only the three familiar world-concepts as they try to incorporate elements of the lifeworld that are operating disfunctionally—incomprehensible utterances, opaque traditions, or at the limit, a not-yet-decoded language—into a common interpretation of the situation. Elements of the lifeworld that fail as resources have to be identified as cultural facts that limit the scope of action.

The situation with institutional orders and personality structures is rather different than with culture; they can indeed restrict the actor's scope for initiative and confront him as elements of a situation. As normative or subjective, they fall by nature, so to speak, under one of the formal world-concepts. This should not mislead us into assuming that norms and experiences (like facts or things and events) can appear *only* as something concerning which participants in interaction reach an understanding. They can occupy a double status—as elements of a social or subjective world, on the one hand, as structural components of the lifeworld, on the other.

Action, or mastery of situations, presents itself as a circular process in which the actor is at once both the *initiator* of his accountable actions and the *product* of the traditions in which he stands, of the solidary groups to which he belongs, of socialization and learning processes to which he is exposed. Whereas *a fronte* the segment of the lifeworld relevant to a situation presses upon the actor as a problem he has to resolve on his own, *a tergo* he is sustained by the background of a life-world that does not consist only of cultural certainties. This background comprises individual skills as well—the intuitive knowledge of *how* one deals with situations—and socially customary practices too—the intuitive knowledge of *what* one can count on in situations—no less than background convictions known in a trivial sense. Society and personality operate not only as restrictions; they also serve as resources. The unquestionable character of the lifeworld from out of which one is acting is also due to the security the actor owes to well-established solidarities and proven competences. Lifeworld knowledge conveys the feeling of absolute certainty only because we do not know *about* it; its paradoxical character is due to the fact that the knowledge of what one can count on and how one does something is still connected with—undifferentiated from—what one prereflectively *knows*. If, then, the solidarities of groups integrated via norms and values and the competences of socialized individuals flow into communicative action *a tergo*, in the way that cultural traditions do, it makes sense for us to correct the culturalistic abridgement of the concept of the lifeworld.

C.—While the communication-theoretic concept of the lifeworld we have been discussing gets us away from the philosophy of consciousness, it nevertheless still lies on the same analytical level as the transcendental lifeworld concept of phenomenology. It is obtained by reconstructing the pretheoretical knowledge of competent speakers: from the perspective of participants the lifeworld appears as a horizon-forming context of processes of reaching understanding; in delimiting the domain of relevance for a given situation, this context remains itself withdrawn from thematization within that situation. The communication-theoretic concept of the lifeworld developed from the participant's perspective is not directly serviceable for theoretical purposes; it is not suited for demarcating an object domain of social science, that is, the region within the objective world formed by the totality of hermeneutically accessible, in the broadest sense historical or sociocultural facts. The *everyday concept of the lifeworld* is better suited for this purpose; it is by this means that communicative actors locate and date their utterances in social spaces and historical times. In the communicative practice of everyday life, persons do not only encounter one another in the attitude of participants; they also give narrative presentations of events that take place in the context of their lifeworld. *Narration* is a specialized form of constative speech that serves to describe sociocultural events and objects. Actors base their narrative presentations on a lay concept of the "world," in the sense of the everyday world or lifeworld, which defines the totality of states of affairs that can be reported in true stories.

This everyday concept carves out of the objective world the region of narratable events or historical facts. Narrative practice not only serves trivial needs for mutual understanding among members trying to coordinate their common tasks; it also has a function in the self-understanding of persons. They have to objectivate their belonging to the lifeworld to which, in their actual roles as participants in communication, they do belong. For they can develop personal identities only if they recognize that the sequences of their own actions form narratively presentable life histories; they can develop social identities only if they recognize that they maintain their membership in social groups by way of participating in interactions, and thus that they are caught up in the narratively presentable histories of collectivities. Collectivities maintain their identities only to the extent that the ideas members have of their lifeworld overlap sufficiently and condense into unproblematic background convictions.

The lay concept of the lifeworld refers to the totality of sociocultural facts and thus provides a jumping-off point for social theory. In my view, one methodologically promising way to clarify this concept would be to analyze the form of narrative statements, as Arthur Danto was one of the first to do,[29] and to analyze the form of narrative texts. In the grammar of narratives we can see how we identify and *describe* states and events that appear in a lifeworld; how we *interlink* and *sequentially organize* into complex unities members' interactions in social spaces and historical times; how we explain the actions of individuals and the events that befall them, the acts of collectivities and the fates they meet with, from the perspective of managing situations. In adopting the narrative form, we are choosing a perspective that "grammatically" forces us to base our descriptions on an everyday concept of the lifeworld as a *cognitive reference system.*

This intuitively accessible *concept of the sociocultural lifeworld* can be rendered theoretically fruitful if we can develop from it a reference system for descriptions and explanations relevant to the lifeworld as a whole and not merely to occurrences within it. Whereas narrative presentation refers to what is innerworldly, theoretical presentation is intended to explain the reproduction of the lifeworld itself. Individuals and groups maintain themselves by mastering situations; but how is the lifeworld, of which each situation forms only a segment, maintained? A narrator is already constrained grammatically, through the form of narrative presentation, to take an interest in the identity of the persons acting as well as in the integrity of their life-context. When we tell stories, we cannot avoid also saying indirectly how the subjects involved in them are faring, and what fate the collectivity they belong to is experiencing. Nevertheless, we can make harm to personal identity or threats to social integration visible only indirectly in narratives. While narrative presentations do point to higher-level reproduction processes—to the maintenance imperatives of lifeworlds—they cannot take as their theme the structures of a lifeworld the way they do with what happens in it. The everyday concept of the lifeworld that we bring to narrative presentation as a reference system has to be worked up for theoretical purposes in such a way as to make possible statements about the reproduction or self-maintenance of communicatively structured lifeworlds.

Whereas the lifeworld is given from the *perspective of participants* only as the horizon-forming context of an action situation, the everyday concept of the lifeworld presupposed in the *perspective of narrators* is already being used for cognitive purposes. To make it theoretically fruitful we have to start from those basic functions that, as we learned from Mead, the medium of language fulfills for the reproduction of the lifeworld. In coming to an understanding with one another about their situation, participants in interaction stand in a cultural tradition that they at once use and renew; in coordinating their actions by way of intersubjectively recognizing criticizable validity claims, they are at once relying on membership in social groups and strengthening the integration of those same groups; through participating in interactions with competently acting reference persons, the growing child internalizes the value orientations of his social group and acquires generalized capacities for action.

Under the functional aspect of *mutual understanding*, communicative action serves to transmit and renew cultural knowledge; under the aspect of *coordinating action*, it serves social integration and the establishment of solidarity; finally, under the aspect of *socialization*, communicative action serves the formation of personal identities. The symbolic structures of the lifeworld are reproduced by way of the continuation of valid knowledge, stabilization of group solidarity, and socialization of responsible actors. The process of reproduction connects up new situations with the existing conditions of the lifeworld; it does this in the *semantic* dimension of meanings or contents (of the cultural tradition), as well as in the dimensions of *social space* (of socially integrated groups), and *historical time* (of successive generations). Corresponding to these processes of *cultural reproduction, social integration,* and *socialization* are the structural components of the lifeworld: culture, society, person.

I use the term *culture* for the stock of knowledge from which participants in communication supply themselves with interpretations as they come to an understanding about something in the world. I use the term *society* for the legitimate orders through which participants regulate their memberships in social groups and thereby secure solidarity. By *personality* I understand the competences that make a subject capable of speaking and acting, that put him in a position to take part in processes of reaching understanding and thereby to assert his own identity. The dimensions in which communicative action extends comprise the semantic field of symbolic contents, social space, and historical time. The interactions woven into the fabric of everyday communicative practice constitute the medium through which culture, society, and person get reproduced. These reproduction processes cover the symbolic structures of the lifeworld. We have to distinguish from this the maintenance of the material substratum of the lifeworld.

Material reproduction takes place through the medium of the purposive activity with which sociated individuals intervene in the world to realize their aims. As Weber pointed out, the problems that actors have to deal with in a given situation can be divided into problems of "inner need" and problems of "outer need." To these categories of tasks as viewed from the perspective of action, there correspond, when the matter is viewed from the perspective of lifeworld maintenance, processes of symbolic and material reproduction.

I would like now to examine how different approaches to interpretative sociology conceive of society as a lifeworld. The structural complexity of a lifeworld, as it has revealed itself to our communication-theoretical analysis, does not come into view along this path. Whenever "the lifeworld" has been made a fundamental concept of social theory— whether under this name, as in Husserl and his followers, or under the title of "forms of life," "cultures," "language communities," or whatever— the approach has remained selective; the strategies of concept formation usually connect up with only one of the three structural components of the lifeworld.

Even the communication-theoretical reading I gave to Schutz's analysis suggests a concept of the lifeworld limited to aspects of mutual understanding and abridged in a culturalistic fashion. On this model, participants actualize on any given occasion some of the background convictions drawn from the cultural stock of knowledge; the process of reaching understanding serves the negotiation of common situation definitions, and these must in turn meet the critical conditions of an agreement accepted as reasonable. Cultural knowledge, insofar as it flows into situation definitions, is thus exposed to a test: it has to prove itself "against the world," that is, against facts, norms, experiences. Any revisions have an indirect effect on nonthematized elements of knowledge internally connected with the problematic contents. From this view, communicative action presents itself as an interpretive mechanism through which cultural knowledge is reproduced. The reproduction of the lifeworld consists essentially in a continuation and renewal of tradition, which moves between the extremes of a mere reduplication of and a break with tradition. In the phenomenological tradition stemming from Husserl and Schutz, the social theory based on such a culturalistically abridged concept of the lifeworld, when it is consistent, issues in a *sociology of knowledge*. This is the case, for instance, with Peter Berger and Thomas Luckmann, who state the thesis of *The Social Construction of Reality* as follows: "The basic contentions of the argument of this book are implicit in its title and subtitle, namely, that reality is socially constructed and that the sociology of knowledge must analyze the processes in which this occurs."[30]

The one-sidedness of the culturalistic concept of the lifeworld becomes clear when we consider that communicative action is not only a process of reaching understanding; in coming to an understanding about something in the world, actors are at the same time taking part in interactions through which they develop, confirm, and renew their memberships in social groups and their own identities. Communicative actions are not only processes of interpretation in which cultural knowledge is "tested against the world"; they are at the same time processes of social integration and of socialization. The lifeworld is "tested" in quite a different manner in these latter dimensions: these tests are not measured directly against criticizable validity claims or standards of rationality, but against standards for the solidarity of members and for the identity of socialized individuals. While participants in interaction, turned "toward the world," reproduce through their accomplishment of mutual understanding the cultural knowledge upon which they draw, they simultaneously reproduce their memberships in collectivities and their identities. When one of these other aspects shifts into the foreground, the concept of the lifeworld is again given a one-sided formulation: it is narrowed down either in an *institutionalistic* or in a *sociopsychological* fashion.

In the tradition stemming from Durkheim, social theory is based on a concept of the lifeworld reduced to the aspect of social integration. Parsons chooses for this expression 'societal community'; he understands by it the lifeworld of a social group. It forms the core of every society,

where 'society' is understood as the structural component that determines the status—the rights and duties—of group members by way of
legitimately ordered interpersonal relations. Culture and personality are
represented only as functional supplements of the 'societal community':
culture supplies society with values that can be institutionalized, and
socialized individuals contribute motivations that are appropriate to
normed expectations.

By contrast, in the tradition stemming from Mead, social theory is
based on a concept of the lifeworld reduced to the aspect of the socialization of individuals. Representatives of symbolic interactionism, such as
Herbert Blumer, A. M. Rose, Anselm Strauss, or R. H. Turner, conceive of
the lifeworld as the sociocultural milieu of communicative action represented as role playing, role taking, role defining, and the like. Culture and
society enter into consideration only as media for the self-formative processes in which actors are involved their whole lives long. It is only
consistent when the theory of society shrinks down then to *social psychology.*[31]

If, by contrast, we take the concept of symbolic interaction that Mead
himself made central and work it out in the manner suggested above—
as a concept of linguistically mediated, normatively guided interaction—
and thereby gain access to phenomenological lifeworld analyses, then
we are in a position to get at the complex interconnection of all three
reproduction processes.

D.—The cultural reproduction of the lifeworld ensures that newly arising situations are connected up with existing conditions in the world in
the semantic dimension: it secures a *continuity* of tradition and *coherence* of knowledge sufficient for daily practice. Continuity and coherence are measured by the *rationality* of the knowledge accepted as
valid. This can be seen in disturbances of cultural reproduction that get
manifested in a loss of meaning and lead to corresponding legitimation
and orientation crises. In such cases, the actors' cultural stock of knowledge can no longer cover the need for mutual understanding that arises
with new situations. The interpretive schemes accepted as valid fail, and
the resource "meaning" becomes scarce.

The social integration of the lifeworld ensures that newly arising situations are connected up with existing conditions in the world in the
dimension of social space: it takes care of coordinating actions by way of
legitimately regulated interpersonal relations and stabilizes the identity
of groups to an extent sufficient for everyday practice. The coordination
of actions and the *stabilization of group identities* are measured by the
solidarity among members. This can be seen in disturbances of social
integration, which manifest themselves in *anomie* and corresponding

conflicts. In such cases, actors can no longer cover the need for coordination that arises with new situations from the inventory of legitimate orders. Legitimately regulated social memberships are no longer sufficient, and the resource "social solidarity" becomes scarce.

Finally the socialization of the members of a lifeworld ensures that newly arising situations are connected up with existing situations in the world in the dimension of historical time: it secures for succeeding generations the acquisition of *generalized competences for action* and sees to it that *individual life histories are in harmony with collective forms of life*. Interactive capacities and styles of life are measured by the *responsibility of persons*. This can be seen in disturbances of the socialization process, which are manifested in psychopathologies and corresponding phenomena of alienation. In such cases, actors' competences do not suffice to maintain the intersubjectivity of commonly defined action situations. The personality system can preserve its identity only by means of defensive strategies that are detrimental to participating in social interaction on a realistic basis, so that the resource "ego strength" becomes scarce.

Once one has drawn these distinctions, a question arises concerning the contribution of the individual reproduction processes to maintaining the structural components of the lifeworld. If culture provides sufficient valid knowledge to cover the given need for mutual understanding in a lifeworld, the contributions of cultural reproduction to maintaining *the two other* components consist, on the one hand, in *legitimations* for existing institutions and, on the other hand, in *socialization patterns* for the acquisition of generalized competences for action. If society is sufficiently integrated to cover the given need for coordination in a lifeworld, the contribution of the integration process to maintaining *the two other* components consist, on the one hand, in *legitimately regulated social memberships* of individuals and, on the other, in moral duties or *obligations*: the central stock of cultural values institutionalized in legitimate orders is incorporated into a normative reality that is, if not criticism-proof, at least resistant to criticism and to this extent beyond the reach of continuous testing by action oriented to reaching understanding. If, finally, personality systems have developed such strong identities that they can deal on a realistic basis with the situations that come up in their lifeworld, the contribution of socialization processes to maintaining *the other two* components consists, on the one hand, in *interpretive accomplishments* and, on the other, in *motivations for actions that conform to norms* (see Figure 21).

The individual reproduction processes can be evaluated according to standards of the *rationality of knowledge*, the *solidarity of members*, and the *responsibility of the adult personality*. Naturally, the measure-

Structural components / Reproduction processes	Culture	Society	Personality
Cultural reproduction	Interpretive schemes fit for consensus ("valid knowledge")	Legitimations	Socialization patterns / Educational goals
Social integration	Obligations	Legitimately ordered interpersonal relations	Social memberships
Socialization	Interpretive accomplishments	Motivations for actions that conform to norms	Interactive capabilities ("personal identity")

Figure 21. Contributions of Reproduction Processes to Maintaining the Structural Components of the Lifeworld

ments within each of these dimensions vary according to the degree of structural differentiation of the lifeworld. The degree of differentiation also determines how great the need for consensual knowledge, legitimate orders, and personal autonomy is at any given time. Disturbances in reproduction are manifested in their own proper domains of culture, society, and personality as loss of meaning, anomie, and mental illness (psychopathology). There are corresponding manifestations of deprivation in the other domains (see Figure 22).

On this basis we can specify the functions that communicative action takes on in the reproduction of the lifeworld (see Figure 23). The highlighted areas along the diagonal in Figure 23 contain the characterizations with which we first demarcated cultural reproduction, social integration, and socialization from one another. In the meantime we have seen that *each* of these reproduction processes contributes in maintaining *all* the components of the lifeworld. Thus we can attribute to the

Structural components / Disturbances in the domain of	Culture	Society	Person	Dimension of evaluation
Cultural reproduction	Loss of meaning	Withdrawal of legitimation	Crisis in orientation and education	Rationality of knowledge
Social integration	Unsettling of collective identity	Anomie	Alienation	Solidarity of members
Socialization	Rupture of tradition	Withdrawal of motivation	Psychopath- ologies	Personal responsibility

Figure 22. Manifestations of Crisis When Reproduction Processes Are Disturbed (Pathologies)

medium of language, through which the structures of the lifeworld are reproduced, the functions set forth in Figure 23.

With these schematically summarized specifications, our communication-theoretical concept of the lifeworld has not yet attained the degree of explication of its phenomenological counterpart. Nonetheless, I shall leave it with this outline to return to the question of whether the concept of the lifeworld proposed here is fit to serve as a basic concept of social theory. Despite his many reservations, Schutz continued to hold to the approach of transcendental phenomenology. If one considers the method developed by Husserl to be unobjectionable, the claim to universality of lifeworld analysis carried out phenomenologically goes without saying. However, once we introduce the concept of the lifeworld in communication-theoretical terms, the idea of approaching any society whatsoever by means of it is not at all trivial. The burden of truth for the universal validity of the lifeworld concept—a validity reaching across

Structural components / Reproduction processes	Culture	Society	Person
Cultural reproduction	Transmission, critique, acquisition of cultural knowledge	Renewal of knowledge effective for legitimation	Reproduction of knowledge relevant to child rearing, education
Social integration	Immunization of a central stock of value orientations	Coordination of actions via intersubjectively recognized validity claims	Reproduction of patterns of social membership
Socialization	Enculturation	Internalization of values	Formation of identity

Figure 23. Reproductive Functions of Action Oriented to Mutual Understanding

cultures and epochs—shifts then to the complementary concept of communicative action.

Mead attempted to reconstruct a sequence of stages of forms of interaction for the transition from the animal to the human. According to this reconstruction, communicative action is anthropologically fundamental; there are empirical reasons—and not merely methodological prejudgments—for the view that the structures of linguistically mediated, normatively guided interaction determine the starting point of sociocultural development. This also determines the range within which historical lifeworlds can vary. Questions of *developmental dynamics* cannot, of course, be answered by identifying structural restrictions of this sort. They can be dealt with only if we take contingent boundary conditions into account and analyze the interdependence between sociocultural transformations and changes in material reproduction. Nevertheless, the fact that sociocultural developments are subject to the structural constraints of communicative action can have a systematic effect. We can speak of a developmental logic—in the sense of the tradition stemming from Piaget, a sense that calls for further clarification—if the structures of historical lifeworlds vary within the scope defined by the structural constraints of communicative action not accidentally but directionally, that is, in dependence on learning processes. For instance, there would be a *directional variation of lifeworld structures* if we could bring evolutionary changes under the description of a structural differentiation between culture, society, and personality. One would have to postulate learning processes for such a structural differentiation of the lifeworld if one could show that this meant an increase in rationality.

The idea of the linguistification of the sacred has served us as a guiding thread for basing an interpretation of this sort on Mead and Durkheim. We can now reformulate this idea as follows: the further the structural components of the lifeworld and the processes that contribute to maintaining them get differentiated, the more interaction contexts come under conditions of rationally motivated mutual understanding, that is, of consensus formation that rests *in the end* on the authority of the better argument. Up to this point, we have considered Mead's utopian projection of a universal discourse in the special form of a communication community that allows for both self-realization and moral argumentation. Behind this, however, stands the more general idea of a situation in which the reproduction of the lifeworld is no longer merely routed *through* the medium of communicative action, but is saddled *upon* the interpretative accomplishments of the actors themselves. Universal discourse points to an idealized lifeworld reproduced through processes of mutual understanding that have been largely detached from normative contexts and transferred over to rationally motivated yes/no positions. This sort of growing autonomy can come to pass only to the extent that the constraints of material reproduction no longer hide behind the mask of a rationally impenetrable, basic, normative consensus, that is to say, behind the authority of the sacred. A lifeworld rationalized in this sense would by no means reproduce itself in conflict-free forms. But the conflicts would appear in their own names; they would no longer be concealed by convictions immune from discursive examination. Such a lifeworld would gain a singular transparence, inasmuch as it would allow only for situations in which adult actors distinguished between success-oriented and understanding-oriented actions just as clearly as between empirically motivated attitudes and rationally motivated yes/no positions.

The—rather rough—historical reference points that Mead and Durkheim cite in support of a rationalization of the lifeworld can be systematized under three perspectives: (*a*) structural differentiation of the lifeworld, (*b*) separation of form and content, and (*c*) growing reflexivity of symbolic reproduction.

(*ad a*) In the relation of culture to society, structural differentiation is to be found in the gradual uncoupling of the institutional system from worldviews; in the relation of personality to society, it is evinced in the extension of the scope of contingency for establishing interpersonal relationships; and in the relation of culture to personality, it is manifested in the fact that the renewal of traditions depends more and more on individuals' readiness to criticize and their ability to innovate. The vanishing point of these evolutionary trends are: for culture, a state in which traditions that have become reflective and then set aflow undergo continuous revision; for society, a state in which legitimate orders are dependent upon formal procedures for positing and justifying norms; and for personality, a state in which a highly abstract ego-identity is continuously stabilized through self-steering. These trends can establish themselves only insofar as the yes/no decisions that carry everyday communicative practice no longer go *back* to an ascribed normative consensus, but issue *from* the cooperative interpretation processes of participants themselves. Thus they signal a release of the rationality potential inherent in communicative action.

(*ad b*) Corresponding to the differentiation of culture, society, and personality, there is a differentiation of form and content. *On the cultural level,* the core, identity-securing traditions separate off from the concrete contents with which they are still tightly interwoven in mythical worldviews. They shrink to formal elements such as world-concepts, communication presuppositions, argumentation procedures, abstract basic values, and the like. *At the level of society,* general principles and procedures crystallize out of the particular contexts to which they are tied in primitive societies. In modern societies, principles of legal order and of morality are established which are less and less tailored to concrete forms of life. *On the level of the personality system,* the cognitive structures acquired in the socialization process are increasingly detached from the content of cultural knowledge with which they were at first integrated in "concrete thinking." The objects in connection with which formal competences can be exercised become increasingly variable.

(*ad c*) To the structural differentiation of the lifeworld, there corresponds finally a functional specification of various reproduction processes. In modern societies, action systems take shape in which specialized tasks of cultural transmission, social integration, and child rearing are dealt with professionally. Weber emphasized the evolutionary significance of *cultural systems of action* (for science, law, and art). Mead and Durkheim further stress the evolutionary significance of democracy: democratic forms of political will-formation are not only the result of a power shift in favor of the carrier strata of the capitalist economic system; *forms of discursive will-formation* are established in them. And these affect the quasi naturalness of traditionally legitimated domination in a similar way, even as modern natural science, jurisprudence with specialized training, and autonomous art break down the quasi naturalness of ecclesiastical traditions. But the rationalization of the lifeworld does not cover only the areas of cultural reproduction and social integration; among the classical thinkers we have considered, Durkheim occupied himself with parallel developments in the area of socialization. Since the eighteenth century, there has been an increasingly pedagogical approach to child-rearing processes, which has made possible a formal system of education free from the imperative mandates of church and family. Formal education today reaches into early childhood socialization. As in the case of cultural systems of action and political processes of will-formation that have been converted to discursive forms, the formalization of education means not only a professional treatment of the symbolic reproduction of the lifeworld, but its *reflective refraction* as well.

Naturally, the progressive rationalization of the lifeworld, as it is described under different aspects by Weber, Mead, and Durkheim, does not at all guarantee that processes of reproduction will be free of disturbances. It is only the level at which disturbances can appear that shifts with the degree of rationalization. As his theses concerning the loss of meaning and freedom indicate, Weber geared his theory of rationalization precisely to diagnosing negative developments. In Mead we find echoes of a critique of instrumental reason,[32] though his studies in the theory of communication are primarily concerned with the orthogenesis of contemporary societies. Their pathogenesis was the stated target of Durkheim's theory of the division of labor. However, he was not able to connect the changing forms of social integration with stages of system differentiation so clearly as to be able to explain the "anomic division of labor," that is, the modern forms of anomie. If we understand the conflicts that Durkheim attributed to social disintegration more generally than he did, that is, as disturbances of reproduction in structurally quite differentiated lifeworlds, "organic solidarity" represents the normal form of social integration in a rationalized lifeworld. It lies on the plane of the symbolic structures of the lifeworld, as do the "abnormal forms" to which Durkheim dedicated Book 3 of *The Division of Labor in Society*.

The systemic mechanisms that Durkheim introduced under the rubric of "the division of labor" lie at another level. This raises the possibility of treating modern forms of anomie in connection with the question of how processes of system differentiation affect the lifeworld and possibly cause disturbances of its symbolic reproduction. In this way, phenomena of reification can also be analyzed along the lines of lifeworld deformations.

The counter-Enlightenment that set in immediately after the French Revolution grounded a critique of modernity that has since branched off in different directions.[33] Their common denominator is the conviction that loss of meaning, anomie, and alienation—the pathologies of bourgeois society, indeed of posttraditional society generally—can be traced back to the rationalization of the lifeworld itself. This backward-looking critique is in essence a critique of bourgeois culture. By contrast, the Marxist critique of bourgeois society is aimed first at the relations of production, for it accepts the rationalization of the lifeworld and explains its deformation by the conditions of material reproduction. This materialist approach to disturbances in the symbolic reproduction of the lifeworld requires a theory that operates on a broader conceptual basis than that of "the lifeworld." It has to opt for a theoretical strategy that neither identifies the lifeworld with society as a whole, nor reduces it to a systemic nexus.

My guiding idea is that, on the one hand, the dynamics of development are steered by imperatives issuing from problems of self-maintenance, that is, problems of materially reproducing the lifeworld; but that, on the other hand, this societal development draws upon structural *possibilities* and is subject to structural *limitations* that, with the rationalization of the lifeworld, undergo systematic change in dependence upon corresponding learning processes. Thus the systems-theoretical perspective is relativized by the fact that the rationalization of the lifeworld leads to a directional variation of the structural patterns defining the maintenance of the system.

E.—A *verstehende* sociology that allows society to be wholly absorbed into the lifeworld ties itself to the perspective of self-interpretation of the culture under investigation; this internal perspective screens out everything that inconspicuously affects a sociocultural lifeworld from the outside. In particular, theoretical approaches that set out from a culturalistic concept of the lifeworld get entangled in the fallacies of "hermeneutic idealism," as Albrecht Wellmer has called it. The other side of this is a methodological descriptivism that denies itself the justified explanatory claims of theory formation in the social sciences.[34] This is true, above all, of the phenomenological, linguistic, and ethnomethodological variants of interpretive sociology, which as a rule do not get beyond reformulations of a more or less trivial everyday knowledge.

From the internal perspective of the lifeworld, society is represented as a network of communicatively mediated cooperation, with strategic relations and ruptures inserted into it. This is not to say that every contingency, every unintended consequence, every unsuccessful coordination, every conflict is expunged from this view. Nevertheless, what binds sociated individuals to one another and secures the integration of society is a web of communicative actions that thrives only in the light of cultural traditions, and not systemic mechanisms that are out of the reach of a member's intuitive knowledge. The lifeworld that members construct from common cultural traditions is coextensive with society. It draws all societal processes into the searchlight of cooperative processes of interpretation. It lends to everything that happens in society the transparency of something about which one can speak—even if one does not (yet) understand it. When we conceive of society in this way, we are accepting three fictions. We are presupposing (*a*) the autonomy of actors, (*b*) the independence of culture, and (*c*) the transparency of communication. These three fictions are built into the grammar of narratives and turn up again in a culturalistically one-sided, interpretive sociology.

(*ad a*) As members of a sociocultural lifeworld, actors satisfy in principle the presuppositions for responsible participation and communication. Responsibility means here that they can orient themselves to criticizable validity claims. It does not follow from this fiction that the web of interactions extending across social spaces and historical times can be explained solely by the intentions and decisions of those involved. Actors never have their action situations totally under control. They control neither the possibilities for mutual understanding and conflict, nor the consequences and side effects of their actions; they are, to borrow a phrase from W. Schapp, "entangled" in their (hi)stories.[35] A given setting presents a situation in which they orient themselves and which they seek to master, according to their insights and opinions. If society consists only of relations entered into by subjects acting autonomously, we get the picture of a process of sociation that takes place with the will and consciousness of adult members.

(*ad b*) The concept of the lifeworld also suggests that culture is independent from external constraints. The imperative force of culture rests on the convictions of the actors who draw upon, test, and further develop transmitted schemes of interpretation, valuation, and expression. From the perspective of subjects who are acting communicatively, no *alien* authority can be hiding behind cultural symbolism. In the situation of action, the lifeworld forms a horizon behind which we cannot go; it is a totality with no reverse side. Accordingly, it is strictly meaningless for members of a sociocultural lifeworld to inquire whether the culture in whose light they deal with external nature, society, and internal nature is empirically dependent on anything *else*.

(*ad c*) Finally, participants in communication encounter one another in a horizon of unrestricted possibilities of mutual understanding. What is represented at a methodological level as hermeneutics' claim to universality, merely reflects the self-understanding of lay persons who are acting with an orientation to mutual understanding. They have to assume that they could, in principle, arrive at an understanding about anything and everything.

As long as they maintain a performative attitude, communicative actors cannot reckon with a systematic distortion of their communication, that is, with resistances built into the linguistic structure itself and inconspicuously restricting the scope of communication. This does not exclude a fallibilistic consciousness. Members know that they can err, but even a consensus that *subsequently* proves to be deceptive rests to start with on uncoerced recognition of criticizable validity claims. From the internal perspective of participants of a sociocultural lifeworld, there can be no pseudoconsensus in the sense of convictions brought about by force; in a basically transparent process of reaching understanding—which is transparent for the participants themselves—no force can gain a footing.

These three fictions become apparent when we drop the identification of society with the lifeworld. They are convincing only so long as we assume that the integration of society can take place *only* on the premises of communicative action—leaving space, of course, for the alternative of acting strategically when consensus breaks down. This is the way things look to the members of a sociocultural lifeworld themselves. In fact, however, their goal-directed actions are coordinated not only through processes of reaching understanding, but also through functional interconnections that are not intended by them and are usually not even perceived within the horizon of everyday practice. In capitalist societies the market is the most important example of a norm-free regulation of cooperative contexts. The market is one of those systemic mechanisms that stabilize nonintended interconnections of action by way of functionally intermeshing action *consequences,* whereas the mechanism of mutual understanding harmonizes the action *orientations* of participants. Thus I have proposed that we distinguish between *social integration and system integration:* the former attaches to action orientations, while the latter reaches right through them. In one case the action system is integrated through consensus, whether normatively guaranteed or communicatively achieved; in the other case it is integrated through the nonnormative steering of individual decisions not subjectively coordinated.

If we understand the integration of society exclusively as *social integration,* we are opting for a conceptual strategy that, as we have seen, starts from communicative action and construes society as a lifeworld. It ties social-scientific analysis to the internal perspective of members of social groups and commits the investigator to hermeneutically connect up his own understanding with that of the participants. The reproduction of society then appears to be the maintenance of the symbolic structures of the lifeworld. Problems of material reproduction are not simply filtered out of this perspective; maintenance of the material substratum of the lifeworld is a necessary condition for maintaining its symbolic structures. But processes of material reproduction come into view only from the perspective of acting subjects who are dealing with situations in a goal-directed manner; what gets filtered out are all the counterintuitive aspects of the nexus of societal reproduction. This limitation suggests an immanent critique of the hermeneutic idealism of interpretive sociology.

If, on the other hand, we understand the integration of society exclusively as *system integration*, we are opting for a conceptual strategy that presents society after the model of a self-regulating system. It ties social-scientific analysis to the external perspective of an observer and poses the problem of interpreting the concept of a system in such a way that it can be applied to interconnections of action. In Chapter VII we shall examine the foundations of social-scientific systems research; for now I want only to note that action systems are considered to be a special case of living systems. Living systems are understood as open systems, which maintain themselves vis-à-vis an unstable and hypercomplex environment through interchange processes across their boundaries. States of the system are viewed as fulfilling functions with respect to its maintenance.[36]

However, the conceptualization of societies cannot be so smoothly linked with that of organic systems, for, unlike structural patterns in biology, the structural patterns of action systems are not accessible to [purely external] observation; they have to be gotten at hermeneutically, that is, from the internal perspective of participants. The entities that are to be subsumed under systems-theoretical concepts from the external perspective of an observer must be identified beforehand as the lifeworlds of social groups and understood in their symbolic structures. The inner logic of the symbolic reproduction of the lifeworld, which we discussed from the standpoints of cultural reproduction, social integration, and socialization, results in *internal limitations* on the reproduction of the societies we view from the outside as boundary-maintaining systems. Because they are structures of a lifeworld, the structures important for the maintenance of a [social] system, those with which the identity of a society stands or falls, are accessible only to a reconstructive analysis that begins with the members' intuitive knowledge.

The fundamental problem of social theory is how to connect in a satisfactory way the two conceptual strategies indicated by the notions of 'system' and 'lifeworld'. I shall leave this to one side for now and take it up again in the context of discussing Parson's work. Until then, we shall have to be content with a provisional concept of society as a system that has to fulfill conditions for the maintenance of sociocultural lifeworlds. The formula—societies are *systemically stabilized* complexes of action of *socially integrated* groups—certainly requires more detailed explanation; for the present, it may stand for the heuristic proposal that we view society as an entity that, in the course of social evolution, gets differentiated both as a system and as a lifeworld. Systemic evolution is measured by the increase in a society's steering capacity,[37] whereas the state of development of a symbolically structured lifeworld is indicated by the separation of culture, society, and personality.

2. The Uncoupling of System and Lifeworld

The provisional concept of society proposed here is radically different in one respect from the Parsonian concept: the mature Parsons reinterpreted the structural components of the lifeworld—culture, society, personality—as action systems constituting environments for one another. Without much ado, he subsumed the concept of the lifeworld gained from an action-theoretical perspective under systems-theoretical concepts. As we shall see below, the structural components of the lifeworld become subsystems of a general system of action, to which the physical substratum of the lifeworld is reckoned along with the "behavior system." The proposal I am advancing here, by contrast, attempts to take into account the methodological differences between the internalist and the externalist viewpoints connected with the two conceptual strategies.

From the participant perspective of members of a lifeworld it looks as if sociology with a systems-theoretical orientation considers only one of the three components of the lifeworld, namely, the institutional system, for which culture and personality merely constitute complementary environments. From the observer perspective of systems theory, on the other hand, it looks as if lifeworld analysis confines itself to one societal subsystem specialized in maintaining structural patterns (pattern maintenance); in this view, the components of the lifeworld are merely internal differentiations of this subsystem which specifies the parameters of societal self-maintenance. It is already evident on methodological grounds that a systems theory of society cannot be self-sufficient. The structures of the lifeworld, with their own inner logic placing internal constraints on system maintenance, have to be gotten at by a hermeneutic approach that picks up on members' pretheoretical knowledge. Furthermore, the objective conditions under which the systems-theoretical objectification of the lifeworld becomes necessary have themselves only arisen in the course of social evolution. And this calls for a type of explanation that does not already move within the system perspective.

I understand social evolution as a second-order process of differentiation: system and lifeworld are differentiated in the sense that the complexity of the one and the rationality of the other grow. But it is not only qua system and qua lifeworld that they are differentiated; they get differentiated from one another at the same time. It has become conventional for sociologists to distinguish the stages of social evolution as tribal so-

153

cieties, traditional societies or societies organized around a state, and modern societies (where the economic system has been differentiated out). From the system perspective, these stages are marked by the appearance of new systemic mechanisms and corresponding levels of complexity. On this plane of analysis, the uncoupling of system and lifeworld is depicted in such a way that the lifeworld, which is at first coextensive with a scarcely differentiated social system, gets cut down more and more to one subsystem among others. In the process, system mechanisms get further and further detached from the social structures through which social integration takes place. As we shall see, modern societies attain a level of system differentiation at which increasingly autonomous organizations are connected with one another via delinguistified media of .communication: these systemic mechanisms—for example, money— steer a social intercourse that has been largely disconnected from norms and values, above all in those subsystems of purposive rational economic and administrative action that, on Weber's diagnosis, have become independent of their moral-political foundations.

At the same time, the lifeworld remains the subsystem that defines the pattern of the social system as a whole. Thus, systemic mechanisms need to be anchored in the lifeworld: they have to be institutionalized. This institutionalization of new levels of system differentiation can also be perceived from the internal perspective of the lifeworld. Whereas system differentiation in tribal societies only leads to the increasing complexity of pregiven kinship systems, at higher levels of integration new social structures take shape, namely, the state and media-steered subsystems. In societies with a low degree of differentiation, systemic interconnections are tightly interwoven with mechanisms of social integration; in modern societies they are consolidated and objectified into norm-free structures. Members behave toward formally organized action systems, steered via processes of exchange and power, as toward a block of quasi-natural reality; within these media-steered subsystems society congeals into a second nature. Actors have always been able to sheer off from an orientation to mutual understanding, adopt a strategic attitude, and objectify normative contexts into something in the objective world, but in modern societies, economic and bureaucratic spheres emerge in which social relations are regulated only via money and power. Norm-conformative attitudes and identity-forming social memberships are neither necessary nor possible in these spheres; they are made peripheral instead.

Niklas Luhmann distinguishes three levels of integration or of system differentiation: the level of simple interactions between present actors; the level of organizations constituted through voluntary and disposable memberships; and finally the level of society in general, encompassing all the interactions reachable, or potentially accessible, in social spaces and historical times.[1] Simple interactions, organizations that have become autonomous and are linked via media, and society form an evolutionarily developed hierarchy of action systems nesting inside one another; this replaces Parsons' conception of a general system of action. It is interesting to note that Luhmann is here reacting to the phenomenon of the uncoupling of system and lifeworld as it presents itself from the perspective of the lifeworld. Systemic interconnections that have consolidated in modern societies into an organizational reality appear as an objectified segment of society, assimilated to external nature, which thrusts itself between given action situations and their lifeworld horizon. Luhmann hypostatizes this lifeworld—which is now pushed back behind media-steered subsystems and is no longer directly connected to action situations, but merely forms the background for formally organized interactions—into "society."

The uncoupling of system and lifeworld cannot be conceived as a *second-order* differentiation process so long as we stick either to the system perspective or to the lifeworld perspective instead of transforming each into the other. I will, therefore, analyze the connections that obtain between the increasing complexity of the system and the rationalization of the lifeworld. I will view tribal societies (A) first as sociocultural lifeworlds and then (B) as self-maintaining systems, in order to show that system integration and social integration are still tightly interwoven at this level of development. Then I will (C) describe four mechanisms that successively take the lead in social evolution, in each case bringing about a new level of differentiation or, in Durkheim's phrase, of the "division of labor." Every new level of system differentiation requires a change in the institutional basis; it is (D) the evolution of law and morality that plays the role of pacemaker in this transformation. The rationalization of the lifeworld can be understood (E) in terms of successive releases of the potential for rationality in communicative action. Action oriented to mutual understanding gains more and more independence from normative contexts. At the same time, ever greater demands are made upon this basic medium of everyday language; it gets overloaded in the end and replaced by delinguistified media. When this tendency toward an uncoupling of system and lifeworld is (F) depicted on the level of a systematic history of forms of mutual understanding, the irresistible irony of the world-historical process of enlightenment becomes evident: the rationalization of the lifeworld makes possible a heightening of systemic complexity, which becomes so hypertrophied that it unleashes system imperatives that burst the capacity of the lifeworld they instrumentalize.

A.—The lifeworld concept of society finds its strongest empirical foothold in archaic societies, where structures of linguistically mediated, normatively guided interaction immediately constitute the supporting social structures. The small, prestate societies, which have been studied above all by English social anthropologists in Africa, Southeast Asia, and Australia, differ from Durkheim's ideal type of an almost homogeneous, and nearly ultrastable, primitive society by their comparatively greater complexity and their surprising social dynamism.[2] Residual tribal societies do, however, resemble Durkheim's picture of *segmental* societies with a pronounced collective consciousness. This is why Thomas Luckmann can base his sociological generalizations concerning archaic societies on the concept of the lifeworld without doing violence to the empirical material. In the words of K. Gabriel, Luckmann's ideal-typical sketch "seeks to establish a high degree of congruence in the relations between institutions, worldviews, and persons. As socially objectivated, worldviews are at the same time close to persons. They integrate institutional orders into unities of meaning and at the same time furnish individual biographies with a situation-transcending context of meaning. There is a high degree of correspondence between socially objectivated structures of meaning and the relevance structures of personal biographies. Worldviews are spread over the social structure as a whole and yet are tightly bound up with daily routines. Institutionally stamped patterns of action and their interpretations ... have their correlate in the construction of subjective relevance structures and their integration into the meaning contexts of personal identities. In turn, the institutionally stabilized worldviews gain in plausibility."[3]

Durkheim's stated views can be smoothly transposed into the model of the lifeworld so long as the supporting structures of society remain intuitively accessible in principle from the action perspectives of adult members of the tribe. This will be the case as long as the social structures do not transcend the horizon of simple interactions interwoven over comprehensible social spaces and relatively short periods (defined by a few generations). It must be possible, naturally, for various interactions to take place simultaneously in different places, with varying participants and themes. Nonetheless, all the interactions that are structurally possible in such a society are enacted within the context of a *commonly* experienced social world. Despite a differential distribution of cultural knowledge, which is already administered by specialists, the universe of possible events and initiatives is well circumscribed spatiotemporally and thematically; thus the collectively available situation interpretations are stored by all participants similarly and can be narratively called upon when needed. Tribal members can still orient their actions *simultaneously* to the present action situation and to expected communications with those not present. A society of this type, which in a certain sense merges into the dimension of the lifeworld, is omnipresent; to put this another way: it reproduces itself as a whole in every single interaction.

This sketch of a collectively shared, homogeneous lifeworld is certainly an idealization, but archaic societies more or less approximate this ideal type by virtue of the kinship structures of society and the mythical structures of consciousness. The *kinship system* is composed of families ordered according to relations of legitimate descent. As a rule, domestic groups form the core, that is, groups composed of parents and children living together in the same place. New families arise through marriage. Marriage has the function of securing for the newborn an identifiable place in the society, an unambiguous status, by way of assignment to socially recognized parents. Status means here one's position within a group formed along the lines of legitimate descent. How these lineages or descent groups get formed depends upon the principles according to which lines of descent are constructed. Descent groups constitute the reference system for the rules of marriage. These are basically exogamous, which is to say, they guarantee that women are exchanged between families of different descent. The rules of marriage vary on the common basis of a prohibition of incest, which covers sexual intercourse between parent and child as well as between siblings.

The system of kinship relations forms something like a total institution. *Social memberships* are defined via these relations, and role differentiations are possible only within the kinship dimensions of sex, generation, and descent. The calculus of kinship relations also defines the *boundary of the social unit.* It divides the lifeworld into areas of interaction with those who are kin and those who are not. This side of the boundary, one is obligated in one's behavior to honesty, loyalty, and mutual support— in short, to act with an orientation toward mutual understanding. The principle of "amity" that M. Fortes introduces in this context can be understood as a metanorm that obliges one to satisfy the presuppositions of communicative action in dealing with one's kin. This does not exclude rivalries, altercations, and latent hostilities, but it normally does exclude manifestly strategic action:

Two of the commonest discriminating indices are the locus of prohibited or prescribed marriage, and the control of strife that might cause bloodshed. Kinship, amity, the regulation of marriage and the restriction of serious fighting form a syndrome. Where kinship is demonstrable or assumed, regardless of its grounds, there amity must prevail and this posits prescription, more commonly proscription, of marriage and ban on serious strife. Conversely, where amity is the rule in the relations of clans or tribes or communities, there kinship or quasi-kinship by myth or ritual allegiance, or by such institutions as the East African joking relationships, is invoked and the kind of fighting that smacks of war is outlawed. By contrast, non-kin, whether or not they are territorially close or distant, and regardless of the social and cultural affinities of the parties, are very commonly identified as being outside the range of prescriptive altruism and therefore marriageable as well as potentially hostile to the point of serious fighting (or, nowadays, litigation) in a dispute. It is as if marriage and warfare are thought of as two aspects of a single constellation, the direct contrary of which is kinship and amity.[4]

On the other hand, the boundary generated by the calculus of kinship relations has to be porous, since small tribes can practice exogamy only under the condition that kinship relations can also be established with alien tribes—we marry those with whom we fight, say the Tallensi:[5] "Different communities, even those of different tribal or linguistic provenance, can exchange personnel by marriage, and can fuse for particular ceremonial occasions by, so to speak, intermeshing their kinship fields. It seems, therefore, that the view that an Australian *community* or *society* is a closed system is in part illusory. It is the kinship calculus that is closed—by its very nature, one might argue—not any community, as such. It is the kinship calculus which, by reason of its exact limitation of range, serves as the basic boundary-setting mechanism for the field of social relations that is at one and the same time the maximum kinship field and the maximum politico-jural field for a specified group."[6]

The lines of legitimate descent and the dictates of exogamy together ensure that there is a clear boundary, not necessarily tied to territories, and that this boundary remains flexible and porous. Boundaries marked out on the level of interaction can remain porous because *mythical worldviews* make it difficult to draw unambiguous social boundaries. As we have seen in Volume 1, mythical interpretive systems assimilate external and internal nature to the social order, natural phenomena to interpersonal relations, events to communicative utterances. On the one hand, the sociocultural lifeworld flows together with the world as a whole and takes on the form of an objective world order; on the other hand, no state, no event, no person is too alien to be drawn into the universal nexus of interactions and transformed into something familiar. In the framework of mythical worldviews, there is no categorical distinction between society and its natural surroundings.[7] Thus there can be no social groups so alien that they could not connect up with a given kinship system.

The norms of the kinship system draw their binding power from their religious foundations. The members of the tribe are thus always a *cultic community*. In tribal societies the validity of social norms has to be maintained without recourse to a state's power of sanction. Social control requires a cultically anchored, religious grounding: violations of central norms of the kinship system count as sacrilege. The place of the missing external sanctions is taken by a mythical worldview that immobilizes the potential of speech for negation and innovation, at least in the domain of the sacred.

I have already indicated how mythical worldviews blur the categorical distinctions between the objective, social, and subjective worlds, and how they do not even draw a clear line between interpretations and the interpreted reality. Internal relations among meanings are fused with external relations among things. There is no concept of the nonempirical validity that we ascribe to symbolic expressions. Concepts of validity such as morality and truth are merged with empirical concepts such as causality and health. To the extent that the mythical understanding of the world actually steers action orientation, action oriented to mutual understanding and action oriented to success cannot yet be separated, and a participant's "no" cannot yet signify the critical rejection of a validity claim. Myth binds the critical potential of communicative action, stops up, so to speak, the source of inner contingencies springing from communication itself. The scope for innovatively intervening in cultural tradition is relatively narrow; culture is orally transmitted and enters into habitual practices almost without much distance. It is still scarcely possible to distinguish between an identity-securing core of tradition and a periphery open to revision; nearly all of the elements of myth support the identity of the tribe and that of its members.

This pronounced homogeneity of the lifeworld should not blind us to the fact that the social structure of tribal societies already provides a relatively large scope for differentiation.[8] Sex, age, descent are the dimensions in which roles are differentiated. Naturally, these are not yet consolidated into professional roles. In small societies with a simple technology, or more generally with a low level of productive forces, the division of labor does not yet rest on specialized skills exercised over an entire lifetime. In general, men engage in activities that take them away from the home and call for physical strength—warfare, hunting, tending the livestock, deep-sea fishing, overseas trade, and the like—whereas women are responsible for working around the home and the garden, and often in the fields as well. There is a corresponding division of labor among the generations: as soon as they can walk, children are taught to do things around the house and yard, whereas the elderly—above all, the old men—take on the "political" (in the broadest sense) tasks. Incentives for differentiating the social structure come first and foremost from the domain of material reproduction.

Social systems regulate their exchanges with their social and natural environments by way of coordinated interventions into the external world. Looked at from *the member's perspective,* this is a matter of maintaining the material substratum of the lifeworld, that is, of producing and distributing goods, of performing military tasks, of settling internal conflicts, and so on. Performance of these tasks calls for cooperation; they can be dealt with more or less economically, more or less effectively. Even simple tasks like preparing for festivities or building a canoe require that the complex activities of different persons be expediently coordinated and that demands be made upon the goods and services of other people. To the extent that *economy of effort* and *efficacy of means* serve as intuitive standards for the successful resolution of such tasks, there are incentives for a *functional specification of activities* with a corresponding *differentiation of their results* or products. In other words, there is a premium on adapting simple action systems to the conditions of *cooperation based on a division of labor.* There are inducements to regulate interaction in such a way that specialized activities can be *authoritatively joined together* and their different results (or products) *exchanged.* The authoritative combination of specialized performances requires delegating the authority to direct, or *power,* to persons who take on the tasks of organization;[9] the functional exchange of products calls for the establishment of *exchange relations.* Thus a progressive division of labor is to be expected only in action systems that make provision for *institutionalizing organizational power and exchange relations.*

When we view a society's interchanges with its social and natural environments from the *system perspective,* we drop the action-theoretical presupposition that a combination of activities on the basis of a division of labor, which enhances the social system's capacity for adaptation and goal attainment, has to be *intended* by all or by some of those involved. What appears from the perspective of participants to be a task-induced division of labor, presents itself from the system perspective as an increase in societal complexity. The adaptive capacity of an action system is measured only by what the aggregate effects of actions contribute to maintaining a system in a given environment; it matters not whether the objective purposiveness of the action consequences can be traced back to purposes of the subjects involved or not. From systemic points of view as well, *power* and *exchange relations* are the dimensions in which action systems adapt themselves to the requirements of the functional specifications of social cooperation. These are, at any rate, the two dimensions we come across in looking for the mechanisms with which tribal societies can expand their complexity within the range for structural variation set by kinship relations.

B.—Relatively small family groups working with simple technologies can increase their complexity either by becoming internally differentiated or by combining themselves into larger social units. Since these groups have *similar structures* and produce *similar products,* exchange between them cannot be economically motivated in the first instance. Rather, there must be some normative constraint that prevents autarky, that is, self-satisfaction through the consumption of their own goods and services, and calls for exchanging even products whose use values would not make this necessary. Exogamous marriage satisfies this condition. Built into the principle of kinship organization, it can be understood as a norm that requires an exchange of marriageable women. The bilateral relations established by marriage create a network of lasting reciprocities that subsequently extends to objects of use and value, to services, immaterial forms of attention, and loyalties.

The exchange of women, normed by rules of marriage, makes possible a *segmental differentiation* of society. Society can gain in complexity when subgroups emerge within given social groups or when similar social units join together in larger units with the same structure. Segmental dynamics develops along the lines either of cell division or of the combination of cells into larger organisms. It can, of course, also react to demographic pressure and other ecological circumstances in an inverse manner, that is, not in the direction of greater complexity but in that of a dedifferentiating splintering off; kinship solidarity continues on and subgroups become self-sufficient.[10] With respect to the establishment of lasting reciprocities between initially alien groups, the ritual exchange of valuables is a functional equivalent for the exchange of women. In his classical study of the circulation exchange of valuable but not really useful gifts in the archipelago of eastern New Guinea,[11] Malinowski showed how the normatively required exchange of two sorts of symbolic objects (bracelets and necklaces not used as ornaments) brought about partnerships (in pairs) among several thousand members of tribes, scattered over a very large area. Like the potlatch observed by Boas among the Kwakiutl and the system of indebtedness observed by Leach among the Kachin, this exchange of valuables can be seen as an example of an *exchange mechanism* that transforms bellicose relations into reciprocal obligations. At any rate, the ritual exchange of valuable objects and the symbolic consumption of useful objects serve less to accumulate wealth than to foster sociation, that is, to stabilize friendly relations with the social environment and to incorporate foreign elements into their own system.[12]

Segmental differentiation via exchange relations increases the complexity of a society by way of horizontally stringing together similarly structured groups. This does not necessarily promote the functional specification of social cooperation. It is only with the *vertical stratification* of unilinear descent groups that power differentials arise that can be used for the authoritative combination of specialized activities, that is, for *organization*. Naturally, in tribal societies organizational power does not yet take the form of political power but that of generalized prestige. The dominant descent groups owe their status, as a rule, to a prestige grounded genealogically, through origins, divine descent, or the like. But, as Shapera observed in connection with the Australian Bushmen, even in small nomadic groups of freebooters (with fifty to one hundred members) a division of labor can develop under the leadership of the chief. "The chief is the leader, not in the sense that he can overrule the opinion of the other men (which would be impossible since he has no means of compelling them to accept his wishes), but in the sense that he is expected to organize the activities that have been decided upon; he tells the hunters where they are to go, when they bring back meat he divides it, he leads them in their moves from one water-hole to the next and in attacks on neighboring bands, and he conducts negotiations with other bands on such matters as permission to enter his territory, or the conclusion of a marriage with one of their members, or the organization of a joint ritual." [13]

Planning the cumulative effects of interdependent actions requires positions with the authority to direct; the decisions of a part have to be attributable to the whole. Collectivities secure their capacity to act through organization when they ensure that the decisions of someone authorized to issue directions are accepted by the other participants as premises for their own decisions. This can also be accomplished through *stratification*. In stratified tribal societies the members of the more distinguished, older descent groups lay claim to positions of leadership. A status system based on prestige allows for integrating tribes of considerable size. The best known example of this is the Nuer studied by Evans-Pritchard. The individual tribe is a unit of up to sixty thousand members which exercises territorial sovereignty. Every tribe identifies itself with a ruling "aristocratic" descent group. Evans-Pritchard emphasizes that while dominant groups enjoy a certain authority in relation to "ordinary" family groups, and while they have a corresponding power of organization at their disposal, they neither exercise political power nor enjoy material advantages. In other cases, tribal stratification also attaches to age-groups. Both in cultic matters and in the profane affairs of production, warfare, the administration of justice, and the like, stratification clears a considerable space for organization.

Just as segmental dynamics did not point only in the direction of growing size and increasing population density, the mechanism of stratification is not linked to any "safety-catch" effect. As Leach's studies in

Burma show,[14] the process of hierarchizing descent groups is reversible. Reports reaching as far back as the beginning of the last century document the low level of stability in the size of the tribal groups in the Kachlin Hills Area; they oscillate between small, autonomous units of some four households to large societies with forty-nine subgroups, some of which comprised in turn one hundred villages each. M. Gluckmann has compared the dynamics of such systems with the fluctuating expansion and contraction of African kingdoms before the European invasion.[15] Apparently, the complexity of these social systems adjusts to changing demographic, ecological, and social conditions in the environments; the processes of differentiation and dedifferentiation take place by way of both segmental differentiation and stratification.

In tribal societies the mechanism of exchange takes on economic functions only to a limited extent. In these societies, organized predominantly as subsistence economies, there are, to be sure, the beginnings of a market commerce in which goods are often exchanged across great distances. There is less trade with objects of daily use than with raw materials, implements, and jewelry. Certain categories of goods—such as livestock or articles of clothing—already serve on occasion as a primitive form of money; Karl Polanyi spoke of "special purpose money." But economic transactions in the narrower sense have no structure-forming effects in tribal societies. Like the mechanism of power formation, the mechanism of exchange gains system-differentiating strength only when it gets tied directly to religion and the kinship system. *Systemic mechanisms have not yet become detached from institutions effective for social integration.* Thus, an important part of the circulation of economic goods is dependent on kinship relations; services circulate primarily in the noneconomic form of normatively required, reciprocal measures of assistance. And as we have seen, the ritual exchange of valuable objects serves the purpose of social integration. In the nonmonetarized economic activities of archaic societies, the mechanism of exchange has so little detached itself from normative contexts that a clear separation between economic and noneconomic values is hardly possible.[16] Only where the mechanism of exchange is at the same time an integral element of the kinship system can it develop its full, complexity-increasing dynamics.

In the exchange of women normed by the rules of marriage, social integration and system integration come together. The same holds for the mechanism of power formation. It operates within the dimensions set by the kinship system: sex, generation, descent. And it allows only for status differentiations based on prestige, not on the possession of political power. This interweaving of system integration and social integration, which is typical of tribal societies, is reflected at the level of methodology.

In archaic societies functional interconnections are peculiarly transparent. When they are not trivially accessible from the perspective of everyday practice, they are encoded in ritual actions. Fortes's account of the great festival of the Tallensi tribe of Talleland provides a nice illustration. In an elaborate arrangement of encounters and ritual agreements, the cooperation, based on a division of labor, among old established groups and immigrant descent groups from which religious and political leaders are recruited, is simultaneously made visible and affirmed.[17] Presumably, social-scientific functionalism was able to establish itself in cultural anthropology because in tribal societies systemic interdependencies are directly mirrored in normative structures.

However, since the social system is largely merged into the sociocultural lifeworld at this stage of development, anthropology is at the same time a hermeneutic science par excellence. Hermeneutic efforts are provoked by the fact that the interweaving of system integration and social integration not only keeps societal processes transparent but also makes them opaque in other respects. On the one hand, it draws all societal processes into the horizon of the lifeworld and gives them the appearance of intelligibility—tribal members know what they are doing when they perform their hunting, fertility, initiation, and marriage rites. On the other hand, the mythical structure of the stories with which they make their lifeworld and their own actions plausible is unintelligible *to us.* The anthropologist is faced with a paradox: the lifeworlds of archaic societies are in principle accessible via their members' intuitive knowledge; at the same time, they stubbornly escape our comprehension owing to our hermeneutic distance from mythical narratives. This situation explains why depth-hermeneutic procedures are popular in anthropology, in both psychoanalytic and structuralist variations. I regard the *hermeneutic paradox* that vexes cultural anthropology as the methodological reflex of a failure to differentiate coordination of action by systemic means from coordination in terms of social integration. It may be that society can be present in the lifeworld, along with its functional interconnections—that is, as a system—only so long as ritual practice, which reduces both purposive activity and communication to a common denominator, supports and shapes the social structure.

To the extent, then, that the structures of the lifeworld get differentiated, the mechanisms of systemic and social integration also get separated from each other. It is this evolutionary process that is the key to Weber's problematic of societal rationalization.

C.—The segmental differentiation of tribal societies via exchange relations and their stratification via power relations mark two different *levels of system differentiation.* Social integration (in the sense of coordinating action *orientations*) is required for system maintenance only insofar as it fixes the boundary conditions for the functionally necessary correlation of action *effects.* But the mechanisms that serve to heighten system complexity are not a priori harmonized with the mechanisms that provide for the social cohesiveness of the collectivity via normative consensus and mutual understanding in language. Systemic mechanisms remain tightly intermeshed with mechanisms of social integration only so long as they attach to *pregiven* social structures, that is, to the kinship system. With the formation of genuinely political power that no longer derives its authority from the prestige of leading descent groups, but from disposition over judicial means of sanction, the power mechanism detaches itself from kinship structures. Organizational complexity constituted at the level of political domination becomes the crystallizing nucleus of a new institution: the state. For this reason I shall refer to the mechanism of *state organization*; it is incompatible with the social structure of societies organized along kinship lines; the social structure appropriate to it is a general political order, within which social strata are assigned their proper places, and to which they are subordinated.

In the framework of societies organized around a state, markets for goods arise that are steered by symbolically generalized relations of exchange, that is, by the medium of money. However, this medium has a structure-forming effect for the social system as a whole only when the economy is separated off from the political order. In Europe during the early modern period, there arose with the capitalist economy a subsystem differentiated out via the money medium—a subsystem that in turn necessitated a reorganization of the state. In the complementary relationship between the subsystems of the market economy and modern administration, the mechanism of steering media—which Parsons referred to as symbolically generalized media of communication—finds its appropriate social structure.

Figure 24 arranges the four mechanisms of system differentiation mentioned above in the order in which they appeared in the course of social evolution. As each mechanism takes the lead in evolution, it characterizes a higher level of interaction at which the preceding mechanisms are at once downgraded, sublated, and refunctionalized. Each new level of system differentiation opens up space for further increases in complexity, that is, for additional functional specifications and a correspondingly more abstract integration of the ensuing subsystems. Mechanisms 1 and 4 operate through exchange relations, mechanisms 2 and 3 through power relations. Whereas mechanisms 1 and 2 remain tied to pregiven kinship structures, mechanisms 3 and 4 give rise to the formation of new social structures. In the process, exchange and power lose the concrete forms of the exchange of women according to marriage rules and the

Coordination of action via / Differentiation and integration of	Exchange	Power
Similarly structured units	1. Segmentary differentiation	2. Stratification
Dissimilar, functionally specified units	4. Steering media	3. State organizations

Figure 24. Mechanisms of System Differentiation

stratification of descent groups measured in differentials of prestige; they are transformed into abstract magnitudes: organizational power and steering media. Mechanisms 1 and 2 bring about the differentiation of kin groups, that is, of similarly structured units, whereas mechanisms 3 and 4 mean a differentiation of propertied classes and organizations, that is, of units that are themselves already functionally specified. The structures that these units take on are already stamped in each case by the mechanisms of the preceding level. The four mechanisms characterize different levels of integration, with which different social formations are connected, as depicted in Figure 25.

Of course, social formations cannot be distinguished by degrees of systemic complexity alone. They are, rather, defined by the *institutional complex* that anchors a newly emerging mechanism of system differentiation in the lifeworld. Thus, segmental differentiation is institutionalized in the form of kinship relations, stratification in that of rank ordering, state organization in forms of political domination, and the first steering medium in the form of relations between private legal persons. The corresponding institutions are sex and generation roles, the status of descent groups, political office, and bourgeois private law.

In archaic societies interactions are determined only by the kinship system's repertoire of roles. The concept of *role* can be unproblematically applied at this level because communicative action is almost en-

Systemic mechanisms / Social structures	Exchange mechanisms	Power mechanisms
Pregiven	1. Egalitarian tribal societies	2. Hierarchical tribal societies
Systemically induced	4. Economically consti- tuted class societies	3. Politically stratified class societies

Figure 25. Social Formations

tirely prejudiced by normative behavior patterns. When a status system arises in stratified tribal societies such that families are ordered hierarchically by prestige, sex and generation roles get relativized; the rank of the family one belongs to is more important for one's social status than one's position within the family. The concept of *status* can be unambiguously applied at this level because society is stratified along one dimension: the prestige a family enjoys owing to its descent. In state-organized societies this status ordering is relativized. When the state rather than kinship determines the structure of society, social stratification is combined with features of participation in political domination and of place in the production process. The concept of the *authority of office* takes on a precise meaning only at this level. The ruler and the political estates vested with the privileges of domination enjoy authority by virtue of offices that still presuppose a unity of public and private spheres of life and thus are understood as their own personal rights. Finally, when money is legally institutionalized as a steering medium for depoliticized economic activity, the authority of the state, political domination in general, is relativized by the private legal order. At this level, *positive law* becomes the guarantor of the calculability of private business activity.[18]

If we take the institutionalization of levels of system differentiation as the mark of social formations, we get a parallel to the Marxist notions of base and superstructure. The impulses toward a differentiation of the social system emanate from the domain of material reproduction. Thus we can understand by "base" the institutional complex that, at a given stage, anchors the evolutionarily leading system mechanism in the life-world and that, therefore, defines the scope for possible increases in complexity in a given social formation. This is all the more plausible if, following Kautsky, we interpret the distinction between base and superstructure with reference to the theory of social evolution.[19] On this account, "base" designates the domain of emerging problems to which an explanation of the transition from one social formation to the next has to make reference. It is in the "basic" domain that we find those system problems that can be resolved only through evolutionary innovations, that is, only when a higher level of system differentiation is institutionalized. It is of course misleading to equate "base" with "economic structure," for not even in capitalist societies does the basic domain, as defined above, coincide with the economic system.

Marx describes the basic institutions of a society in terms of the mode of production; it has to be kept in mind, however, that every social formation allows for various modes of production (and combinations thereof). As is well known, Marx characterizes modes of production by the stage of development of productive forces and by certain forms of social intercourse—the relations of production. The *forces of production* comprise (a) the labor power of those active in production, the producers; (b) technically useful knowledge insofar as it is converted into productivity-enhancing tools of labor, into techniques of production; and (c) organizational knowledge insofar as it is used to set labor power efficiently into motion, to qualify labor power, and to coordinate effectively the cooperation of workers on the basis of a division of labor (mobilization, qualification, and organization of labor power). The forces of production determine the extent of a society's possible disposition over natural resources. The *relations of production* comprise those institutions and societal mechanisms that determine the ways in which labor power is combined with the available means of production at a given stage of the forces of production. Regulation of access to the means of production, the manner of controlling socially employed labor power, also indirectly determines the distribution of socially produced wealth. Relations of production express the distribution of social power; with their pattern of distribution of social rewards, that is, of socially recognized opportunities for need satisfaction, they determine the interest structure that obtains in a given society.

In tribal societies, whether stratified or not, the kinship system takes on the role of relations of production, as M. Godelier has rightly emphasized.[20] These societies consist of base and superstructure both in one;

not even religion is sufficiently differentiated off from kinship institutions that it could be characterized as superstructural. In traditional societies the relations of production are incorporated into the general political order, while religious worldviews take on ideological functions. It is only with capitalism, where the market also serves the function of stabilizing class relations, that production relations assume an economic shape. There is a corresponding differentiation of base from superstructure: first the traditional political order is differentiated off from the religious worldviews that legitimate the state; then the complementary subsystems of an economy specialized in "adaptation" and a state administration specialized in "goal attainment" (to use Parsonian terms) are differentiated off from domains of action that primarily serve the needs of cultural reproduction, social integration, and socialization. Base and superstructure can separate off from one another only when the kinship system breaks down as the basic social structure, thus bursting apart the clamps that held systemic and socially integrative mechanisms tightly together. In what follows, I shall comment on the levels of system differentiation which politically stratified and economically constituted class societies attain by means of state organization and the monetary medium.

(a) In *hierarchized tribal societies,* functional specification increases along with organizational activities; special roles can be differentiated out for leadership functions in war and peace, for ritual actions and healing practices, for settling legal conflicts, and so on. But this specialization remains within the bounds of a kinship system whose units have basically similar structures. It is in *societies organized around a state* that functional specification first encroaches upon the very way of life of social groups. Under the conditions of political domination, social stratification detaches itself from the substratum of the kinship system. Social units can themselves become functionally specified via participation and exclusion from political power. The dominant-status groups—officials, military men, landowners—and the mass of the population—fishermen, farmers, mine workers, craftsmen, and so forth—change from classifications based on birth to politically guaranteed social classes based on possessions. The different strata are no longer differentiated only by the extent of their possessions, but by the way they acquire them, their position in the production process. Socioeconomic classes arise, even if they do not yet appear in economic form—that is, as classes based on source of income. They are stratified according to political power and criteria relating to particular modes of life. On the basis of an increasingly sharp dichotomy between high and popular culture,[21] classes develop their own milieus, lifeworlds, and value orientations specific to the various strata. In place of the stratification of similar social units, we find a

political organization of dissimilar social units, in place of hierarchized descent groups, stratified classes.

As the large empires of antiquity impressively demonstrate, social systems with the mechanism of state organization can develop incomparably greater complexity than tribal societies. Anthropological field studies of the political systems in African tribal cultures show that societies at a precivilization (or preliterary) level, which acquire some form of state organization, are already more complex than the most complex of those societies organized along kinship lines.[22] Social anthropologists distinguish these social formations on the basis of the appearance of "governments"—that is, organizations for central rule, which have administrative staffs, however rudimentary, that are maintained by taxes and tribute, and have jurisdiction to ensure that the rulers' demands are followed. What is decisive from a systemic point of view is disposition over the power to sanction, for this makes binding decisions possible:

> In our judgment, the most significant characteristic distinguishing the centralized, pyramidal, state-like forms of government of the Ngwato, Bemba, etc., from the segmentary political systems of the Logoli, the Tallensi, and the Nuer is the incidence and function of organized force in the system. In the former group of societies, the principle sanction of a ruler's rights and prerogatives, and the authority exercised by his subordinate chief, is the command of organized force. This may enable an African to rule oppressively for a time, if he is inclined to do so, but a good ruler uses the armed forces under his control in the public interest, as an accepted instrument of government—that is, for the defense of the society as a whole or of any sections of it, for offense against a common enemy, and as a coercive sanction to enforce the law or respect for the constitution.[23]

Disposition over the means to sanction binding decisions provides the basis for an authority of office with which organizational power is institutionalized for the first time *as such*—and not merely as an appendix to, and filling out of, pregiven social structures. In the state, organizations that secure the collectivity's capacity to act as a whole take on a directly institutional shape. Society as a whole can now be understood as an organization. Social affiliation with the collectivity is interpreted through the fiction of a membership that is in principle contingent; it is interpreted, in short, as citizenship in a state. Whereas one is born into a family, citizenship is based on a legal act. One does not "have" it in the way that one has a family background; it can be acquired and lost. Citizenship in a state presupposes voluntary—at least in principle—recognition of the political order; for political rule means that citizens commit themselves, at least in principle, to a general willingness to obey those who hold office. In this way, the many cede to the few the competence to act on behalf of all. They relinquish the right that participants in simple interactions can claim for themselves: the right to orient their actions only by actual agreement with those present.

(b) In traditional societies the state is an organization in which is concentrated the collectivity's capacity for action—that is, the capacity for action of society as a whole; by contrast, modern societies do without the accumulation of steering functions within a single organization. Functions relevant to society as a whole are distributed among different subsystems. With an administration, military, and judiciary, the state specializes in attaining collective goals via binding decisions. Other functions are depoliticized and given over to nongovernmental subsystems. The capitalist economic system marks the breakthrough to this level of system differentiation; it owes its emergence to a new mechanism, the steering medium of money. This medium is specifically tailored to the economic function of society as a whole, a function relinquished by the state; it is the foundation of a subsystem that grows away from normative contexts. The capitalist economy can no longer be understood as an institutional order in the sense of the traditional state; it is the medium of exchange that is institutionalized, while the subsystem differentiated out via this medium is, as a whole, a block of more or less norm-free sociality.

Money is a special exchange mechanism that transforms use values into exchange values, the natural economic exchange of goods into commerce in commodities. Traditional societies already allow for internal and external markets; it is only with capitalism, however, that we have an economic system such that both the internal commerce among business enterprises and the interchange with noneconomic environments, private households, and the state are carried out through monetary channels. The institutionalization of wage labor, on the one hand, and of a state based on taxation,[24] on the other, is just as constitutive for the new mode of production as the emergence of the capitalist enterprise. Money has structure-forming effects only when it becomes an *intersystemic medium of interchange.* The economy can be constituted as a monetarily steered subsystem only to the degree that it regulates its interchanges with its social environments via the medium of money. Complementary environments take shape as the production process is converted over to wage labor and the state apparatus is connected up with production via the yield from taxes on those employed. The state apparatus becomes dependent upon the media-steered subsystem of the economy; this forces it to reorganize and leads, among other things, to an assimilation of power to the structure of a steering medium: power becomes assimilated to money.

Within a subsystem that has been differentiated out for a single function relevant to society as a whole, the scope for organizational accomplishments expands once again. Now, the activities of different organizations for the same function and the activities of the same organization for different functions can be clustered together. Under these conditions, organizations are institutionalized as private enterprises and public institutions, that is, in such as way that what had to remain largely a fiction when applied to the state as a political organization of the whole, actually becomes true of them: private enterprises and public institutions actualize the principle of voluntary membership, which is first made possible by autonomous forms of organization. In Luhmann's words: "We shall designate as 'formally organized' ... those social systems which make recognizing certain expectations of behavior a condition of membership in the system. Only those who accept certain specifically marked out expectations can become and remain members of formally organized social systems."[25] The traditional state is an organization that structures society as a whole; in defining its membership, shaping its program, and recruiting its personnel, it therefore has to link up with the established lifeworlds of a stratified class society and with the corresponding cultural traditions. By contrast, the capitalist enterprise and the modern administration are systemically independent units within norm-free subsystems. As Luhmann has shown, what distinguishes *autonomous organizations* is that, by means of membership conditions that have to be accepted all at once, they can make themselves independent from communicatively structured lifeworld relations, from the concrete value orientations and action dispositions—susceptible to conflict as they are—of persons who have been pushed out into the environment of the organization.[26]

D.—To this point I have been viewing social evolution from the perspective of increasing systemic complexity, but the institutionalization of new levels of system differentiation is also visible from the internal perspective of the lifeworld involved. In tribal societies, system differentiation is linked to existing structures of interaction through the exchange of spouses and the formation of prestige; for this reason it does not yet make itself noticeable by intervening in the structures of the lifeworld. In politically stratified class societies, a new level of functional interconnection, in the form of the state, rises above the level of simple interactions. This difference in levels is reflected in the relation of the whole to its parts—a relation that is at the heart of classical political theory from the time of Aristotle, although the corresponding images of society as polity that arise in the spectrum from popular to high culture are considerably different. The new level of system differentiation has the form of a general political order that needs to be legitimated; this order can be brought into the lifeworld only at the cost of an illusory interpretation of class society, that is, through religious worldviews taking on ideological functions. Finally, a third level of functional interconnection arises in modern societies with interchange processes that operate via media. These systemic interconnections, detached from normative contexts and rendered independent as subsystems, challenge the assimilative powers of an all-encompassing lifeworld. They congeal into the "second nature" of a norm-free sociality that can appear as something in the objective world, as an *objectified* context of life. The uncoupling of system and lifeworld is experienced in modern society as a particular kind of objectification: the social system definitively bursts out of the horizon of the lifeworld, escapes from the intuitive knowledge of everyday communicative practice, and is henceforth accessible only to the counterintuitive knowledge of the social sciences developing since the eighteenth century.

What we have already found in the system perspective seems to be confirmed from this internal perspective: the more complex social systems become, the more provincial lifeworlds become. In a differentiated social system the lifeworld seems to shrink to a subsystem. This should not be read causally, as if the structures of the lifeworld changed in dependence on increases in systemic complexity. The opposite is true: increases in complexity are dependent on the structural differentiation of the lifeworld. And however we may explain the dynamics of this structural transformation, it follows the inner logic of communicative rationalization. I have developed this thesis with reference to Mead and Durkheim and have carried it over to lifeworld analysis. Now I shall make systematic use of it.

As we have seen, the level of possible increases in complexity can be raised only by the introduction of a new system mechanism. Every new leading mechanism of system differentiation must, however, be anchored in the lifeworld; it must be *institutionalized* there via family status, the authority of office, or bourgeois private law. In the final analysis, social formations are distinguished by the institutional cores that define society's "base," in the Marxian sense. These basic institutions form a series of evolutionary innovations that can come about only if the lifeworld is sufficiently rationalized, above all only if law and morality have reached a corresponding stage of development. The institutionalization of a new level of system differentiation requires reconstruction in the core institutional domain of the moral-legal (i.e., consensual) regulation of conflicts.

Morality and law are specifically tailored to check open conflict in such a way that the basis of communicative action—and with it the social integration of the lifeworld—does not fall apart. They secure the next level of consensus to which we can have recourse when the mechanism of reaching understanding fails in the normatively regulated communication of everyday life, that is, when the coordination of actions anticipated in the normal case does not come to pass and the alternative of violent confrontation becomes a reality. Moral and legal norms are, in this sense, *second-order norms of action;* the different forms of social integration can be profitably studied in regard to them. As we have seen, Durkheim analyzed the transformation of social integration in connection with the development of law and morality; he noted a long-term trend toward heightened abstractness and universality in law and morality, with a simultaneous differentiation between the two. Taking our cue from ontogenesis, it is now possible to construct stages of development for morality and law, with the underlying sociocognitive concepts of 'expectation', 'norm' (= generalized expectation), and 'principle' (= higher-level norm) as our measure. Lawrence Kohlberg distinguishes three levels of moral consciousness:[27] the preconventional level, on which only the consequences of action are judged, the conventional level, on which the orientation to norms and the intentional violation of them are already judged, and finally the postconventional level, on which norms themselves are judged in the light of principles. Klaus Eder has shown that there are homologous structures of consciousness in the moral and legal developments of archaic, traditional, and modern societies.[28] And as we have seen in Volume 1, Wolfgang Schluchter has interpreted Weber's historically supported typology of law from this point of view.[29] I shall confine myself here to the schematic presentation in Figure 26.

In the first row, morality and law are not separated; in the second row, they are separated by a broken line to mark the processes of differentiation that will lead to a separation of law and morality at the postconventional level. At the level of principled moral consciousness, morality is deinstitutionalized to such an extent that it is now anchored only in the personality system as an *internal* control on behavior. Likewise, law develops into an *external* force, imposed from without, to such an extent that modern compulsory law, sanctioned by the state, becomes an institution detached from the ethical motivations of the legal person and dependent upon abstract obedience to the law. This development is part of the structural differentiation of the lifeworld. It reflects both the growing independence of the societal component of the lifeworld—the system of institutions—in relation to culture and personality, and the trend toward the growing dependence of legitimate orders on formal procedures for positing and justifying norms.

My thesis is that higher levels of integration cannot be established in social evolution until legal institutions develop in which moral consciousness on the conventional, and then postconventional, levels is em-

Stages of moral consciousness	Basic socio-cognitive concepts	Ethics	Types of law
Preconventional	Particular expectations of behavior	Magical ethics	Revealed law
Conventional	Norm	Ethics of the law	Traditional law
Postconventional	Principle	Ethics of conviction and responsibility	Formal law

Figure 26. Stages in the Development of Law

bodied.[30] So long as the kinship system represents some sort of total institution, which it does in tribal societies, there is no place for the administration of justice as a *meta*institution. The practices of administering justice are developed not as superordinate, but as coordinate institutions. This explains the continuing debate among anthropologists as to how the concept of law is appropriately defined. There are rights [*Rechte*] following from all socially recognized norms of action, but law [*das Recht*] refers only to the treatment of norm violations considered to be so serious that they can neither be made good directly nor tolerated without further ado. At the other end, the modern concept of compulsory law as a system of laws covered by the state's power to sanction is too narrow. Law in tribal societies is not yet compulsory law. The self-help of the disputing parties remains the *ultima ratio*; it cannot be replaced by judicial decisions in any obligatory fashion. There are not even institutions in all societies that specialize in the administration of justice (or the infliction of punishment). But even where there are no courts, there are routines for peacefully settling disputes that affect the interests of an individual and his family or the welfare of the collective as a whole.

Recent work done by anthropologists has concentrated on the careful recording of cases, as far as possible in the context of what is already known about the disputants, their relative status, and the events that led up to a "trouble case". P. H. Gulliver, a London anthropologist who has done much work of this kind in Tanzania, maintains what is implicit in Hoebel, that when we are studying law what we should really be looking for is *the process of dispute settlement.* By a dispute he means a quarrel that has reached the point where the man who thinks he is injured demands some kind of third party intervention to establish what his rights are and give him the satisfaction due to him. He reminds us that "settlement" does not necessarily dispose of the issue. But once a *quarrel* has been treated by either party as a *dispute* something has to be done.[31]

Durkheim's distinction between offenses or crimes that are avenged through penal law and crimes that require compensation for the injured party was picked up by Radcliffe-Brown, but it could not be sustained in relation to the empirical material in quite the way Durkheim had expected. For our purposes, what is important is that the idea of restoring an integral state or a normal order also has application to situations in which Durkheim's distinction between penal and civil laws holds. "There are two main ways of dealing with a complaint that somebody has broken the law. One is to persuade or compel him to make restitution to the person he has robbed. The other is to punish the law-breaker; if that method is chosen, it could be argued that he is making restitution to the community as a whole, being held by his action to have injured them all."[32] The facts of the case are judged from a preconventional perspective of restitution for harm done; it is the consequences of action that are morally relevant and not the intentions of the wrongdoer. Thus, for example, a violation of the incest prohibition counts as a crime that results in the spiritual contamination of society, a kind of pollution of the environment—and the punishment attached to it is not meant to avenge a norm violation for which an individual is accountable, but rather functions to ward off imminent harm to the collectivity. The validity of norms is directly rooted in the ritual action of the cultic community. It is not based on external sanctions under the exclusive control of some supreme legal authority. The punishment for trespasses against the sacred order has the character of an atonement that cannot, in the end, be forced by social authority.

The moment of accepting a punishment is even clearer in civil-law conflicts between opposing parties. Against the background of the right of self-defense or other self-help routines (e.g., blood vengeance), the court of arbitration can at most exert pressure upon the disputants to come to some agreement; it cannot impose its judgment upon them, that is, against the will of one or the other party.

One cannot divide society neatly into those in which disputes are fought out, and those in which they are argued out before an impartial authority which decides who is right and what is to be done. The latter type indubitably have legal institutions; some of the former might be said to go only part of the way. Thus, among the Luhya of Western Kenya, the heads of descent groups were traditionally held to be responsible for the actions of their members, and if someone was involved in a dispute the elders of the two groups got together and tried to agree on a solution. Except within the narrowest descent group, no solution could be imposed unless the party agreed. In the case of a dispute between members of a larger lineage, it was not considered permissible to fight the matter out, but if no reconciliation could be attained the weaker party numerically (who could not have won in a fight) moved away and broke off relations with the rest of the lineage.[33]

Things work differently in societies organized around a state. The basis of political authority is disposition over centralized means of sanction, which gives to the decision of officeholders a binding character. The ruler gets this authority not from a merely factual power to sanction, but from a power of sanction recognized as legitimate by citizens. According to a hypothesis advanced by Klaus Eder, legitimate disposition over power, which represents the core of political domination, can be traced back to the royal judgeship. The latter could take shape only after the institutions for the administration of justice had been cognitively changed over to another stage of moral consciousness, namely, the conventional. From a conventional perspective, an offense appears as a violation of intersubjectively recognized norms for which an individual is held accountable. Normative deviation is measured against the intentions of a responsibly acting subject, and punishment is aimed not merely at compensating for disadvantageous consequences of action, but at blameworthy actions. At this stage of moral judgment, the consensual regulation of conflict is guided not by the idea of restoring a violated status quo ante, but by that of making amends for a wrong that has been responsibly committed, of healing an intentional breach of norms. With this, the function of administering justice and the position of the judge change in the minds of legal subjects. The judge protects the integrity of the legal order, and the force he avails himself of in exercising this function derives its legitimacy from a legal order respected as valid. Judicial power is no longer based on the prestige of one's status, but on the legitimacy of a legal order in which the position of someone who safeguards the law and is equipped with the required power of sanction becomes structurally necessary. *Because judicial office is itself a source of legitimate power, political domination can first crystallize around this office.*

Upon the basis of traditional law, the separation between penal and civil law only implicitly drawn in archaic legal institutions is carried through clearly. Civil law derives from converting arbitration proceedings understood in preconventional terms over to the conventional stage of moral consciousness. Furthermore, law now has the position of a metainstitution; it serves as a kind of insurance against breakdown, covering situations in which the binding power of first-order institutions fails to work. The political order as a whole is constituted as a legal order, but it is laid like a shell around a society whose core domains are by no means legally organized throughout. Social intercourse is institutionalized much more in forms of traditional mores than through law. This changes in modern societies.

With an economy differentiated out via the medium of money, there emerges an ethically neutralized system of action that is institutionalized *directly* in forms of bourgeois private law. The system of social labor gets transferred from first-order institutions (which are themselves guaranteed by law) *directly* over to the norms of civil law. Insofar as actions are coordinated through a delinguistified medium such as money, normatively embedded interactions are turned into success-oriented transactions among private legal subjects. As civil law largely loses the position of a metainstitution, a functionally equivalent gradation of first-order and second-order norms takes shape within the legal system itself.

Beyond the differentiation of penal and civil law, there is now a separation of private and public law. Whereas civil society is institutionalized as a sphere of legally domesticated, incessant competition between strategically acting private persons, the organs of state, organized by means of public law, constitute the level on which consensus can be restored in cases of stubborn conflict. This helps clarify how the problem of justification is both displaced and intensified. Inasmuch as law becomes positive, the paths of legitimation grow longer. The legality of decisions, which is measured by adherence to formally unobjectionable procedures, relieves the legal system of justification problems that pervade traditional law in its entirety. On the other hand, these problems get more and more intensive where the criticizability and need for justification of legal norms are only the other side of their positivity—the principle of enactment and the principle of justification reciprocally require one another. The legal system *as a whole* needs to be anchored in basic principles of legitimation. In the bourgeois constitutional state these are, in the first place, basic rights and the principle of popular sovereignty; they embody postconventional structures of moral consciousness. Together with the moral-practical foundations of penal and civil law, they are in the bridges between a de-moralized and externalized legal sphere and a deinstitutionalized and internalized morality.

I have roughly sketched out these two stages in the evolution of law and morality to show that the transitions to conventional and postconventional legal and moral representations fulfill *necessary* conditions for the emergence of the institutional frameworks of political and economic class societies. I understand the connection between them as follows: new levels of system differentiation can establish themselves only if the rationalization of the lifeworld has reached a corresponding level. But then I have to explain why the development toward universalism in law and morality *both* expresses a rationalization of the lifeworld *and* makes new levels of integration possible. This becomes clearer in the light of two *countertendencies* that establish themselves on the level of interactions and action orientations in the wake of increasing "value generalization."

E.—Parsons applies the phrase "value generalization" to the tendency for value orientations that are institutionally required of actors to become more and more general and formal in the course of social evolution. This trend is the structurally necessary result of a legal and moral development that, as we saw, shifts the securing of consensus in cases of conflict to more and more abstract levels. Naturally, even the simplest interaction systems cannot function without a certain amount of *generalized* action orientations. Every society has to face the basic problem of coordinating action: how does ego get alter to continue interaction in the desired way? How does he avoid conflict that interrupts the sequence of action? If we begin with simple interactions within the framework of everyday communicative practice and inquire after *generalized motives* that might move alter to a *blanket* acceptance of ego's interaction offers, we come across trivial elements not tied to any special presuppositions: the prestige ego enjoys and the influence he exercises. When a prestigious or influential person takes the initiative, he can count on receiving a certain "advance" of trust or confidence, which may be paid out in a readiness for consensus and obedience that goes beyond any single situation. We might also say: the generalized action orientations of the other participants correspond to the prestige and influence disposed over by some persons.

In stratified tribal societies, the social structure is stamped by prestige and influence. The advance of trust is transferred from person to group. The situation-transcending readiness to accept extends now to dominant descent groups; members of higher-status groups meet with obedience to expectations that no longer need to be covered by their personal status. In politically constituted societies, the rulers' authority of office expands the scope for generalized value orientations; in certain spheres of action, they are detached from particular kinship relations. The readiness to agree and to follow is accorded in the first instance not to influential families but to the legal authorities of the state. Political rule means the competence to carry out decisions on the basis of binding norms; the political order is legitimate insofar as it is based on the citizens' fidelity to the law. This duty of obedience to officeholders is less particularistic than the readiness to follow members of a leading social stratum. Modern bourgeois society, finally, requires an even higher level of value generalization. Insofar as traditional morals [*Sittlichkeit*] split up into legality and morality, an autonomous application of general principles is required in private affairs, while in the occupational and public spheres obedience to positively enacted laws is demanded. Actors' motives were at first under the control of the concrete value orientations of kinship rules; in the end, the generalization of motives and values goes so far that *abstract obedience to law* becomes the only normative condition that actors have to meet in formally organized domains of action.

The trend toward value generalization gives rise to two tendencies on the plane of interaction. The further motive and value generalization advance, the more communicative action gets detached from concrete and traditional normative behavior patterns. This uncoupling shifts the burden of social integration more and more from religiously anchored consensus to processes of consensus formation in language. The transfer of action coordination to the mechanism of reaching understanding permits the structures of communicative action to appear in an ever purer form. In this respect, value generalization is a necessary condition for releasing the rationality potential immanent in communicative action. This fact by itself would entitle us to understand the development of law and morality, from which value generalization originates, as an aspect of the rationalization of the lifeworld.

On the other hand, freeing communicative action from particular value orientations also forces the separation of action oriented to success from action oriented to mutual understanding. With the generalization of motives and values, space opens up for subsystems of purposive rational action. The coordination of action can be transferred over to delinguistified media of communication only when contexts of strategic action get differentiated out. While a deinstitutionalized, only internalized morality ties the regulation of conflict to the idea of justifying normative validity claims—to the procedures and presuppositions of moral argumentation—a de-moralized, positive, compulsory law exacts a deferment of legitimation that makes it possible to steer social action via media of a different type.

This polarization reflects an uncoupling of system integration from social integration, which presupposes a differentiation on the plane of interaction not only between action oriented to success and to mutual understanding, but between the corresponding mechanisms of action coordination—the ways in which ego brings alter to continue interaction, and the bases upon which alter forms generalized action orientations. On the basis of increasingly generalized action orientations, there arises an ever denser network of interactions that do without directly normative steering and have to be coordinated in another way. To satisfy this growing need for coordination, there is either explicit communication or relief mechanisms that reduce the expenditure of communication and the risk of disagreement. In the wake of the differentiation between action oriented to mutual understanding and to success, two sorts of *relief mechanisms* emerge in the form of communication media that either condense or replace mutual understanding in language. We have already come across prestige and influence as primitive generators of a willingness to follow; the formation of media begins with them.

Prestige is attributed rather to the person, influence to the flow of communication itself. Although prestige and influence are interdependent variables—prestige enhances influence, influence enhances prestige—we can separate them analytically in respect to their sources. In the simplest case, prestige is based on personal attributes, influence on disposition over resources. In the catalog of qualities relevant to prestige, we find physical strength and attractiveness, technical-practical skills, intellectual abilities, as well as what I call the responsibility of a communicatively acting subject. By this I understand strength of will, credibility, and reliability, that is to say, cognitive, expressive, and moral-practical virtues of action oriented to validity claims. On the other hand, property and knowledge are the two most important sources of influence. The term 'knowledge' is used here in a broad sense covering anything that can be acquired through learning and appropriating cultural traditions, where the latter are understood to include both cognitive and socially integrative (i.e., expressive and moral-practical) elements.

Alter's generalized readiness to accept can now be traced to specific sources of ego's prestige or influence: in the cases of physical strength and attractiveness, cognitive-instrumental skills and disposition over property, it can be traced to ties that are motivated empirically, by inducement or intimidation; in the cases of interactive responsibility and disposition over knowledge, by contrast, it goes back to a trust or confidence that is rationally motivated, by agreement based on reasons. This yields a provisional classification of the generalized acceptability induced by prestige and influence (see Figure 27).

I do not mean to raise a systematic claim with this schema; it is intended merely to illustrate that a differentiation along the lines of empirically motivated ties and rationally motivated trust can be found in the sources of prestige and influence. Alter takes up ego's offer either because he is oriented to the rewards and sanctions ego can dispense, or because he is confident that ego has the requisite knowledge and is suf-

Motivation \ Attribution of prestige and influence	Attributes	Resources
Empirical	*Strength:* Deterrence through the fear of punishment, inducement through the expectation of protection *Know-how:* Inducement through the expectation of success *Physical attractiveness:* Emotional ties	*Property:* Inducement through the expectation of reward
Rational	*Responsibility:* Trust in autonomy	*Knowledge:* Trust in valid knowledge

Figure 27. Sources of Generalized Acceptability

ficiently autonomous to guarantee the redemption of the validity claims he raises in communication.

The problem of reducing the expenditure of communication and the risk of dissensus can be resolved on the next level when prestige and influence no longer only induce a readiness for consensus and a willingness to follow, but are themselves generalized. They come to form generalized media.

One condition for the formation of different types of media is a differentiation of sources of influence, in particular, a separation of empirically motivated trust. Media such as money and power attach to empirically motivated ties, while generalized forms of communication such as professional reputation or "value commitment" (i.e., moral-practical leadership) rest on specific kinds of trust that are supposedly rationally motivated.

We can clarify the difference in type as follows. Everyday communicative practice is, as we have seen, embedded in a lifeworld context defined by cultural tradition, legitimate orders, and socialized individuals. Interpretive performances draw upon and advance consensus.[34] The rationality potential of mutual understanding in language is actualized to the extent that motive and value generalization progress and the zones of what is unproblematic shrink. The growing pressure for rationality that a problematic lifeworld exerts upon the mechanism of mutual understanding increases the need for achieved consensus, and this increases the expenditure of interpretive energies and the risk of dissensus. It is these demands and dangers that can be headed off by media of communication. The way these media function differs according to whether they focus consensus formation in language through specializing in certain aspects of validity and hierarchizing processes of agreement, or whether they uncouple action coordination from consensus formation in language altogether, and neutralize it with respect to the alternatives of agreement or failed agreement.

The transfer of action coordination from language over to steering media means an uncoupling of interaction from lifeworld contexts. Media such as money and power attach to empirical ties; they encode a purposive-rational attitude toward calculable amounts of value and make it possible to exert generalized, strategic influence on the decisions of other participants while *bypassing* processes of consensus-oriented communication. Inasmuch as they do not merely simplify linguistic communication, but *replace* it with a symbolic generalization of rewards and punishments, the lifeworld contexts in which processes of reaching understanding are always embedded are devalued in favor of media-steered interactions; the lifeworld is no longer needed for the coordination of action.

Societal subsystems differentiated out via media of this kind can make themselves independent out of the lifeworld, which gets shunted aside into the system environment. Hence the transfer of action over to steering media appears from the lifeworld perspective both as reducing the costs and risks of communication and as conditioning decisions in expanded spheres of contingency—and thus, in this sense, as a *technicizing of the lifeworld.*

The generalization of the influence that attaches to rationally motivated trust in the possession of knowledge—whether cognitive-instrumental, moral-practical, or aesthetic-practical—cannot have the same effect. Where reputation or moral authority enters in, action coordination has to be brought about by means of resources familiar from consensus formation in language. Media of this kind cannot uncouple interaction from the lifeworld context of shared cultural knowledge, valid norms, and accountable motivations, because they have to make use of the resources of consensus formation in language. This also explains why they need no special institutional reconnection to the lifeworld and remain dependent upon rationalization of the lifeworld.

Influence that is specialized in cognitive matters—that is, scientific reputation—can take shape only insofar as cultural value spheres (in Weber's sense) have been differentiated out, making it possible to treat the cognitive tradition exclusively under the validity aspect of truth. Normatively specialized influence—for example, moral leadership—can take shape only insofar as moral and legal development have reached the postconventional level at which moral consciousness is anchored in the personality system through internal behavior controls. Both kinds of influence require, in addition, technologies of communication by means of which a public sphere can develop. Communicative action can be steered through specialized influence, through such media as professional reputation and value commitment, only to the extent that communicative utterances are, in their original appearance, already embedded in a virtually present web of communicative contents far removed in space and time but accessible in principle.

Writing, the printing press, and electronic media mark the significant innovations in this area; by these means speech acts are freed from spatiotemporal contextual limitations and made available for multiple and future contexts. The transition to civilization was accompanied by the invention of writing; it was used at first for administrative purposes, and later for the literary formation of an educated class. This gives rise to the role of the author who can direct his utterances to an indefinite, general public, the role of the exegete who develops a tradition through teaching and criticism, and the role of the reader who, through his choice of reading matter, decides in which transmitted communications he wants to take part. The printing press gained cultural and political significance only in modern society. It brought with it a freeing of communicative action from its original contexts; this was raised again to a higher power by the electronic media of mass communication developed in the twentieth century.

The more consensus formation in language is relieved by media, the more complex becomes the network of media-steered interaction. However, the two different kinds of relief mechanism promote quite different types of multiple communication. Delinguistified media of communication such as money and power, connect up interactions in space and time into more and more complex networks that no one has to comprehend or be responsible for. If by 'responsibility' we mean that one orients one's actions to criticizable validity claims, then a "deworlded" coordination of action that is unhinged from communicatively established consensus does not require that participants be responsible actors. By contrast, those media of communication such as reputation and value commitment, which decontextualize and focus, but do not replace, processes of reaching understanding, relieve interaction from yes/no positions of criticizable validity claims only *in the first instance.* They are dependent on technologies of communication, because these technologies make possible the formation of public spheres, that is, they see to it that even concentrated networks of communication are connected up to the cultural tradition and, *in the last instance,* remain dependent on the actions of responsible actors.

F.—These two contrary tendencies clearly mark a polarization between two types of action-coordinating mechanisms and an extensive uncoupling of system integration and social integration. In subsystems differentiated out via steering media, systemic mechanisms create their own, norm-free social structures jutting out from the lifeworld. These structures do, of course, remain linked with everyday communicative practice via basic institutions of civil or public law. We cannot directly infer from the mere fact that system and social integration have been largely uncoupled to linear dependency in one direction or the other. Both are conceivable: the institutions that anchor steering mechanisms such as power and money in the lifeworld could serve as a channel *either* for the influence of the lifeworld on formally organized domains of action *or,* conversely, for the influence of the system on communicatively structured contexts of action. In the one case, they function as an institutional framework that subjects system maintenance to the normative restrictions of the lifeworld, in the other, as a base that subordinates the lifeworld to the systemic constraints of material reproduction and thereby "mediatizes" it.

In theories of the state and of society, both models have been played through. Modern natural law theories neglected the inner logic of a functionally stabilized civil society in relation to the state; the classics of political economy were concerned to show that systemic imperatives were fundamentally in harmony with the basic norms of a polity guaranteeing freedom and justice. Marx destroyed this practically very important illusion; he showed that the laws of capitalist commodity production have the latent function of sustaining a structure that makes a mockery of bourgeois ideals. The lifeworld of the capitalist carrier strata, which was expounded in rational natural law and in the ideals of bourgeois thought generally, was devalued by Marx to a sociocultural superstructure. In his picture of base and superstructure he was also raising the methodological demand that we exchange the internal perspective of the lifeworld for an observer's perspective, so that we might grasp the systemic imperatives of an independent economy as they act upon the bourgeois lifeworld *a tergo.* In his view, only in a socialist society could the spell cast upon the lifeworld by the system be broken, could the dependence of the superstructure on the base be lifted.

In one way, the most recent systems functionalism is an heir-successor to Marxism, which it radicalizes and defuses at the same time. On the one hand, systems theory adopts the view that the systemic constraints of material production, which it understands as imperatives of self-maintenance of the general social system, reach right through the symbolic structures of the lifeworld. On the other hand, it removes the critical sting from the base-superstructure thesis by reinterpreting what was intended to be an empirical diagnosis as a prior analytical distinction. Marx took over from bourgeois social theory a presupposition that we found again in Durkheim: it is not a matter of indifference to a society whether and to what extent forms of social integration dependent on consensus are repressed and replaced by anonymous forms of system-integrative sociation. A theoretical approach that presents the lifeworld merely as one of several anonymously steered subsystems undercuts this distinction. Systems theory treats accomplishments of social and system integration as functionally equivalent and thus deprives itself of the standard of communicative rationality. And without that standard, increases in complexity achieved *at the expense* of a rationalized lifeworld cannot be identified *as costs.* Systems theory lacks the analytic means to pursue the question that Marx (also) built into his base-superstructure metaphor and Weber renewed in his own way by inquiring into the paradox of societal rationalization. For us, this question takes on the form of whether the rationalization of the lifeworld does not become paradoxical with the transition to modern societies. The rationalization of the lifeworld makes possible the emergence and growth of subsystems whose independent imperatives turn back destructively upon the lifeworld itself.

I shall now take a closer look at the conceptual means by which this hypothesis might be given a more exact formulation. The assumption regarding a "mediatization" of the lifeworld refers to "interference" phenomena that arise when system and lifeworld have become differentiated from one another to such an extent that they can exert mutual influence upon one another. The mediatization of the lifeworld takes effect on and with the structures of the lifeworld; it is not one of those processes that are available as themes *within* the lifeworld, and thus it cannot be read off from the intuitive knowledge of members. On the other hand, it is also inaccessible from an external, systems-theoretical perspective. Although it comes about counterintuitively and cannot easily be perceived from the internal perspective of the lifeworld, there are indications of it in the formal conditions of communicative action.

The uncoupling of system integration and social integration means at first only a differentiation between two types of action coordination, one coming about through the consensus of those involved, the other through functional interconnections of action. System-integrative mechanisms attach to the effects of action. As they work through action orientations in a subjectively inconspicuous fashion, they may leave the socially integrative contexts of action which they are parasitically utilizing structurally unaltered—it is this sort of intermeshing of system with social integration that we postulated for the development level of tribal societies. Things are different when system integration intervenes in the very forms of social integration. In this case, too, we have to do with latent functional interconnections, but the subjective inconspicuousness of systemic constraints that *instrumentalize* a communicatively structured lifeworld takes on the character of deception, of objectively false consciousness. The effects of the system on the lifeworld, which change the structure of contexts of action in socially integrated groups, have to remain hidden. The reproductive constraints that instrumentalize a lifeworld without weakening the illusion of its self-sufficiency have to hide, so to speak, in the pores of communicative action. This gives rise to a *structural violence* that, without becoming manifest as such, takes hold of the forms of intersubjectivity of possible understanding. Structural violence is exercised by way of systematic restrictions on communication; distortion is anchored in the formal conditions of communicative action in such a way that the interrelation of the objective, social, and subjective worlds gets prejudged for participants in a typical fashion. In analogy to the cognitive a priori of Lukacs's "forms of objectivity," I shall introduce the concept of a *form of understanding* [*Verständigungsform*].

Lukacs defined forms of objectivity as principles that, through the societal totality, preform the encounters of individuals with objective nature, normative reality, and their own subjective nature. He speaks of a priori forms of objectivity because, operating within the framework of the philosophy of the subject, he starts from the basic relation of a knowing and acting subject to the domain of perceptible and manipulable objects. After the change of paradigm introduced by the theory of communication, the formal properties of the intersubjectivity of possible understanding can take the place of the conditions of the objectivity of possible experience. A form of mutual understanding represents a compromise between the general structures of communicative action and reproductive constraints unavailable as themes within a given lifeworld. Historically variable forms of understanding are, as it were, the sectional planes that result when systemic constraints of material reproduction inconspicuously intervene in the forms of social integration and thereby mediatize the lifeworld.

I shall now (*a*) illustrate the concept of a form of understanding with those civilizations in which religious-metaphysical worldviews take on ideological functions, in order (*b*) to gain an analytic perspective on the hypothetical sequence of forms of mutual understanding.

(a) In societies organized around a state, a need for legitimation arises that, for structural reasons, could not yet exist in tribal societies. In societies organized through kinship, the institutional system is anchored ritually, that is, in a practice that is interpreted by mythical narratives and that stabilizes its normative validity all by itself. By contrast, the authority of the laws in which a general political order is articulated has to be guaranteed, in the first instance, by the ruler's power of sanction. But political domination has socially integrating power only insofar as disposition over means of sanction does not rest on naked repression, but on the authority of an office anchored in turn in a legal order. For this reason, laws need to be intersubjectively recognized by citizens; they have to be legitimated as right and proper. This leaves culture with the task of supplying reasons why an existing political order deserves to be recognized. Whereas mythical narratives interpret and make comprehensible a ritual practice of which they themselves are part, religious and metaphysical worldviews of prophetic origin have the form of doctrines that can be worked up intellectually and that explain and justify an existing political order in terms of the world-order they explicate.[35]

The need for legitimation that arises, for structural reasons, in civilizations is especially precarious. If one compares the ancient civilizations with even strongly hierarchized tribal societies, one finds an unmistakable increase in social inequality. In the framework of state organization, units with different structures can be functionally specified. Once the organization of social labor is uncoupled from kinship relations, resources can be more easily mobilized and more effectively combined. But this expansion of material reproduction is gained at the price of transforming the stratified kinship system into a stratified class society. What presents itself from a system perspective as an integration of society at the level of an expanded material reproduction, means, from the perspective of social integration, an increase in social inequality, wholesale economic exploitation, and the juridically cloaked repression of dependent classes. The history of penal law provides unmistakable indicators of the high degree of repression required in all ancient civilizations. Social movements that can be analyzed as class struggles—although they were not carried on as such—pose a threat to social integration. For this reason, the functions of exploitation and repression fulfilled by rulers and ruling classes in the systemic nexus of material reproduction have to be kept latent as far as possible. Worldviews have to become ideologically efficacious.

Weber showed how the world religions were dominated by a basic question, namely, the legitimacy of the unequal distribution of earthly goods among humankind. Theocentric worldviews put forward theodicies so as to reinterpret the need for a religious explanation of suffering perceived as unjust into an individual need for salvation, and thus to satisfy it. Cosmocentric worldviews offered equivalent solutions to the same problem. What is common to religious and metaphysical world-views is a more or less clearly marked, dichotomous structure that makes it possible to relate the sociocultural world to a world behind it. The world behind the visible world of this life, behind the world of appear-ances, represents a fundamental order; when it is possible to explain the orders of a stratified class society as homologous to that world-order, worldviews of this kind can take on ideological functions. The world religions pervaded both popular and high cultures; they owed their over-whelming efficacy to the fact that with the same set of assertions and promises they could satisfy the need for justification at very different levels of moral consciousness simultaneously.

At first glance, it strikes one as puzzling that ideological interpreta-tions of the world and society could be sustained *against all appear-ances* of barbaric injustice. The constraints of material reproduction could not have reached so effectively and relentlessly through the class-specific lifeworlds of civilizations if cultural traditions had not been im-munized against dissonant experiences. I would explain this unassailabil-ity by the systemic restrictions placed on communication. Although religious-metaphysical worldviews exerted a strong attraction on in-tellectual strata; although they provoked the hermeneutic efforts of many generations of teachers, theologians, educated persons, preachers, man-darins, bureaucrats, citizens, and the like; although they were reshaped by argumentation, given a dogmatic form, systematized and rationalized in terms of their own motifs, the basic religious and metaphysical con-cepts lay at a level of undifferentiated validity claims where the rational-ity potential of speech remains more tightly bound than in the profane practice of everyday life, which had not been worked through intellec-tually. Owing to the fusion of ontic, normative, and expressive aspects of validity, and to the cultically rooted fixation of a corresponding belief attitude, the basic concepts that carried, as it were, the legitimation load of ideologically effective worldviews were immunized against objections already within the cognitive reach of everyday communication. The im-munization could succeed when an institutional separation between the sacred and the profane realms of action ensured that traditional founda-tions were not taken up "in the wrong place"; within the domain of the sacred, communication remained *systematically restricted* due to the lack of differentiation between spheres of validity, that is, *as a result of the formal conditions of possible understanding.*[36]

The mode of legitimation in civilizations is thus based on a form of understanding that systemically limits possibilities of communication owing to its failure to differentiate sufficiently among the various validity claims. Earlier we placed mythical, religious-metaphysical, and modern worldviews in a hierarchy, according to the degree of decentration of the world-understandings they make possible. Analogously, we can order action orientations, and the realms of action they define, according to the degree of differentiation of validity aspects, and in this way we can get at the relative a priori of the form of understanding dominant at a given ·time and place. These *forms of the intersubjectivity of mutual understanding* do not reflect the structures of dominant worldviews in any symmetrical manner, for established interpretive systems do not pervade all areas of action with the same intensity. As we have seen, in civilizations the immunizing power of the form of understanding derives from a peculiar, structurally describable differential between two realms of action: in comparison to profane action orientations, sacred ones enjoy a greater authority, even though validity spheres are less differentiated and the potential for rationality is less developed in sacred than in profane domains of action.

(b) With a systematic investigation of forms of understanding in mind, I shall distinguish four domains of action: (1) the domain of cultic practice; (2) the domain in which religious systems of interpretation have the power directly to orient everyday practice; and finally the profane domains in which the cultural stock of knowledge is utilized for (3) communication and (4) purposive activity, without the structures of the worldview directly taking effect in action orientations.

Since I regard (1) and (2) as belonging to the sacred realm of action, I can avoid difficulties that result from Durkheim's oversimplified division.

Magical practices carried on by individuals outside of the cultic community should not be demoted, as Durkheim proposed they should, to the profane realm. Everyday practice is permeated throughout with ceremonies that cannot be understood in utilitarian terms. It is better not to limit the sacred realm of action to cultic practice, but to extend it to the class of actions based on religious patterns of interpretation.[37]

Furthermore, there are internal relations between the structures of worldviews and the kinds of cultic actions: to myth there corresponds a *ritual* practice (and sacrificial actions) of tribal members; to religious-metaphysical worldviews a *sacramental* practice (and prayers) of the congregation; to the religion of culture [*Bildungsreligion*] of the early modern period, finally, a *contemplative* presentation of auratic works of art. Along this path, cultic practice gets "disenchanted," in Weber's sense; it loses the character of compelling the gods to some end, and it is less and less carried on in the consciousness that a divine power can be *forced* to do something.[38]

Within the realm of profane action I shall distinguish between communicative and purposive activity; I shall assume that these two *aspects* can be distinguished even when corresponding *types* of action (not to mention *domains* of action defined by these types) have not yet been differentiated. The distinction between communicative and purposive activity is not relevant to the sacred realm. In my view, there is no point in contrasting religious cults and magical practices from this perspective.[39]

The next step would be to place the practices in different domains of action in a developmental-logical order according to the degree to which aspects of validity have been differentiated from one another. At one end of the scale stands ritual practice, at the other end the practice of argumentation. If we further consider that between the sacred and the profane domains there are differentials in authority and rationality—and in the opposite directions—we then have the points of view relevant to ordering the forms of understanding in a systematic sequence. The following schema (Figure 28) represents four forms of mutual understanding ordered along the line of a progressive unfettering of the rationality potential inherent in communicative action. The areas (1–2) and (3–4) stand for the form of understanding in archaic societies, the areas (5–6) and (7–8) for that in civilizations, the areas (9–10) and (11–12) for that in early modern societies.

Taking the archaic form of understanding as an example, I shall next give a somewhat more detailed account of the contrasting directions of the differentials in authority and rationality between the sacred and the profane domains of action. Following that I shall comment more briefly on the forms of understanding typical of civilizations (5–8) and of early modern societies (9–12).

(ad 1 and *2)* We find ritualized behavior already in vertebrate societies; in the transitional field between primate hordes and paleolithic societies, social integration was probably routed primarily through those strongly ritualized modes of behavior we counted above as symbolically mediated interaction. Only with the transformation of primitive systems of calls into grammatically regulated, propositionally differentiated speech was the sociocultural starting point reached at which ritualized *behavior* changed into ritualized *action;* language opened up, so to speak, an interior view of rites. From this point on, we no longer have to be content with *describing* ritualized behavior in terms of its observable features and hypothesized functions; we can try to *understand* rituals—insofar as they have maintained a residual existence and have become known to us through field studies.

A modern observer is struck by the extremely irrational character of ritual practices. The aspects of action that we cannot help but keep apart today are merged in one and the same act. The element of purposive

Domains of action — Differentiation of validity spheres	Sacred		Profane	
	Cultic practice	Worldviews that steer practice	Communication	Purposive activity
Confusion of relations of validity and effectiveness: performative-instrumental attitude	1. Rite (institutionalization of social solidarity)	2. Myth	—	—
Differentiation between relations of validity and effectiveness: orientation to success vs. to mutual understanding	5. Sacrament/prayer (institutionalization of paths to salvation and knowledge)	6. Religious and metaphysical worldviews	3. Communicative action bound to particular contexts and with a holistic orientation to validity	4. Purposive activity as a task-oriented element of roles (utilization of technical innovations)
Differentiation of specific validity claims at the level of action: objectivating vs. norm-conformative vs. expressive attitudes	9. Contemplative presentation of auratic art (institutionalization of the enjoyment of art)	10. Religious ethics of conviction, rational natural law, civil religion	7. Normatively regulated communicative action with an argumentative handling of truth claims	8. Purposive activity organized through legitimate power (utilization of specialized practical-professional knowledge)
Differentiation of specific validity claims at the level of discourse: communicative action vs. discourse	—	—	11. Normatively unbound communicative action with institutionalized criticism	12. Purposive activity as ethically neutral purposive-rational action (utilization of scientific technologies and strategies)

Figure 28. Forms of Mutual Understanding

activity comes out in the fact that ritual practices are supposed magically to bring about states in the world; the element of normatively regulated action is noticeable in the quality of obligation that emanates from the ritually conjured, at once attracting and terrifying, powers; the element of expressive action is especially clear in the standardized expressions of feeling in ritual ceremonies; finally an assertoric aspect is also present inasmuch as ritual practice serves to represent and reproduce exemplary events or mythically narrated original scenes.

Ritual practice is, of course, already part of a sociocultural form of life in which a higher form of communication has emerged with grammatical speech. Language [in the strict sense] breaks up the unity of teleological, normative, expressive, and cognitive aspects of action. Yet mythical thought shields ritual practice from the tendencies toward decomposition that appear at the level of language (with the differentiation between action oriented to mutual understanding and to success, and the transformation of adaptive behavior into purposive activity). Myth holds the same aspects together on the plane of interpretation that are fused together in ritual on the plane of practice. An interpretation of the world that confuses internal relations of meaning with external relations among things, validity with empirical efficacy, can protect ritual practice against rips in the fabric woven from communicative and purposive activity indistinguishably. This explains its coexistence with profane contexts of cooperation in which goal-oriented actions are effectively coordinated within the framework of kinship roles. The experience gained in everyday practice is worked up in myth and connected with narrative explanations of the orders of the world and of society. In this regard, myth bridges over the two domains of action.

We can see in the formal structures of the relevant action orientations that there is a rationality differential between sacred and profane domains. At the heart of the sacred realm is ritual practice, which stands or falls with the interweaving of purposive activity and communication, of orientations to success with orientations to mutual understanding. It is stabilized by a mythical understanding of the world that, while it develops in narrative form, that is, at the level of grammatical speech, nonetheless exhibits similar categorial structures. In the basic categories of myth, relations of validity are still confused with relations of effectiveness. On the other hand, the mythical worldview is opened to the flow of experience from the realm of profane action. Everyday practice already rests on a difference between aspects of validity and reality.

(*ad 3* and *4*) It is above all in the areas of production and warfare that cooperation based on a division of labor develops and requires action oriented to success. From the standpoint of developmental history as well, efficacy is the earliest aspect of the rationality of action. As long as truth claims could barely be isolated on the level of communicative action, the "know-how" invested in technical and strategic rules could not yet take the form of explicit knowledge. In contrast to magic, the profane practice of everyday life already calls for differentiating between orientations to success and to mutual understanding. However, within communicative action the claims to truth, to truthfulness, and to rightness likely flowed together in a whole that was first broken up in a methodical fashion when, with the advent of writing, a stratum of literati arose who learned to produce and process texts.

The normative scope of communicative action was relatively narrowly restricted by particularistic kinship relations. Under the aspect of fulfilling standardized tasks, goal-directed cooperative actions remained embedded in a communicative practice that itself served to fulfill narrowly circumscribed social expectations. These expectations issued from a social structure regarded as part of a mythically explained and ritually secured world-order. The mythical system of interpretation closed the circuit between profane and sacred domains.

(ad 5 and *6)* When a holistic concept of validity was constituted, internal relations of meaning could be differentiated from external relations among things, though it was still not possible to discriminate among the various aspects of validity. As Weber has shown, it is at this stage that religious and metaphysical worldviews arise. Their basic concepts proved to be resistant to every attempt to separate off the aspects of the true, the good, and the perfect. Corresponding to such world views is a sacramental practice with forms of prayer or exercises and with demagicalized communication between the individual believer and the divine being. These worldviews are more or less dichotomous in structure; they set up a "world beyond" and leave a demythologized "this world" or a desocialized "world of appearances" to a disenchanted everyday practice. In the realm of profane action, structures take shape that break up the holistic concept of validity.

(ad 7 and *8)* On the level of communicative action, the syndrome of validity claims breaks up. Participants no longer only differentiate between orientations to success and to mutual understanding, but between the different basic pragmatic attitudes as well. A polity with a state and conventional legal institutions has to rely on obedience to the law, that is, on a norm-conforming attitude toward legitimate order. The citizens of the state must be able to distinguish this attitude—in everyday actions as well—from an objectivating attitude toward external nature and an expressive attitude vis-à-vis their own inner nature. At this stage, communicative action can free itself from particularistic contexts, but it stays in the space marked out by solid traditional norms. An argumentative treatment of texts also makes participants aware of the differences be-

tween communicative action and discourse. But specific validity claims are differentiated only on the plane of action. There are not yet forms of argumentation tailored to specific aspects of validity.[40]

Purposive activity also attains a higher level of rationality. When truth claims can be isolated, it becomes possible to see the internal connection between the efficiency of action oriented to success and the truth of empirical statements, and to make sure of technical know-how. Thus practical professional knowledge can assume objective shape and be transmitted through teaching. Purposive activity gets detached from unspecific age and sex roles. To the extent that social labor is organized via legitimate power, special activities can define occupational roles.

(ad 9 and *10)* That validity claims are not yet fully differentiated at this stage can be seen in the cultural tradition of the early modern period. Independent cultural value spheres do take shape, but to begin with only science is institutionalized in an unambiguous fashion, that is, under the aspect of exactly one validity claim. An autonomous art retains its aura and the enjoyment of art its contemplative character; both features derive from its cultic origins. An ethics of conviction remains tied to the context of religious traditions, however subjectivized; postconventional legal representations are still coupled with truth claims in rational natural law and form the nucleus of what Robert Bellah has called "civil religion." Thus, although art, morality, and law are already differentiated value spheres, they do not get wholly disengaged from the sacred domain so long as the internal development of each does not proceed unambiguously under precisely one specific aspect of validity. On the other hand, the forms of modern religiosity give up basic dogmatic claims. They destroy the metaphysical-religious "world beyond" and no longer dichotomously contrast this profane world to Transcendence, or the world of appearances to the reality of an underlying essence. In domains of profane action, structures can take shape that are defined by an unrestricted differentiation of validity claims on the levels of action *and* argumentation.

(ad 11 and *12)* It is here that discourse becomes relevant for profane spheres of action, too. In everyday communication, participants can keep apart not only different basic pragmatic attitudes, but also the levels of action and discourse. Domains of action normed by positive law, with posttraditional legal institutions, presuppose that participants are in a position to shift from naïvely performing actions to reflectively engaging in argumentation. To the extent that the hypothetical discussion of normative validity claims is institutionalized, the critical potential of speech can be brought to bear on existing institutions. Legitimate orders still appear to communicatively acting subjects as something normative, but this normativity has a different quality insofar as institutions are no

longer legitimated per se through religious and metaphysical world-views.

Purposive activity is freed from normative contexts in a more radicalized sense. Up to this point, action oriented to success remained linked with norms of action and embedded in communicative action within the framework of a task-oriented system of social cooperation. But with the legal institutionalization of the monetary medium, success-oriented action steered by egocentric calculations of utility loses its connection to action oriented by mutual understanding. This strategic action, which is disengaged from the mechanism of reaching understanding and calls for an objectivating attitude even in regard to interpersonal relations, is promoted to the model for methodically dealing with a scientifically objectivated nature. In the instrumental sphere, purposive activity gets free of normative restrictions to the extent that it becomes linked to flows of information from the scientific system.

The two areas on the left in the bottom row of Figure 28 have been left empty because, with the development of modern societies, the sacred domain has largely disintegrated, or at least has lost its structure-forming significance. At the level of completely differentiated validity spheres, art sheds its cultic background, just as morality and law detach themselves from their religions and metaphysical background. With this *secularization of bourgeois culture,* the cultural value spheres separate off sharply from one another and develop according to the standards of the inner logics specific to the different validity claims. Culture loses just those formal properties that enabled it to take on ideological functions. Insofar as these tendencies—schematically indicated here—actually do establish themselves in developed modern societies, the structural force of system imperatives intervening in the forms of social integration can no longer hide behind the rationality differential between sacred and profane domains. The modern form of understanding is too transparent to provide a niche for this structural violence by means of inconspicuous restrictions on communication. Under these conditions it is to be expected that the competition between forms of system and social integration would become more visible than previously. In the end, systemic mechanisms suppress forms of social integration even in those areas where a consensus-dependent coordination of action cannot be replaced, that is, where the symbolic reproduction of the lifeworld is at stake. In these areas, the *mediatization* of the lifeworld assumes the form of a *colonization.*

In the concluding chapter I shall take the modern form of understanding, which has been crystallizing in the West since the eighteenth century, as my point of departure for a theory of modernity linked to Weber's rationalization thesis. Before doing so, I want to pick up again the thread of the history of social theory. Through the work of Talcott Parsons we can get clear about how to interrelate the basic concepts of systems theory and action theory, which we have until now merely conjoined in an abstract way. In the process we can also look at the present state of discussions concerning the foundations of social science, and we can take up the problem of reification once more, at the level of contemporary standards of theory formation, and reformulate it in terms of systemically induced lifeworld pathologies.

VII

Talcott Parsons: Problems in Constructing a Theory of Society

Owing in part to the writings of Talcott Parsons, Weber, Mead, and Durkheim now count as undisputed classics in the history of sociological theory. It requires no explicit justification to deal with these authors today as if they were our contemporaries. However highly one may rank Parsons, his status as a classic is not so beyond dispute that any justification for taking his work as the reference point for the systematic discussion that follows would be superfluous.

To begin with the obvious, none of his contemporaries developed a social theory of comparable complexity. The autobiographical account of his work that Parsons published in 1974 gives a first impression of the continuity and cumulative success of the efforts that this scholar devoted to constructing a single theory over the course of more than fifty years.[1] The body of work he left us is without equal in its level of abstraction and differentiation, its social-theoretical scope and systematic quality, while at the same time it draws upon the literatures of specialized research. Interest in Parsons' theory has been on the wane since the middle of the 1960s, and his later work was even pushed into the background for a time by hermeneutically and critically oriented approaches to social inquiry. Nevertheless, no theory of society can be taken seriously today if it does not at least situate itself with respect to Parsons. To deceive oneself on this point is to be held captive by questions of topicality rather than being sensitive to them. This holds as well for any neo-Marxism that wants to bypass Parsons. Errors of this sort are usually corrected rather quickly in the history of scientific inquiry.

Furthermore, among the productive theorists of society no one else has equaled Parsons' intensity and persistence in conducting a dialogue with the classics and connecting up his own theory to them. One need not share his conviction that the convergence of the great theoretical traditions and agreement with them are a touchstone for the truth of one's own theoretical approach,[2] but the ability to appropriate and work up the best traditions is indeed a sign of a social theory's powers of comprehension and assimilation—though such theories aim as well to establish a specific paradigm of society rooted in a collective self-understanding. From beginning to end, the theories of Durkheim, Weber, and Freud formed a reference system for Parsons which he used as a check on his own thought.[3] Of course, along with this went not only the constant demarcation from philosophical empiricism, but a shield against Marx and Mead, against materialist and symbolic interactionist varieties of critical social theory receptive to Kant and Hegel.[4] Moreover, the fact that Parsons remained, on the whole, closed to philosophy—with the exception of Whitehead's influence on his earlier work, and the rather vague references to Kant in one of his later works[5]—does not fit well with the ecumenical style of this all-incorporating systematic thinker. Nor did he make use of analytic philosophy, even where it suggested itself, as in the theories of language and action.

The main reason for occupying ourselves with Parsons, in both an instructive and a critical vein, has to do with the theme of our second set of intermediate reflections. The competition between action-theoretical and systems-theoretical paradigms was of decisive significance in the development of Parsons' thought. He was the first to make a technically rigorous concept of system fruitful for social-theoretical reflection. The most important problem for him was linking the theory of action to a conceptual strategy indicated by the model of a boundary-maintaining system. He had already developed a system of categories for describing the object domain of ordered social action before the cybernetic model presented itself at the end of the 1940s as a way of re-formulating social-scientific functionalism. Unlike many systems theorists of a more recent vintage, Parsons was not tempted to forget the *constitution* of the object domain "action" or "society" in the process of *applying* the systems model to it. What is instructive in his work is precisely the tension between the two paradigms, which persisted till the end.[6] His orthodox disciples flatly deny any such tension,[7] whereas the less orthodox endeavor to resolve it, and in two opposing directions: a self-sufficient systems functionalism,[8] and a reversion to neo-Kantian positions.[9]

Parsons himself was convinced that he succeeded in connecting up action theory with the conceptual strategy suggested by the systems model, at the very latest in his response to Dubin's critique.[10] By contrast, interpreters such as Ken Menzies have come to the conclusion that "at the center of [Parsons'] world lies a fundamental confusion. His voluntarism is too eclectic to reconcile positivism and idealism. Running throughout his work are two different programs—a social action one in the idealist tradition and a social system one in the positivist tradition. The action program focuses on the meaning of an action to an actor, while his social systems program focuses on the consequences of an activity or a system of activity. Parsons does not have an action system, as he claims, but only a behavioral system and a separate action theory."[11] One can see a peculiar tension between systems theory and action theory in the history of Parsons' influence as well. Most of his older disciples and readers who approach him from the side of his writings on socialization theory assert (or tacitly assume) a methodological primacy for basic action-theoretical concepts. Most of his younger disciples and readers who approach him from the side of his macrosociological works assert that systems-theoretical concepts are fundamental to his theory construction. To illustrate these different assessments: for the one group the key to understanding his work as a whole is *Toward a General Theory of Action* and the relations between culture, society, and person (with institutionalization and internalization as the most important mechanisms of interconnection); for the other it is *Economy and Society* (with the schema of intersystemic interchange relations). When Parsons reprinted his two encyclopedia articles entitled "Social Interaction" and "Social System" one after the other, he justified the order by noting that "the subject of social interaction is in a fundamental sense logically prior to that of social system."[12] If, however, one looks at his theory construction itself, he seems to have answered the question otherwise.

Orthodox Parsonians glide over the inconsistencies that, as we shall see, can be found in his theoretical development. On the other hand, the view that Parsons pursued two incompatible theoretical programs misses the central intention without which his theory of society would collapse. The same can be said of the selective readings that isolate out of his work either a systems-theoretical or an action-theoretical strand. We can learn something from this large-scale endeavor only if we take seriously Parsons' intent and examine how, in realizing this aim, he became entangled in instructive contradictions.

My point of departure, then, is that the problem for theory construction of how to combine the basic concepts of systems and action theory is a genuine one. My provisional formula, to the effect that societies be conceived as systemically stabilized complexes of action of socially integrated groups, already includes these two aspects. The question with which Parsons starts, how is society possible as an ordered complex of action, warrants beginning with the problem of coordinating action. By what sort of mechanisms are alter's actions connected up with ego's in such a way that conflicts that might threaten a given action interrelation can either be avoided or sufficiently checked? We have drawn a distinction between mechanisms of social integration, which attach to action orientations, and mechanisms of system integration, which reach right through action orientations. In the one case, the agents' actions are coordinated through a harmonizing of action orientations that is present to them; in the other, through a functional intermeshing of action consequences that remain latent, that is, that can go beyond the participants' horizon of orientation. According to Parsons, the social integration of action contexts is established via normatively secured consensus, and their system integration via a nonnormative regulation of self-maintenance processes. In short, the orientation of acting subjects toward values and norms is constitutive for establishing order through social integration but not for system integration.

The anonymous sociative mechanism of the market has served as a model for the latter ever since the eighteenth century, when political economy took as the object of its scientific analysis an economic system differentiated out of the general political order. A problem till then unknown to natural law theorists also dates from that time: what is the relation between the two forms of integrating action contexts, one that takes effect, so to speak, with the consciousness of actors and is present as a lifeworld background, whereas the other silently penetrates right through actors' orientations? In his *Philosophy of Right* Hegel resolved this problem through an idealist transition from subjective to objective spirit. And Marx brought in the theory of value so as to be able to connect economic statements about a system's anonymous interdependencies with historical statements about the lifeworld contexts of actors, individual or collective. These strategies have since lost their plausibility. Thus systems theory and action theory can be viewed as the *disjecta membra* of this Hegelian-Marxist heritage. The older German sociology—whose points of departure were Dilthey, Husserl, and (with Weber) especially the Southwest German school of neo-Kantianism—set out its basic concepts in action-theoretical terms. At the same time, the foundations were being laid for an economic theory that took over from Hobbes and utilitarianism the idea of an instrumental order and developed it into the conception of a system steered by the money medium.

The history of social theory since Marx might be understood as the unmixing of two paradigms that could no longer be integrated into a two-level concept of society connecting system and lifeworld. Critical tools such as the concept of ideology have become dull because it has not been possible to develop a sufficiently complex metatheoretical framework within one or the other of these two—now separate—paradigms. With this in mind, it is of considerable interest to examine how the two lines of theoretical development come together again in Parsons' work. In what follows I shall elaborate on three theses:

1. The framework of his action theory proved too narrow for Parsons to develop a concept of society from that perspective; thus he felt it necessary to represent complexes of action directly as systems and to convert social theory from the conceptual primacy of action theory over to that of systems theory.

2. In the course of this systems-theoretical turn, however, action theory did not get unreservedly reinterpreted and assimilated. The Parsonian variant of systems functionalism remained freighted with a theory of culture carried along with his inheritance from Durkheim, Freud and, above all, Weber.

3. The theory of modernity developed by Parsons in this framework suggests, on the whole, too harmonious a picture, because it does not have the wherewithal to provide a plausible explanation of pathological patterns of development.

1. From a Normativistic Theory of Action to a Systems Theory of Society

If we begin, as Durkheim did, with "collective representations," or as Mead did, with "symbolically mediated interaction," or as I have proposed, with the basic concept of "communicative action," society can be conceived, to start with, as the lifeworld of the members of a social group. Along this path the concept of social order can be introduced in action-theoretical terms, that is, without having recourse to a technical concept of system. There is in Parsons nothing equivalent; as I shall try to show, his action theory was not sufficiently complex to permit the derivation of a concept of society. As a result, Parsons was forced to link the conceptual transition from the level of action to that of action complexes with a shift of analytic perspective and correspondingly of the basic conceptual apparatus.

This gave the false impression that the functionalist analysis of action complexes referred per se to the conception of society as a self-regulating system. But if we introduce 'lifeworld' as a concept complementary to that of 'communicative action', and understand it as the context-forming background of processes of reaching understanding, the reproduction of the lifeworld can already be analyzed from different functional perspectives. Above we distinguished the symbolic reproduction of the lifeworld from its material reproduction and then viewed communicative action as the medium via which the symbolic structures of the lifeworld are reproduced. In doing so, we proposed a functional differentiation between processes of cultural reproduction, social integration, and socialization, which did not at all necessitate changing our basic conceptual perspective. In my view, Parsons underestimated the capacity and degree of self-sufficiency of action-theoretical concepts and strategies; as a consequence, in constructing his theory of society he joined the system and action models too soon.

Parsons also fails to see the methodological point of attempting to transform the two conceptual standpoints into one another. The action-theoretical approach ties social-scientific analysis to the internal perspective of the members of a social group. For the social scientist this poses the methodological problem of hermeneutically connecting up his own understanding to that of the participants. By contrast, systems theory ties social-scientific analysis to the external perspective of an observer. Thus, the metatheoretical question of the relationship between systems and action theory cannot be resolved independent of the methodological question of how an objectivistic conceptual apparatus can be linked up with a reconstructive conceptual apparatus developed from an internal perspective. Parsons did not concern himself with hermeneutics, that is to say, with the problem of gaining access to the object domain of social science through an understanding of meaning. This is not only a matter of leaving himself open to criticism from competing approaches of interpretive sociology—to which Victor Lidz drew attention, albeit rather late in the game.[1] Most important, Parsons fails to see the methodological point of the question, whether systems theory has to be coordinated with and subordinated to action theory.

In what follows, I shall (A) first take up the action-theoretical project of 1937 and discuss the construction problem that forced Parsons to rebuild his theory in the following years. I shall then (B) examine the status of the pattern variables in the conception he developed in 1951, and (C) show why he felt it necessary also to drop this second version of his theory of action in favor of a systems functionalism.

A.—In his first great work, *The Structure of Social Action,* Parsons develops the main features of a normativist theory of action via a critical treatment of the empiricist tradition. He attacks the latter from two sides. On the one hand, he analyzes the concept of purposive rational action in order to show that utilitarianism cannot ground the acting subject's freedom of choice (the utilitarian dilemma). On the other hand, he focuses on the concept of instrumental order to show that the question of how social order is possible cannot be resolved under empiricist presuppositions (the Hobbesian problem). With reference to the two central categories, 'unit act' and 'action system', Parsons subdivides each of the two opposing parties into two warring camps, neither of which can resolve their respective problem. Rationalist and empiricist concepts of action can no more grasp the autonomy of action than materialist and idealist concepts of order can comprehend the legitimacy of an action system based on interests. Parsons opposes to these (a) a voluntaristic concept of action and (b) a normativist concept of order.

(a) As the motto for his investigation into the structure of social action, Parsons chose a line from Weber (which he left in the original German): "All serious reflection about the ultimate elements of meaningful human conduct is oriented primarily in terms of the categories 'end' and 'means'."[2] With Weber, Parsons takes the teleological structure of purposiveness immanent in all action as the guiding thread in his analysis of the concept of social action. In doing so he directs his attention to the most general determinations of the smallest thinkable units of possible action.

He hopes in this way to obtain an action-theoretical framework that will define in basic concepts the object domain of the sciences of action.[3]

The teleological model of action depicts the actor as one who, in a given situation, sets ends and then chooses and applies means that appear suited to achieve them. As usual, Parsons defines an "end" as a future state of affairs that the actor wants to bring about; the "situation" is composed of elements that, from the actor's point of view, either can be brought under control or are beyond his control—that is to say, it is composed of "means" and "conditions." Underlying the actor's decisions between alternative means are maxims; underlying his setting of ends are orientations to values and norms. Parsons brings the two together under the concept of "normative standards." Thus, at an elementary level actions can be analyzed in terms of the *action orientations* ascribed to an *actor* in an action *situation.*

This action frame of reference has a number of conceptual implications important for Parsons. First, the model presupposes not only that the actor has cognitive capacities, but also that he can make normatively oriented decisions in the dimensions of setting ends and selecting means. Under this aspect Parsons speaks of a "voluntaristic" theory of action. Furthermore, his concept of a situation presupposes that the means and conditions entering into action orientations are interpreted from the perspective of the agents themselves, but they can also be judged from the perspective of a third person. In this respect the theory of action is set out in "subjectivistic" terms; at least it excludes the objectivism of reformulating action concepts in behaviorist terms. Finally, the concept of an action orientation is fashioned in such a way that the temporal reference or process character of action can be viewed under two aspects. Action is represented as a process of attaining goals while taking normative standards into account. Under the aspect of *goal attainment,* it requires an effort or expenditure that is rewarded by satisfaction or yield (the motivational dimension: instrumental/consummatory). Under the second aspect, that of *taking normative standards into account,* action bridges the gap between the regions of the "is" and the "ought," between facts and values, between the *conditions* of a given situation and the agents' orientations as defined by *values* and *norms* (the ontological dimension: conditions/norms). The "effort" that an action requires does not have the empirical sense of striving for gratification. It is rather "a name for the relating factor between the normative and conditional elements of action. It is necessitated by the fact that norms do not realize themselves automatically but only through action, so far as they are realized at all."[4]

This implication, that action requires a, as it were, moral effort, is obviously connected with the "voluntarism" of the proposed action frame of reference, but Parsons cannot explain the latter so long as he restricts his analysis to the basic unit act. The concept of a normative action orientation cannot be clarified in an action-theoretical framework that extends only to the orientations of isolated actors.

The elements of "ends," "means," and "conditions" suffice to specify the *function* of value standards: they are supposed to *regulate decisions* in the dimensions of setting ends and choosing means. But Parsons cannot explain what it means for an actor to orient his decisions to values so long as he restricts his analysis to the basic unit of action.

The main part of the book is devoted to the basic concepts of social order as developed by Durkheim and Weber.

(*b*) Parsons answers the question of how social order is possible with reference to the debate between Durkheim and Spencer. He accepts Durkheim's view that the actions of a plurality of actors can be satisfactorily coordinated only on the basis of intersubjectively recognized norms. This *social integration* demands of individual actors respect for a moral authority upon which the validity claim of collectively binding rules can rest. Parsons is already developing here the idea of a morally imperative—and in this sense ultimate—value system, which is, on the one hand, embodied in social norms and, on the other, anchored in the motives of acting subjects: "Applied to the permanent regulation of conduct in a set of relatively settled conditions, such a value system also becomes embodied in a set of normative rules. They not only serve directly as the ends of a specific act, and chains of them, but they govern as a whole, or in large part, the complex action of the individual."[5] This process requires, in turn, building up internal behavior controls: "The normal concrete individual is a morally disciplined personality. This means above all that the normative elements have become 'internal', 'subjective' to him. He becomes, in a sense, 'identified' with them."[6]

Parsons is not yet interested in processes of embodying and anchoring values, that is, of institutionalizing and internalizing them (though he already refers to Freud's concept of introjection and to the buildup of superego structures).[7] He is content, at first, to characterize the normative dimension by the attitude in which an acting subject can follow or violate binding commands. He regards Durkheim's distinction between moral and causal constraints, between the constraint of conscience and constraint by external circumstances, as a decisive break with empiricist prejudices. Durkheim arrived at this distinction as it became clear to him that "fear of sanctions constitutes only the secondary motive for adherence to institutional norms; the primary is the sense of moral obligation. With this the primary meaning of constraint becomes moral obligation and a clear distinction is drawn between social constraint and that of natural facts."[8] Of course an agent may adopt the same attitude toward values and norms that he does toward facts, but he would not even *understand* what values and norms meant if he were *unable* to adopt toward them a conformative attitude based on a recognition of their claim to be valid. It is only in *this* attitude that the actor experiences the moral constraint that manifests itself in feelings of obligation as well as in reactions of guilt and shame—a constraint that is not only *compatible* with the autonomy of the actor, but is even constitutive of it in a certain sense. It is a constraint that the actor makes his own, in such a way that it no longer affects him as an external force, but pervades his motives and brings them into line.

Thus, Parsons attempts to give a sociological twist to the Kantian idea of freedom as obedience to laws that one gives to oneself—or rather, he attempts to find this idea of autonomy turning up again in the basic sociological concepts of Durkheim and Weber. For this it is essential that there be a symmetrical relation between the authority of valid norms the actor encounters and the self-control anchored in his personality, a correspondence between the institutionalization and the internalization of values. This reflects the dual character of a freedom constituted by the *personal* recognition of being bound to a *suprapersonal* order.

What Durkheim calls the moral authority of an order, Weber terms its legitimacy. Parsons works out the convergence between these basic concepts in connection with two modes of action coordination distinguished by Weber: complementarity of interests and value consensus. In the one case, a de facto order of empirically regular sequences of action is established; it may, in certain circumstances, be produced through purposive action orientations. In the other case, an institutional order of legitimately regulated interpersonal relations takes shape; it may, in certain circumstances, require value-rational action orientations. Parsons is concerned, however, that social orders cannot be stabilized through interests *alone*. Orders that are stripped of their normative power and reduced to an artificial interlocking of interests lead to anomic states of affairs: "A social order resting on interlocking of interests alone, and thus ultimately on sanctions, is hardly empirically possible though perhaps theoretically conceivable given the order as an initial assumption."[9] Thus, his answer to the question of how social order is possible is that institutions not only embody values, but *integrate* values with interests. Actors' orientations to legitimate orders must not exclude their orientations to their own interests.

With this, Parsons comes—on the analytical level of order—to the same problem that he was unable to clear up in the framework of his analysis of the unit act. Insofar as, in legitimate orders, ultimate ends or values are already selectively related to existing interests and made compatible with them, institutionalized action can be conceived of as a process of *realizing values under existing conditions.* This would suggest linking the concepts of action and order developed under (a) and (b) above, but Parsons isolates the two levels of analysis and thereby exacerbates the construction problem that will later force him to modify his approach. This becomes clearer when we recall the context in which he was developing his theory of action.

(c) *The utilitarian dilemma.* There are chiefly three elements of the concept of purposive rational action interpreted along utilitarian lines that Parsons stresses. The actor stands over against exactly one objective world of existing states of affairs and has more or less precise empirical knowledge of events and states in it. Empiricism assimilates the acting subject to the representing and judging subject at the center of modern theories of knowledge and science. "The starting point is that of conceiving the actor as coming to know the facts of the situation in which he acts, and thus the conditions necessary and the means available for the realization of his ends."[10] The only category of knowledge allowed is that of scientifically testable, empirical knowledge. Thus Parsons calls the concept of action "rationalistic."

Parsons further emphasizes that the success of purposive activity oriented to facts is measured exclusively by whether the action leads to the goal. Apart from maxims of increasing utility, the only norms permissible in the model of purposive rationality have to do with the effectiveness of the means selected, that is, with the efficiency of the intervention carried out with them. "There has been an ... overwhelming stress upon one particular type [of normative element] which may be called the 'rational norm of efficiency.'"[11] Normative standards are restricted to regulating the relations between the ends set, the means available, and the conditions given. Thus this action model leaves the choice of ends undetermined; Parsons speaks of the "randomness of ends," in the sense that the ends of action vary according to contingent probabilities.[12]

The third element is connected with this. The concept of purposive-rational action does not provide for any mechanism through which the actions of different actors might be coordinated with one another. Thus Parsons also calls the concept of strategic action "atomistic." If the actor confronts only a world of existing states of affairs, the decisions of other actors are relevant to him exclusively from the point of view of his own success. A stable relation among a number of actors can come about only contingently—for example, owing to the fact that the interests of those involved are complementary and mutually stabilizing.

If one is interested, as Parsons is, in how to conceive freedom of choice as the core of freedom of action, the utilitarian concept of action gives rise to a dilemma. His somewhat tortuous reflections on this dilemma can be summarized more or less as follows. The utilitarian concept of action fulfills a necessary condition for adequately conceptualizing the actor's freedom of choice: ends can vary independent of means and conditions. Parsons seeks to show that this is indeed necessary, but not sufficient, for the concept of freedom of choice he has in mind. So long as normative orientations relate only to the effectiveness of means and the success of action, so long as, beyond such decision maxims, no *values* are permitted to regulate the selection of ends themselves, the utilitarian model of action leaves room for two opposed interpretations, which are equally deterministic, that is to say, incompatible with the postulate of freedom of choice. Both *positivistic* and *rationalistic* attempts to explain the process of setting ends lead to an assimilation of ends to conditions that empirically determine actions. In the one case, ends are reduced either to innate or to acquired dispositions: "they are assimilated to ... elements analyzable in terms of non-subjective categories, principally heredity or environment."[13] In the other case, setting ends is viewed as a function of the knowledge an actor has of his situation: "If ends were not random, it was because it must be possible for the actor to base his choice of ends on scientific knowledge of some empirical reality ... action becomes a process of rational adaptation to conditions. The active role of the actor is reduced to one of the understanding of his situation and forecasting of its future course of development."[14] Neither the rationalistic nor the positivistic interpretation of the utilitarian model of action can explain how the actor can make mistakes *in a sense other than the purely cognitive.*

It becomes clear at this point what conceptual dimension Parsons finds lacking: he understands freedom of choice in the sense of an autonomy characterized by *moral fallibility*. He is not satisfied with free choice in the sense of a decision between alternatives that is determined either empirically through heredity and environment, or cognitively, through knowledge and calculation. Thus he expands the concept of normative standards, which acquire the status of noninstrumentalizable value standards or ultimate ends, so that the corresponding value orientations can regulate the setting of ends themselves: "The term 'normative' will be used as applicable to an ... element of a system of action if and only insofar as it may be held to manifest ... a sentiment that something is an end in itself."[15]

(*d*) *The Hobbesian problem.* Parsons also develops the concept of a legitimate order in opposition to the empiricist tradition. In this instance he takes Hobbes's social philosophy as his point of reference. He sees in Hobbes a thinker who consistently posed the question of how social order is possible under empiricist assumptions, thus providing a suitable jumping-off point for his own immanent critique. Like the utilitarians after him, Hobbes begins with solitary subjects equipped with the ability to act in a purposive-rational way. He assumes, further, that rational capacities are in the service of the passions, which dictate the ends of action. Since the passions of individuals vary by chance and are not coordinated by nature, the rational pursuit of their own interests has to degenerate into a war of all against all for security and for scarce goods. If one considers only the quasi-natural equipment of individuals who have interests and act purposive-rationally, social relations cannot assume from the start the form of peaceful competition. Rather, from the concept of action oriented to success it follows that each actor can view the decisions of every other actor only as means or conditions for realizing his own ends. Thus, prior to any artificial regulations, we have the natural maxim that everyone strives to exercise influence on everyone else and seeks to acquire generalized influence, that is to say, power.

Parsons formulates the Hobbesian problem as follows. If we start from the concept of purposive-rational action, "it is inherent in the latter that the actions of men should be potential means to each other's ends. Hence, as a proximate end it is a direct corollary of the postulate of rationality that all men should desire and seek power over one another. Thus the concept of power comes to occupy a central position in the analysis of the problem of order. A purely utilitarian society is chaotic and unstable, because in the absence of limitations on the use of means, particularly force and fraud, it must, in the nature of the case, resolve itself into an unlimited struggle for power; and in the struggle for the immediate end, power, all prospect of attainment of the ultimate, of what Hobbes called the diverse passions, is irreparably lost." [16] The solution Hobbes proposes—in the form of a contract through which all unconditionally subordinate themselves to the absolute power of a single person—presupposes a situation in which subjects acting purposive-rationally are already prepared to meet the necessary conditions for concluding a contract. This is a situation "where the actors come to realize the situation as a whole instead of pursuing their own ends in terms of their immediate situation, and then take the action necessary to eliminate force and fraud, purchasing security at the sacrifice of the advantages to be gained by their future employment." [17]

Parsons regards this solution as unconvincing, for two reasons. The model of purposive-rational action cannot explain how actors can make an agreement that is "*rational*" in the sense of taking *everyone's* interests into account. Hobbes has to explicitly expand—or, as Parsons put it, "stretch"—the concept of purposive rationality,[18] so that actors can pursue their interests rightly understood not only through *exercising a calculated force upon one another,* but also by way of *forming a rational will with one another.* Hence Parsons draws a sharp distinction between the *technical* and the *practical* concepts of *rationality,* and between two corresponding methods of pursuing interests. Indirectly influencing

another actor's action situation means attempting to condition his decisions by means of sanctions, including force and deception. By contrast,
directly influencing another actor's action orientations means attempting
to convince him with argumentative means of consensus formation.
"Force" and "fraud" stand opposed to "rational persuasion." [19]

Parsons discusses this alternative in connection with Lockean theory.
Locke lays claim to a practical reason that forbids us to follow only imperatives of purposive rationality in rationally pursuing our own interests. He already conceives of the state of nature from the perspective of
the *intersubjective* validity of a *natural right* to the rational pursuit of
one's own interests. The right of each to behave in this way is limited by
the fact that from the start everyone else also has the same right: "By
employing the term 'reason' Locke apparently implies that this attitude
is something at which men arrive by a cognitive process. It includes the
recognition that all men are equal and independent and that they have a
reciprocal obligation to recognize each other's rights and thus take upon
themselves sacrifices of their own immediate interests." [20]

Thus the point of Parsons' first, Lockean, objection to Hobbes is that
obligation—including even the unique act of submission to an absolute
power—has to rest on a normative consensus that cannot itself be the
result of purposive-rational considerations *alone.* Aggregating the various calculations of means-ends relations, which every actor undertakes
on the basis of his empirical knowledge and with an orientation to his
own success, can at best result in everyone regarding it as *desirable* that
a common norm be followed. But a norm's desirability does not yet explain the *obligating force* of valid norms, which is based not on sanctions
but on an intersubjective recognition, motivated by reasons, of reciprocal expectations of behavior. As Parsons puts it, "At the basis of (Locke's)
position lies the postulate of rational recognition." [21]

Even if we assumed that the often-tried and often-failed attempt within
the empiricist tradition to reduce practical reason to a competence for
the purposive-rational choice of means could succeed,[22] this would not
meet another, essentially empirical, objection. Parsons agrees with Weber
and Durkheim that the artificial order of constraint Hobbes envisioned,
which was to secure the observance of norms through external sanctions
alone, could not be made to last and is, therefore, unsuitable as a model
for explaining how social order is possible. In his view, this is true of
every merely de facto, norm-free social order based *solely* on interests—
no matter whether the conditioned behavior patterns are maintained, as
in the Hobbesian model, by the power of authority and the fear of negative sanctions, or, as in theories of political economy, by an exchange of
goods and a striving for positive sanctions, or by some combination of
the two mechanisms. Even in the sphere of market-regulated economic

behavior, to which empiricist accounts from Locke to Spencer were chiefly oriented, we can show, using the Durkheimian arguments analyzed earlier, that de facto patterns of social behavior cannot be stabilized in the absence of norms limiting actors' interest-guided actions through an orientation to values.[23] Social orders cannot be explained in terms of some collective instrumentalism; a de facto order issuing from the competition between purposive-rational actors for power and/or wealth remains unstable so long as the moral moment of conscience and obligation—that is to say, the orientation of action to binding values—is missing.

Here again, Parsons constructs a symmetrical relationship between two contrary, and equally false, positions. Sociological *materialism* does not deny the fact that interpersonal relations in general are normatively regulated, but it reduces norms to externally imposed regulations and fails to see that the institutionalization of behavioral expectations attaches to agents' orientations, normatively binding them, and does not merely exert an influence upon them by manipulating the consequences of action. On the other hand, sociological *idealism* falls into the error of underestimating the selective force issuing from the nonnormative components of action situations, from the material substratum of the lifeworld in general. This explains Parsons' reservations concerning Durkheim.[24] From his symmetrical critique of these two positions, Parsons develops a concept of social order based on an idea of institutions that follows the neo-Kantian model of realizing values, that is, that adheres to the Weberian concept of an order integrating values and interests. As we have seen: "Action must always be thought of as involving a state of tension between two different orders of elements, the normative and the conditional."[25]

(e) *Social Interaction.* It would have made sense at this point to connect the concept of action with that of order so that they complemented one another at the same analytical level and thus yielded a concept of social interaction. The concept of *normative agreement* could have served as a bridge between the concepts of value-oriented purposive activity and an order integrating values with interests. This would have placed at the center of action theory the interpretations and yes/no positions of the participants in interaction who are the bearers of value consensus and norm recognition. Center stage would no longer have been occupied by the means-ends structure of action, but by a language-dependent building of consensus as the mechanism that harmonizes the plans of action of different actors and thereby first makes social interaction possible. But Parsons does not take this path.[26] He remains tied to the empiricist traditions from which he is distancing himself. Although he views purposive activity as bounded by value standards and corresponding value orientations, the individualistic approach of a theory oriented to the teleology of action comes through inasmuch as the singular actions of solitary actors remain the ultimately decisive point of reference. I would like now to elaborate Parsons' *first important decision in theory construction* against the background of the theory of communicative action.

Parsons begins with the monadic actor and seeks to establish a conceptual transition from the unit act to the nexus of action by viewing elementary interaction as made up of the actions—introduced independently, to begin with—of two actors. The point of departure for his analysis is the *singular* action orientation conceived of as resulting from *contingent decisions between alternatives.* A value orientation gives expression to the fact that the corresponding values set a preference for one or the other of the given alternatives. Since the regulative force of cultural values does not negate the contingency of these decisions, every interaction between two actors entering into a relation takes place under the condition of "double contingency."[27] This is treated as a fact that generates a problem: it makes ordering accomplishments functionally necessary. In the logical construction of interaction, the double contingency of free choice by ego and alter is prior to the ordering mechanisms that coordinate actions. At the analytical level of the unit act, value standards are attributed to individual actors as something subjective; thus they need to be intersubjectively harmonized. The element of value orientation is meant only to exclude the postulation of contingent processes of setting ends and to prevent any retraction of the autonomy to set ends in favor of a rationalistic or positivistic assimilation of action orientations to determinants of the action situation.

Parsons held on to the core of the utilitarian concept of action, interpreting the actor's freedom of decision as a choice between alternative means for given ends. Perhaps he felt he could rescue voluntarism only by conceiving freedom of decision as a contingent freedom of choice—in the language of German idealism, as *Willkür.*

This view stands in contrast to the idea of a cultural system of values that is intersubjectively shared from the start. And this is precisely the problem in theory construction: how should Parsons connect the monadic concept of action with the intersubjective concept of order he borrowed from Durkheim? The problem could be solved if he made the interpretive accomplishments of participants in interaction, which make consensus possible, central to the concept of social order. As shown above, language-dependent processes of reaching understanding take place against the background of an intersubjectively shared tradition, especially of values accepted in common. The context to which a text refers might serve here as a model for what establishes order. On this model the problem of coordinating action posed by the doubly contingent relation between actors capable of decisions would be solved by an orientation to the validity claims of norms intended for intersubjective recognition.

Yes/no positions on normative validity claims do not spring from a contingent freedom of choice but from moral-practical convictions; they are subject, at least implicitly, to the binding force of good reasons. If we begin, as Parsons does, by setting out action-orienting decisions as the product of the private choices [*Willkür*] of solitary actors, we have no mechanism that could explain how action systems get constructed out of action units.[28] It is this embarrassment that explains Parsons' rearrangement of his theory of action in two works that appeared in 1951: *The Social System* and *Toward a General Theory of Action.*

B.—In this *early middle period* Parsons no longer confines himself to grasping the unit act in terms of the orientation of a subject acting in a situation. Instead, he now attempts to conceive of the action orientation itself as a product of the combined operations of culture, society, and personality.[29] He analyzes action orientations *a tergo,* as it were, from the point of view of what those three components contribute to the occurrence of a concrete action. This places the actor in the perspective of an agent who is both motivated by needs and controlled by values. The personality system plays a part in orienting action through motivational orientations; the social system makes itself felt in normative orientations.

In the meantime, Parsons had familiarized himself with Freud's personality theory and with cultural anthropology—especially Malinowski's. That also contributed to the shift in theoretical perspective. In the new approach we can no longer construct action systems out of their elementary units; we have to begin with them. From now on, Parsons begins his construction with the concept of culture and explains the action systems of society and personality as the institutional embodiment and motivational anchoring of cultural patterns. The elementary units are no longer unit acts but cultural patterns or symbolic meanings. They come together to form configurations, culturally transmissable systems of values and interpretations. The part of cultural tradition directly relevant to the constitution of action systems is the value patterns. They are the raw materials that get worked up into binding role expectations and intersubjectively valid norms along the path of institutionalization, or into personal motives and character-forming dispositions along the path of internalization. In this way Parsons conceives of the two action systems as complementary channels through which cultural values are converted into motivated actions: "social systems are systems of motivated action organized about the relations of actors to each other: personalities are systems of motivated action organized about the living organism."[30]

This manner of proceeding raises two problems. (*a*) First, we need an account of how the cultural determination of action orientations is to be understood; (*b*) and we need an account of how the three concepts of order—the cultural, social, and personality systems—can be joined together with a concept of action out of which they cannot be constructed. I shall approach these two questions aporetically, so that we can get clear about the difficulties plaguing a monological action theory that begins with solitary actors and does not take the coordinating mechanism of reaching understanding in language systematically into account.

(*a*) In the various presentations of his action theory at the start of the 1950s, Parsons no longer restricts himself to dissecting action orientations into their analytic components from the perspective of the value-oriented realization of ends. It is now a question of conceptually analyzing the connection between motivations and value orientations. Parsons develops this *second version of his theory of action* in four steps.

With respect to the motivational orientation of an actor who has to decide between alternative means in view of the ends adopted and the conditions given, Parsons distinguishes two aspects: a *cathectic orientation* to the goals and objects toward which the actor directs his feelings and interests, and a *cognitive orientation* to the states of affairs and alternatives that he comprehends and calculates. The two aspects can be separated only analytically, for every cathected object has to be recognized, and every cognitively comprehended object is relevant from the standpoint of satisfying needs. Both modes of orientation extend equally to subjective goal projections and objective elements of the situation.

But the process of orientation could not be understood as a decision between alternatives if there were not a third aspect of the motivational action orientation—an *evaluative orientation*, the aim of which is to establish as advantageous a relation as possible between attainable gratification and unavoidable deprivation: "The evaluative mode involves the cognitive act of balancing out the gratification-deprivation significances of various alternative courses of action with a view to maximizing gratification in the long run."[31] The only standards that can be derived from the dimensions of cathexis and cognition themselves are utility and efficiency—just the standards permitted in the utilitarian concept of action. However, if the evaluative orientation is to gain any independence from cathectic and cognitive orientations, the balance of gratification has to be secured through the mediation of standards of nonutilitarian origin: *cultural standards* exert—via the evaluative orientation—a decisive, primarily regulative influence on the motivations for action.[32]

The evaluative orientation is the switching station where culture gets coupled to actors' motivational orientations. This gives Parsons occasion to derive a classification of value standards and corresponding value orientations from the classification of motivational orientations. He distinguishes cognitive, appreciative, and moral standards. In the cognitive dimension, we have to do with criteria of truth, objectivity, logical inference, and the like; in the cathectic dimension, with aesthetic standards, with criteria of sincerity, authenticity, appropriateness, and so forth; and in the evaluative dimension, with questions of the normative standpoints from which cognitive and appreciative standards can be derived and integrated with one another—Parsons introduces the term moral standards for the higher-level standards of this type.

These three kinds of standards represent only one segment of cultural tradition, that of cultural values or the evaluative element of culture. In addition to these, culture also includes cognitive schemata for *interpreting* what is actually the case, and *expressive* forms of symbolism for presenting aesthetic-expressive experiences.

Thus, the following components are decisive in the cultural determination of action: elements of the *cultural system*—cognitive schemata of interpretation, expressive forms of symbolism, and standards of value; included among these *value standards* are standards for solving cognitive-instrumental problems, appreciative standards, and standards for resolving moral-practical problems; the corresponding *normative orientations* are cognitive, appreciative, and moral; and, finally, *motivational orientations* are cognitive, cathectic, and evaluative. Figure 29 provides a schematic representation of the relations between these elements.

Although Parsons starts from the motivational orientations, so as to construct the schema from bottom to top, Figure 29 has to be read in the opposite direction and understood as illustrating the penetration of cultural regulatives into the motives of action. For the idea of a cultural determination of action orientations is supposed to solve the problem of coordination with which the first version of the theory of action struggled in vain. Value standards are no longer ascribed to individual actors as subjective properties; instead, cultural value patterns are introduced as intersubjective from the start. Of course, at first they count only as elements of cultural traditions; they are not normatively binding to start with. Thus, if we want to identify the conditions for normatively regulated and motivationally anchored interactions, it will not do to connect the elements of action orientations *directly* to elements of the cultural system. I shall return to this problem later. First I will take up the matter of how Parsons conceives the actor's orienation to cultural values.

(*b*) In this scheme culture only comes into connection with action orientations via its evaluative components; it develops regulative power only through the actor's orientation to cultural standards of value. These

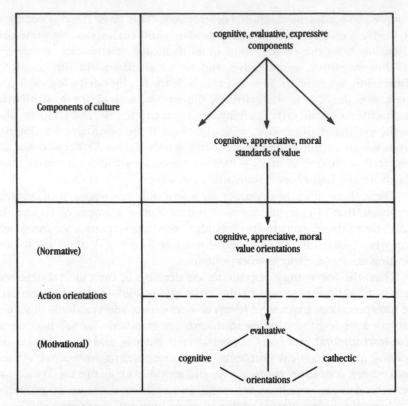

Figure 29. The Cultural Determinants of Action Orientations. *Source:* T. Parsons, *Toward a General Theory of Action* (New York, 1951).

standards extend beyond the evaluative sphere in the narrower sense; in addition to standards for what counts as "good" (or as better or worse), Parsons takes into account standards for the resolution of cognitive-instrumental and moral-practical problems. Evidently it is a question of the *standards* against which the *validity* of descriptive, normative, evaluative, and expressive statements are measured within the framework of a given cultural tradition. But the *substantive* richness of a culture is not exhausted by such *abstract standards of value and validity.* Figure 29 makes it seem as if neither cognitive patterns of understanding nor expressive forms of symbolism could find their way into action orientations. This could not have been Parsons' intention, and yet it is no accident that we get this impression. In dealing with the question of what it means for an actor to orient his action in the context of a tradition, Parsons uses too simple a model. The idea behind it is that an actor acts within the framework of his culture by orienting himself to *cultural ob-*

jects. Though Parsons mentions that language is the exemplary medium for cultural transmission, he does not exploit this insight in his theory of action. He plays down the communicative aspect of coordinating action, and this comes through in Figure 29.

Acting within the framework of a culture means that participants draw interpretations from a culturally secured and intersubjectively shared stock of knowledge in order to come to an understanding about their situation and to pursue their respective aims on this basis. From the conceptual perspective of action oriented to mutual understanding, the interpretive appropriation of transmitted cultural contents appears as the act through which the cultural determination of action takes place. Parsons closes off this path of analysis because he conceives of the orientation to values as an orientation to *objects.*

At first Parsons classified the objects to which actors can relate from the perspective of purposive activity—as means (or resources) and conditions (or restrictions). Now he offers another classification from the standpoint of the interactive structure of an action context. Ego distinguishes social objects that can assume the role of an alter from nonsocial objects. Among the latter, he distinguishes further between physical objects, which can appear only as means or conditions, and cultural objects. The key to this distinction between physical and cultural objects is the conditions under which they can be identified. Physical objects are entities in space and time; symbolic objects represent cultural patterns that can be transmitted—that is, passed on and appropriated—without changing their meaning. Spatiotemporal individuation does not affect the semantic content but only the material substratum in which a meaning pattern takes symbolic shape.

Thus Parsons gives an ontological characterization of physical and cultural objects from the viewpoint of the *knowing* subject; he thereby lets a difference slip that is more important from the perspective of *speaking* and *acting* subjects: the difference between spatiotemporally individuated *objects* and symbolic *meanings.* The former can be observed and manipulated, that is to say, changed by goal-oriented interventions; the latter can only be understood, that is, generated or made accessible by means of (at least virtual) participation in communication processes. Parsons fails to recognize this difference; *he assimilates transmissible cultural patterns to situation elements* that an actor relates to as if to objects. This reification distorts his view of the role that cultural tradition plays as a context and background for communicative action. The idea that an actor can develop motivational orientations vis-à-vis cultural objects in the same way as he does vis-à-vis other situation elements—be they opponents, means, or conditions—already exhibits this *reification of transmissible cultural contents.* Of course, an actor can upon occasion also behave reflectively toward his cultural tradition; he can, so to speak, turn around and make ideas, values, or expressive symbols the object of analysis, positively or negatively cathect them as objectified, evaluate them in the light of corresponding standards, and so on. But this does not hold for the normal case in which someone acting communicatively makes use of his cultural tradition in a performative attitude.

Communicatively acting subjects face the task of finding a common definition of their action situations and of coming to some understanding about topics and plans within this interpretive framework. In their interpretive work they make use of a transmitted stock of knowledge. As we have seen, cultural patterns of interpretation, evaluation, and expression have a twofold function in this process. Taken as a whole, they form the context of background knowledge accepted without question; at the same time, however, individual cultural patterns enter into the semantic content of *actual* utterances. Culture then no longer remains at the backs of communicative actors; it sheds the mode of background certainty and assumes the shape of knowledge that is in principle criticizable. However, neither in their context-forming function nor in their text-generating function do cultural patterns attain the status of objects that the actor might relate to as he does to the elements of the action situation.

Drawing interpretations from the fund of their tradition, participants in interaction seek to bring about a consensus regarding something in the world. In doing so, they refer to identifiable objects in the world; the latter can be, on the one hand, things and events in a world of existing states of affairs (i.e., physical objects) or, on the other hand, elements of a social world of legitimately regulated interpersonal relations or elements of a subjective world of experiences to which someone has privileged access (i.e., social objects in a wider sense). The ideas, values, or symbolic forms of expression that enter into the process of reaching understanding serve communication *about* such objects; they are not themselves objects of a comparable kind. At most, one can say of interpreters and translators, of scientists, moral and legal theorists, artists and art critics, that they refer to cultural objects when they are working reflectively with ideas, values, and symbolic forms of expression.

Parsons places the cultural patterns of meaning that supposedly appear as "objects" in action situations over against those elements of culture that have been internalized or institutionalized. But this distinction does not reverse his reification of culture; rather, by posing a false contrast, it actually makes it fast. The underlying idea is the following: When cultural patterns of value are internalized and institutionalized, when they shape motives on the one hand and define role expectation on the other, they are transformed into empirical—that is, spatiotemporally individuated—elements of personalities or interaction systems. By contrast, cultural objects remain external to actors and their orientations. Although a certain kind of controlling function is attributed to these cultural objects as well, they develop neither the propelling motive force nor the steering normative force of those values incorporated in persons or institutions: "Unlike need-disposition and role-expectations, the *symbols* which are the postulated controlling entities in this case are not internal to the systems whose orientations they control. Symbols control systems of orientation, just as do need-dispositions and role-expectations, but they exist not as postulated internal factors but as objects of orientations (seen as existing in the external world alongside of the other objects oriented by a system of action.)"[33]

This attempt to delimit *free-floating* cultural contents from *incorporated* value patterns, along the dimension 'objective versus nonobjective,' only adds to the confusion. As we have seen, the object-oriented subject of the theory of knowledge is just the wrong model [for a theory of interaction]. The structure of action oriented to reaching understanding is a better model for studying how culture, society, and personality work together in determining action orientations. By attending to the formal properties of the interpretive performances of actors who harmonize their actions via communicative acts, we can show how cultural traditions, institutional orders, and personal competences—in the form of diffuse taken-for-granted features of the lifeworld—make possible the communicative interweaving and stabilizing of action systems.

Like cultural traditions, the competences of socialized individuals and the solidarities of groups integrated through values and norms represent resources for the background of lifeworld certainties. At the same time they also form the context of action situations. With regard to culture's contribution to action oriented to mutual understanding, we distinguished its context-forming from its text-generating function. However specific the contribution of the cultural stock of knowledge to producing a text, the contributions of personality and society, of competences acquired in socialization, and of institutional orders are no less significant. The background, against which interaction scenes are played out and out of which, as it were, the situation of action oriented to mutual understanding issues, consists not only of cultural certainties, but equally, as we have seen, of individual *skills*—the intuitive *knowledge* of *how* to deal with a situation—and of customary social *practices*—the intuitive *knowledge* of *what* one can count *on* in a situation. The certainties of the lifeworld have not only the cognitive character of familiar cultural traditions, but also the, so to speak, psychic character of acquired and proven competences, as well as the social character of tried and true solidarities. The "beyond all question" character of the lifeworld out of which one acts communicatively derives not only from the kind of security based on *what* one trivially *knows,* but also from the kinds of certainty based on the consciousness of *knowing how* to do something or of being able to *count on* someone. The specific indubitability of what is known—which, paradoxically, denies it the character of knowledge that may possibly turn out to be false—seems to be due to the fact that ·in lifeworld certainties all three components are still more or less diffusely interconnected. The knowledge of *how* one goes about something and the knowledge of *what* one can count *on* are interwoven with *what* one knows. It separates off as "know that" from "know how" when cultural certainties are transformed into contents of communication and thereby enter into a knowledge connected with criticizable validity claims.[34]

(*c*) The concept of communicative action not only provides us with a point of reference for analyzing the contributions made by culture, society, and personality to the formation of action orientations; this model also enables us to get clear about how culture, society, and personality hang together as components of a symbolically structured lifeworld. To understand Parsons' construction problem here, we have to see that he first introduces these three orders in a wholly unspecific manner—as "systems." He is still working with the idea that society can be conceived from the perspective of action theory as a complex of action divided up into these components. Our idea, that the symbolic structures of the lifeworld are reproduced by communicative action, points the way now to a fruitful analysis of the *interconnections between culture, society, and personality.* If we inquire how cultural reproduction, social integration, and socialization can draw upon the same mechanism of mutual understanding, in different ways, the interdependencies among the three lifeworld components come into view. Because Parsons neglected this mechanism in constructing his theory of action, he had to try to find something equivalent to the lifeworld concept, but *under different premises.*

As we saw, his first important decision for theory construction established the model of the actor's value-oriented decision between action alternatives. With this as a point of departure, he has now to provide the conceptual means to comprehend how an action orientation issues from the joint operations of cuture, society, and personality. To this end, he introduces the so-called "pattern variables of value orientation,"[35] and with that he makes his *second important decision for theory construction.* Cultural values function as patterns for a choice between action alternatives; they determine the actor's orientation by establishing preferences, without affecting the contingency of a decision. Parsons maintains that in any action situation there are precisely five problems that every actor *unavoidably* faces, and they have the form of universal abstract alternatives schematized in a binary fashion.[36] In a certain sense he is attributing a transcendental status to his pattern variables: every action orientation is supposedly conceivable as the result of simultaneous decisions among five universal and unavoidable dichotomies.

There is, however, no trace of a "transcendental deduction" or of any other systematic justification; the catalog of problems and the corresponding table of alternatives derive a certain plausibility from the contrast introduced by Tönnies between *Gemeinschaft* and *Gesellschaft*. The pattern variables are located in the dimension in which the older sociology described the transition from traditional to modern society, that is, the process of societal rationalization. Parsons himself points this out.[37] *Gemeinschaft* and *Gesellschaft* designate types of social structures to which typical value orientations correspond on the level of social action. The combination of preferences for collectivity orientation, affectivity, particularism, ascription, and diffuseness is the choice characteristic of *Gemeinschaften;* the contrary combination of preferences is typical of *Gesellschaften*. On this account, the process of societal rationalization that interested Weber can be understood as a progressive institutionalization of value orientations that guarantee actors (e.g., in economic exchange) will follow their own (rightly understood) interest, adopt an affectively neutral attitude, show preference for universalistic regulations, judge social counterparts according to their functions, and specify action situations in a purposive-rational manner—in terms of means and conditions. Parsons can thus reformulate in terms of pattern variables what Weber conceptualized as the institutionalized purposive rationality of economic and administrative action.

This reformulation has two advantages. First, Parsons can take up Weber's insight that the utilitarian model of action, which directly attributes to the actor the purposive-rational pursuit of his own enlightened self-interest and thus places it at a psychological level, is not adequate for explaining capitalist economic activity. Commercial intercourse regulated by markets can become established only to the extent that the orientation pattern of purposive rational action is made binding as a *cultural value,* that is, as a choice pattern, independent of qualities of personality such as egoism and the ability to carry things through, and is placed on an ethical foundation. Second, Parsons can free himself from the concretism of the *Gemeinschaft-Gesellschaft* typology and show—by appealing to instances of academic-professional orientations, particularly in the medical profession—that Weber's "rationally controlled action" (*Gesellschaftshandeln*) is only one among several types of purposive-rational and value-rational actions. The modern physician typically acts in just as universalistic and functionally specific a manner as the businessman in the capitalist economy; at the same time, however, he is subject to the rules of a professional ethic that prevents him from pursuing his own economic interests with all legally permitted means.

The early essays in which Parsons developed these two arguments shed light on the context in which the pattern variables arose.[38] It is clear there that Parsons singled out just those problem situations and alternative possibilities of choice that could be combined into different types of purposive-rational *and* value-rational behavior.[39] It is for this reason that the pattern variables are suited to describing social structures and action orientations from the viewpoint of rationalization. Modern societies exhibit a high structural differentiation of spheres of action; this forces actors to choose among the fundamental dichotomies in general and, when necessary, consciously to adopt contrary choice patterns in different areas of life and to be able to switch from one combination of preferences to the opposite.

Perhaps it is possible to derive the pattern variables from dimensions characteristic of the decentered understanding of the world in the modern era. For my part, I can see no other way of justifying the claim that the table of pattern variables forms a *system.*

Be that as it may, the pattern variables are supposed to put us in a position to examine how any given set of cultural values structures an actor's scope for choice through one of the a priori possible combinations of basic choices. Furthermore, the preference patterns described in terms of the pattern variables can be regarded as the structural nucleus that links action orientations not only with transmitted culture but also with society and personality.[40] For example, the "instrumental activism" that Parsons developed in the forties and fifties in connection with the action orientations of American businessmen and physicians—and which he viewed as determined by basic choices for an affectively neutral attitude, universalism, performance orientation, and a field-independent cognitive style directed to specifics—is reflected on three levels simultaneously, namely, structurally analogous action motives, professional roles, and cultural values.[41]

But if the pattern variables describe a structural core *common* to all three components, they cannot simultaneously serve *to elucidate the specific differences in the ways that personality, society, and culture influence action orientations.* From the global idea that contingent choices are regulated by preferences, we can gain *no* standpoint for differentiating between the motivational drives to action, the normative bonds of action, and the orientation of action to cultural values. It is again evident that *a pendant to the mechanism of mutual understanding is lacking.*

The scope for choice regulated by preference patterns does not get filled in by the actors' interpretive accomplishments. The model does not allow for such initiatives that could be examined to see how the various resources of the lifeworld—acquired competences, recognized norms, and transmitted cultural knowledge—flow together to form a reservoir out of which interaction participants construct common action orientations. The pattern variables serve only to identify structurally analogous components, that is, sectors in which the three systems overlap and mutually penetrate one another—in which they "interpenetrate," as Parsons puts it.[42] From the perspective of action conceived as value-regulated purposive activity, we cannot explain how culture, society, and personality hang together. That concept does not yield the complementary concept of an intersubjectively shared world. *Without the brackets of a lifeworld centered on communicative action, culture, society, and personality fall apart.* It is precisely this that leads Parsons to treat these three orders as autonomous systems that directly act upon and partially interpenetrate one another.

Parsons gave up the attempt to provide an *action-theoretical* account of the idea that cultural values are incorporated into society and personality via the channels of institutionalization and internalization. Instead, he moved the model of *the interpenetration of analytically separate systems* into the foreground.

C.—Parsons' *third important decision in constructing his theory of society* has to do with the refinement of his concept of system, which was at the start rather loose. Until 1951 he used the functionalist concept familiar in cultural anthropology. It did not say much more than that a system was an ordered set of elements that tended to maintain existing structures. States of the system were to be analyzed from the viewpoint of whether and how they fulfilled functions in the maintenance of system structures. 'Structure' and 'function' were the two central concepts. In an essay entitled "Values, Motives, and Systems of Action" which he and Shils wrote for *Toward a General Theory of Action*, Parsons made some inconspicuous revisions in his notion of a "system." From that point on he characterized systems of action in terms of the basic concepts of general systems theory. The central idea was that systems have to secure their continued existence under conditions of a variable and hypercomplex— that is, never more than partly under control—environment. The long-influential model of a self-maintaining organism suggested the formulation that self-regulating systems maintain their boundaries relative to a hypercomplex environment. What he earlier understood as the tendency to maintain equilibrium, Parsons now conceived in terms of boundary maintenance.[43] Instead of the structural functionalism inspired by cultural anthropology, he now pursued a systems functionalism inspired by biocybernetics. The concepts of 'function' and 'structure' were no longer viewed as being on the same level. Rather, the functional imperatives of a boundary-maintaining system were fulfilled by structure as well as by process—structure and process could in certain cases serve as functional equivalents.[44]

This more rigorous concept was, however, first applied only to "society" and "personality," whereas the peculiarly free-floating system of transmissable cultural meanings was a complex regulated "grammatically" in the broadest sense of the term; it was at most a "system" in the structuralist sense of the term as used from Saussure to Lévi-Strauss. When Parsons speaks now of the structure of a tradition, of a cultural system of values, he means the order of internal relations between meaning components and *not* the order found in external (e.g., functional) relations between the empirical elements of an organized whole. Thus he also distinguishes the logical sense in which complexes of meaning are "integrated" from the empirical sense in which boundary-maintaining systems are "integrated."[45] The coherence of symbolic structures produced according to rules is to be judged under aspects of validity, whereas the coherence of systems subject to environmental influences is to be assessed from the standpoint of self-maintenance. Parsons reserves the expression "integration" for empirical interconnections of system components; he understands the coherence of meaning complexes as "consistency."[46]

However, when cultural values are connected with interests or motives through being incorporated in action systems, their status changes: they thereby become functioning components of empirically identifiable systems of action. The background for this way of thinking is the dualism found in Rickert's and Weber's theory of values. Values belong to the sphere of validity and gain empirical status only by entering into relation with facts and being actualized as values in cultural objects. Moreover, Parsons outfits sociocultural reality with systemic properties; hence he sets up the spheres of validity and existence rather differently than the spheres of mere being and functioning: "a cultural system does not 'function' except as part of a concrete system; it just is."[47]

This ambiguity in Parsons' use of the concept of 'system' marks his ambivalent combination of Weber's idea of value realization with the cybernetic idea of a boundary-maintaining system. The special status of culture over against the empirical system of action makes it possible for him to import the neo-Kantian dualism of values and facts into systems functionalism. And it is this value-theoretical boundary that marks off the Parsonian systems functionalism from that of Luhmann. System maintenance is defined by a set of cultural values embodied in the institutional orders of the society in question or anchored in the motivational basis of personality. As these values are taken from the cultural system, which *belongs to a different sphere from that of*—to put it pointedly—*the struggle for survival,* they have the power to define a system's basic structures in ways that resist the supreme system imperative to surrender any structure whatsoever for the sake of system self-maintenance.

This can be seen in the two basic problems that societies and personalities have to solve when they are understood as culturally structured, boundary-maintaining systems. On the one hand, they have to fulfill the functional imperatives that arise from the constraints of the system's environment; on the other hand, they have to integrate and uphold the structure-defining patterns that result from the institutionalization and internalization of values. Parsons distinguishes between these two basic tasks of preserving the integrity of an action system internally and externally; he discusses the corresponding basic function under the catchwords "allocation" and "integration."[48] Allocation has to do with functions of adaptation and goal attainment—with the creation, mobilization, distribution, and effective employment of scarce resources. In this context, Parsons repeatedly mentions the restrictions of time, space, and natural factors, as well as the limitations set by the organic nature of human beings. The *functional integration* of an action system is secured by solving these problems of allocation in the broadest sense; Parsons is careful to distinguish from this *social integration.*[49] The latter has to do with functions of maintaining and integrating the cultural values incorporated into an action system. Social integration is not measured against the functional imperatives resulting from a system's relation to its environment but against consistency requirements deriving from internal—as a rule, semantic—relations within a cultural system of values. As *boundary-maintaining systems,* society and personality are subject to imperatives that result from system-environment relations; as *culturally structured action systems,* they are at the same time subject to requirements of consistency that arise from the dependence of institutionalized and internalized value patterns on the independent logic of culture.

This double relation of an action system to environment and culture is depicted in Figure 30, where the arrows represent external system-environment relations characterized by differentials in complexity, and the broken lines represent internal relations constitutive of structural similarities.

This construction suffers from an unclear fusion of basic concepts behind which stand two different paradigms. The cultural system is a kind of placeholder for the missing concept of the lifeworld; as a result, it has the ambiguous status of an environment that is at once *superordinate* and *internal* to action systems, and that is stripped, so to speak, of the

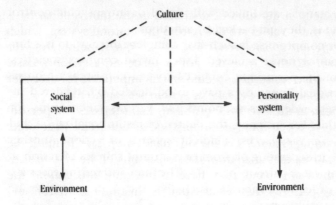

Figure 30.

empirical properties of a system environment. The instability of this construction becomes evident when we examine the ways in which the different requirements on action systems deriving from culture and environment compete with one another and are brought into harmony. Parsons understands the structures and processes of an action system as a continually renewed compromise between the imperatives of—as they are still called here—functional and social integration, both of which must be fulfilled simultaneously: "Integration, both within an individual's value system and within the value system prevailing in a society is a compromise between the functional imperatives of the situation and the dominant value-orientation patterns of the society. Every society is of necessity shot through with such compromises."[50] He transfers the concept of value realization underlying Weber's notion of a legitimate order to self-regulating systems. The process of institutionalizing and internalizing values is dealt with from the perspective of achieving compromises between the consistency requirments of culture and the pressure of functional imperatives. These compromises can in turn be viewed under two aspects. From the perspective of the cultural system, the institutionalization and internalization of values is a matter of specifying general, at first context-free, meanings for typical action situations. In norms and roles, in superego structures and motives for action, values lose their generalized meanings; they are related to restricted contexts and differentiated into meanings specific to situations. From the perspective of the hypercomplex environment that compels an action system to react adaptively, the institutionalization and internalization of values are not matters of cutting generalized meanings down to size, but of empirically anchoring meanings that have been tailored to situations. The specified behavioral expectations are linked with social or intrapsychic control mechanisms, that is, they get backed by sanctions.

The scope for compromise is such that complete integration is a limiting case seldom or never achieved. Especially in complex societies, manifestations of the permanent conflict between consistency requirements and functional imperatives have to be headed off, rendered innocuous, and set aside. Parsons points out various mechanisms for accomplishing this. For instance, the degree of institutionalization and internalization can vary across different spheres of action. Another method consists in separating off from one another spheres of action in which conflicting value patterns prevail.[51] The more interesting cases are conflicts of an order of magnitude such that they can no longer be checked in the usual manner.

Parsons refers here to historical events, sudden changes of constellation that come into *stubborn* opposition to the cultural value system and are in this sense problematic: "Problematical facts in the present sense are those which it is functionally imperative to face and which necessitate actions with value implications incompatible with the paramount value system."[52] Conflicts of this sort call into play mechanisms that save the integration of an action system only *at the cost of* social or individual *pathologies:* "Where this order of strain exists, the accommodation will often be facilitated by 'rationalization' or ideological 'masking' of a conflict. This reduces awareness of the existence of a conflict and its extent and ramifications. Mechanisms of the personality and mechanisms of social control in the social system operate in these areas of strain to bring the system into equilibrium. Their inadequacy to reestablish such equilibrium constitutes a source of change."[53] Mechanisms that *repress* an actual conflict by excluding it from the realm of situation interpretations and action orientations and covering it up with illusions have pathological side effects. They lead to solutions that are unstable in the long run but that temporarily secure the integration—however *compulsively*—of the action system.

Parsons is here drawing upon the psychoanalytic model of dealing with instinctual conflicts unconsciously and in a way that produces symptoms. But it is just such pathologies of society and personality that make manifest the fragility of his dualistic construction of the action system. While this construction enables Parsons to recognize pathological forms of conflict resolution, it is not clear how he can accommodate such phenomena within his framework.

Parsons recognizes the *limiting cases of an illusory resolution of conflicts* because they express the resistance of culture's independent logic over against the functional imperatives of system maintenance. If these imperatives enjoyed an unconditional primacy, then any structures would have to be open to revision for the sake of maintaining the system. *Ultrastable* systems of this sort maintain themselves through changes from which *no* components of the system are in principle exempt. They do not even allow for pathological forms of stabilization, since the system-environment relation provides no standpoint from which we could speak of pathological side effects or of symptoms. This is possible only if the identity of the action system is tied, via the definition of its basic structures, to a value sphere that sets its "own" kind of imperatives against the pressure to adapt exerted by a hypercomplex environment. It is in this manner that Parsons characterizes culture: it makes itself felt in claims that are subject to standards different from those governing a system's successful adaptation to its environment. Problems that have to be dealt with in the area of *internal* relations between symbolic expressions cannot be surmounted through solutions in the area of *external* relations.

Pathological forms of conflict resolution draw upon the special circumstances that the inner logic of culture is not infallible; phenomena of deception and self-deception can appear in the sphere of validity claims—and only in this sphere. In such cases, the stabilization of action systems is accompanied by symptoms that can be understood as *the price to be paid for objectively violating validity claims* that, from the *subjective* point of view of participants, appear to be *vindicated.* Symptoms are the tribute exacted for the deceptions with which stability is bought. Symptomatic side effects are experienced as pathological because they express the revenge taken on action systems by culture's independent logic when deception results from the pressure of functional imperatives. Deception is the mode in which the demands of a rationality expressing itself in the inner logic of culture are circumvented, that is to say, *inconspicuously disregarded.* If this intuition makes intelligible why Parsons recognizes manifestations of symptom-forming conflict resolution, the analysis of these manifestations reveals the ambiguity of a construction that interprets boundary-maintaining systems in terms of neo-Kantian cultural theory.

The question that arises is how a culture that transcends society and personality in a certain way, without being able to exert any influence upon them in the mode of a hypercomplex environment, can, so to speak, put backbone into the validity claims derived from it, how it can lend facticity and efficacy to such claims. If the consistency requirements of culture did not become empirically effective, the integration of action systems could be secured through an illusory satisfaction of validity claims, without risk and without side effects. According to Parsons, the facticity of validity claims is due to the external and internal sanctions with which institutionalized and internalized values are connected. But then it is difficult to see why a complex of values that has become dysfunctional and is giving rise to conflict should not, under the pressure of the self-maintenance imperatives of a system threatened by its environment, be discontinued and replaced by a more functional complex of values to which sanctions get attached. To what internal barriers against a value transformation induced by altered system-environment relations could Parsons appeal? If the pattern variables have only the elementaristic significance of making different cultures conceivable as different combinations of the same patterns of choice, if they do not also describe a structure that sets internal limits to the transformation of these patterns, then Parsons has no theoretical tools at his disposal with which to explain *the resistance that cultural patterns with their own independent logics offer to functional imperatives.* By contrast, the pathogenic treatment of conflicts between requirements of social and of functional integration can be made comprehensible in a two-level concept of society that connects lifeworld and system.

Through the concept of lifeworld, the sphere of validity claims, which is, according to Parsons, located in a transcendent realm of free-floating cultural meanings, would be incorporated from the start into empirical, spatiotemporally identifiable contexts of action. If, as proposed above, we view consensus formation as a mechanism for coordinating actions and if we further assume that the symbolic structures of the lifeworld are reproduced through the medium of communicative action, then the independent logics of cultural value spheres are built into the validity basis of speech and thus into the mechanism whereby complexes of communicative action are reproduced. If validity claims function, so to speak, as pulleys over which consensus formation and thus the symbolic reproduction of the lifeworld pass, they are, without prejudice to their normative content, installed as social facts—their facticity needs no further foundation. On this conception, culture is, together with society and personality, part of the lifeworld; it is not set off from the other components as something transcendent. The dualism between cultural requirement and survival imperatives does not thereby fully vanish, but it assumes a different shape when the system concept is developed from the concept of the lifeworld and not *directly* superimposed upon the action concept. I shall now briefly characterize this alternative conceptual strategy.

At the level of simple interactions, actors, in carrying out their plans of action, are subject to the temporal, spatial, and material restrictions set by the situation in which they find themselves. The lifeworld of a social group is subject to corresponding restrictions. Through its material substratum, every lifeworld is in an exchange with its surroundings [*Umgebung*], formed by the ecology of external nature, the organisms of its members, and the structures of alien lifeworlds. It is the *situation of action* rather than the environment [*Umwelt*] of a system that serves as a model for the *surroundings of a sociocultural lifeworld.* With its material substratum the lifeworld stands under contingent conditions that appear from the perspective of its members as barriers to the realization of plans of action rather than as constraints on self-steering. This substratum has to be maintained by social labor drawing upon scarce resources. Parsons described the corresponding tasks as allocation problems. Whereas the aspect of social action most relevant to the symbolic reproduction of the lifeworld is that of *mutual understanding,* the aspect of *purposive activity* is important for material reproduction, which takes place through the medium of goal-directed interventions into the objective world.

To be sure, the material reproduction of the lifeworld does not, even in limiting cases, shrink down to surveyable dimensions such that it might be represented as the intended outcome of collective cooperation. Normally it takes place as the fulfillment of latent functions *going beyond the action orientations* of those involved. Insofar as the aggregate effects of cooperative actions fulfill imperatives of maintaining the material substratum, these complexes of action can be stabilized functionally, that is, through feedbck from functional side effects. This is what Parsons means by "functional," in contrast to "social," integration.

These reflections—from within the paradigm of the lifeworld—suggest a change of method and of conceptual perspective, namely, an *objectivating conception of the lifeworld as a system.* Insofar as we are considering the material reproduction of the lifeworld, it is not a question of the symbolic structures of the lifeworld itself, but only of those processes of exchange with its surroundings on which, by our definitions, the maintenance of the material substratum depends. With respect to these "metabolic processes" (Marx), it makes sense to *objectify* the lifeworld as a boundary-maintaining system, for functional interdependencies come into play here that cannot be gotten at adequately via members' intuitive knowledge of lifeworld contexts. Survival imperatives require a functional integration of the lifeworld, which reaches right through the symbolic structures of the lifeworld and therefore cannot be grasped without further ado from the perspective of participants. Rather, they require a counterintuitive analysis from the standpoint of an observer who objectivates the lifeworld.

From this *methodological point of view,* we can separate the two aspects under which the integration problems of a society may be thematized. *Social integration* presents itself as part of the symbolic reproduction of a lifeworld that, besides the reproduction of memberships (or solidarities), is dependent upon cultural traditions and socialization processes; by contrast, *functional integration* is equivalent to a material reproduction of the lifeworld that is conceived as system maintenance. The transition from one problem area to the other is tied to a change of methodological attitude and conceptual apparatus. Functional integration cannot be adequately dealt with by way of lifeworld analysis undertaken from an internal perspective; it only comes into view when the lifeworld is objectified, that is to say, represented in an objectivating attitude as a boundary-maintaining system. The systems model is no mere artifact in this context. Rather, the change in attitude follows from our reflective awareness of the limits of applicability of the lifeworld concept, which, however, we cannot, for hermeneutic reasons, simply leap over. The latent functions of action call for the concept of a systemic interdependency that goes beyond the communicative intermeshing of action orientations.

Once we get clear about this methodological step, the social and individual pathologies that could not be properly accommodated in Parsons' construction no longer present any difficulties. The intuition that led him to remark upon symptom-forming conflicts can readily be explicated in terms of a concept of society as a systematically stabilized complex of actions of socially integrated groups. The functions that the various domains of action within a differentiated lifeworld take on with regard to maintaining its material substratum generally remain latent: they are not present as ends in the orientations of the actors involved. The special case that Parsons has in mind comes to pass *when the social integration of these action domains would be endangered if those functions were to become manifest.*

Following Parsons, we can conceive of the integration of a society as a continuously renewed compromise between two series of imperatives. The conditions for the social integration of the lifeworld are defined by the validity basis of action-coordinating processes of reaching understanding in connection with the structures of the prevailing worldview; the conditions for the functional integration of society are set by the relations of a lifeworld objectified as a system to an environment only partially under control. If a compromise between internal validity claims and external survival imperatives can be achieved only at the cost of institutionalizing and internalizing value orientations not in keeping with the actual functions of the corresponding action orientations, the compromise holds only so long as those functions remain latent. Under circumstances such as these, the illusory character of the fulfillment of validity claims that carry a value consensus and make social integration possible must not be seen through. What is needed is a systematic restriction on communication, so that the illusion of satisfied validity claims can assume objective force. The facticity of validity claims, without which convictions—even false convictions—do not become settled, expresses itself in the fact that illusion exacts a price that is at once discrete and palpable. *False consciousness,* whether collective or intrapsychic, in the form of ideologies or self-deceptions, is accompanied by symptoms, that is, by restrictions that participants attribute not to the environment but to the social life-context itself, and that, therefore, they *experience* as repression, however unacknowledged.

By pursuing this alternative conceptual strategy Parsons could have avoided the fusion of paradigms to which the second version of his theory, developed in the early 1950s, succumbed. But, as we have seen, the basis of this action theory was too narrow to permit his developing a concept of society from the concept of action. Thus Parsons had to make action complexes *directly* conceivable as systems, without becoming aware of the change in attitude through which the concept of an action *system* is first generated methodologically by way of *an objectification of the lifeworld.* Parsons did, to be sure, start from the primacy of action theory, but because he did not carry that through in a radical fashion, the methodologically derivative status of basic systems-theoretical concepts remained in the dark. After the failure of his attempt to make a conceptual transition from the unit act to the context of action, Parsons dispensed with introducing the systems concept via the theory of action. As the placeholder for the missing concept of the lifeworld, the cultural system took on the untenable, ambiguous status of an environment at once superordinate to the action system and internal to it, and was, as it were, stripped of all empirical properties of a system environment.

Parsons rid himself of the difficulties arising from his dualistic view of culturally structured action systems by abruptly ceding basic conceptual primacy to systems theory.

2. The Development of Systems Theory

The shift from the primacy of action theory to that of systems theory was signaled by the fact that Parsons no longer claimed a special status for culture. This was the only instance in which he acknowledged undertaking a revision of great significance for his construction as a whole. We can characterize this break in his theoretical development in terms of three decisions concerning theory construction. Parsons himself was less clear about some of them than others.

First, Parsons conceives of action systems as a special case of living systems, which have to be understood as boundary-maintaining systems and analyzed in systems-theoretical concepts. At the sociocultural stage of development, "action," or meaningfully oriented behavior, makes its appearance as an emergent complex of properties. To define these emergent properties Parsons draws on his action frame of reference. He distinguishes between the actor as an abstract placeholder and the action system; the latter does not act but functions. The relation between actor and action system cannot be assimilated to that between action system and environment. What is constitutive for an action system are the analytical relations among the elements of an action orientation: values, norms, goals, and resources. Luhmann captures this point in a sentence: "Action is a system by virtue of its internal analytical structure."[1] This determines the four references for the detailed analysis of action systems. These systems are composed of subsystems, each of which specializes in producing and maintaining one component of action: culture in values, society in norms, personality in goals, and the behavioral system [organism] in means or resources. "Each of these primary action subsystems is defined on the basis of theoretical abstraction. Concretely, every empirical system is all of them at once; thus, there is no concrete human individual who is not an organism, a personality, a member of a social system, and a participant in a cultural system."[2]

In the concept of an action system, actors disappear as acting subjects; they are abstracted into units to which the decisions and thus the effects of action are attributed. In so far as actions are viewed in terms of their internal analytical structure and conceived of as the outcome of a complex joint operation among the specific subsystems, actors are merely circumscribed by the places they can occupy—in each instance under different aspects—in the four subsystems.

Second, this basic decision leads to the reinterpretation of the cultural system mentioned above. Up to this point Parsons had reserved a kind of extramundane position for culture as the sphere of values and validity. It is now lowered to the same level on which society and personality already had their places as empirical action systems. Supplemented by the organism or behavioral system, these three systems are subordinated as subsystems to *the newly introduced general action system.* Parsons now stresses the difference between cultural objects standing in internal relation to one another and culture as a system of action: "A body of knowledge, though a cultural object, is more specifically a complex of meanings symbolized within a code. A cultural system as a system of action, however, consists not only of cultural objects but, as a system, of all the components of action insofar as they are oriented in terms of cultural objects."[3] The cultural system comes to light when we view action systems from the standpoint of how an actor's decisions are steered by living traditions.

Society, personality, and behavioral system issue from similar abstractions. These subsystems *are* the action system viewed under its different aspects. The four aspects are not, however, merely conventional; they are by no means simply reflections of the theoretician's arbitrary points of view. Because the reference points correspond to the elements of which action itself is made up, the arrangement into subsystems has more than analytical significance. Viewed empirically as well, the subsystems disclosed under the four aspects have a certain independence. Though personalities can no more exist outside of a social milieu than persons and societies can without culture, these subsystems are able, within bounds, to *vary independent of one another.*

It is culture's empirical independence from society that is most characteristic of this revised version.

A cultural system can die out through the extinction of the personalities and societies which are its heirs, but it can also survive its bearers. Culture is not only transmitted from generation to generation through teaching and learning; it can be embodied in externalized symbols, for example, works of art, the printed page, or storage devices such as computer tapes. Though there are differences between hearing Plato philosophize in the Academy of Athens and reading the *Republic,* especially in a language other than classical Greek, there is a sense in which the meaning of the cultural object is the same. Hence persons living in the twentieth century can share with Plato's contemporaries parts of the culture of Athens in the fourth century B.C. This is temporal continuity that no person can approach. Thus, a cultural system can be stable over time and relatively insulated from the effects of its environments, which include not only the physical-organic world but social, psychological, and organic subsystems of action.

This stability enables a cultural system to serve as the prototype of an *autonomous action system*.[4]

From this point on, culture is understood as a system that follows its *own* imperatives of self-maintenance, that itself has to manage with scarce resources, and that interpenetrates other subsystems only in the sense that systems that form environments for one another can overlap and intermesh in border zones.

Third, this revision entails a break, however tacit, with the methodological views that Parsons has characterized as "analytical realism." Officially, he continued into the 1960s to reaffirm the basic proposition that "scientific theory is a body of interrelated generalized propositions about empirical phenomena within a frame of reference."[5] This frame of reference has the status of basic concepts and basic assumptions which are not to be confused with the empirical theories constructed by means of them. (Compare the protophysical framework of classical mechanics.) In this sense the action frame of reference is supposed also to *constitute* the object domain of the social sciences. Parsons did not introduce it as a theoretical model; it was not supposed to represent basic features analytically abstracted from reality itself. Analytical realism insists rather on a graduated ordering of problems that establishes internal, nonempirical relations between categorial frameworks, empirical theories, scientific prognoses and explanations, and facts. This hierarchy does not take us outside the linguistic universe of the scientific community.

Once Parsons identified the action frame of reference with emergent properties that appeared in the evolution of natural systems at the stage of sociocultural forms of life, analytical realism retained rhetorical value only. From that point on the action frame of reference has served to characterize a specific type of boundary-maintaining system. The task of building models to simulate relevant segments of reality falls now to systems theory. Statements about analytical relations between values, norms, goals, and resources get quietly transformed into statements about empirical relations between the elements of a system. *The action unit, reinterpreted in empiricist terms, is formed in interchange processes among its components.* Only under this essentialist presupposition can the organism or behavioral system be smoothly annexed to the triad: person, society, culture. What was once understood as a construction of the scientist, now takes on the connotation of a reconstruction of properties of self-regulating action systems.[6]

If these observations are correct, it is difficult to comprehend how Parsons and many of his disciples can deny this systems-theoretical turn and maintain that there is an unbroken continuity in the development of his thought. In what follows I will argue that this break could remain inconspicuous because Parsons pursued the construction of a systems theory of society only with certain *characteristic reservations*. His *Working Papers in the Theory of Action* (1953) inaugurated a period of transition that came to a close with his response to Dubin's criticism (1960).[7] During these years Parsons constructed his theory of society with the help of basic systems-theoretical concepts. He developed the four-function scheme and the idea of reciprocal interchange relations among four functionally specified subsystems. In the two principal works of this period, *Family, Socialization and Interaction Process* (1955) and *Economy and Society* (1956), he unabashedly drew upon these new theoretical tools for the first time to sketch a theory of personality and socialization in the former work, and a theory of the economy embedded in social systems in the latter. The basic features of his theory of society were set in those works; the theories of communication media and social evolution developed in the 1960s were only supplements to it. In the 1970s, anthropological problems moved into the foreground, motivating Parsons to take up again the previously neglected theme of the general system of action. In this late phase of his work, Parsons drew the metaphysical consequences from the theoretical program he had launched at the start of the 1950s with a *decision concerning theory construction that was inherently ambivalent*.

Since that time Parsons held fast to his aim of converting social theory from the conceptual primacy of action theory to that of systems theory, but under the proviso of retaining the view he had gained from the history of social theory, in which action systems were conceived as embodiments of cultural value patterns. Thus the theoretical developments that set in with the *Working Papers* and extended across more than two-and-one-half decades can be characterized by *three contemporaneous features:* the construction of a systems theory of society, a corresponding assimilation and reinterpretation of the categorial frame of action theory, and a recoupling of functionalism to the culture-theoretical freight that Parsons had carried off from the estates of Durkheim, Freud, and Weber. In what follows, I shall (A) document these tendencies with a few important examples, and then go on to demonstrate the fragility of this theoretical compromise with regard to (B) Parsons' later anthropological philosophy, and especially (C) his theory of communications media.

A.—In the introduction to the first volume of his theory of social evolution,[8] Parsons presents a concept of society that characterizes quite well the theoretical approach developed since 1953. *First,* society is understood as a *system in an environment,* which, through its capacity for self-steering, achieves autarchy or self-sufficiency and can maintain its existence in the long run. "The self-sufficiency of a society is a function of the balanced combination of its controls over its relations with the environment and of its own state of internal integration."[9] A society's stage of development is measured by the degree of autonomy that it can maintain as an integrated whole vis-à-vis its environments. Integration is spoken of here only in the sense of function integration.

Second, Parsons specifies society as an *action system;* it is culture and language, and not value-oriented purposive activity, that furnish the constitutive determinations: "We prefer the term 'action' to 'behavior' because we are interested not in the physical events of behavior for their own sake, but in their patterning, their patterned meaningful products ... human action is cultural in that meanings and intentions concerning acts are formed in terms of symbolic systems."[10] In action systems, transmitted cultural patterns interpenetrate, via the medium of language, with the genetically inherited organic equipment of individual members. Collectivities composed of sociated individuals are the bearers of action systems; they develop their own structures within the limits set by culture and species-specific endowments.

Third, Parsons thus conceives of every action system as a zone of interaction and of reciprocal interpenetration among *four subsystems:* culture, society, personality, and organism. Each of these subsystems is specialized in one basic function of the societal reproduction of action complexes. Action systems can be viewed under precisely four functional aspects: "Within action systems, cultural systems are specialized around the function of pattern-maintenance, social systems around the integration of acting units (human individuals or, more precisely, personalities engaged in roles), personality systems around goal attainment, and the behavioral organism around adaptation."[11]

Since the subsystems possess in turn a relative self-sufficiency—that is, since they are not merely different points of reference—they have contingent relations to one another. The relations between subsystems are, however, prejudiced in a certain way by their belonging to a common action system. While subsystems do form environments for one another, their interchange relations are *regulated.*

Fourth, the mutually attuned, reciprocal performances that subsystems provide for one another can be analyzed as flows of intersystemic interchange. In the border zones of subsystems with a common boundary, such relations condense into new structures; in that case Parsons speaks of "interpenetration."

Fifth, Parsons does not restrict himself to assumptions concerning horizontal relations on the same level, but postulates a *hierarchy of control* that involves an assessment of the four basic functions (see Figure 31).

Parsons explains the right side of Figure 31 as follows: "The upward-

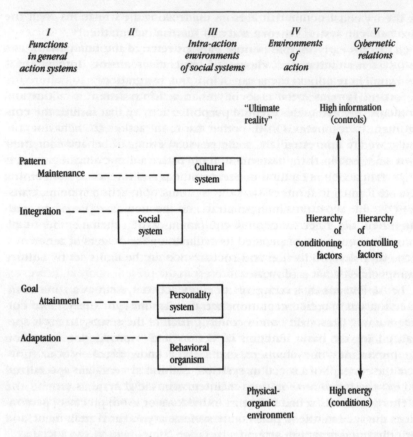

Figure 31. Subsystems of Action

pointed arrow indicates the hierarchy of conditions, which at any given cumulative level in the upward series is, in the common formula, 'necessary but not sufficient'. The downward-pointed arrow designates the hierarchy of controlling factors, in the cybernetic sense. As we move downward, control of more and more necessary conditions makes the implementation of patterns, plans, or programs possible. Systems higher in the order are relatively high in information while those lower down are relatively high in energy."[12]

With the exception of the intersystemic interchange relations (to which I shall return when discussing the theory of steering media), the basic features of Parsons' systems-theoretical concept of society as he understood it in the mid-1960s are represented in Figure 31. However, this snapshot tells us nothing about the theoretical dynamics that led to this static picture. In what follows I shall identify the decisions concerning theory construction that Parsons made along the way to his compromise between systems theory and neo-Kantian culture theory.

(*a*) In his early middle period, Parsons referred the functions of action systems to the two classes of imperatives arising from system-environment relations on the one hand, and from relations to culture on the other. He treated the tasks of "functional integration" as allocation problems, involving the creation, mobilization, and goal-directed employment of resources. On the other hand, the tasks of "social integration" directly concerned the maintenance of solidarities and memberships, and indirectly the transmission of culture and socialization. In our terms, functional integration concerned the material reproduction of the lifeworld, and social integration the reproduction of its symbolic structures. As of 1953 this dichotomous construction is replaced by the scheme of four basic functions—the famous AGIL scheme.[13] The functions of allocation are specified as "adaptation" and "goal attainment"; both cultural reproduction and socialization are hidden under "pattern maintenance." What is of greater interest in the present context, however, is the simultaneous leveling of the once central distinction between functional and social integration; the two are brought together under "integration." This shift *makes unrecognizable* the seams that resulted from joining the two paradigms of "action" and "system." Parsons makes the important—but nowhere explicitly acknowledged—decision to drop the concept of a social integration established via values and norms and to speak from now on only of "integration" in general.

This decision is veiled by the intuitive manner in which Parsons introduces the systems-theoretical concept of society. As previously, he begins with the integrative subsystem as the core component of the social system and describes it in terms of the legitimate order of interpersonal relations.[14] This *societal community* stands first for the diffuse complex of society as a whole; it suggests the features of a lifeworld, all the more since Parsons immediately presents the complementary relations between the societal community on the one hand, and culture and personality on the other.[15] The categories in terms of which 'societal community' is analyzed—'values', 'norms', 'collectivity', 'roles'—first give the impression that this subsystem is, in the manner of a symbolically structured lifeworld, specialized in *social* integration, in integration established via normative consensus.

But this picture changes when Parsons goes on to describe the differentiation of the societal community into four subsystems of the social system along the lines of the four-function scheme.[16]

The function attributed to the societal community, as one of four subsystems (along with the economy, the polity, and cultural reproduction/socialization), now takes the abstract meaning of "integration" in the sense of securing the cohesiveness of a system whose continued existence is threatened by hypercomplex environments and that, under this pressure, has to ward off the permanent danger of falling apart into its individual components. But this tacitly gives precedence to the idea that Parsons earlier connected with the phrase '*functional* integration'. The functional imperatives in which the societal community is now said to be specialized *can* still be fulfilled by way of normative consensus, but in modern societies the areas of "norm-free sociality" have so expanded that the need for integration *has to* be met largely through bypassing the mechanism of reaching understanding.

The societal community is first introduced from a structural viewpoint as the core of society, but the subsystems differentiated out of this diffuse whole are then specified exclusively from a functional perspective. In the course of his *presentation,* Parsons repeats the paradigm shift from an action-theoretically based concept of society to a concept of the social system.

Its subsystems can indeed be *illustrated* by significant institutions, such as the business enterprise (economy), public administration (polity), law (integrative subsystem), church and family (maintenance of cultural patterns), but they cannot be identified with these prototypical institutional orders. Every institution has to *adapt* to changing boundary conditions by drawing on its own resources; every institution has to *select and pursue goals* in order to mediate between external limitations and the value orientation of its members; every institution has to *order* interactions *normatively* via membership conditions; and every one relies upon *legitimation* through recognized values. Because each institution belongs to *all* societal subsystems under its different aspects, none of them is suited to be the defining mark of any *one* of those subsystems. Rather, they have to be distinguished according to their functions.

Parsons defines the functions at a relatively abstract level as adaptation, goal attainment, integration, and positive maintenance. At the level of sociological theory, on which Parsons first *introduces* the functions, they can be *concretely illustrated* by references to the productive performances of the economy, the organizational performances of public administration, the integrative performances of law, and the normalizing performances of tradition and family socialization. The correlation Parsons makes between his four-function scheme and the basic concepts of action theory can also be rendered intuitively comprehensible on this level. The action frame of reference, reified now into the general action system, breaks down into subsystems, each of which is specialized in producing one component of action orientations. The function of the subsystem in question can be read off of these products: values, norms, goals, and resources (see Figure 32). On the level of the general action

Components of action orientations	Subsystems	Funtions
Values	Culture	Pattern maintenance
Norms	Society	Integration
Goals	Personality	Goal attainment
Means, resources	Behavioral system	Adaptation

Figure 32. Functions and Action Orientations

system this correlation appears to be rather arbitrary, or at least in need of further justification; on the level of the social system, and connected with ideas from the history of social theory, it becomes somewhat more plausible (see Figure 33).

Naturally, these illustrations cannot themselves resolve the two problems arising from Parsons' introduction of the four-function scheme. He has to explain why precisely these four functional points of view are necessary and sufficient for analyzing action systems. And he has, further, to reinterpret the basic concepts of action theory in the light of systems theory.

(*b*) Parsons understands social systems theory as a special case of the theory of living systems; thus, though the four-function scheme has to be applicable to social systems and to action systems, it is conceived with a considerably wider range of application in mind. Parsons starts from the formal properties of a system in an environment in order to ground the *universal validity* of the four-function scheme. He begins with the process of system formation itself and differentiates the overall problem of self-maintenance into aspects of space and time. Along the axis internal/external there arises the problem of demarcating the processes and structures that count as belonging to the system from the events and states that the system encounters in the environment. Along the axis

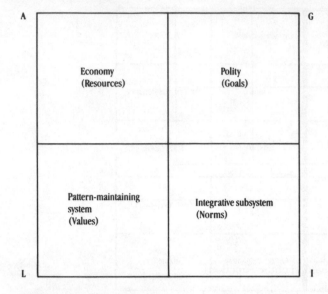

Figure 33. The Social System

present/future—systems have pasts only as properties in the present—there arises the problem of purposively utilizing actually available resources in pursuit of anticipated goals. The combination of both problems yields the desired four functions (see Figure 34).

Parsons defines the problem of boundary maintenance in terms of the differences in complexity between system and environment: "It is assumed that the system of reference is characterized by a pattern of functioning by virtue of which its internal states are at any given time different from those of the environment in significant respects. The direction of these differences is toward greater stability and a higher level of organization than that of the environment in the respects relevant to the system of reference."[17]

Parsons connects the problem of attaining goals with the dimension "instrumental-consummatory," which has its origin in action theory and represents a special interpretation of the temporal axis: "This is a somewhat narrow designation but in the right direction. A pattern does not in the real world actualize itself. The system for which it is a template must meet conditions and utilize environmentally available resources. Meeting conditions and utilization are possible only through processes which are inherently time-extended. Time is *one* aspect of processes which include energy input and utilization, organization or combination of components, and evaluation of stages."[18]

The simultaneous mastery of both problems has to be analyzed in the

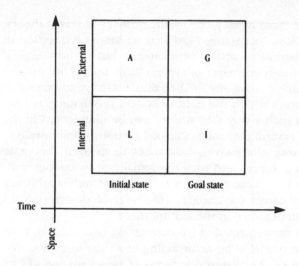

Figure 34. Deduction of the Functions

spatial and temporal dimensions *at once;* this means that a system has to maintain itself in relation to the environment and to itself (external/internal), as well as in the relation of existing initial states to anticipated goal states (instrumental/consummatory). Combining these reference points we get exactly four functional aspects of self-maintenance; they can be ordered in pairs if we distinguish functions according to whether they refer to exchanges with the environment as against to the system itself (adaptation/goal attainment versus pattern maintenance/integration), or to goal-oriented initial states as against the goal states themselves—for which existing states then represent only potentials (adaptation/pattern maintenance versus goal attainment/integration). In this way Parsons arrives at a general justification of the AGIL schema, and one that is *independent* of concepts of society fashioned in action-theoretical terms.

(c) Once the scheme of the four basic functions has been *torn from its roots* in action theory and applied to living systems in general, the analytical components of action must now be conceived in turn as solutions to systemic problems. As pointed out above, Parsons correlates values, norms, goals, and resources each to one of the basic functions. This decision concerning theory construction creates a pressure to *reinterpret* the heretofore central *pattern variables.* Parsons undertakes this revision in the course of his exchange with Dubin. The abstract alternatives for choice were introduced to explain how, from a universalistic point of view, cultural values can be reduced to a finite number of preference patterns. Once Parsons has given up the primacy of action theory, the pattern variables lose that status. Now it is no longer a question of the cultural determination of action orientations, but of how actors' choices issue directly from processes of system formation. If the pattern variables are to be carried along any further, they will have to be useful, at best, as lenses through which the light of system problems gets prismatically refracted in such a way that actions can be illuminated in the reflected splendor of system dynamics. Parsons abruptly eliminates one of the five pairs of basic alternatives,[19] detaches them from the value orientations of acting subjects, and uses the remaining twice-four variables to describe the four basic functions by means of rather arbitrary combinations of alternatives for choice. This level of description no longer has any great significance in the mature theory.

Dubin stylizes this reinterpretation by contrasting two models. "Parsons I" starts from the model of an actor acting in a situation, such that his action orientations can be analyzed in terms of an orientation to (social or nonsocial) objects. The pure types of action orientation (intellectual, expressive, responsive, instrumental) can be characterized, with the help of the pattern variables, by corresponding choice patterns. "Parsons II," by contrast, starts from the most general problems of action systems. These correspond to the four functional aspects under which the basic problem of self-maintenance can be analyzed: "A radical departure from Model I was presented by Parsons when he turned his attention to analyzing the social act from the standpoint of social system problems. Perceiving the need to articulate social action with the requirement of a social system, Parsons started with problems of social structure and attempted to move from there to the level of the individual actor in the system. Parsons' Model I essentially 'looks out' to the social system from the vantage point of the actor; his Model II 'looks down' at the individual actor from the perspective of the social system."[20] System problems get transposed into action orientations via the pattern variables, so the reference point for analysis is no longer the actor's choices but the problem-solving dynamics of a self-stabilizing action system: "The essential difference between these two solutions lies in the units out of which the models are constructed. In Model I the social act is seen as the product of the actor's evaluation of objects and of his orientations towards them—both of which are subjective or social-psychological units. In Model II the social act is viewed as a product of *role definitions peculiar to the four presumably universal social system problems.* Hence the primary analytical unit becomes the system's modalities from which the actor's evaluation of objects and orientations toward them are uniquely derived."[21] Dubin sums up these relations in the schema represented in Figure 35.

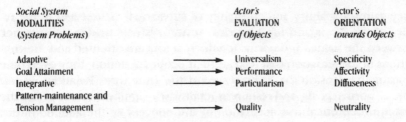

Social System MODALITIES (*System Problems*)		Actor's EVALUATION *of Objects*	Actor's ORIENTATION *towards Objects*
Adaptive	⟶	Universalism	Specificity
Goal Attainment	⟶	Performance	Affectivity
Integrative	⟶	Particularism	Diffuseness
Pattern-maintenance and Tension Management	⟶	Quality	Neutrality

Figure 35. Parsons' Model II of the Social Act

Dubin bases his interpretation on suggestions made by Parsons in *Economy and Society* as he reviewed the results of his collaboration with Robert Bales.[22] In that passage Parsons refers to Chapters III and V of *Working Papers.* But there was no indication in that work that the correlation of dichotomous choices with basic functions could be arrived at through *logical* or *conceptual* analysis. At that time, in 1953, Parsons claimed instead that he had *empirically* established the connection between specific action orientations and each of four system problems—through an interpretation of the results of Bales's research with small groups. In addition, he brought in some vague analogies with the basic assumptions of thermodynamics.

This vacillation shows the arbitrary nature of an interconnection that is indeed central to the subsumption of action theory under the now dominant systems theory, but that can be justified neither logically nor empirically. Parsons' arbitrary correlations cannot even stand the test of simple intuitive reflection. Jeffrey Alexander is right to ask why integration problems could not just as well be resolved by universalistic as by particularistic action orientations, or problems of maintaining cultural patterns by an orientation to performance as well as by an orientation to the intrinsic qualities of one's interaction partner.

(*d*) Parsons' reinterpretation of the concept of cultural values provides a further example of how he melts down basic action-theoretical concepts with the help of systems theory. He interprets the validity of cultural values in the cybernetic terms of control functions attributed to the goal values of self-regulating systems. *Semantic relations* between cultural values are tacitly reinterpreted as *empirical relations* between controlling variables. This shift, however, already exemplifies the tendencies running counter to the eradication of all traces of action theory.

From his critique of utilitarianism, Parsons got the idea of a choice of ends regulated by values and maxims; from Weber he took the idea of value realization. Together, these two ideas lead to the conception that cultural values are related to action systems and connected with sanctions by way of institutionalization and internalization; by these means they gain the stablity and constancy of substantial *Sittlichkeit* in the reality of life-forms and life histories. Action systems bridge the distance between the values and norms to which actors are oriented and the conditions of the situation that restrict their scope for action; they overcome a normative tension that is preserved at the same time. Relations among values, norms, goals, and resources retain their significance even after the systems-theoretical transformation of the concept of the action system. But now that culture has been demoted to the status of one subsystem among others, the differential between the sphere of values and norms claiming validity and the domain of the de facto conditions gets leveled down. To avoid this consequence, Parsons retranslates the tension between the normative and the factual by drawing upon the cybernetic analogies mentioned above. Whereas controlled processes in a physical system require the usual input of energy, the control itself requires a flow of information that consumes relatively little energy. Parsons equates cultural values with governing control-values and views the organic basis of the action system as a source of energy. He then sets up a hierarchy among behavioral system, personality, social system, and culture, such that lower-level systems are superior to higher-level ones as regards energy expended, while higher-level systems are superior to lower-level ones as regards information and steering performances. This linear ordering of the four subsystems on the model of a *hierarchy of control* reserves to the cultural system a sovereign status in matters of steering; at the same time, it remains dependent upon energy inputs from the other subsystems.

With this move Parsons not only paves the way for cultural determinism, but also gives a surprising twist to the use of systems-theoretical models in the construction of social theory: he differentiates between *two categories of environments.*

At the lower end of the hierarchy of control, the action system is bounded by a natural or empirical environment; at the opposite end by a nonempirical environment of a supranatural sort:

Neither the individual personality nor the social system has any direct relation to the physical environment; their relations with the latter are mediated entirely through the organism, which is action's primary link with the physical world. This, after all, is now a commonplace of modern perceptual and epistemological theory ... In essentially the same sense, neither personalities nor social systems have direct contact with the ultimate objects of reference, with the 'ultimate reality' which poses 'problems of meaning' in the sense sociologists associate above all with the works of Max Weber. The objects that personalities and social systems know and otherwise directly experience are in our terminoogy cultural objects, which are human artifacts in much the same sense as are the objects of empirical cognition. Hence, the relations of personalities and social systems with ultimate 'non-empirical reality' are in a basic sense mediated through the cultural system.[23]

Through this singular combination of the cybernetic concept of a control hierarchy with the idea of value realization, Parsons translates the idea of the transcendence of values and validity claims into the empiricist conceptual apparatus of systems theory; the structure that results is not, however, free of cracks. In the early middle period the intuition concerning value realization was taken into account by assigning a special status to culture; now, a culture incorporated into the action system is supposed to draw its steering power from contact with a "non-empirical environment." But this latter concept is foreign to systems theory, which conceives of *self*-regulated system maintenance in such a way that the boundary of the system is threatened in basically *the same way* on *all* fronts, and has *everywhere* to be defended against invasions from hypercomplex environments. Processes of system maintenance are controlled exclusively by values intrinsic to the system itself; *outside* of the system's boundaries there are only conditioning—not steering—variables.

Parsons is aware that his system concept diverges from the usual one in this crucial respect: "Of course, directionality may be conceived as internal to the system of reference. However, at the action level what is more prevalant are attempts to legitimate selections among alternative paths by invoking some source of authority outside the system of action as currently conceived by the acting units."[24] But he makes no effort to show how the model of self-regulating systems can be fitted to the needs of a culture theory of entirely different provenance, and in such a way that the systems paradigm remains unaltered in the process.

(e) With the introduction of a hierarchy of control, the four basic functions lose their equality of rank. The axis along which the functions are located one after the other has, above and beyond its temporal significance, a hierarchical meaning. The idea of value realization gets sublimated into an abstract rank-ordering that guarantees a priori that the functionally specified subsystems cannot act upon one another in just any way, but only in the LIGA direction of cultural determinism. This bias is inconspicuously built into the technique of cross-tabulation. The latent sense of this formalism is that the aspect of the validity of symbolic expressions gets reinterpreted in empiricist terms,[25] while at the same time value change gets immunized against materialist assumptions.[26] We can see how the technique of cross-tabulation secures the concealed idealism of Parsonian systems functionalism by looking, for example, at how the cultural system itself gets divided up. Parsons had first followed Weber's tripartite division into cognitive patterns of interpretation, moral-practical patterns of value, and aesthetic-expressive patterns of expression. Now his formalism requires a fourfold division. The fourth square is earmarked for constitutive symbolism—read "religion"—even though in the modern age science and technology, law and morality, and autonomous art have been differentiated out of the context of religious-metaphysical traditions and therefore do not stand on the same level— either structurally or historically—as religious symbolism.

In Parsons' "late philosophy," the secret hidden in the formalism of his cross-tabulation is fully disclosed: the general action system is subordinated to the reified transcendence of a "telic system."[27] It becomes clear here what Parsons had slipped into the theory of society with his hierarchy of control.

B.—When the general action system, encompassing culture, society, personality, and behavioral system, is viewed in turn as only one of four subsystems and correlated in its entirety with the I (integration) function, it becomes necessary to construct a system of the most comprehensive aspects of human existence, to which Parsons gives the name "the human condition." With the L function is correlated a so-called *telic system,* which is connected to the action system at its highest pole and thus occupies the place of a supraempirical environment. It is instructive to note the construction problem that arises symmetrically, as it were, at the lower pole of the action system.

Parsons had originally thought of the lowest subsystem of action in the hierarchy of control as the organic bearer of personality, as the human organism. But this can hardly be added to the action system, especially as regards its genetically fixed, species-specific equipment. Thus Parsons subsequently adopted a suggestion by Charles and Victor Lidz and gave priority to a psychological interpretation of the behavioral system.[28] In relation to the personality, which Parsons still understands in terms of the psychoanalytic tradition, the behavioral system no longer encompasses the natural substratum of the person; rather, it comprises the general competences of knowing, speaking, and acting as understood in a Piagetian sense. Then, however, the human organism occupies the position of an environment of the action system; through the behavioral system, the action system borders on organic nature.

By the same logic, the cultural system is conceived so narrowly that everything that hitherto had the connotation of a highest level of control or, in the theological language of Paul Tillich, of an "ultimate reality" is now put in the position of an environment of the action system. Through its cultural subsystem, the action system borders on a transcendent realm reified into the "telic system." As Parsons puts it: "Clearly, we think of the telic system, standing as it does in our treatment in a relation of

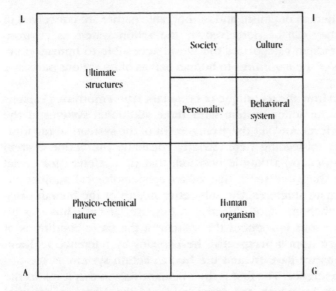

Figure 36. The Human Condition

cybernetic superordination to the action system, as having to do especially with religion. It is primarily in the religious context that throughout so much of cultural history belief in some kind of 'reality' of the non-
empirical world has figured prominently."[29]

This speculative step lands Parsons in his *late philosophy*. He rounds
off the action system with three additional subsystems (see Figure 36).

Looked at methodologically, the system of the basic conditions of human existence has a status different from all the other systems with
which social theory or the individual social sciences are concerned. To
begin with, the telic system, traditionally regarded as the domain of religious belief, cannot be introduced as an object domain of science as the
other systems can—unless it be as an object domain of social science;
but then religion would have to take its place within the framework of
the cultural system. Parsons insists that any talk of a telic system *presupposes* belief in a sphere of ultimate reality. (This strategy is not at all
unlike that with which the late Schelling, who took the experience of
God's existence as his basic point of departure, introduced his "positive"
philosophy.) In Parsons' words: "With full recognition of the philosophical difficulties of defining the nature of that reality we wish to affirm our
sharing the age-old belief in its existence."[30] Another reason this system
of the human condition has a unique status is that it has to be interpreted
in epistemological terms; it represents the world as a whole from the
perspective of the action system. Not only the religious sphere, but the

spheres of the human organism and of inorganic nature are conceived in the way that they can be perceived by the action system as environments: "the paradigm categorizes the world accessible to human experience in terms of the *meanings* to human beings of its various parts and aspects.[31]

We have seen how the technique of cross-tabulation motivates Parsons to supplement the action system with three additional systems at the same analytical level. And yet the arrangement of the systems in the four-field scheme is misleading here. Strictly speaking, the action system would have to occupy a double position: that of a referent for social theory and, at the same time, that of an epistemological subject *for* which the ultimate stuctures, the subjective nature of the human organism, and the phenomena of objective nature are "given." Thus it is no accident that Parsons introduces the system of the basic conditions of human existence from a perspective he explains by reference to Kant: "For two reasons we have treated the human action system as the primary point of reference. The first is the mundane reason that it marks the intellectual path by which the formulation of the larger conceptual scheme has been reached. There is something to be said, as investigative policy, for proceeding from the relatively well known to the unknown rather than vice versa. The second reason, however, is that ... we conceive the human condition as a version of whatever universe may in some sense be knowable and which is quite specifically and self-consciously formulated and organized *from the perspective of its significance to human beings* and indeed relatively contemporary ones. From this point of view it is the system of action that constitutes the necessary reference base for such an enterprise."[32]

Parsons takes the general action system, which was hitherto the subject of his systems theory of society, as the *point of departure* for a *reflexive* examination of the system of the human condition. With this move, however, *the theoretician gives up any standpoint independent of that subsystem—he cannot break out of the perspective of the action system*. At all the other systemic levels social theory can approach its objects *intentione recta;* at the anthropological level theory becomes self-referential. For this self-referencial theory of society Parsons has in mind the model of Kant's critique of knowledge: "We have already maintained that human 'orientation' to the world takes the form of treating the world, including that of action itself, as composed of entities that have symbolically apprehendable *meaning* to human actors. We therefore think it appropriate to call these entities 'objects' and to speak of a subject-object relationship ... We think it legitimate to adopt the Kantian account of *knowing* as the prototype of a mode of relation between human actors and worlds outside the action system as well as objects within it."[33] It is interesting to note that Parsons does not consistently hold to this approach. He mixes his *quasi-transcendental* account of the human condition with an *objectivistic* account forced upon him by his systems-theoretical approach.

In the transcendental interpretation,[34] the telic system sets the universal and necessary conditions under which the action system can relate to external nature, to internal nature, and to itself; in this regard, it determines the "transcendental orders" under which objective nature, subjective nature, and the action system stand *for* the action system itself: "The general proposition is that for each of the modes of human orientation there is a *meta*-level that is concerned with 'conditions' or 'assumptions' that are necessary in order for an orientation to be meaningful, to 'make sense.'"[35] The function Parsons attributes to the ultimate structures is similar to that Weber ascribed to religious-metaphysical worldviews insofar as, like Weber, he infers abstract attitudes toward the world from worldviews. On this account, only certain attitudes toward the world make possible the decentered understanding of the world that developed in the modern age; it is with this understanding of the world that Parsons' version of "the human condition" is connected.[36]

Parsons makes cursory reference to Kant's three critiques; he understands them as attempts to reconstruct the transcendental conditions for the objectivation of external nature (from cognitive-instrumental points of view), for the constitution of contexts of action (from moral-practical points of view), and for nonobjectivating dealings with one's own internal nature (from aesthetic points of view).[37]

From this perspective, religion emerges as the more or less hybrid result of objectifying transcendental achievements in establishing order; the latter are reified into something transcendent, in the sense of the existence of a divine being. One might also interpret Kant's "religion within the bounds of reason alone" in this way. But Parsons does not rest satisfied with this: "There is according to our paradigm a fourth sphere of transcendental ordering to which Kant did not devote a special critique. We think it has particularly to do with religion. It seems possible that Kant, as a good child of the Enlightenment, was sufficiently skeptical in this sphere so that he did not venture to say anything positive but rested content with stating his famous denial of the *probability* of the existence of God. There is, however, a logical gap here that demands to be filled."[38]

Parsons' filling of this gap is a result not only of his religious needs and experiences, but, as he rightly notes, of the demands of his system construction as well. It is not only that there is a fourth cell here to be occupied; his systems-theoretical approach itself blocks any transcendental account of the human condition; it requires an objectivistic under-

standing. *The system of ordering accomplishments* has to be reinterpreted into *a system of highest controlling values* or of ultimate
structures in such a way that, as a world of supraempirical entities, it can
interact with the other worlds, that is, the physicochemical, organic, and
sociocultural worlds. This way of viewing the matter leads to specu-
lations I do not wish to take up here. As with Comte and the Saint-
·Simonians, Parsons' theoretical development lands him in the attempt to
create a social-theoretical substitute for the socially integrating functions
of a religion whose very substance was being snapped.[39]

Another aspect of Parsons' late philosophy is more instructive. In our
analysis, his theory of society is based on an ambiguous assimilation of
action theory to systems theory. It has the shape of a theoretical compromise between two competing conceptual frames, a compromise that
covers over but does not resolve the conflict. After the construction of
his systems theory had been completed, this repressed conflict broke out
again when Parsons turned once more to the problems of the general
action system that had issued from a reification of the action frame of
reference developed in *The Structure of Social Action.* At the end of his
complex intellectual development, Parsons found himself face to face
with the resulting problems.

With the transcendental status of the ultimate structures, an action-
theoretical meaning gets mixed into the system of the basic conditions
of human existence: the action system is represented as a subject that
takes up relations to external nature, to internal nature, and to itself
under determinate transcendental conditions. In keeping with his monological concept of action, Parsons looks to the epistemological model
of the *knowing* subject à la Kant. This model penetrated social theory at
the time of Georg Simmel and Max Adler; in the neo-Kantian and phenomenological variants of *verstehenden* sociology going back to Rickert
and Husserl, it has been a source of confusion. The communications-
theoretical model of speaking and acting subjects is better suited for
laying the foundations of social theory than is the epistemological model.
For this reason, it is worth our effort to try and decode the transcendental version of Parsons' late philosophy in terms of the model of communicative action. This will lead to the discovery that behind the system of
the basic conditions of human existence, behind the four subsystems of
the "human condition," can be found the structures of the lifeworld complementary to communicative action—in a somewhat irritating version,
to be sure.

If we understand "the human condition" as the analytical level on
which actions coordinated through reaching understanding are to be located, then the upper left square (ultimate structures) contains the general structures of world understanding that determine how participants

can relate to something in a world with their communicative expressions. The lower left square (physicochemical nature) represents the objective world of possible relations of this sort, the lower right square (human organism) the subjective world, and the upper right square (society, culture, personality, behavioral system) the social world. Parsons himself speaks of "worlds" here, of the physical world, the world of the human organism, and the world of interpersonal relations. In this version the telic system represents the reference system on which communicatively acting subjects base their processes of reaching understanding, whereas each of the three remaining subsystems represents the totality of that about which mutual understanding is possible insofar as communicative actors relate exclusively to something in the objective, the subjective, or the social world. On this reading, the four-field schema introduced under the title "the human condition" might be viewed as a variation on the scheme of world relations of communicative acts depicted in Figure 20. What we then find vexing is the fact that Parsons introduces the system of the basic conditions of human existence *intentione recta* by way of supplementing the action system with three additional subsystems. Allowing for this objectivating perspective, the action system would have to coincide with the lifeworld, which, with its components—culture, society, and person—provides the *background* and the *resources* for communicative action. Then the other three subsystems, as well as the lifeworld itself, could be conceived as *regions* that play their part in the generation of communicative actions, *but not in the same direct way* as the components of the lifeworld.

In discussing the interdependence of the lifeworld and communicative action, we have made clear what it means to say that the components of the lifeworld are "directly" involved in the production and communicative interweaving of interactions. Communicative action not only depends upon cultural knowledge, legitimate orders, and competences developed through socialization; it not only feeds off of the resources of the lifeworld; it is itself the medium through which the symbolic structures of the lifeworld are reproduced. *But this is not true of the material substratum of the lifeworld*—neither the physical nor the chemical components of the external nature with which society is connected via the metabolic processes of the human organism, nor the genetic makeup of the human organism with which society is connected via processes of sexual reproduction. Of course, social processes intervene in organic nature as well as in processes of distributing human genetic potentials. But unlike the lifeworld, nature does not need the medium of communicative action for its own reproduction; human action merely reacts back upon it.

In this *second version,* the two lower squares represent regions upon which communicative action is dependent "indirectly," that is, via the material substratum of the lifeworld. Organic and inorganic nature figure here in their functional connection with the material reproduction of the lifeworld and not as object domains of possible knowledge or as reference domains of communicative action.

The telic system is supposed to occupy an analogous position. Parsons conceives of it as a region that *indirectly* influences communicative action via the symbolic reproduction of the lifeworld. He is evidently postulating *a supernatural counterpart to physicochemical nature and to the genetic nature of the human species.* The ultimate structures supposedly enjoy the same autarchy, the same independence from the structures of the lifeworld as inorganic and organic nature. But there are no indicators accessible to social-theoretical analysis for a transcendence that is *independent* in this way from the communicative practice of human beings, from their sacrifices, entreaties, prayers, no indicators for a god who, to borrow an image from Jewish mysticism, does not himself have to be redeemed through the efforts of human beings. Thus the autarchic position that the telic system is supposed to occupy in the second version is due to an *unjustified reduplication of the cultural components of the action system,* which takes the place of the lifeworld in Parsons' scheme. Only the first version, in which the transcendental perspective is transferred from the subject-object model of knowledge to intersubjective understanding between speaking and acting subjects, can give the ultimate structures and their ordering accomplishments a theoretically defensible meaning that can be cashed in empirically.

C.—It is not only the paradoxes arising from the constraints placed on construction by the technique of cross-tabulation that show the fragility of Parsons' conceptual compromise between action theory and systems theory. The pressure to reduce the forms of social integration, which are established through consensus in the last analysis, to instances of system integration is no less problematic. Parsons has to *reduce* the structures of linguistically generated intersubjectivity, on which both culture as a shared possession and norms as socially valid are based, to mechanisms such as exchange and organization, which secure the cohesiveness of a system over the heads of the actors involved. The most striking example of this sort of reduction is Parsons' notion of intersystemic interchange relations and his introduction of media of communication to regulate them. With these two moves, the systems-theoretical act of reformulation penetrates the inner regions of the theory of communicative action. Parsons hopes thereby to base the integrative accomplishments of linguistic communication itself on interchange mechanisms that undercut the structures of linguistic intersubjectivity and thereby to abolish, once and for all, the distinction between social integration and system integration.

In his autobiographical reflections on the development of his thought,[40] Parsons described the problem situation that gave rise to his media theory. The "interchange paradigm" first set out in 1956 represents the complex exchange relations among the four societal subsystems as mediated through six "markets." It emerged from an attempt to integrate into the theory of society the methodologically most advanced area of social science, namely, economics.[41] The aim was to show that the economic system represented one of several functionally specialized subsystems of society.

Neoclassical economic theory had conceived of the economy as a system, with porous boundaries, that exchanges input from its environments against its own output. It had preferred to concentrate on the case of exchange between private households and private firms, and had analyzed the relations between capital and labor from the point of view of a systemic exchange between real units of labor power and consumer goods, on the one hand, and corresponding monetary units of wages and private expenditures, on the other. As a social theorist rather than an economist, Parsons was interested not so much in the internal dynamics of the economic system as in the relations of the economy to the other social subsystems; he wanted to explain the noneconomic parameters of the economic process. This gave rise to two problems: first, what is the conceptual status of money as a medium that steers intersystemic exchanges between real units such as, for example, labor power and consumer goods? And second, do the *other* social subsystems regulate exchanges with their environments via *similar* media? "The major problem has been, whether the same principle ... could be generalized beyond the case of money to that of other media."[42]

Parsons wrestled with the latter problem in the 1960s. In 1963 he published an essay on the concept of power in which he attempted to conceive of *power* as a steering medium anchored in the political system and exhibiting structural analogies to money.[43] He saw this as a successful test of the generalizability of the concept of a medium. His work on the concept of *influence* appeared in the same year and was followed a few years later by his analysis of the concept of *value commitment.*[44]

Thus, in the sequence of money, power, influence, and value commitment, Parsons analyzed the basic features of four media, each of which was correlated with one social subsystem: money with the economic system, power with the political, influence with the system of social integration, and value commitment with that of maintaining structural patterns. *This first round of generalizing the concept of a medium,* which extended to the level of the social system, was followed by a second

round. Parsons introduced four *additional* media (intelligence, performance capacity, affect, and interpretation) for the level of the action system
in general, as composed of the behavioral system, personality, society,
and culture.[45] Systemic considerations require that four additional media
each be specified for the behavioral system, person, and culture, at the
same level of generality as money, power, influence, and value commitment. This rounding off is still underway.[46]

Looking closely at this path of generalizing the media concept from
money to value commitment, from societal media to media of the action
system in general, and from here to media at the levels of the behavioral
system, person and culture, we see that the structural analogies to the
money medium become increasingly unclear and the conceptual specifications increasingly abstract and imprecise—in the end, merely metaphorical. This is true above all for the media that Parsons eventually correlated with the subsystems of the all-encompassing system of the human
condition (transcendental order, symbolic meaning, health, empirical order).[47] It could be that these speculative features have a trivial source,
namely, that we are dealing with work in progress. It would be less trivial
if they were due to the overgeneralization of a model that cannot bear
the weight of the entire construction. With this in mind, I shall take up
the question that Parsons himself posed early in the 1960s: can the same
principles be generalized beyond the case of money?

In doing so I shall limit myself to what I called the "first round" of
generalization. Is the temporal sequence in which Parsons adopted and
analyzed the concept of media at the level of the social system a matter
of chance, or does it reflect a substantive problematic? Naturally, the fact
that economics had already analyzed money as a medium regulating the
optimal use of scarce resources offered a heuristic opportunity of which
Parsons took advantage. But this fact itself is worthy of note; it shows
that with the emergence of the capitalist mode of production the economy was the first functionally specified subsystem to be differentiated
out. Money was the first medium to be institutionalized. Thus one might
surmise that Parsons worked up the steering media in the order of their
historical appearance and according to the degree to which they were
institutionally established. Then there would be a good reason for the
increasing imprecision of the media concept. On this reading, the structural qualities of a medium appear *in recognizable form* only to the
extent that they get normatively anchored and make it possible for a
societal subsystem to be differentiated out. In other words, social evolution must itself satisfy necessary conditions if the systemic interconnections of media are to be recognized and worked out. This conjecture
provides no grounds for criticizing Parsons' bold strategy of generalizing;
one might even level the contrary criticism at him, namely, that he did

not proceed boldly enough, that is, sufficiently deductively. For if money is only one of sixty-four media important for social theory, then we cannot know which of its structural features are characteristic of media as such.[48]

However, the increasing imprecision of the media concepts, the order in which Parsons dealt with them, and the incompleteness of his systematic treatment of them might also be explicable in another way: the concept of a medium can only be used in certain domains of action, because the structure of action permits a media-steered formation of subsystems *only for certain functions*—for example, for that of adaptation, but not for that of cultural reproduction. If this conjecture is correct, the attempt to generalize the case of the money medium to society and the action system, even to the system of the human condition, is open to the objection of overgeneralization. The problem would not be the incompleteness of the system of media, but the claim that there is any such *system of steering media* at all. I will now suggest a few arguments in favor of this charge of overgeneralization.

The exchanges between system and environment and the exchanges among functionally specified units within a system—be it an organism or a society—have to take place by way of some medium or other. It seems obvious that communication in language is such a medium, and that special "languages" such as money and power derive their structures from it. At the same time, mutual understanding in language is such an important mechanism for coordinating action that where action theory has methodological primacy, it can elucidate the concept of action only in connection with that of language.

Parsons first used the concept of language in a sense taken from cultural anthropology: language as a medium that makes intersubjectivity possible and carries the value consensus important for normative order. He used the model of language to explain what it meant for actors to *share* value orientations. The communicative sharing of identical meanings, the consensus of a linguistic community, served him as a model for the common possession of cultural values and for the collective obligation to a normative order. "The concept of a shared basis of normative order is basically the same as that of a common culture or a symbolic system. The prototype of such an order is language."[49] But when Parsons faced the task of representing steering media such as money and power as specializations of linguistic communication, the culturistic concept of language proved unsatisfactory for two reasons. On the one hand, we are no longer dealing here with that peculiar kind of commonality represented by the intersubjectivity of mutual understanding in language, but with structural analogies between language and media such as money and power. Parsons finds these analogies in the structure of code and message. On the other hand, after the turn toward systems theory, it was difficult to avoid the previously neglected question of the systematic place of linguistic communication.

Language seemed at first to belong to the cultural system. Parsons understood it as the medium through which traditions were reproduced. To be sure, the ideas of institutionalization and internalization—those mechanisms of systemic intermeshing that anchor cultural patterns in the social and personality systems—had already suggested the question of whether language is central *to the action system in general* and has to be analyzed at the *same* level as the concept of action. The theory of steering media made this question unavoidable. Victor Lidz addressed the following programmatical remarks to this problem:

> Language has often been discussed as a prototypical instance of the media. Indeed, it has stood second only to money in being treated as a prototypical medium. Yet, no convincing analysis has been put forward of the precise functional location within action systems that should be attributed to language. It has remained something of a "free floating" medium, therefore, and the value of holding it up as a prototypical medium has perhaps been considerably reduced on that account. Here, a functional location for language will be proposed, and it will be maintained, moreover, that this functional location makes clear why language should be given high theoretical priority as a model for the treatment of other media. Language will be discussed as comprising the core of the generalized mechanism of the whole system of action. It stands "over" the media which have been treated as specialized about regulation of the combinatorial and interchange processes of each of the four primary subsystems of action. Thus it provides the basis in common meaning by which the processes generated by the respective action subsystem media may be coordinated with one another.[50]

There are, of course, two opposed strategies for dealing with this task. On the one hand, we can, as Lidz does, carry out the analysis of language at the level of a theory of communication. In this case we can link up with general linguistics and with the philosophy of language, as well as with sociological action theories that analyze interpretation and mutual understanding as mechanisms for coordinating action. This is no longer possible if, on the other hand, one cuts beneath the level of language theory and action theory, pursues a systems-theoretical strategy, and brings the mechanism of linguistic understanding into social theory only from the functionalist perspective of system formation. In that case, the features of communicative action captured by reconstructive analysis—features characterizing a specific emergent level of social evolution—are replaced by elements in which the abstract determinations of general processes of system formation are merely reduplicated.

This is the strategy Luhmann is following when he writes that "the emergent orders must themselves constitute the elements they connect (though in the process they tie into the prior performances of lower orders and build upon them) . . . One would not then construct a theory of the action system . . . from an analysis of action to which general systems-theoretical viewpoints were attached; one would start with general systems-theoretical considerations concerning theory construction, and *infer* from them how systems constitute actions on the emergent level in question."[51] Among the disciples of Parsons, R. C. Baum has adopted this option and attempted to derive the four basic functions from basic processes of reducing and enhancing complexity, in order then to characterize the linguistic level of communication by means of a four-function scheme of meaning production.[52] In relating language, via the four-function scheme, to general processes of system formation, thereby leaping over the *internally accessible* structures of communication in language, Baum makes a highly problematic prior decision at the analytical level. Because linguistic communication and, consequently, mutual understanding as a mechanism for coordinating action come into view *only under aspects of steering,* systems theorists proceed on the assumption that any steering medium whatever can be differentiated out of language. They do not so much as consider the *possibility* that the structure of language might itself set limits to this process.

In opposition to that strategy, I will show that the only functional domains that can be differentiated out of the lifeworld by steering media are those of material reproduction. The symbolic structures of the lifeworld can be reproduced only via the basic medium of communicative action; action systems keyed to cultural reproduction, social integration, and socialization remain tied to the structures of the lifeworld and of ordinary language.

In what follows, I shall (*a*) take another look at the concept of a steering medium introduced above, and then show (*b*) how Parsons elucidates this concept and (*c*) what difficulties arise when it is extended to power relations or (*d*) to the other spheres of the social system in general. These reflections will lead us back to (*e*) the distinction suggested above between generalized forms of communication and steering media.

(*a*) The money medium replaces linguistic communication in certain situations and in certain respects; this substitution decreases both the expenditure of intepretive energy and the risk of a breakdown in mutual understanding. I will now compare this paradigm case of media-steered interaction with a case of communicative action in order to identify more precisely what substitutions are involved.

Commands normally appear in the course of the communicative (though not always explicitly linguistic) practice of everyday life. The elementary unit in question consists of an utterance by ego and a response by alter. Under its communicative aspect, their interaction can be described as a process of coming to an understanding; with respect to the interaction problem they have to solve, mutual understanding serves to coordinate the goal-directed actions of the two actors. When ego issues a command to alter and alter accepts it, the two reach an understanding regarding how to bring about something in the world and thereby coordinate their actions. Their communication serves both to inform and to coordinate action. The latter takes place when alter says "yes" to the validity claim ego raises with his utterance, that is, when alter responds affirmatively. Parsons pointed out the double contingency of actors' decisions. It is present in communicative action because each participant can raise (or refrain from raising) claims that are criticizable in principle, and can accept (or reject) such claims; he makes his decisions on the presupposition that the same is true for the other participants. *The doubly contingent process of reaching understanding* rests on the interpretive accomplishments of actors who—so long as they are not oriented egocentrically to their own success but to mutual understanding, and so long as they want to achieve their goals by way of communicative agreement—must endeavor to arrive at a common definition of a situation. It might be well to remind ourselves here that actions can be coordinated via consensus formation in language only if every communicative practice is embedded in a lifeworld context defined by cultural traditions, institutional orders, and competences. Actors' interpretive performances feed on these lifeworld resources.

The rationality potential of achieving understanding in language must be actualized to the extent that the shared lifeworld context in which communicative action is embedded loses its quasi naturalness. With this, the need for reaching understanding, the expenditure of interpretive energy, and the risk of disagreement are all increased. However, these demands and dangers can be reduced through media that replace mutual understanding in language as a mechanism of coordination in certain well-defined contexts. "Instead of negotiating to consensus ad idem on all four elements of action ... men rely on symbols 'promising' the experience of meaning as a statistical probability over many acts. They are free from the efforts to negotiate basics all the time."[53] Such media serve not only to reduce the expenditure of interpretive energy but also to overcome the risk of action sequences falling apart. Media such as money

or power can largely spare us the costs of dissensus because they uncouple the coordination of action from consensus formation in language
and neutralize it against the alternatives of achieved versus failed agreement.

In this regard, steering media may not be understood as a functional
specification of language; rather, they are a substitute for special functions of language. Language serves as a model for such media in other
respects as well. Media simulate some of its features—for example, the
symbolic embodiment of semantic contents or the structure of raising
and redeeming claims—while others are not reproduced—above all, the
internal structure of mutual understanding which terminates in the recognition of criticizable validity claims and is embedded in a lifeworld
context. The transfer of action coordination from ordinary language to
steering media has the effect of uncoupling interaction from lifeworld
contexts.

In this connection Luhmann speaks of a "technizing of the lifeworld";
by this he means "relieving the interpretation processes of experience
and action from having to take up, formulate, and communicatively explicate all meaning relations that are implied [in the lifeworld context of
communicative action—J.H.]."[54] Media-steered interactions can be spatially and temporally interconnected in increasingly complex webs, without it being necessary for anyone to survey and stand accountable for
these communicative networks—even if only in the manner of collectively shared background knowledge. If responsibility means that one
can orient one's actions to criticizable validity claims, then action coordination that has been detached from communicatively achieved consensus no longer requires responsible participants. This is one side of the
matter. The other side is that relieving interaction from yes/no positions
on criticizable validity claims—which actors themselves have to defend
and for which they hold one another accountable—also enhances the
degrees of freedom of action oriented to success. "Encoding and symbolizing unburden consciousness and thus enhance the capacity to orient oneself to contingencies."[55] This is what Weber had in mind when he
understood the rise of the capitalist economy and the modern state administration—that is, of subsystems that, according to Parsons, could be
differentiated out only via the media of money and power—as an institutionalization of purposive rational action.

Starting from the level of action theory, I shall now consider the
question of what a steering medium must look like if the conversion of
communicative action over to media-steered interaction is to "technicize" the lifeworld in the sense that the expenditure and risk of consensus-forming processes are obviated while the prospects for purposive-
rational action are enhanced.

(*b*) Parsons develops this concept from the example of the money medium. He stresses four sets of features.

Structural features. Money has the properties of a code by means of which information can be transmitted from a sender to a receiver. The monetary medium makes it possible to produce and transmit messages with a built-in preference structure. They can inform the receiver about an offer and induce him to accept it. But since this acceptance is not to rest on an affirmative response to a criticizable validity claim, but is supposed to issue from an automatic process independent of processes of consensus building, the media code is good only

· for a narrowly circumscribed class of standard situations,
· which is defined by clear interest positions, such that
· the action orientations of those involved can be covered by a generalized value,
· alter can basically choose one of two alternative responses,
· ego can steer alter's responses through offers, and
· the actors are oriented only to the consequences of actions, that is, they have the freedom to make their decisions depend only on calculating the success of their actions.

In the exemplary case of money, the *standard situation* is defined by the process of exchanging goods. The parties to the exchange are pursuing economic *interests* in that they seek to optimize the relation of expenditure to payoff in utilizing scarce resources for alternative ends. Utility is the *generalized value* in question; the modifier 'generalized' means here that this value binds every actor taking part in monetary exchanges, everywhere and at all times, and in the same way. The money code *schematizes* alter's possible responses in such a way that he either accepts ego's offer to exchange or rejects it, and thus either acquires a possession or does without it. Under these conditions, the parties to the exchange can reciprocally condition their responses through their offers without having to rely on the willingness to cooperate presupposed by communicative action. Instead, what is expected of the actors is an objectivating attitude toward the action situation and a rational orientation to action consequences. *Profitability* serves as the measure by which success is calculated.

Through this switchover to media-steered interactions, the actors gain new degrees of freedom.[56]

Qualitative properties. It is not on the basis of a suitable media code alone that a medium is able to fulfill its two functions; the medium must itself exhibit certain properties. It must be such

· that it can be measured,
· that it can be alienated in whatever amounts, and
· that it can be stored.

These conditions are trivially entailed by the requirements that in media-steered interaction, ego must be able to affect the decisions of alter *in a purposive-rational manner,* and that the medium itself is the only permissible means of influence and the measure of its success. Parsons' formulation is that the medium is at once the "measure and store of value." Whereas a linguistic utterance gets a measurable information value only in relation to the context-dependent state of information of the sender and the receiver, media have to embody measurable amounts of value to which all participants can relate as something objective, independent of particular contexts. And whereas the semantic content of a linguistic utterance cannot be *exclusively* appropriated by individual actors (except when exclusivity is established by means of special barriers to communication), steering media have to incorporate amounts of value that can be taken into exclusive possession in variable quantities, that can pass from hand to hand—in short, that can *circulate.* Finally, the amounts of value embodied in media must be *depositable* in banks, must allow for the creation of credit, must be *capable of being invested* in accord with the entrepreneurial model proposed by Schumpeter—another property that is lacking in language. In a monetarized economic system there are basically four options; money can be hoarded or spent, saved or invested.

The structure of claim and redemption. The phenomenon of "banking" takes us to another aspect. Money is neither a commodity nor a production factor; though it symbolizes amounts of value, as a medium it has no intrinsic value. In this respect it is not unlike the medium of language. We express knowledge in communicative utterances, but the symbolic expressions are not themselves this knowledge. Now the monetary medium is supposed to replace language not only as a carrier of information but above all for purposes of achieving coordination. In communicative action this is achieved through ego raising a criticizable validity claim with his utterance and motivating alter to accept it. For this task there are no other means at ego's disposal than the *reasons* with which he could try, if necessary, to redeem the validity claim, so as to move alter to an affirmative response. In the ideal-typical case, acts of reaching understanding owe their power to coordinate action to criticizable validity claims that can be redeemed through reasons and that carry a consensus when they are intersubjectively recognized. The *real value* of reaching understanding consists therefore in a communicatively produced agreement that is measured against validity claims and is *backed* by potential reasons (reasons that could be set out if necessary).

The money medium mirrors this structure of claim and redemption. The nominal claims set by the code and issued in exchange values can be redeemed in real use values; they are backed by reserves of a particular kind, namely, money or drawing rights on the world bank. Of course, there are unmistakable differences as well. The real values, or "intrinsic satisfiers," are in the one case reasons that develop a capacity to *motivate rationally* on the basis of internal relations, and in the other case physical components of the action system, or "real things," that have the capacity to *motivate empirically* with a view to opportunities for need satisfaction. Moreover, language is a medium that needs no additional certification, because communicative actors always already find themselves involved in ordinary language and have no alternative to it, whereas money is a medium that does not arouse adequate "confidence in the system" merely by virtue of its functioning but needs to be *institutionally* anchored. This takes place via the basic institutions of civil law (property and contract).

This point is of great significance. We cannot mistrust our mother tongue (limiting cases such as mystical experience and creative linguistic innovation aside). For it is through the medium of consensus formation in ordinary language that cultural transmission and socialization as well as social integration come about, in the course of which communicative action is always embedded in lifeworld contexts. By contrast, the monetary medium functions in such a way that interaction is detached from these contexts. And it is this uncoupling that makes it necessary to *recouple the medium back to the lifeworld* This recoupling takes the form of legally defining exchange relations through property and contract.

I shall not discuss in any detail the *system-building effect* that the money medium can have under certain evolutionary conditions, as we saw above. It is no accident that the discussions of media theory were sparked by the major historical event of the emergence of the capitalist mode of production. Some of the important indicators of successful system formation are

- · on the one hand, critical fluctuations in the quantitative relation of the values embodied in the medium and the real values they represent (i.e., the dynamics of inflation and deflation);
- · on the other hand, a self-referential extension of money that, for instance, makes capital markets possible.

In the present context another aspect is of greater importance. A societal subsystem like the economy can be differentiated out via the money medium only if markets and forms of organization emerge that bring under monetary control the transactions within the system and, more important, its transactions with the relevant environments. Interchange relations with private households and the administrative system become monetarized, as can be seen in such evolutionary innovations as wage labor and the state based on taxation. This monetary regulation of external relations does not necessarily require a *double relation* in the sense of an interchange of pairs of factors and products taking place via two different media. If power is a medium like money, the relations between the economy and the state can indeed be conceived according to the Parsonian model as a *double* interchange. But for the relation between the economy and the domain of private households it is by no means certain that labor power exchanged for wages enters into the economic system via a nonmonetary medium such as value commitments. In fact, the point of departure for the whole critique of capitalism was the question of whether the transfer of prebourgeois, normatively organized labor relations over to the money medium—that is, whether the *monetarization of labor power*—constituted an intrusion into living conditions and interaction spheres that were not themselves integrated via media and that could not be painlessly—that is, without sociopathological consequences—cut loose from structures of action oriented to mutual understanding. For a medium-steered subsystem to take shape, it appears to be sufficient that boundaries arise across which a simple interchange, steered by a *single* medium, can take place with *every* environment. This induces readjustments in the spheres of interaction that form the environments for the medium-steered subsystem; as the example of monetarized labor power shows, the foreign medium has a certain appropriative effect. Parsons' idea is that the environments react to this challenge by transforming themselves into media-steered subsystems so as to raise the interchange to the media level from the other side as well. I want to argue against this—that in the areas of life that primarily fulfill functions of cultural reproduction, social integration, and socialization, mutual understanding cannot be replaced by media as the mechanism for coordinating action—that is, it *cannot be technicized*— though it can be expanded by technologies of communication and organizationally mediated—that is, it can be *rationalized.*

(c) Parsons transferred the medium concept he developed from the model of money to the concept of power. In what follows, I will note the structural analogies between money and power that justify his generalization and then, noting as well the unmistakable differences between them, identify the media properties favorable to institutionalization. The other two media that Parsons introduces on the level of the social system, "influence" and "value commitment," can then serve as test cases for the results of our comparison.

Considered as a steering medium, power represents the symbolic embodiment of amounts of value without itself possessing any intrinsic value. It consists neither in effective performances nor in the use of physical force. The medium of power also mirrors the structure of claim and redemption. Nominal claims to compliance with binding decisions can be redeemed in real values and are backed by reserves of a particular kind. According to Parsons, what corresponds to power as a "value in exchange" is the "value in use" of realizing collective goals; what backs power claims is the disposition over means of enforcement that can be used to threaten sanctions or to apply direct force.[57] Like the money code, the power code can be characterized by a series of *structural features*. It holds for the standard situation of following imperatives. More clearly than in the case of interaction between parties to an exchange, it is here supposed that alter and ego, the one with the power and the one subject to him, belong to the same collectivity. For it is definitive of power interests that performance potentials are to be mobilized for achieving *collectively* desired goals. As utility was in the case of money, so effectiveness of goal attainment is the generalized value here. The power code schematizes alter's possible responses in a binary fashion: he can either submit to or opppose ego's demands. A preference for compliance is built into the code through the prospect ego holds out for sanctioning alter in case the latter fails to carry out orders. Under these conditions, the person in power can condition the responses of those subordinate to him, without having to depend primarily on their willingness to cooperate. From both sides is expected an objectivating attitude toward the action situation and an orientation to the possible consequences of action. The party in power is provided with a measure—analogous to profitability—with which he can calculate the success of his decisions. Parsons vacillates between "sovereignty" and "success"; the former is a standard in the struggle for power, the latter in the use of power.

Whatever the criterion of rationality, the power medium not only guarantees a certain automatic quality to the continuation of interactions, but also creates new degrees of freedom of rational choice for those who possess power (and those who compete for it). The claims set in the code and embodied in the medium—claims to gain compliance with binding decisions—form, however, a mass of value that *cannot* be manipulated *to the same extent* as exchange values.

This is already evident in the fact that there is no sign system equivalent to money available here. There is a discrete multiplicity of symbols of power—ranging from uniforms and emblems of authority to official seals and the signatures of those authorized to sign—but there is nothing that could be compared with syntactically well organized prices. The problem of measurement is connected with this. It is not possible to quantify power; even a nonnumerical assignment of measuring units to amounts of political value is no simple matter. As a substitute for more precise measurements of power we find a hierarchical ordering of the formal competence to decide, a recourse to status orderings in general. As we know from everyday experience and from empirical investigations, these indicators are often misleading.

Furthermore, though power is something that can be transferred, it cannot circulate in so *unrestricted* a manner as money. Naturally, power can take the shape of a medium only because and insofar as it is not tied to specific persons and specific contexts. But there is a stronger tendency for power to get bound up symbiotically with the person of the powerful and the context of the exercise of power than there is for money with the person of the wealthy and his business. The advantage of incumbency enjoyed by a head of government in an election campaign may serve to illustrate this phenomenon. Finally, power cannot be so reliably deposited as money in a bank. There are indeed analogies. For example, the mandate of the voters to party leaders that they should take over the government for a term of office can be *interpreted* as an institutionalized procedure for depositing power. But there seems to be an inherent tendency for power potential deposited in this way to degenerate—and not only in the way that the value of uninvested, nonworking capital may decline.

A party in power has not only to husband its deposit of power; it must keep it fresh by realizing it in action and engaging in confrontations of power from time to time; it must demonstrate it has power through testing it. The use of success in foreign affairs for domestic purposes is an example of this demonstrative use of power; it is necessary because those in power cannot be so sure of their disposition over a deposit as can the directors of a solvent bank.

Thus, money and power do not differ in regard to their susceptibility of being measured, circulated, and deposited to such an extent that the concept of power as a medium is wholly without value. But we are correct in making the comparative judgment that power cannot be calculated as well as money.

There are also differences in regard to the *systemic effects* of power. In this domain, the phenomena of media dynamics familiar from the economy are not so clearly marked that we could study them as empirical regularities of power inflation and deflation. Moreover, reflexivity leads to quite the opposite consequences in the two media domains. Whereas financing money—that is, the credit system—is a mechanism that usually heightens the internal complexity of the economic system, superimposing power is a mechanism that creates counterpower and normally dedifferentiates the power system.[58]

Our comparison of the two media thus yields a series of differences concerning which we might ask: can they be explained by an as yet *insufficient institutionalization* of power as a medium that might be remedied under more favorable conditions? Or does the power relation itself harbor *structural barriers* to farther-reaching institutionalization? With this in mind, we move now to a comparison of *the ways in which the two media are normatively anchored in the lifeworld.*

Money is institutionalized via institutions of bourgeois civil law such as property and contract, power via the public-legal organization of offices. Two differences leap to the eye. (*a*) Parsons dealt with the first under the rubric of the hierarchical aspect of the organization of public offices. (*b*) The second has to do with the aspect of legitimation.

(*ad a*) The right to possess money implies access to markets in which transactions are possible; the right to exercise power implies, as a rule, having a position in the framework of an organization in which power relations are ordered hierarchically. Unlike money, it is only through organization that power can be rendered permanent and used for collective goals. Unlike property rights, directive authority requires some organization that channels the flow of binding decisions through positions and programs.[59]

The fact that power can be exercised at a societal level only as *organized power* throws light on the different evolutionary paths of the two media, money and power. Long before it had system-building effects, money was already a circulating medium under primitive conditions. By contrast, before power was differentiated out under the modern conditions of legal domination and rational administration as a medium that could circulate within limits, it appeared in the form of an authority of office tied to certain persons and positions. Unlike money, therefore, power is not "by nature" a circulating medium.

(*ad b*) This brings us to a more important difference: power not only needs to be backed like money (e.g., by gold or means of enforcement); it not only needs to be legally normed like money (e.g., in the form of property rights or official positions); power needs an *additional* basis of confidence, namely, *legitimation.* There is no structural analogy to this in the case of money. It is true that the order of private law has in turn to be safeguarded against conflict through the administration of justice and the infliction of punishment, but this is equally true of public law. And when conflicts about specific property relations expand into con-

flicts about the foundations of the very property order defined by property law, the legitimacy of the legal order as a component of the *political*
order is placed in question. Parsons did, of course, take into consideration the fact that power needs to be legitimated. In his model of intersystemic interchanges, the political system draws legitimations, as a production factor, from the system of cultural pattern maintenance. But we
are here viewing the matter at the analytical level of comparing media,
particularly the institutionalization of money and power.

What Parsons misses here is the asymmetry consisting in the fact that
confidence in the power system has to be secured *on a higher level* than
confidence in the monetary system. The institutions of civil law are said
to secure the functioning of market-governed monetary transactions in
the same way as the organization of public office does the exercise of
power. But the latter requires an advance of trust that signifies not only
"compliance"—a de facto obedience to laws—but "obligation"—a duty
based on the recognition of normative validity claims. It is precisely this
asymmetry that has all along been behind socialist reservations regarding
the organizational power of owners of capital, a power secured only in
private-legal terms.

Explaining this asymmetry leads us to consider the conditions under
which different media can be institutionalized. We can make clear why
power needs to be legitimated—and therefore calls for a *more demanding normative anchoring* than money—by looking at the *underlying
standard situations*. Whereas the exchange relation does not in its very
definition disadvantage anyone involved in his calculation of utility, and
whereas the process of exchange may well be, as we say, in the interest
of both parties, a person taking orders is structurally disadvantaged in
relation to a person with the power to give them. The latter relies upon
the possibility of causing harm to those who disobey; if need be, he can
actualize alternatives that those subject to his orders dread more than
carrying them out. This *disadvantage* to one of the parties [in a power
relation], which is built into the standard situation and enters into the
power code, can be compensated for by reference to collectively desired
goals. As the person in power uses his definitional power to establish
which goals are going to count as collective ones, the structural disadvantage can be offset only if those subject to him can themselves examine the goals and either endorse or repudiate them. They have to be
in a position to contest [the claim] that the goals set are collectively
desired or are, as we say, in the general interest. *It is only the reference
to legitimizable collective goals that establishes the balance in the
power relation built into the ideal-typical exchange relation from the
start.* Whereas no agreement among the parties to an exchange is required for them to make a judgment of interests, the question of what

lies in the *general* interest calls for a consensus among the members of a collectivity, no matter whether this normative consensus is secured in advance by tradition or has first to be brought about by democratic processes of bargaining and reaching understanding. In the latter case, *the connection to consensus formation in language,* backed only by potential reasons, is clear. To put the matter in terms of speech-act theory: power as a medium evidently retains something of the power to command that is connected with the authority behind commands in contrast to simple imperatives. This connection seems to leave power less suited for the role of a steering medium designed to relieve us of the burdens and risks of consensus formation in language than is money, which needs no legitimation. I will now to sum up the results of our comparison of media in three theses:

(i) The symbolically embodied amounts of value expended in exchange values or in binding decisions are backed by reserves of gold or means of enforcement and can be redeemed in the form either of use values or of the effective realization of collective goals. Both the reserves that back them and the real values they are redeemed for are such that they have empirically motivating power and can *replace* rational motivation through reasons.

(ii) Money and power are manipulable items toward which actors can adopt an objectivating attitude oriented directly to their own success. Money and power can be calculated and are tailored to purposive-rational action. For this it must be possible to activate the reserves that back them (e.g., gold or weapons), to concentrate such reserves, and to hold them in safekeeping. It is also a necessary condition that the values embodied in the media be such that they can be measured, circulated, and deposited. In this respect there are, however, gradual differences: power cannot be measured as well as money; it is less flexible as regards alienation, and it cannot be deposited with equal security.

(iii) I have explained these differences by the fact that the money medium, while it does get connected back to the communicatively structured lifeworld via legal institutions, is not made *dependent* on processes of consensus formation in language as is the medium of a power still in need of legitimation.

(*d*) From this comparison of media properties we can infer the conditions required for an optimal institutionalization of media: the real values and reserve backings ["security bases"] have to be such that they have empirically motivating power. It must be possible to have physical control over the reserves. The media must be susceptible of being measured, alienated, and deposited. The normative anchoring of the media should not give rise to *new* expenditures of communication and should not create *additional* risks of disagreement. If we take these as our criteria, we can see that the generalization of the media concept runs up against limits already at the level of the social system. Of course we can always find *names* for one new medium after another, but these are only postulates to begin with—they have to prove themselves fruitful. In economics the medium concept of money has held up empirically at least as an approach; in political science attempts have been made at least to make the medium concept of power fruitful in voting studies and comparative studies of different political systems. Similar efforts with other media have gotten bogged down right away in the attempt to find operational definitions.[60]

The first cases that offer themselves for testing the generalizability of the media concept are those spheres functionally specialized in the symbolic reproduction of the lifeworld, that is, the "societal community" insofar as it fulfills tasks of social integration, and the "patterns maintenance" system, which fulfills tasks of cultural reproduction and socialization. The foregoing media comparison puts us in a position to demonstrate, by way of immanent critique, that the steering media postulated for these two domains of action fail already at the level of conceptual analysis to satisfy the necessary conditions for institutionalization. My remarks will be based on the properties Parsons attributes to "influence" and "value commitment," as summarized in Figure 37.

If we consider the proposal to apply the media concept to influence and value commitment in the light of our intuitive understanding of these things, our first reaction is ambivalent. It has a certain prima facie plausibility; persons and institutions can have a kind of prestige that enables them to exert influence on the convictions of others, even on collective opinion formation, by their statements—without giving detailed reasons for demonstrating competence. Influential persons and institutions meet with a willingness in their audience to take advice. The utterances of the influential are not authorized by an official position, but they function as authoritative in virtue of a persuasive power that is manifested in the communicative achievement of consensus. Something similar is true of the *moral authority* of leaders or leading bodies that are in a position to evoke in others a willingness to accept concrete obligations by their moral appeals, without giving detailed reasons or demonstrating legitimacy. Their utterances are not authorized, but function as authoritative in virtue of their critical-appellative power. In both cases we have to do with *generalized forms of communication* (see Figure 37).

On the other hand, it is not particularly plausible to place influence and value commitment on a par with money and power, for they cannot be calculated like the latter. It is possible to wield influence and value commitment strategically only when they are treated like deposits of

Components / Medium	Standard situation	Generalized value	Nominal claim	Rationality criteria	Actors' attitude	Real value	Reserve backing	Form of institution-alization
Money	Exchange	Utility	Exchange value	Profitableness	Oriented to success	Use value	Gold	Property and contract
Power	Directives	Effectiveness	Binding decisions	Success (sovereignty)	Oriented to success	Realization of collective goals	Means of enforcement	Organization of official positions
Influence	Advice	Loyalty	Authoritative explanations (declarations, interpretations, judgments, etc.)	Consensus	Oriented to mutual understanding	Reasons for convictions	Cultural traditions and forms of social life	Prestige orderings
Value commitment	Moral appeals	Integrity	Authoritative admonitions (criticism and encouragement)	Pattern consistency	Oriented to mutual understanding	Justifications for obligations	Internalized values, internal sanctions	Moral leadership

Figure 37. Steering Media at the Level of the Societal System

money or power, that is, only *when we make manipulative use of non-manipulable goods.* Influence and value commitments can, naturally, be *interpreted as media.* The amount of value embodied by a medium is expended in nominal claims, that is, in authoritative statements and moral appeals; these can be redeemed in such real values as reasons or justifications, and they are backed by such reserves as a shared cultural stock of knowledge or way of life, or by internalized and internally sanctioned values. But there is something forced about this interpretation, as we can see by running through, in reverse order, the above-mentioned conditions for institutionalizing media.

Obviously we have no institutions that, in analogy to property and offices, would permit a well-circumscribed normative anchoring of influence or value commitment. The concepts invoked for that purpose—prestige ordering and moral leadership—are more an expression of embarrassment, for they scarcely allow a differentiation between the media themselves and their institutionalizations: 'influence' can be more or less translated as 'prestige' or 'reputation', 'value commitment' as 'moral authority'. It is interesting to note that the possession of prestige or moral authority is less clearly normed in modern societies, where, on Parsons' assumptions, the differentiation of these media would have to be farther along than in premodern societies, where prestige orderings were well anchored in social stratification and moral leadership in sacred institutions. There are some exceptions: in the science system, which specializes in producing validated knowledge, reputation has a controlling function, and linked with it the academic professions, in which highly specialized knowledge finds application. But these examples do not support the assertation that the medium of influence is institutionalized in the system of social integration, that is, in a public sphere established through the mass media, where the influence of journalists, party leaders, intellectuals, artists, and the like is of primary importance.

Furthermore, it is evident that influence and value commitment are less susceptible of being measured, alienated, and stored than money or even power. The charismatic leader Parsons points to as an example of a "banker" who accumulates and invests influence and moral authority suggests, rather, that these media remain strongly tied to persons and particular contexts. We can see this, for example, in papal visits, which are intended to raise "investments" in the form of religious ties. The always present danger of the routinization of charisma is a sign that the "banks" for influence and moral authority operate in a highly unreliable manner, if at all. Things are no better with the control of the reserves that back them. The assumption that a shared cultural background, or motives and guilt feelings, can be sheltered like money or weapons seems more appropriate to premodern societies, in which the administration of sacred values rests firmly in the hands of churches.

Finally, we have to get clear about the significance of the fact that the real values and reserve backings (security bases) of influence and value commitment have no underlying *empirically* motivating power. The standard situations of giving advice and making a moral appeal represent communicative relationships, special cases of consensus formation in language, in which, to be sure, one party is outfitted with a preponderance of competence (of knowledge, moral-practical insight, persuasive power, or autonomy). Unlike the situations of exchange or imperatives, these situations do not contain any elements that could *induce* an addressee oriented to his own success to accept ego's offers. Ego has at his disposal nothing equivalent to consumable values or threatened sanctions, upon which he might rely to move alter to the desired continuation of interaction *without having recourse to the resources of reaching understanding.*

In exerting influence or mobilizing engagement, the coordination of action has to be brought about by means of the *same* resources familiar from first-order processes of consensus formation in language. The "security base" is a shared cultural background or inculcated value orientations and behavioral controls; the "intrinsic satisfiers" are grounds for justifications in which convictions or obligations are rooted. Influential persons or persons with moral authority at their disposal claim the competence of "initiates," of experts in matters of knowledge or of morality. For this reason they can make use of the mechanism of reaching understanding *at a higher level:* that which counts as backing in communicative action—the potential reasons with which ego could, if necessary, defend his validity claim against alter's criticisms—assumes the status of the "real value" in interaction steered via influence and moral authority, whereas the "security base" gets pushed into the cultural and socializing background. These observations lead me to the thesis that, though influence and value commitment are indeed forms of generalized communication that bring about a reduction in the expenditure of energy and in the risks attending mutual understanding, they achieve this relief effect in a *different way* than do money and power. They cannot uncouple interaction from the lifeworld context of shared cultural knowledge, valid norms, and responsible motivations, because they remain second-order processes of consensus formation in language. This also explains why they need no special institutional reconnection to the lifeworld. Influence and value commitment are not neutral in relation to the alternatives of agreement and failed consensus; rather, *they merely elevate to generalized values two cases of consensus* that are based on the intersubjective recognitiion of cognitive and normative validity claims. Unlike media such as money and power, they cannot replace ordinary language in its coordinating function, but only provide it with relief through abstraction from lifeworld complexity. In a sentence: *media of this kind cannot technicize the lifeworld.*

(*e*) I have distinguished the steering media that replace language as a mechanism for coordinating action from the forms of generalized communication that merely simplify an overly complex nexus of communicative action, and that in doing so remain dependent on language and on a lifeworld, however rationalized. I shall now sharpen this distinction by examining Parsons' own attempts to ground media theory in action theory, for his distinction between modes of interaction ran parallel at first to my contrasting of money and power with influence and value commitment: "My suggestion is that there is a very simple paradigm of modes by which one acting unit—let us call him ego—can attempt to get results by bringing to bear on another unit, which we may call alter, some kind of communicative operation: call it pressure if that term is understood in a nonpejorative sense. It can be stated in terms of two variables. The first variable is whether ego attempts to work through potential control over the *situation* in which alter is placed and must act, or through an attempt to have an effect on alter's *intentions,* independently of changes in his situation.⁶¹

The point of departure here is the problem of coordinating actions: how does ego get alter to continue interaction in the desired manner, so that no conflict arises to interrupt the sequence of action. Parsons relies on the model of interaction familiar from learning theory: there is a message exchanged between sender and receiver that says both that the sender expects a certain behavior of the receiver and that the sender will reward/punish the receiver if the expected behavior does/does not take place. Interaction proceeding according to the stimulus/response scheme gets complicated by the fact that ego and alter can act in a goal-directed manner, interpret their action situation in the light of values, norms, and goals, and distinguish in the process between boundary conditions and resources. In addition, they know about one another that they possess these competences, and thus must understand their actions as resulting from a choice between action alternatives. Every choice is contingent: it could have turned out otherwise. Thus ego and alter each has to *condition* the freedom of the other so that the other's choices turn out to be favorable to his own interests. If only a choice between positive and negative sanctions is allowed, and if two channels of "pressure" are opened up—either for affecting alter's beliefs and obligations, or for affecting his situation—there result four *conditioning strategies.* Parsons calls them modes of interaction and correlates one medium with each of them (see Figure 38).

Influence on actors': Sanctions	Intention	Situation
Positive	Persuasion (influence)	Inducement (money)
Negative	Admonition (value commitment)	Deterrence (power)

Figure 38. Grounding of the Media in Action Theory

This scheme has been criticized from different angles.[62] What I find most vexing is the fact that the peculiar asymmetry between strategic and consensual influence is tacitly relied upon in this scheme, while at the same time it is made to disappear behind empiricist concepts. The strategies of "inducement" and "deterrence" can easily be subsumed under positive rewarding sanctions and negative punishing sanctions and used to characterize situations of exchanging goods and issuing directives—that is, those standard situations on which Parsons bases the media of money and power. But this is not true of the other two strategies: ego can infuence alter's beliefs and obligations through informing, explaining, and criticizing as well as through encouraging and critically admonishing. J. J. Loubser illustrates this by correlating both positive and negative expressions with both strategies at once. He characterizes the positive strategies of persuading with verbs such as agree, approve, support, assent, recognize, and so forth, and the negative with verbs such as disagree, disapprove, protest, dissent, and so forth. As to strategies of encouragement, he lists verbs such as praise, accept, and so forth; strategies of admonition are characterized by verbs such as deplore, blame, and so forth. This problem cannot be solved through a more differentiated cross-tabulation, as Loubser thinks. Parsons' error lies elsewhere. He does not consider that *the concept of sanction cannot be applied to yes/no responses to criticizable validity claims*—and within the framework of his action theory that cannot be given proper consideration. This becomes clear when we try to pinpoint the differences between the two pairs of strategies: inducement/deterrence and persuasion/moral appeal. In the first case, ego intervenes in alter's action situation in order to induce the latter to make a decision favorable to ego's own aims. This can take place through instrumental action or by verbal means, but always in such a way that ego is oriented exclusively to the consequences of his action. In the other case, ego has to speak with alter with the aim of bringing about a consensus; there is no other way open to him than coming to an understanding with alter. If he wishes to influence alter's beliefs and obligations, he has to convince the latter of the existence of certain states of affairs or make clear to him that in a given situation he ought to act in such and such a manner. Ego has to bring alter to accept the truth claims he is raising with his constative speech acts or the rightness claims he is raising with his normative recommendations. For this reason he cannot orient himself exclusively to the consequences of his action, but must endeavor to reach an understanding with alter. In the former case, ego is behaving with an orientation to success, in the latter with an orientation to mutual understanding. This can again be seen in the expressions that Loubser associates with the two pairs of strategies. As noted above, for the strategies of persuasion and moral appeal he points to verbs that can be used to build performative sentences and to reach illocutionary goals; by contrast he characterizes the other two strategies with expressions that cannot be used to carry out illocutionary acts but only to describe perlocutionary effects that can be elicited in a hearer: bribe, keep ignorant, withhold, blackmail, threaten, submit, and so forth. Sanctions belong to a class of actions that ego threatens for the sake of their impact or, when they are linguistic in nature, for the sake of their perlocutionary effect. Sanctions cannot be directly attached to illocutionary acts that enable ego and alter to take up an interpersonal relation and come to a mutual understanding about something. For this reason, the modes of interaction described as intentional—persuasion and moral appeal—which Parsons attaches to the media influence and value commitment, do not fit into a scheme of sanctions.

When we say that an affirmative response to a criticizable validity claim—for example, concurring with an assertion or recommendation—is elicited by sanctions, by rewards or punishments, this description renders the affirmative response in categories under which the actor himself could not have taken his "yes" seriously. The scheme of sanctions can cover only modes of interaction in which ego endeavors *empirically* to move alter to continue an interaction. Motivation by reasons is not analytically provided for; in the proposed categorial framework, the freedom that is moved to recognize criticizable validity claims only by reasons gets *reinterpreted* from the start into the contingency of choices that can be conditioned. In other theoretical contexts there may be good reasons for employing an empiricist concept of freedom of choice; in the present context, however, we are concerned with the differences between two types of media. Generalized forms of communication such as influence and value commitment require illocutionary acts and thus remain dependent on the binding effects of using language with an orientation to mutual understanding. Steering media such as money and power guide interaction through ego's intervention in the situation of alter, through perlocutionary effects if need be. The differentiation Parsons has in mind at the level of action theory cannot be *carried through* within his scheme of sanctions, since that has no room for ties other than those that are empirically motivated.

I proposed an alternative approach above, in section VI.2. On that account we can trace alter's generalized acceptance to specific sources of ego's prestige or influence, in such a way as to permit a strict distinction between *ties that are motivated empirically* through inducement and deterrence and *trust that is motivated rationally* through agreement based on reasons. Alter takes up ego's offer either because he is oriented to the punishments and rewards that ego can allot, or because he trusts that ego possesses the required knowledge and is sufficiently autonomous to guarantee the redemption of the validity claims he has raised in communication.

One might conjecture that prestige and influence, which are attached to specific persons to begin with, themselves get generalized once again. The generalization of prestige has more of a *structure-forming* effect: it leads to the formation of status systems that can develop along the axis of differentials of prestige between collectivities—between family groups to start with. The generalization of influence has a *media-forming* effect in which even physical attributes get transformed into resources and shaped into media. Thus, for instance, strength and skill can be transformed into power; on the other hand, attributes such as reliability, physical good looks, or sexual attractiveness evidently cannot be transformed into generalized resources. Furthermore, not all resources provide an equally suitable basis for generalizing some specialized mode of influencing the responses of a partner in interaction. Talk of love as a medium remains hopelessly metaphorical. But media can be clearly distinguished by whether they attach to empirically motivated ties or to forms of rationally motivated trust.

Steering media such as money and power attach to empirically motivated ties. They encode purposive-rational dealings with calculable amounts of value and make it possible to exert generalized strategic influence on the decisions of other participants while bypassing processes of consensus formation in language. Because they not only simplify communication in language but *replace it with a symbolic generalization of negative and positive sanctions,* the lifeworld context in which processes of reaching understanding always remain embedded gets *devalued:* the lifeworld is no longer necessary for coordinating actions.

Societal subsystems differentiated out via such media can render themselves independent of a lifeworld pushed out into the system environment. Thus, from the perspective of the lifeworld the transfer of action over to steering media appears both as a relief from the expenditures and risks of communication and as a conditioning of decisions in expanded fields of contingency—and in this latter sense, as a *technicizing of the lifeworld.*

The generalization of influence cannot have such an effect, whether the influence rests on rationally motivated trust in the cognitive-instrumental knowledge of others, or in their moral insight or aesthetic judgment. Interactions guided by generalized rational motivation represent only a higher-order specialization of processes of consensus formation in language. Via the mechanism of reaching understanding, they remain dependent on recourse to the cultural background and to elements of the personality structure. These forms of generalized communication make it possible to locate communicative action at a greater distance from institutional orders, from normative contexts in general. But their resources remain, from start to finish, those upon which consensus formation in language draws. Cognitively specialized influence—for example, scientific reputation—can take shape to the extent that cultural value spheres (in Weber's sense) are differentiated out, thus making it possible to deal with a cognitive tradition exclusively under the validity aspect of truth. Normatively specialized influence—for example, moral leadership—can take shape to the extent that moral and legal development reaches the postconventional stage at which a morality separated from legality is largely deinstitutionalized, and to the extent that a moral consciousness guided by principle is anchored via internal behavioral roles almost exclusively in the personality system. Both types of influence require, in addition, technologies of communication that free speech acts from spatiotemporal contextual restrictions and make them available for multiple contexts.

We began with the question of the extent to which the media concept developed on the model of money can be generalized and carried over to other spheres of action. The path of immanent critique has led us in the end to two contrary types of communication media; this media dualism explains the resistance that structures of the lifeworld offer in certain domains to being converted over from social integration to system integration. We can thus see in Parsons' theory of communication media what we earlier found in his anthropological "late philosophy": even in its mature form, his theory did not really resolve, but at most concealed, the conflict between two competing conceptual frames that is inherent in it.

3. The Theory of Modernity

The systems theory of society developed by Parsons rests on a compromise that, while it preserves the memory of neo-Kantian problematics in culture theory, excludes a concept of society with room for such problems. His compromise does not allow for separating the aspects under which action complexes can be analyzed now as a system, now as a lifeworld. The reproduction of the lifeworld accessible from the internal perspective is distantiated into an external view of system maintenance, without this methodological step of objectivation leaving behind any visible trace. Let us recall the two theses I developed in the second set of intermediate reflections: the far-reaching uncoupling of system and lifeworld was a necessary condition for the transition from the stratified class societies of European feudalism to the economic class societies of the early modern period; but the capitalist pattern of modernization is marked by a deformation, a reification of the symbolic structures of the lifeworld under the imperatives of subsystems differentiated out via money and power and rendered self-sufficient. If these two theses are correct, the weaknesses of a theory that *retracts* the basic conceptual distinction between system and lifeworld should show up especially in dealing with this topic.

Like his theory as a whole, Parsons' theory of modernity is Janus-faced. On the one side, it differs from a systems functionalism that highlights only the features of complexity in modern societies. [In this latter view,] such societies owe their high level of complexity to the pronounced differentiation of subsystems that are relatively independent from one another and yet form environments for one another, and that enter into regulated interchanges with one another such that zones of reciprocal penetration (or interpenetration) emerge. It is along this path that we would find, for instance, Luhmann's theory of evolution, which definitively does away with the neo-Kantian idea of value realization, sweeps clean the heaven of cultural values, undoes the corset of the four-function scheme, and thereby undoubtedly gives to the theory of modernity much more freedom of movement—anything might have been possible. At any rate, Luhmann now wants to explain in historical terms what Parsons still predicted on theoretical grounds—for instance, the fact that the development of modern societies is marked by exactly three revolutions.

Differentiation counts only as one of four evolutionary mechanisms.

The other three are expansion of adaptive capacity, generalization of memberships or inclusion, and generalization of values.[1] Parsons deduces from the four-function scheme what the heightening of complexity and steering capacity can mean for social systems. By doing so he also gains some advantages in comparison to a more consistent systems functionalism that does not pin itself down so strongly. Inclusion and value generalization are correlated with the two functions into which the concept of value realization—the institutionalization and internalization of values—was absorbed, but in which it is also preserved. Unlike Luhmann, Parsons can *translate* the increase in system complexity grasped from the outside, from the observation of modern societies, into the internal perspective of the lifeworld-bound self-understanding of system members. He can connect the growing system autonomy with the developing autonomy of moral-practical understanding and can interpret the increasing inclusion and value generalization as a progressive approximation to universalistic ideals of justice.[2]

Thus we can see, on the one hand, that on the basis of his compromise between neo-Kantianism and systems theory, Parsons holds open the possibility of connecting up a functionalist approach to the theory of modernity with the Weberian problematic of occidental rationalism—he conceives of societal modernization not only as systemic rationalization but as a rationalization of action orientations. On the other hand, however, as we have shown, Parsons failed to develop a concept of society from the action perspective; as a result, he cannot describe the rationalization of the lifeworld and the increasing complexity of systems as separate, interacting processes that often run counter to one another. So far as modernity is concerned, he holds only to connecting new levels of system differentiation and correlative increases in system autonomy with the self-understanding of modern culture by means of such catch phrases as 'institutional individualism' and 'secularization', and also to *interpreting* them in Weber's sense as an expanded institutionalization of value-rational, norm-rational, and purposive-rational action orientations.[3]

Because he does not resolve the competition between lifeworld and system but only quiets it down with a compromise, Parsons has to *bring* the rationalization of the lifeworld conceptually *into line* with the growth of system complexity. Hence he is unable to grasp the dialectic inherent in modernization processes, the burdens placed on the internal structures of the lifeworld by growing system complexity. He has to reduce these phenomena to the scale of crisis manifestations explicable on the model of inflation and deflation. Media dynamics of this kind relate only to accidental and temporary disturbances of the equilibrium in intersystemic interchange processes. Parsons cannot explain the systemic tendencies toward the sorts of pathologies that Marx, Durkheim, and Weber had in view. I am referring here to the deformations that inevitably turn up when forms of economic and administrative rationality encroach upon areas of life whose internal communicative structures cannot be rationalized according to those criteria.

I shall now (A) show why Parsons' theory of modernity is blind to the social pathologies Weber wanted to explain with his rationalization thesis. In turning to systems theory, Parsons relinquished the possibility of justifying in terms of action theory a reasonable criterion for societal modernization conceived of as rationalization. (B) This deficit cannot be made good by suspending the Parsonian compromise, abandoning the elements of systems functionalism, and moving in the direction of a neo-Kantian theory of culture.

A.—Parsons orders the phenomena of modernization in the West from the point of view of structural differentiation, to begin with. In doing so he takes the integrative subsystem as his reference point, and this is by no means a trivial decision for his construction: it makes moral and legal development the key evolutionary variables, whereas the dynamics of the material reproduction of the lifeworld recede into the background, and with them the conflicts that arise from class structures and the political order. This thesis is summed in a sentence: "What is thought of as *modern* society took shape in the 17th century in the northwest corner of the European system of societies, in Great Britain, Holland, and France. The subsequent development of modern society included three processes of revolutionary structural change: the industrial revolution, the democratic revolution, and the educational revolution."[4]

These three revolutions can be explained in systems-theoretical terms as the developmental thrusts in which the integrative system detached itself from the other three subsystems, one after the other. Parsons understands the industrial revolution that got underway in late-eighteenth-century England, the French Revolution of 1789 (and the upheavals oriented to that model), as well as the educational revolution—the expansion of formal schooling that is rooted in the ideas of the eighteenth century but was not radically carried out until the middle of the twentieth—as structural differentiations of the subsystem of the societal community from the economic, the political, and the cultural subsystems.[5]

These three revolutions divide the *early* period from *advanced* modernity. They fulfilled the initial conditions for an international system of highly complex societies that fit Parsons' standard description of social systems with four subsystems apiece. The latter stand in a reciprocal interchange of "products" and "factors," which takes place via four media and six "markets." Each of them is specialized in one of four general societal functions. The degree of modernization is measured by an overall societal complexity that can be grasped not only from the perspective of structural differentiation. Modern societies owe their increased adaptive capacity to a capitalist economy that is geared to mobilizing performance potentials and natural resources; they owe the subordination and incorporation of all merely particular membership relations to a societal community that is tailored to abstract and universal norms, and they owe the generalization of cultural, especially moral, values to a culture that has been secularized.[6] Parsons understands the developments emanating from the "spearhead" of modernity, northwestern Europe, since the eighteenth century essentially as an exemplification of his schematically presented system concept of society. His basic assumptions regarding evolutionary theory become clearer if one looks at the status he accords to the Reformation and Renaissance, those two major events of the early modern period. They are the precursor revolutions that made the transition to the modern age possible by unleashing the cognitive potentials contained in the traditions of Christianity and of ancient Rome and Greece—but previously worked up only by cultural elites in monastic orders and universities—and by allowing them to exert an influence on an institutional level. Parsons is here picking up on Weber's theory of societal rationalization; just as the Reformation abolished the barriers between clergy, religious orders, and laity and set the impulses of religious ethics of conviction free to shape profane realms of action, the humanism of the Renaissance made the Roman-Greek heritage accessible to the science, jurisprudence, and art that were emancipating from the church—above all, it cleared a path for the modern legal system. Parsons views the cultural traditions of the West as a code that needs to be implemented if it is to manifest itself phenotypically, at the level of social institutions. The Reformation and the Renaissance figure as those processes of societal implementation. The *direction* in which occidental rationalism *developed* was set by the cultural code that had formed in the rationalization of worldviews, but the institutional framework in which a rationalization of society could get underway took shape only in the wake of the Reformation and the Renaissance. Parsons traces the gradual institutionalization and internalization of purposive-rational economic and administrative action in the development of law in England since the late sixteenth century.[7] The institutions of a legal domination based on religious tolerance and an agricultural production based on wage labor provided the basis for the three above-mentioned "revolutions" by which modernization burst the shell of a stratified, still estate-bound society. Parsons explains the fact that it was in early modern Europe that culturally stored rationality potentials were exploited by appealing to those boundary conditions that Weber had already mentioned. The canon law of the Roman Catholic church, the republican constitutions of medieval cities, the sharp tension between orientations to need and to gain among urban tradesmen and craftsmen, the competition between church and state, in general the decentralization of powers in central Europe are said to provide a favorable starting point for this period.

Parsons' substantive account of the transition to the modern age and the development of modern societies relies heavily on Weber's account of occidental rationalism. At the same time, he takes the latter out of the framework of a theory of rationalization. By the end of the 1960s, borrowings from the biological theory of evolution already show up in his terminology. He regards cultural development as an equivalent for *changes in the genetic code.* The societal implementation of cognitive potential stored in worldviews is said to correspond to a *selection from the range of cultural variations,* while the different national paths of development among modern societies are regarded as indications of the conditions under which structure-forming innovations can best be *stabilized.* What Weber viewed as a transfer of cultural to societal rationalization—as the institutional embodiment and motivational anchoring of cognitive structures that first emerged from the rationalization of worldviews—Parsons explains in terms of evolution theory as resulting from the cooperation of mechanisms of selection and stabilization with a mechanism of variation located on the level of the cultural code. At the same time, he intertwines the theory of social evolution with systems theory in such a way as to reduce the modernization that Weber presented as societal rationalization to a heightening of systemic complexity—that is, to the increase in complexity that comes about when a society differentiates out the subsystems of the economy and the state administration via special steering media.

Parsons thereby assimilates the rationalization of the lifeworld to processes of system differentiation. And he accounts for the latter in accordance with his four-function paradigm, into which the idea of value realization has been built. Thus there is an analytical connection between the growing steering capacity of the social system and increasing inclusion and value generalization. This connection at the analytical level leaves the theoretical interpretation of modernity ambivalent: (*a*) on the one hand, it makes it *possible* to conceive of modernization processes described in systems-theoretical terms not only as a growing autonomy of society in relation to its environments but at the same time as a rationalization of the lifeworld; (*b*) on the other hand, it makes it *necessary* to identify the one with the other—increasing system complexity means *eo ipso* progress in the rational shaping of the conditions of life. As we shall see, this dilemma cannot be avoided by swerving over into a neo-Kantian reading of Parsons' theory of modernity.

(*a*) I developed the concept of a rationalization of the lifeworld in connection with the history of social theory by offering an interpretation of the approaches of Mead and Durkheim. The concept refers to trends in the alteration of lifeworld structures that spring from a growing differentiation between culture, society, and personality. Durkheim understands the generalization of values, the universalization of law and morality, and the individuation and growing autonomy of the individual as the consequences of a changeover from social integration through faith to integration established through communicative agreement and cooperation. From Mead's and our point of view, the same trends can be understood as a linguistification of the sacred, as an unfettering of the rationality potential of action oriented to mutual understanding. This potential gets converted into a rationalization of the lifeworld of social groups to the extent that language takes over the functions of achieving understanding, coordinating action, and socializing individuals, and thus becomes the medium through which cultural reproduction, social integration, and socialization take place. I traced these tendencies to the fact that the basic religious consensus was set communicatively aflow; Parsons treats them under the rubrics of 'secularization' and 'institutionalized individualism'.

By *institutionalized individualism* he understands two complementary, intermeshing patterns of social integration and socialization. The development of ego-identities corresponds to the universalization of law and morality, to the separation of *Sittlichkeit* into law and morality, and to the release of communicative action from normative contexts that become increasingly abstract. Thus the pattern of institutionalized individualism is simultaneously characterized both by expanded ranges of alternatives and by bonds of generalized memberships: "I have in a number of places referred to the conception of 'institutionalized individualism' by deliberate contrast to the utilitarian version. In the pattern of institutionalized individualism the keynote is not the direct utilitarian conception of 'the rational pursuit of self-interest' but a much broader conception of the self-fulfillment of the individual in a social setting in which the aspect of solidarity ... figures at least as prominently as does that of self-interest in the utilitarian sense."[8]

'Institutionalized individualism' is a concept that should be developed from the viewpiont of a dialectic of the universal and the particular. Of course, Parsons himself does not emphasize the wealth of individual options so much as the capacity for value realization, which can grow for collectivities only to the degree that it does for the individuals socialized within them: "Institutionalized individualism means a mode of organization of the components of human action which, on balance, enhance the capacity of the average individual and of collectivities to which he belongs to implement the values to which he and they are committed. This enhanced capacity at the individual level has developed concomitantly with that of social and cultural frameworks of organization and institutional norms, which form the framework of order for the realization of individual and collective unit goals and values."[9]

The concept of *secularization* is connected with the generalization of values at the level of the general action system. Parsons does not understand the secularization of religious values and ideas as the loss of their binding character. As the religious ethics of conviction take root in the world, their moral-practical contents do not get uprooted. Secularized value orientations do not necessarily detach themselves from their religious ground; more typically, a confessional faith exercising tolerance arranges itself ecumenically in the circle of other confessions (including the radically secularized, nonreligious variants of humanistically based ethics): "The contemporary Catholic, Protestant or Jew may, with variations within his broader faith, even for Catholics, be a believer in the wider societal moral community. This level he does not share in regard to specifics with those of other faiths. He has, however ... come to respect the religious legitimacy of these other faiths. The test of this legitimacy is that he and the adherents of these other faiths recognize that they can belong to the same moral community—which may be a predominantly secular, politically organized society—and that this common belongingness means sharing a religious orientation at the level of *civil religion.*"[10]

Parsons illustrates this concept of a "civil religion," which he took from Robert Bellah, in connection with the political attitudes that underlie the United States Constitution:

The new society became a secular society in which religion was relegated to the private sphere. The other theme is no less important: the building of the Kingdom of God on earth. The establishment of the new American nation was a culmination of this process. The very facts of independence and a new constitution "conceived in liberty and dedicated to the proposition that all men are created equal" were developments that could not fail to carry with them a religious dimension. This took a form that was relatively consistent with traditional Christian conceptions and definitions, and it is this that is the core of what Bellah calls the American civil religion. There was no radical break with the primary religious heritage, though there was a careful avoidance of any attempt to define civil religion as Christian in a specifically dogmatic sense. Bellah documents, for example, how many official statements—notably presidential inaugural addresses—that use the term 'God' or various synonyms such as 'Supreme Being' carefully avoid reference to Christ." [11]

For Parsons, this secularization of religious forces means a dedogmatization that makes it possible for confessions, whose rivalry was once a matter of life and death, to coexist on the basis of shared basic convictions. In this respect, secularization conveys and promotes a value generalization through which the process of societal implementation—paradigmatically studied in the case of the Protestant ethic—continues on. The secularization of religious value orientations means a deepening of their institutional influence. By means of this concept of secularization, Parsons arrives at an assessment of moral and legal development in modern societies that differs from that of Weber. Weber thought the Protestant ethic could not persist in developed capitalism because the religious foundations of ethics of conviction could not meet the challenges of a scientized culture and, without any dialectical twists, would fall prey to a secularization that did not merely universalize religious value orientations but cut the ground from under them *as* ethically deracinated value orientations. Weber's argument offers both an empirical prediction and a theoretical justification.

The latter is based on his skeptical view that a principled moral consciousness not embedded in a religious worldview can be neither philosophically explained nor socially stabilized. This view is difficult to maintain in the face of cognitivist approaches to ethics from Kant to Rawls. It is just as little in accord with empirical evidence for the spread of a humanistically enlightened moral consciousness from the time of the Enlightenment. In this regard, Parsons' secularization thesis is the more plausible: insofar as we must have recourse to moral-practical convictions, there is no alternative in developed modern societies to posttraditional legal and moral consciousness or to the corresponding level of justification. Naturally, this says nothing against the empirical side of Weber's argument concerning the end of the Protestant ethic of the calling.

According to him, the vocational ethic that was, in the early phase, particularly influential among capitalist entrepreneurs and juristically trained expert officials, did not establish itself in the occupational system of developed capitalism; it was driven out by instrumentalist attitudes right into the core of the academic profession. The positivistic hollowing out of legal domination and the dislodging of the moral basis of modern law could be seen as parallel phenomena. But Parsons emphatically rejects these empirical statements as well: "In my opinion the Protestant ethic is far from dead. It continues to form our orientations to a very important sector of life today as it did in the past. We do value systematic rational work in 'callings', and we do so out of what is at some level a religious background. In my opinion the instrumental apparatus of modern society could not function without a generous component of this kind of evaluation."[12]

(b) In the face of the massive critique of civilization with which Parsons saw himself confronted as a university professor during the years of student protest, he generally took the opposite position to Weber's in questions concerning the diagnosis of the age. He did not believe that the disintegration of religious and metaphysical worldviews in modern societies threatened the solidary relations and the identity of individuals who could no longer orient their lives to "ultimate ideas." He was convinced, rather, that modern societies had brought about an incomparable increase in freedom for the great mass of their populations.[13] He rejects *both* elements of the Weberian diagnosis—the thesis of a loss of meaning as well as that of a loss of freedom. There would be no need here to examine this difference of opinion if it were only a question of competing global (and difficult to verify) assertions regarding trends. It is worth taking note of Parsons' position, however, because it follows deductively from his description of modernization processes. If one accepts his theoretical description, one is unable to assert any *different* view of highly complex societies. If developed modern societies are characterized by their high degree of internal complexity, and if this complexity can only rise in all four dimensions at once—steering capacity, differentiation of media-steered subsystems, inclusion, and value generalization—then there is an *analytical* relation between a high level of system complexity on the one hand and, on the other, universalistic forms of social integration and an individualism institutionalized in a noncoercive manner. It is this analytical scheme that forces Parsons to project a harmonious picture of everything that falls under his description of a modern society.

The arguments he adduces against Weber's bureaucratization thesis are indicative:

> We have argued that the main trend is actually not toward increasing bureaucracy, but rather toward associationism. But many sensitive groups clearly *feel* that bureaucracy has been increasing . . . There are in the expression of this sense of deprivation two especially prominent positive symbols. One is *"community"*, which is widely alleged to have grossly deteriorated in the course of modern developments. It is pointed out that the residential community has been "privatized" and that many relationships have been shifted to the context of large formal organizations. We should note again, however, that bureaucratization in its most pejorative sense is not threatening to sweep all before it. Furthermore, the whole system of mass communications is a functional equivalent of some features of *Gemeinschaft* and one that

enables an individual selectively to participate according to his own standards and desires. The second positive symbol is *"participation"*, especially in the form of "participatory democracy". Demands for it are often stated as if "power", in a specific technical sense were the main disideratum, but the very diffuseness of these demands casts doubt on this conclusion. We suggest that the demands are mainly another manifestation of the desire for inclusion, for full "acceptance" as members of solidary groups.[14]

This diagnosis grandly ignores two facts: neither is the network of modern mass communications set up in such a way as to work against the "privatization" of life-styles, nor can the universalization of formal and legal claims be understood without further ado as an expansion of democratic processes of will formation. Parsons deploys his categories in such a way that the *same* phenomena that Weber could interpret as signs of social pathologies count as further evidence for the view that modern Western societies have developed the forms of solidarity appropriate to their complexity. Precisely those distinctions we have to make if we are to grasp the pathologies that emerge in the modern age are blocked by *this basic conceptual harmonizing of the rationalization of the lifeworld with the increasing complexity of the social system.*

Parsons has to reduce sociopathological phenomena to systemic disequilibria; what is specific to social crises gets lost in the process. *Internal disequilibria are normal* for self-regulating systems that have constantly to secure their risky self-maintenance by adapting to conditions in a contingent and hypercomplex environment. From his perspective as an observer, the systems analyst can judge whether these disequilibria reach a critical point only if he can refer to clearly identifiable survival limits, as he can with organisms. There is no comparably clear-cut problem of death in the case of social systems.[15] The social scientist can speak of crises only when relevant social groups *experience* systematically induced structural changes as critical to their continued existence and feel their identities threatened.[16] When Weber conceives of modernization as societal rationalization, he establishes a connection with identity-securing worldviews and with structures of the lifeworld that set the conditions for the consistency of social experiences. He can find in his complex concept of rationality itself the criteria for those structurally generated "aporetic" or "paradoxical" experiences that, in certain circumstances, get worked up in the form of social pathologies. Parsons does not have these, or similar, conceptual means at his disposal; he applies the concept of crisis in the sense of a disturbance of intersystemic interchange relations, independent of the experiences of those involved and without reference to identity problems. On this approach the crises that arise in modern societies can only be grasped in terms of media dynamics, the model for which is supplied by economic inflation and deflation.[17]

It did not go unnoticed in Parsonian circles that analyses of this type cannot get at the conspicuous symptomatic aporias of modernity—the crisis phenomena that characterized the growth pattern of capitalist modernization. Thus R. C. Baum has made an interesting attempt to do justice, with Parsonian means, to the global social pathologies that appeared in wake of modernization. To start with, he defines "conflations" of single media as subprocesses of a dynamic involving several media; then he traces the phenomena that Marx had conceived as a loss of freedom through monetarization and Weber as a loss of freedom through bureaucratization to a *categorial confusion of the provinces of different media.*

Baum assumes that even in the economically most advanced societies, all four media could not yet be adequately developed and institutionalized; even there the exchange of products and factors through six markets, as it is described and theoretically predicted in the "interchange paradigm," has not yet happened. Only one of these media, namely, money, has been institutionally anchored to an extent where it can function both as a "measure of value" and as a "store of value." But if media are unequally developed, there is an inclination to define steering problems, wherever they arise, in terms of the medium or media that can be managed best:

> The tremendous trend towards increasing rationalization in the Western world so brilliantly exposed by Max Weber amounts to a net preference to use the most rational yardsticks available in legitimating social action. Relative to the other media and in measurement efficacy this is money. Men, therefore, may prefer to use money as a yardstick even in efforts which do not have the aim of making additions to a society's stock of utility. Even where the aim is to add to solidarity, collective effectiveness, or societal authenticity, men, once committed to rationalization, deployed a variety of cost-benefit analyses to measure their performance. As neither power, influence nor value commitments as media have as yet proved usable as measures of account, they use money instead. But money, designed, so to speak, to measure utility cannot measure adequately what it is supposed to reflect—additions to the other realities of societal functions. A whole host of social problems from urban renewal to delinquency prevention projects remain a mess in part because of the use of money for ends that money alone cannot serve.[18]

In this way the destruction of urban environments as a result of uncontrolled capitalist growth, or the overbureaucratization of the educational system, can be explained as a "misuse" of the media of money and power. Such misuses spring from the false perception of those involved that rational management of steering problems is possible only by way of calculated operations with money and power.

Media theory is supposed to criticize this distorted perception, push for a more careful use of the most advanced media, and raise awareness that the underdeveloped media of influence and value commitment have to do some catching up. Of course, Baum could argue in this way only if he were prepared to single out systemic equilibrium states—in this case, the balanced development of the four steering media postulated for society—in a normative way. But Parsons always refused to make social systems theory dependent on normative premises. This may explain why Baum brings into play here the normative ideas and ideals contained in the cultural traditions of the societies themselves.

He too explains the systematically flawed reception that leads to dangerous media preferences by pointing to the selectivity of prevalent worldviews. Depending on the type of "good" society that a worldview projects and suggests, one or another function has a privileged position in the members' perception. This priority can lead to overloading the corresponding medium with problems that have been erroneously assigned to it. But views of the world and of society are themselves subject to media dynamics; thus it is not easy to understand why worldviews are now supposed to be able—in the face of the cumulative pressure of unresolved problems—to maintain the normative barriers they erect against a balanced use of media and a categorically appropriate assignment of problems. Only an independent, *internal* resistence to functionally required revisions of one-sided views of the world and of society could explain crises, that is, disturbances that have a systematic character and represent something more than temporary disequilibria. Baum has no more analytical means at his disposal than Parsons to identify such internal limitations of cultural development. This is the advantage of the Weberian theory of rationalization, which, owing to its neo-Kantian presuppositions, operates with a nonfunctionalist concept of rationality and a nonempirical concept of validity. Thus, those disciples of Parsons to whom it has become clear that the theory of modernity cannot do without a standard for evaluating crisis-ridden processes of modernization are only drawing the conclusions when they try to take his theory of culture out of its systems-theoretical casing again.

B. Excursus on an Attempt to Re-Kantianize Parsons.—Richard Münch has made a straightforward attempt to connect up Parsons' social systems theory with Weber's theory of rationalization. He distinguishes cultural from societal rationalization more sharply than did Weber himself:

If we want to reconstruct Weber's question of how to explain the rationalization process peculiar to the Occident then we have to distinguish two parts of the explanation. In one part, Weber tried to work out the methodical-rational lifestyle peculiar to the Occident. This is supposed to explain the impetus to rationalization and its general direction. The latter is set by the worldviews institutionalized within cultural milieus. From this perspective Weber studied Confucianism, Hinduism and Jewish-Christian religion—especially its most consistently developed form: ascetic Protestantism—as interpretations of the world that generate three different attitudes toward it, thereby setting the overall courses of the rationalization of life conduct. These three *general directions* enter in turn into connections with the so called inner logics of individual social spheres. From this combination of general attitudes toward the world and the specific inner logics of social spheres, there result specific directions of rationalization within individual social spheres such as, for example, economics, politics, law, administration, science. The "inner logic" of each of these spheres stems from the way in which its problems are defined within the frame of a specific attitude toward the world.[19]

The "direction" definitive of the Occident is, in Münch's view, set by the attitude of active mastery of the world. Taking his cue from Parsons, he makes do with such characterizations as "individualist-universalist" and "rationalist-activist," and focuses on the question of how we can conceive of the transposition of cultural rationalization into societal rationalization.

Weber's version of this problem was that religious ethics and the world mutually permeated one another in the methodical-rational conduct of life of the carrier strata of capitalism; this "interpenetration" led to an ethical restructuring of everyday action reaching into all profane areas of life and, in the end, to the institutionalization of purposive-rational economic and administrative action. To be sure, Weber did not provide a convincing model of the release of cognitive potential significant for social evolution. Münch turns to Parsons at this point. He describes the institutional embodiment and motivational anchoring of the cognitive structures that issued from the rationalization of religious worldviews in the language of systems theory and understands the rise of occidental rationalization as an example of the *interpenetration of action systems*: "For Weber, what is specific to modern development in the Occident is the mutual penetration of religious ethics and the world, which has to be seen in a dual perspective: on the one side, as an interpenetration of the fiduciary-cultural religious sphere and the community, through which the ethics of the community was systematized and universalized, and on the other hand, as an interpenetration of the community with the economic and political spheres, through which the economic and political orders could first arise and through which the ethics of the community took on an increasingly practical and formal-legal character."[20]

In Münch's version of the Weberian theory, modern law and the Protestant ethic are the result of a *vertical* interpenetration between culture and society (or its integrative subsystem), whereas the capitalist economy and rational public administration are due to a *horizontal* interpenetration between a societal community already revolutionized by universalistic legal and moral representations and those domains that follow the inner logics of economic and administrative problems. From an evolutionary perspective, this process can then be described as follows: "If we start from the genetic code of Occidental societies and want to explain their development, we have to ask how this code becomes phenotypic via the institutionalization and internalization of genotypic information. We have to explain the concrete normative structures by the degree to which it gets anchored in communities and interpenetrates with adaptive action."[21]

Two things are noteworthy about the terminology in which this reformulation is couched. First, Münch still uses the expressions 'institutionalization' and 'internalization' for the embodiment and anchoring of cognitive structures. Parsons used them to designate the incorporation of cultural patterns of value, that is, of cultural *contents*, but modern law and the Protestant ethic are expressions of societal rationalization only insofar as they embody or anchor the *formal structures* of a higher level of moral consciousness. Second, Münch uses the expression 'interpenetration' not only for the "vertical" process in which an objectified, decentered understanding of the world gets implemented, but at the same time for the "horizontal" intermeshing of an institutional framework transferred over to posttraditional morality with the subsystems of the economy and state. The institutionalization of purposive-rational economic and administrative action is a result of the two "interpenetrations" working together. But only the vertical interpenetration is equivalent in meaning to the mutual permeation of ethics and the world, that is, to the evolutionary learning process in which cultural rationalization was transposed with innovative force into the rationalization of society. It is only under *this* aspect that we have to do with a rationalization of the *lifeworld* that can be seen in the rationality of *life conduct*. The vertical interpenetration fulfills necessary conditions for the horizontal; modern law and the Protestant ethic further the institutionalization of money and power as the steering media, with the help of which modern societies achieve a higher level of integration. But Münch lumps both "processes of interpenetration" together; he does not distinguish the growth in complexity of the social system from the progressive rationalization of the lifeworld, any more than Parsons did. Münch is able seriously to pursue his aim of bringing Weber's explanation of occidental rationalism into Parsons' theory only because he twists the latter back onto the premises of the former and extracts the core of neo-Kantian culture theory from the husks of systems theory. In a certain sense, he revokes Parsons' turn toward systems functionalism. He removes from the latter any essentialist connotations and treats 'system' only as an analytical frame of reference. Not only do action systems not "act"—they also do not "function." On Münch's interpretation of Parsons, the four-function paradigm is no longer supposed to serve the purpose of functionalist explanation. It does not even permit us to assert that "every social system depends on the fulfillment of the four AGIL functions. This is not the explanatory direction to take in applying the analytical scheme. Application is guided rather, by the core thesis that we can explain a given aspect of reality only by the way in which the energic and steering systems differentiated in the scheme work together."[22] Münch sees himself forced to advance this bold thesis because he wants to preserve the genuine content of the rationalization thesis. He understands "structural differentiation . . . as the result of . . . interpenetration and not as the result of the functional adaptation of a system to a more complex environment."[23] He conceives interpenetration in the sense of the value realization that Parsons had built into his concept of value-regulated, purposive activity.[24]

Thus he sees in the concept of a steering hierarchy the essential element in a theory of action systems understood in structuralist terms. This seems all the more plausible as Münch wants, with the concept of interpenetration, to actualize the philosophical content that Parsons had simultaneously accommodated and made unrecognizable in his concept of a hierarchy of control. The hierarchical ordering of the four functions and the corresponding subsystems made sense only on the premise that the self-maintenance processes of action systems are at the same time processes of value realization. On this view, every social state of affairs can be analyzed as resulting from the conjunction of energic (conditioning) and steering (controlling) action subsystems. The position of a subsystem in the steering hierarchy is determined by the proportion between its steering and energic contributions to the process of value realization. By contrast, the functional specification of subsystems retains only subordinate significance.

This arrangement permits Münch to use the concept of interpenetration in more than a descriptive fashion. Since it is meant to provide an equivalent for Weber's concept of rationalization, it has to incorporate a normative content. The expression 'interpenetration' refers simultaneously to the *empirical process* of the reciprocal penetration of action systems *and* to the *normatively privileged state* that two systems attain when they penetrate one another *in a balanced way* and to a degree that is *optimal* for the problem-solving needs of both. Münch distinguishes this case of *successful interpenetration* from cases of *mutual isolation,* of *adaptation* (of the steering systems to the energic, less ordered systems), and of *constriction* (of the energic systems by the predominance of the steering systems). These normative ideas are presented in the jargon of systems theory, but they express something more than a normatively upgraded idea of systemic equilibrium under conditions of high internal complexity. The intuition behind them is, rather, that of an unfolding of the potentials residing in culture. The modernization of society counts as the phenotypic realization of a cultural code that is presented not as some arbitrary potential of value orientations, but—drawing on Weber's theory of religious rationalization—as the result of learning processes and as a new learning level.

Münch is unable to give adequate account of this intuition with his normative interpretation of the concept of interpenetration. Weber was able to conceive of modernization as societal *rationalization* because he first explained the rationality of the modern understanding of the world developed in the West. This step is missing in Münch; he reverses things by calling a cultural code rational when it is suitable for the mutual penetration of ethics and the world: "Through this form of institutionalizing and internalizing a value system, societies and personalities achieve an increasingly higher degree of interconnection between two opposed orientations: they combine an extensive preservation of scopes for freedom and possibilities of change with orderliness."[25] With the expression "interpenetration," Münch is proposing a program of mediation; lacking any dialectic, he is convinced of the value of dialectical mediation. Instead of working out the complex concept of rationality that at least implicitly guided Weber, he falls back into the reifying world of systems-theoretical ideas. His justification of the normative upgrading of interpenetration is as follows: "(Through interpenetration) the world becomes more and more complex while preserving its orderliness; that is, there arises more and more *ordered complexity.* This is a definition of the direction of evolution which is, in the end anchored in the telic code of the human condition—in the aprioristic necessity of constituting meaning under the conditions of a complex world that is not immediately meaningful."[26]

What happpens, in fact, is that Münch starts by painting a harmonious picture of European-American modernity and then represents Parsons' systems-theoretically conceived state of differentiated equilibrium from the perspective of value realization as a successful interpenetration. It is in the light of Parsons' interpretation of modernity that Münch conceptualizes processes of societal rationalization as interpenetration. In doing so, he keeps Parsons' idealism in the shadows. What Weber maintained in regard to the beginnings of the modern world is supposed to be all the more true of its development since the eighteenth century: "The interpenetration of community and economy makes possible both the expansion of solidarity and the spread of economic rationality at once, without the one happening at the expense of the other. In this sense, action can become simultaneously more moral, more solidary, and more economically rational; the increase in solidarity is even a condition of economically rational action, which is no longer purely utilitarian action but ethically regulated economic action."[27] In projecting this asceptic picture of developed capitalist societies, purified of all social pathologies, Münch falls in with Parsons—and not by chance. They owe their agreement to complementary weaknesses in a theoretical construction that retracts the distinction between system and lifeworld and thus bypasses the indications pointed to by Weber of a modernity at variance with itself. Parsons brings the rationalization of the lifeworld conceptually into line with the increasing complexity of the action system in such a way that the phenomena of the stubborn resistance to functional imperatives offered by communicatively structured spheres of life escape him. In the theory of interpenetration, on the other hand, modernization appears so much the actualization of a cultural potential that Münch waters down the constraints of material reproduction into conditions for realizing values, and no longer comprehends their internal systemic dynamics.

VIII

Concluding Reflections:
From Parsons via Weber to Marx

The basic conceptual structure of our two-level concept of society, combining the aspects of lifeworld and system, has been elucidated with reference to construction problems in Parsons' social theory. The very object of the theory of society changes in the course of social evolution. The more the material reproduction of the communicatively structured lifeworld is expanded and differentiated, the more it calls for a systems-theoretical analysis to get at the counterintuitive aspects of sociation. This shift in perspective must, of course, be undertaken with methodological care and without confusing the two paradigms. Parsons toiled with this problem, but to no avail. It is precisely the phenomena of contradictory rationalization investigated along the path from Marx to Weber that call for a theoretical approach sufficiently sensitive to the analytic separation of social and system integration. As much as Parsons learned from Weber's investigations, he was unable to exploit fully the potentials of the *Zwischenbetrachtung*, to whose central importance Wolfgang Schluchter has recently alerted us. Neither of the principal components of Weber's diagnosis of the times has become any less relevant in the six or seven decades since he formulated them.

This holds true for the thesis of a loss of meaning no less than for that of a loss of freedom. Weber saw the noncoercive, unifying power of collectively shared convictions disappearing along with religion and metaphysics, along with the forms of objective reason in Horkheimer's sense. A reason restricted to the cognitive-instrumental dimension was placed at the service of a merely subjective self-assertion. It is in this sense that Weber spoke of a polytheism of impersonal forces, an antagonism of ultimate orders of value, a competition of irreconcilable gods and demons. To the degree that objective reason shrunk down to subjective reason, culture was losing the power to reconcile particular interests through convictions.[1] As to the other thesis, concerning a loss of freedom, in a famous passage Weber conjures up that "shell of bondage which men will perhaps be forced to inhabit someday, as powerless as the fellahs of ancient Egypt. This could happen if a technically superior administration were to be the ultimate and sole value in the ordering of their affairs, and that means: a rational bureaucratic administration with the corresponding welfare benefits."[2] The illuminating power of this diagnosis can best be appreciated if we understand the bureaucratization of spheres of action as the model for a technicizing of the lifeworld that robs actors of the meaning of their own actions.[3]

I shall (1) take up again Weber's reflections on the paradoxes of societal rationalization, in light of the hypothesis I have developed—in a global manner, to be sure—under the catch phrase 'mediatization of the lifeworld'; after our critical examination of Parsons' theory of society, it will be possible to give this hypothesis a sharper formulation. This second attempt to appropriate Weber in the spirit of Western Marxism is inspired by the concept of communicative reason developed in connection with Durkheim and Mead. In this respect, it is (2) also critical of the Marxist tradition itself. In the advanced industrial societies of the West, containment of class conflict by the welfare state sets in motion the dynamics of a reification of communicatively structured areas of action, which, while still conditioned by capitalist relations, works itself out in ways that are less and less class-specific. This critical development of basic Marxist assumptions provides a view of the currently conspicuous aporias of societal modernization. In the concluding section, I shall (3) characterize the tasks in relation to which critical social theory will have to measure itself against competing approaches.

1. A Backward Glance: Weber's Theory of Modernity

Our analysis (in Volume 1, Chapter II) of Weber's theory of rationalization led to conflicting results. On the one hand, his approach still holds out the best prospect of explaining the social pathologies that appeared in the wake of capitalist modernization. On the other hand, we ran into a number of inconsistencies, which indicates that the systematic content of his theory can today be appropriated only through reconstructing it with improved conceptual tools.

One problem arose from the fact that Weber studies the rationalization of action systems only under the aspect of purposive rationality. If now, consistent with his approach, we want to arrive at a more adequate description and explanation of the pathologies of modernity, we shall have to deploy a more complex concept of rationality that enables us to delineate the scope for modernizing society opened up by the rationalization of worldviews in the West. Then we could analyze the rationalization of action systems not only under the cognitive-instrumental aspect, but by bringing in moral-practical and aesthetic-expressive aspects across the whole spectrum. I have attempted to meet this desideratum, analytically and in terms of the history of social theory, by elucidating such concepts as 'action oriented to mutual understanding', 'symbolically structured lifeworld', and 'communicative rationality'.

A second problem arose from the fact that Weber, hampered by bottlenecks in the formation of his action-theoretical concepts, equated the capitalist pattern of modernization with societal rationalization generally. Thus, he could not trace the symptomatic manifestations he noted back to the selective exploitation of culturally available cognitive potentials. If we want now to make Weber's diagnosis fruitful, we shall have to take account of the pathological side effects of a class structure that cannot be satisfactorily grasped by action-theoretical means alone. This places the rise of subsystems of purposive rational action in another light. The rationalization of contexts of communicative action and the emergence of subsystems of purposive rational economic and administrative action are processes that have to be sharply distinguished analytically. Accordingly, another desideratum was to resituate analysis from the level of conflicting action orientations to that of an opposition between principles of societal integration. For purposes of conceptual clarification, we discussed the trend toward an uncoupling of system and lifeworld; we then turned to Parsons to examine the problem in theory construction of how the two paradigms can be connected at a basic conceptual level. We shall now have to see whether this has given us an interpretive perspective from which the inconsistencies in Weber's explanation of Occidental rationalism might be resolved.

Our analysis turned up the following difficulties:

—Weber correctly described the Protestant ethic of the calling and the corresponding methodical-rational conduct of life as embodiments of a moral consciousness guided by principles; but he was unable to give a systematic account of the fact that an egocentric vocational asceticism, based on a particularism of grace, represented a highly irrational embodiment of the religious ethic of neighborliness.

—Weber noted the erosion of ethical orientations toward work in one's calling and the spread of instrumental orientations, but his reasoning that secularization processes were responsible for this disintegration of the vocational ethic is not convincing. Principled moral consciousness is not necessarily connected with a personal interest in salvation; it has in fact been stabilized in secularized form, even if, to begin with, only in certain social strata.

—Weber observed a drift of life-styles toward a polarization between specialists and hedonists; here too, his reasoning that this resulted from an antagonism between cultural value spheres with their own linear logics is unconvincing. In principle, when substantive reason comes apart into its different moments, reason can retain its unity in the form of procedural rationality.

—Finally, Weber considered a systematic opposition between formal and substantive rationalization to be endemic to the modern development of law; but, as we have seen, he was unable consistently to bring the legitimation problems generated by a postivistically hollowed out legal domination under the pattern of rationalization of modern societies, because he remained himself tied to legal-positivistic views.

Weber's explanatory strategy can be rid of these and similar difficulties if we assume that

(p) the emergence of modern, to begin with capitalist, societies required the institutional embodiment and motivational anchoring of postconventional moral and legal representations; but

(q) capitalist modernization follows a pattern such that cognitive-instrumental rationality surges beyond the bounds of the economy and state into other, communicatively structured areas of life and achieves dominance there at the expense of moral-political and aesthetic-practical rationality, and (*r*) this produces disturbances in the symbolic reproduction of the lifeworld.

Weber's explanation of the emergence of modern societies focuses on the proposition (*p*); his diagnosis of the times refers to the pathological side effects asserted in (*r*); he does not put forward the proposition (*q*), which is nevertheless compatible with the interpretation of his *Zwischenbetrachtung* proposed above in Volume 1. The propositions (*p*), (*q*), and (*r*) can be connected together in a loose argument sketch if we expand the theoretical framework in the manner suggested, that is, if we (1) extend our action-theoretical foundations in the direction of a theory of communicative action tailored to the lifeworld concept of society and to the developmental perspective of the differentiation of lifeworld structures; and (2) develop our own basic social-theoretical concepts in the direction of a two-level concept of society that suggests the developmental perspective of a growing autonomy of systemically integrated action contexts over against the socially integrated lifeworld.

From this there follows a global assumption regarding the analysis of modernization processes, to wit, that a progressively rationalized lifeworld is both uncoupled from and made dependent upon increasingly complex, formally organized domains of action, like the economy and the state administration. This dependency, resulting from the *mediatization* of the lifeworld by system imperatives, assumes the sociopathological form of an *internal colonization* when critical disequilibria in material reproduction—that is, systemic crises amenable to systems-theoretical analysis—can be avoided only at the cost of disturbances in the symbolic reproduction of the lifeworld—that is, of "subjectively" experienced, identity-threatening crises or pathologies.

Using this as our guide, we can connect the propositions (*p*) and (*q*) by interpreting the institutionalization of purposive-rational economic and administrative action as the anchoring of the money and power media in the lifeworld. The proposition (*q*) then says that the subsystems differentiated out via the media of money and power make possible a level of integration higher than that in traditional class societies, and that they force a restructuring of such societies into economically constituted class societies. Finally, the propositions (*q*) and (*r*) can be connected by means of the assumption that in developed capitalist societies, mechanisms of system integration encroach upon spheres of action that can fulfill their functions only under conditions of social integration. If this rough sketch is filled in with Weber's arguments, new light is thrown on the rise and development of the modern age. In what follows, I shall (*A*) begin with Weber's thesis on bureaucratization, (*B*) return to his explanation of the emergence of capitalist societies and, with the help of this reconstruction, (*C*) take up again his diagnosis of the times.

A.—For Weber, bureaucratization is a key to understanding modern societies. The latter are marked by the appearance of a new type of organization: economic production is organized in a capitalist manner, with rationally calculating entrepreneurs; public administration is organized in a bureaucratice manner, with juristically trained, specialized officials— that is, they are organized in the form of private enterprises and public bureaucracies. The relevant means for carrying out their tasks are concentrated in the hands of owners and leaders; membership in these organizations is made independent of ascriptive properties. By these means, organizations gain a high degree of internal flexibility and external autonomy. In virtue of their efficiency, the organizational forms of the capitalist economy and the modern state administration establish themselves in other action systems to such an extent that modern societies fit the picture of "a society of organizations," even from the standpoint of lay members. For sociologists, this new type of organization also provides an illustration of the concept of a self-regulating social system. It is no accident that the basic concepts of systems theory were first applied in the sociology of organizations.[1]

Weber represented the activities of organizations as a kind of purposive-rational action writ large. In his view, the rationality of an organization was measured by the degree to which an enterprise or institution made purposive-rational action by members both possible and secure. This purposive model has been dropped in more recent approaches to organization theory, for it cannot explain the fact that it is not only (or even chiefly) by way of the purposive-rational action of members that organizations resolve problems of self-maintenance. We may not assume, even in the cases of the capitalist economic organization and the modern state organization, any linear dependency of organizational rationality on the rationality of members' actions. Thus, functionalism in social science no longer ties into the rationality of the actors' knowledge. In studying processes of societal rationalization, functionalism adopts the reference point of systems rationality: rationalizable "knowledge" is expressed in the capacity of social systems to steer themselves. Weber understood societal rationalization as an institutionalization of purposive-rational economic and administrative action in the organizational forms of the private enterprise and public bureaucracy. The purposive-rational action of organization members is of less importance to systems theory; what is of chief interest are the functional contributions that positions, programs, and decisions—any state of affairs or element—make to solving system problems.[2]

Weber held that the tendencies toward bureaucratization in society as a whole established two things at once: the highest form of societal rationality and the most effective subsumption of acting subjects under the objective force of an apparatus operating autonomously, above their heads. Upon closer analysis, this thesis of a loss of freedom owes its plausibility to an ambiguous use of the expression 'rationalization'. Depending upon the context, its meaning shifts unnoticeably from action rationality to system rationality. Weber is full of admiration for the organizational accomplishments of modern bureaucracies, but when he adopts the perspective of members and clients, and analyzes the objectification of social relations in organizations as depersonalizing, he describes the rationality of bureaucracies that have been cut loose from vocational-ethical attitudes, from value-rational attitudes in general, and have developed their own internal dynamics, in terms of the image of a rationally operating machine: "An inanimate machine is mind objectified. Only this provides it with the power to force men into its service and to dominate their everyday working life as completely as is actually the case in the factory. Objectified intelligence is also that animated machine, the bureaucratic organization, with its specialization of trained skills, its division of jurisdiction, its rules and hierarchical relations of authority."[3] In union with the inanimate machine, the animate machine of the self-sufficient bureaucracy works toward establishing that "shell of bondage" of which Weber spoke. Only inanimate machines "work" in the sense of the physical concept of work; in other cases we say that machines "function" more or less well. This metaphor of an animate machine creates some distance from the purposive model and already suggests the idea of a system stabilizing itself in relation to a contingent environment. The distinction between systemic and purposive rationality was, of course, introduced only later, but Weber already had some such notion in mind; however vaguely and intuitively. At any rate, the thesis of a loss of meaning can be made more plausible if we regard bureaucratization as the sign of a new level of system differentiation. Via the media of money and power, the subsystems of the economy and the state are differentiated out of an institutional complex set within the horizon of the lifeworld; *formally organized domains of action* emerge that—in the final analysis—are no longer integrated through the mechanism of mutual understanding, that sheer off from lifeworld contexts and congeal into a kind of norm-free sociality.

With these new organizations, system perspectives arise from which the lifeworld is distantiated and perceived as an element of system environments. Organizations gain autonomy through a neutralizing demarcation from the symbolic structures of the lifeworld; they become peculiarly indifferent to culture, society, and personality. Luhmann describes these effects as the "dehumanization of society." Social reality seems to shrink down to an objectified organizational reality cut loose from normative ties. Actually, "dehumanization" means any splitting off from the lifeworld of formally organized domains of action which is made possible by steering media; it does not mean only "depersonalization" in the sense of the separation of organized action systems from personality structures; there are corresponding neutralizations of the other two components of the lifeworld as well.

To begin with the indifference between organization and personality: modern enterprises and institutions take the principle of voluntary membership seriously. From their standpoint, functionally necessary motives, value orientations, and performances are viewed as contributions that members bring to the organization. Through blanket acceptance of membership conditions and members' generalized willingness to follow orders, organizations render themselves independent from concrete dispositions and goals, in general from the particular contexts of life that might otherwise flow into them from the socializatory background of personality traits and impede their steering capacity: "The differentiation of the membership role constitutes a buffer zone between system and person and makes it possible largely to uncouple the meaning relations of action adequate to the system from personal structures of meaning and motivation. By means of this role, motivation for participating in the system, independent of the requirements of action internal to the system, can be secured and, in generalized form, made useful for an objectively complex and temporally flexible, internal structure of the system."[4]

The capitalist enterprise, detached from the family household of the entrepreneur, can serve as a historically significant example of the indifference between an organization and those who belong to it, when the latter are neutralized into "members." For a business enterprise, the private life-contexts of all of its employees become part of the environment.

There is not only a zone of indifference between organization and personality; the same holds for an organization's relation to culture and society. As illustrated by the historical example of the separation of a secularized state from the church, that is, by the emergence of a secular state power exercising tolerance, modern forms of organization also need to be independent from legitimating worldviews, in general from cultural traditions that could previously be used only through interpretively continuing and developing them. Organizations use ideological neutrality to escape the force of traditions that would otherwise restrict the scope and the sovereign exercise of their competence to shape their own programs. Just as persons are, as members, stripped of personality structures and neutralized into bearers of certain performances, so too cultural traditions, as ideologies, are robbed of their binding power and converted into raw material for purposes of ideology planning, that is, for an administrative processing of meaning constellations. Organizations have to provide for their own legitimation needs. It is again Luhmann who has given the most suggestive description of how culture, reified into the environment of a system, is instrumentalized for purposes of system maintenance: "Organizational systems are especially adept at organizing even the consequences of action and the neutralizing accomplishments of their ends, at 'ideologically' constituting in this way contexts of interpretation and valuation that wear their contingency and relativity openly."[5]

Organizations not only disconnect themselves from cultural commitments and from attitudes and orientations specific to given personalities; they also make themselves independent from lifeworld contexts by neutralizing the normative background of informal, customary, morally regulated contexts of action. The social is not absorbed as such by organized action systems; rather, it is split up into spheres of action constituted as the lifeworld and spheres neutralized against the lifeworld. The former are communicatively structured, the latter formally organized. They do not stand in any *hierarchical* relationship between levels of interaction and organization; rather, they stand *opposite* one another as socially and systemically integrated spheres of action. In formally organized domains, the mechanism of mutual understanding in language, which is essential for social integration, is partially rescinded and relieved by steering media. Naturally, these media have to be anchored in the lifeworld by means of formal law. Thus, as we shall see, the types of legal regulation of social relations are good indicators of the boundaries between system and lifeworld.

I call "formally organized" all social relations located in media-steered subsystems, so far as these relations are *first generated by positive law*. They also include exchange and power relations constituted by private and public law but going beyond the boundaries of organizations. In premodern societies, social labor and political domination are still based on first-order institutions that are *merely overlaid and guaranteed by law*; in modern societies, they are replaced by orders of private property and legal domination that appear *directly* in forms of positive law. Modern compulsory law is uncoupled from ethical motives; it functions as a means for demarcating areas of legitimate choice for private legal persons and scopes of legal competence for officeholders (for incumbents of organized power positions generally). In these spheres of action, legal norms replace the prelegal substratum of traditional morals to which previously, in their metainstitutional role, legal norms had reference. The law no longer starts from previously existing structures of communication; it generated forms of commerce and chains of command suited to media of communication. In the process, traditionally customary contexts of action oriented to mutual understanding get shoved out into the environments of systems. Using this criterion, we can locate the boundaries between system and lifeworld, in a rough and ready way, such that the subsystems of the economy and the bureaucratic state administration are on one side, while on the other side we find private spheres of life (connected with family, neighborhood, voluntary associations) as well as public spheres (for both private persons and citizens). I shall come back to this.

The formal-legal constitution of action systems and the expulsion of webs of communicative action into system environments show up in the social relations within organizations. To what extent the scope of disposition cleared by a formal organization is utilized in a purposive-rational manner, instructions are carried out in a purposive-rational way, and internal conflicts are dealt with in a purposive-rational fashion; to what extent the imperatives of profitableness in business, which capitalist enterprises must (more or less) follow, leave their mark on the action orientations of the operating staff—these are questions that, as empirical studies have shown, can by no means be answered deductively. The basic characteristic of the action orientations of members is not purposive-rationality, but the fact that all their actions fall under the conditions of organizational membership, that is to say, under the premises of a legally regulated domain of action. When we understand business concerns as self-regulating systems, it is the aspect of legal organization that comes to the fore.

The idealized background assumptions of the classical model of bureaucracy have rightly been criticized on the grounds that the organizational structure expressed in programs and positions certainly does not get translated automatically and without distortion into organizational activity that is calculated, impersonal, open to objective check, and independent of situation.[6]

Even within formally organized domains of action, interactions are still connected via the mechanism of mutual understanding. If all processes of genuinely reaching understanding were banished from the interior of organizations, formally regulated social relations could not be sustained, nor could organizational goals be realized. Nevertheless, the classical model of bureaucracy is right in one respect: action within organization falls *under the premises* of formally regulated domains of action. Because the latter are ethically neutralized by their legal form of organization, *communicative action forfeits its validity basis in the interior of organizations.*

Members of organizations act communicatively only *with reservation.* They know they *can* have recourse to formal regulations, not only in exceptional but in routine cases; there is no *necessity* for achieving consensus by communicative means. Under conditions of modern law, the formalization of interpersonal relations means the legitimate demarcation of scopes for decision making that can, if necessary, be utilized in a strategic manner. Innerorganizational relations constituted via membership do not replace communicative action, but they do *disempower* its validity basis so as to provide the legitimate possibility of redefining at will spheres of action oriented to mutual understanding into action situations stripped of lifeworld contexts and no longer directed to achieving consensus. Of course, the externalization of lifeworld contexts cannot be carried through without remainder, as the informal organization upon which all formal organization relies amply demonstrates. Informal organization covers those legitimately regulated, innerorganizational relations that, notwithstanding the juridification of the framework, may be moralized. The lifeworlds of members, never completely husked away, penetrate here into the reality of organizations.

We can sum up by saying that tendencies toward bureaucratization are represented from the internal perspective of organizations as a growing *independence* from elements of the lifeworld that have been shoved out into system environments. From the opposite perspective of the lifeworld, the same process presents itself as one of increasing *autonomization,* for areas of action converted over to communication media and systemically integrated are *withdrawn* from the institutional orders of the lifeworld. This constitution of action contexts that are no longer socially integrated means that social relations are separated off from the identities of the actors involved. The objective meaning of a functionally stabilized nexus of action can no longer be brought into the intersubjective context of relevance of subjectively meaningful action. At the same time, as Luckmann notes, it makes itself felt as a causality of fate in the experiences and sufferings of actors: "The course of action is 'objectively' determined by the 'purposive-rational' context of meaning of the specialized institutional domain in question; but it no longer fits unproblematically into the 'subjective' context of meaning of the individual biography. In other words, in most of the areas of everyday life important for maintaining a society, the objective meaning of an action no longer coincides as a matter of course with the subjective sense of acting."[7] Whether identity problems result from the fact that action systems grow out of the horizon of the lifeworld and can no longer be experienced by actors as a totality is another question altogether.[8] Identity problems are unavoidable only if there is an *irresistible* tendency to an *ever-expanding* bureaucratization.

Luhmann's systems functionalism is actually based on the assumption that in modern societies the symbolically structured lifeworld has already been driven back into the niches of a systemically self-sufficient society and been colonized by it. As against this, the fact that the steering media of money and power have to be anchored in the lifeworld speaks prima facie for the primacy of socially integrated spheres of action over objectified systemic networks. There is no doubt that the coordinating mechanism of mutual understanding is put partially out of play within formally organized domains, but the relative weights of social versus system integration is a different question, and one that can be answered only empirically.

Whether the tendencies toward bureaucratization described by Weber will ever reach the Orwellian state in which all integrative operations have been converted from the—in my view, still fundamental—sociative mechanism of reaching understanding in language over to systemic mechanisms, and whether such a state is at all possible without a transformation of anthropologically deep-seated structures—these are open questions. I see the methodological weakness of an absolutized systems functionalism precisely in the fact that it formulates its basic concepts *as if* that process, whose beginnings Weber perceived, had already been concluded—*as if* a total bureaucratization had dehumanized society as a whole, consolidated it into a system torn from its roots in a communicatively structured lifeworld, and demoted the lifeworld to the status of one subsystem among many. For Adorno, this "administered world" was a vision of extreme horror; for Luhmann it has become a trivial presupposition.[9]

B.—I shall consider Weber's diagnosis of the times from the perspective of the mediatization of the lifeworld; before doing so, however, I shall see how this reformulation of his bureaucratization thesis in system-lifeworld terms might be connected to his rationalization thesis.

The differentiation of the economic system out of the political order of European feudalism was constitutive for emerging capitalist society. For its part, the political order was reorganized under the functional imperatives of the new mode of production, namely, in the form of the modern state. Production in the capitalist economy was both decentralized and regulated unpolitically via markets. The state, which was not itself a producer and drew off the resources for its ordering accomplishments from private income, organized and secured the legal commerce of competing private persons who carried the production process. Thus, for Weber, the two institutional nuclei, the capitalist enterprise and the modern administrative apparatus, were the phenomena calling for explanation. In the case of the capitalist enterprise, the conspicuous evolutionary advance was not the institutionalization of wage labor but the planfulness of economic decision making oriented to profit and based on rational bookkeeping. Weber's explanation refers in the first instance not to the establishment of the labor markets that turned abstract labor power into an expense in business calculations, but to the "spirit of capitalism," that is, to the mentality characteristic of the purposive-rational economic action of the early capitalist entrepreneurs. Whereas Marx took the mode of production to be the phenomenon in need of explanation, and investigated capital accumulation as the new mechanism of system integration, Weber's view of the problem turns the investigation in another direction. For him the explanans is the conversion of the economy and state administration over to purposive-rational action orientations; the changes fall in the domain of forms of *social integration*. At the same time, this new form of social integration made it possible to institutionalize the money mechanism, and thereby new mechanisms of system integration.

Marx starts from problems of system integration, Weber from problems of social integration. If these two analytic levels are kept separate, Weber's theory of rationalization can be incorporated into an explanatory model that I have sketched elsewhere.[10] Its basic lines are as follows:

(*a*) Learning capacities first acquired by individual members of a society or by marginal groups make their way into the society's interpretive system via exemplary learning processes. Collectively shared structures of consciousness and stocks of knowledge represent a *cognitive potential*—in terms of empirical knowledge and moral-practical insight—that can be utilized for societal purposes.

(*b*) Societies learn through resolving system problems that present evolutionary challenges. By this I mean problems that overload the steering capcity available within the limits of a given social formation. Societies can *learn in an evolutionary sense* by drawing upon moral and legal representations contained in worldviews to reorganize systems of action and shape new forms of social integration. This process can be understood as an institutional embodiment or rationality structures already developed at the cultural level.

(*c*) The establishment of a *new form of social integration* makes it possible to implement available (or to produce new) technical-organizational knowledge, that is to say, it makes possible a *heightening of productive forces* and an expansion of systemic complexity. Thus learning processes in the area of moral-practical consciousness function as a pacemaker in social evolution.

According to this theory, evolutionary advances are marked by institutions that make it possible to solve whatever system problems are producing a crisis, and to do so in virtue of features that derive from their embodiment of rationality structures. This institutional embodiment of rationality structures that were already developed within the culture of the old society means a new *level of learning.* 'Institutionalization' does not refer here to making cultural patterns obligatory, that is, to making certain *substantive* orientations binding, but rather to opening new *structural* possibilities for rationalizing action. Evolutionary learning processes are understood as the implementation of a learning potential. And this process can in turn be causally explained in terms of structures and events. I shall not go into the thorny methodological question of how to conceptualize the reciprocal influence of structures and events, the impetus provided by problem-generating events, and the challenge afforded by structurally open possibilities.[11]

Adopting these hypothetical orientations, we can reconstruct the outline of Weber's explanatory strategy as follows. With regard to the institutional complexes characteristic of the modern level of development, we must be able to show (*i*) that they are functional for resolving previously unresolved system problems and (*ii*) that they embody higher-level structures of moral consciousness. The causal explanation then consists (*iii*) in demonstrating the existence of a corresponding cognitive potential within rationalized worldviews, (*iv*) specifying the conditions under which the institutional embodiment of structures of consciousness already developed at the cultural level can first be tried out and then stabilized, and finally (*v*) identifying the phases of the learning process itself with reference to historical processes. In short, causal explanation requires in this case that we combine functionalist and structuralist explanations. I cannot fill in this explanatory model here, not even by way of illustrating it, but I will suggest how it might be "occupied" by the points of view from which Weber investigated Occidental rationalism.

(*ad i*) It would be the task of functional analysis to identify the *system problems* in the feudal society of the high Middle Ages that could not be resolved on the basis of agricultural production regulated by feudal law, handicrafts centered in the cities, local markets, and foreign trade oriented to luxury consumption—that is, to show that certain problems overloaded the steering capacities and learning abilities of political class societies. It is not the *kind* of system problems that is distinctive of developments in Europe, for other civilizations had to struggle with such problems as well. What is distinctive is the fact that they were taken up as *evolutionary challenges.* Further tasks of functional analysis would be to explain why the mode of production that grew up around the institutional nucleus of the capitalist enterprise was able to solve those problems once the modern state developed. The latter secured the bourgeois private legal order and thereby the institutionalization of the money medium. More generally, it secured the prerequisites for sustaining a depoliticized economic process, cut loose from moral norms and use-value orientations, in markets of a certain size—precisely that of the territorial state.[12]

(*ad ii*) It would then be the task of *structural analysis* to clarify the formal properties of the action orientations functionally required by the capitalist enterprise and the modern administration. Weber investigated the norming of purposive-rational action under both *vocational-ethical* and *legal* aspects. The systematizing power of principled moral consciousness was needed for a motivational anchoring of purposive-rational action orientations so constant and so encompassing as to be able to constitute vocational roles. Thus, structural analysis aimed at the "elective affinity" between the "Protestant ethic" and the "spirit of capitalism" that had congealed into the modern occupational culture. Weber explained, in terms of its structure, why a deinstitutionalized ethic of conviction based on a particularism of grace could penetrate all spheres and stages of life, dramatize work in one's calling generally, and simultaneously lead to the unbrotherly consequence of objectifying interpersonal relations. In another vein, a conception of *law based on principles of enactment and justification* was needed for the value-rational anchoring of purposive-rational action. Here structural analysis was directed to the validity bases of modern law, which were supposed to replace traditional validity with agreements arrived at rationally. The positivizing, legalizing, and formalizing of law that was required for the institutionalization of money and power and for the corresponding organization of economic and administrative action meant, at the same time, separating legality from morality. Thus the legal system as a whole had to rely upon an autonomous justification possible only in terms of posttraditional morality.

(*ad iii*) Once the institutions that mark the transition to modern society as an evolutionary learning process have been identified, it must be shown that the rationality structure they embody were previously *available as structures of worldviews*. As a matter of fact, in his comparative studies on the economic ethics of world religions, Weber wanted to show that the rationalization of worldviews led along the Jewish-Christian line of tradition, and only along this occidental line of development, to the differentiation of cultural value spheres with their own inner logics, and thereby to posttraditional legal and moral representations. This was a *necessary condition* for that "interpenetration of ethics and the world" in the course of which the profane orders of society were transformed.

(*ad iv*) However, the *causal explanation* of the transition to the modern age could succeed only with the discovery of the conditions *sufficient* for utilizing—however selectively—the available cognitive potential, so as to bring about the *characteristic* institutional innovations. As sketched under point (*i*) above, the latter evince a new form of social integration; they make possible a new level of system differentiation and permit the expansion of steering capacity beyond the limits of a politically constituted, stratified class society. A number of factors that Weber discussed at length and Parsons reexamined belong in this context: the special position of medieval trading cities and the political rights of their citizens, the strict organization of the Catholic church, the exemplary role of canon law, the competition between religious and secular powers, the decentralization of political power within a culturally almost homogeneous society, and so forth. Other factors must be brought in to explain why the new institutional complexes could get established and stabilized. It is only with the expansion and consolidation of the market economy within the territorial state that capitalist society entered upon the stage of a self-sufficient reproduction steered by its own driving mechanisms. And only when legal domination developed into the bourgeois legal and constitutional order did the relationship of functional complementarity and reciprocal stabilization between a capitalist economy and an unproductive state get established.

(*ad v*) If this explanatory sketch could be worked out to the point where we could order historical events from a theoretical point of view, the main task outstanding would be to describe the evolutionary learning process in terms of social movements and political upheavals. Weber concentrated almost exclusively on the Reformation and some of the sectarian movements emanating from it; he neglected the bourgeois revolution and the mass movements of the nineteenth century. But he was on the interesting track of the institutionalization of new, posttraditional structures of consciousness. This process began with the transformation of ethical attitudes, culminated in the formal-legal institutionalization of market commerce and political domination, and continued on in the imperial expansion of formally organized domains of action (and in the sociopathological side effects of bureaucratization). This trail is interesting in that it captures the development of media-steered subsystems *from the viewpoint of the lifeworld.* In studying ethical attitudes, Weber discovered that evolutionary learning processes began with a rationalization of the lifeworld that first affected culture and personality structures and only then took hold of institutional orders.

He relied on historical materials showing that the process of anchoring the money medium in the lifeworld had *begun* with the motivational anchoring of rational action orientations in the carrier strata of early capitalism; it was first carried along by *ethical* orientations before it could take on *legal-institutional* form. The path led from the Protestant ethic of the calling to the bourgeois order of private law. The capitalist economic system, which regulated both internal exchange (between capitalist enterprises) and external exchange (with wage-dependent households and a tax-dependent state) via the money medium, did not arise from any fiat of a lawgiver using legal means of organization to establish a new mode of production. The rise of the absolutist state, within which the establishment of the new mode of production could be furthered by mercantilist measures, was itself part of the process of primitive accumulation [of capital]. That process, made possible at first by the purposive-rational action of independent entrepreneurs in the early stages of capitalism, later required the purposive-rational administrative action of juristically trained expert officials no less than the repressive molding of deracinated and impoverished strata to proletarian life-forms and capitalist work discipline. In any case, the institutionalization of economic exchange regulated by markets came only at the *end* of this development. It was only the legal institutionalization of the money medium in the bourgeois private legal order since the late eighteenth century that made the economic system independent from the externally generated, special, and improbable motives of particular groups. Once the capitalist economy was established as a media-steered subsystem, it no longer required an ethical—that is, value-rational—anchoring of rational action orientations. This expressed itself in the growing autonomy of enterprises and organizations vis-à-vis the motives of their members.

The path of rationalization suggested by Weber can be explained by the fact that formally organized spheres of action can only detach themselves from lifeworld contexts after the symbolic structures of the lifeworld have themselves been sufficiently differentiated. The juridification of social relations requires a high degree of value generalization, an extensive loosening of social action from normative contexts, and a splitting up of concrete ethical life into morality and legality. The lifeworld has to be rationalized to a point where ethically neutralized spheres of action can be legitimately regulated by means of formal processes for enacting and justifying norms. Cultural tradition must already have thawed to the point where legitimate orders can do without dogmatic foundations firmly fixed in tradition. And persons must already be able to act autonomously within the scopes for contingency marked out by abstractly and generally normed spheres of action, so that they can switch from morally defined contexts of action oriented to mutual understanding over to legally organized spheres of action without endangering their own identities.[13]

C.—If we work Weber's theory into our explanatory model in this way, the paradox of societal rationalization that he saw in the manifestations of bureaucratization also appears in a different light. The loss of freedom that Weber attributed to bureaucratization can no longer be explained by a shift from purposive rationality that is grounded value rationally to purposive rationality without roots. In our model, the pertinent phenomena can no longer appear under the description of highly rationalized action orientations. They now count as *effects of the uncoupling of system and lifeworld.* The paradoxical relation no longer holds between different types of action orientations, but between different principles of sociation. Rationalization of the lifeworld makes it possible to convert societal integration over to language-independent steering media and thus to separate off formally organized domains of action. As objectified realities, the latter can then work back upon contexts of communicative action and set their own imperatives against the marginalized lifeworld. On this reading, the neutralization of vocational-ethical attitudes does not count per se as a sign of social pathology. The bureaucratization that sets in when ethics is replaced by law is, in the first instance, only an indication that the institutionalization of a steering medium is coming to its conclusion.

This interpretation has the advantage of rendering superfluous the questionable secularization hypothesis that is supposed to explain the erosion of ethical attitudes. It also throws a different light on the irrational aspects of the Protestant ethic, which remain incomprehensible so long as they are viewed only as necessary conditions for the motivational anchoring of purposive-rational action. If bureaucratization has to be viewed, to begin with, as a normal component of modernization processes, the question arises of how to distinguish from this those pathological variants to which Weber referred with his thesis of a loss of freedom. In order to locate, at least in analytic terms, the threshold at which *the mediatization of the lifeworld turns into its colonization,* I shall characterize more precisely the interchange relations between system and lifeworld in modern societies.

(*a*) We have conceptualized capitalism and the apparatus of the modern state as subsystems differentiated off from the system of institutions, that is, from the societal components of the lifeworld, via the media of money and power. The lifeworld reacts in a characteristic fashion. In bourgeois society, over against those areas of action that are systemically integrated in the economy and the state, socially integrated areas of action take the shape of private and public spheres, which stand in a com-plementary relation to one another. The institutional core of the private sphere is the nuclear family, relieved of productive functions and special-ized in tasks of socialization; from the systemic perspective of the econ-omy, it is viewed as the environment of *private households*. The institu-tional core of the public sphere comprises communicative networks amplified by a cultural complex, a press and, later, mass media; they make it possible for a public of art-enjoying private persons to participate in the reproduction of culture, and for a public of citizens of the state to participate in the social integration mediated by public opinion. From the systemic perspective of the state, the cultural and political public spheres are viewed as the environment relevant to *generating legitima-tion.*[14]

From the standpoint of the subsystems of the economy and the state, their interactions with the respectively contiguous spheres of the life-world take the form of interchange relations connected in parallel. The economic system exchanges wages against labor (as in input factor), as well as goods and services (as the output of its own products) against consumer demand. The public administration exchanges organizational performances for taxes (as an input factor), as well as political decisions (as the output of its own products) for mass loyalty.

The schema represented in Figure 39 takes into account only the in-terchanges between areas of action governed by different principles of societal integration, that is to say, it ignores the interchange relations between spheres of the lifeworld and those between subsystems. Parsons held that all systems of action constitute environments for one another, develop their own media, and regulate intersystemic interchange via these media; by contrast, our two-level concept of society requires that we distinguish between the perspectives of system and lifeworld. The interchanges schematized in Figure 39 represent the perspective of the economic and administrative subsystems. Because the private and public spheres are communicatively structured spheres of action, which are not held together by systemic means—that is, not by steering media—inter-change relations can develop only by way of two such media. *From the perspective of the lifeworld,* various social roles crystallize around these interchange relations: the roles of the employee and the consumer, on the one hand, and those of the client and the citizen of the state, on the other. (For the sake of simplicity, I shall leave to one side here the role structures of the artistic enterprise and of the artistic-literary public sphere.)

In categories (1) and (1a), relations are defined by *organization-dependent roles.* The employment system regulates its interchanges with the lifeworld via the role of a member of an organization, the public

Institutional orders of the lifeworld	Interchange relations	Media-steered subsystems
Private sphere	1) P' $\longrightarrow$ Labor power M $\longleftarrow$ Income from employment 2) M $\longleftarrow$ Goods and services M' $\longrightarrow$ Demand	Economic system
Public sphere	1a) M' $\longrightarrow$ Taxes P $\longleftarrow$ Organizational accomplishments 2a) P $\longleftarrow$ Political decisions P' $\longrightarrow$ Mass loyalty	Administrative system

M = Money medium

P = Power medium

Figure 39. Relations between System and Lifeworld from the Perspective of the System

administration its interchanges via the role of the client. Both roles are constituted in legal form and with reference to organizations. Actors who assume the roles of employees or of clients of the public administration detach themselves from lifeworld contexts and adapt themselves to formally organized domains of action. Either they make some organization-specific contribution and are compensated for it (normally in the form of wages or salaries), or they are the recipients of organization-specific services and make compensation therefore (normally in the form of taxes).

Viewed historically, the monetarization and bureaucratization of labor power and government performance is by no means a painless process; its price is the destruction of traditional forms of life. The path to capitalist modernization is strewn with resistance to the uprooting of the plebian rural population and the urban proletariat, with revolts against the establishment of the absolutist state; against taxes, price decrees, and trade regulations; against the recruitment of mercenaries, and the like.[15] Since the nineteenth century, these—at first more defensive—reactions have been replaced by the struggles of organized labor. In spite of the destructive side effects of the violent processes of capital accumulation and state formation, the new organizational forms gained wide acceptance and considerable permanency on the strength of their greater effectiveness and superior level of integration. The capitalist mode of production and bureaucratic-legal domination can better fulfill the tasks of materially reproducing the lifeworld—in Parsons' terms, the functions of adaptation and goal attainment—than could the institutions of the feudal order that preceded them. This is the functionalist "rationality" of organizationally structured private enterprises and public institutions, which Weber never tired of calling to our attention.

Things are different with the second category of interchange relations. The roles of consumer (2) and of participant in processes of public opinion formation (2a) are also defined *with reference to* formally organized domains of action, but not as *dependent upon* them. Consumers do enter into exchange relations, and members of the public are, insofar as they are exercising the functions of citizens, even members of the political system. However, their roles were not first constituted by legal fiat in the same way as were those of the employee and the client of the state. The relevant legal norms have the form of contractual relations and civil rights. These norms have to be filled in with action orientations expressing a private way of life or the cultural and political form of life of sociated individuals. Thus, the roles of consumer and citizen refer to prior self-formative processes in which preferences, value orientations, attitudes, and so forth have taken shape. Such orientations are developed in the private and public spheres; unlike labor power and taxes, they cannot be "bought" or "collected" by private or public organizations. This might explain why bourgeois ideals attach principally to these roles. The autonomy of the individual consumer and the sovereignty of the individual citizen are, to be sure, only postulates of economic and political theory. But these fictions express the fact that cultural patterns of demand and legitimation evince their own independent structures; they are tied to lifeworld contexts and cannot be taken over economically or politically as can abstract quantities of labor power and taxes.

At the same time, labor power is not by nature an abstract quantity. The transformation of concrete work activities into abstract labor power that can be sold as a commodity even served Marx as the model for the process of real abstraction. A process of this type sets in whenever the lifeworld, in its interchanges with the economic or administrative systems, has to adapt itself to steering media. Just as concrete work has to be transformed into abstract labor so that it can be exchanged for wages, use-value orientations have to be transformed, in a certain sense, into demand preferences, and publicly articulated opinions and collective expressions of will have to be transformed into mass loyalty, so that they can be exchanged for consumer goods and political leadership. The media of money and power can regulate the interchange relations between system and lifeworld only to the extent that the products of the lifeworld have been *abstracted, in a manner suitable to the medium in question,* into input factors for the corresponding subsystem, which can relate to its environment only via its own medium.

We shall see that a corresponding abstraction process is also to be found in the relationship of clients to the administrations of the welfare state. This is even the model case for the colonization of the lifeworld that is behind reification phenomena in advanced capitalist societies. It sets in when the destruction of traditional forms of life can no longer be offset by more effectively fulfilling the functions of society as a whole. The functional ties of money and power media become noticeable only to the degree that elements of a private way of life and a cultural-political form of life get split off from the symbolic structures of the lifeworld through the monetary redefinition of goals, relations and services, life-spaces and life-times, and through the bureaucratization of decisions, duties and rights, responsibilities and dependencies. As our examination of Parsons' media theory made clear, only domains of action that fulfill economic and political functions can be converted over to steering media. The latter fail to work in domains of cultural reproduction, social integration, and socialization; they cannot replace the action-coordinating mechanism of mutual understanding in these functions. Unlike the material reproduction of the lifeworld, its symbolic reproduction cannot be transposed onto foundations of system integration without pathological side effects.

Monetarization and bureaucratization appear to overstep the boundaries of normality when they instrumentalize an influx from the lifeworld that possesses its own inner logic. Weber was interested chiefly in the constraints generated when a private way of life was adapted to organized labor relations, or a [shared] form of life was adjusted to the penetrating directives of juridically organized authorities. He understood this changeover to the organizational membership of employees and the organizational dependence of clients as a threat to individual freedom, as a potential *loss of freedom.*

(*b*) We can use the same theoretical framework to explain the phenomena of a *loss of meaning* that drew Weber's critical attention: a one-sided style of life and a bureaucratic desiccation of the political public sphere. Our interpretation would lead us to predict just the interference phenomena he observed whenever the functional imperatives of highly formalized domains penetrate into the private and public spheres, that is, into spheres of the lifeworld in which sociation proceeds mainly by communicative means.

To the degree that the Protestant ethic of the calling ceased to place its stamp on the private conduct of life, the methodical-rational way in which bourgeois strata led their lives was displaced by the utilitaraian life-style of "specialists without spirit" and the aesthetic-hedonistic life-style of "sensualists without heart," that is, by two complementary ways of life that soon became mass phenomena. The two life-styles can be strikingly represented by different personality types, but they can also take hold of the same person. With this fragmentation of the person, individuals lose their ability to give their life histories a certain degree of consistent direction.

To the extent that methodical-rational conduct of life gets uprooted, purposive-rational action orientations become self-sufficient; technically intelligent adaptation to the objectified milieu of large organizations is combined with a utilitarian calculation of the actor's own interests. The life conduct of specialists is dominated by cognitive-instrumental attitudes toward themselves and others. Ethical obligations to one's calling give way to instrumental attitudes toward an occupational role that offers the opportunity for income and advancement, but no longer for ascertaining one's personal salvation or for fulfilling oneself in a secular sense. Weber notes that the idea of the calling is now a *caput mortuum.* The life-style of sensualists, on the other hand, is shaped and occupied by expressive attitudes. Weber views this type from the standpoint of compensating for the denials required by a rational conduct of life. Artistic-creative expression of a sensitive subjectivity, devotion to aesthetic experience, heightening the capacity for sexual and erotic experience—these become the center of a mode of life that promises a "this-worldly salvation . . . from the routines of everyday life and especially from the increasing pressures of theoretical and practical rationalism."[16]

Weber feared that the orienting power of the private sphere would become weaker and weaker. Neither an instrumentally nor an expressively one-sided style of life—nor any alternating from one to the other—could provide the inner strength needed for replacing the intersubjective unity of a traditionally based lifeworld with a subjectively produced and morally centered unity of private life-conduct based on conviction.

Corresponding to these problems of orientation, problems of legitimation arise in the public sphere. In Weber's view, every bureaucratic-legal domination always brings with it an objectively unavoidable but subjectively unbearable loss of legitimacy. Political action is reduced to the struggle for and exercise of legitimate power. Weber notes "the complete elimination of ethics from political reasoning."[17] The legitimacy of the power monopolized by the modern state consists in the legality of its decisions, in its keeping to legally established procedures, where legality depends in the end on the power of those who can define what counts as legally established procedure.

Weber drew these consequences not only for himself, as a social scientist; he thought that they also set the premises for the actions of citizens involved in the legitimation process. In their eyes, a political order not amenable to normative justification, a struggle for political power carried out only in the name of subjective gods and demons, had to appear in the end as wanting legitimation. A political system that no longer had at its disposal the binding power of religious-metaphysical worldviews was threatened by the withdrawal of legitimation. Above all, Weber feared exorbitant demands created by false legitimation expectations that could no longer be made good, unsatisfied needs for material justice on the part of those who could not come to terms with the "fundamental fact" that we are "destined to live in a godless and prophetless time,"[18] who demanded surrogates and false prophets. In his view, only a heroic nihilism was adequate for legitimating a type of domination based on value skepticism, but he doubted that such an outlook could have broad socializing impact—the more so since, "with the emergence of the modern class problem," workers came to support legal ideologies, thus strengthening those general motives "by which legal formalism is weakened." Legal domination rests on a formalism that is weak in legitimation and subjectively difficult to bear; it flies in the face of "the emotional demands of those underprivileged classes which clamor for social justice."[19]

Weber wanted to trace both private orientation problems and political legitimation problems back to the disintegration of substantive reason, to the "loss of meaning." But he was unable to explain the polarization between specialists and sensualists as the result of an antagonism between value spheres with their own inner logics; he could not consistently fit the legitimation weaknesses of a positivistically hollowed out legal domination into the pattern of rationalization of modern societies. Both these difficulties disappear if we connect the phenomena he described critically with our revised version of the bureaucratization thesis, and attribute them to a colonization of the lifeworld by system imperatives that drive moral-practical elements out of private and political-public spheres of life. It is not the irreconcilability of cultural value spheres—or the clash of life-orders rationalized in their light—that is the cause of one-sided life-styles and unsatisfied legitimation needs; their cause is the monetarization and bureaucratization of everyday practices both in the private and public spheres. This places Weber's critical diagnoses in a different light.

To the degree that the economic system subjects the life-forms of private households and the life conduct of consumers and employees to its imperatives, consumerism and possessive individualism, motives of performance, and competition gain the force to shape behavior. The communicative practice of everyday life is one-sidedly rationalized into a utilitarian life-style; this media-induced shift to purposive-rational action orientations calls forth the reaction of a hedonism freed from the pressures of rationality. As the private sphere is undermined and eroded by the economic system, so too is the public sphere by the administrative system. The bureaucratic disempowering and desiccation of spontaneous processes of opinion- and will-formation expands the scope for engineering mass loyalty and makes it easier to uncouple political decision-making from concrete, identity-forming contexts of life. Insofar as such tendencies establish themselves, we get Weber's (stylized) picture of a legal domination that redefines practical questions as technical ones and dismisses demands for substantive justice with a legalistic reference to legitimation through procedure.

If, however, we do not attribute orientation and legitimation problems to the destruction of those cognitive conditions under which religious and metaphysical principles could develop their power to create meaning; if we explain them instead by the disintegration of socially integrated contexts of life and their assimilation to the formally organized domains of the capitalist economy and the bureaucratic state apparatus—then what happens to the status of Weber's loss-of-meaning thesis? Owing to the instrumentalization of the lifeworld by systemic constraints, the communicative practice of everyday life suffers from a forced adjustment to cognitive-instrumental action orientations and tends to corresponding reaction-formations. But this one-sided rationalization or reification of everyday practice, a practice that is wholly reliant upon the interplay of cognitive with moral-practical and aesthetic-expressive elements, should not be confused with a, in my view, *different* phenomenon: the complementary manifestation of cultural impoverishment that threatens a lifeworld whose traditional substance has been devalued. The thesis of a loss of meaning can be applied to this, albeit in a modified form.

(*c*) Weber characterized cultural modernity by the fact that the substantive reason expressed in religious and metaphysical worldviews falls apart into moments that are held together only procedurally, that is, through the form of argumentative justification. As traditional problems are divided up under the specific viewpoints of truth, normative rightness, and authenticity or beauty, and are dealt with respectively as questions of knowledge, justice, or taste, there is a differentiation of the value spheres of science, morality, and art. In the corresponding cultural action systems, scientific discourse, studies in moral and legal theory, and the production and criticism of art are all institutionalized as the affairs of experts. Professionalized treatment of cultural tradition under only *one* abstract aspect of validity *at a time* permits the inner logics of cognitive-instrumental, moral-practical, and asethetic-expressive complexes of knowledge to manifest themselves. From this point on, there are also *internal histories* of science, of moral and legal theory, of art—not linear developments, to be sure, but learning processes nonetheless.

In consequence of this professionalization, the distance between expert cultures and the broader public grows greater. What accrues to a culture by virtue of specialized work and reflection does not come *as a matter of course* into the possession of everyday practice. Rather, cultural rationalization brings with it the danger that a lifeworld devalued in its traditional substance will become impoverished. This problem was first seen in all its acuteness in the eighteenth century; it called into being the project of the Enlightenment. Eighteenth-century philosophers still hoped to develop unflinchingly the objectivating sciences, universalistic foundations of morality and law, and art, each according to its own inner logic, and *at the same time* to free the cognitive potentials built up in this way from their esoteric forms and to use them in practice, that is, in rationally shaping the conditions of daily life. Enlighteners cast in the mold of a Condorcet had the extravagant expectation that the arts and sciences would promote not only the control of natural forces, but also interpretations of the world and of ourselves, moral progress, the justice of social institutions, even the happiness of humankind.

The twentieth century has left little of this optimism intact; but now, as then, there is a difference of opinion as to whether we should hold fast to the intentions of the Enlightenment, in however refracted a form, or should give up the project of modernity as lost—whether, for instance, cognitive potentials that do not flow into technical progress, economic growth, and rational administration should be dammed up in the enclaves of their high-cultural forms so that habits dependent on blind tradition can remain untouched by them.

The processes of reaching understanding upon which the lifeworld is centered require a cultural tradition across the whole spectrum. In the communicative practice of everyday life, cognitive interpretations, moral expectations, expressions, and valuations have to interpenetrate and form a rational interconnectedness via the transfer of validity that is possible in the performative attitude. This communicative infrastructure is threatened by two interlocking, mutually reinforcing tendencies: *systemically induced reification* and *cultural impoverishment.*

The lifeworld is assimilated to juridified, formally organized domains of action and simultaneously cut off from the influx of an intact cultural tradition. In the deformations of everyday practice, symptoms of rigidification combine with symptoms of desolation. The former, the one-sided rationalization of everyday communication, goes back to the growing autonomy of media-steered subsystems, which not only get objectified into a norm-free reality beyond the horizon of the lifeworld, but whose imperatives also penetrate into the core domains of the lifeworld. The latter, the dying out of vital traditions, goes back to a differentiation of science, morality, and art, which means not only an increasing autonomy of sectors dealt with by experts, but also a splitting-off from traditions; having lost their credibility, these traditions continue along on the basis of everyday hermeneutics as a kind of second nature that has lost its force.

Working Weber's diagnosis of the times into our interpretive framework has the advantage of elucidating, in terms of communication theory, the sense in which the phenomena he observed, when they appear with broad effect, should be regarded as pathologies, that is, as symptoms of a distorted everyday practice. This does not explain, however, why pathologies of this kind appear in the first place. Our reconstruction of Weber's paradox of societal rationalization is by no means complete. We have not explained, for instance, why the differentiation of economic and administrative systems of action at all pushes beyond the bounds of what is necessary for the institutionalization of money and power, why the subsystems build up irresistible internal dynamics and systematically undermine domains of action dependent upon social integration. Nor have we explained why cultural rationalization not only sets free the inner logics of cultural value spheres, but also remains encapsulated in expert cultures; why modern science serves technical progress, capitalist growth, and rational administration, but not the understanding that communicating citizens have of themselves and the world; why, in general, the explosive contents of cultural modernity have been defused. In such matters, Weber himself had recourse only to the inner logics of cultural value spheres and the effectiveness of new forms of organization.

But this does not explain why modernization follows a highly selective pattern that appears to exclude two things at once: building institutions of freedom that protect communicatively structured areas of the private and public spheres against the reifying inner dynamics of the economic and administrative systems,[20] and reconnecting modern culture to an everyday practice that, while dependent on meaning-bestowing traditions, has been impoverished with traditionalist, left-overs.[21]

It is no mere accident that Parsons can base his rather too harmonious picture of modernity on Weber's analyses. In comparison to Parsons, Weber was, to be sure, sensitive to the price that the capitalist modernization of the lifeworld exacted for a new level of system differentiation, but he too failed to investigate the drive mechanism behind the autonomized expansion of the economic system and its governmental complement.

Perhaps an explanation of the Marxian type could help here. It points us in the direction of an economically constituted class domination, which withdraws into the anonymous internal dynamics of valorization processes uncoupled from orientations to use values. And this might explain why the imperatives Weber connected with the idea of "bureaucratization" penetrate into communicatively structured domains of action, so that the space opened up by the rationalization of the lifeworld for moral-practical will-formation, expressive self-presentation, and aesthetic satisfaction does not get utilized.

(*d*) If we appropriate Weber's diagnosis of the times from this Marxian perspective, the paradox of societal rationalization looks rather different. The rationalization of the lifeworld makes it possible to differentiate off autonomized subsystems and at the same time opens up the utopian horizon of a bourgeois society in which the formally organized spheres of action of the *bourgeois* (the economy and the state appartus) form the foundation of the posttraditional lifeworld of the *homme* (the private sphere) and the *citoyen* (the public sphere). Since the eighteenth century, the features of a form of life in which the rational potential of action oriented to mutual understanding is set free have been reflected in the self-understanding of the humanistically imbued European middle classes—in their political theories and educational ideals, in their art and literature.[22] Metaphysical-religious worldviews ceded the function of legitimating domination to the basic ideas of rational natural law, which offered a justification for the modern state from the perspective of a social order free of violence and centered on markets organized by private law. At the same time, bourgeois ideals penetrated private spheres of life; they stamped the individualism of relationships of love and friendship as well as the culture of morality and feeling in intensified family relations. From this point of view, the subject of private law, who was wholly absorbed by the functional interconnections of material reproduction, could be unceremoniously identified with the *human being* who was formed in the private sphere and realized himself there, and with the *private person* who, together with others, formed the *public* of citizens of the state.

To be sure, this *utopia of reason, formed in the Enlightenment,*[23] was persistently contradicted by the realities of bourgeois life and shown to be a *bourgeois ideology.* But it was never a mere illusion; it was an objective illusion that arose from the structures of differentiated lifeworlds which, while certainly limited in class-specific ways, were nonetheless rationalized. To the extent that culture, society, and personality separated off from one another as Mead and Durkheim said they did, and the validity basis of communicative action replaced the sacred foundations of social integration, there was at least *an appearance of posttraditional everyday communication* suggested by the structures of the lifeworld. It was, so to speak, a transcendental apparition—determining bourgeois ideology, while yet surpassing it. In it, communication was represented as standing on its own feet, setting limits to the inner dynamics of autonomous subsystems, bursting encapsulated expert cultures, and thus as escaping the combined threat of reification and desolation.

The paradox, however, is that the rationalization of the lifeworld simultaneously gave rise to *both* the systemically induced reification of the lifeworld *and* the utopian perspective from which capitalist modernization has always appeared with the stain of dissolving traditional life-forms without salvaging their communicative substance. Capitalist modernization destroys these forms of life, but does not transform them in such a way that the intermeshing of cognitive-instrumental with moral-practical and expressive moments, which had obtained in everyday practice prior to its rationalization, could be retained at a higher level of differentiation. Against this background, images of traditional forms of life—of rural and peasant life, or the life of town dwellers and craftsmen, even the plebian way of life of the agricultural laborers and cottage industry pieceworkers recently dragged into the accumulation process[24]—retained the melancholy charm of irretrievable pasts and the radiance of nostalgic remembrance of what had been sacrificed to modernization. But more than this, modernization processes have been followed, as if by a shadow, by what might be called an instinct formed by reason: the awareness that, with the one-sided canalization and destruction of possibilities for expression and communication in private and in public spheres, changes are fading that we can bring together again, in a posttraditional everyday practice, those moments that, in traditional forms of life, once composed a unity—a diffuse one surely, and one whose religious and metaphysical interpretations were certainly illusory.

In understanding Weber's paradox of societal rationalization in this way, we are making two decisive changes in his argument. Since its beginnings in the late eighteenth century, bourgeois cultural criticism has always wanted to attribute the pathologies of modernity to one of two causes: either to the fact that secularized worldviews lose their socially integrating power, or to the fact that society's high level of complexity overtaxes the individual's power to integrate. Like an echo, bourgeois cultural apologetics has furnished two mirror-arguments, maintaining that disenchantment and alienation are structurally necessary conditions of freedom (where the latter is always represented merely as individual choice among institutionally guaranteed possibilities). Weber tried to combine both pairs of arguments and counterarguments through the idea of a paradox built into Occidental development itself. His theses of the loss of meaning and freedom pick up on themes of bourgeois cultural criticism; he varies them, however, with the idea that it is precisely in these phenomena that the reason of Occidental rationalism establishes itself—and thus tries to meet apologetic needs.

The modifications I have made in Weber's thesis do not fit into this pattern of argumentation without bourgeois cultural theory. They run counter to the critical and apologetic lines of argument no less than their paradoxical combination. The deformations that interested Marx, Durkheim, and Weber—each in his own way—ought not be attributed either to the rationalization of the lifeworld as such or to increasing system complexity as such. Neither the secularization of worldviews nor the structural differentiation of society has unavoidable pathological side effects per se. It is not the differentiation and independent development of cultural value spheres that lead to the cultural impoverishment of everyday communicative practice, but an elitist splitting-off of expert cultures from contexts of communicative action in daily life. It is not the uncoupling of media-steered subsystems and of their organizational forms from the lifeworld that leads to the one-sided rationalization or reification of everyday communicative practice, but only the penetration of forms of economic and administrative rationality into areas of action that resist being converted over to the media of money and power because they are specialized in cultural transmission, social integration, and child rearing, and remain dependent on mutual understanding as a mechanism for coordinating action. If we assume, further, that the phenomena of a loss of meaning and freedom do not turn up by chance but are structurally generated, we must try to explain why media-steered subsystems develop *irresistible inner dynamics* that *bring about* both the colonization of the lifeworld and its segmentation from science, morality, and art.

2. Marx and the Thesis of Internal Colonization

There are a number of reasons for going back to Marx, or more precisely, to the interpretation of Marx stemming from Western Marxism's reception of Weber. On the one hand, the dynamics of class opposition might explain the inner dynamics of bureaucratization—the hypertrophic growth of media-steered subsystems, resulting in the encroachment of administrative and monetary steering mechanisms upon the lifeworld. On the other hand, the reification of communicatively structured domains of action does not, in the first instance, produce effects distributed in any class-specific manner. The phenomena that Weber traced to bureaucratization are by no means characteristic of specific class situations but of modernized societies as a whole. Lukacs connected Weber's theory of rationalization with Marx's political economy in such a way that he could understand the *class-unspecific* side effects of modernization processes as the results of an underlying class conflict. Whereas in Marx there was a direct path from the analysis of the commodity form to the material impoverishment of proletarian forms of life, Lukacs derived from the subsumption of labor power under the commodity form a form of objectivity with which he hoped to decode all "the forms of subjectivity in bourgeois society." He already had in view an objectivistic deformation of subjectivity generally, a reification of consciousness that embraced bourgeois culture and science and the mentality of bourgeois strata, as well as the economistic and reformist self-understanding of the labor movement. For this reason he could assert that the bourgeoisie shares with the proletariat the reification of all its expressions of life; their positions in the production process, which separate the two classes, privilege the wage laborer only in respect to the possibility of recognizing the cause of alienation, namely, the subsumption of life-relations under the commodity form. It is only in connection with this theory of class consciousness that the theory of reification could trace an all-encompassing rationalization back to the conditions of class struggle under which modernization took place in capitalist societies.

As we saw in Volume 1, this Hegelianizing philosophy of history leads to untenable consequences that induced Horkheimer and Adorno to give up the theory of class consciousness. They solved the problem of connecting Marx and Weber by leaning all the more heavily on Weber. If, following Weber, one conceives of the rationalization of life's orders as the institutionalization of purposive rational action, it is only a small step to generalizing the reification of consciousness into an expression of instrumental reason. And if, like him, one sees the subsystems of purposive rational action irresistably congealing into an iron cage, it is only a small step from Lukacs's theory of reification to the critique of instrumental reason, that is, to the vision of an administered, totally reified world in which means-ends rationality and domination are merged. This theory has the advantage of directing our attention to the symptoms of the systemically induced deformation of communicatively structured life-contexts, which is no longer localizable in any class-specific way. Its weakness consists in deriving the erosion of the lifeworld from the spell of a means-ends rationality that has been demonized as instrumental reason. The critique of instrumental reason thereby falls into the same error as the Weberian theory and, in addition, forfeits the fruits of an approach nonetheless directed to systemic effects.

The concept of instrumental reason suggests that the rationality of knowing and acting subjects is systemically expanded into a purposive rationality of a higher order. Thus the rationality of self-regulating systems, whose imperatives override the consciousness of the members integrated into them, appears in the shape of a totalized purposive rationality. This confusion of system rationality and action rationality prevented Horkheimer and Adorno, as it did Weber before them, from adequately separating the rationalization of action orientations within the framework of a structurally differentiated lifeworld from the expansion of the steering capacity of differentiated social systems. As a result, they could locate the spontaneity that was not yet in the grips of the reifying force of systemic rationalization only in irrational powers—in the charismatic power of the leader or in the mimetic power of art and love.

Horkheimer and Adorno failed to recognize the communicative rationality of the lifeworld that had to develop out of the rationalization of worldviews before there could be any development of formally organized domains of action at all. It is only this communicative rationality, reflected in the self-understanding of modernity, that gives an inner logic—and not merely the impotent rage of nature in revolt—to resistance against the colonization of the lifeworld by the inner dynamics of autonomous systems. Horkheimer and Adorno were unable to appropriate the systematic content of Weber's diagnosis of the times and to make it fruitful for social-scientific inquiry, because

> they did not take seriously enough Weber's studies on the rationalization of worldviews, or the independent logic of cultural modernity; but also because they were uncritical in two directions;

· vis-à-vis Marx, in that they held fast to the basic assumptions of the theory of value as the core of their tacit orthodoxy, and in this way they blinded themselves to the realities of a developed capitalism based on the pacification of class conflict through welfare-state measures;

· vis-à-vis Weber, in that they remained fixated on the model of purposive rationality and, for that reason, did not expand the critique of instrumental reason into a critique of functionalist reason.

There is no need to say any more about this last point. I will deal now with the other two by (*A*) examining what Marx's theory of value can contribute to a theory or reification translated into system-lifeworld concepts, and then pointing out its weaknesses, in order (*B*) to see how we might explain the pacification of class conflict in welfare-state mass democracies and how we could combine the Marxian view of ideology with Weber's reflections on cultural modernity. Finally, I will (*C*) develop the thesis of internal colonization and support it with some examples from current tendencies toward juridification.

A.—The Marxian approach owes its theoretical superiority over proposals subsequently developed at the same level of abstraction to an ingenious coup de main: the analysis of the commodity form. Through his analysis of the double character of the commodity, Marx arrived at basic value-theoretical assumptions that enabled him both to describe the process of the development of capitalist society from the economic perspective of an observer as a crisis-ridden process of the self-realization of capital and, at the same time, to represent it from the historical perspective of those involved (or of a virtual participant) as a conflict-ridden interaction between social classes. In the concepts of value theory, the exchange relation between labor power and variable capital—a relation that, institutionalized in the labor contract, is fundamental to this mode of production—can be explained simultaneously as the steering mechanism of a self-regulating process of production and as a reflexive relation that makes the whole accumulation process intelligible as an objectified and anonymous process of exploitation. Marx starts from the idea that the *form* of the conflict bred in all class societies by the privileged appropriation of socially produced wealth had changed in a characteristic way with the establishment of the capitalist mode of production. Whereas the dynamics of class in politically constituted, stratified societies were manifested directly on the level of conflicts of interest between social groups, in bourgeois society they are objectivistically concealed and objectivated through the medium of exchange value. The mechanism of the labor market, institutionalized in private law, takes over functions that had previously been performed by politically institutionalized relations of social force and economic exploitation. The monetarization of labor power becomes the basis of class relations. The analysis of these relations has to begin therefore with the double character of the commodity.

On the one hand, labor power is expended in *concrete* actions and cooperative relationships; on the other hand, it is absorbed as an *abstract* performance by a labor process that is formally organized for purposes of valorization. In this respect, the labor power sold by producers is the site of an encounter between the imperatives of system integration and those of social integration: as an *action* it belongs to the lifeworld of the producers, as a *performance* to the functional nexus of the capitalist enterprise and of the economic system as a whole. Marx was concerned to uncover the illusion that labor power is a commodity like any other. As Claus Offe has put it:

> The institution of the labor "market" and "free wage labor" is a fiction, since what is of interest positively and negatively in the commodity called labor power is indeed what distinguishes it from all other commodities, namely, that it is in fact a "living" labor power that (1) does not arise for the purpose of salability, (2) cannot be separated from its owner, and (3) can be set in motion only by its owner. This inextirpable subject-rootedness of labor power implies that in wage labor the categories of action and functioning, of social and system integration are inextricably intertwined.[1]

The wage-labor relation neutralizes the performances of producers vis-à-vis the lifeworld contexts of their actions. It sets the conditions of organizational membership under which wage laborers declare their general willingness to expend their labor power as a suitably programmed contribution to maintaining the capitalist enterprise. It is this monetarized labor power, which is appropriated as a commodity and alienated from the life context of producers, that Marx calls "abstract labor." "It is indifferent to the natural-material object of use and to the need that it satisfies; it is indifferent to the particular kinds of activity, as well as to the working individuals and their social situations. These marks of indifference find expression in the determinations of labor which produces exchange value; it is characterized as 'human labor' that is 'the same', 'without difference', 'without individuality', 'abstract', 'universal'. These same features continue on in the relations of indifference that mark the workers' behavior toward others and toward himself."[2] The analysis of the double character of the commodity "labor power" follows step by step the neutralizations through which labor power is constituted as abstract, "indifferent to the lifeworld," and available for systemic imperatives.

Marx explains this process of *real abstraction* by means of the objectification of socially integrated contexts of action, which takes place when interactions are no longer coordinated via norms and values, or via processes of reaching understanding, but via the medium of exchange value. In this case, participants are primarily interested in the consequences of their actions. Inasmuch as they orient themselves to "values" in a purposive-rational manner, as if the latter were objects in a second nature, they adopt an objectivating attitude to each other and to themselves, and they transform social and intrapsychic relations into instrumental relations. In this respect, the transformation of concrete into abstract labor power is a process in which communal and individual life become reified. In what follows, I will first emphasize the strengths of this theoretical approach (*a*); and then discuss its weaknesses (*b*).

(*a*) The Marxian theory of value is of methodological and substantive interest for the path that we have followed from Parsons back to Weber. It specifies rules for the fundamental interchange relations between the economic system and the lifeworld, that is, for the market-regulated appropriation of labor power. Using these rules, systematic statements about anonymous processes of valorization can be translated into historical statements about interaction relations between social classes. In this way, problems of system integration—that is to say, the crisis-ridden pattern of accumulation—can be reflected at the level of social integration and connected with the dynamics of class conflict. Taking up from the illuminating Marx interpretation of E. M. Lange,[3] Hauke Brunkhorst has distinguished two pairs of theory languages and observation languages, which, depending on the pragmatic roles of their basic concepts, refer either to states and events in the lifeworlds of capitalists and wage laborers, or to systemic contexts of valorization.[4] The language of classes (*Lc*) is constructed from such action-theoretical concepts as 'concrete labor', 'class interests', and the like; the language of valorization (*Lv*) from such systems-theoretical concepts as 'abstract labor' and 'value'.

Within each of these two languages, the theoretical concepts have first to be operationalized and correlated with concepts of an observation language.[5] Furthermore, statements expressed in one theory or observation language have to be translated into statements of the other. The theory of value can now be understood as an attempt to explicate these translation rules. The metaphor of the transformation of concrete into abstract labor is tied to the basic intuition by which Marx wants to make clear how statements from *Lct* can be translated into *Lvt*. On this basis, and with the aid of the correlation rules linking each of the theory languages to an observation language, correspondences can then be worked

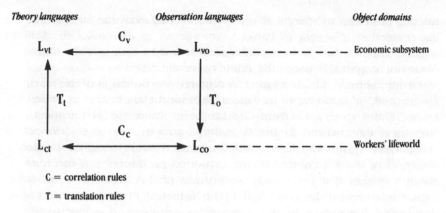

Figure 40. Brunkhorst's Model of the Structure of Scientific Language in *Capital*

out between statements in *Lvo* and *Lco*. This would make it possible, for example, to infer from economic crises to risks affecting the lives of the workers. From statements of this sort—referring to pathologies and deformations of practical forms of life—and with the aid of certain empirical hypotheses—for instance, about the solidarizing effects of the forms of cooperation developed under the factory system—Marx derives statements about the political organization of the labor movement and the dynamics of class struggle, that is, propositions having to do with the theory of revolution, which are also formulated in *Lco*.

To the extent that the structure of Marxian theory is characterized by this connecting of systems-theoretic and action-theoretic concepts, the central position of value theory can be seen in Figure 40, a scheme of rules for correlating expressions and translating statements.

If we represent the theory advanced in *Capital* in this way, that is, in terms of the language of science, then it is the task of value theory to explain the "translation rules" (*Tt*) by which we can pass from a hermeneutically developed, class-theoretical description (of concrete labor relations, embedded in lifeworld contexts) to an objectivating description (of value relations in the economic system). In this translation from one theoretical description to the other, the references have to be retained to a degree sufficient for retranslating (using *To*) from statements about problems of system integration into statements about problems of social integration.

Viewed *methodologically,* the theory of value had for Marx a status similar to that which the action-theoretical introduction of steering media had for Parsons. From a *substantive* perspective, however, Marx's con-

necting of systems theory and action theory had from the start a critical sense that is absent in Parsons: he wanted to *denounce* the self-
maintainance of the economic subsystem as a dynamics of exploitation
made unrecognizable under the veil of objectification.

Georg Lohmann has developed an original interpretation of the Marxian method, in particular of the intention behind Marx's "critical presentation." Drawing on texts from *Capital,* he explains the relation of the
"historical excursuses" to the "economic passages" in the narrower
sense. Only against the historically illuminated background of the destruction of the life-context of the exploited producers can the truth
about a system that transcends the horizon of this lifeworld come to
light. Capital reveals its secret only in the historically preserved traces of
destruction left behind by the autonomous capitalist economic system
in a lifeworld subjected to its imperatives. The further it consolidates the
production of social wealth into a system steered autonomously via the
medium of exchange value and has, in that respect, become an end unto
itself, and the further the social reality of the sphere of social labor
thereby gets adapted to the basic categories of systems theory, all the
more does "the whole" reveal itself to be "the untrue." The historical
excursuses reveal "the subsumption of precapitalist modes of labor and
life under the domination of capital, the acts of resistance and struggle
of the workers for a life more in line with their demands, as well as the
formation of the processes and conditions of their lives."[6]

Because Marx uses the theory of value to get from the lifeworld of
concrete labor to the economic valorization of abstract labor, he can
return from this level of systems analysis to the level of a historical and
class-theoretical presentation of everyday practice, and can there reckon
up the costs of capitalist modernization. The "bilingual" character of the
theoretical presentation gives to the dialectical conceptual framework in
which Marx brings together systems and action theory its critical point:
"Whereas for Hegel the move toward more developed categories is at the
same time an advance in the manifestation of 'Truth', for Marx the further
categorial conceptualization of the whole is an advance in uncovering
the *truth about* capital: that, as a whole, it is something 'negative', something that is historically changeable."[7]

(*b*) At this point we can see a first weakness in the theory of value.
My reconstruction tacitly began with the problem of connecting the
action/lifeworld and system paradigms—a problem that became explicit
only with Parsons. This was a marked stylization. Marx does move at the
two analytical levels of "system" and "lifeworld," but their separation is
not really presupposed in his basic economic concepts, which remain
tied to Hegelian logic. On the contrary, the interconnection between the
two types of theoretical *statements* could be explained through a *se-*

mantic explication of the shifts in meaning involved in using these basic terms only if it is assumed that there is a logical (in the Hegelian sense) connection between the development of the system and the structural transformation of the lifeworld. It is only under this assumption that Marx could hope to grasp a totality comprising both moments at one blow, so to speak, by means of a theory of value that proceeds in terms of semantic analysis. Otherwise it would have been necessary to engage in empirical investigations of real abstraction, that is, of the transformation of concrete into abstract labor.

As matter of fact, the young Marx conceives of the unity of system and lifeworld as did the young Hegel, on the model of a ruptured ethical totality whose abstractly divided moments are condemned to pass away. Under these premises, an accumulation process that has broken away from orientations to use value literally amounts to an illusion—the capitalist system is *nothing more* than the ghostly form of class relations that have become perversely anonymous and fetishized. The systemic autonomy of the production process has the character of an enchantment. Marx is convinced a priori that in capital he has before him *nothing more* than the mystified form of a class relation. This interpretation excludes from the start the question of whether the systemic interconnection of the capitalist economy and the modern state administration do not *also* represent a higher and evolutionarily advantageous level of integration by comparison to traditional societies. Marx conceives of capitalist society so strongly as a totality that he fails to recognize the *intrinsic* evolutionary *value* that media-steered subsystems possess. He does not see that the differentiation of the state apparatus and the economy *also* represents a higher level of system differentiation, which simultaneously opens up new steering possibilities *and* forces a reorganization of the old, feudal, class relationships. The significance of this level of integration goes beyond the institutionalization of a new class relationship.

Marx's misperception also has consequences for his theory of revolution. He does not want merely to describe how the systemically autonomous process of capital's self-realization is experienced from the lifeworld perspective of the wage laborer as a continual exploitation, how the subsumption of labor power under the commodity form tears the workers out of their traditional conditions of life, uproots feudal modes of existence in a plebian fashion, and then shapes them into proletarian forms. Rather, he projects a *practical-political* perspective for action, which, in its assumptions, is exactly contrary to the perspective tacitly adopted by systems functionalism. Systems theory presupposes that the world-historical process of instrumentalizing the lifeworld, particularly the sphere of social labor, in line with the imperatives of self-regulating systems—the process that Marx denounces—has already come to a close. The marginalized lifeworld can, it is supposed, survive only if it transforms itself in turn into a media-steered subsystem and leaves behind the communicative practice of everyday life as the empty shell of formally organized domains of action. As opposed to this, Marx has in view a future state of affairs in which the objective semblance of capital has dissolved and the lifeworld, which had been held captive under the dictates of the law of value, gets back its spontaneity. He foresees that the forces of the industrial proletariat, at first merely in revolt, will, under the leadership of a theoretically enlightened avant-garde, form themselves into a movement that seizes political power for the purpose of revolutionizing society. Along with the private ownership of the means of production, the movement will also destroy the institutional foundations of the medium through which the capitalist economic system was differentiated out, and will bring the systemically autonomous process of economic growth back again into the horizon of the lifeworld.

System and lifeworld appear in Marx under the metaphors of the "realm of necessity" and the "realm of freedom." The socialist revolution is to free the latter from the dictates of the former. It seems as if theoretical critique has only to lift the spell cast by abstract labor (subsumed under the commodity form). The intersubjectivity of workers associated in large industries is crippled under the self-movement of capital; theoretical critique has only to free it of its stiffness for an avant-garde to mobilize living—critically enlivened—labor against dead labor and to lead it to the triumph of the lifeworld over the system of deworlded labor power.

As against these revolutionary expectations, Weber's prognosis has proven correct: the abolition of private capitalism would not at all mean the destruction of the iron cage of modern industrial labor.[8] Marx's error stems in the end from dialectically clamping together system and lifeworld in a way that does not allow for a sufficiently sharp separation between the *level of system differentiation* attained in the modern period and the *class-specific forms* in which it has been *institutionalized.* Marx did not withstand the temptations of Hegelian totality-thinking; he construed the unity of system and lifeworld dialectically as an "untrue whole." Otherwise he could not have failed to see that *every* modern society, whatever its class structure, has to exhibit a high degree of structural differentiation.

This failure is connected with a second weakness of the value-theoretical approach. Marx has no criteria by which to distinguish the destruction of traditional forms of life from the reification of posttraditional lifeworlds.

In Marx and the Marxist tradition the concept of "alienation" has been applied above all to the wage laborer's mode of existence. In the Paris Manuscripts it is still the expressivist model of creative productivity, in which the artist develops his own essential powers as he shapes his works, that furnishes the standard for criticizing alienated labor. This perspective is retained in the more strongly phenomenologically and anthropologically oriented versions of contemporary praxis philosophy.[9] Marx himself, however, broke free of this ideal of self-formation inherited from Herder and Romanticism[10] when he moved on to the theory of value. In the idea of an exchange of equivalents, the latter retains only a formal perspective of distributive justice from which to judge the subsumption of labor power under the commodity form. With the idea of transforming concrete into abstract labor, the concept of alienation loses its determinacy. It no longer refers to deviations from the model of an exemplary praxis, but to the instrumentalization of a life that is represented as an end in itself: "The wage laborer has to orient himself to the possibilities of life as a whole by abstracting from them a part so reduced that they get specified as capacities to work, and these in turn are redefined in such a way that they get expressed as objectified powers ... Life is no longer lived for its own sake; instead, the totality of life's accomplishments is used to realize a certain type of activity, namely the sale of one's labor power. What is posited through capitalist integration, in the 'buying and selling of labor power', only as a possibility—namely, the gradual reduction of the whole of life's possibilities to the capacity to work and their abstraction into labor power—realizes itself backwards, so to speak, in the development of the capitalist production process."[11]

This concept of alienation remains indeterminate insofar as there is no historical index for the underlying concept, at times Aristotelian, at times Hegelian, of a "life" that is reduced in its possibilities as a result of violating the ideal of justice inherent in the exchange of equivalents. Marx speaks in the abstract about life and life's possibilities; he has no concept of a rationalization to which the lifeworld is subject to the extent that its symbolic structures get differentiated. Thus, in the historical context of his investigations, the concept of alienation remains peculiarly ambiguous.

Marx uses it to criticize the conditions of life that arose with the proletarianizing of craftsmen, farmers, and rural plebians in the course of capitalist modernization. But he is unable to distinguish in this repressive uprooting of traditional forms of life between the aspect of *reification* and that of *structural differentation of the lifeworld.* For this, the concept of alienation is not sufficiently selective. The theory of value provides no basis for a concept of reification, enabling us to identify syndromes of alienation relative to the degree of rationalization attained in a lifeworld. At the stage of posttraditional forms of life, the pain that the separation of culture, society, and personality *also* causes those who grow into modern societies and form their identities within them counts as a process of individuation and not alienation. In an extensively rationalized lifeworld, reification can be measured only against the conditions of communicative sociation, and not against the nostalgically loaded, frequently romanticized past of premodern forms of life.

I find the third, and decisive, weakness of the theory of value to be the overgeneralization of a specific case of the subsumption of the lifeworld under the system. Even if we trace the dynamics of class conflict back to the "fundamental contradiction" between wage labor and capital, processes of reification need not appear only in the sphere in which they were caused—in the sphere of social labor. As we have seen, the economy steered by money depends on being functionally supplemented by an administrative system differentiated out via the medium of power. Thus, formally organized domains of action are able to absorb communicative contexts of life through both media—money and power. The process of reification can manifest itself just as well in public as in private domains, and in the latter areas it can attach to consumer as well as to occupational roles. By contrast, the theory of value allows for only *one* channel through which the monetarization of labor power expropriates from producers work activities abstracted into performances.

There is in the action-theoretic foundations of the theory of value an error similar to the one found in Weber and in two lines of Weber reception, Western Marxism and Parsons: the model of purposive rationality is viewed as fundamental for social action as well. Marx was unable to conceive the transformation of concrete into abstract labor as a special case of the systemically induced reification of social relations in general because he started from the model of the purposive actor who, along with his products, is robbed of the possibility of developing his essential powers. The theory of value is carried through in action-theoretic concepts that make it necessary to approach the genesis of reification *below* the level of interaction, and to treat as derived phenomena the de-formation of interaction relations themselves—the deworlding of communicative action that is transferred over to media and the technicizing of the lifeworld that follows upon this. "The one-sided interpretation of basic action concepts, according to which action can be understood only as productive-objectifying activity, takes its revenge in underestimating the extent of neutralization that comes with the reduction of abstract labor. Marx is too harmless, in categorial terms, when it comes to determining the neutralizations of action required for system integration."[12]

The three weaknesses of the theory of value that we have analyzed here explain why, despite its two-level concept of society combining system and lifeworld, the critique of political economy has been unable to produce a satisfactory account of late capitalism. The Marxian approach requires an economistically foreshortened interpretation of developed capitalist societies. Marx was right to assign an evolutionary primacy to the economy in such societies: the problems in this subsystem determine the path of development of the society as a whole. But this primacy should not mislead us into tailoring the complementary relationship between the economy and the state apparatus to a trivial notion of base and superstructure. As opposed to the monism of the theory of value, we have to allow for two steering media and four channels through which the two complementary subsystems subject the lifeworld to their imperatives. Reification effects can result in like manner from the bureaucratization and monetarization of public and private areas of life.

B.—Our critical discussion of the theory of value gives occasion to build the dynamics of an accumulation process that has become an end in itself into the model developed earlier for interchange relations between the economy and state, on the one side, and the private and public spheres, on the other (Figure 39). This model protects us against an economistically narrowed interpretation, directs our attention to the interaction between state and economy, and provides an explanation for the characteristic features of political systems in developed capitalist societies. Marxian orthodoxy has a hard time explaining government interventionism, mass democracy, and the welfare state. The economistic approach breaks down in the face of the pacification of class conflict and the long-term success of reformism in European countries since World War II, under the banner of a social-democratic program in the broader sense. In what follows, I shall (*a*) indicate the theoretical deficits detrimental to Marx's attempts to explain late capitalism, in particular state interventionism, mass democracy, and the welfare state; and then (*b*) introduce a model that explains the compromise structures of late capitalism and the cracks within them; and finally (*c*) go back to the role of culture, to which the Marxian theory of ideology does not do justice.

(*a*) *Government Interventionism.* If we take as a basis the model of two complementary subsystems, one of which presents the problems to the other, a crisis theory that proceeds only in economic terms proves to be unsatisfactory. Even if system problems arise in the first place from the crisis-ridden course of economic growth, economic disequilibria can be balanced through the state jumping into the functional gaps of the market. Of course, the substitution of governmental for market functions takes place under the proviso that the sovereign right of private enterprise in matters of investment be fundamentally safeguarded. Economic growth would lose its intrinsic capitalist dynamics and the economy would forfeit its primacy if the production process were *controlled* through the medium of power. The intervention of the state may not affect the division of labor between a market-dependent economy and an economically unproductive state. In all three central dimensions—guaranteeing by military and legal-institutional means the presuppositions for the continuance of the mode of production; influencing the business cycle; and attending to the infrastructure with a view to the conditions of capital realization—government intervention has the *indirect* form of manipulating the boundary conditions for the decisions of private enterprise, and the *reactive* form of strategies for avoiding its side effects or compensating for them. This refracted mode of employing administrative power is determined by the propelling mechanism of an economy steered via the money medium.

As a result of this structural dilemma, economically conditioned crisis tendencies are not only administratively processed, flattened out, and intercepted, but also are inadvertently displaced into the administrative system. They can appear in various forms there—for example, as conflicts between business-cycle policy and infrastructure policy, as an overuse of the resource "time" (national debt), as an overloading of bureaucratic planning capacities, and so forth. This can, in turn, call forth relief strategies aimed at shifting the burden of problems back onto the economic system. Claus Offe has been particularly concerned to explain this complicated pattern of crises and of maneuvers to deal with them—oscillating from one subsystem to the other, pushed from one dimension to the other.[13]

Mass democracy. If we start from a model with two steering media, namely, money and power, then an economic theory of democracy developed in terms of Marxist functionalism is inadequate. In comparing these two media, we saw that the institutionalization of power is more demanding than that of money. Money is anchored in the lifeworld by the institutions of bourgeois private law; for this reason the theory of value can start from the contractual relation between the wage laborer and the owner of capital. By contrast, the public-legal (in the sense of the law applying to public bodies) pendant of an organization of offices does not suffice for power; above and beyond this, a legitimation of the political order is needed. And only democratic procedures of political will-formation can in principle generate legitimacy under conditions of a rationalized lifeworld with highly individuated members, with norms that have become abstract, positive, and in need of justification, and with traditions that have, as regards their claim to authority, been reflectively refracted and set communicatively aflow.[14] In this respect, the organized labor movement aimed in the same direction as the bourgeois emancipation movements. In the end, the legitimation process is regulated—on the basis of freedom of organization and of belief, and by way of competition between parties—in the form of free, secret, and general elections. Of course, the political participation of citizens takes place under certain structural restrictions.

Between capitalism and democracy there is an *indissoluble* tension; in them two opposed principles of societal integration compete for primacy. If we look at the self-understanding expressed in the basic principles of democratic constitutions, modern societies assert the primacy of a lifeworld in relation to the subsystems separated out of its institutional orders. The normative meaning of democracy can be rendered in social-theoretical terms by the formula that the fulfillment of the functional necessities of *systemically* integrated domains of action shall find its limits in the integrity of the lifeworld, that is to say, in the requirements of domains of action dependent on *social* integration. On the other hand, the internal dynamics of the capitalist economic system can be preserved only insofar as the accumulation process is uncoupled from orientations to use value. The propelling mechanism of the economic system has to be kept as free as possible from lifeworld restrictions as well as from the demands for legitimation directed to the administrative system. The internal systemic logic of capitalism can be rendered in social-theoretical terms by the formula that the functional necessities of systemically integrated domains of action shall be met, if need be, even at the cost of *technicizing* the lifeworld. Systems theory of the Luhmannian sort transforms this practical postulate into a theoretical one and thus makes its normative content unrecognizable.

Offe has expressed the tension between capitalism and democracy, from the standpoint of the competition between two contrary principles of societal integration, in the following paradox:

> Capitalist societies are distinguished from all others not by the problem of their reproduction, that is, the reconciliation of social and system integration, but by the fact that they attempt to deal with what is in fact the basic problem of all societies in a way that simultaneously entertains two solutions which logically preclude one another: the differentiation or privatization of production and its politicization or "socialization" (in the Marxian sense). The two strategies thwart and paralyze each other. As a result the system is constantly confronted with the dilemma of having to abstract from the normative rules of action and the meaning relations of subjects without being able to disregard them. The political neutralization of the spheres of labor, production, and distribution is simultaneously confirmed and repudiated.[15]

This paradox also manifests itself in the fact that if parties want to gain or retain the power of office, they have to secure the trust of private investors and of the masses simultaneously.

Above all, the two imperatives clash in the political public sphere, where the autonomy of the lifeworld has to prove itself in the face of the administrative system. The "public opinion" that gets articulated there has a different meaning from the perspective of the lifeworld than it does from the systemic perspective of the state apparatus.[16] One or the other of these perspectives is adopted by political sociologists according to whether they take an action-theoretic or a systems-theoretic approach; the chosen perspective is then applied to support a pluralistic, or ideology-critical, or authoritarian approach. Thus, from one point of view, what opinion polls report as public opinion or the will of the voters, of parties and associations, counts as a pluralistic expression of a general interest; social consensus is regarded as the *first link* in the chain of political will-formation and as the *basis* of legitimation. From the other point of view, the same consensus counts as the *result* of engineering legitimation; it is regarded as the *last link* in the chain of production of mass loyalty, with which the political system outfits itself in order to make itself independent from lifeworld restrictions. These two lines of interpretation have been falsely opposed to one another as the normative versus the empirical approach to democracy. In fact, however, each of the two views contains only one aspect of mass democracy. The formation of will that takes place via competition between parties is a result of both—the pull of communication processes in which norms and values are shaped, on the one hand, and the push of organizational performances by the political system, on the other.

The political system produces mass loyalty in both a positive and a selective manner: positively through the prospect of making good on social-welfare programs, selectively through excluding themes and contributions from public discussion. This can be accomplished through a sociostructural filtering of access to the political public sphere, through a bureaucratic deformation of the structures of public communication, or through manipulative control of the flow of communication.

By a combination of such variables we can explain how the symbolic self-presentation of political elites in the public sphere can be largely uncoupled from real decision-making processes within the political system.[17] Corresponding to this, we find a segmenting of the role of the voter, to which political participation is generally restricted. In general, electoral decisions have influence only on the recruitment of leadership personnel; as far as the motives behind them are concerned, they are removed from the grasp of discursive will-formation. This arrangement amounts to a neutralization of the possibilities for political participation opened up by the role of citizen.[18]

Welfare state. If we begin with a model of the interchange of the formally organized domains of economics and politics, on the one side, and communicatively structured domains of the private and public spheres on the other, then we have to consider that problems arising in the sphere of social labor get shifted from private to public spheres of life and, under the conditions of competitive-democratic will-formation, are there transformed into mortgages on legitimation. The social burdens resulting from class conflict—and these are in the first instance private burdens—cannot be kept away from the political sphere. Thus does social welfare become the political content of mass democracy. This shows that the political system cannot emancipate itself without a trace from its citizens' orientations to use values. It cannot produce mass loyalty in any desired amount, but must, in its social-welfare programs, also make offers that can be checked as to fulfillment.

The legal institutionalization of collective bargaining became the basis of a reform politics that has brought about a pacification of class conflict in the social-welfare state. The core of the matter is the legislation of rights and entitlements in the spheres of work and social welfare, making provision for the basic risks of the wage laborers' existence and compensating them for handicaps that arise from the structurally weaker market positions (of employees, tenants, consumers, etc.). Social-welfare policy heads off extreme disadvantages and insecurities without, naturally, affecting the structurally unequal property, income, and power relations. The regulations and performances of the social-welfare state are, however, not only oriented to goals of social adjustment through individual compensations, but also to overcoming collectively experienced, external effects—for example, in the ecologically sensitive areas of town planning and highway construction, energy and water policy, protection of the countryside, or in the areas of health, culture, and education.

Politics directed to expanding the social-welfare state is certainly faced with a dilemma, which is expressed at the fiscal level in the zero-sum game between pubic expenditures for social-welfare measures, on the one side, and expenditures aimed to promote business and to improve the infrastructure in ways that foster economic growth, on the other side. The dilemma consists in the fact that the social-welfare state is supposed to head off immediately negative effects on the lifeworld of a capitalistically organized occupational system, as well as the dysfunctional side effects thereupon of economic growth that is steered through capital accumulation, and it is supposed to do so without encroaching upon the organizational form, the structure, or the drive mechanism of economic production. Not the least among the reasons why it may not impair the conditions of stability and the requirements of mobility of capitalist growth is the following: adjustments to the pattern of distribution of social compensations trigger reactions on the part of privileged groups unless they can be covered by increases in the social product and thus do not affect the propertied classes; when this is not the case, such measures cannot fulfill the function of containing and mitigating class conflict.

Thus, not only is the *extent* of social-welfare expenditures subject to fiscal restrictions, the *kind* of social-welfare performances, the *organized way* in which life is provided for, has to fit into the structure of an interchange, via money and power, between formally organized domains of action and their environments.

(*b*) Insofar as the political system in developed capitalist societies manages to overcome the structural dilemmas accompanying government interventionism, mass democracy, and the welfare state, structures of late capitalism take shapes that have to appear as paradoxical from the perspective of a Marxian theory with a narrowly economic approach. The welfare-state pacification of class conflict comes about under the condition of a continuation of the accumulation process whose capitalist drive mechanism is protected and not altered by the interventions of the state. In the West, under both social-democratic and conservative governments, a reformism relying on the instruments of Keynesian economics has made this development into a program; since 1945, especially in the phase of reconstructing and expanding destroyed productive capacity, it has achieved unmistakable economic and sociopolitical successes. The societal structures that have crystallized out in the process should not, however, be interpreted in the manner of Austro-Marxist theoreticians such as Otto Bauer or Karl Renner, that is, as the result of a class compromise. For with the institutionalization of class conflict, the social antagonism bred by private disposition over the means of producing social wealth increasingly loses its structure-forming power for the lifeworlds of social groups, although it does remain constitutive for the structure of the economic system. Late capitalism makes use in its own way of the relative uncoupling of system and lifeworld. A class structure shifted out of the lifeworld into the system loses its historically palpable shape. The unequal distribution of social rewards reflects a structure of privilege that can no longer be traced back to class positions in any unqualified way. The old sources of inequality are, to be sure, not sealed off, but now there is interference with both welfare-state compensations and inequalities of another sort. Disparities and conflicts among marginal groups are characteristic of this. The more the class conflict that is built into society through the private economic form of accumulation can be dammed up and kept latent, the more problems come to the fore that do not *directly* violate interest positions ascribable on a class-specific basis.

Here I shall not go into the difficult problem of how the composition rules for the pattern of social equality in late capitalism undergo change; I am interested rather in how a new type of reification effect arises in class-unspecific ways, and why these effects—filtered, naturally, through the pattern of social inequality and spread around in a differential fashion—are today found above all in communicatively structured domains of action.

The welfare-state compromise alters the conditions of the four existing relations between system (economy and state) and lifeworld (private and public spheres), around which the roles of the employee and the consumer, the client of public bureaucracies and the citizen of the state, crystallize. In his theory of value Marx concentrated solely on the exchange of labor power for wages and found the symptoms of reification in the sphere of social labor. Before his eyes he had that historically limited type of alienation that Engels, for example, had described in *The Condition of the Working Class in England.*[19] From the model of alienated factory work in the early stages of industrialization, Marx developed a concept of alienation that he carried over to the proletarian lifeworld as a whole. This concept makes no distinction between the dislocation of traditional lifeworlds and the destruction of posttraditional lifeworlds. And it also does not discriminate between impoverishment, which concerns the material reproduction of the lifeworld, and disturbances in the symbolic reproduction of the lifeworld—in Weber's terms, between problems of outer and of inner need. But this type of alienation recedes further and further into the background as the welfare state becomes established.

In the social-welfare state, the roles provided by the occupational system become, so to speak, normalized. Within the framework of post-traditional lifeworlds, the structural differentiation of employment within organizations is no foreign element in any case; the burdens resulting from the character of heteronomously determined work are made at least subjectively bearable—if not through "humanizing" the work place, through providing monetary rewards and legally guaranteed securities—and are largely headed off in this way, along with other disadvantages and risks stemming from the status of workers and employees. The role of employee loses its debilitating proletarian features with the continuous rise in the standard of living, however differentiated by stratification. As the private sphere is shielded against palpable consequences of the system imperatives at work, conflicts over distribution also lose their explosive power; it is only in dramatic, exceptional cases that they go beyond the institutional boundaries of collective bargaining and become a burning issue.

This new equilibrium between normalized occupational roles and upgraded consumer roles is, as we have seen, the result of a welfare arrangement that comes about under the legitimation conditions of mass democracy. The theory of value was wrong to ignore the interchange relations between the political system and the lifeworld. For the pacification of the sphere of social labor is only the counterpart to an equilibrium established on the other side, between an expanded, but at the same time neutralized, citizen's role and blown-up client's role. The establishment of basic political rights in the framework of mass democracy means, on the one hand, a universalization of the role of citizen and, on the other hand, a segmenting of this role from the decision-making process, a cleansing of political participation from any participatory content. Legitimacy and mass loyalty form an alloy that is not analyzed by those involved and cannot be broken down into its critical components.

For this neutralization of the generalized role of citizen, the welfare state also pays in the coin of use values that come to citizens as clients of welfare-state bureaucracies. "Clients" are customers who enjoy the rewards of the welfare state; the client role is a companion piece that makes political participation that has been evaporated into an abstraction and robbed of its effectiveness acceptable. The negative side effects of institutionalizing an alienated mode of having a say in matters of public interest are passed off onto the client role in much the same way as the burdens of normalizing alienated labor are passed off onto the consumer role. It is primarily in these two channels that new conflict potentials of late capitalist society are gathering. With the exception of critical theorists such as Marcuse and Adorno, Marxists have found these new potentials vexing. Of course, the framework of the critique of instrumental reason within which those critical theorists operated has turned out to be too narrow. Only in the framework of a critique of functionalist reason can we give a plausible account of why, under the cover of a more or less successful welfare-state compromise, there should still be any conflicts breaking out at all—conflicts that do not appear primarily in class-specific forms and yet go back to a class structure that is displaced into systemically integrated domains of action. The explanation suggested by our model of late capitalist society—a model that is admittedly very stylized and that works with only a few, idealized assumptions—is the following.

Welfare-state mass democracy is an arrangement that renders the class antagonism still built into the economic system innocuous, under the condition, however, that the capitalist dynamics of growth, protected by measures of state intervention, do not grow weak. Only then is there a mass of compensation available that can be distributed according to implicitly agreed upon criteria, in ritualized confrontations, and channeled into the roles of consumer and client in such a way that the structures of alienated labor and alienated political participation develop no explosive power. However, the politically supported, internal dynamics of the economic system result in a more or less continuous increase in system complexity—which means not only an *extension* of formally organized domains of action, but an increase in their internal *density* as well. This is true, in the first place, for relations within the subsystems of the economy and the public administration and for their relations with each other. It is this internal growth that explains the processes of concentration in commodity, capital, and labor markets, the centralization of private firms and public agencies, as well as part of the expansion in the functions and activities of the state (as manifested by the correlative rise in government budgets).

However, the growth of this whole complex has as much to do with the interchange of the subsystems with those spheres of the lifeworld that have gotten redefined as system environments—in the first instance, private households that have been converted over to mass consumption, and client relations that are coordinated with bureaucratic provisions for life.

On the basic assumptions of our model, these are the two channels through which the compensations flow, which the welfare state offers for the pacification of the sphere of social labor and the neutralization of participation in political decision-making processes. If we ignore for the moment crisis-laden disequilibria of the system that are passed on to the lifeworld in administratively processed forms, capitalist growth triggers conflicts within the lifeworld chiefly as a consequence of the expansion and the increasing density of the monetary-bureaucratic complex; this happens, first of all, where socially integrated contexts of life are redefined around the roles of consumer and client and assimilated to systemically integrated domains of action. Such processes have always been part of capitalist modernization; historically, they have been successful in overriding the defensive reaction of those affected so long as it was primarily a question of transferring the material reproduction of the lifeworld over to formally organized domains of action. Along the front between system and lifeworld, the lifeworld evidently offers stubborn and possibly successful resistance only when functions of symbolic reproduction are in question.

(c) Before getting into these empirical matters, we have to pick up a thread that we earlier laid aside. We interpreted Weber's thesis of the loss of freedom in terms of a systemically induced reification of communicatively structured domains of action; then, from our critical discussion of the theory of value, we arrived at hypotheses that might explain why there are reification tendencies at all in developed capitalist societies, even if in an altered form. But how does Weber's second cultural-critical thesis—which had to do with the disintegration of religious-metaphysical worldviews and with phenomena of a loss of meaning—fit together with this reception of Marx? In Marx and Lukacs the theory of reification is supplemented and supported by a theory of class consciousness. The latter is directed, in an ideology-critical fashion, against the dominant form of consciousness and reclaims for the other side certain privileged opportunities for critical insight. In the face of a class antagonism pacified by means of welfare-state measures, however, and in the face of the growing anonymity of class structures, the theory of class consciousness loses its empirical reference. It no longer has application to a society in which we are increasingly unable to identify strictly class-specific lifeworlds. Consistent with this, Horkheimer and his collaborators replaced it with a theory of mass culture.

Marx developed his dialectical concept of ideology with an eye to eighteenth-century bourgeois culture. These ideals of self-formation, which had found classic expression in science and philosophy, in natural right and economics, in art and literature, had entered into the self-understanding and the private life-styles of the bourgeoisie and of an increasingly bourgeois nobility, as well as into the principles of public order. Marx recognized the ambivalent content of bourgeois culture. In its claims to autonomy and scientific method, to individual freedom and universalism, to radical, romantic self-disclosure, it is on the one hand, the result of cultural rationalization—having ceased to rely on the authority of tradition, it is sensitive to criticism and self-criticism. On the other hand, however, the normative contents of its abstract and unhistorical ideas, overshooting as they do existing social realities, not only support a critically transforming practice by providing some initial guidance, but also support an affirming and endorsing practice by providing a measure of idealistic transfiguration. The utopian-ideological double character of bourgeois culture has been worked out again and again from Marx to Marcuse.[20] This description applies to just those structures of consciousness that we would expect under the conditions of a modern form of understanding.

We designated as a "modern form of understanding" a structure of communication characterized in profane domains of activity by the facts that (a) communicative actions are increasingly detached from normative contexts and become increasingly dense, with an expanded scope for contingencies; and (b) forms of argumentation are institutionally differentiated, namely, theoretical discourse in the scientific enterprise, moral-practical discourse in the political public sphere and in the legal system, and aesthetic criticism in the artistic and literary enterprise. (See Figure 28 above). In the early modern period, the realm of the sacred was not completely leveled down; in secularized form it lived on in the contemplation of an art that had not shed its aura, as well as in practically effective religious and philosophical traditions, in the transitional forms of a not yet fully secularized bourgeois culture. As this residue of the sacred gets flattened out, however, as the syndrome of validity claims gets disentangled here as well, the "loss of meaning" that occupied Weber makes itself felt. The rationality differential that had always existed between the realms of the sacred and the profane now disappears. The rationality potential released in the profane realm had previously been narrowed down and neutralized by worldviews. Considered in structural terms, these worldviews were at a lower level of rationality than everyday consciousness; at the time, however, they were intellectually better worked through and articulated. What is more, mythical or religious worldviews were so deeply rooted in ritual or cultic practices that the motives and value orientations formed without coercion in collective convictions were sealed off from the influx of dissonant experiences, from the rationality of everyday life. This all changes with the secularization of bourgeois culture. The irrationally binding, sacrally preserved power of a level of rationality that had been superseded in everyday practice begins to wane. The substance of basic convictions that were culturally sanctioned and did not need to be argued for begins to evaporate.

From the logic of cultural rationalization we can project the vanishing point toward which cultural modernity is heading; as the rationality differential between the profane realm of action and a definitively disenchanted culture gets leveled out, the latter will lose the properties that made it capable of taking on ideological functions.

Of course, this state of affairs—which Daniel Bell has proclaimed as "The End of Ideology"—was a long time coming. The French Revolution, which was fought under the banner of bourgeois ideals, inaugurated the epoch of ideologically determined mass movements. The classical bourgeois emancipation movements gave rise to traditionalist reactions with the characteristics of a regression to the prebourgeois level of imitated substantiality. On the other hand, there was also a syndrome of heterogeneous modern reactions, ranging across a broad spectrum of scientific—mostly pseudoscientific—popular views, from anarchism, communism, and socialism, through syndicalist, radical-democratic, and conservative-revolutionary orientations, to fascism and National Socialism. This was the second generation of ideologies that arose on the ground of bourgeois society. All differences in formal level and synthetic power notwithstanding, they have one thing in common. Unlike the classical bourgeois ideology, these worldviews, rooted in the nineteenth century, work up specifically modern manifestations of withdrawal and deprivation—that is to say, deficits inflicted upon the lifeworld by societal modernization. This is the direction indicated, for instance, by the visionary desires for a moral or aesthetic renewal of the political public sphere or, more generally, for revitalizing a politics that has shrunk to administration. Thus, tendencies to moralization are expressed in the ideals of autonomy and participation that usually predominate in radical-democratic and socialist movements. Tendencies to aestheticization are expressed in needs for expressive self-presentation and authenticity; they can predominate in both authoritarian movements (like fascism) and antiauthoritarian movements (like anarchism). Such tendencies are in keeping with modernity inasmuch as they do not turn to metaphysically or religiously satisfying worldviews to "salvage" the moral-practical and expressive moments suppressed or neglected by the capitalist pattern of modernization; they seek, instead, to establish them practically in the new life forms of a society revolutionized in some way or other.

In spite of the differences in content, these worldviews still share with the ideologies of the first generation—the offspring of rational natural law, of utilitarianism, of bourgeois social philosophy and philosophy of history in general—the *form* of totalizing conceptions of order addressed to the political consciousness of comrades and partners in struggle. It is just this form of a global interpretation of the whole, drawn up from the perspective of the lifeworld and capable of integration, that had to break down in the communication structures of a developed modernity. When the auratic traces of the sacred have been lost and the products of a synthetic, world-picturing power of imagination have vanished, the form of understanding, now fully differentiated in its validity basis, becomes so transparent that the communicative practice of everyday life no longer affords any niches for the structural violence of ideologies. The imperatives of autonomous subsystems then have to exert their influence on socially integrated domains of action from the outside, and *in a discernible fashion.* They can no longer hide behind the rationality differential between sacred and profane realms of action and reach inconspicuously through action orientations so as to draw the lifeworld into intuitively inaccessible, functional interconnections.

If, however, the rationalized lifeworld more and more loses its structural possibilities for ideology formation, if the facts that speak for an instrumentalizing of the lifeworld can hardly be interpreted away any longer and ousted from the horizon of the lifeworld, one would expect that the competition between forms of social and system integration would openly come to the fore. But the late capitalist societies fitting the description of "welfare-state pacification" do not confirm this conjecture. They have evidently found some functional equivalent for ideology formation. In place of the positive task of meeting a certain need for interpretation by ideological means, we have the negative requirement of preventing holistic interpretations from coming into existence. The lifeworld is always constituted in the form of a global knowledge intersubjectively shared by its members; thus, the desired equivalent for no longer available ideologies might simply consist in the fact that the everyday knowledge appearing in totalized form remains diffuse, or at least never attains that level of articulation at which alone knowledge can be accepted as valid according to the standards of cultural modernity. *Everyday consciousness* is robbed of its power to synthesize; it becomes *fragmented.*

Something of this sort does in fact happen; the differentiation of science, morality, and art, which is characteristic of occidental rationalism, results not only in a growing autonomy for sectors dealt with by specialists, but also in the splitting off of these sectors from a stream of tradition continuing on in everyday practice in a quasi-natural fashion. This split has been repeatedly experienced as a problem. The attempts at an *Aufhebung* of philosophy and art were rebellions against structures that subordinated everyday consciousness to the standards of exclusive expert cultures developing according to their own logics and that yet cut it off from any influx from them.[21] Everyday consciousness sees itself thrown back on traditions whose claims to validity have already been suspended; where it does escape the spell of traditionalism, it is hopelessly splintered. In place of "false consciousness" we today have a "fragmented consciousness" that blocks enlightenment by the mechanism of reification. It is only with this that the conditions for a *colonization of the lifeworld* are met. When stripped of their ideological veils, the imperatives of autonomous subsystems make their way into the lifeworld from the outside—like colonial masters coming into a tribal society—and force a process of assimilation upon it. The diffused perspectives of the local culture cannot be sufficiently coordinated to permit the play of the metropolis and the world market to be grasped from the periphery.

Thus, the theory of late-capitalist reification, reformulated in terms of system and lifeworld, has to be supplemented by an analysis of cultural modernity, which replaces the now superseded theory of consciousness. Rather than serving a critique of ideology, this analysis would have to explain the cultural impoverishment and fragmentation of everyday consciousness. Rather than hunting after the scattered traces of revolutionary consciousness, it would have to examine the conditions for recoupling a rationalized culture with an everyday communication dependent on vital traditions.

C.—Tendencies toward Juridification.—I have explained the symptoms of reification appearing in developed capitalist societies by the fact that the media-controlled subsystems of the economy and the state intervene with monetary and bureaucratic means in the symbolic reproduction of the lifeworld. According to our hypothesis, a "colonialization of the lifeworld" can come about only

  · when traditional forms of life are so far dismantled that the structural components of the lifeworld (culture, society, and personality) have been differentiated to a great extent;
  · when exchange relations between the subsystems and the lifeworld are regulated through differentiated roles (for employment at organized work places, for the consumer demand of private households, for the relation of clients to government bureaucracies, and for formal participation in the legitimation process);
  · when the real abstractions that make available the labor power of the employed and make possible the mobilization of the vote of the electorate are tolerated by those affected as a trade-off against social rewards (in terms of time and money);
  · where these compensations are financed according to the welfare-state pattern from the gains of capitalist growth and are canalized into those roles in which, withdrawn from the world of work and the public sphere, privatized hopes for self-actualization and self-determination are primarily located, namely, in the roles of consumer and client.

Statements about an internal colonialization of the lifeworld are at a relatively high level of generalization. This is not so unusual for social-theoretical reflection, as can be seen in the example of systems functionalism as well. But such a theory is always exposed to the danger of overgeneralization and so must be able to specify at least *the type* of empirical research that is appropriate to it. I shall therefore provide an example of the evidence by which the thesis of internal colonialization can be tested: the juridification of communicatively structured areas of action. I choose this example because it offers no particularly serious problems in method or content. The development of law belongs to the undisputed and, since Durkheim and Weber, classical research areas of sociology.

If it is true that the symbolic reproduction of the lifeworld cannot be transposed onto the base of systemic integration without pathological consequences, and if precisely this trend is the unavoidable side effect of a successful welfare-state program, then in the areas of cultural reproduction, social integration, and socialization an assimilation to formally organized domains of action would have to take place under the conditions mentioned above. The social relations we call "formally organized" are those that are first constituted in forms of modern law. Thus it is to be expected that the changeover from social to system integration would take the form of juridification processes. The predicted reification effects would have to be demonstrated at the analytical level and, indeed, as being the symptomatic consequence of *a specific kind* of juridification.

I shall analyze this specific juridification process in connection with German examples from the spheres of family and school law. It is only the late offshoot of a juridification process that has accompanied bourgeois society since its beginnings. The expression 'juridification' [*Verrechtlichung*] refers quite generally to the tendency toward an increase in formal (or positive, written) law that can be observed in modern society. We can distinguish here between the *expansion* of law, that is the legal regulation of new, hitherto informally regulated social matters, from the *increasing density* of law, that is, the specialized breakdown of global statements of the legally relevant facts [*Rechtstatbestände*] into more detailed statements.[22] Otto Kirchheimer introduced the term *Verrechtlichung* into academic discussion during the Weimar Republic. At that time he had in mind primarily the institutionalization of class conflict through collective bargaining law and labor law, and in general the juristic containment of social conflicts and political struggles. This development toward the welfare state, which found expression in the participatory social rights [*soziale Teilhaberechte*] of the Weimar Constitution and received great attention in the constitutional law theories of the time (above all from Heller, Smend, and Carl Schmitt), is but the last link in a chain of juridification thrusts. In rough outline, we can distinguish four epochal juridification processes. The first wave led to *the bourgeois state*, which, in western Europe, developed during the period of Absolutism in the form of the European state system. The second wave led to the *constitutional state* [*Rechtsstaat*], which found an exemplary form in the monarchy of nineteenth-century Germany. The third wave led to the *democratic constitutional state* [*demokratischer Rechtsstaat*], which spread in Europe and in North America in the wake of the French Revolution. The last stage (to date) led finally to the *democratic welfare state* [*soziale und demokratische Rechtsstaat*], which was achieved through the struggles of the European workers' movement in the course of the twentieth century and codified, for example, in Article 21 of the Constitution of the Federal Republic of Germany. I will characterize

these *four global waves of juridification* from the viewpoint of the uncoupling of system and lifeworld and the conflict of the lifeworld with
the inner dynamics of autonomous subsystems.

(*a*) The European development of law during the phase of Absolutism
can be understood basically as an institutionalization of the two media
through which the economy and state were differentiated off into subsystems. The *bourgeois state* formed the political order within which
early modern, occupationally structured society was transformed into a
capitalist market society. On the one hand, relations among individual
commodity owners were subjected to legal regulation in a code of civil
law tailored to strategically acting legal persons who entered into contracts with one another. As we have seen, this legal order is characterized
by positivity, generality, and formality; it is constructed on the basis of
the modern concept of statutory law and the concept of the legal person
as one who can enter into contracts, acquire, alienate, and bequeath
property. The legal order is supposed to guarantee the liberty and property of the private person, the security of the law [*Rechtssicherheit*], the
formal equality of all legal subjects before the law, and thereby the calculability of all legally normed action. On the other hand, public law
authorizes a sovereign state power with a monopoly on coercive force as
the sole source of legal authority. The sovereign is absolved from orientation toward any particular policies or from specific state objectives and
becomes defined instrumentally, that is, only in relation to the means for
the legal exercise of bureaucratically organized domination. The means
of effectively allocating power become the only goal.

With this first wave of juridification, "civil society" was constituted, if
we use this expression in the sense of Hegel's philosophy of right. The
self-understanding of this phase found its most consistent expression in
Hobbes's *Leviathan*. This is of special interest in our context inasmuch
as Hobbes constructs the social order exclusively from the system perspective of a state that constitutes civil society; he defines the lifeworld
negatively—it encompasses everything excluded from the administrative system and left to private discretion. The lifeworld is that from
which civil law and legal authority emancipate the citizen; its essence
lies in the corporatively bound, status-dependent conditions of life that
had found their particularistic expression in feudal [*ständisch*] laws concerning person, profession, trade, and land. What remains of this in
Hobbes's rational state is attributed to the sphere of the private, which
indeed can now only be characterized privately—by the minimum of
peace that ensures physical survival, and by the unfettering of the empirical needs of isolated subjects who compete for scarce resources according to the laws of the market. The lifeworld is the unspecific reservoir

from which the subsystems of the economy and state extract what they need for their reproduction: performance at work and obedience.[23]

The Hobbesian construction hits exactly at the level of abstraction at which the innovations of the bourgeois state—namely, legal provisions for the institutionalization of money and power—can be characterized. Hobbes, in abstracting from the historical substratum of premodern life-forms, anticipates in his theory what Marx will later ascribe to reality as "real abstractions." Without this lifeworld substratum, the state in its absolutist form could not have found a basis for its legitimation, nor could it have functioned. Certainly, the bourgeois state accelerated the dissolution of this substratum on which it tacitly fed. However, out of the exhausted traditional life forms, and out of the premodern life-contexts in the process of dissolution, there arose—at first in class-specific forms—the structures of a modern lifeworld, which Hobbes could not see because he exclusively adopted the system perspective of the bourgeois state. From this perspective, everything that is not constituted in the forms of modern law must appear *formless*. But the modern lifeworld is no more devoid of its own structures than are historical forms of life. *Subsequent* juridification thrusts can be understood in these terms: a lifeworld that at first was placed at the disposal of the market and of absolutist rule little by little makes good its claims. After all, media such as power and money need to be anchored in a modern lifeworld. Only in this way can the bourgeois state gain a nonparasitic legitimacy appropriate to the modern level of justification. Today the structurally differentiated lifeworld, upon which modern states are functionally dependent, remains as the only source of legitimation.

(*b*) *The bourgeois constitutional state* found a prototypical form in nineteenth-century German constitutionalism and was conceptualized by theoreticians of the *Vormärz* period (1815–48), such as Karl von Rotteck or Robert von Mohl,[24] and later by F. J. Stahl.[25] Used as an analytical concept, it refers to more general aspects of a wave of juridification that by no means coincides with the specific legal developments in Germany.[26] This second wave means the constitutional regulation of administrative authority which up to then was limited and bound only by the legal form and the bureaucratic means of exercising power. Now, as private individuals, citizens are given actionable civil rights against a sovereign—though they do not yet democratically participate in forming the sovereign's will. Through this kind of constitutionalization of the state [*Verrechtsstaatlichung*], the bourgeois order of private law is coordinated with the apparatus for exercising political rule in such a way that the principle of the legal form of administration can be interpreted in the sense of the "rule of law." In the citizens' sphere of freedom the administration may interfere neither *contra* nor *praeter* nor *ultra legem*. The guarantees of the life, liberty, and property of private persons no longer arise only as functional side effects of a commerce institutionalized in civil law. Rather, with the idea of the constitutional state, they achieve the status of morally justified constitutional norms and mark the structure of the political order as a whole.

In terms of social theory, this process can again be seen from two sides: from the perspectives of the system and the lifeworld. The absolutist state had understood itself exclusively as an agent of subsystems that were differentiated out via money and power; it had treated the lifeworld, pushed into the private sphere, as unformed matter. This legal order was now enriched by elements that acknowledged the entitlement to protection of the citizens' modern lifeworld. Viewed from the outside, this can also be understood as a first step by which the modern state acquired a legitimacy in its own right: legitimation *on the basis* of a modern lifeworld.

(c) The *democratic constitutional state* took shape during the French Revolution and, since Rousseau and Kant, has occupied political theory to the present day. Again, I am using the term analytically to refer to the wave of juridification in which the idea of freedom already incipient in the concept of law as developed in the natural law tradition was given constitutional force. Constitutionalized state power was democratized; the citizens, as citizens of the state, were provided with rights of political participation. Laws now come into force only when there is a democratically backed presumption that they express a general interest and that all those affected could agree to them. This requirement is to be met by a procedure that binds legislation to parliamentary will-formation and public discussion. The *juridification of the legitimation process* is achieved in the form of general and equal suffrage and the recognition of the freedom to organize political associations and parties. This heightens the problem of the separation of powers, that is, of the relations among the functionally differentiated governmental institutions of the legislature, the executive, and the judiciary. In the constitutional state this problem had existed only for the relationship between the executive and the judiciary.

In terms of social theory, this wave of democratization lies along the same path as the previous constitutionalization. Once again the modern lifeworld asserts itself against the imperatives of a structure of domination that abstracts from all concrete life-relations. At the same time, this brings to a certain close the process of anchoring the medium of power in a lifeworld that is rationalized and differentiated, and no longer only among the bourgeoisie.

The first juridification wave constitutive of bourgeois society was still dominated by those ambivalences that Marx exposed in connection with "free" wage labor. The irony of this freedom was that the social emancipation of wage laborers, that is, the freedom of movement and freedom of choice upon which the labor contract and membership in organizations were based, had to be paid for with the proletarianization of the wage laborers' mode of life, of which normatively no account was taken at all. The next two waves of juridification were already carried forward by the pathos of bourgeois emancipation movements. Along the way to the constitutionalization and democratization of the bureaucratic authority that at first appeared in absolutist form, we find the unambiguously freedom-guaranteeing character of legal regulations. Wherever bourgeois law visibly underwrites the demands of the lifeworld against bureaucratic domination, it loses the ambivalence of realizing freedom at the cost of destructive side effects.

(*d*) The *welfare state* (which I need not characterize once again) that developed in the framework of the democratic constitutional state continues this line of *freedom-guaranteeing juridification.* Apparently it bridles the economic system in a fashion similar to the way in which the two preceding waves of juridification bridled the administrative system. In any case, the achievements of the welfare state were politically fought for and vouchsafed in the interest of guaranteeing freedoms. The parallels leap to the eye: in the one case the inner dynamics of the bureaucratic exercise of power, in the other the inner dynamics of economic accumulation processes were reconciled with the obstinate structures of a lifeworld that had itself become rationalized.

The development toward a *democratic welfare state* can in fact be understood as the institutionalizing in legal form of a social power relation anchored in class structure. Classic examples would be limitations placed upon working hours, the freedom to organize unions and bargain for wages, protection from layoffs, social security, and so forth. These are instances of juridification processes in a sphere of social labor previously subordinated to the unrestricted power of disposition and organization exercised by private owners of the means of production. Here too we are dealing with power-balancing juridifications within an area of action that is *already constituted by law.*

Norms that contain class conflict and enforce social-welfare measures have, from the perspective of their beneficiaries as well as from that of democratic lawgivers, a freedom-guaranteeing character. However, this does not apply unambiguously to all welfare-state regulations. From the start, the *ambivalence of guaranteeing freedom and taking it away* has attached to the policies of the welfare state.[27] The first wave of juridification constitutive of the relation between capital and wage labor owed its ambivalence to a contradiction between, on the one hand, the socially emancipatory intent of the norms of bourgeois civil law and, on the other, its socially repressive effects on those who were forced to offer their labor power as a commodity. The net of welfare-state guarantees is meant to cushion the external effects of a production process based on wage labor. Yet the more closely this net is woven, the more clearly ambivalences of *another sort* appear. The negative effects of this—to date, final—wave of juridification do not appear as side effects; they result *from the form of juridification itself.* It is now the very means of guaranteeing freedom that endangers the freedom of the beneficiaries.

In the area of *public welfare policy* this situation has attracted wide attention under the title "juridification and bureaucratization as limits to welfare policy."[28] In connection with social-welfare law, it has been shown repeatedly that although legal entitlements to monetary income in case of illness, old age, and the like definitely signify historical progress when compared with the traditional care of the poor,[29] this juridification of life-risks exacts a noteworthy price in the form of *restructuring interventions in the lifeworlds* of those who are so entitled. These costs ensue from the bureaucratic implementation and monetary redemption of welfare entitlements. The structure of bourgeois law dictates the formulation of welfare-state guarantees as *individual* legal entitlements under precisely *specified* general legal conditions.

In social-welfare law, *individualization*—that is, the attribution of entitlements to strategically acting legal subjects pursuing their private interests—may be more appropriate to the life situations requiring regulation than is the case, for instance, in family law. Nevertheless, the individualizing definition of, say, geriatric care has burdensome consequences for the self-image of the person concerned, and for his relations with spouse, friends, neighbors, and others; it also has consequences for the readiness of solidaric communities to provide subsidiary assistance. A considerable compulsion toward the redefinition of everyday situations comes above all from the *specification of legal conditions*—in this case, the conditions under which social security will provide compensation: "An insured case is normally understood as a 'typical example of the particular contingency against which social security is supposed to provide protection'. Compensation is made in the event of a valid claim to benefit. The juridification of social situation-definitions means introducing into matters of economic and social distribution an if-then structure of conditional law that is 'foreign' to social relations, to social causes, dependencies and needs. This structure does not, however, allow for appropriate, and especially not for preventive, reactions to the causes of the situations requiring compensation."[30]

In the end, the *generality* of legal situation-definitions is tailored to *bureaucratic implementation,* that is, to the administration that deals with the social problem as presented by the legal entitlement. The situation to be regulated is embedded in the context of a life history and of a concrete form of life; it has to be subjected to violent abstraction, not merely because it has to be subsumed under the law, but so that it can be dealt with administratively. The implementing bureaucracies have to proceed very selectively and *choose* from among the legally defined conditions of compensation those social exigencies that can at all be dealt with by means of bureaucratic power exercised according to law. Moreover, this suits the needs of a centralized and computerized handling of social exigencies by large, distant organizations. These organizations add a spatial and temporal element to the social and psychological distance of the client from the welfare bureaucracy.

Furthermore, the indemnification of the life-risks in question usually takes the *form of monetary compensation.* However, in such cases as reaching retirement or losing a job, the typical changes in life situation and the attendant problems cannot as a rule be subjected to consumerist redefinition. To balance the inadequacy of these system-conforming compensations, *social services* have been set up to lend *therapeutic assistance.*

With this, however, the contradictions of welfare-state intervention are only reproduced at a higher level. The form of the administratively prescribed treatment by an expert is for the most part in contradiction with the aim of the therapy, namely, that of promoting the client's independence and self-reliance. "The process of providing social services takes on a reality of its own, nurtured above all by the professional competence of public officials, the framework of administrative action, biographical and current 'findings', the readiness and ability to cooperate of the person seeking the service or being subjected to it. In these areas too there remain problems connected with a class-specific utilization of such services, with the assignments made by the courts, the prison system and other offices, and with the appropriate location and arrangement of the services within the network of bureaucratic organizations of the welfare state; but beyond this, such forms of physical, psycho-social and emancipatory aid really require modes of operation, rationality criteria and organizational forms that are foreign to bureaucratically structured administration."[31]

The ambivalence of the last juridification wave, that of the welfare state, can be seen with particular clarity in the paradoxical consequences of the social services offered by the therapeutocracy—from the prison system through medical treatment of the mentally ill, addicts and the behaviorally disturbed, from the classical forms of social work through the newer psychotherapeutic and group-dynamic forms of support, pastoral care and the building of religious groups, from youth work, public education, and the health system through general preventive measures of every type. The more the welfare state goes beyond pacifying the class conflict lodged in the sphere of production and spreads a net of client relationships over private spheres of life, the stronger are the anticipated pathological side effects of a juridification that entails both a bureaucratization and a monetarization of core areas of the lifeworld. The *dilemmatic structure of this type of juridification* consists in the fact that, while the welfare-state guarantees are intended to serve the goal of social integration, they nevertheless promote the disintegration of life-relations when these are separated, through legalized social intervention, from the consensual mechanisms that coordinate action and are transferred over to media such as power and money. In this sense, R. Pitschas speaks of the crisis of public-welfare policy as a crisis of social integration.[32]

For an empirical analysis of these phenomena, it is important to clarify the criteria on the basis of which the aspects of guaranteeing and taking away freedom can be separated. From the legal standpoint the first thing that presents itself is the classical division of fundamental rights into liberties and participatory rights; one might presume that the structure of bourgeois formal law becomes dilemmatic precisely when these means are no longer used to negatively demarcate areas of private discretion, but are supposed to provide positive guarantees of membership and participation in institutions and benefits. If this presumption proved true, then one would already expect a change from guaranteeing to taking away freedom at the third (democratizing) stage of juridification and not only at the fourth (welfare state) stage. There are indeed indications that the *organization of the exercise of civil liberties* considerably restricts the possibilities for spontaneous opinion formation and discursive will-formation through a segmentation of the voter's role, through the competition of leadership elites, through vertical opinion formation in bureaucratically encrusted party apparatuses, through autonomized parliamentary bodies, through powerful communication networks, and the like. However, such arguments cannot be used to deduce aspects of taking away freedom from the very *form* of participatory rights, but only from the bureaucratic ways and means of their *implementation.* One can scarcely dispute the unambiguously freedom-guaranteeing character of the *principle* of universal suffrage, nor of the *principles* of freedom of assembly, of the press, and of opinion—which, under the conditions of modern mass communication, must also be interpreted as democratic participatory rights.

A different criterion, more sociological in nature and open to social-theoretic interpretation, takes us further: that is, the classification of legal norms according to whether they can be legitimized only through procedure in the positivist sense, or are amenable to substantive justification. If the legitimacy of a legal norm is brought into question, it is, in many cases, sufficient to refer to the formally correct genesis of the law, judicial decision, or administrative act. Legal positivism has conceptualized this as legitimation through procedure, though, of course, without seeing that this mode of legitimation is insufficient in itself and merely points to the need for justification of the legitimizing public authorities.[33] In the face of the changing and steadily increasing volume of positive law, modern legal subjects content themselves in actual practice with legitimation through procedure, for in many cases substantive justification is not only not possible, but is also, from the viewpoint of the lifeworld, meaningless. This is true of cases where the *law* serves *as a means for organizing media-controlled subsystems* that have, in any case, become autonomous in relation to the normative contexts of action oriented by mutual understanding. Most areas of economic, commercial, business, and administrative law fit here:[34] the law is combined with the media of power and money in such a way that it takes on the role of a steering medium itself. Law as a medium, however, remains bound up with *law as an institution.* By legal *institutions* I mean legal norms that cannot be sufficiently legitimized through a positivistic reference to procedure. Typical of these are the bases of constitutional law, the principles of criminal law and penal procedure, and all regulation of punishable offenses close to morality (e.g., murder, abortion, rape, etc.). As soon as the validity of *these* norms is questioned in everyday practice, the reference to their legality no longer suffices. They need substantive justification, because they belong to the legitimate orders of the lifeworld itself and, together with informal norms of conduct, form the background of communicative action.

We have characterized modern law through a combination of principles of enactment and justification. This structure simultaneously makes possible a positivistic prolongation of the paths of justificatory reasoning and a moralizing intensification of the justification problematic, which is thereby shifted into the foundations of the legal system. We can now see how the uncoupling of system and lifeworld fits in with this legal structure. Law used as a steering medium is relieved of the problem of justification; it is connected with the body of law whose substance requires legitimation only through formally correct procedure. By contrast, legal institutions belong to the societal components of the lifeworld. Like other norms of conduct not covered by the sanctioning authority of the state, they can become moralized under appropriate circumstances. Admittedly, changes in the basis of legitimation do not directly affect the stock of legal norms, but they may provide the impetus for a legal (or, in the limiting case, a revolutionary) change in existing law.

As long as the law functions as a complex medium bound up with money and power, it extends to formally organized domains of action that, as such, are directly constituted in the forms of bourgeois formal law. By contrast, legal institutions have no *constitutive* power, but only a *regulative* function. They are embedded in a broader political, cultural, and social context; they stand in a continuum with moral norms and are superimposed on communicatively structured areas of action. They give to these informally constituted domains of action a binding form backed by state sanction. From this standpoint we can distinguish processes of juridification according to whether they are linked to antecedent institutions of the lifeworld and juridically superimposed on socially integrated areas of action, or whether they merely increase the density of legal relationships that are constitutive of systemically integrated areas of action. Here, the question of the appropriate mode of legitimation may serve as a first test. The technicized and de-moralized areas of law that grow along with the complexity of the economic and administrative systems have to be evaluated with respect to functional imperatives and in accordance with higher-order norms. Looked at historically, the continuous growth in positive law largely falls into this category and merely indicates an increased recourse to the medium of law. The epochal juridification waves are, on the other hand, characterized by *new legal institutions,* which are also reflected in the legal consciousness of everyday practice. Only with respect to this second category of juridification do questions of normative evaluation arise.

The first wave of juridification had a freedom-guaranteeing character to the extent that bourgeois civil law and a bureaucratic domination exercised by legal means at least meant emancipation from premodern relations of power and dependence. The three subsequent juridification waves guaranteed an increase in freedom insofar as they were able to restrain, in the interests of citizens and of private legal subjects, the political and economic dynamics that had been released by the legal institutionalization of the media of money and power. The step-by-step development toward the democratic welfare state is directed against those modern relations of power and dependence that arose with the capitalist enterprise, the bureaucratic apparatus of domination, and, more generally, the formally organized domains of action of the economy and the state. The inner dynamics of these action systems also unfold within the organizational forms of law, but in such a way that law here takes on the role of a steering medium rather than supplementing institutional components of the lifeworld.

In its role as a medium, existing law can be more or less functional, but outside of the horizon of the lifeworld it is meaningless to question the freedom-guaranteeing or freedom-reducing character of these norms. The ambivalence of guaranteeing/taking away freedom cannot be reduced to a dialectic between law as an institution and law as a medium, because the alternative between guaranteeing or taking away freedom is posed only from the viewpoint of the lifeworld, that is, only in relation to legal institutions.

So far we have proceeded on the assumption that law is used as a medium only within formally organized domains of action, and that as a steering medium it remains indifferent in relation to the lifeworld and to the questions of substantive justification that arise within its horizons. Welfare-state interventionism has since rendered this assumption invalid. Public welfare policy has to use the law precisely as a medium to regulate those exigencies that arise in communicatively structured areas of action. To be sure, the principle of social participation and social compensation is, like freedom of association, a constitutionally anchored institution that can connect up easily with the legitimate orders of the modern lifeworld. But social-welfare law, through which social compensation is implemented, differs from, for instance, the laws governing collective bargaining, through which freedom of association becomes effective, in one important respect: measures of social-welfare law (as a rule, compensatory payments) do not, like collective wage and salary agreements, intervene in an area that is *already* formally organized. Rather, they regulate exigencies that, as lifeworld situations, belong to a communicatively structured area of action. Thus, I should like to explain the type of reification effect exhibited in the case of public welfare policy by the fact that the *legal institutions* that guarantee social compensation become effective only through *social-welfare law used as a medium.* From the standpoint of action theory the paradox of this legal structure can be explained as follows. As a medium, social-welfare law is tailored to domains of action that are first constituted in legal forms of organization and that can be held together only by systemic mechanisms. At the same time, however, social-welfare law applies to situations embedded in informal lifeworld contexts.

In our context, government welfare policy serves only as an illustration. The thesis of internal colonization states that the subsystems of the economy and state become more and more complex as a consequence of capitalist growth, and penetrate ever deeper into the symbolic reproduction of the lifeworld. It should be possible to test this thesis sociologically wherever the traditionalist padding of capitalist modernization has worn through and central areas of cultural reproduction, social integration, and socialization have been openly drawn into the vortex of economic growth and therefore of juridification. This applies not only to such issues as protection of the environment, nuclear reactor security, data protection, and the like, which have been successfully dramatized in the public sphere. The trend toward juridification of informally regulated spheres of the lifeworld is gaining ground along a broad front—the more leisure, culture, recreation, and tourism recognizably come into the grip of the laws of the commodity economy and the definitions of mass consumption, the more the structures of the bourgeois family manifestly become adapted to the imperatives of the employment system, the more the school palpably takes over the functions of assigning job and life prospects, and so forth.

The structure of juridification in school and family law is marked by ambivalences similar to those in the area of welfare law. In the Federal Republic of Germany these problems, which dominate discussions of legal policy, have been worked out for particular aspects of the development of school[35] and family law.[36] In both cases juridification means, in the first place, the establishment of basic legal principles: recognition of the child's fundamental rights against his parents, of the wife's against her husband, of the pupil's against the school, and of the parents', teachers', and pupils' against the public school administration. Under the headings of "equal opportunity" and "the welfare of the child" the authoritarian position of the paterfamilias—which is still anchored in, among other things, matrimonial-property law in the German Civil Code—is being dismantled in favor of a more equal distribution of the competencies and entitlements of other family members. To the juridification of this traditional, economically grounded, patriarchal power relation in the family, there corresponds, in the case of the schools, a legal regulation of the special power relation (which persisted into the 1950s) between government bureaucracy and the schools. While the core areas of family law (governing marriage, support, matrimonial property, divorce, parental care, guardianship) have been reformed via adjudication (i.e., court decisions) and via legislation, bringing schools under the rule of law—that is, the legal regulation of areas outside the law as specified in the official prerogatives of the schools—was initially stimulated by adjudication and then carried forward by the government educational bureaucracy through administrative channels.[37] The bureaucracy had to ensure that instructional procedures and school measures, as far as they were relevant to the pupil's later life and the parents' wishes, were given a form in which they were accessible to judicial review. It is only more recently that the judiciary has called upon the legislature to act so as to guide the overflowing bureaucratic juridification into statutory channels.[38]

The expansion of legal protection and the enforcement of basic rights in the family and the schools require a high degree of differentiation of specific conditions, exceptions, and legal consequences. In this way, these domains of action are opened up to bureaucratic intervention and judicial control. In no way are family and school formally organized spheres of action. If they were, *to begin with*, already constituted in legal form, the increasing density of legal norms could lead to a redistribution of money and power without altering the basis of social relations. In fact, however, in these spheres of the lifeworld, we find, *prior to* any juridification, norms and contexts of action that by functional necessity are based on mutual understanding as a mechanism for coordinating action. Juridification of these spheres means, therefore, not increasing the density of an already existing network of formal regulations, but, rather, legally supplementing a communicative context of action through the superimposition of legal norms—not through legal institutions but through law as a medium.

The formalization of relationships in family and school means, for those concerned, an objectivization and *removal from the lifeworld* of (now) formally regulated social interaction in family and school. As legal subjects they encounter one another in an objectivizing, success-oriented attitude. S. Simitis describes the complementary role played by the law in socially integrated areas of action: "Family law *supplements* a morally secured system of social rules of conduct, and to that extent is strictly complementary."[39] The same is true of the schools. Just as the socialization process in the family *exists prior to and conditions* legal norms, so too does the pedagogical process of teaching. These formative processes in family and school, which take place via communicative action, must be able to function independent of legal regulation. If, however, the structure of juridification requires administrative and judicial controls that do not merely *supplement* socially integrated contexts with legal institutions, but *convert* them over to the medium of law, then functional disturbances arise. This is the action-theoretic explanation for the negative effects of juridification stressed in juristic and sociological discussions.

Simitis and his collaborators have carried out empirical research on the dilemmatic structure of the juridification of the family in connection with child custody laws.[40] The group has concentrated on the decision-making practices of wardship courts. The protection of the welfare of the child as a basic right can be implemented only by giving the state possibilities to intervene in parental privileges, once regarded as untouchable. It was the dialectic of this juridification that inspired Simitis to undertake his study: "However indispensable state services may be, they not only bring advantages for individual family members, but simultaneously bring about increasing dependence. Emancipation within the family is achieved at the cost of a new bond. In order to constitute himself as a person, the individual family member sees himself compelled to make claims on the assistance of the state. What therefore, at first sight, is sometimes presented as an instrument for breaking up domination structures within the family, proves on closer examination to be also a vehicle for another form of dependence."[41] The study shows that the wardship judges surveyed based their judgments on insufficient information and oriented themselves predominantly to the child's "physical" rather than "spiritual" well-being. The psychological shortcomings of judicial decision-making practice result, however, not so much from an inadequate professional training of jurists for such tasks, as from juristic formalization of matters that require a *different type* of treatment: "Initiatives to ascertain the facts or to suggest better ways of resolving conflicts are scarcely to be found. There are perhaps reasons for this on the side of the parents themselves; but it is also a result of their position in respect to the legal process (and in reality), which tends to turn them into 'objects' of negotiation between the judge and the youth-welfare office and thus to make them 'subordinated subjects of the proceedings' rather than 'participants' in them."[42] In almost all cases one can see "how little the judge is able to accomplish with his specifically juridical means, whether it is a question of communication with the child that is essential for the proceedings, or of understanding the factors important for the child's development."[43] It is the medium of the law itself that violates the communicative structures of the sphere that has been juridified.

From this viewpoint, one can understand the policy recommendation to the effect that legislators keep to a minimum the state interventions necessary to protect children's rights. "Among the various possible solutions, the one to be preferred is that which leaves the judge the least amount of discretion in making decisions. Legislative regulation, therefore, ought not to favor far-reaching judicial intervention, as has hitherto increasingly been the case. On the contrary, it must, first and foremost, do everything possible to de-judicialize the conflict."[44]

Of course, replacing the judge with the therapist is no panacea; the social worker is only another expert, and does not free the client of the welfare-state bureaucracy from his or her position as an object. Remodeling wardship law in a therapeutic direction would merely accelerate the assimilation of family law to child welfare law: "In this para-law of the family, it is a governmental authority, the Division of Child Welfare, which sets the tone. Here child-rearing takes place under state supervision, and parents are held accountable for it. The language, particularly of many older commentaries, shows better than any regulation what the goal is. State intervention compensates for disrupted normality."[45]

Nevertheless, the intuition that lies behind the paradoxical proposal to dejudicialize juridified family conflict is instructive: the juridification of communicatively structured areas of action should not go beyond the enforcement of principles of the rule of law, beyond the legal institutionalization of the *external* consititution of, say, the family or the school. The place of law as a medium is to be taken by procedures for settling conflicts that are appropriate to the structures of action orientated by mutual understanding—discursive processes of will-formation and consensus-oriented procedures of negotiation and decision making. This demand may seem more or less acceptable for private realms such as the family, and it may well be in line with the educational orientations specific to the middle class. For a public domain such as the schools, the analogous demand for deregulation and debureaucratization meets with resistance.[46] The call for a more strictly pedagogical approach to instruction and for a democratization of decision-making structures is not immediately compatible with the neutralization of the citizen's role;[47] it is even less compatible with the economic system-imperative to uncouple the school system from the fundamental right to education and to close-circuit it with the employment system. From the perspective of social theory, the present controversy concerning the basic orientations of school policy can be understood as a fight for or against the colonization of the lifeworld. However, I shall confine myself to the analytical level of juridification; this manifests itself no less ambivalently in the schools than in the family.

The protection of pupils' and parents' rights against educational measures (such as promotion or nonpromotion, examinations and tests, and so forth), or from acts of the school or the department of education that restrict basic rights (disciplinary penalties), is gained at the cost of a judicialization and bureaucratization that penetrates deep into the teaching and learning process. For one thing, responsibility for problems of educational policy and school law overburdens government agencies, just as responsibility for the child's welfare overburdens the wardship courts. For another, the medium of the law comes into collision with the form of educational activity. Socialization in schools is broken up into a mosaic of legally contestable administrative acts. Subsuming education under the medium of law produces an "abstract grouping together of those involved in the educational process and individualized legal subjects in a system of achievement and competition. The abstractness consists in the fact that the norms of school law apply without consideration of the persons concerned, of their needs and interests, cutting off their experiences and splitting up their life relationships."[48] This has to endanger the pedagogical freedom and initiative of the teacher. The compulsion toward litigation-proof certainty of grades and the over-regulation of the curriculum lead to such phenomena as depersonalization, inhibition of innovation, breakdown of responsibility, immobility, and so forth.[49] G. Frankenberg has studied the consequences of the juridification of teaching practice from the viewpoint of how teachers, as those to whom the legal norms are addressed, perceive the demands of law and react to them.

There are structural differences between the legal form in which courts and school administrations exercise their powers, on the one hand, and an educational task that can be accomplished only by way of action oriented to mutual understanding, on the other. Frankenberg captures these differences well: "We can take as dominant characteristics of the political-legal dimension of the teaching task: (1) a discrepancy between behavioral prescriptions and concrete action situations; (2) a 'double coverage' for the government's 'educational mandate', through the school administration's responsibility for setting guidelines and through the authority of administrative courts to interpret and specify general norms; (3) an unclear demarcation of the teacher's pedagogic scope of action; and (4) possible threats, whether open or disguised, of sanctions for behavior that conflicts with the norms. To the opacity of the normative complex of school law this adds the incalculability of the normative demands decisive for educational practice."[50] These structural differences leave the teacher insecure and evoke reactions that Frankenberg describes as over- or underutilization of the pedagogical scope of action, that is, as overattention to or concealed disobedience of the law.

The legal regulation of the special power relation of the school removes some relics of absolutist state power. However, the normative remolding of this communicatively structured action area is accomplished in the form of welfare-state interventionist regulations. Controlled by the judiciary and the administration, the school changes imperceptibly into a welfare institution that organizes and distributes schooling as a social benefit. As in the case of the family, the result for legal policy is the call to dejudicialize and above all to debureaucratize the pedagogical process. The framework of a school constitution under the rule of law, which transposes "the private law of the state into a genuinely public law," is to be filled, not by the medium of law, but through consensus-oriented procedures for conflict resolution—through "decision-making procedures that treat those involved in the pedagogical process as having the capacity to represent their own interests and to regulate their affairs themselves."[51]

If one studies the paradoxical structure of juridification in such areas as the family, the schools, social-welfare policy, and the like, the meaning of the demands that regularly result from these analyses is easy to decipher. The point is to protect areas of life that are functionally dependent on social integration through values, norms, and consensus formation, to preserve them from falling prey to the systemic imperatives of economic and administrative subsystems growing with dynamics of their own, and to defend them from becoming converted over, through the steering medium of the law, to a principle of sociation that is, for them, dysfunctional.

3. The Tasks of a Critical Theory of Society

My purpose in discussing the thesis of internal colonization in connection with recent tendencies toward juridification in the Federal Republic of Germany was, among other things, to show by example how processes of real abstraction, to which Marx directed his attention, can be analyzed without our having any equivalent for his theory of value. This brings us back to the central question of whether, in the present state of the social sciences, it is necessary and possible to replace the theory of value, at least insofar as it enables us to connect theoretical statements about lifeworld and system to each other. As we have seen, Marx conceived the systemic context of capital self-realization as a fetishistic totality; from this there followed the methodological requirement that we decipher anything that might correctly be brought under a systems-theoretical description simultaneously as a process of reification of living labor. This far-reaching claim has to be dropped, however, if we see in the capitalist economic system not only a new formation of class relationships but an advanced level of system differentiation in its own right. Under these premises, the *semantic question* of how something can be translated from one language into the other can be converted into the *empirical question* of when the growth of the monetary-bureaucratic complex affects domains of action that cannot be transferred to system-integretive mechanisms without pathological side effects. The analysis of Parsonian media theory led me to the assumption that this boundary is overstepped when systemic imperatives force their way into domains of cultural reproduction, social integration, and socialization. This assumption needs to be tested empirically in connection with "real abstractions" detected in the core zones of the lifeworld. The semantic problem of connecting systems-theoretic and action-theoretic descriptions requires a solution that does not prejudge substantive questions.

I introduced the system concept of society by way of a *methodological objectification* of the lifeworld and justified the shift in perspective connected with this objectification—a shift from the perspective of a participant to that of an observer—in action-theoretic terms. Like the theory of value, this justification has the form of a conceptual explication. It is supposed to explain what it means for the symbolic reproduction of the lifeworld when communicative action is replaced by media-steered interaction, when language, in its function of coordinating action, is replaced by media such as money and power. Unlike the transformation of concrete into abstract labor, this does not *eo ipso* give rise to reifying effects. The conversion to another mechanism of action coordination, and thereby to another principle of sociation, results in reification—that is, in a pathological de-formation of the communicative infrastructure of the lifeworld—only when the lifeworld cannot be withdrawn from the functions in question, when these functions cannot be painlessly transferred to media-steered systems of action, as those of material reproduction sometimes can. In this way phenomena of reification lose the dubious status of facts that can be inferred from economic statements about value relations by means of semantic transformations alone. "Real abstractions" now make up instead an object domain for empirical inquiry. They become the object of a research program that no longer has need of value theory or any similar translation tool.

In other respects a theory of capitalist modernization developed by means of a theory of communicative action does follow the Marxian model. It is *critical* both of contemporary social sciences and of the social reality they are supposed to grasp. It is critical of the reality of developed societies inasmuch as they do not make full use of the learning potential culturally available to them, but deliver themselves over to an uncontrolled growth of complexity. As we have seen, this increasing system complexity encroaches upon nonrenewable supplies like a quasi-natural force; not only does it outflank traditional forms of life, it attacks the communicative infrastructure of largely rationalized lifeworlds. But the theory is also critical of social-scientific approaches that are incapable of deciphering the paradoxes of societal rationalization because they make complex social systems their object only from one or another abstract point of view, without accounting for the historical constitution of their object domain (in the sense of a reflexive sociology).[1] Critical social theory does not relate to established lines of research as a competitor; starting from its concept of the rise of modern societies, it attempts to explain the specific limitations and the relative rights of those approaches.

If we leave to one side the insufficiently complex approach of behaviorism, there are today three main lines of inquiry occupied with the phenomenon of modern societies. We cannot even say that they are in competition, for they scarcely have anything to say to one another. Efforts at theory comparison do not issue in reciprocal critique; fruitful critique that might foster a common undertaking can hardly be developed across these distances, but at most within one or another camp.[2] There is a good reason for this mutual incomprehension: the object domains of the competing approaches do not come into contact, for they are the result of one-sided abstractions that unconsciously cut the ties between system and lifeworld constitutive for modern societies.

Taking as its point of departure the work of Max Weber, and also in part Marxist historiography, an approach—sometimes referred to as the history of society [*Gesellschaftsgeschichte*]—has been developed that is comparative in outlook, typological in procedure, and, above all, well informed about social history. The dynamics of class struggle are given greater or lesser weight according to the positions of such different authors as Reinhard Bendix, R. Lepsius, C. Wright Mills, Barrington Moore, and Hans-Ulrich Wehler; however, the theoretical core is always formed by assumptions about the structural differentiation of society in functionally specified systems of action. Close contact with historical research prevents the *theory of structural differentiation* from issuing in a more strongly theoretical program, for instance, in some form of systems functionalism. Rather, analysis proceeds in such a way that modernization processes are referred to the level of institutional differentiation. The functionalist mode of investigation is not so widely separated from the structuralist mode that the potential competition between the two conceptual strategies could develop. The modernization of society is, to be sure, analyzed in its various ramifications, but a one-dimensional idea of the whole process of structural differentiation predominates. It is not conceived as a second-order differentiation process, as an uncoupling of system and lifeworld that, when sufficiently advanced, makes it possible for media-steered subsystems to react back on structurally differentiated lifeworlds. As a result, the pathologies of modernity do not come into view as such from this research perspective; it lacks the conceptual tools to distinguish adequately between (*a*) the structural differentiation of the lifeworld, particularly of its societal components, (*b*) the growing autonomy of action systems that are differentiated out via steering media, as well as the internal differentiation of these subsystems, and finally (*c*) those differentiation processes that simultaneously dedifferentiate socially integrated domains of action in the sense of colonizing the lifeworld.

Taking as its point of departure neoclassical economic theory, on the one hand, and social-scientific functionalism, on the other, a *systems-theoretical approach* has established itself above all in economics and in the sciences of administration. These system sciences have, so to speak, grown up in the wake of the two media-steered subsystems. As long as they were occupied chiefly with the internal complexity of the economic and administrative systems, they could rest content with sharply idealized models. To the extent that they had to bring the restrictions of the relevant social environments into their analyses, however, there arose a need for an integrated theory that would also cover the interaction between the two functionally intermeshed subsystems of state and economy.

It is only with the next step in abstraction, which brought society as a whole under systems-theoretical concepts, that the system sciences overdrew their account. The systems theory of society first developed by Parsons and consistently carried further by Luhmann views the rise and development of modern society solely in the functionalist perspective of growing system complexity. Once systems functionalism is cleansed of the dross of the sociological tradition, it becomes insensitive to social pathologies that can be discerned chiefly in the structural features of socially integrated domains of action. It hoists the vicissitudes of communicatively structured lifeworlds up to the level of media dynamics; by assimilating them, from the observer perspective, to disequilibria in intersystemic exchange relations, it robs them of the significance of identity-threatening deformations, which is how they are experienced from the participant perspective.

Finally, from phenomenology, hermeneutics, and symbolic interactionism there has developed an *action-theoretical approach*. To the extent that the different lines of *interpretive sociology* proceed in a generalizing manner at all, they share an interest in illuminating structures of worldviews and forms of life. The essential part is a theory of everyday life, which can also be linked up with historical research, as it is in the work of E. P. Thompson. To the extent that this is done, modernization processes can be presented from the viewpoint of the lifeworlds specific to different strata and groups; the everyday life of the subcultures dragged into these processes are disclosed with the tools of anthropological research. Occasionally these studies condense to fragments of history written from the point of view of its victims. Then modernization appears as the sufferings of those who had to pay for the establishment of the new mode of production and the new system of states in the coin of disintegrating traditions and forms of life. Research of this type sharpens our perception of historical asynchronicities; they provide a stimulus to critical recollection in Benjamin's sense. But it has as little place for the internal systemic dynamics of economic development, of nation and state building, as it does for the structural logics of rationalized lifeworlds. As a result, the subcultural mirrorings in which the sociopathologies of modernity are refracted and reflected retain the subjective and accidental character of *uncomprehended* events.

Whereas the theory of structural differentiation does not sufficiently separate systemic and lifeworld aspects, systems theory and action theory, each isolates and overgeneralizes one of the two aspects. The methodological abstractions have the same result in all three cases. The theories of modernity made possible by these approaches remain insensitive to what Marx called "real abstractions"; the latter can be gotten at through an analysis that at once traces the rationalization of lifeworlds *and* the growth in complexity of media-steered susbystems, and that keeps the paradoxical nature of their interference in sight. As we have seen, it is possible to speak in a nonmetaphorical sense of paradoxical conditions of life if the structural differentiation of lifeworlds is described as rationalization. Social pathologies are not to be measured against "biological" goal states but in relation to the contradictions in which communicatively intermeshed interaction can get caught because deception and self-deception can gain objective power in an everyday practice reliant on the facticity of validity claims.

By "real abstractions" Marx was referring not only to paradoxes experienced by those involved as deformations of their lifeworld, but above all to paradoxes that could be gotten at only through an analysis of reification (or of rationalization). It is in this latter sense that we call "paradoxical" those situations in which systemic relief mechanisms made possible by the rationalization of the lifeworld turn around and overburden the communicative infrastructure of the lifeworld. After attempting to render a fourth approach to inquiry—the *genetic structuralism* of developmental psychology—fruitful for appropriating Weber's sociology of religion, Mead's theory of communication, and Durkheim's theory of social integration,[3] I proposed that we read the Weberian rationalization thesis in that way. The basic conceptual framework I developed by these means was, naturally, not meant to be an end in itself; rather, it has to prove itself against the task of explaining those pathologies of modernity that other approaches pass right by for methodological reasons.

It is just this that critical theory took as its task before it increasingly distanced itself from social research in the early 1940s. In what follows I will (A) recall the complex of themes that originally occupied critical theory, and (B) show how some of these intentions can be taken up without the philosophy of history to which they were tied. In the process, I shall (C) go into one topic at somewhat greater length: the altered significance of the critique of positivism in a postpositivist age.

A.—The work of the Institute for Social Research was essentially dominated by six themes until the early 1940s when the circle of collaborators that had gathered in New York began to break up. These research interests are reflected in the lead theoretical articles that appeared in the main part of the *Zeitschrift für Sozialforschung*. They have to do with (*a*) the forms of integration in postliberal societies, (*b*) family socialization and ego development, (*c*) mass media and mass culture, (*d*) the social psychology behind the cessation of protest, (*e*) the theory of art, and (*f*) the critique of positivism and science.[4] This spectrum of themes reflects Horkheimer's conception of an interdisciplinary social science.[5] In this phase the central line of inquiry, which I characterized with the catchphrase "rationalization as reification," was to be worked out with the differentiated means of various disciplines.[6] Before the "critique of instrumental reason" contracted the process of reification into a topic for the philosophy of history again, Horkheimer and his circle had made "real abstractions" the object of empirical inquiry. From this theoretical standpoint it is not difficult to see the unity in the multiplicity of themes enumerated above.

(*a*) To begin with, after the far-reaching changes in liberal capitalism the concept of reification needed to be specified.[7] National Socialism, above all, provided an incentive to examine the altered relationship between the economy and the state, to tackle the question of whether a new principle of social organization had arisen with the transition from the Weimar Republic to the authoritiarian state, of whether fascism evinced stronger similarities to the capitalist societies of the West or, given the totalitarian features of its political system, had more in common with Stalinism. Pollock and Horkheimer were inclined to the view that the Nazi regime was like the Soviet regime, in that a state-capitalist order had been established in which private ownership of the means of production retained only a formal character, while the steering of general economic processes passed from the market to planning bureaucracies; in the process the management of large concerns seemed to merge with party and administrative elites. In this view, corresponding to the authoritarian state we have a totally administered society. The form of societal integration is determined by a purposive rational—at least in intention—exercise of centrally steered, administrative domination.

Neumann and Kirchheimer opposed to this theory the thesis that the authoritarian state represented only the totalitarian husk of a monopoly capitalism that remained intact, in that the market mechanism functioned the same as before. On this view, even a developed fascism did not displace the primacy of economic imperatives in relation to the state. The compromises among the elites of economy, party, and adminstration came about *on the basis* of an economic system of private capitalism. From this standpoint, the structural analogies between developed capitalist societies—whether in the political form of a totalitarian regime or a mass democracy—stood out clearly. Since the totalitarian state was not seen as the center of power, societal integration did not take place exclusively in the forms of technocratically generalized, administrative rationality.[8]

(*b and c*) The relation between the economic and administrative systems of action determined how society was integrated, which forms of rationality the life-contexts of individuals were subjected to. However, the subsumption of sociated individuals under the dominant pattern of social control, the process of reification itself, had to be studied elsewhere: in the family, which, as the agency of socialization, prepared coming generations for the imperatives of the occupational system; and in the political-cultural public sphere, where, via the mass media, mass culture produced compliance in relation to political institutions. The theory of state capitalism could only explain the *type* of societal integration. The analytical social psychology that Fromm,[9] in the tradition of left Freudianism,[10] linked with questions from Marxist social theory was supposed, on the other hand, to explain the *processes* through which individual consciousness was adjusted to the functional requirements of the system, in which a monopolistic economy and an authoritarian state had coalesced.

Institute co-workers investigated the structural change of the bourgeois nuclear family, which had led to a loss of function and a weakening of the authoritarian position of the father, and which had at the same time mediatized the familial haven and left coming generations more and more in the socializing grip of extrafamilial forces. They also investigated the development of a culture industry that desublimated culture, robbed it of its rational content, and functionalized it for purposes of the manipulative control of consciousnsess. Meanwhile, reification remained, as it was in Lukacs, a category of the philosophy of consciousness; it was discerned in the attitudes and modes of behavior of individuals. The phenomena of reified consciousness were to be explained empirically, with the help of psychoanalytic personality theory. The authoritarian, easily manipulable character with a weak ego appeared in forms typical of the times; the corresponding superego formations were traced back to a complicated interplay of social structure and instinctual vicissitudes.

Again there were two lines of interpretation. Horkheimer, Adorno, and Marcuse held on to Freudian instinct theory and invoked the dynamics of an inner nature that, while it did react to societal pressure, nevertheless remained in its core resistant to the violence of socialization.[11] Fromm, on the other hand, took up ideas from ego psychology and shifted the process of ego development into the medium of social interaction, which permeated and structured the natural substratum of instinctual impulses.[12] Another front formed around the question of the ideological character of mass culture, with Adorno on one side and Benjamin on the other. Whereas Adorno (along with Löwenthal and Marcuse) implacably opposed the experiential content of authentic art to consumerized culture, Benjamin steadfastly placed his hopes in the secular illuminations that were to come from a mass art stripped of its aura.

(*d*) Thus in the course of the 1930s the narrower circle of members of the institute developed a consistent position in regard to all these themes. A monolithic picture of a totally administered society emerged; corresponding to it was a repressive mode of socialization that shut out inner nature and an omnipresent social control exercised through the channels of mass communication. Over against this, the positions of Neumann and Kirchheimer, Fromm and Benjamin are not easily reduced to a common denominator. They share a more differentiated assessment of the complex and contradictory character both of forms of integration in postliberal societies and of family socialization and mass culture. These competing approaches might have provided starting points for an analysis of potentials still resistant to the reification of consciousness. But the experiences of the German émigrés in the contemporary horizon of the 1930s motivated them rather to investigate the mechanisms that might explain the suspension of protest potentials. This was also the direction of their studies of the political consciousness of workers and employees, and especially of the studies of anti-Semitism begun by the institute in Germany and continued in America up to the late 1940s.[13]

(*e and f*) Processes of the reification of consciousness could be made the object of a wide-ranging program of empirical research only after the theory of value had lost its foundational role. With this, of course, also went the normative content of rational natural law theory that was preserved in value theory.[14] As we have seen, its place was then occupied by the theory of societal rationalization stemming from Lukacs. The normative content of the concept of reification now had to be gotten from the rational potential of modern culture. For this reason, in its classical period critical theory maintained an emphatically affirmative relation to the art and philosophy of the bourgeois era. The arts—for Lowenthal and Marcuse, classical German literature above all; for Benjamin and Adorno, the literary and musical avant-garde—were the preferred object of an ideology critique aimed at separating the transcendent contents of authentic art—whether utopian or critical—from the affirmative, ideologically worn-out components of bourgeois ideals. As a result, philosophy retained central importance as the keeper of those bourgeois ideals. "Reason," Marcuse wrote in the essay that complemented Horkheimer's programmatic demarcation of critical theory from traditional theory, "is the fundamental category of philosophical thought, the only one by means of which it has bound itself to human destiny."[15] And further on: "Reason, mind, morality, knowledge, and happiness are not only categories of bourgeois philosophy, but concerns of mankind. As such they must be preserved, if not derived anew. When critical theory examines the philosophical doctrines in which it was still possible to speak of man, it deals first with the camouflage and misinterpretation that characterized the discussion of man in the bourgeois period."[16]

This confrontation with the tradition through the critique of ideology could aim at the truth content of philosophical concepts and problems, at appropriating their systematic content, only because critique was guided by theoretical assumptions. At that time critical theory was still based on the Marxist philosophy of history, that is, on the conviction that the forces of production were developing an objectively explosive power. Only on this presupposition could critique be restricted to "bringing to consciousness potentialities that have emerged within the maturing historical situation itself."[17] Without a *theory* of history there could be no immanent critique that applied to the manifestations of objective spirit and distinguished what things and human beings could be from what they actually were.[18] Critique would be delivered up to the reigning standards in any given historical epoch. The research program of the 1930s stood and fell with its historical-philosophical trust in the rational potential of bourgeois culture—a potential that would be released in social movements under the pressure of developed forces of production. Ironically, however, the critiques of ideology carried out by Horkheimer, Marcuse, and Adorno confirmed them in the belief that culture was losing its autonomy in postliberal societies and was being incorporated into the machinery of the economic-administrative system. The development of productive forces, and even critical thought itself, was moving more and more into a perspective of bleak assimilation to their opposites. In the totally administered society only instrumental reason, expanded into a totality, found embodiment; everything that existed was transformed into a real abstraction. In that case, however, what was taken hold of and deformed by these abstractions escaped the grasp of empirical inquiry.

The fragility of the Marxist philosophy of history that implicitly serves as the foundation of this attempt to develop critical theory in interdisciplinary form makes it clear why it had to fail and why Horkheimer and Adorno scaled down this program to the speculative observations of the *Dialectic of Enlightenment.* Historical-materialist assumptions regarding the dialectical relation between productive forces and productive relations had been transformed into pseudonormative propositions concerning an objective teleology in history. This was the motor force behind the realization of a reason that had been given ambiguous expression in bourgeois ideals. Critical theory could secure its normative foundations only in a philosophy of history. But this foundation was not able to support an empirical research program.

This was also evident in the lack of a clearly demarcated object domain like the communicative practice of the everyday lifeworld in which rationality structures are embodied and processes of reification can be traced. The basic concepts of critical theory placed the consciousness of individuals directly vis-à-vis economic and administrative mechanisms of integration, which were only extended inward, intrapsychically. In contrast to this, the theory of communicative action can ascertain for itself the rational content of anthropologically deep-seated structures by means of an analysis that, *to begin with,* proceeds reconstructively, that is, unhistorically. It describes structures of action and structures of mutual understanding that are found in the intuitive knowledge of competent members of modern societies. There is no way back from them to a theory of history that does not distinguish between problems of developmental logic and problems of developmental dynamics.

In this way I have attempted to free historical materialism from its philosophical ballast.[19] Two abstractions are required for this: (i) abstracting the development of cognitive structures from the historical dynamic of events, and (ii) abstracting the evolution of society from the historical concretion of forms of life. Both help in getting beyond the confusion of basic categories to which the philosophy of history owes its existence.

A theory developed in this way can no longer start by examining concrete ideals immanent in traditional forms of life. It must orient itself to the range of learning processes that is opened up at a given time by a historically attained level of learning. It must refrain from critically evaluating and normatively ordering totalities, forms of life and cultures, and life-contexts and epochs *as a whole.* And yet it can take up some of the intentions for which the interdisciplinary research program of earlier critical theory remains instructive.

B.—Coming at the end of a complicated study of the main features of a theory of communicative action, this suggestion cannot count even as a "promissory note." It is less a promise than a conjecture. So as not to leave it entirely ungrounded, in what follows I will comment briefly on the theses mentioned above, and in the same order. With these illustrative remarks I also intend to emphasize the fully open character and the flexibility of an approach to social theory whose fruitfulness can be confirmed only in the ramifications of social and philosophical research. As to what social theory can accomplish in and of itself—it resembles the focusing power of a magnifying glass. Only when the social sciences no longer sparked a single thought would the time for social theory be past.

(*a*) *On the forms of integration in postliberal societies* Occidental rationalism arose within the framework of bourgeois capitalist societies. For this reason, following Marx and Weber I have examined the initial conditions of modernization in connection with societies of this type and have traced the capitalist path of development. In postliberal societies there is a fork in this path: modernization pushes forward in one direction through endogenously produced problems of economic accumulation, in the other through problems arising from the state's efforts at rationalization. Along the developmental path of organized capitalism, a political order of welfare-state mass democracy took shape. In some places, however, under the pressure of economic crises, the mode of production, threatened by social disintegration, could be maintained for a time only in the political form of authoritarian or fascist orders. Along the developmental path of bureaucratic socialism a political order of dictatorship by state parties took shape. In recent years Stalinist domination by force has given way to more moderate, post-Stalinist regimes; the beginnings of a democratic workers' movement and of democratic decision-making processes within the Party are for the time visible only in Poland. Both the fascist and the democratic deviations from the two dominant patterns depend rather strongly, it seems, on national peculiarities, particularly on the political culture of the countries in question. At any rate, these branchings make historical specifications necessary even at the most general level of types of societal integration and of corresponding social pathologies. If we permit ourselves to simplify in an ideal-typical manner and limit ourselves to the two dominant variants of postliberal societies, and if we start from the assumption that alienation phenomena arise as systemically induced deformations of the lifeworld, then we can take a few steps toward a comparative analysis of principles of societal organizations, kinds of crisis tendencies, and forms of social pathology.

On our assumption, a considerably rationalized lifeworld is one of the initial conditions for modernization processes. It must be possible to anchor money and power in the lifeworld as media, that is, to institutionalize them by means of positive law. If these conditions are met, economic and administrative systems can be differentiated out, systems that have a complementary relation to one another and enter into interchanges with their environments via steering media. At this level of system differentiation modern societies arise, first capitalist societies, and later—setting themselves off from those—bureaucratic-socialist societies. A capitalist path of modernization opens up as soon as the economic system develops its own intrinsic dynamic of growth and, with its endogenously produced problems, takes the lead, that is, the evolutionary primacy, for society as a whole. The path of modernization runs in another direction when, on the basis of state ownership of most of the means of production and an institutionalized one-party rule, the administrative action system gains a like autonomy in relation to the economic system.

To the extent that these organizational principles are established, there arise interchange relations between the two functionally interlocked subsystems and the societal components of the lifeworld in locked subsystems and the societal components of the lifeworld in which the media are anchored (see Figure 39, p. 320). The lifeworld, more or less relieved of tasks of material reproduction, can in turn become more differentiated in its symbolic structures and can set free the inner logic of development of cultural modernity. At the same time, the private and public spheres are now set off as the environments of the system. According to whether the economic system 'or the state apparatus attains evolutionary primacy, either private households or politically relevant memberships are the points of entry for crises that are shifted from the subsystems to the lifeworld. In modernized societies disturbances in the material reproduction of the lifeworld take the form of stubborn systemic disequilibria; the latter either take effect directly as *crises* or they call forth *pathologies* in the lifeworld.

Steering crises were first studied in connection with the business cycle of market economies. In bureaucratic socialism, crisis tendencies spring from self-blocking mechanisms in planning administrations, as they do on the other side from endogenous interruptions of accumulation processes. Like the paradoxes of exchange rationality, the paradoxes of planning rationality can be explained by the fact that rational action orientations come into contradiction with themselves through unintended systemic effects. These crisis tendencies are worked through not only in the subsystem in which they arise, but also in the complementary action system into which they can be shifted. Just as the capitalist economy relies on organizational performances of the state, the socialist planning bureaucracy has to rely on self-steering performances of the economy. Developed capitalism swings between the contrary policies of "the market's self-healing powers" and state interventionism.[20] The structural dilemma is even clearer on the other side, where policy oscillates hopelessly between increased central planning and decentralization, between orienting economic programs toward investment and toward consumption.

These *systemic disequilibria* become *crises* only when the performances of economy and state remain manifestly below an established level of aspiration and harm the symbolic reproduction of the lifeworld by calling forth conflicts and reactions of resistance there. It is the societal components of the lifeworld that are directly affected by this. Before such conflicts threaten core domains of social integration, they are pushed to the periphery—before anomic conditions arise there are appearances of withdrawal of legitimation or motivation (see Figure 22, p. 143). But when steering crises—that is, perceived disturbances of material reproduction—are successfully intercepted by having recourse to lifeworld resources, pathologies arise in the lifeworld. These resources appear in Figure 21 (p. 142) as contributions to cultural reproduction, social integration, and socialization. For the continued existence of the economy and the state, it is the resources listed in the middle column as contributing to the maintenance of society that are relevant, for it is here, in the institutional orders of the lifeworld, that subsystems are anchored.

We can represent the replacement of steering crises with lifeworld pathologies as follows: anomic conditions are avoided, and legitimations and motivations important for maintaining institutional orders are secured, at the expense of, and through the ruthless exploitation of, other resources. Culture and personality come under attack for the sake of warding off crises and stabilizing society (first and third columns versus middle column in Figure 21). The consequences of this substitution can be seen in Figure 22: instead of manifestations of anomie (and instead of the withdrawal of legitimation and motivation in place of anomie), phenomena of alienation and the unsettling of collective identity emerge. I have traced such phenomena back to a colonization of the lifeworld and characterized them as a reification of the communicative practice of everyday life.

However, deformations of the lifeworld take the form of a reification of communicative relations only in capitalist societies, that is, only where the private household is the point of incursion for the displacement of crises into the lifeworld. This is not a question of the overextension of a single medium but of the monetarization and bureaucratization of the spheres of action of employees and of consumers, of citizens and of clients of state bureaucracies. Deformations of the lifeworld take a different form in societies in which the points of incursion for the penetration of crises into the lifeworld are politically relevant memberships. There too, in bureaucratic-socialist societies, domains of action that are dependent on social integration are switched over to mechanisms of system integration. But instead of the reification of communicative relations we find the shamming of communicative relations in bureaucratically desiccated, forcibly "humanized" domains of pseudopolitical intercourse in an overextended and administered public sphere. This pseudopoliticization is symmetrical to reifying privatization in certain respects. The lifeworld is not directly assimilated to the system, that is, to legally regulated, formally organized domains of action; rather, systemically self-sufficient organizations are fictively put back into a simulated horizon of the lifeworld. While the system is draped out as the lifeworld, the lifeworld is absorbed by the system.[21]

(b) *Family socialization and ego development.* The diagnosis of an uncoupling of system and lifeworld also offers a different perspective for judging the structural change in family, education, and personality development. For a psychoanalysis viewed from a Marxist standpoint, the theory of the Oedipus complex, interpreted sociologically, was pivotal for explaining how the functional imperatives of the economic system could establish themselves in the superego structures of the dominant social character. Thus, for example, Löwenthal's studies of drama and fiction in the ninetenth century served to show in detail that the constraints of the economic system—concentrated in status hierarchies, occupational roles, and gender stereotypes—penetrated intó the innermost aspects of life history via intrafamilial dependencies and patterns of socialization.[22] The intimacy of highly personalized relations merely concealed the blind force of economic interdependencies that had become autonomous in relation to the private sphere—a force that was experienced as "fate."

Thus the family was viewed as the agency through which systemic imperatives influenced our instinctual vicissitudes; its communicative internal structure was not taken seriously. Because the family was always viewed only from functionalist standpoints and was never given its own weight from structuralist points of view, the epochal changes in the bourgeois family could be misunderstood; in particular, the results of the leveling out of paternal authority could be interpreted wrongly. It seemed as if systemic imperatives now had the chance—by way of a mediatized family—to take hold directly of intrapsychic events, a process that the soft medium of mass culture could at most slow down. If, by contrast, we *also* recognize in the structural transformation of the bourgeois family the inherent rationalization of the lifeworld; if we see that, in egalitarian patterns of relationship, in individuated forms of intercourse, and in liberalized child-rearing practices, some of the potential for rationality ingrained in communicative action is *also* released; then the changed conditions of socialization in the middle-class nuclear family appear in a different light.

Empirical indicators suggest the growing autonomy of a nuclear family in which socialization processes take place through the medium of largely deinstitutionalized communicative action. Communicative infrastructures are developing that have freed themselves from latent entanglements in systemic dependencies. The contrast between the *homme* who is educated to freedom and humanity in the intimate sphere and the *citoyen* who obeys functional necessities in the sphere of social labor was always an ideology. But it has now taken on a different meaning. Familial lifeworlds see the imperatives of the economic and administrative systems coming at them from outside, instead of being mediatized by them from behind. In the families and their environments we can observe a polarization between communicatively structured and formally organized domains of action; this places socialization processes under different conditions and exposes them to a different type of danger. This view is supported by two rough sociopsychological clues: the diminishing significance of the Oedipal problematic and the growing significance of adolescent crises.

For some time now, psychoanalytically trained physicians have observed a symptomatic change in the typical mainfestations of illness. Classical hysterias have almost died out; the number of compulsion neuroses is drastically reduced; on the other hand, narcissistic disturbances are on the increase.[23] Christopher Lasch has taken this symptomatic change as the occasion for a diagnosis of the times that goes beyond the clinical domain.[24] It confirms the fact that the significant changes in the present escape sociopsychological explanations that start from the Oedipal problematic, from an internalization of societal repression which is simply masked by parental authority. The better explanations start from the premise that the communication structures that have been set free in the family provide conditions for socialization that are as demanding as they are vulnerable. The potential for irritability grows, and with it the probability that instabilities in parental behavior will have a comparatively strong effect—a subtle neglect.

The other phenomenon, a sharpening of the adolescence problematic, also speaks for the socializatory significance of the uncoupling of system and lifeworld.[25] Systemic imperatives do not so much insinuate themselves into the family, establish themselves in systematically distorted communication, and inconspicuously intervene in the formation of the self as, rather, openly come at the family from outside. As a result, there is a tendency toward disparities between competences, attitudes, and motives, on the one hand, and the functional requirements of adult roles on the other. The problem of detaching oneself from the family and forming one's own identity have in any case turned adolescent development (which is scarcely safeguarded by institutions anymore) into a critical test for the ability of the coming generation to connect up with the preceding one. When the conditions of socialization in the family are no longer functionally in tune with the organizational membership conditions that the growing child will one day have to meet, the problems that young people have to solve in their adolescence become insoluble for more and more of them. One indication of this is the social and even political significance that youth protest and withdrawal cultures have gained since the end of the 1960s.[26]

This new problem situation cannot be handled with the old theoretical means. If we connect the epochal changes in family socialization with the rationalization of the lifeworld, socializatory interaction becomes the point of reference for the analysis of ego development, and systematically distorted communication—the reification of interpersonal relations—the point of reference for investigating pathogenesis. The theory of communicative action provides a framework within which the structural model of ego, id, and superego can be recast.[27] Instead of an instinct theory that represents the relation of ego to inner nature in terms of a philosophy of consciousness—on the model of relations between subject and object—we have a theory of socialization that connects Freud with Mead, gives structures of intersubjectivity their due, and replaces hypotheses about instinctual vicissitudes with assumptions about identity formation.[28] This approach can (i) appropriate more recent developments in psychoanalytic research, particularly the theory of object relations[29] and ego psychology,[30] (ii) take up the theory of defense mechanisms[31] in such a way that the interconnections between intrapsychic communication barriers and communication disturbances at the interpersonal level become comprehensible,[32] and (iii) use the assumptions about mechanisms of conscious and unconscious mastery to establish a connection between orthogenesis and pathogenesis. The cognitive and sociomoral development studied in the Piagetian tradition[33] takes place in accord with structural patterns that provide a reliable foil for intuitively recorded clinical deviations.

(c) *Mass media and mass culture.* With its distinction between system and lifeworld, the theory of communicative action brings out the independent logic of socializatory interaction; the corresponding distinction between two contrary types of communication media makes us sensitive to the ambivalent potential of mass communications. The theory makes us skeptical of the thesis that the essence of the public sphere has been liquidated in postliberal societies. According to Horkheimer and Adorno, the communication flows steered via mass media *take the place of* those communication structures that had once made possible public discussion and self-understanding by citizens and private individuals. With the shift from writing to images and sounds, the electronic media—first film and radio, later television—present themselves as an apparatus that completely permeates and dominates the language of everyday communication. On the one hand, it transforms the authentic content of modern culture into the sterilized and ideologically effective stereotypes of a mass culture that merely replicates what exists; on the other hand, it uses up a culture cleansed of all subversive and transcending elements for an encompassing system of social controls, which is spread over individuals, in part reinforcing their weakened internal behavioral controls, in part replacing them. The mode of functioning of the culture industry is said to be a mirror image of the psychic apparatus, which, as long as the internalization of paternal authority was still functioning, had subjected instinctual nature to the control of the superego in the way that technology had subjected outer nature to its domination.

Against this theory we can raise the empirical objections that can always be brought against stylizing oversimplifications—that it proceeds ahistorically and does not take into consideration the structural change in the bourgeois public sphere; that it is not complex enough to take account of the marked national differences—from differences between private, public-legal, and state-controlled organizational structures of broadcasting agencies, to differences in programming, viewing practices, political culture, and so forth. But there is an even more serious objection, an objection in principle, that can be derived from the dualism of media discussed above.[34]

I distinguished two sorts of media that can ease the burden of the (risky and demanding) coordinating mechanism of reaching understanding: on the one hand, steering media, via which subsystems are differentiated out of the lifeworld; on the other hand, generalized forms of communication, which do not replace reaching agreement in language but merely condense it, and thus remain tied to lifeworld contexts. Steering media uncouple the coordination of action from building consensus in language altogether and neutralize it in regard to the alternative of coming to an agreement or failing to do so. In the other case we are dealing with a specialization of linguistic processes of consensus formation that remains dependent on recourse to the resources of the lifeworld background. The mass media belong to these generalized forms of communication. They free communication processes from the provinciality of spatiotemporally restricted contexts and permit public spheres to emerge, through establishing the abstract simultaneity of a virtually present network of communication contents far removed in space and time and through keeping messages available for manifold contexts.

These media publics hierarchize and at the same time remove restrictions on the horizon of possible communication. The one aspect cannot be separated from the other—and therein lies their ambivalent potential. Insofar as mass media one-sidedly channel communication flows in a centralized network—from the center to the periphery or from above to below—they considerably strengthen the efficacy of social controls. But tapping this authoritarian potential is always precarious because there is a counterweight of emancipatory potential built into communication structures themselves. Mass media can simultaneously contextualize and concentrate processes of reaching understanding, but it is only in the first instance that they relieve interaction from yes/no responses to criticizable validity claims. Abstracted and clustered though they are, these communications cannot be reliably shielded from the possibility of opposition by responsible actors.

When communications research is not abridged in an empiricist manner and allows for dimensions of reification in communicative everyday practice,[35] it confirms this ambivalence. Again and again reception research and program analysis have provided illustrations of the theses in culture criticism that Adorno, above all, developed with a certain over-statement. In the meantime, the same energy has been put into working out the contradictions resulting from the facts that

- · the broadcasting networks are exposed to competing interests; they are not able to smoothly integrate economic, political and ideological, professional and aesthetic viewpoints;[36]
- · normally the mass media cannot, without generating conflict, avoid the obligations that accrue to them from their journalistic mission and the professional code of journalism;[37]
- · the programs do not only, or even for the most part, reflect the standards of mass culture;[38] even when they take the trivial forms of popular entertainment, they may contain critical messages—"popular culture as popular revenge";[39]
- · ideological messages miss their audience because the intended meaning is turned into its opposite under conditions of being received against a certain subcultural background;[40]
- · the inner logic of everyday communicative practice sets up defenses against the direct manipulative intervention of the mass media;[41] and
- · the technical development of electronic media does not necessarily move in the direction of centralizing networks, even though "video pluralism" and "television democracy" are at the moment not much more than anarchist visions.[42]

(*d*) *Potentials for protest.* My thesis concerning the colonization of the lifeworld, for which Weber's theory of societal rationalization served as a point of departure, is based on a critique of functionalist reason, which agrees with the critique of instrumental reason only in its intention and in its ironic use of the word 'reason'. One major difference is that the theory of communicative action conceives of the lifeworld as a sphere in which processes of reification do not appear as mere reflexes—as manifestations of a repressive integration emanating from an oligopolistic economy and an authoritarian state. In this respect, the earlier critical theory merely repeated the errors of Marxist functionalism.[43] My references to the socializatory relevance of the uncoupling of system and lifeworld and my remarks on the ambivalent potentials of mass media and mass culture show the private and public spheres in the light of a rationalized lifeworld in which system imperatives *clash with* independent communication structures. The transposition of communicative action to media-steered interactions and the deformation of the structures of a damaged intersubjectivity are by no means predecided processes that might be distilled from a few global concepts. The analysis of lifeworld pathologies calls for an (unbiased) investigation of tendencies *and* contradictions. The fact that in welfare-state mass democracies class conflict has been institutionalized and thereby pacified does not mean that protest potential has been altogether laid to rest. But the potentials for protest emerge now along different lines of conflict—just where we would expect them to emerge if the thesis of the colonization of the lifeworld were correct.

In the past decade or two, conflicts have developed in advanced Western societies that deviate in various ways from the welfare-state pattern of institutionalized conflict over distribution. They no longer flare up in domains of material reproduction; they are no longer channeled through parties and associations; and they can no longer be allayed by compensations. Rather, these new conflicts arise in domains of cultural reproduction, social integration, and socialization; they are carried out in sub-institutional—or at least extraparliamentary—forms of protest; and the underlying deficits reflect a reification of communicatively structured domains of action that will not respond to the media of money and power. The issue is not primarily one of compensations that the welfare state can provide, but of defending and restoring endangered ways of life. In short, the new conflicts are not ignited by distribution problems but by questions having to do with the grammar of forms of life.

This new type of conflict is an expression of the "silent revolution" in values and attitudes that R. Inglehart has observed in entire populations.[44] Studies by Hildebrandt and Dalton, and by Barnes and Kaase, confirm the change in themes from the "old politics" (which turns on questions of economic and social security, internal and military security) to a "new politics."[45] The new problems have to do with quality of life, equal rights, individual self-realization, participation, and human rights. In terms of social statistics, the "old politics" is more strongly supported by employers, workers, and middle-class tradesmen, whereas the new politics finds stronger support in the new middle classes, among the younger generation, and in groups with more formal education. These phenomena tally with my thesis regarding internal colonization.

If we take the view that the growth of the economic-administrative complex sets off processes of erosion in the lifeworld, then we would expect old conflicts to be overlaid with new ones. A line of conflict forms between, on the one hand, a center composed of strata *directly* involved in the production process and interested in maintaining capitalist growth as the basis of the welfare-state compromise, and, on the other hand, a periphery composed of a variegated array of groups that are lumped together. Among the latter are those groups that are further removed from the "productivist core of performance" in late capitalist societies,[46] that have been more strongly sensitized to the self-destructive consequences of the growth in complexity or have been more strongly affected by them.[47] The bond that unites these heterogeneous groups is the critique of growth. Neither the bourgeois emancipation movements nor the struggles of the organized labor movement can serve as a model for this protest. Historical parallels are more likely to be found in the social-romantic movements of the early industrial period, which were supported by craftsmen, plebians, and workers, in the defensive movements of the populist middle class, in the escapist movements (nourished by bourgeois critiques of civilization) undertaken by reformers, the *Wandervögel*, and the like.

The current potentials for protest are very difficult to classify, because scenes, groupings, and topics change very rapidly. To the extent that organizational nuclei are formed at the level of parties or associations, members are recruited from the same diffuse reservoir.[48] The following catchphrases serve at the moment to identify the various currents in the Federal Republic of Germany: the antinuclear and environmental movements; the peace movement (including the theme of north-south conflict); single-issue and local movements; the alternative movement (which encompasses the urban "scene," with its squatters and alternative projects, as well as the rural communes); the minorities (the elderly, gays, handicapped, and so forth); the psychoscene, with support groups and youth sects; religious fundamentalism; the tax-protest movement, school protest by parents' associations, resistance to "modernist" reforms; and, finally, the women's movement. Of international significance are the autonomy movements struggling for regional, linguistic, cultural, and also religious independence.

In this spectrum I will differentiate emancipatory potentials from potentials for resistance and withdrawal. After the American civil rights movement—which has since issued in a particularistic self-affirmation of black subcultures—only the feminist movement stands in the tradition of bourgeois-socialist liberation movements. The struggle against patriarchal oppression and for the redemption of a promise that has long been anchored in the acknowledged universalistic foundations of morality and law gives feminism the impetus of an offensive movement, whereas the other movements have a more defensive character. The resistance and withdrawal movements aim at stemming formally organized domains of action for the sake of communicatively structured domains, and not at conquering new territory. There is an element of particularism that connects feminism with these movements; the emancipation of women means not only establishing formal equality and eliminating male privilege, but overturning concrete forms of life marked by male monopolies. Furthermore, the historical legacy of the sexual division of labor to which women were subjected in the bourgeois nuclear family has given them access to contrasting virtues, to a register of values complementary to those of the male world and opposed to a one-sidedly rationalized everyday practice.

Within resistance movements we can distinguish further between the defense of traditional and social rank (based on property) and a defense that already operates on the basis of a rationalized lifeworld and tries out new ways of cooperating and living together. This criterion makes it possible to demarcate the protest of the traditional middle classes against threats to neighborhoods by large technical projects, the protest of parents against comprehensive schools, the protest against taxes (patterned after the movement in support of Proposition 13 in California), and most of the movements for autonomy, on the one side, from the core of a new conflict potential, on the other: youth and alternative movements for which a critique of growth sparked by themes of ecology and peace is the common focus. It is possible to conceive of these conflicts in terms of resistance to tendencies toward a colonization of the lifeworld, as I hope now to indicate, at least in a cursory way.[49] The objectives, attitudes, and ways of acting prevalent in youth protest groups can be understood, to begin with, as reactions to certain problem situations that are perceived with great sensitivity.

"Green" problems. The intervention of large-scale industry into ecological balances, the growing scarcity of nonrenewable natural resources, as well as demographic developments present industrially developed societies with major problems; but these challenges are abstract at first and call for technical and economic solutions, which must in turn be globally planned and implemented by administrative means. What sets off the protest is rather the tangible destruction of the urban environment; the despoliation of the countryside through housing developments, industrialization, and pollution; the impairment of health through the ravages of civilization, pharmaceutical side effects, and the like—that is, developments that noticeably affect the organic foundations of the lifeworld and make us drastically aware of standards of livability, of inflexible limits to the deprivation of sensual-aesthetic background needs.

Problems of excessive complexity. There are certainly good reasons to fear military potentials for destruction, nuclear power plants, atomic waste, genetic engineering, the storage and central utilization of private data, and the like. These real anxieties are combined, however, with the terror of a new category of risks that are literally invisible and are comprehensible only from the perspective of the system. These risks invade the lifeworld and at the same time burst its dimensions. The anxieties function as catalysts for a feeling of being overwhelmed in view of the possible consequences of processes for which we are morally accountable—since we do set them in motion technically and politically—and yet for which we can no longer take moral responsibility—since their scale has put them beyond our control. Here resistance is directed against abstractions that are forced upon the lifeworld, although they go beyond the spatial, temporal, and social limits of complexity of even highly differentiated lifeworlds, centered as these are around the senses.

Overburdening the communicative infrastructure. Something that is expressed rather blatantly in the manifestations of the psychomovement and renewed religious fundamentalism is also a motivating force behind most alternative projects and many citizens' action groups—the painful manifestations of deprivation in a culturally impoverished and one-sidedly rationalized practice of everyday life. For this reason, ascriptive characteristics such as gender, age, skin color, neighborhood or locality, and religious affilitation serve to build up and separate off communities, to establish subculturally protected communities supportive of the search for personal and collective identity. The revaluation of the partic-ular, the natural, the provincial, of social spaces that are small enough to be familiar, of decentralized forms of commerce and despecialized activ-ities, of segmented pubs, simple interactions and dedifferentiated public spheres—all this is meant to foster the revitaliztion of possibilities for expression and communication that have been buried alive. Resistance to reformist interventions that turn into their opposite, because the means by which they are implemented run counter to the declared aims of social integration, also belongs in this context.

The new conflicts arise along the seams between system and life-world. Earlier I described how the interchange between the private and public spheres, on the one hand, and the economic and administrative action systems, on the other, takes place via the media of money and power, and how it is institutionalized in the roles of employees and con-sumers, citizens and clients of the state. It is just these roles that are the targets of protest. Alternative practice is directed against the profit-dependent instrumentalization of work in one's vocation, the market-dependent mobilization of labor power, against the extension of pres-sures of competition and performance all the way down into elementary school. It also takes aim at the monetarization of services, relationships, and time, at the consumerist redefinition of private spheres of life and personal life-styles. Furthermore, the relation of clients to public service agencies is to be opened up and reorganized in a participatory mode, along the lines of self-help organizations. It is above all in the domains of social policy and health policy (e.g., in connection with psychiatric care) that models of reform point in this direction. Finally, certain forms of protest negate the definitions of the role of citizen and the routines for pursuing interests in a purposive-rational manner—forms ranging from the undirected explosion of disturbances by youth ("Zurich is burning!"), through calculated or surrealistic violations of rules (after the pattern of the American civil rights movement and student protests), to violent provocation and intimidation.

According to the programmatic conceptions of some theoreticians, a partial disintegration of the social roles of employees and consumers, of clients and citizens of the state, is supposed to clear the way for counterinstitutions that develop from within the lifeworld in order to set limits to the inner dynamics of the economic and political-administrative action systems. These institutions are supposed, on the one hand, to divert out of the economic system a second, informal sector that is no longer oriented to profit and, on the other hand, to oppose to the party system new forms of a "politics in the first person," a politics that is expressive and at the same time has a democratic base.[50] Such institutions would reverse just those abstractions and neutralizations by which in modern societies labor and political will-formation have been tied to media-steered interaction. The capitalist enterprise and the mass party (as an "ideology-neutral organization for acquiring power") generalize their points of social entry via labor markets and manufactured public spheres; they treat their employees and voters as abstract labor power and voting subjects; and they keep at a distance—as environments of the system—those spheres in which personal and collective identities can alone take shape. By contrast, the counterinstitutions are intended to dedifferentiate some parts of the formally organized domains of action, remove them from the clutches of the steering media, and return these "liberated areas" to the action-coordinating mechanism of reaching understanding.

However unrealistic these ideas may be, they are important for the polemical significance of the new resistance and withdrawal movements reacting to the colonization of the lifeworld. This significance is obscured, both in the self-understanding of those involved and in the ideological imputations of their opponents, if the communicative rationality of cultural modernity is rashly equated with the functionalist rationality of self-maintaining economic and administrative action systems—that is, whenever the rationalization of the lifeworld is not carefully distinguished from the increasing complexity of the social system. This confusion explains the fronts—which are out of place and obscure the real political oppositions—between the antimodernism of the Young Conservatives[51] and the neoconservative defense of postmodernity[52] that robs a modernity at variance with itself of its rational content and its perspectives on the future.[53]

C.—In this work I have tried to introduce a theory of communicative action that clarifies the normative foundations of a critical theory of society. The theory of communicative action is meant to provide an alternative to the philosophy of history on which earlier critical theory still relied, but which is no longer tenable. It is intended as a framework within which interdisciplinary research on the selective pattern of capitalist modernization can be taken up once again. The illustrative observations (*a*) through (*d*) were meant to make this claim plausible. The two additional themes (*e*) and (*f*) are a reminder that the investigation of what Marx called "real abstraction" has to do with the social-scientific tasks of a theory of modernity, not the philosophical. Social theory need no longer ascertain the normative contents of bourgeois culture, of art and of philosophical thought, in an indirect way, that is, by way of a critique of ideology. With the concept of a communicative reason ingrained in the use of language oriented to reaching understanding, it again expects from philosophy that it take on systematic tasks. The social sciences can enter into a cooperative relation with a philosophy that has taken up the task of working on a theory of rationality.

It is no different with modern culture as a whole than it was with the physics of Newton and his heirs: modern culture is as little in need of a philosophical grounding as science. As we have seen, in the modern period culture gave rise of itself to those structures of rationality that Weber then discovered and described as value spheres. With modern science, with positive law and principled secular ethics, with autonomous art and institutionalized art criticism, three moments of reason crystallized without help from philosophy. Even without the guidance of the critiques of pure and practical reason, the sons and daughters of modernity learned how to divide up and develop further the cultural tradition under these different aspects of rationality—as questions of truth, justice, or taste. More and more the sciences dropped the elements of worldviews and do without an interpretation of nature and history as a whole. Cognitive ethics separates off problems of the good life and concentrates on strictly deontological, universalizable aspects, so that what remains from the Good is only the Just. And an art that has become autonomous pushes toward an ever purer expression of the basic aesthetic experiences of a subjectivity that is decentered and removed from the spatiotemporal structures of everyday life. Subjectivity frees itself here from the conventions of daily perception and of purposive activity, from the imperatives of work and of what is merely useful.

These magnificent "one-sidednesses," which are the signature of modernity, need no foundation and no justification in the sense of a transcendental grounding, but they do call for a self-understanding regarding the character of this knowledge. Two questions must be answered: (i) whether a reason that has objectively split up into its moments can still preserve its unity, and (ii) how expert cultures can be mediated with everyday practice. The reflections offered in the first and third chapters [of Volume 1] are intended as a provisional account of how formal pragmatics can deal with these questions. With that as a basis, the theory of science, the theory of law and morality, and aesthetics, in cooperation with the corresponding historical disciplines, can then reconstruct both the emergence and the internal history of those modern complexes of knowledge that have been differentiated out, each under a different single aspect of validity—truth, normative rightness, or authenticity.

The mediation of the moments of reason is no less a problem than the separation of the aspects of rationality under which questions of truth, justice, and taste were differentiated from one another. The only protection against an empiricist abridgement of the rationality problematic is a steadfast pursuit of the tortuous routes along which science, morality, and art communicate with one another. In each of these spheres, differentiation processes are accompanied by countermovements that, under the primacy of one dominant aspect of validity, bring back in again the two aspects that were at first excluded. Thus nonobjectivist approaches to research within the human sciences bring viewpoints of moral and aesthetic critique to bear[54]—without threatening the primacy of questions of truth; only in this way is critical social theory made possible. Within universalistic ethics the discussion of the ethics of responsibility and the stronger consideration given to hedonistic motives bring the calculation of consequences and the interpretation of needs into play[55]—and they lie in the domains of the cognitive and the expressive; in this way materialist ideas can come in without threatening the autonomy of the moral.[56] Finally, post-avant-garde art is characterized by the coexistence of tendencies toward realism and engagement with those authentic continuations of classical modern art that distilled out the independent logic of the aesthetic[57]; in realist art and *l'art engagé*, moments of the cognitive and of the moral-practical come into play again in art itself, and at the level of the wealth of forms that the avant-garde set free. It seems as if the radically differentaited moments of reason want in such countermovements to point toward a unity—not a unity that could be had at the level of worldviews, but one that might be established *this side* of expert cultures, in a nonreified communicative everyday practice.

How does this sort of affirmative role for philosophy square with the reserve that critical theory always maintained in regard to both the established scientific enterprise and the systematic pretensions of philosophy? Is not such a theory of rationality open to the same objections that pragmatism and hermeneutics have brought against every kind of foundationalism?[58] Do not investigations that employ the concept of communicative reason without blushing bespeak universalistic justificatory claims that will have to fall to those—only too well grounded—meta-philosophical doubts about theories of absolute origins and ultimate grounds? Have not both the historicist enlightenment and materialism forced philosophy into a self-modesty for which the tasks of a theory of rationality must already appear extravagant? The theory of communicative action aims at the moment of unconditionality that, with criticizable validity claims, is built into the conditions of processes of consensus formation. *As claims* they transcend all limitations of space and time, all the provincial limitations of the given context. Rather than answer these questions here with arguments already set out in the introductory chapter [to Volume 1], I shall close by adding two methodological arguments that speak against the suspicion that the theory of communicative action is guilty of foundationalist claims.

First we must see how philosophy changes its role when it enters into cooperation with the sciences. As the "feeder" [*Zubringer*] for a theory of rationality, it finds itself in a division of labor with reconstructive sciences; these sciences take up the pretheoretical knowledge of competently judging, acting, and speaking subjects, as well as the collective knowledge of traditions, in order to get at the most general features of the rationality of experience and judgment, action and mutual understanding in language. In this context, reconstructions undertaken with philosophical means also retain a hypothetical character; precisely because of their strong universalistic claims, they are open to further, indirect testing. This can take place in such a way that the reconstructions of universal and necessary presuppositions of communicative action, of argumentative speech, of experience and of objectivating thought, of moral judgments and of aesthetic critique, enter into empirical theories that are supposed to explain *other* phenomena—for example, the ontogenesis of language and of communicative abilities, of moral judgment and social competence; the structural transformation of religious-metaphysical worldviews; the development of legal systems or of forms of social integration generally.

From the perspective of the history of theory, I have taken up the work of Mead, Weber, and Durkheim and tried to show how in their approaches, which are simultaneously empirical and reconstructive, the operations of empirical science and of philosophical conceptual analysis intermesh. The best example of this cooperative division of labor is Piaget's genetic theory of knowledge.[59]

A philosophy that opens its results to indirect testing in this way is guided by the fallibilistic consciousness that the theory of rationality it once wanted to develop on its own can now be sought only in the felicitous coherence of different theoretical fragments. Coherence is the sole criterion of considered choice at the level on which mutually fitting theories stand to one another in relations of supplementing and reciprocally presupposing, for it is only the individual propositions derivable from theories that are true or false. Once we have dropped foundation- alist claims, we can no longer expect a hierarchy of sciences; theories— whether social-scientific or philosophical in origin—have to fit with one another, unless one puts the other in a problematic light and we have to see whether it suffices to revise the one or the other.

The test case for a theory of rationality with which the modern under- standing of the world is to ascertain its own universality would certainly include throwing light on the opaque figures of mythical thought, clari- fying the bizarre expressions of alien cultures, and indeed in such a way that we not only comprehend the learning processes that separate "us" from "them," but also become aware of what we have *unlearned* in the course of this learning. A theory of society that does not close itself off a priori to this possibility of unlearning has to be critical also in relation to the preunderstanding that accrues to it from its own social setting, that is, it has to be open to self-criticism. Processes of unlearning can be gotten at through a critique of deformations that are rooted in the selec- tive exploitation of a potential for rationality and mutual understanding that was once available but is now buried over.

There is also another reason why the theory of society based on the theory of communicative action cannot stray into foundationalist by- ways. Insofar as it refers to structures of the lifeworld, it has to explicate a background knowledge over which no one can dispose at will. The lifeworld is at first "given" to the theoretician (as it is to the layperson) as his or her own, and in a paradoxical manner. The mode of preunder- standing or of intuitive knowledge of the lifeworld from within which we live together, act and speak with one another, stands in peculiar con- trast, as we have seen, to the explicit knowledge of something. The hor- izontal knowledge that communicative everyday practice *tacitly* carries with it is paradigmatic for the *certainty* with which the lifeworld back- ground is present; yet it does not satisfy the criterion of knowledge that stands in internal relation to validity claims and can therefore be criti- cized. That which stands beyond all doubt seems as if it could never become problematic; as what is simply unproblematic, a lifeworld can at most fall apart. It is only under the pressure of approaching problems that relevant components of such background knowledge are torn out of their unquestioned familiarity and brought to consciousness as some- thing in need of being ascertained. It takes an earthquake to make us aware that we had regarded the ground on which we stand everyday as unshakable. Even in situations of this sort, only a small segment of our background knowledge becomes uncertain and is set loose after having been enclosed in complex traditions, in solidaric relations, in compe- tences. If the objective occasion arises for us to arrive at some understanding about a situation that has become problematic, background knowledge is transformed into explicit knowledge only in a piecemeal manner.

This has an important methodological implication for sciences that have to do with cultural tradition, social integration, and the socialization of individuals—an implication that became clear to pragmatism and to hermeneutic philosophy, each in its own way, as they came to doubt the possibility of Cartesian doubt. Alfred Schutz, who so convincingly depicted the lifeworld's mode of unquestioned familiarity, nevertheless missed just this problem: whether a lifeworld, in its opaque take-for-grantedness, eludes the phenomenologist's inquiring gaze or is opened up to it does not depend on just *choosing* to adopt a theoretical attitude. The totality of the background knowledge constitutive for the construction of the lifeworld is no more at his disposition than at that of any social scientist—unless an objective challenge arises, in the face of which the lifeworld as a whole becomes problematic. Thus a theory that wants to ascertain the general structures of the lifeworld cannot adopt a transcendental approach; it can only hope to be equal to the *ratio essendi* of its object when there are grounds for assuming that the objective context of life in which the theoretician finds himself is opening up to him its *ratio cognoscendi.*

This implication accords with the point behind Horkheimer's critique of science in his programmatic essay "Traditional and Critical Theory": "The traditional idea of theory is abstracted from scientific activity as it is carried on within the division of labor at a particular stage in the latter's development. It corresponds to the activity of the scholar which takes place alongside all the other activities of a society, but in no immediately clear connection with them. In this view of theory, therefore, the real social function of science is not made manifest; it conveys not what theory means in human life, but only what it means in the isolated sphere in which, for historical reasons, it comes into existence."[60] As opposed to this, critical social theory is to become conscious of the self-referentiality of its calling; it knows that in and through the very act of knowing it belongs to the objective context of life that it strives to grasp. The context of its emergence does not remain external to the theory; rather, the theory takes this reflectively up into itself: "In this intellectual activity the needs and goals, the experiences and skills, the customs and tendencies of the contemporary form of human existence have all played their part."[61] The same holds true for the context of application: "As the influence of the subject matter on the theory, so also the application of the theory to the subject matter is not only an intrascientific process but a social one as well."[62]

In his famous methodological introduction to his critique of political economy of 1857, Marx applied the type of reflection called for by Horkheimer to one of his central concepts. He explained there why the basic assumptions of political economy rest on a seemingly simple abstraction, which is in fact quite difficult:

> It was an immense step forward for Adam Smith to throw out every limiting specification of wealth-creating activity—not only manufacturing, or commercial, or agricultural labor, but one as well as the others, labor in general. With the abstract universality of wealth-creating activity we now have the universality of the object defined as wealth, the product as such or again labor as such, but labor as past objectified labor. How difficult and great this transition was may be seen from how Adam Smith himself from time to time still falls back into the Physiocratic system. Now it might seem that all that had been achieved thereby was to discover the abstract expression for the simplest and most ancient relation in which human beings—in whatever form of society—play the role of producers. This is correct in one respect. Not in another ... Indifference toward specific labors corresponds to a form of society in which individuals can with ease transfer from one labor to another, and where the specific kind is a matter of chance for them, hence of indifference. Not only the category 'labor', but labor in reality has here become the means of creating wealth in general, and has ceased to be organically linked with particular individuals in any specific form. Such a state of affairs is at its most developed in the modern form of existence of bourgeois society—in the United States. Here, then, for the first time, the point of departure of modern economics, namely the abstraction of the category 'labor', 'labor as such', labor pure and simple, becomes true in practice.[63]

Smith was able to lay the foundations of modern economics only after a mode of production arose that, like the capitalist mode with its differentiation of an economic system steered via exchange value, forced a transformation of concrete activities into abstract performances, intruded into the world of work with this real abstraction, and thereby created a problem for the workers themselves: "Thus the simplest abstraction which modern economics places at the head of its discussions and which expresses an immeasurably ancient relation valid in all forms of society, nevertheless achieves practical truth as an abstraction only as a category of the most modern society."[64]

A theory of society that claims universality for its basic concepts, without being allowed simply to bring them to bear upon their object in a conventional manner, remains caught up in the self-referentiality that Marx demonstrated in connection with the concept of abstract labor. As I have argued above, when labor is rendered abstract and indifferent, we have a special case of the transference of communicatively structured domains of action over to media-steered interaction. This interpretation decodes the deformations of the lifeworld with the help of another category, namely, 'communicative action'. What Marx showed to be the case in regard to the category of labor holds true for this as well: "how even the most abstract categories, despite their validity—precisely because of their abstractness—for all epochs, are nevertheless, in the specific character of this abstraction, themselves likewise a product of historical relations, and possess their full validity only for and within these relations."[65] The theory of communicative action can explain why this is so: the development of society must *itself* give rise to the problem situations that *objectively* afford contemporaries a privileged access to the general structures of the lifeworld.

The theory of modernity that I have here sketched in broad strokes permits us to recognize the following: In modern societies there is such an expansion of the scope of contingency for interaction loosed from normative contexts that the inner logic of communicative action "becomes practically true" in the deinstitutionalized forms of intercourse of the familial private sphere as well as in a public sphere stamped by the mass media. At the same time, the systemic imperatives of autonomous subsystems penetrate into the lifeworld and, through monetarization and bureaucratization, force an assimilation of communicative action to formally organized domains of action—even in areas where the action-coordinating mechanism of reaching understanding is functionally necessary. It may be that this provocative threat, this challenge that places the symbolic structures of the lifeworld as a whole in question, can account for why they have become accessible to us.

Notes

Chapter V. The Paradigm Shift in Mead and Durkheim

Section V.1: The Foundations of Social Science in the Theory of Communication

1. Mead makes note of this on p. 2 of the methodological introduction to his lectures on social psychology, in *Mind, Self, and Society*, ed. C. Morris (Chicago, 1962): "Historically, behaviorism entered psychology through the door of animal psychology."
2. For an excellent account of his work as a whole, see H. Joas, *G. H. Mead: A Contemporary Re-Examination of His Thought* (Cambridge, Mass., 1985). See also M. Natanson, *The Social Dynamics of G. H. Mead* (Washington, D.C., 1956); A. H. Reck, "The Philosophy of G. H. Mead," *Tulane Studies in Philosophy* 12 (1963): 5–51; H. Blumer, "Sociological Implications of the Thought of G. H. Mead," *American Journal of Sociology* 71 (1866): 535–44; G. A. Cook, "The Self as Moral Agent," Ph.D. diss., Yale, 1966; K. Raiser, *Identität und Sozialität* (Munich, 1971). On Blumer's influential development of symbolic interactionism, see C. McPhail and C. Rexroat, "Mead vs. Blumer," *American Journal of Sociology* 44 (1979): 449ff.; D. Miller, *G. H. Mead: Self, Language, and the World* (Chicago, 1980).
3. Mead, *Mind, Self, and Society*, p. 244; henceforth cited as *MSS*.
4. Ibid., p. 7.
5. Ibid.
6. Ibid., p. 6.
7. See vol. 1, chap. 3, this work.
8. On the theory of singular terms, see E. Tugendhat, *Traditional and Analytical Philosophy: Lectures on the Philosophy of Language* (Cambridge, 1982).

9. *MSS,* pp. 42–43. Elsewhere Mead explains gesture-mediated interaction between animals as follows: "There exists thus a field of conduct even among
animals below man, which in its nature may be classed as gesture. It consists
of the beginning of those actions which call out instinctive responses from
other forms. And these beginnings of acts call out responses which lead to
readjustments of acts which have been commenced, and these readjustments lead to still other beginnings of response which again call out still
other readjustments. Thus there is a conversation of gesture, a field of palaver
within the social conduct of animals. Again the movements which constitute
this field of conduct are themselves not the complete acts which they start
out to become. They are the glance of the eye that is the beginning of the
spring or the flight, the attitude of body with which the spring or flight
commences, the growl or cry, or snarl with which the respiration adjusts
itself to oncoming struggle, and they all change with the answering attitudes,
glances of the eye, growls and snarls which are the beginnings of the actions
which they themselves arouse." G. H. Mead, *Selected Writings,* ed. A. Reck
(Chicago, 1964), p.124.
10. *MSS,* p. 76.
11. Ibid., p. 47. L. S. Vygotsky takes a similar position in *Thought and Language*
(Cambridge, Mass., 1962). Vygotsky's book first appeared in Moscow in
1934, a year after the death of its author, and at the same time as the post-
humous publication of *Mind, Self, and Society.*
12. This is the point of departure for Ernst Tugendhat's treatment of Mead in
Self-Consciousness and Self-Determination (Cambridge, Mass., 1986), pp.
219–62.
13. *MSS,* p. 47.
14. Ibid., pp. 117–18.
15. Ibid., p. 100.
16. Mead, *Selected Writings,* p. 131.
17. Referring to the thought of Wilhelm von Humboldt, Arnold Gehlen emphasizes "the double givenness of the sound, which is both a motoric accomplishment of the language instrument and itself a sound that is returned and
heard." *Der Mensch* (Bonn, 1950), p. 144; compare pp. 208–9.
18. See *MSS,* pp. 61ff., and Mead, *Selected Writings,* pp. 136–37.
19. Tugendhat, *Self-Consciousness and Self-Determination,* p. 228.
20. Ibid., pp. 229–30.
21. The only passage Tugendhat cites in support of it appears on pp. 108–9 of
MSS.
22. Ibid., p. 108.
23. Ibid., p. 139. My emphasis.
24. Ibid., pp. 147–49.
25. D. S. Shwayder, *The Stratification of Behavior* (London, 1965), pp. 21ff.
26. Charles Morris, "Foundations of the Theory of Signs," in *International Encyclopedia of Unified Science,* vol. 1, no. 2 (Chicago, 1938); and idem, *Signs,
Language and Behavior* (New York, 1946).
27. J. Habermas, *Zur Logik der Sozialwissenschaften* (Frankfurt, 1970), pp.
150ff. English trans. forthcoming, MIT Press, 1987.
28. L. Wittgenstein, *Philosophiche Grammatik II, Schriften* (Frankfurt, 1969),
pp. 24ff.
30. L. Wittgenstein, *Philosophical Investigations* (New York, 1953), p. 81.
31. From this standpoint, Mead's efforts at reconstruction also serve to elucidate

Wittgenstein's explication of the concept of a rule: the concept he develops holds, to start with, only for meaning conventions and not for norms of action. See 1:421–22, n. 37, this work.

32. See E. W. Count, *Das Biogramm* (Frankfurt, 1970); E. Morin, *Das Rätsel des Humanen* (Munich, 1973).
33. *MSS,* p. 162.
34. Tugendhat, *Traditional and Analytical Philosophy.*
35. G. H. Mead, *The Philosophy of the Act,* ed. C. Morris (Chicago, 1938), p. 147.
36. Ibid., pp. 151–52.
37. *MSS,* pp. 377–78.
38. Joas, *Mead,* chap. 7, pp. 145–66.
39. This is emphasized by U. Oevermann in "Programmatische Überlegungen zu einer Theorie der Bildungsprozesse," in K. Hurrelmann, ed., *Sozialisation und Lebenslauf* (Heidelberg, 1976), pp. 134ff. See the following studies inspired by Oevermann's work: M. Miller, *Zur Logik der frühkindlichen Sprachentwicklung* (Stuttgart, 1976); W. van de Voort, "Die Bedeutung der sozialen Interaktion für die Entwicklung der kognitiven Strukturen," diss., Frankfurt, 1977; H. Harten, *Der vernünftige Organismus oder die gesellschaftliche Evolution der Vernunft* (Frankfurt, 1977); F. Maier, *Intelligenz als Handlung* (Stuttgart, 1978). See also W. Doise, G. Mugney, and A. N. Perret-Clermont, "Social Interaction and Cognitive Development," *European Journal of Social Psychology* 6 (1976): 245ff.; J. Youniss, "Dialectical Theory and Piaget on Social Knowledge," *Human Development* (1978):234ff.; and idem, "A Revised Interpretation of Piaget," in I. E. Sigel, ed., *Piagetian Theory and Research* (Hillsdale, N.J., 1981).
40. Tugendhat, *Self-Consciousness and Self-Determination,* p. 161.
41. See the preface to the third German edition of this work for modifications of this view.
42. Imperatives and declarations of intention can of course be criticized and defended from the standpoint of the practicability of the action demanded or intended—see M. Schwab, *Redehandeln* (Königstein, 1980), pp. 65ff. and 79ff.—but they are first connected to criticizable validity claims though secondary norming; see 1:305ff., this work.
43. *MSS,* pp. 150–51.
44. Ibid., pp. 153–54.
45. Since Mead, the sociocognitive development of the child has been well researched in a tradition that stems from the work of J. Flavell and combines the theoretical perspectives of Mead and Piaget. See J. Flavell, *The Development of Role-Taking and Communicative Skills in Children* (New York, 1968); M. Keller, *Kognitive Entwicklung und soziale Kompetenz* (Stuttgart, 1976); R. Döbert, J. Habermas, and G. Nunner-Winkler, eds., *Entwicklung des Ichs* (Cologne, 1977), pp. 20ff.; R. Selman and D. F. Byrne, "Stufen der Rollenübernahme," in Döbert, Habermas, and Nunner-Winkler, *Entwicklung des Ichs,* pp. 109ff.; J. Youniss, "Socialization and Social Knowledge," in R. Silbereisen, ed., *Soziale Kognition* (Technische Universität Berlin, 1977), pp. 3ff.; R. Selman and D. Jacquette, "Stability and Oscillation in Interpersonal Awareness," in C. B. Keasy, ed., *Nebraska Symposium on Motivation* (Lincoln, 1977), pp. 261ff.; R. Selman, *The Growth of Interpersonal Understanding* (New York, 1980); J. Youniss, *Parents and Peers in Social Development* (Chicago, 1980).

46. *MSS,* p. 261. On the ontogenesis of socionormative concepts, see E. Turiel, "The Development of Social Concepts," in D. De Palma and J. Foley, eds., *Moral Development* (Hillsdale, N.J., 1975); E. Turiel, "Social Regulations and Domains of Social Concepts," in W. Damon, ed., *New Directions for Child Development,* 2 vols. (San Francisco, 1978); W. Damon, *The Social World of the Child* (San Francisco, 1977); H. G. Furth, *The World of Grown-ups: Children's Conceptions of Society* (New York, 1980).
47. Mead, *Selected Writings,* p. 284.
48. Ibid., p. 291.
49. *MSS,* p. 140.
50. Ibid., p. 174. On the relation between perspective-taking and moral consciousness, see the review of the literature by L. A. Kurdek, "Perspective Taking as the Cognitive Basis of Children's Moral Development," *Merrill-Palmer Quarterly* 24 (1978): 3ff.
51. *MSS,* p. 178.
52. Ibid., p. 204.
53. Ibid., p. 212.
54. Ibid., p. 213.

Section V.2: *The Authority of the Sacred and the Normative Background of Communicative Action*

1. Marked in the text by the break between parts 3 and 4 of *MSS.*
2. *MSS,* pp. 227ff.
3. Ibid., p. 233.
4. Ibid., p. 253.
5. Ibid., p. 237.
6. M. Heidegger, *Being and Time* (New York, 1962), pp. 115ff.
7. *MSS,* p. 248.
8. In this respect Scheler is closer to Mead's pragmatism; see his study on cognition and work in *Die Wissensformen und die Gesellschaft* (Bern, 1960), pp. 191ff.
9. *MSS,* p. 255.
10. Ibid., p. 256.
11. "I have illustrated this by the ball game, in which the attitudes of a set of individuals are involved in a cooperative response in which the different roles involve each other. In so far as a man takes the attitude of one individual in the group, he must take it in its relationship to the action of the other members of the group; and if he is fully to adjust himself, he would have to take the attitudes of all involved in the process." Ibid., p. 256.
12. Ibid., p. 273.
13. See the very thorough intellectual biography by Steven Lukes, *Emile Durkheim: His Life and Work* (London, 1973), which contains an extensive bibliography of Durkheim's publications (pp. 573ff.) as well as of writings on or directly relevant to Durkheim (pp. 591ff.). See also R. König, "E. Durkheim," in D. Käsler, ed., *Klassiker des soziologischen Denkens* (Munich, 1976), 1:312ff.
14. It is above all under this aspect that Parsons appropriated Durkheim's thought in *The Structure of Social Action* (New York, 1937), pp. 302ff. See also Parsons, "Durkheim's Contribution to the Theory of Integration of Social Systems," in T. Parsons, *Sociological Theory and Modern Society* (New York,

1967), pp. 3–34; Robert Nisbet, *The Sociology of Emile Durkheim* (New York, 1964); and R. König, *E. Durkheim zur Diskussion* (Munich, 1978).

15. E. Durkheim, *The Elementary Forms of the Religious Life* (New York, 1965).
16. E. Durkheim, "The Determination of Moral Facts," in Durkheim, *Sociology and Philosophy* (New York, 1974), pp. 35ff.
17. Ibid., pp. 35–36.
18. Ibid., p. 42. This was the point of departure for my distinction between labor and interaction in "Technology and Science as 'Ideology,'" in *Toward a Rational Society* (Boston, 1970), pp. 90ff.
19. Ibid., p. 43.
20. For a comparison of Durkheim and Weber see R. Bendix, "Two Sociological Traditions," in R. Bendix and G. Roth, *Scholarship and Partisanship* (Berkeley, 1971).
21. Durkheim, *Sociology and Philosophy*, p. 73.
22. Durkheim, "Determination of Moral Facts," p. 43.
23. Ibid., p. 37.
24. Ibid., p. 55.
25. Ibid., p. 45.
26. Durkheim, *Sociology and Philosophy*, p. 70.
27. Durkheim, "Determination of Moral Facts," p. 36.
28. Similarly, Walter Benjamin describes the aura of the work of art as a "unique phenomenon of distance," in "The Work of Art in the Age of Mechanical Reproduction," in *Illuminations* (New York, 1969), p. 243.
29. Durkheim, "Determination of Moral Facts," p. 48.
30. Durkheim, *Sociology and Philosophy*, p. 69.
31. "Spencer's morality, for example, betrays a complete ignorance of the nature of obligation. For him punishment is no more than the mechanical consequence of the act. (This is most apparent in his *Education,* on the subject of school punishments.) But this is completely to misunderstand the character of moral obligation." Ibid., p. 44. [The last sentence does not appear in the English translation—Trans.]
32. Durkheim, "Determination of Moral Facts," p. 51.
33. Durkheim, *Elementary Forms of the Religious Life*
34. Ibid., pp. 456–57.
35. E. Durkheim, "The Dualism of Human Nature and Its Social Conditions," in Kurt Wolff, ed., *Essays on Sociology and Philosophy* (New York, 1960), p. 335.
36. Ibid., pp. 335–36.
37. Durkheim, *Elementary Forms,* p. 22.
38. Parsons rightly refers to a "positivistic residue" here, in *Structure of Social Action,* pp. 427–49.
39. Durkheim, *Elementary Forms,* pp. 474–75.
40. Ibid., p. 306.
41. Ibid., p. 262.
42. I. Eibl-Eibesfeld, *Grundriss der vergleichenden Verhaltensforschung* (Munich, 1967), pp. 109ff. and 179ff.
43. Durkheim, *Elementary Forms,* p. 466.
44. Ibid., p. 481.
45. Parsons is critical of Durkheim on this point. He finds no clear differentiation between the level of cultural values and the level of institutionalized values, that is, of norms related to situations via social roles. See "Durkheim's Con-

tribution." See also G. Mulligan and B. Lederman, "Social Facts and Rules of Practice," *American Journal of Sociology* 83 (1977): 539ff.

46. Durkheim, *Elementary Forms,* p. 29.
47. Durkheim, "Dualism of Human Nature," p. 337.
48. Durkheim, *Elementary Forms,* p. 307.
49. Ibid., pp. 415ff.
50. *MSS,* p. 200. In his essays on the sociology of education Durkheim develops a concept of internalization akin to those of Freud and Mead. See Parsons' foreword in Durkheim's *Education and Sociology* (New York, 1956).
51. *MSS,* p. 175.
52. Ibid., p. 177.
53. Hannah Arendt explicates this insight in *The Human Condition* (Chicago, 1958).
54. *MSS,* p. 178.
55. Stanley Cavell, *Must We Mean What We Say?* (New York, 1969).
56: Compare the theory of the original illocutions developed by G. Beck in *Sprechakte und Sprachfunktionen* (Tübingen, 1980). Beck traces the illocutionary binding effect back to the commanding power of the sacred, which is drawn upon by rulers in declarative speech acts, to begin with, and which the addressees encounter with acts of subordination, of worship, homage, praise, and the like.
57. Durkheim, *Elementary Forms,* p. 469.
58. Ibid., p. 470.
59. Ibid., pp. 484–85.
60. Ibid., p. 485.
61. At this point Durkheim comes close to the idea of truth developed by C. S. Peirce. As can be seen in his lectures on pragmatism, Durkheim is aware that his critique of the empiricist bases of the pragmatist theory of truth in William James and F. C. Schiller accords with the views of the founder of the pragmatist tradition. See E. Durkheim, *Pragmatisme et sociologie* (Paris, 1955).
62. E. Tugendhat, *Vorlesungen zur Einführung in der sprachanalytischen Philosophie* (Frankfurt, 1976), pp. 66ff. and 517ff.
63. From Herder through Nietzsche to Heidegger and Gehlen, being able to say no has been repeatedly stressed as an anthropological monopoly of ours. The thesis put forward by Popper and Adorno in different versions, to the effect that reliable knowledge can only be gained through the negation of statements, is based on the same insight.

Section V.3: The Rational Structure of the Linguistification of the Sacred

1. E. Durkheim, *The Division of Labor in Society* (New York, 1933).
2. E. Durkheim, *Professional Ethics and Civic Morals* (London, 1957).
3. Durkheim, *Division of Labor,* p. 100.
4. Durkheim, *Professional Ethics,* pp. 147–48.
5. "Individual property came into being only when an individual split off from the family aggregate who embodied in himself all the sacred life diffused amongst the people and things of the family, and who became the holder of all the rights of the group." Ibid., p. 171.

6. Ibid., p. 177.
7. Durkheim, *Division of Labor,* p. 215.
8. Durkheim, *Professional Ethics,* p. 178.
9. Ibid., p. 207.
10. E. Durkheim, *Montesquieu and Rousseau: Forerunners of Sociology* (Ann Arbor, 1960).
11. Durkheim, *Professional Ethics,* p. 92.
12. Ibid., p. 50.
13. Ibid., p. 89.
14. Ibid., p. 91.
15. Ibid., p. 182.
16. Durkheim, *Division of Labor,* p. 131.
17. Ibid., pp. 288–89.
18. Ibid., p. 348.
19. Ibid., p. 290.
20. Ibid., p. 289.
21. Ibid., p. 290.
22. Ibid., p. 400.
23. Ibid., p. 405.
24. Ibid., p. 403.
25. See chap. 6 in this volume.
26. Durkheim, *Division of Labor,* p. 209.
27. Ibid., pp. 407–8.
28. Ibid., p. 409.
29. Luhmann raises this charge of moralism in his introduction to the German edition of *Division of Labor—Über die Teilung der sozialen Arbeit* (Frankfurt, 1977), pp. 17ff.—but he does so under the premises of a research strategy that, with an eye to the analytical level of "norm-free sociality," undercuts Durkheim's way of posing the problem.
30. See above, pp. 58–60, this volume.
31. G. H. Mead, "Fragments on Ethics," in *MSS,* pp. 379–89. See also G. Mead, "The Philosophical Basis of Ethics," in *George Herbert Mead: Selected Writings,* ed. Andrew Reck (Chicago, 1964), pp. 82–93. On this point see Gary A. Cook, "The Self as Moral Agent," Ph.D. diss., Yale, 1966, pp. 156ff.; and Hans Joas, *G. H. Mead: A Contemporary Re-examination of His Thought* (Cambridge, Mass., 1985), pp. 121ff.
32. On this point see R. Wimmer, *Universalisierung in der Ethik* (Frankfurt, 1980), which deals with the universalistic approaches of Kurt Baier, Marcus Singer, R. M. Hare, John Rawls, Paul Lorenzen, Fr. Kambartel, K.-O. Apel, and myself.
33. *MSS,* pp. 381–82.
34. Ibid., p. 379.
35. G. H. Mead, "Philanthropy from the Point of View of Ethics," in *Selected Writings,* p. 404.
36. *MSS,* p. 380.
37. Ibid.
38. Ibid., 388–89.
39. Ibid., p. 386.
40. Mead, "Philanthropy," pp. 404–5.
41. *MSS,* p. 387.
42. Ibid., 384.

43. Ibid., p. 385.
44. Ibid., p. 381.
45. G. H. Mead, "Scientific Method and the Moral Sciences," in *Selected Writings,* pp. 257ff.
46. See my remarks on Hegel's Jena "Philosophy of Spirit," in *Theory and Practice* (Boston, 1973), pp. 142ff.
47. *MSS,* p. 199.
48. Ibid., p. 326.
49. Ibid., pp. 167–68.
50. Ibid., p. 389.
51. See my "Notizen zum Begriff der Rollenkompetenz," in *Kultur und Kritik* (Frankfurt, 1973), pp. 195ff.; I develop there some thoughts of U. Oevermann.
52. D. J. de Levita, *Der Begriff der Identität* (Frankfurt, 1971); L. Krappmann, *Soziologische Dimensionen der Identität* (Stuttgart, 1971). Various theoretical approaches converge in this normative perspective on ego development: H. S. Sullivan, *The Interpersonal Theory of Psychiatry* (New York, 1953); E. Jacobson, *The Self and the Object World* (New York, 1964); D. W. Winnicott, *The Maturational Process and the Facilitating Environment* (New York, 1965); J. Loevinger, *Ego Development* (San Francisco, 1976); R. Döbert, J. Habermas, and G. Nunner-Winkler, eds., *Entwicklung des Ichs* (Cologne, 1977); J. Broughton, "The Development of Self, Mind, Reality and Knowledge," in W. Damon, ed., *New Directions for Child Development,* 2 vols. (San Francisco, 1978); R. G. Kegan, "The Evolving Self," *Counseling Psychologist* 8(179).
53. Dieter Henrich, "Identität," in O. Marquard and K. Stierle, eds., *Identität, Poetik und Hermeneutik* (Munich, 1979), 8:371ff.
54. Ibid., 8:372–73.
55. D. Locke, "Who I Am," *Philosophical Quarterly* 29 (1979): 302ff.
56. E. Tugendhat, *Self-Consciousness and Self-Determination* (Cambridge, Mass., 1986),pp. 254ff.
57. Ibid., p. 59.
58. Cf. H. N. Castaneda, "Indicators and Quasi-Indicators," *American Philosophical Quarterly* 17 (1967): 85ff.
59. E. Tugendhat, *Vorlesungen zur Einführung in die sprachanalytischen Philosophie* (Frankfurt, 1976), pp. 358ff.
60. Peter Geach, "Ontological Relativity and Relative Identity," in M. K. Munitz, *Logic and Ontology* (New York, 1973).
61. Henrich, "Identität," p. 382.
62. The rough distinction between role-identity and ego-identity needs to be differentiated further. Even the growing child who does not yet identify himself via the role structure of his family and his place in it says "I" to himself as soon as he learns to speak. This only confirms my thesis that at each stage of development of personal identity, the identity conditions for persons in general, as well as the basic identity criteria for specific persons, change. Even small children and infants can, when necessary, be identified by their parents through names and passports; but they are identified, on the basis of the same kind of data, *in a different sense* than youths or adults who can identify themselves. The presuppositions for numerically identifying an infant are comparatively less demanding, because the possibilities of deception and self-deception are also fewer. Thus, for example, difficulties with identi-

fication caused by mental confusion, loss of identity, and the like are still excluded.

63. For example: G. Rohrmoser, *Herrschaft und Versöhnung* (Freiburg, 1972); O. Marquard, *Schwierigkeiten mit der Geschichtsphilosophie* (Frankfurt, 1973); H. Lübbe, *Fortschritt als Orientierungsproblem* (Freiburg, 1975); R. Spaemann, *Zur Kritik der politischen Utopie* (Stuttgart, 1977). See R. Lederer, *Neokonservative Theorie und Gesellschaftsanalyse* (Frankfurt, 1979).

64. Michel Foucault, *The Archaeology of Knowledge* (New York, 1972); idem, *Madness and Civilization* (New York, 1965). On the theory of modernity, see my lecture "Modernity versus Postmodernism," *New German Critique* 22 (1981): 3–14.

65. Cf. Niklas Luhmann's objections to a theory of communicative action in J. Habermas and N. Luhmann, *Theorie der Gesellschaft oder Sozialtechnologie: Was Leistet die Systemforschung?* (Frankfurt, 1971), pp. 291ff.

66. Albrecht Wellmer, "Praktische Philosophie und Theorie der Gesellschaft" (Konstanz, 1979), and B. C. Birchall, "Moral Life as the Obstacle to the Development of Ethical Theory," *Inquiry* 21 (1978): 409ff., both press for a renewal of the Hegelian distinction between *Moralität and Sittlichkeit* in terms of the analysis of language.

67. *MSS,* pp. 221–22.

68. See my reply to Steven Lukes's and Seyla Benhabib's criticisms of the formalism of communicative ethics: "A Reply to My Critics," in J. Thompson and D. Held, eds., *Habermas: Critical Debates* (Cambridge, Mass., 1982), pp. 252ff.

Chapter VI.   Intermediate Reflections

1. See, for instance, E. Durkheim, *The Division of Labor in Society* (New York, 1933), p. 39.

2. "But the division of labor is not peculiar to the economic world; we can observe its growing influence in the most varied fields of society. The political, administrative and judicial functions are growing more and more specialized." Ibid., p. 40.

3. "The division of labor varies in direct ratio with the volume and density of societies, and, if it progresses in a continuous manner in the course of social development, it is because societies become regularly denser and generally more voluminous." Ibid., p. 262.

4. Ibid., p. 181.

5. Ibid., p. 41.

6. Cf. Luhmann's introduction to E. Durkheim, *Über die Teilung der sozialen Arbeit* (Frankfurt, 1977), pp. 17–34.

7. Durkheim, *Division of Labor,* p. 226.

8. Ibid., pp. 202–3.

9. Ibid., p. 41.

10. Ibid., p. 217.

11. Ibid., pp. 203–4.

12. Ibid., p. 228.

13. Ibid., p. 354.

14. Ibid., p. 365.

15. Ibid., p. 368.

Section VI.1: The Concept of the Lifeworld and the Hermeneutic Idealism of Interpretive Sociology

1. On the phenomenological concept of the lifeworld see L. Landgrebe, *Phänomenologie und Metaphysik* (Heidelberg, 1949), pp. 10ff.; and idem, *Philosophie der Gegenwart* (Bonn, 1952), pp. 65ff.; A. Gurwitsch, *The Field of Consciousness* (Pittsburg, 1964); G. Brand, *Welt, Ich und Zeit* (The Hague, 1955); H. Hohl, *Lebenswelt und Geschichte* (Freiburg, 1962); W. Lippitz, "Der phänomenologische Begriff der Lebenswelt," *Zeitschrift für Philosophische Forschung* 32 (1978): 416ff.; K. Ulmer, *Philosophie der modernen Lebenswelt* (Tübingen, 1972).

2. On the sociological analysis of forms of life see P. Winch, *The Idea of a Social Science* (London, 1958); R. Rhees, *Without Answers* (New York, 1969); D. L. Phillips and H. O. Mounce, *Moral Practices* (London, 1970); H. Pitkin, *Wittgenstein and Justice* (Berkeley, 1972); P. McHugh et al., *On the Beginning of Social Inquiry* (London, 1974).

3. See 1:99ff., 305ff., and 325ff., this work.

4. Alfred Schutz, *Collected Papers I: The Problem of Social Reality,* ed. M. Natanson (The Hague, 1962).

5. Cf. H. Kuhn, "The Phenomenological Concept of Horizon," in M. Farber, ed., *Philosophical Essays in Memory of E. Husserl* (Cambridge, Mass., 1940), pp. 106ff.

6. E. Husserl, *Experience and Judgment* (Evanston, 1973). For a critique of the foundation in consciousness of Schutz's phenomenological ontology of the social, see Michael Theunissen, *The Other: Studies in the Social Ontology of Husserl, Heidegger, Sartre and Buber* (Cambridge, Mass., 1984), pp. 345–52.

7. L. Weisgerber, *Die Muttersprache im Aufbau unserer Kultur* (Düsseldorf, 1957); R. Hoberg, *Die Lehre vom sprachlichen Feld* (Düsseldorf, 1970); H. Gipper, *Gibt es ein sprachliches Relativitätsprinzip?* (Frankfurt, 1972).

8. A. Schutz and T. Luckmann, *The Structures of the Lifeworld* (Evanston, 1973). See also A. Schutz, *Reflections on the Problem of Relevance,* ed. R. Zaner (New Haven, 1970); and W. M. Sprondel and R. Grathoff, eds., *A. Schütz und die Idee des Alltags in den Sozialwissenschaften* (Stuttgart, 1979).

9. Schutz and Luckmann, *Structures of the Lifeworld,* p. 6.

10. Ibid., pp. 114–15.

11. Ibid., pp. 99–100.

12. Ibid., pp. 103–4.

13. Ibid., p. 104.

14. G. W. Allport, *Personality* (New York, 1937); T. Parsons, *The Structure of Social Action* (New York, 1949); T. M. Newcomb, *Social Psychology* (New York, 1950); K. Lewin, *Field Theory in the Social Sciences* (New York, 1951); R. Dahrendorf, *Homo Sociologicus* (Tübingen, 1958); F. H. Tenbruck, "Zur deutschen Rezeption der Rollentheorie," *Kölner Zeitschrift für Soziologie und Sozialpsychologie* 13 (1961): 1ff.

15. In German sociology, phenomenological approaches have been developed by K. Stavenhagen and H. Plessner. Cf. H. P. Bahrdt, *Industriebürokratie* (Stuttgart, 1958); H. Popitz, *Der Begriff der sozialen Rolle als Element der soziologischen Theorie* (Tübingen, 1967); H. P. Dreitzel, *Das gesellschaftliche Leiden und das Leiden an der Gesellschaft* (Stuttgart, 1968). On the

reception in German psychology, see C. F. Graumann, *Zur Phänomenologie und Psychologie der Perspektivität* (Berlin, 1960).

16. J. Markowitz, *Die soziale Situation* (Frankfurt, 1980). See also L. Eley, *Transzendentale Phänomenologie und Systemtheorie* (Freiburg, 1972).

17. A. Schutz, "Das Problem der transzendentalen Intersubjektivität bei Husserl," *Philosophische Rundschau* 5 (1957):81ff.; Theunissen, *The Other,* pp. 109ff.; and idem, *Kritische Theorie der Gesellschaft* (Berlin, 1981); D. M. Carr, "The Fifth Meditation and Husserl's Cartesianism," *Philosophy and Phenomenological Research* 34 (1973): 14ff.; P. Hutcheson, "Husserl's Problem of Intersubjectivity," *Journal of the British Society for Phenomenology* 11 (1980): 144ff.

18. N. Luhmann, "Interpenetration," *Zeitschrift für Soziologie* (1977): 62ff.

19. Luckmann rightly emphasizes this influence in his introduction to *Structures of the Lifeworld,* p. xx.

20. Ibid., pp. 3–4.

21. John Searle, "Literal Meaning," in *Expression and Meaning* (Cambridge, 1979), pp. 177ff.; see 1:335–37, this work.

22. Schutz and Lukmann, *Structure of the Lifeworld,* p. 4.

23. Ibid.

24. Ibid., pp. 7–8.

25. Ibid., p. 9.

26. Ibid., p. 170.

27. Ibid., p. 7.

28. Ibid., p. 11.

29. Arthur Danto, *Analytical Philosophy of History* (Cambridge, 1968). See also P. Gardiner, ed., *The Philosophy of History* (Oxford, 1974). For the German discussion, see H. M. Baumgartner, *Kontinuität und Geschichte* (Frankfurt, 1972); R. Koselleck and W. Stempel, eds., *Geschichte, Ereignis und Erzählung* (Munich, 1973); K. Acham, *Analytische Geschichtsphilosophie* (Freiburg, 1974); J. Rüsen, *Für eine erneuerte Historik* (Stuttgart, 1976); H. Baumgartner and J. Rüsen, eds., *Geschichte und Theorie* (Frankfurt, 1976).

30. P. Berger and T. Luckmann, *The Social Construction of Reality* (Garden City, N.Y., 1967), p. 1.

31. Cf. A. M. Rose, ed., *Human Behavior and Social Processes* (Boston, 1962). The above-mentioned debate between ethnomethodology and symbolic interactionism can be traced back to the competition between one-sided, culturalistic and socialization-theoretical concepts of the lifeworld; see N. K. Denzin, "Symbolic Interactionism and Ethnomethodology," in Jack D. Douglas, ed., *Understanding Everyday Life* (London, 1971), pp. 259–84, versus D. H. Zimmerman and D. L. Wieder, "Ethnomethodology and the Problem of Order," ibid., pp. 285–98.

32. G. H. Mead, *Selected Writings,* ed. A. Reck (Chicago, 1964), p. 296.

33. Between the world wars this tradition was represented by such thinkers as Heidegger, Gehlen, Konrad Lorenz, and Carl Schmitt; today it is continued at a comparable level only in French poststructuralism.

34. See J. Habermas, *Zur Logik der Sozialwissenschaften* (Frankfurt, 1970), English trans. forthcoming, MIT Press; A. Ryan, "Normal Science or Political Ideology?" in P. Laslett, W. G. Runciman, and Q. Skinner, eds., *Philosophy, Politics and Society,* vol. 4 (Cambridge, 1972).

35. W. Schapp, *In Geschichten Verstrickt* (Wiesbaden, 1976).

36. T. Parsons, "Some Problems of General Theory," in J. C. McKinney and E. A. Tiryakian, eds., *Theoretical Sociology* (New York, 1970), p. 34. See also H. Willke, "Zum Problem der Interpretation komplexer Sozialsysteme," *Kölner Zeitschrift für Soziologie und Sozialpsychologie* 30 (1978): 228ff.
37. A. Etzione, "Elemente einer Makrosoziologie," in W. Zapf, ed., *Theorien des Sozialen Wandels* (Cologne, 1969), pp. 147ff.; and idem, *The Active Society* (New York, 1968), pp. 135ff.

Section VI.2: The Uncoupling of System and Lifeworld

1. N. Luhmann, "Interaction, Organization, and Society," in *The Differentiation of Society* (New York, 1982), pp. 69–89.
2. "Segmentary societies are not 'primitive societies', nor are they simple; it does not make sense to think of them as societies in the beginning stages of development. On the other hand, neither are they in some dead-end of societal development. They are dynamic in respect both to their structural reproduction and to their geographical expansion." Christian Sigrist, "Gesellschaften ohne Staat und die Entdeckungen der Sozialanthopologie," in F. Kramer and C. Sigrist, eds., *Gesellschaften ohne Staat* (Frankfurt, 1978), 1:39.
3. K. Gabriel, *Analysen der Organisationsgesellschaft* (Frankfurt, 1979), pp. 151–52. Cf. P. Berger, *Zur Dialektik von Religion und Gesellschaft* (Frankfurt, 1973), pp. 60ff.; T. Luckmann, "Zwänge und Freiheiten im Wandel der Gesellschaftsstruktur," in H. G. Gadamer and P. Vogler, *Neue Anthropologie* (Stuttgart, 1972), 3:168ff.
4. M. Fortes, *Kinship and Social Order* (Chicago, 1969), p.234.
5. Ibid.
6. Ibid., p. 104.
7. T. Luckmann, "On the Boundaries of the Social World," in M. Natanson, eds., *Phenomenology and Social Reality* (The Hague, 1970).
8. A summary account can be found in L. Mair, *An Introduction to Social Anthropology,* rev. ed. (Oxford, 1972), pp. 54ff.
9. On the elements of social organization in tribal societies see R. Firth, *Elements of Social Organization* (London, 1971), pp. 35ff.
10. On segmental dynamics, see C. Sigrist, *Regulierte Anarchie* (Frankfurt, 1979), pp. 21ff.
11. B. Malinowski, "The Circulation Exchange of Valuables in the Archipelago of Eastern New Guinea," *Man* (1920): 97ff.
12. Cf. the classical study by M. Mauss, *The Gift* (London, 1954), with an introduction by E. E. Evans-Pritchard.
13. Mair, *Social Anthropology,* p. 115.
14. E. Leach, *Political Systems of Highland Burma* (London, 1964).
15. M. Gluckmann, "Rituals of Rebellion in South East Africa," in *Order and Rebellion in Tribal Africa* (London, 1963), pp. 110ff.
16. F. Steiner, "Notiz zur vergleichenden Ökonomie," in Kramer and Sigrist, *Gesellschaften ohne Staat,* pp. 85ff.
17. Cf. the interpretation by Mair in *Social Anthropology,* pp. 237–38.
18. This sequence explains the evolutionary content of the basic sociological concepts: role, status, office, formal law. They become blunt, or at least in need of sharpening, when used to analyze phenomena that do not appertain to the corresponding social formation. For example, the concept of role is

central to explaining socialization processes, since the child grows into its social world by appropriating the system of familial roles. And yet it is precisely research into socialization that has given the strongest impulse to reformulating the role concept. This concept is not only derived from the kinship system, it can be *smoothly* applied only to phenomena in societies organized along kinship lines; socialization processes in modern societies escape the grasp of a social psychology tailored to the internalizing of roles. Cf. L. Krappmann, *Soziologische Dimensionen der Identität* (Stuttgart, 1971). On the historicity of basic sociological concepts, see D. Zaret, "From Weber to Parsons and Schütz: The Eclipse of History in Modern Social Theory," *American Journal of Sociology* 85 (1980): 1180ff.

19. J. Habermas, *Communication and the Evolution of Society* (Boston, 1979), pp. 143–44.
20. M. Godelier, *Perspectives in Marxist Anthropology* (Cambridge, 1976); and idem, "Infrastructures, Societies, and History," *Current Anthropology* 19 (1978): 763ff.
21. Luckmann, "Zwänge und Freiheiten," pp. 191–92.
22. M. Fortes and E. Evans-Pritchard, eds., *African Political Systems* (Oxford, 1970).
23. Ibid., p. 14.
24. On this concept see R. Goldscheid and O. Schumpeter, *Die Finanzkrise des Steuerstaats,* ed. R. Hickel (Frankfurt, 1976).
25. N. Luhmann, *Zweckbegriff und Systemrationalität* (Tübingen, 1969), p. 339.
26. N. Luhmann, "Allgemeine Theorie organisierter Sozialsysteme," in *Soziologische Aufklärung,* vol. 2 (Opladen, 1975). Cf. pp. 306ff., in this volume.
27. L. Kohlberg, *Essays on Moral Development,* vols. 1 and 2 (San Francisco, 1981, 1984).
28. K. Eder, *Die Entstehung staatlich organisierter Gesellschaften* (Frankfurt, 1976).
29. W. Schluchter, *The Rise of Western Rationalism* (Berkeley, 1981).
30. I developed this thesis in more detail in *Communication and the Evolution of Society* (Boston, 1979), chaps. 3 and 4.
31. Mair, *Social Anthropology,* pp. 145–46.
32. Ibid., p. 146.
33. Ibid., pp. 148–49.
34. "Normally we do not have to think about the foundations of our corporate life or the conditions of its continued existence, nor to justify actions or expressly to find and display appropriate motives. Problematizing and thematizing are not excluded; they are always possible; but normally this non-actualized possibility already suffices as a basis for interaction. If no one calls it into question, then 'everything's o.k.'" N. Luhmann, *Macht* (Stuttgart, 1975).
35. N. Eisenstadt, "Cultural Traditions and Political Dynamics: The Origins and Modes of Ideological Politics," *British Journal of Sociology* 32 (1981): 155ff. Naturally, the world religions appear only relatively late. Other bases of legitimation are required in archaic societies that have attained the level of state organization. In this connection M. Bloch's studies of kingdoms in central Madagascar are of particular interest: M. Bloch, "The Disconnection of Power and Rank as a Process," in S. Friedman and M. J. Rowland, eds., *The Evolution of Social Systems* (London, 1977); and idem, "The Past and the

TABLE N. 1

Everyday Speech Acts	Formalized Speech Acts
Choice of loudness	Fixed loudness patterns
Choice of intonation	Extremely limited choice of intonation
All syntactic forms available	Some syntactic forms excluded
Complete vocabulary	Partial vocabulary
Flexibility of sequencing of speech acts	Fixity of sequencing of speech acts
Few illustrations from a fixed body of accepted parallels	Illustrations only from certain limited sources, e.g., scriptures, proverbs
No stylistic rules consciously held to operate	Stylistic rules consciously applied at all levels

Source: M. Bloch, "Symbols, Song, Dance and Features of Articulation," *Archives Européennes de Sociologie* 15 (1974): 55ff.

Present in the Present," *Man* 13 (1978): 278ff. Bloch shows that in the transition from stratified tribal societies to class societies organized by a state, certain rites and ritually secured social rank-orderings get refunctionalized for purposes of legitimation. The hierarchical structures of the superseded tribal societies remain standing as a facade behind which the class structures of the new state-organized kingdoms hide, so to speak.

36. M. Bloch also uses a communications-theoretical approach to explain the ideological functions that actions passed down from the period of tribal society can take on in class societies. The formalism according to which ritual practices can assume such functions may be characterized in terms of restrictions on communication, as Table n.1 illustrates.

37. See for example Mair, *Social Anthropology,* p. 229: "In fact Leach's distinction between the technical and the ritual—between acts that we, as observers with some knowledge of scientific principles, can see produce the ends they aim at and those which do not—though it is not the same as Durkheim's distinction between sacred and profane, is the one that all anthropologists have made in distinguishing the magico-religious from the field of everyday life. As we see it, there is an aspect of life in which people seek to attain ends that are either not attainable by any human action or not attainable by the means they are using. They purport to be calling in aid beings or forces which *we* consider to be outside the course of nature as we understand it, and so call 'supernatural'. To this field of activity belong both the religious and the magical."

38. On the contrast between ritual and sacramental practice see Mary Douglas, *Natural Symbols* (London, 1973), p. 28l: "Ritualism is taken to be a concern that efficacious symbols be correctly manipulated and that the right words be pronounced in the right order. When we compare the sacraments to magic there are two kinds of view to take into account: on the one hand the official doctrine, on the other the popular form it takes. On the first view the Christian theologian may limit the efficacy of sacraments to the internal working of grace in the soul. But by this agency external events may be changed since decisions taken by a person in a state of grace will presumably

differ from those of others. Sacramental efficacy works internally; magical efficacy works externally."
39. Mair, *Social Anthropology*, p. 229.
40. Strictly speaking, not even the philosophical discourse of Greek philosophy was specialized about the isolated validity claim of propositional truth.

Chapter VII. Talcott Parsons

1. T. Parsons, "On Building Social System Theory: A Personal History," in *Social Systems and the Evolution of Action Theory* (New York, 1977), pp. 22ff.
2. For the convergence thesis, see T. Parsons, *The Structure of Social Action*, 2d ed. (New York, 1949), pp. 722ff. The first edition was published in 1937.
3. He came back again and again to Durkheim in particular. See T. Parsons, "Durkheim's Contribution to the Theory of Integration of Social Systems," in *Sociological Theory and Modern Society* (New York, 1967), pp. 3ff.; and idem, "Durkheim on Religion Revisited: Another Look at *The Elementary Forms of the Religious Life,*" in C. Y. Glock and P. E. Hammond, eds., *Beyond the Classics? Essays in the Scientific Study of Religions* (New York, 1973), pp. 156ff.
4. It was only in 1968 in his article on "Social Interaction" for the *International Encyclopaedia of the Social Sciences* that Parsons established a smooth connection to symbolic interactionism. The article is reprinted in *Social Systems and the Evolution of Action Theory*, pp. 145ff.
5. T. Parsons, "A Paradigm of the Human Condition," in *Action Theory and the Human Condition* (New York, 1978), pp. 352ff. This global reference to Kant's *Critiques* scarcely justifies talk of a "Kantian core" to Parsons' theory; cf. R. Münch, "T. Parsons und die Theorie des Handelns," pts. 1 and 2, *Soziale Welt* 30 (1979): 385ff. and 31 (1980): 3ff.
6. K. Menzies, *Talcott Parsons and the Social Image of Man* (London, 1976).
7. For example, R. Münch in the essay cited in n. 5. H. P. M. Adriaansens emphasizes the continuity of Parsons' theoretical development, in "The Conceptual Dilemma," *British Journal of Sociology* 30 (1979): 7ff.
8. The very titles of his last two books show that Parsons always held on to the idea of interpreting the model of open, boundary-maintaining systems (developed in general systems theory and presented in the language of information theory) from the conceptual perspective of action theory specific to his discipline, and of doing so empirically, as had already been done for the biology in which he came of age scientifically, so to speak. Unlike Luhmann, Parsons never had the idea of *deriving* the basic social-scientific concepts that serve the empirical explanation of systems at the level of development of human society—and thus serve to constitute the object domain of social science—from the basic concepts of systems theory (such as choice, information, selection, complexity, and so on). Cf. R. C. Baum, "Communication and Media," in J. S. Loubser, R. C. Baum, A. Effrat, and V. M. Lidz, eds., *Explorations in General Theory in Social Science*, 2 vols. (New York, 1976), pp. 533ff., esp. 540ff. (Hereafter cited as *Festschrift*.)
9. This tendency is clear in Jeffrey Alexanders's comprehensive reconstruction of Parsons' thought: *Theoretical Logic in Sociology*, vol. 4, *The Modern Reconstruction of Classical Thought: Talcott Parsons* (Berkeley, 1983), which

also contains an intensive and extensive discussion of the secondary literature. One also finds a neo-Kantian reading of Parsons in W. Schluchter, "Gesellschaft und Kultur," in W. Schluchter, ed., *Verhalten, Handeln und System*
(Frankfurt, 1980), pp. 106ff.

10. T. Parsons, "Pattern Variables Revisited: A Response to R. Dubin," in *Sociological Theory and Modern Society,* pp. 192ff.
11. Menzies, *Talbott Parsons and the Social Image of Man,* p. 160.
12. Parsons, *Social Systems and the Evolution of Action Theory,* p. 145.

Section VII.1: From a Normativistic Theory of Action to a Systems Theory of Society

1. C. W. Lidz and V. M. Lidz, "Piaget's Psychology of Intelligence and the Theory
   of Action," in *Festschrift,* 1:195–239, here p. 231.
2. The quote is from Weber's essay "'Objectivity' in Social Science and Social
   Policy," in *The Methodology of the Social Sciences* (New York, 1949), pp.
   50–112, here p. 52.
3. "Just as the units of a mechanical system in the classical sense, particles, can
   be defined only in terms of their properties, mass, velocity, location in space,
   direction of motion, etc., so the units of action systems also have certain
   basic properties without which it is not possible to conceive of the unit as
   'existing'. Thus, to continue the analogy, the conception of a unit of matter
   which has mass but which cannot be located in space is, in terms of the
   classical mechanics, nonsensical. It should be noted that the sense in which
   the unit is here spoken of as an existent entity is not that of concrete spa-
   tiality or otherwise separate existence, but of conceivability as a unit in
   terms of a frame of reference." T. Parsons, *The Structure of Social Action,* 2d
   ed., (New York, 1949), pp. 43–44; see also pp. 76ff.
4. Ibid., p. 719.
5. Ibid., p. 400.
6. Ibid., pp. 385–86.
7. See T. Parsons, *Essays in Sociological Theory* (New York, 1949), p. 386n.
8. Parsons, *Structure of Social Action,* p. 709.
9. Ibid., p. 404. Thomas Burger takes issue with this thesis in "Talcott Parsons:
   The Problem of Order in Society," *American Journal of Sociology* 83
   (1978): 320ff.
10. Parsons, *Structure of Social Action,* p. 58.
11. Ibid., p. 56.
12. Ibid., p. 59.
13. Ibid., p. 64.
14. Ibid., pp. 63–64. A contemporary example of the positivistic conceptual
    strategy is Niklas Luhmann's proposal to regard normative and cognitive ex-
    pectations basically as functional equivalents and to distinguish them only
    according to whether an actor (or action system) "decides" to stabilize a
    given expectation counterfactually or to hold it open for revision. See N.
    Luhmann, "Normen in soziologischer Perspektive," *Soziale Welt* 20 (1969):
    28ff.
15. Ibid., p. 75.
16. Ibid., pp. 93–94.
17. Ibid., p. 93. On this point, see R. Martin, "Hobbes and the Doctrine of Natural

Rights: The Place of Consent in His Political Philosophy," *Western Political Quarterly* (1980): 380ff.

18. Ibid., p. 93.
19. Ibid., p. 101.
20. Ibid., p. 96.
21. Ibid.
22. Noteworthy efforts to this end have been made by David Lewis, *Conventions* (Cambridge, Mass., 1969); and Jon Elster, *Ulysses and the Sirens* (Cambridge, 1979). What we find here, once again, are proposals for resolving a problem that has already been *redefined in empiricist terms;* in the process, the phenomenon in need of explanation, namely, the obligating character of valid norms, gets lost.
23. "A contractual agreement brings men together only for a limited purpose, for a limited time. There is no adequate motive given why men should pursue even this limited purpose by means which are compatible with the interests of others, even though its attainment as such should be so compatible. There is a latent hostility between men which this theory does not take account of. It is as a framework of order that the institution of contract is of primary importance. Without it, men would, as Durkheim explicitly says, be in a state of war. But actual social life is not war. In so far as it involves the pursuit of individual interests it is such interests, pursued in such a manner as greatly to mitigate this latent hostility, to promote mutual advantage and peaceful cooperation rather than mutual hostility and destruction. Spencer and others who think like him have entirely failed to explain how this is accomplished. And in arriving at his own explanation Durkheim first points to an empirical fact: this vast complex of action in the pursuit of individual interests takes place within the framework of a body of rules, independent of the immediate motives of the contracting parties. This fact the individualists have either not recognized at all, or have not done justice to. It is the central empirical insight from which Durkheim's theoretical development starts, and which he never lost." Parsons, *Structure of Social Action,* pp. 313–14.
24. Ibid., p. 446.
25. Ibid., p. 732. The fact that Parsons based this concept on Durkheim and Weber has, several decades after the fact, set off a lively controversy. See W. Pope, J. Cohen, and E. Hazelrigg, "On the Divergence of Weber and Durkheim: A Critique of Parsons' Convergence Thesis," *American Sociological Review* 40 (1975): 417ff.; R. S. Warner, "Towards a Redefinition of Action Theory," *American Journal of Sociology* 83 (1978): 1317ff.; W. Pope and J. Cohen, "On R. S. Warner's Redefinition of Action Theory," *American Journal of Sociology* 83 (1978): 1359ff.; T. Parsons, "Comment on R. S. Warner's Redefinition of Action Theory," *American Journal of Sociology* 83 (1978): 1351ff.
26. In The *Structure of Social Action* Parsons does not place the concepts of action and order in a complementary relation but locates them at different levels. He proposes two dimensions in which unit acts can be aggregated and joined together into systems of action: connecting the actions of different actors, and connecting different actions by the same actor. Interpersonal aggregation gives rise to social systems, which can range from simple interactions to whole societies. In the other dimension we get personality systems, which can also combine into collectivities of whatever complexity.

While the historical considerations set forth in *The Structure of Social Action* suggest a symmetry between the concepts of action and order, it becomes clear at the end of the book that the conceptual distance between action and the personality system is no greater than that between action and the interaction system. See *Structure of Social Action,* pp. 737–48.

27. T. Parsons, *The Social System* (Glencoe, 1951), p. 36.

28. I shall pass over the attempt to invoke ideas from learning theory for this purpose. The so-called sanctions model can at most explain how nonnormative expectations get conditionally connected with each other.

29. Parsons, *Social System,* pp. 3–23; and idem, *Toward a General Theory of Action* (New York, 1951), pp. 3–25 and 53–109.

30. Parsons, *Toward a General Theory of Action,* p. 54.

31. Ibid., p. 71.

32. "We say that the evaluative mode designates the point in the system of motivation at which these values or cultural standards of the value orientation become effective ... The evaluative mode itself concerns the weighing of alternatives and the act of choosing. When this evaluation is made with an eye to any standards for guiding choice, then the evaluative mode has brought in some aspect of the value orientation. It should be remembered that the act of choosing is essentially the aspect of orientation implied by the term evaluative mode; the standards on which choices are based are the aspects of orientation implied by the term value orientations." Ibid., pp. 71–72.

33. Ibid., p. 160.

34. A seminar on "Background Knowledge" offered by John Searle and Hubert Dreyfus at the University of California, Berkeley, in the spring semester of 1980, provided valuable suggestions in this regard. Language-analytic attempts to get at the structure of the lifeworld background using the "context" model strike me as more promising than phenomenological attempts at reconstruction. See however M. Polanyi, *Personal Knowledge* (London, 1958); and idem, *The Tacit Dimension* (New York, 1966); Marjorie Grene, "Tacit Knowing," *Journal of the British Society for Phenomenology* 8 (1977): 164ff.; Rom Harre, "The Structure of Tacit Knowledge," *Journal of British Phenomenology* 8 (1977): 672ff.

35. Parsons, *Social System,* pp. 58ff.; and idem, *Toward a General Theory of Action,* pp. 78ff.

36. Parsons derives the table of pattern variables from the following problems: (1) Should the actor directly pursue his own interests or should he allow for normative considerations in which general interests are brought to bear? The alternative here is between orientation to interests of one's own or to general interests. (2) Should the actor straightway follow his affects and desires or should he restrain his impulses and put off immediate gratification. The alternative here is between an impulsive, affect-laden attitude and a disciplined, affectively neutral one. (3) Should the actor analyze the situation, in which he finds himself in a distanced manner, from points of view covering everyone, or should he, as an involved party, give priority to the particular constellations of the given situation? The alternative here is between an orientation to general standards and a consideration of particular, context-dependent relations. These three problems have to do with stances the actor adopts toward himself. There are two additional problems concerning the manner in which the actor categorizes objects, particularly the other partic-

ipants in interactions. (4) Should the actor judge and treat other actors in the light of their performances, that is, of the functions they fulfill, or in the light of their intrinsic values, their given qualities? The actor has to decide whether he will give priority to relational or to qualitative aspects. (5) Should the actor respond to concrete objects and actors in all their complexity, or should he confine himself to specific, relevant, analytically circumscribed aspects? The alternative here is between diffusely responding to nonanalyzed wholes and specifying certain aspects.

From these problems Parsons derives a table of the alternatives for choice through which cultural values, as preference patterns, regulate an actor's orientations without thereby detracting from the contingency of his choices:

1. The private versus collective interest dilemma: self versus collectivity orientation.
2. The gratification-discipline dilemma: affectivity versus affective neutrality.
3. The dilemma of transcendence versus immanence: universalism versus particularism.
4. The choice between object modalities: performance versus quality (achievement versus ascription).
5. The definition of the scope of interest in the object: specificity versus diffuseness.

Parsons never really vindicated his claim that this table represents a *system.* He once attempted to derive the choice alternatives from the analysis of action orientations represented in Figure 29 (see *Toward a General Theory of Action,* pp. 88ff.), but he never came back to these rather implausible suggestions. Thus he did not really get beyond the dogmatic assertion that "the actor must make a series of choices before the situation will have a determinate meaning. Specifically, we maintain, the actor must make five specific dichotomous choices before any situation will have a determinate meaning. The five dichotomies which formulate these choice alternatives are called pattern variables because any specific orientation (and consequently any action) is characterized by a pattern of five choices." Ibid., p. 76.

37. Ibid., pp. 41ff.
38. T. Parsons, "The Professions and Social Structure," and "The Motivation of Economic Activities," in *Essays in Sociological Theory,* pp. 34ff. and 50ff.
39. Parsons, "Professions and Social Structure," pp. 45–46.
40. Parsons, *Toward a General Theory of Action,* pp. 76ff.
41. Ibid., p. 78.
42. This term appears simultaneously in *Toward a General Theory of Action* and *The Social System,* both published in 1951.
43. "This is the tendency to maintain equilibrium ... within certain boundaries relative to an environment—boundaries which are not imposed from outside but which are self maintained by the properties of the constituent variables as they operate within the system." Parsons, *Toward a General Theory of Action,* p. 108.
44. T. Parsons, "Some Problems of General Theory in Sociology," in J. C. McKinney and E. A. Tiryakan, eds., *Theoretical Sociology* (New York, 1970), p.35.
45. Parsons, *Social System,* p. 15.

46. Parsons, *Toward a General Theory of Action*, p. 173.
47. Parsons, *Social System*, p. 17.
48. Ibid., pp. 114ff.
49. Parsons, *Toward a General Theory of Action*, pp. 107ff.
50. Ibid., p. 203.
51. Ibid., pp. 174, 178.
52. Ibid., p. 173, n.14.
53. Ibid., p. 174.

Section VII.2: The Development of Systems Theory

1. N. Luhmann, "T. Parsons: Die Zukunft eines Theorieprogramms," *Zeitschrift für Soziologie* 9 (1980): 8.
2. T. Parsons, "Some Problems of General Theory in Sociology," in J. C. McKinney and E. A. Tiryakan, eds., *Theoretical Sociology* (New York, 1970), p. 44.
3. T. Parsons and M. Platt, *The American University* (Cambridge, Mass., 1973), p. 17.
4. Ibid., p. 16 (my emphasis).
5. T. Parsons, E. Shils, K. D. Naegele, and J. D. Pitts, eds., *Theories of Society* (New York, 1961), p. 1965.
6. Those disciples of Parsons who adhere to his earlier, neo-Kantian understanding of science (e.g., J. Alexander, R. Münch) fail to appreciate this essentialist element in the Parsonian—and not only in the Luhmannian—version of systems functionalism.
7. See R. Dubin, "Parsons' Actor: Continuities in Social Theory," in T. Parsons, *Sociological Theory and Modern Society* (New York, 1967), pp. 521ff.; and Parsons' response in the same volume, pp. 192ff.
8. T. Parsons, *Societies* (Englewood Cliffs, N.J., 1966).
9. Ibid., p. 9.
10. Ibid., p. 5.
11. Ibid., p. 7.
12. Ibid., p.28.
13. T. Parsons, Robert Bales, and Edward Shils, *Working Papers in the Theory of Action* (New York, 1953), pp. 183ff.
14. "The core of a society, as a system, is the patterned normative order through which the life of a population is collectively organized. As an order, it contains values and differentiated and particularized norms and rules, all of which require cultural references in order to be meaningful and legitimate. As a collectivity it displays a patterned conception of membership which distinguishes between those individuals who do and do not belong. Problems involving the 'jurisdiction' of the normative system may make impossible an exact coincidence between the status of 'coming under' normative obligations and the status of membership, because the enforcement of a normative system seems inherently linked to the control (e.g., through the 'police function') of sanctions exercised by and against the people actually residing within a territory." Parsons, *Societies*, p. 10.
15. Ibid., pp. 10–15.
16. Ibid., pp. 24ff.; and T. Parsons, *The System of Modern Societies* (Englewood Cliffs, N.J., 1971), pp. 10ff.

17. Parsons and Platt, *American University,* p. 10.
18. Ibid., p. 11.
19. At one time the pair "self- vs. collectivity-orientation" represented the most important dimension for choosing between the equally "rational" action orientations of businessmen and professionals. In T. Parsons and N. J. Smelser, *Economy and Society* (New York, 1956), this dimension is removed from the catalog of pattern variables with an argument that tacitly presupposes the shift from an action-theoretical to a systems-theoretical perspective: owing to their different system references, self-orientation and collectivity orientation are no longer to be located in the same dimension. "In the course of time it became apparent that the categories of this pair were not significant as defining characteristics of one specific action system; rather they defined the relations between two systems placed in a hierarchical order. Self-orientation defined a state of relative independence from involvement of the lower-order in the higher-order system, leaving the norms and values of the latter in a regulatory, i.e., limit-setting relation to the relevant courses of action. Collectivity orientation, on the other hand, defined a state of positive membership whereby the norms and values of the higher-order system are positively prescriptive for the action of the lower." Ibid., p. 36.
20. Dubin, "Parsons' Actor," p. 530.
21. Ibid.
22. "It was then discovered that these correspondences converged logically with Bales' fourfold classification of the functional problems of systems of action. In the terminology finally adopted, the adaptive problem was defined from the attitudinal point of view in terms of specificity, from the object-categorization point of view in terms of universalism; the goal-attainment problem from the attitudinal point of view in terms of affectivity, from that of object-categorization in terms of performance; the integrative problem from the attitudinal point of view in terms of diffuseness, from the object-categorization point of view in terms of particularism; finally, the pattern maintenance and tension-management problem from the attitudinal point of view in terms of affective neutrality, from the object-categorization point of view in terms of quality." Parsons and Smelser, *Economy and Society,* p. 36.
23. T. Parsons, "Social Systems," in *Social Systems and the Evolution of Action Theory* (New York, 1977), p. 181.
24. Parsons and Platt, *American University,* p. 32.
25. Parsons applies the AGIL scheme to all objects without distinction. Thus, for example, a scientific theory is treated no differently than an empirical system of action, as indicated in figure 41 (p. 426), taken from ibid., p. 65.
26. M. Gould, "Systems Analysis, Macrosociology, and the Generalized Media of Social Action," in *Festschrift,* 2:470ff.
27. T. Parsons, "A Paradigm of the Human Condition," in *Action Theory and the Human Condition* (New York, 1978), pp. 352ff., here p. 382.
28. C. W. Lidz and V. M. Lidz, "Piaget's Psychology of Intelligence and the Theory of Action," in *Festschrift,* 1.195ff.
29. Parsons, "Paradigm of the Human Condition," p. 356.
30. Ibid.
31. Ibid., p. 361.
32. Ibid., pp. 382–83.
33. Ibid., pp. 367–68.

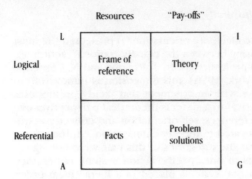

Figure 41. Components of Knowledge as Cultural Object-Types

34. This is how R. Münch understands the system of the human condition; see his "T. Parsons und die Theorie des Handelns," pts. 1 and 2, *Soziale Welt* 30 (1979): 385ff. and 31 (1980): 3ff.
35. Parsons, "Paradigm of the Human Condition," p. 370.
36. Ibid., p. 383.
37. Ibid., pp. 370–71.
38. Ibid., p. 371.
39. A. Gouldner, *The Coming Crisis of Western Sociology* (New York, 1970).
40. T. Parsons, "On Building Social Systems: A Personal History," in *Social Systems and the Evolution of Action Theory* (New York, 1977), pp. 22ff.
41. See the "Technical Note" appended to T. Parsons, "On the Concept of Political Power," in *Sociological Theory and Modern Society,* pp. 347ff. Parsons and Smelser, *Economy and Society.*
42. T. Parsons, "Review of Harold J. Bershady, *Ideology and Social Knowledge,*" in *Social Systems and the Evolution of Action Theory,* pp. 122–34, here p. 128.
43. Parsons, "On the Concept of Political Power."
44. T. Parsons, "On the Concept of Value Commitment," *Social Inquiry* 38 (1968): 135ff.
45. Parsons, "Some Problems of General Theory in Sociology"; and Parsons and Platt, *American University,* "Technical Appendix," pp. 423ff.
46. R. C. Baum, "On Societal Media Dynamics," in *Festschrift,* 2:579ff.
47. Parsons, "Paradigm of the Human Condition," p. 393.
48. This is the view of R. C. Baum in his introduction to "Part IV: Generalized Media in Action," in *Festschrift,* 2:448ff.: "One cannot go into extensive detail mapping of the components unless one has the general action media worked out. In the reverse case, as for instance starting with the societal level, which actually happened, there is the danger of premature detail specification" (p. 449).
49. T. Parsons, "Social Interaction," in *Social Systems and the Evolution of Action Theory,* pp. 154ff., here p. 168.
50. V. M. Lidz, introduction to "Part II: General Action Analysis," in *Festschrift,* 1:124ff., here p. 125.
51. N. Luhmann, *Soziologische Aufklärung* (Opladen, 1981), 3:50ff.
52. R. C. Baum, "Communication and Media," in *Festschrift,* 2:533ff.

53. Baum, "On Societal Media Dynamics," p. 580.
54. N. Luhmann, *Macht* (Stuttgart, 1975), p. 71.
55. Ibid., p. 72.
56. Parsons specifies these degrees of freedom of rational choice in four respects: "In exchange for its lack of direct utility money gives the recipient four important degrees of freedom in his participation in the total exchange system. (1) He is free to spend his money for any *item* or combination of items available on the market which he can afford, (2) he is free to *shop around* among alternative sources of supply for desired items, (3) he can choose his own *time* to purchase, and (4) he is free to consider *terms* which, because of freedom of time and source, he can accept or reject or attempt to influence in the particular case. By contrast, in the case of barter, the negotiator is bound to what his particular partner has or wants in relation to what he has and will part with at the particular time. On the other side of the gain in degrees of freedom is of course the risk involved in the probabilities of the acceptance of money by others and the stability of its value." Parsons, "On the Concept of Political Power," p. 307.
57. T. Parsons, "Some Reflections on the Place of Force in Social Process," in *Sociological Theory and Modern Society,* pp. 264ff.
58. N. Luhmann, "Zur Theorie symbolisch generalisierter Kommunikationsmedien," *Zeitschrift für Soziologie* (1974): 236ff.; and idem, *Macht,* pp. 112ff.
59. Parsons, "On the Concept of Political Power," p. 98.
60. For an attempt to introduce the media concept 'value commitment' into educational theory, see S. Jensen and J. Naumann, "Commitments: Medienkomponente einer Kulturtheorie?" *Zeitschrift für Soziologie* 9 (1980): 79–80. In this interesting article we can see how the concept of value commitment, when it is tailored to the analysis of circulation processes in the educational system, has to be assimilated to the media concept of money as employed in the economics of education.
61. Parsons, "On the Concept of Political Power," p. 361.
62. M. Gould, "Development and Revolution in Science," Max Planck Institut zur Erforschung der Lebensbedingungen der wissenschaftlich-technischen Welt, Starnberg, 1977. See also, Baum, "Communication and Media," 544ff.; and J. J. Loubser's general introduction to *Festschrift,* 1:10ff.

Section VII.3: The Theory of Modernity

1. T. Parsons, *Societies* (Englewood Cliffs, N.J., 1966), pp. 21ff.
2. T. Parsons, *The System of Modern Societies* (Englewood Cliffs, N.J., 1971), pp. 114ff.
3. See the corresponding value standards for the various media of the general action system in T. Parsons and M. Platt, *The American University* (Cambridge, Mass., 1973), p. 446.
4. Ibid., p. 1.
5. Parsons, *System of Modern Societies,* p. 101. This construction is not at all convincing. At times Parsons seems also to understand the three "revolutions" as processes in the course of which, one by one, each subsystem sets itself off from all the others. If, following this line, we correlate the three revolutions mentioned above with the economic, political, and cultural subsystems, we should expect one further revolution for the integrative subsystem—perhaps this is what Parsons calls the "Expressive Revolution" in

"Religion in Postindustrial America," in *Action Theory and the Human Condition* (New York, 1978), pp. 300–322, here pp. 320–22.

6. Parsons mentions the increasing reflexivity of steering media as a further evolutionary mechanism; he illustrates this through the example of bank credit. *System of Modern Societies*, p. 27.

7. Ibid., pp. 50ff.

8. Parsons, "Religion in Postindustrial America," p. 321.

9. Parsons and Platt, *American University*, p. 1.

10. T. Parsons, "Belief, Unbelief, and Disbelief," in *Action Theory and the Human Condition*, p. 240.

11. Parsons, "Religion in Postindustrial America," p. 309.

12. Ibid., p. 320. "In part I am being deliberately paradoxical in attributing to the concept secularization what has often been held to be its opposite, namely not the loss of commitment to religious values and the like, but the institutionalization of such values, and other components of religious orientation in evolving cultural and social systems." Parsons, "Belief, Unbelief, and Disbelief," p. 241, n. 11. Referring to Weber's studies on the Protestant ethic, Parsons adds: "Put into sociological terminology, there is the possibility that religious values should come to be institutionalized, by which we mean that such values come to be the focus of the definition of the situation for the conduct of members of secular societies, precisely in their secular roles." Ibid., p. 241. See also Parsons' introduction to *Max Weber: The Sociology of Religion* (Boston, 1964), pp. xix*ff.*; R. K. Fenn, "The Process of Secularization: A Post-Parsonian View," *Scientific Study of Religion* 9 (1970): 117ff.; F. Ferrarotti, "The Destiny of Reason and the Paradox of the Sacred," *Social Research* 46 (1979): 648ff.

13. Parsons, "Religion in Postindustrial America," pp. 320ff.; and idem, *System of Modern Societies*, pp. 114–15.

14. Parsons, *System of Modern Societies*, pp. 116–17.

15. R. Döbert, *Systemtheorie und die Entwicklung religiöser Deutungssysteme* (Frankfurt, 1973).

16. J. Habermas, *Legitimation Crisis* (Boston, 1973), pp. 1ff.

17. Parsons and Platt, *American University*, pp. 304ff. In this fashion Parsons himself traced the crisis in higher education back to cyclical swings and corresponding panic reactions in the domains of "intelligence" and "influence."

18. R. C. Baum, "On Societal Media Dynamics," in *Festschrift*, 2: 604ff.

19. R. Münch, "Max Webers Anatomie des okzidentalen Rationalismus," *Soziale Welt* 29 (1978): 217ff., here p. 220.

20. R. Münch, "Über Parsons zu Weber, von der Theorie der Rationalisierung zur Theorie der Interpenetration," *Zeitschrift für Soziologie* 1 (1980): 18ff., here p. 47.

21. R. Münch, "Rationalisierung und Interpenetration," manuscript, 1980, p. 35.

22. Ibid., p. 33.

23. Ibid.

24. R. Münch, "T. Parsons und die Theorie des Handelns," pt. 1, *Soziale Welt* 30 (1979): 397.

25. Münch, "Über Parsons zu Weber," p. 30.

26. Ibid.

27. Münch, "Rationalisierung und Interpenetration," pp. 38–39.

Chapter VIII.   Concluding Reflections

1. On the so-called crisis of meaning, see D. Bell, *The Cultural Contradictions of Capitalism* (New York, 1976); and idem, *The Winding Passage* (Cambridge, 1980).
2. Max Weber, *Economy and Society,* 3 vols., ed. G. Roth and C. Wittich (New York, 1968), p. 1402.
3. On dispossessing the actor of his own actions, see R. P. Hummel, *The Bureaucratic Experience* (New York, 1977).

Section VIII. 1: Weber's Theory of Modernity

1. R. Mayntz, ed., *Bürokratische Organisation* (Cologne, 1968).
2. N. Luhmann, "Zweck—Herrschaft—System," *Der Staat* (1964): 129ff.
3. M. Weber, *Economy and Society,* 3 vols., ed. G. Roth and C. Wittich (New York, 1968), p. 1402.
4. K. Gabriel, *Analysen der Organisationsgesellschaft* (Frankfurt, 1979), p.107; J. Grünberger, *Die Perfektion des Mitglieds* (Berlin, 1981).
5. Gabriel, *Organisationsgesellschaft,* p. 102.
6. With regard to the work situation in government organizations, for example, S. Wolff comes to the following conclusion: "We have been able to show, in various ways, that such an objectivation is problematic in view of concrete practice within government:

    · in the *cognitive* dimension, the local-historical situatedness of social action conditions active accomplishments of defining and typifying;
    · in the *social* dimension, the application of regulations has to be oriented by the (narrower and broader) societal contexts of the action situation;
    · in the *motivational* dimension, the assumption that social actors are oriented exclusively to exchange values, that their motivation is wholly ego-alien, proves—particularly for government organizations—to be untenable."

    S. Wolff, "Handlungsformen und Arbeitssituationen in staatliche Organisationen," in E. Treutner, S. Wolff, and W. Bonss, *Rechtsstaat und situative Verwaltung* (Frankfurt, 1978), p. 154.

7. T. Luckmann, "Zwänge und Freiheiten im Wandel der Gesellschaftsstruktur," in H. G. Gadamer and P. Vogler, eds., *Neue Anthropologie* (Stuttgart, 1972), 3: 190.
8. Gabriel, *Organisationsgesellschaft,* pp. 168ff.
9. Gabriel develops this as the point on which everything turns in the controversy between Weber and Luhmann, ibid., p. 114.
10. J. Habermas, *Communication and the Evolution of Society* (Boston, 179), pp. 116ff. and 160ff
11. Cf. W. Schluchter, *Die Entwicklung des okzidentalen Rationalismus* (Tübingen, 1979), pp. 256ff.
12. The strength of Marxist explanatory approaches still resides in the fact that they trace new modes of production back to the internal dynamics of the economic system rather than to external factors. In this connection, see the interesting discussion of the approaches of P. Sweezy, I. Wallerstein, and A. G.

Frankby R. Brenner, "The Origins of Capitalist Development: A Critique of Neo-Smithian Marxism," *New Left Review* 104 (1977): 25ff.; B. Fine, "On the Origins of Capitalist Development," *New Left Review* 109 (1978): 88ff.

13. See S. Seidman and M. Gruber, "Capitalism and Individuation in the Sociology of Max Weber," *British Journal of Sociology* 28 (1977): 498ff.

14. I have analyzed the social structure of bourgeois society in greater detail in *Strukturwandel der Öffentlichkeit* (Neuwied, 1962); English translation forthcoming, MIT Press. On the history of the ideas of the private sphere and the public sphere see L. Hölscher, *Öffentlichkeit und Geheimnis* (Stuttgart, 1979). On the social history of the public sphere, see H. U. Gumbrecht, R. Reichardt, and T. Schleich, eds., *Sozialgeschichte der Aufklärung in Frankreich*, 2 vols. (Munich, 1981).

15. C. Tilly, "Reflections on the History of European State-Making," in C. Tilly, ed., *The Formation of National States in Western Europe* (Princeton, 1975), pp. 3ff.; A. Griessinger, *Das symbolische Kapital der Ehre: Streikbewegungen und kollektives Bewusstsein deutscher Handwerksgesellen im 18. Jahrhundert* (Frankfurt, 1981).

16. Max Weber, "Religious Rejections of the World and Their Directions," in H. Gerth and C. W. Mills, eds., *From Max Weber* (New York, 1946), pp. 323–59, here p. 342.

17. Ibid., 334.

18. M. Weber, "Science as a Vocation," in *From Max Weber*, pp. 129–56, here p. 153.

19. Weber, *Economy and Society*, p. 892.

20. This is the basic guiding intention of Hannah Arendt, *The Human Condition* (New York, 1958); and idem, *The Life of the Mind*, vols. 1 and 2 (New York, 1978). Cf. J. Habermas, "Hannah Arendt on the Concept of Power," in *Philosophical-Political Profiles* (Cambridge, Mass., 1983), pp. 171–87; J. T. Knauer, "Motive and Goal in Hannah Arendt's Concept of Political Action," *American Political Science Review* 74 (1980): 721ff.

21. On this basic intention of Benjamin's theory of art, see J. Habermas, "Consciousness-Raising or Rescuing Critique," in *Philosophical-Political Profiles*, pp. 129–63.

22. Theorists inspired by Marxism, such as Adorno, Bloch, Lukacs, Lowenthal, and Hans Mayer, have worked up this utopian content in the classical works of bourgeois art and literature. See, for instance, L. Lowenthal, *Das bürgerliche Bewusstsein in der Literatur*, vol. 2 of *Gesammelte Schriften* (Frankfurt, 1981).

23. P. Kondylis, *Die Aufklärung im Rahmen des neuzeitlichen Rationalismus* (Stuttgart, 1981).

24. E. P. Thompson, *The Making of the English Working Class* (Harmondsworth, 1968); P. Kriedte, H. Medick, and J. Schimbohm, *Industrialisierung vor der Industrialisierung* (Göttingen, 1978).

Section VIII.2: Marx and the Thesis of Internal Colonization

1. Claus Offe, "Ungovernability," in J. Habermas, ed., *Observations on "The Spiritual Situation of the Age"* (Cambridge, Mass., 1984), pp. 67–88, here p. 84.

2. Georg Lohmann, "Gesellschaftskritik und normativer Massstab," in A. Honneth and U. Jaeggi, eds., *Arbeit, Handlung, Normativität* (Frankfurt, 1980), pp. 270–72.

3. E. M. Lange, "Wertformanalyse, Geldkritik und die Konstruktion des Fetischismus bei Marx," *Neue Philosophische Hefte* 13 (1978): 1ff.

4. Hauke Brunkhorst, in an unpublished manuscript, "Zur Dialektik von Verwertungssprache und Klassensprache," Frankfurt, 1980.

5. One well-known problem of correlation concerns the relation of objectively ascribed class positions (class in itself) to empirically identifiable attitudes and actions; another has to do with the transformation problem that arises in correlating values to prices.

6. Lohmann, "Gesellschaftskritik," p. 259.

7. Ibid., p. 251.

8. Max Weber, *Economy and Society* (New York, 1968), 3:1401–2.

9. See the contributions by J. P. Arnason, A. Honneth, and G. Markus to Honneth and Jaeggi, *Arbeit, Handlung, Normativität.*

10. Charles Taylor, *Hegel* (Cambridge, 1975), pp.5–29.

11. Lohmann, "Gesellschaftskritik," p. 275.

12. Ibid., p. 271.

13. Claus Offe, *Contradictions of the Welfare State* (Cambridge, Mass., 1984); and idem, *Disorganized Capitalism* (Cambridge, Mass., 1985).

14. J. Habermas, "Legitimation Problems in the Modern State," in *Communication and the Evolution of Society* (Boston, 1979), pp. 178–205.

15. Offe, "Ungovernability," p. 85.

16. Niklas Luhmann, "Öffentliche Meinung," in *Politische Planung* (Opladen, 1971), pp. 9ff.

17. M. Edelmann, *The Symbolic Uses of Politics* (Urbana, Ill., 1964); D. O.Sears, R. R. Lau,T. R. Tyler, and H. M. Allen, "Self-Interest vs. Symbolic Politics," *American Political Science Review* 74 (1980): 670ff.

18. This neutralization is normally sufficient at least to prevent a basic empirical question that would affect the normative self-understanding of democracies from making its way into everyday political consciousness: "Whether a process moving along institutional lines yields up results of a consensus arrived at free from domination and for that reason vouchsafing legitimacy, or whether this process itself produces and enforces a passive mass loyalty more or less accepting of its institutional restrictions, and thus props itself up on a self-generated foundation of formally democratic (*scheindemokratischer*) acclamation." W. D. Narr and C. Offe, "Einleitung," in *Wohlfahrtsstaat und Massenloyalität* (Cologne, 1975), p. 28.

19. S. Marcus, *Engels, Manchester, and the Working Class* (London, 1974).

20. Herbert Marcuse, "The Affirmative Character of Culture," in *Negations* (Boston, 1968), pp. 88–133; idem, *An Essay on Liberation* (Boston, 1969); idem, *Counterrevolution and Revolt* (Boston, 1972). See J. Habermas, "Herbert Marcuse: On Art and Revolution," in *Philosophical-Political Profiles* (Cambridge, Mass., 1983), pp. 165–70.

21. Corresponding to this direct intervention of experts into everyday life, and to the technocratic scientization of practice, are tendencies toward deprofessionalization, for which U. Oevermann is attempting to develop a theoretical explanation.

22. R. Voigt, "Verrechtlichung in Staat und Gesellschaft," in R. Voigt, ed., *Verrechtlichung* (Frankfurt, 1980), p. 16.

23. U. K. Preuss, "Der Staat und die indirekten Gewalten," paper delivered at the Berlin Hobbes Colloquium, October 12–14, 1980. See also Franz Neumann's ground-breaking study, "The Governance of the Rule of Law," 1936.

24. H. Boldt, *Deutsche Staatslehre im Vormärz* (Düsseldorf, 1975).
25. I. Maus, "Entwicklung und Funktionswandel der Theorie des bürgerlichen Rechtsstaats," in M. Tohidipur, ed., *Der bürgerliche Rechtsstaat* (Frankfurt, 1978), 1: 13ff. The famous definition reads: "The state should be a constitutional state based on the rule of law (*Rechtsstaat*)—that is the slogan and the developmental thrust of modern times. It should precisely define, by way of the law, the paths and limits of its efficacy and the free sphere of its citizens, and it should unswervingly guarantee these; it should not realize (enforce) moral ideas through the state, i.e. directly, any further than is proper to the legal sphere, i.e. only as far as the really necessary demarcations. This is the concept of the *Rechtsstaat*—not that the state should merely manage the legal order without administrative objectives, or merely protect the rights of the individual; it does not at all refer to the aim and content of the state, but only to the ways and means of realizing these." F. J. Stahl, *Die Philosophie des Rechts* (Darmstadt, 1963), 2: 137–38.
26. E. W. Böckenförde, "Entstehung und Wandel des Rechtsstaatsbegriffs," in *Staat, Gesellschaft, Freiheit* (Frankfurt, 1976), pp. 65ff.
27. T. Guldimann, M. Rodenstein, U. Rödel, and F. Stille, *Sozialpolitik als soziale Kontrolle* (Frankfurt, 1978).
28. For the relevant literature, see E. Reidegeld, "Vollzugsdefizite sozialer Leistungen," in Voigt, *Verrechtlichung*, pp. 275ff.
29. Christian v. Ferber, *Sozialpolitik in der Wohlstandsgesellschaft* (Hamburg, 1967).
30. Reidegold, "Vollzugsdefizite," p. 277.
31. Ibid., p. 281.
32. "In the area where the constitutional state and the welfare state meet, social policy that uses 'active' social intervention in the state's organization of freedom threatens to overwhelm the individual's right to help himself. The state benefit system thereby not only undoes the distribution of responsibilities between state and society; by shaping social benefits, it moulds *whole patterns of life*. If the citizen's life is insured in legalized form against all vicissitudes, from before birth to after death—as the law governing survivors' benefits teaches—then the individual fits himself into these social shells of his existence. He lives his life free of material worries, but simultaneously suffers from an excess of government provisions and from a fear of losing them." R. Pitschas, "Soziale Sicherung durch fortschreitende Verrechtlichung," in Voigt, *Verrechtlichung*, p. 155.
33. See vol. 1 of this work, *Reason and Rationalization of Society* (Boston, 1984), 1: 264ff.
34. [In American usage, 'administrative law' includes the law governing the operation of the social welfare bureaucracies. Habermas clearly uses *Verwaltungsrecht* in a narrower sense. I am indebted for this and other information regarding the legal terminology employed in this chapter to Robert Burns and Carol Rose—TRANS.]
35. A. Laaser, "Die Verrechtlichung des Schulwesens," in Projektgruppe Bildungsbericht, ed., *Bildung in der BRD* (Hamburg, 1980); I. Richter, *Bildungsverfassungsrecht* (Stuttgart, 1973); and idem, *Grundgesetz und Schulreform* (Weinheim, 1974).
36. S. Simitis and G. Zenz, eds., *Familie und Familienrecht*, vols. 1 and 2 (Frankfurt, 1975). See P. Finger, *Familienrecht* (Königstein, 1979); G. Beitzke, *Familienrecht* (Munich, 1979).

37. On the increasing recourse to the courts in regulating the schools, see Laaser, "Die Verrechtlichung des Schulwesens," pp. 1348ff.
38. On school legislation, see ibid., pp. 1357ff.
39. Simitis and Zen, *Familie und Familienrecht,* 1:48.
40. S. Simitis et al., *Kindeswohl* (Frankfurt, 1979); G. Zenz, *Kindesmisshandlung und Kindesrecht* (Frankfurt, 1979).
41. Simitis and Zen, *Familie und Familienrecht,* 1:40.
42. Simitis et al., *Kindeswohl,* p. 39.
43. Simitis and Zenz, *Familie und Familienrecht,* 1:55.
44. Ibid., 1:51–52.
45. Ibid., 1:36.
46. In this connection, L. R. Reuter speaks of a "reconstruction of the pedagogical mission in the pedagogical responsibility of educational institutions." "Bildung zwischen Politik und Recht," in Voigt, *Verrechtlichung,* p. 130.
47. See U. Scheuner, *Das Mehrheitsprinzip in der Demokratie* (Opladen, 1973), pp. 61–62.
48. G. Frankenberg, "Elemente einer Kritik und Theorie des Schulrechts," diss., University of Munich, 1978, p. 217.
49. Reuter, "Bildung," pp. 126–27.
50. Frankenberg, *Elemente einer Kritik,* pp. 227–28.
51. Ibid., p. 248. This is also the direction taken in the draft of a provincial law put forward by the Commission on School Law of the Deutscherjuristentag, entitled *Schule im Rechtstaat,* vol. 1 (Munich, 1981).

Section VIII.3: *The Tasks of a Critical Theory of Society*

1. A. Gouldner, *The Coming Crisis of Western Sociology* (New York, 1970), pp. 25ff.; B. Gruenberg, "The Problem of Reflexivity in the Sociology of Science," *Philosophy of Social Science* 8 (1978): 321ff.
2. See the contributions by K. O. Hondrich, K. Eder, J. Habermas, N. Luhman, J. Matthes, K. D. Opp, and K. H. Tjaden to "Theorienvergleich in der Soziologie," in R. Lepsius, ed., *Zwischenbilanz der Soziologie* (Stuttgart, 1976), pp. 14ff.
3. W. Mayrl, "Genetic Structuralism and the Analysis of Social Consciousness," *Theory and Society* 5 (1978): 20ff.
4. See the nine-volume reprint of *Zeitschrift für Sozialforschung* by Kösel Verlag (Munich, 1979).
5. The state of the program is discussed in W. Bonss and A. Honneth, eds., *Sozialforschung als Kritik* (Frankfurt, 1982).
6. H. Dubiel, *Theory and Politics: Studies in the Development of Critical Theory* (Cambridge, Mass., 1985), pt. 2.
7. On what follows, see H. Dubiel and A. Söllner, "Die Nationalsozialismusforschung des Instituts fur Sozialforchung," in Dubiel and Söllner, eds., *Recht und Staat im Nationalsozialismus* (Frankfurt, 1981), pp. 7ff.
8. As Marcuse presented it even then: "Social Implications of Modern Technology," *Zeitschrift fur Sozialforschung* 9 (1941): 414ff.
9. E. Fromm, "Über Methode und Aufgabe einer analytischen Sozialpsychologie," *Zeitschrift für Sozialforschung* 1 (1932): 28ff. English translation in E. Fromm, *The Crisis of Psychoanalysis* (Greenwich, Conn., 1971).
10. H. Dahmer, *Libido und Gesellschaft* (Frankfurt, 1973); H. Dahmer, ed., *Analytische Sozialpsychologie* (Frankfurt, 1980).

11. They did not change their position. See T. W. Adorno, "Sociology and Psychology," *New Left Review* 46 (1967): 67–80, and 47 (1968): 79–90.; H. Marcuse, *Eros and Civilization* (Boston, 1955); and idem, *Five Lectures* (Boston, 1970).

12. E. Fromm, *Escape from Freedom* (New York, 1942).

13. E. Fromm, *Arbeiter und Angestellte am Vorabend des Dritten Reiches: Eine sozialpsychologische Untersuchung,* ed. W. Bonss (Stuttgart, 1980).

14. E. M. Lange, "Wertformanalyse, Geldkritik und die Konstruktion des Fetischismus bei Marx," *Neue Philosophische Hefte* 13 (1978): 1ff.

15. H. Marcuse, "Philosophy and Critical Theory," in *Negations* (Boston, 1968), pp. 134–58, here p. 135.

16. Ibid., p. 147.

17. Ibid., p. 158.

18. Ibid.

19. See J. Habermas, *Communication and the Evolution of Society* (Boston, 1979), esp. chaps. 3 and 4.

20. On the discussion of the breakdown of Keynesian econonic policy in the West, see P. C. Roberts, "The Breakdown of the Keynesian Model," *Public Interest* (1978): 20ff.; J. A. Kregel, "From Post-Keynes to Pre-Keynes," *Social Research* 46 (1979): 212ff.; J. D. Wisman, "Legitimation, Ideology-Critique and Economics," *Social Research* 46 (1979): 291ff.; P. Davidson, "Post Keynesian Economics," *Public Interest* (1980): 151ff.

21. A. Arato, "Critical Sociology and Authoritarian State Socialism," in D. Held and J. Thompson, eds., *Habermas: Critical Debates* (Cambridge, Mass., 1982), pp. 196–218.

22. L. Löwenthal, *Gesammelte Schriften,* vol. 2 (Frankfurt, 1981).

23. H. Kohut, *Narzissmus, eine Theorie der Behandlung narzistischer Persönlichkeitsstörungen* (Frankfurt, 1973); and idem, *Die Heilung des Selbst* (Frankfurt, 1979).

24. Christopher Lasch, *The Culture of Narcissism* (New York, 1978).

25. P. Blos, *On Adolescence* (New York, 1962); Erik Erikson, *Identity and the Life Cycle* (New York, 1959).

26. See R. Döbert and G. Nunner-Winkler, *Adoleszenzkrise and Identitätsbildung* (Frankfurt, 1975); T. Ziehe, *Pubertät und Narzissmus* (Frankfurt, 1975); R. M. Merelman, "Moral Development and Potential Radicalism in Adolescence," *Youth and Society* 9 (1977): 29ff.; C. A. Rootes, "Politics of Moral Protest and Legitimation Problems of the Modern Capitalist State," *Theory and Society* 9 (1980): 473ff.

27. See J. Habermas, *Knowledge and Human Interests* (Boston, 1971), esp. chaps. 10–12; A. Lorenzer, *Sprachzerstörung und Rekonstruktion* (Frankfurt, 1970); K. Menne, M. Looser, A. Osterland, K. Brede, and E. Moersch, *Sprache, Handlung und Unbewusstes* (Frankfurt, 1976).

28. J. Habermas, "Moral Development and Ego Identity," in *Communication and the Evolution of Society,* pp. 69–94; R. Keagan, *The Evolving Self* (Cambridge, Mass., 1981·).

29. W. R. D. Fairbane, *An Object Relations Theory of Personality* (London, 1952); D. W. Winnicott, *The Maturational Process and the Facilitating Environment* (New York, 1965).

30. See E. Jacobson, *The Self and the Object World* (New York, 1964); M. Mahler, *Symbiose und Individuation,* 2 vols. (Stuttgart, 1972); Kohut, *Narzissmus;* H. Kohut, *Introspektion, Empathie und Psychoanalyse* (Frankfurt, 1976);

O. Kernberg, *Borderline-Störungen und pathologischer Narzissmus* (Frankfurt, 1978).

31. A. Freud, *The Ego and the Mechanisms of Defense* (New York, 1946); D. R. Miller and G. E. Swanson, *Inner Conflict and Defense* (New York, 1966); L. B. Murphy, "The Problem of Defense and the Concept of Coping," in E. Antyony and C. Koipernik, eds., *The Child in His Family* (New York, 1970); N. Haan, "A Tripartite Model of Ego-Functioning," *Journal of Neurological Mental Disease* 148 (1969): 14ff.
32. R. Dobert, G. Nunner-Winkler, and J. Habermas, eds., *Entwicklung des Ichs* (Cologne, 1977); R. L. Selman, *The Growth of Interpersonal Understanding* (New York, 1980).
33. W. Damon, ed., *New Directions for Child Development*, 2 vols. (San Francisco, 1978); H. Furth, *Piaget and Knowledge* (Chicago, 1981).
34. See pp. 277ff., this volume.
35. C. W. Mills, *Politics, Power and People* (New York, 1963); B. Rosenberg and D. White, eds., *Mass Culture* (Glencoe, Ill., 1957); A. Gouldner, *The Dialectics of Ideology and Technology* (New York, 1976); E. Barnouw, *The Sponser* (New York, 1977); D. Smythe, "Communications: Blind Spot of Western Marxism," *Canadian Journal of Political and Social Theory* 1 (1977); T. Gitlin, "Media Sociology: The Dominant Paradigm," *Theory and Society* 6 (1978): 205ff.
36. D. Kellner, "Network Television and American Society: Introduction to a Critical Theory of Television," *Theory and Society* 10 (1981): 31ff.
37. Ibid., pp. 38ff.
38. A. Singlewood, *The Myth of Mass Culture* (London, 1977).
39. D. Kellner, "TV, Ideology and Emancipatory Popular Culture," *Socialist Review* 45 (1979): 13ff.
40. D. Kellner, "Kulturindustrie und Massenkommunikation: Die kritische Theorie und ihre Folgen," in W. Bonss and A. Honneth, eds., *Sozialforschung als Kritik* (Frankfurt, 1982), pp. 482–515.
41. From Lazarfeld's early radio studies on the dual character of communication flows and the role of opinion leaders, the independent weight of everyday communication in relation to mass communication has been confirmed again and again: "In the last analysis it is people talking with people more than people listening to, or reading, or looking at the mass media that really causes opinions to change." Mills, *Power, Politics and People*, p. 590. See P. Lazarsfeld, B. Berelson, and H. Gaudet, *The People's Choice* (New York, 1948); P. Lazarsfeld and E. Katz, *Personal Influence* (New York, 1955). Compare O. Negt and A. Kluge, *Öffentlichkeit und Erfahrung* (Frankfurt, 1970), and, by the same authors, *Geschichte und Eigensinn* (Munich, 1981).
42. H. M. Enzenberger, "Baukasten zu einer Theorie der Meiden," in *Palaver* (Frankfurt, 1974), pp. 91ff.
43. S. Benhabib, "Modernity and the Aporias of Critical Theory," *Telos* 49 (1981): 30–60.
44. R. Inglehart, "Wertwandel und politisches Verhalten," in J. Matthes, ed., *Sozialer Wandel in Westeuropa* (Frankfurt, 1979).
45. K. Hildebrandt and R. J. Dalton, "Die neue Politik," *Politische Vierteljahresschrift* 18 (1977): 230ff.; S. H. Barnes, M. Kaase et al., *Political Action* (Beverly Hills/London, 1979).
46. J. Hirsch, "Alternativbewegung: Eine politische Alternative," in R. Roth, ed., *Parlamentarisches Ritual und politische Alternativen* (Frankfurt, 1980).

47. On this point I found a manuscript by K. W. Brand very helpful: "Zur Diskussion um Entstehung, Funktion und Perspektive der "Ökologie- und Alternativbewegung," Munich, 1980.
48. Hirsch, "Alternativbewegung"; J. Huber, *Wer soll das alles ändern?* (Berlin, 1980).
49. J. Rraschke, "Politik und Wertwandel in den westlichen Demokratien," supplement to the weekly paper *Das Parlament,* September 1980, pp. 23ff.
50. On the dual economy, see A. Gorz, *Abschied vom Proletariat* (Frankfurt, 1980); J. Huber, *Wer soll das alles ändern?* Concerning the effects of democratic mass parties on the lifeworld contexts of voters, see Claus Offe, "Konkurrenzpartei und kollektive politische Identität," in Roth, *Paralmentarisches Ritual.*
51. See, for example, B. Guggenberger, *Bürgerinitiativen in der Parteindemokratie* (Stuttgart, 1980).
52. See, for example, P. Berger, B. Berger, and H. Kellner, *Das Unbehagen in der Modernität* (Frankfurt, 1975).
53. J. Habermas, "Modernity versus Postmodernity," *New German Critique* 22 (1981): 3–14; L. Baier, "Wer unsere Köpfe kolonisiert," in *Literaturmagazin* 9 (1978).
54. R. Bernstein, *The Restructuring of Social and Political Theory* (Philadelphia, 1976).
55. In "The Methodological Illusions of Modern Political Theory," *Neue Hefte für Philosophie* 21 (1982): 47–74, Seyla Benhabib stresses the fact that the discourse theory of ethics proposed by K. O. Apel and myself treats calculations of consequences and, above all, interpretations of needs as essential elements of moral argumentation. See K. O. Apel, "Sprechakttheorie und transzendentale Sprachpragmatik, zur Frage ethischer Normen," in K. O. Apel, ed., *Sprachpragmatik und Philosophie* (Frankfurt, 1976), pp. 10–173; J. Habermas, *Moralbewusstsein und kommunikatives Handeln* (Frankfurt, 1983).
56. On this point, Max Horkheimer's essay "Materialismus und Moral," *Zeitschrift fur Sozialforschung* 2 (1933): 263ff. is still worth reading.
57. P. Bürger, *Theory of the Avant-Garde* (Minneapolis, 1984).
58. R. Rorty, *Philosophy and the Mirror of Nature* (Princeton, 1979).
59. R. F. Kitchener, "Genetic Epistemology, Normative Epistemology, and Psychologism," *Synthese* 45 (1980): 257ff.; T. Kesselring, *Piagets genetische Erkenntnistheorie und Hegels Dialektik* (Frankfurt, 1981). I have examined the methodological peculiarities of reconstructive sciences in connection with the division of labor between philosophy and psychology in Kohlberg's theory of the development of moral consciousness, in "Interpretive Sociale Wetenschap versus Radicale Hermeneutiek," *Kennis en Method* 5 (1981): 4ff.
60. In M. Horkheimer, *Critical Theory* (New York, 1972), pp. 188–243, here p. 197.
61. Ibid., p. 205.
62. Ibid., p. 196. I once characterized the relation between social theory and social practice in the same way: "Historical materialism aims at achieving an explanation of social evolution which is so comprehensive that it encompasses the theory's own contexts of origin and application. The theory specifies the conditions under which a self-reflection of the history of the species has become objectively possible. At the same time it names those to whom

the theory is addressed, who can with its help gain enlightenment about themselves and their emancipatory role in the process of history. With this reflection on the context of its origin and this anticipation of the context of its application, the theory understands itself as a necessary catalytic moment in the very complex of social life that it analyzes; and it analyzes this complex as an integral network of coercion, from the viewpoint of its possible transformation." *Theory and Practice* (Boston, 1973), pp. 2–3.

63. K. Marx, *Grundrisse* (Harmondsworth, Eng., 1973), pp. 104–5.
64. Ibid., p. 105.
65. Ibid.

Index

439

Analytical Table of Contents

VI. Intermediate Reflections: System and Lifeworld

VII. Talcott Parsons: Problems in Constructing a Theory of Society